American Women Regionalists 1850–1910

A Norton Anthology

American Women Regionalists 1850–1910

A Norton Anthology

JUDITH FETTERLEY
THE UNIVERSITY AT ALBANY, STATE UNIVERSITY OF NEW YORK

MARJORIE PRYSE
STATE UNIVERSITY OF NEW YORK COLLEGE AT PLATTSBURGH

W. W. NORTON & COMPANY • *New York* • *London*

Chopin: "A Little Country Girl" from *The Complete Works of Kate Chopin*, edited by Per Seyersted. Copyright © 1969 by Louisiana State University Press.

Chopin: "The Storm" reprinted by permission of Louisiana State University Press from *The Complete Works of Kate Chopin*, edited by Per Seyersted. Copyright © by Louisiana State University Press.

Dunbar-Nelson: "The Stones of the Village" by Alice Dunbar-Nelson from *The Works of Alice Dunbar-Nelson*, Vol. 3., edited by Gloria T. Hull. The Schomburg Library of Nineteenth-Century Black Women Writers. Copyright © 1988 by Oxford University Press, Inc. Used by permission.

Cather: "Old Mrs. Harris" from *Obscure Destinies* by Willa Cather. Copyright © 1930, 1932 by Willa Cather and renewed 1958, 1960 by the Executors of the Estate of Willa Cather. Reprinted by permission of Alfred A. Knopf, Inc.

Printed in the United States of America.
The text of this book is composed in Electra,
with the display set in Bernhard Modern.
Composition by Com Com.
Manufacturing by Haddon Craftsmen.
Book design by Antonina Krass.

First Edition

Library of Congress Cataloging-in-Publication Data

American women regionalists 1850-1910 / edited by Judith Fetterley, and Marjorie Pryse.
     p. cm.
"A Norton anthology."
Includes bibliographical references and index.
    1. American Literature—Women authors. 2. Regionalism—United States—Literary collections. 3. Women—United States—Literary collections.
4. American Literature—19th century. I. Fetterley, Judith, 1938-   . II. Pryse, Marjorie, 1948- .
PS508.W7A48 1992
810.8'09287'0903—dc20   91-11583

ISBN 0-393-96137-0

W.W. Norton & Company, Inc., 500 Fifth Avenue, New York, N.Y. 10110
W.W. Norton & Company, Ltd., 10 Coptic Street, London WCIA 1PU

1 2 3 4 5 6 7 8 9 0

Contents

Acknowledgments

We would like to thank our students at the University at Albany, State University of New York, and at the University of Tennessee, who first read with us many of the works included in this anthology and confirmed for us their value for readers. We would also like to thank colleagues who have attended our several "dialogues" about regionalism—at the Modern Language Association, the National Women's Studies Association, and the Sarah Orne Jewett Conference held in June 1985 at Westbrook College—for beginning to engage with us in discussion. In particular we acknowledge early support for our work on these writers from Elizabeth Ammons and Sarah Way Sherman, and we are grateful for conversations with Joanne Dobson and Sandra Zagarell. We thank the John C. Hodges Better English Fund at the University of Tennessee, the National Endowment for the Humanities, and the University at Albany, all of which provided released time that enabled us to continue our work on regionalism. Most of all, we thank John Benedict, our editor at W. W. Norton, who shared our interest in regionalism for almost a decade until his death in July 1990.

Introduction

Most editors who create an anthology begin with an established genre, literary tradition, national literature, or period boundaries, and within those guidelines proceed to select texts based on their own assumptions about what constitutes the best, most representative, or most diverse set of texts for that genre, tradition, or period. In our own case, while we have accepted certain conditions for categorizing texts—the writers in this anthology belong to the larger tradition of nineteenth-century American prose writers—we have made our primary assumption in establishing the category itself. For, in creating this anthology, we are asserting the existence of a tradition among nineteenth-century American women writers that we term regionalism. We began our project by reading extensively both in little-known or unknown American nineteenth-century women writers and in nineteenth-century writers of both sexes working within the traditions already identified in American literary history as "local color" or "regional realism." We began to observe that white men did not write the same kinds of regional texts that some white women or some members of minority groups did. Based on these observations, developed within the context of evolving women's studies research and feminist theory of the 1970s and 1980s, we have tried to reconstruct a regionalist women's tradition in American literature that might both possess historical foundations and also speak to our own needs as late-twentieth-century women readers and professional critics.

In using the term "regionalism" to describe the body of literature collected here, we are aware that we may be more self-conscious about the connections between these texts than were the writers themselves. They would probably not have objected to those terms more prevalent during the late nineteenth century to describe fiction which took as its setting an identifiable American region—terms such as "local color" or "regional realism." The phrase "local colorist" (which implies a literary analogy to painters of so-called "genre" scenes) refers to numerous post–Civil War writers, including, for example, Sherwood Bonner, Alice Brown, George Washington Cable, Hamlin Garland, Bret Harte, Ruth McEnery Stuart, Mark Twain, and Constance Fenimore Woolson. These writers depicted "local" scenes, often from regions more newly opened to settlement and statehood than New England, from the perspective of a narrator defined as superior to and outside of the region of the fiction, and often to entertain and satisfy the curiosity of late-nineteenth-century urban readers in Boston and New York.

We acknowledge that the writers we here term "regionalists" would not have claimed a distinction between their own writing and the fiction of their contemporaries. Many of the regionalists contributed their work to the *Atlantic Monthly* and other eastern magazines in the same issues in which writers such as Bret Harte and Hamlin Garland also published, and Mary Wilkins Freeman, at least, corresponded with Garland and expressed admiration for his work. And, like their "local colorist" contemporaries, the regionalists wrote about life in the South and the West, as well as about life in New England. Nevertheless, we find implicit evidence in several of the sketches and stories collected here that in practice the regionalists did differentiate themselves from the "local colorists," primarily in their desire not to hold up regional characters to potential ridicule by eastern urban readers but rather to present regional experience from within, so as to engage the reader's sympathy and identification. In making this observation, we think in particular of the following works anthologized here: Jewett's "The Circus at Denby" and "A White Heron"; Murfree's "The Star in the Valley"; Chopin's "A Gentleman of Bayou Têche"; Dunbar-Nelson's "M'sieu Fortier's Violin"; and Sui Sin Far's " 'Its Wavering Image.' "

These women also share writing careers that included work in many other forms in addition to regional fiction—poetry, novels, children's literature, autobiography, and religious and didactic literature. However, the regionalist prose of these writers differs significantly from the work they produced in other forms with respect to their conception of character, language, plot, and the relationship of the author or narrator to her material. Thus, although we have found no evidence that the writers in this volume were conscious of inventing a literary form— among these writers only Mary Austin wrote essays that might be considered literary theory—they do seem to have recognized the distinctiveness of the regional mode of writing and the possibilities it presented for articulating a particular perspective on American life.

The writers in this volume frequently knew each other and admired each other's work. Writing to Annie Fields, her life partner in what the late nineteenth century recognized as a "Boston marriage," Jewett described her experience of rereading *The Pearl of Orr's Island*, a book she first encountered as an adolescent and that she remembered as an experience significant to her own development as a writer: "It is classical—historical—anything you like to say, if you can give it high praise enough" (Jewett, *Letters*, 47). Stowe clearly influenced Jewett, and later Jewett clearly influenced Cather; our organization of this anthology takes this line of influence as central to explicating the literary tradition of regionalism. In the case of Stowe and Jewett, the bonds were literary rather than personal, although Annie Fields served as a personal link between Jewett and the older writer, with whom Fields had long shared a friendship. In the case of Jewett and Cather, the bonds were personal as well as literary; Jewett served as a mentor for Cather, and after Jewett's death Cather continued to visit Jewett's home in South Berwick, Maine.

Biographical evidence suggests an even larger network among these writers than we may clearly measure as literary influence. In addition to mentoring Cather, Jewett formed a close friendship with Celia Thaxter and met Mary Wilkins Freeman and Mary Noailles Murfree. Through her relationship with Annie Fields, she knew Rose Terry Cooke and admired her work. Kate Chopin claimed that Freeman was a "great genius" and that she knew of "no one better than Miss Jewett to study for technique and nicety of construction" (Seyersted 52). Although we have not found any evidence that Alice Cary and Harriet Beecher Stowe knew each other when they were both living in Cincinnati, Ohio, they did publish in the pages of the *National Era* together, and in some of the same issues. Years after Alice Cary's death, her friend Mary Louise Booth served as Freeman's editor at *Harper's Bazar*, and we have speculated that the young Mary E. Wilkins, on one of her visits to Booth's home in New York City, might have inquired about the portrait of Alice Cary which Booth hung in her library. Paul Dunbar, in a letter to the young Alice Ruth Moore, associated her sketches with the work of Grace King. Mary Austin's mentor Charles Lummis, editor of the California magazine *The Land of Sunshine*, also published Sui Sin Far and was host to both writers at his Southern California ranch. Willa Cather wrote part of her novel *Death Comes for the Archbishop* in Mary Austin's house in Santa Fe, New Mexico. And although we have not found specific evidence to support it, it seems likely that Mary Austin might have known Zitkala-Sä, for both were involved in organizations dedicated to promoting Native American culture.

These writers also shared an historical context. They were all American women who became adults and produced fiction during the latter half of the nineteenth century. Here we recall that the dominant ideology of the American nineteenth century believed in essential differences between women and men, promoted the existence of a "woman's sphere," and accepted "woman's sphere" as culturally productive. To the extent that "woman's sphere" attributed to women essential characteristics which "naturally" fitted them for motherhood, and which delineated domesticity, child-rearing, and spiritual life as their arenas of influence, it is conceivable that the writers represented in this volume possessed a certain self-consciousness that their own values, and the fiction that emerged from these values, was "different" from that of men, and of some other women writers. Because, as Nancy Cott observes in her discussion of "woman's sphere" in *The Bonds of Womanhood*, the concept of "woman's sphere" was liberating as well as constraining for nineteenth-century women's development, regionalism may reflect the possibilities as well as the limitations of the sex-segregated culture of the nineteenth century.

In tracing the origins of regionalism, we begin the anthology with Harriet Beecher Stowe's "Uncle Lot," first published in 1834 in the *Western Monthly Magazine* under the title "A New England Sketch," even though Stowe's story falls outside the chronological boundaries of our subtitle, 1850–1910. Stowe was one of a number of earlier writers, including Catharine Sedgwick, Caroline Kirkland, and Lydia Huntley Sigourney, whose work of the 1820s and 1830s included regional elements. We have chosen "Uncle Lot" from among other possible origin texts to illustrate the inception of regionalism for two reasons. First, although Stowe locates her sketch in the New England tradition of didactic literature, and categorizes her "main story" as a conventional love story, "Uncle Lot" derives its energy from the character after whom Stowe eventually named her story, and from the narrative line she develops through him. Second, we have included "Uncle Lot" rather than other early sketches with regional elements because through this sketch, Stowe initiates a dialogue with some of the assumptions of early American fiction as Washington Irving delineated these in "Rip Van Winkle" and "The Legend of Sleepy Hollow," and she associates her part of this dialogue with the vision and values that characterized "woman's sphere." Thus, the dual impulse to bring regional elements into the center of the fictional sketch and to search for alternative values and forms to express American identity makes "Uncle Lot" a rich and significant text with which to preface a collection that illustrates the tradition of regionalism.

The elements of regionalism take shape in "Uncle Lot" both as Stowe's response to the dilemma of national identity that early-nineteenth-century American writers faced and as her attempt to find a form in fiction to express the "woman's" vision that other early-nineteenth-century writers, particularly Irving, had dismissed. Although James Benton, the young protagonist of the sketch, and Uncle Lot are male, they contrast markedly with the frontier "heroes" of Stowe's contemporaries, characters such as Sut Lovingood, in the fiction of George Washington Harris, the Mike Fink of early American folk legend, or the Lyman Hall of Augustus Baldwin Longstreet's *Georgia Scenes* (1835). The values Stowe explores in "Uncle Lot" more closely resemble the values of domesticity, stability, and community than the values of separation and "rugged individualism" associated with life on the frontier. Specifically, in Stowe's "revision" of "The Legend of Sleepy Hollow," not Brom Bones but the Ichabod Crane figure, James Benton, becomes the hero of the sketch, as Stowe asserts the value of what Irving had dismissed as the "sleepy region," with its base in the authority of the kitchen, the schoolroom, and the pulpit.

Those imitators of Irving who created "ring-tailed roarers" in the image of Brom Bones masculinized the literary portrait of American region and provided the primary influence for the "Old Southwest humorist" school of American fiction (which included such figures as Thomas Bangs Thorpe, George Washington Harris, Augustus Baldwin Longstreet, and the male writers who contributed to the "sporting magazine" of the 1830s, *The Spirit of the Times*). This "school" later evolved into the "local color" and humorist writing of late-nineteenth-century writers such as Harte, Garland, and Mark Twain. In taking a different path and reconstructing the "sleepy" region that Irving disparages in "The Legend of Sleepy Hollow," Stowe provided the germinal influence for the writers included in this volume who continued to develop what she began.

In describing James Benton as possessed of a "natural tact for seeing into others," Stowe provides an early portrayal of the empathy that became one of the most significant features of regionalism. While Stowe connects empathy with Christian values, and accords James the status of minister, in "Uncle Lot" she nevertheless transforms empathy from purely religious uses into literary purpose. In the narrative line that traces James Benton's conversion of Uncle Lot from roughness to kindness, Stowe identifies the narrative elements that will inform the work of later regionalists. James uses empathy to engage Uncle Lot so that he can persuade him to recognize and reveal the "latent kindness" he holds within his "rough exterior" and to act more in congruence with his feelings; he directs his attention to an old man, thus shifting the center of perception to Uncle Lot; and he conducts his work of "conversion" as part of a visit to Uncle Lot's house.

In exploring the possibilities of character rather than plot as her fiction's organizing principle in "Uncle Lot," Stowe opened up the possibility of the sketch as the ideal form for conveying regionalist values. As we noted above, Stowe subsequently changed the title of her first published fiction from "A New England Sketch" to "Uncle Lot," suggesting her desire to bring into focus the depiction of character. A fictional form that takes its energy from character creates an opening for storytelling that makes plot a lesser concern; women writers could—and did—readily appropriate this form, the sketch, to portray their culture. For example, in Jewett's "The Foreigner," two women wait for a storm to pass; in Freeman's "A New England Nun," a woman decides not to marry; in Chopin's "Odalie Misses Mass," a child doesn't go to church; and in Dunbar-Nelson's "The Praline Woman," a woman offers pralines for sale. In these sketches, the depiction of character clearly takes precedence over plot. Furthermore, only a few regionalist texts even approach novel-length, and, when they do, the structure of these longer works seems significantly different from that of other nineteenth-century works we would more easily recognize as novels. Sarah Orne Jewett's *Deephaven* and *The Country of the Pointed Firs* and Mary Austin's *The Land of Little Rain* present a series of related sketches, but all conspicuously lack the integrated plot we associate with the nineteenth-century novel. Kate Chopin's *The Awakening* is certainly a novel, but, as the excerpt we have anthologized illustrates, Chopin explores regionalism primarily in her portrait of a secondary character, Mademoiselle Reisz, while her larger plot-line moves beyond the identifiable features of regionalist fiction.

Regionalist writers frequently connect their interest in character to an interest in development or discovery of identity, specifically in relation to home, region, and community. While not all protagonists in regionalist fiction are orphans, some works begin with a female character's search for a mother or for a connection with other women that allows her to return in some derivative way to the world of her maternal origins. Jewett's "A White Heron," Freeman's "On the Walpole Road" and "Sister Liddy," King's "The Balcony," Chopin's "Lilacs," and Dunbar-Nelson's "Sister Josepha" all focus on orphans, or on the desire of female characters to seek out a connection with "mother." Celia Thaxter's narrator substitutes a relationship with nature for her original relationship with mother. Through interactions with other women, and with their stories, often enfolded as narratives-within-narratives, female protagonists and narrators in regionalist fiction often develop further within the context of a particular community of women located in a specific place, and define identity as collective, connected, and collaborative. Community between women becomes a particularly strong presence in Stowe's *The Pearl of Orr's Island*, Cooke's "Miss Beulah's Bonnet," Jewett's "The Circus at Denby" and "The Foreigner," Freeman's "Sister Liddy" and "A Church Mouse," Sui Sin Far's "Mrs. Spring Fragrance" and "The Inferior Woman," and Cather's "Old Mrs. Harris." As a consequence of her series of returns to the world of women and of her increasing awareness of her connection to other women, the female protagonist in regionalist fiction becomes capable of an adult identity, for which she finds models in those older women who serve as teacher, guide, storyteller, hoodoo priestess—as in Jewett's *The Country of the Pointed Firs* or Dunbar-Nelson's "The Goodness of Saint Rocque"—or—as in Mary Austin's "The Basket Maker"—artist-healer. Jewett accords this role to her narrator, who passes on what she has learned from Mrs. Todd and Mrs. Blackett to the successive generations who will read her fiction. Several works included here also extend this model of development, particularly the values of connection with "mother," to male characters, as in Stowe's "The Minister's Housekeeper," Cooke's "Freedom Wheeler's Controversy with Providence," Jewett's "The Old Singers," Murfree's "The 'Harnt' That Walks Chilhowee," and Chopin's "Ozème's Holiday."

Since the regionalist character tends to develop within her community of origin, her relationship to place—to the regional landscape—is central to her discovery of self. Indeed, for some writers included in this anthology—Celia Thaxter, Mary Austin, and Zitkala-Sä serve as examples—the regional landscape literally serves to mirror the narrator, providing her with a source of nurturance and a point of reference essential to the establishment of her identity. Yet even in those instances in which the region is not literally or specifically associated with mother, regionalist fiction asserts an essential connection between character and place. In "Uncle Lot" we see Stowe initiating the pattern of identifying specific aspects of character with specific features of regional topography. Uncle Lot is old, quirky, a study in lights and contrast, a chestnut burr, and, in noting that "all the strata of his character were crossed by a vein of surly petulance," she uses language to describe his character that could as easily be used to describe the New England landscape. Characters in regional fiction are rooted; they don't leave home in search of their identity. Even Austin's "The Walking Woman" confines her walking to her region. Regional characters gain their identity from the regions they inhabit; for regional characters, living for a long time in the same place affects character. As Mary Austin writes, in *The Land of Little Rain*, "the manner of the country makes the usage of life there, and the land will not be lived in except in its own fashion." Regional writers respect and cherish the actual places that provide the environmental contexts for their characters. Other works which demonstrate the strong connection between regionalist characters and the regions they inhabit include Thaxter's *Among the Isles of Shoals*, Jewett's "The Outer Island" and "Green Island" from *The Country of the Pointed Firs*, Murfree's "The Star in the Valley" and "Over on the T'Other Mounting," Freeman's "On the Walpole Road" and "A Mistaken Charity," King's "The Balcony," Chopin's "At the 'Cadian Ball" and "A Gentleman of Bayou Têche," and Sui Sin Far's "The Sing Song Woman."

Another significant feature of regionalist fiction concerns the role of the narrator. In the regional text, the narrator does not distance herself from the inhabitants of the region, as is the case in "local color" fiction; indeed, she frequently appears to be an inhabitant herself. The regionalist narrator empowers the voice of regional characters, viewing them as agents of their own lives, rather than undermining them with the ironic perspective characteristic of "local color" writing. And the narrator's stance of careful listening fosters an empathic connection between the reader of the work and the lives the work depicts. We believe empathy as a feature of narration is particularly evident in works such as Stowe's "The Minister's Housekeeper," Cary's "Passages from the Married Life of Eleanor Homes," Cooke's "How Celia Changed Her Mind," Jewett's "The Circus at Denby" and "The Queen's Twin," King's "'One of Us'" and "Pupasse," Dunbar-Nelson's "The Stones of the Village," Austin's "The Return of Mr. Wills," and Sui Sin Far's "'Its Wavering Image.'"

Because regional narrators identify with rather than distance themselves from the material of their stories, regionalist texts allow the reader to view the regional speaker as subject and not as object and to include empathic feeling as an aspect of critical response. Regionalist texts illustrate this process through a phenomenon that we call shifting the center of perception. Jewett explores this phenomenon in "The Circus at Denby." When the narrator enters the tent containing the Kentucky Giantess, she expects to see a freak in the circus sideshow; discovering that the giantess is Marilly, a woman her companion used to know, and hearing Marilly's story transforms her encounter into an empathic experience in which she gains an insider's perception of what it feels like to be an outsider or a freak. This shift in perception provides the dramatic moment in the fiction, and offers empathy as a model for the relationship between reader and character as well. Reading becomes a synonym for listening; regional writers create regional characters in order to enlarge the hearts and perspectives of their readers, not to reinforce the reader's sense of superiority. We also find evidence of shifting the center of perception in Cary's "Uncle Christopher's," Cooke's "How Celia Changed Her Mind," Thaxter's portrait of learning to "listen" and to "read" the landscape of *Among the Isles of Shoals*, Freeman's "Sister Liddy" and "A Church Mouse," Chopin's portrait of Mademoiselle Reisz in *The Awakening*, and Sui Sin Far's "The Inferior Woman."

The shift in the center of perception that transforms a circus sideshow into someone with a name, a story, and a personal connection also creates a climate within which writers can avoid reliance on sexist, racist, or classist stereotypes in the depiction of character. Readers familiar with some of these writers will note exceptions to this statement. For example, Kate Chopin silences the black women who appear in *The Awakening*, and even though in her portraits of Creoles she writes empathically, her portraits of black persons in her short fiction may seem to emerge more from stereotype than from empathy. Sarah Orne Jewett allows class distinctions to shape her narrator's perception in *Deephaven*. And Mary Wilkins Freeman's "The Poetess" may strike some readers as sexist in its stereotypic portrait of the nineteenth-century woman poet. Nor are these writers free from the casual racism of their culture, apparent, for example, in Cooke's reference to "a slatternly Negress" ("How Celia Changed Her Mind") or in Jewett's creation of a character who specifies as the thief of her money "a Negro" ("The Foreigner"). Nevertheless, in general the regionalist writers incorporated inclusivity as a cultural value. Cary and King demonstrate compassion for children in "Uncle Christopher's" and "Pupasse"; Cooke and Murfree write sympathetically about characters who are weak and have difficulty surviving, such as Lowly in "Freedom Wheeler's Controversy With Providence" or the "harnt" in "The 'Harnt' That Walks Chilhowee"; Jewett, Thaxter, and Austin promote respect for animals; Freeman's characters often include poor, elderly, homeless, and lower-class women, as well as women others might deem "crazy," as in "Sister Liddy"; Jewett extends her narrator's sympathy to foreigners in "The Foreigner"; King empathizes with the wealthy dispossessed in "A Drama of Three," "The Grande Demoiselle," and "The Old Lady's Restoration"; Cooke in "How

Celia Changed Her Mind," Freeman in "A New England Nun," and King in " 'One of Us' " include spinsters as women whose lives matter; Chopin portrays Cajun characters in "At the 'Cadian Ball" and "The Storm"; Dunbar-Nelson writes about characters of mixed racial origins in "Mr. Baptiste" and "The Stones of the Village"; Zitkala-Sä writes directly from within the experience of growing up Native American; Austin creates a Native-American woman in "The Basket Maker" as her prototype of the artist-healer; Sui Sin Far's Mrs. Spring Fragrance wants to write a book to explain American women to her Chinese-American friends; and Cather grants her Jewish character Mrs. Rosen the fullest achievement of empathy in "Old Mrs. Harris."

We have intended our "Introduction" to sketch out rather than to fully explicate the tradition of regionalism, and therefore we have not considered the influence of regionalism on twentieth-century fiction. However, the reader familiar with the literary tradition of twentieth-century African-American women writers—Toni Morrison, Alice Walker, Toni Cade Bambara, and others—and with other minority traditions that have become particularly significant in recent decades may want to explore the relationship between regionalism in Dunbar-Nelson, Sui Sin Far, and Zitkala-Sä, and the development of twentieth-century fiction by minority writers. Other lines of influence may lead the reader to compare and contrast the features of nineteenth-century regionalism with the features of southern fiction, especially by women writers such as Flannery O'Connor, Eudora Welty, and Carson McCullers, as we know it in the twentieth century.

We have chosen to end our anthology with Willa Cather's "Old Mrs. Harris." Like "Uncle Lot," "Old Mrs. Harris," published in 1932, also falls outside the chronological range we have identified for the regionalist tradition. As we discuss more fully in our headnote introduction to Cather, "Old Mrs. Harris" serves as a postscript to this anthology, a work that marks the limit of the development of nineteenth-century regionalism. Thus, regionalism as we have represented it here possesses a critical narrative of its own, its own "story" of the development of a women's tradition in American fiction, a story that possesses a beginning, a middle, and an end. We invite our readers to conclude their own reading of this anthology by considering the larger questions that continue to intrigue us, namely, to what extent does the tradition of regionalism actually emerge from the ideology of separate spheres, and to what extent did it fail to survive the dissolution of that ideology early in the twentieth century? We end with "Old Mrs. Harris" in part because we believe Cather's work holds some answers to these questions.

∘ ∘ ∘

The process of creating this anthology has taken place over the course of nearly a decade. When we began to collaborate on this project, we had each experienced the power of Sarah Orne Jewett's *The Country of the Pointed Firs* and had begun to wonder what, both in individual and cultural history, had made this book possible. We shared an interest in Jewett's life, with her "Boston marriage" to Annie Adams Fields, as well as her extensive circle of close friends, most of whom were women, and many of whom were writers or artists. We had also both read widely in the fiction of other nineteenth-century American women writers. We had found ourselves drawn to the short fiction of Alice Cary, Rose Terry Cooke, Mary Wilkins Freeman, Mary Austin; and when together we tried to answer the question of origins, and later influences, for Sarah Orne Jewett, we concluded that the work of these and other writers included in this anthology provided the context we were seeking.

As our collaboration developed, we created with each other and with our students and interested colleagues a community of readers able to share in the evolving inquiry into a body of meaningful texts. Recognizing the importance to this tradition of physical place, we personally began to journey to some of the actual places the writers collected here had recognized as the source of their own inspiration and had recreated in their fiction. We visited the Cary Cottage near Cincinnati, Ohio, where Alice Cary lived as a young adult, and saw the early stages of the renovation of the Beecher house, where the young Harriet Beecher lived when her family moved to Cincinnati; we took the ferry nine miles out to Celia Thaxter's Isles of Shoals and saw White Island, where Thaxter had spent her childhood; we explored Beersheba Springs in Tennessee, where Mary Murfree had summered, and about whose inhabitants she had written; we visited Jewett's house in South Berwick, Maine, and the site where she wrote *The Country of the Pointed Firs*—Martinsville, Maine, near Port Clyde and Tenant's Harbor; one of us had lived for a time near Brattleboro, Vermont, where Mary Wilkins Freeman began her life as a writer; together we explored Walnut Canyon, Arizona, and Mesa Verde, Colorado, two places which Willa Cather responded to in her fiction; and we visited San Francisco's Chinatown, one of the sites of Sui Sin Far's *Mrs. Spring Fragrance*. Thus our collaborative relationship shared with the writers we valued a common connection to place.

Over the past decade, then, regionalism has emerged for us as a rich, complex, and powerful set of texts, capable of answering our need for tradition, for literary mothers, and for a place of our own in American literary history. Regionalism has also provided us with a literature responsive to the issues affecting our personal and professional lives and the lives of many of our contemporaries: our relation to place; our connection to mothers; the effort to create community in a world defined by the nuclear family and geographic mobility; the desire to find a model for our own development and for the development of our children; the struggle to find voice and authority; and the power of a feminist literary theory that has evolved from literary practice.

A Note on the Text

We have based the order in which writers appear in this anthology on the dates when they published their first significant works of regionalism. At the end of this volume, we have included the chronology of first regional publications that has generated this order. We have based the order of texts by individual writers on the dates when they were first published, where we have been able to identify these. Following each of the texts included, we have provided the information concerning its publication history; the first date refers to magazine publication, the second to book publication. We have in general taken our texts from books in which the sketches later appeared.

At the end of this volume, we supply for each writer a bibliography of regional works, along with selected biographical and critical studies. While we refer to some of these texts in the general introduction and in the individual headnotes (see *List of Works Cited*), following the editorial format for Norton anthologies we have limited our footnotes to linguistic, historical, or critical annotations.

Although we have included Willa Cather's "Old Mrs. Harris" as the final text in this anthology, for reasons we discuss in our introduction to this story we do not locate her within the nineteenth-century tradition of regionalism as we illustrate it here. Therefore we have not included Cather on the "Chronology of First Regional Publications" and have not provided a bibliography for her. We have based our biographical sketch of Cather on Sharon O'Brien, *Willa Cather: The Emerging Voice* (New York: Oxford University Press, 1987).

In accordance with the publisher's editorial practice, some slight changes in orthography and punctuation have been made to regularize the text, although we have been careful to preserve the spelling and punctuation of the various dialect prose included in this anthology.

American Women Regionalists
1850–1910

A Norton Anthology

HARRIET BEECHER STOWE
1811–1896

Born June 14, 1811, in Litchfield, Connecticut, Harriet Beecher Stowe was the daughter of the Congregationalist minister Lyman Beecher, one of the most notable preachers of his day. Like Alice Cary, Stowe lost her mother, Roxana Foote, early in life, at the age of four. And, like Cary, she carried her mother's memory into adulthood, possibly creating Mara Lincoln, the protagonist of *The Pearl of Orr's Island,* whose mother dies giving birth to her, in remembrance of her own childhood grief. Although her older sister Catharine would offer support to Harriet and enlist her aid as a teacher in her Hartford Female Seminary and later in her Western Female Institute, Stowe turned primarily to her father for guidance. The profession of minister and the work of spiritual conversion served as the only model for adult life the evangelical Lyman could offer his children, and Stowe's biographers view Stowe's writing, with its emphasis on Christian conversion, as her attempt to create a vocation that would—in a feminine way—imitate that model.

In 1832 Lyman moved his family to Cincinnati, and there Stowe began to write, producing a children's geography that was published under her sister's name in 1833 and winning a literary prize in 1834 for "A New England Sketch," later retitled "Uncle Lot." In 1836 she married the widower Calvin Stowe, minister and professor at Lane Theological Seminary. When Calvin accepted a position at Bowdoin College in 1850, the family moved east to Brunswick, Maine. There, Stowe conceived and wrote *Uncle Tom's Cabin* and began *The Pearl of Orr's Island.* Later, when Calvin retired from Andover Theological Seminary in 1864, the Stowes settled in Hartford, Connecticut, where they would become next-door neighbors to Samuel and Olivia Clemens.

In light of the conditions under which she worked, Stowe was a strikingly productive and successful writer, achieving wide popularity both at home and abroad with the publication of *Uncle Tom's Cabin* (1851–52). Annie Fields, Stowe's close friend and biographer, describes Stowe writing her novels while simultaneously supervising the cooking and attending to household chores. In addition, despite her own periods of physical ill health and psychological depression, Stowe provided emotional support for the chronically depressed Calvin and financial stability for both her husband and children (six survived infancy). Stowe spent the last years of her life, widowed after 1886, in her Florida home; no longer writing, her mind wandering, she died July 1, 1896, the same year that Sarah Orne Jewett would publish *The Country of the Pointed Firs.* She included among her friends her publisher James T. Fields, Nathaniel Hawthorne and his wife, Lady Byron, and George Eliot.

° ° °

While Harriet Beecher Stowe has always been best known for her antislavery novel, she wrote equally fine fiction as a regionalist. In *Uncle Tom's Cabin,* and in her second antislavery novel, *Dred* (1856), Stowe found a way to "preach" like her father, brothers, and husband. In her regional fiction, however, she develops a different kind of storytelling power. We can see the origins of her interest in regional subjects in "Uncle Lot" and in the series of sketches collected in *The Mayflower* (1843). And in "Uncle Lot" we can see as well her association of regional material with the issue of storytelling. "And so I am to write a story—but of what, and where?" Stowe asks at the beginning of "Uncle Lot." She chooses to answer this question by writing about New England, and by introducing into her fiction a character who is not "our hero," who is neither young, nor charming, nor marriageable. Her interest in the character of Uncle Lot displaces romance as the inevitable subject of women's writing; instead she identifies the marginal, the peculiar, the regional as a space within which women might begin to tell some truths about their lives. Yet Stowe stops short of giving voice to women in "Uncle Lot"; she portrays Uncle Lot's daughter Grace Griswold as "lively and chatty," yet Grace does not really speak in the sketch. Later writers, such as Rose Terry Cooke, would do more than create a space for women to speak. In "Miss Beulah's Bonnet," for example, Cooke gives to a female character, Aunt Beulah, the distinctive regional interest Stowe locates in Uncle Lot. However, she also makes her the central focus of the sketch and creates her as a character who feels free to say "I never did like boys," thus giving Aunt Beulah a literary authority Stowe stops short of granting to either Lot or Grace Griswold.

Stowe did not return to regional fiction until she had moved back to New England and written *Uncle Tom's Cabin*. She began work on *The Pearl of Orr's Island* in 1852, the same year that Alice Cary published her first volume of Clovernook sketches. Called on to defend the veracity of *Uncle Tom's Cabin*, Stowe interrupted work on what she called her "Maine story" to write *A Key to "Uncle Tom's Cabin"* (1853), in which she identified the factual sources for her fiction; she did not return to *The Pearl of Orr's Island* until 1860, the year after she published the first of her New England fictions, *The Minister's Wooing* (1859). *The Pearl of Orr's Island* was published serially in *The Independent* from January 3, 1861 until April 4, 1861, and then again from December 1, 1861, until April 24, 1862; again Stowe had interrupted work on her Maine story, this time in favor of completing *Agnes of Sorrento*, which was appearing concurrently with *The Pearl of Orr's Island*.

Both Annie Fields and Sarah Orne Jewett saw *The Pearl of Orr's Island* as flawed, although Jewett called the book "divine," "exquisite," and "perfectly original and strong" (*Letters* 46). While Stowe's story obviously suffers from the interruptions surrounding the composition of the text, one might argue that Stowe interrupted her work on *The Pearl of Orr's Island* because she had difficulty imagining how to continue it. Unlike her contemporary, Alice Cary, who gave narrative agency and authority to women's voices in her regional fiction and who saw regionalism as the opportunity to speak subjectively about her own and other women's lives, Stowe could not imagine a female character as storyteller; she could not fully locate or imagine herself within her fiction. Perhaps class associations that she could not overcome are at issue here. While Roxy and Ruey talk freely and tell stories, they are clearly of a different class from either the heroine or the narrator. When faced with the possibility of telling about her feelings or experience, Mara Lincoln falls silent "for it was not the little maiden's way to speak when anything thwarted or hurt her, but rather to fold all her feelings and thoughts inward." Working class women speak, middle class women keep quiet; and Stowe as writer cannot find her way out of this dilemma. Annie Fields writes in her biography that Stowe "loved to gather a small circle of friends around a fireside, when she easily took the lead in fun and storytelling. This was her own ground, and upon it she was not to be outdone" (376). In her fiction only men—Captain Kittridge, Horace Holyoke, Sam Lawson—occupy this ground that in life was her own.

Though she was unable to establish woman as storyteller, going so far as to sign the Preface to *Oldtown Folks* "H.H." for Horace Holyoke, the novel's male narrator, Stowe contributed much to the development of the themes and images that recur in regionalist writing. *The Pearl of Orr's Island* tells the story of a motherless child who longs always for her mother; many later regional writers would structure their fiction around finding a lost mother. In "Uncle Lot" Stowe associates New England landscape and masculine character; in *The Pearl of Orr's Island* Roxy and Ruey reflect "that cold, clear, severe climate of the North" where, once rooted, people never age and, like the Toothacre sisters, "can always be found, like last year's mullein stalks, upright, dry and seedy, warranted to last for any length of time." Moreover, in this text many of Stowe's descriptions of place and landscape can be read as referring to women's experience and particularly to the female body.

Additionally, in texts like *Oldtown Folks* (1869) and "The Minister's House-keeper" (1872), Stowe begins the process, central to regional fiction, of shifting the center of perception from viewing the lives of rural women as objects of a narrator's story to viewing them as subjects of their own lives and stories, a shift that begins to locate sympathy for women as a feature of regionalism. Based on her husband's memories of growing up in Natick, Massachusetts, *Oldtown Folks* introduces Sam Lawson, do-nothing and raconteur, whom Stowe would invoke throughout the 1870s to tell still more New England stories like the one anthologized here. Stowe models Sam and his wife, Hepsy, on Rip and Dame Van Winkle, but Stowe revises Irving's tale. Like Rip, Sam treats boys and animals kindly and for his handiness and gossip finds a "warm corner" in most households except his own; indeed Sam has kindness for everyone except his wife and time for everything except the work of supporting his family. The narrator of *Oldtown Folks*, Horace Holyoke, makes it clear that although he likes and even admires Sam Lawson he does not endorse Sam's behavior or attitude towards Hepsy. Though Hepsy is a scold, Horace does not make her the story's scapegoat but rather directs our sympathies toward her. In Stowe's interpretation of New England life, every village must have its do-nothing as compensation for the general Yankee emphasis on work. The woman with six children to feed, however, like Hepsy, cannot choose the pleasures of this role, and therefore Stowe defends herself in standing up for Hepsy.

Indeed, the work of the woman of "faculty"—the woman who, like Roxy and Ruey, has a genius for managing the practical side of life—increases according to her ability, as witness the instance of Huldy, in "The Minister's House-keeper." In telling this story from Huldy's perspective, Sam reveals his sympa-thy for women who are not his wife and shifts the center of perception to a position inside women's culture. From this position we get a rather different view of the relative value of male and female creatures, with their respective commitments to "larning" and "temporals," from that usually afforded by the pulpit or the Hebrew text. The vehicle of a male narrator freed Stowe to write about a character probably modeled on her husband Calvin, who was notoriously useless to Stowe in the practical work of raising her own six children. Implicitly "The Minister's Housekeeper" takes the process of shifting values even further by suggesting that Huldy serves as a more effective spiritual force than the parson. With her flowers and her singing, she provides the material and inspiration for the parson's invigorated sermons and the occasion for his vision of the "New Jerusalem."

Uncle Lot

And so I am to write a story—but of what, and where? Shall it be radiant with the sky of Italy? or eloquent with the beau ideal[1] of Greece? Shall it breathe odor and languor from the orient, or chivalry from the occident? or gayety from France? or vigor from England? No, no; these are all too old—too romance-like—too obviously picturesque for me. No; let me turn to my own land—my own New England; the land of bright fires and strong hearts; the land of deeds, and not of words; the land of fruits, and not of flowers; the land often spoken against, yet always respected; "the latchet of whose shoes the nations of the earth are not worthy to unloose."[2]

Now, from this very heroic apostrophe, you may suppose that I have something very heroic to tell. By no means. It is merely a little introductory breeze of patriotism, such as occasionally brushes over every mind, bearing on its wings the remembrance of all we ever loved or cherished in the land of our early years; and if it should seem to be rodomontade[3] to any people in other parts of the earth, let them only imagine it to be said about "Old Kentuck," old England, or any other corner of the world in which they happened to be born and they will find it quite rational.

But, as touching our story, it is time to begin. Did you ever see the little village of Newbury, in New England? I dare say you never did; for it was just one of those out-of-the-way places where nobody ever came unless they came on purpose: a green little hollow, wedged like a bird's nest between half a dozen high hills, that kept off the wind and kept out foreigners; so that the little place was as straitly *sui generis*[4] as if there were not another in the world. The inhabitants were all of that respectable old standfast family who make it a point to be born, bred, married, to die, and be buried all in the selfsame spot. There were just so many houses, and just so many people lived in them; and nobody ever seemed to be sick, or to die either, at least while I was there. The natives grew old till they could not grow any older, and then they stood still, and *lasted* from generation to generation. There was, too, an unchangeability about all the externals of Newbury. Here was a red house, and there was a brown house, and across the way was a yellow house; and there was a straggling rail fence or a tribe of mullein

1. Beautiful ideal, model of perfection.
2. See Mark 1.7; Luke 3.16; John 1.27.
3. Boasting, bragging, big talk.
4. Of its own kind; in a class by itself; unique.

stalks between. The minister lived here, and Squire Moses lived there, and Deacon Hart lived under the hill, and Messrs. Nadab and Abihu Peters lived by the crossroad, and the old "widder" Smith lived by the meeting-house, and Ebenezer Camp kept a shoemaker's shop on one side, and Patience Mosely kept a milliner's shop in front; and there was old Comfort Scran, who kept store for the whole town, and sold axeheads, brass thimbles, licorice balls, fancy handkerchiefs, and everything else you can think of. Here, too, was the general post-office, where you might see letters marvelously folded, directed wrong side upward, stamped with a thimble, and superscribed to some of the Dollys, or Pollys, or Peters, or Moseses aforenamed or not named.

For the rest, as to manners, morals, arts, and sciences, the people in Newbury always went to their parties at three o'clock in the afternoon, and came home before dark; always stopped all work the minute the sun was down on Saturday night; always went to meeting on Sunday; had a schoolhouse with all the ordinary inconveniences; were in neighborly charity with each other; read their Bibles, feared their God, and were content with such things as they had—the best philosophy, after all. Such was the place into which Master James Benton made an irruption in the year eighteen hundred and no matter what. Now, this James is to be our hero, and he is just the hero for a sensation—at least, so you would have thought, if you had been in Newbury the week after his arrival. Master James was one of those whole-hearted, energetic Yankees, who rise in the world as naturally as cork does in water. He possessed a great share of that characteristic national trait so happily denominated "cuteness," which signifies an ability to do everything without trying, and to know everything without learning, and to make more use of one's ignorance than other people do of their knowledge. This quality in James was mingled with an elasticity of animal spirits, a buoyant cheerfulness of mind, which, though found in the New England character, perhaps, as often as anywhere else, is not ordinarily regarded as one of its distinguishing traits.

As to the personal appearance of our hero, we have not much to say of it—not half so much as the girls in Newbury found it necessary to remark, the first Sabbath that he shone out in the meeting-house. There was a saucy frankness of countenance, a knowing roguery of eye, a joviality and prankishness of demeanor, that was wonderfully captivating, especially to the ladies.

It is true that Master James had an uncommonly comfortable opinion of himself, a full faith that there was nothing in creation that he could not learn and could not do; and this faith was maintained with an abounding and triumphant joyfulness, that fairly carried your sympathies along with him, and made you feel quite as much delighted with his qualifications and prospects as he felt himself. There are two kinds of self-sufficiency: one is amusing, and the other is provoking. His was the amusing kind. It seemed, in truth, to be only the buoyancy and overflow of a vivacious mind, delighted with everything delightful, in himself or others. He was always ready to magnify his own praise, but quite as ready to exalt his neighbor, if the channel of discourse ran that way: his own perfections being more completely within his knowledge, he rejoiced in them more constantly; but, if those of any one else came within the same range, he was quite as much astonished and edified as if they had been his own.

Master James, at the time of his transit to the town of Newbury, was only eighteen years of age; so that it was difficult to say which predominated in him most, the boy or the man. The belief that he could, and the determination that he would, be something in the world had caused him to abandon his home, and, with all his worldly effects tied in a blue cotton pocket-handkerchief, to proceed to seek his fortune in Newbury. And never did stranger in Yankee village rise to promotion with more unparalleled rapidity, or boast a greater plurality of employment. He figured as schoolmaster all the week, and as chorister[5] on Sundays, and taught singing and reading in the evenings, besides studying Latin and Greek with the minister, nobody knew when; thus fitting for college, while he seemed to be doing everything else in the world besides.

James understood every art and craft of popularity, and made himself mightily at home in all the chimney-corners of the region round about; knew the geography of everybody's cider barrel and apple bin, helping himself and every one else therefrom with all bountifulness; rejoicing in the good things of this life, devouring the old ladies' doughnuts and pumpkin pies with most flattering appetite, and appearing equally to relish every body and thing that came in his way.

The degree and versatility of his acquirements were truly wonderful. He knew all about arithmetic and history, and all about catching squirrels and planting corn; made poetry and hoe-handles with equal celerity; wound yarn and took out grease spots for old ladies, and made nosegays and knick-knacks for young ones; caught trout Saturday afternoons, and discussed doctrines on Sundays, with equal adroitness and effect. In short, Mr. James moved on through the place

> "Victorious,
> Happy and glorious,"[6]

welcomed and privileged by everybody in every place; and when he had told his last ghost story, and fairly flourished himself out of doors at the close of a long winter's evening, you might see the hard face of the good man of the house still phosphorescent with his departing radiance, and hear him exclaim, in a paroxysm of admiration, that "Jemeses talk re'ly did beat all; that he was sartainly most a miraculous cre'tur!"

It was wonderfully contrary to the buoyant activity of Master

---

5. Member of a church choir; also choir leader.
6. From "God Save the Queen," the British national anthem.

James's mind to keep a school. He had, moreover, so much of the boy and the rogue in his composition, that he could not be strict with the iniquities of the curly pates[7] under his charge; and when he saw how determinately every little heart was boiling over with mischief and motion, he felt in his soul more disposed to join in and help them to a frolic than to lay justice to the line, as was meet.[8] This would have made a sad case, had it not been that the activity of the master's mind communicated itself to his charge, just as the reaction of one brisk little spring will fill a manufactory[9] with motion; so that there was more of an impulse towards study in the golden, good-natured day of James Benton than in the time of all that went before or came after him.

But when "school was out," James's spirits foamed over as naturally as a tumbler of soda water, and he could jump over benches and burst out of doors with as much rapture as the veriest little elf in his company. Then you might have seen him stepping homeward with a most felicitous expression of countenance, occasionally reaching his hand through the fence for a bunch of currants, or over it after a flower, or bursting into some back yard to help an old lady empty her washtub, or stopping to pay his devoirs[1] to Aunt This or Mistress That, for James well knew the importance of the "powers that be," and always kept the sunny side of the old ladies.

We shall not answer for James's general flirtations, which were sundry and manifold; for he had just the kindly heart that fell in love with everything in feminine shape that came in his way, and if he had not been blessed with an equal facility in falling out again, we do not know what ever would have become of him. But at length he came into an abiding captivity, and it is quite time that he should; for having devoted thus much space to the illustration of our hero, it is fit we should do something in behalf of our heroine; and, therefore, we must beg the reader's attention while we draw a diagram or two that will assist him in gaining a right idea of her.

Do you see yonder brown house, with its broad roof sloping almost to the ground on one side, and a great, unsupported sunbonnet of a piazza shooting out over the front door? You must often have noticed it; you have seen its tall wellsweep,[2] relieved against the clear evening sky, or observed the feather beds and bolsters lounging out of its chamber windows on a still summer morning; you recollect its gate, that swung with a chain and a great stone; its pantry window, latticed with little brown slabs,[3] and looking out upon a forest of beanpoles. You remember the zephyrs[4] that used to play among its pea brush, and shake the long tassels of its corn patch, and how vainly any zephyr

---

7. Heads.
8. Fit.
9. Something that is manufactured.
1. Pay his respects.
2. A long pole, pivoted on the top of a high post, by means of which water is raised in a bucket attached

to the end of the pole.
3. Rough outside planks of timber cut from a log or tree trunk before it is sawed into planks or squared for a beam.
4. Breezes.

might essay to perform similar flirtations with the considerate cabbages that were solemnly vegetating near by. Then there was the
whole neighborhood of purple-leaved beets and feathery parsnips;
there were the billows of gooseberry bushes rolled up by the fence,
interspersed with rows of quince-trees; and far off in one corner was
one little patch, penuriously devoted to ornament, which flamed with
marigolds, poppies, snappers, and four-o'clocks. Then there was a little
box by itself with one rose geranium in it, which seemed to look around
the garden as much like a stranger as a French dancing-master in a
Yankee meeting-house.

That is the dwelling of Uncle Lot Griswold. Uncle Lot, as he was
commonly called, had a character that a painter would sketch for its
lights and contrasts rather than its symmetry. He was a chestnut burr,
abounding with briers without and with substantial goodness within.
He had the strong-grained practical sense, the calculating worldly
wisdom of his class of people in New England; he had, too, a kindly
heart; but all the strata of his character were crossed by a vein of surly
petulance, that, halfway between joke and earnest, colored everything
that he said and did.

If you asked a favor of Uncle Lot, he generally kept you arguing half
an hour, to prove that you really needed it, and to tell you that he could
not all the while be troubled with helping one body or another, all
which time you might observe him regularly making his preparations
to grant your request, and see, by an odd glimmer of his eye, that he
was preparing to let you hear the "conclusion of the whole matter,"
which was, "Well, well—I guess—I'll go, on the *hull*[5] —I s'pose I must,
at least;" so off he would go and work while the day lasted, and then
wind up with a farewell exhortation "not to be a-callin' on your neighbors when you could get along without." If any of Uncle Lot's neighbors were in any trouble, he was always at hand to tell them that "they
should n't 'a' done so;" that "it was strange they could n't had more
sense;" and then to close his exhortations by laboring more diligently
than any to bring them out of their difficulties, groaning in spirit,
meanwhile, that folks would make people so much trouble.

"Uncle Lot, father wants to know if you will lend him your hoe
today," says a little boy, making his way across a cornfield.

"Why don't your father use his own hoe?"

"Ours is broke."

"Broke! How came it broke?"

"I broke it yesterday, trying to hit a squirrel."

"What business had you to be hittin' squirrels with a hoe?—say!"

"But father wants to borrow yours."

"Why don't you have that mended? It's a great pester to have
everybody usin' a body's things."

"Well, I can borrow one somewhere else, I suppose," says the

---

5. Whole.

suppliant. After the boy has stumbled across the ploughed ground, and is fairly over the fence, Uncle Lot calls,—

"Hallo, there, you little rascal! what are you goin' off without the hoe for?"

"I did n't know as you meant to lend it."

"I did n't say I would n't, did I? Here, come and take it—stay, I'll bring it; and do tell your father not to be a-lettin' you hunt squirrels with his hoes next time."

Uncle Lot's household consisted of Aunt Sally, his wife, and an only son and daughter; the son, at the time our story begins, was at a neighboring literary institution. Aunt Sally was precisely as clever, as easy to be entreated, and kindly in externals, as her helpmate was the reverse. She was one of those respectable, pleasant old ladies whom you might often have met on the way to church on a Sunday, equipped with a great fan and a psalm-book, and carrying some dried orange peel or a stalk of fennel, to give to the children if they were sleepy in meeting. She was as cheerful and domestic as the teakettle that sung by her kitchen fire, and slipped along among Uncle Lot's angles and peculiarities as if there never was anything the matter in the world; and the same mantle of sunshine seemed to have fallen on Miss Grace, her only daughter.

Pretty in her person and pleasant in her ways, endowed with native self-possession and address, lively and chatty, having a mind and a will of her own, yet good-humored withal, Miss Grace was a universal favorite. It would have puzzled a city lady to understand how Grace, who never was out of Newbury in her life, knew the way to speak, and act, and behave, on all occasions, exactly as if she had been taught how. She was just one of those wild flowers which you may sometimes see waving its little head in the woods, and looking so civilized and garden-like, that you wonder if it really did come up and grow there by nature. She was an adept in all household concerns, and there was something amazingly pretty in her energetic way of bustling about, and "putting things to rights." Like most Yankee damsels, she had a longing after the tree of knowledge, and, having exhausted the literary fountains of a district school, she fell to reading whatsoever came in her way. True, she had but little to read; but what she perused she had her own thoughts upon, so that a person of information, in talking with her, would feel a constant wondering pleasure to find that she had so much more to say of this, that, and the other thing than he expected.

Uncle Lot, like every one else, felt the magical brightness of his daughter, and was delighted with her praises, as might be discerned by his often finding occasion to remark that "he didn't see why the boys need to be all the time a-comin' to see Grace, for she was nothing so extraor'nary, after all." About all matters and things at home she generally had her own way, while Uncle Lot would scold and give up with a regular good grace that was quite creditable.

"Father," says Grace, "I want to have a party next week."

"You sha'n't go to havin' your parties, Grace. I always have to eat bits and ends a fortnight after you have one, and I won't have it so." And so Uncle Lot walked out, and Aunt Sally and Miss Grace proceeded to make the cake and pies for the party.

When Uncle Lot came home, he saw a long array of pies and rows of cakes on the kitchen table.

"Grace—Grace—Grace, I say! What is all this here flummery[6] for?"

"Why, it is to eat, father," said Grace, with a good-natured look of consciousness.

Uncle Lot tried his best to look sour; but his visage began to wax comical as he looked at his merry daughter; so he said nothing, but quietly sat down to his dinner.

"Father," said Grace, after dinner, "we shall want two more candlesticks next week."

"Why, can't you have your party with what you've got?"

"No, father, we want two more."

"I can't afford it, Grace—there's no sort of use on't—and you sha'n't have any."

"Oh, father, now do," said Grace.

"I won't, neither," said Uncle Lot, as he sallied out of the house, and took the road to Comfort Scran's store.

In half an hour he returned again; and fumbling in his pocket, and drawing forth a candlestick, leveled it at Grace.

"There's your candlestick."

"But, father, I said I wanted two."

"Why, can't you make one do?"

"No, I can't; I must have two."

"Well, then, there's t'other; and here's a fol-de-rol[7] for you to tie round your neck." So saying, he bolted for the door, and took himself off with all speed. It was much after this fashion that matters commonly went on in the brown house.

But having tarried long on the way, we must proceed with the main story.

James thought Miss Grace was a glorious girl; and as to what Miss Grace thought of Master James, perhaps it would not have been developed had she not been called to stand on the defensive for him with Uncle Lot. For, from the time that the whole village of Newbury began to be wholly given unto the praise of Master James, Uncle Lot set his face as a flint against him—from the laudable fear of following the multitude. He therefore made conscience of stoutly gainsaying everything that was said in his behalf, which, as James was in high favor with Aunt Sally, he had frequent opportunities to do.

So when Miss Grace perceived that Uncle Lot did not like our hero as much as he ought to do, she, of course, was bound to like him well

---

6. Trifles, useless trappings or ornaments, non-sense; also the name given to various sweet dishes made with milk, flour, eggs, and sugar.
7. A gewgaw, trifle; a flimsy thing.

enough to make up for it. Certain it is that they were remarkably happy in finding opportunities of being acquainted; that James waited on her, as a matter of course, from singing-school; that he volunteered making a new box for her geranium on an improved plan; and above all, that he was remarkably particular in his attentions to Aunt Sally—a stroke of policy which showed that James had a natural genius for this sort of matters. Even when emerging from the meeting-house in full glory, with flute and psalm-book under his arm, he would stop to ask her how she did; and if 't was cold weather, he would carry her foot-stove[8] all the way home from meeting, discoursing upon the sermon and other serious matters, as Aunt Sally observed, "in the pleasantest, prettiest way that ever ye see." This flute was one of the crying sins of James in the eyes of Uncle Lot. James was particularly fond of it, because he had learned to play on it by intuition; and on the decease of the old pitchpipe, which was slain by a fall from the gallery, he took the liberty to introduce the flute in its place. For this and other sins, and for the good reasons above named, Uncle Lot's countenance was not towards James, neither could he be moved to him-ward by any manner of means.

To all Aunt Sally's good words and kind speeches, he had only to say that "he didn't like him; that he hated to see him a-manifesting and glorifying there in the front gallery Sundays, and a-acting everywhere as if he was master of all: he didn't like it and he wouldn't." But our hero was no whit cast down or discomfited by the malcontent aspect of Uncle Lot. On the contrary, when report was made to him of divers[9] of his hard speeches, he only shrugged his shoulders, with a very satisfied air, and remarked that "he knew a thing or two for all that."

"Why, James," said his companion and chief counselor, "do you think Grace likes you?"

"I don't know," said our hero, with a comfortable appearance of certainty.

"But you can't get her, James, if Uncle Lot is cross about it."

"Fudge! I can make Uncle Lot like me if I have a mind to try."

"Well then, Jim, you'll have to give up that flute of yours, I tell you now."

"Fa, sol, la—I can make him like me and my flute too."

"Why, how will you do it?"

"Oh, I'll work it," said our hero.

"Well, Jim, I tell you now, you don't know Uncle Lot if you say so: for he is just the *settest* crittur in his way that ever you saw."

"I do know Uncle Lot, though, better than most folks; he is no more cross than I am; and as to his being set, you have nothing to do but make him think he is in his own way when he is in yours—that is all."

"Well," said the other, "but you see I don't believe it."

8. A box with a pan for live coals, used to keep the feet warm.   9. Various, sundry.

"And I'll bet you a gray squirrel that I'll go there this very evening, and get him to like me and my flute both," said James.

Accordingly the late sunshine of that afternoon shone full on the yellow buttons of James as he proceeded to the place of conflict. It was a bright, beautiful evening. A thunder-storm had just cleared away, and the silver clouds lay rolled up in masses around the setting sun; the raindrops were sparkling and winking to each other over the ends of the leaves, and all the bluebirds and robins, breaking forth into song, made the little green valley as merry as a musical box.

James's soul was always overflowing with that kind of poetry which consists in feeling unspeakably happy; and it is not to be wondered at, considering where he was going, that he should feel in a double ecstasy on the present occasion. He stepped gayly along, occasionally springing over a fence to the right to see whether the rain had swollen the trout brook, or to the left to notice the ripening of Mr. Somebody's watermelons—for James always had an eye on all his neighbors' matters as well as his own.

In this way he proceeded till he arrived at the picket fence that marked the commencement of Uncle Lot's ground. Here he stopped to consider. Just then four or five sheep walked up, and began also to consider a loose picket, which was hanging just ready to drop off; and James began to look at the sheep. "Well, mister," said he, as he observed the leader judiciously drawing himself through the gap, "in with you—just what I wanted;" and having waited a moment to ascertain that all the company were likely to follow, he ran with all haste towards the house, and swinging open the gate, pressed all breathless to the door.

"Uncle Lot, there are four or five sheep in your garden!" Uncle Lot dropped his whetstone and scythe.

"I'll drive them out," said our hero; and with that, he ran down the garden alley, and made a furious descent on the enemy; bestirring himself, as Bunyan[1] says, "lustily and with good courage," till every sheep had skipped out much quicker than it skipped in; and then, springing over the fence, he seized a great stone, and nailed on the picket so effectually that no sheep could possibly encourage the hope of getting in again. This was all the work of a minute, and he was back again; but so exceedingly out of breath that it was necessary for him to stop a moment and rest himself. Uncle Lot looked ungraciously satisfied.

"What under the canopy set you to scampering so?" said he; "I could 'a' driv out them critturs myself."

"If you are at all particular about driving them out yourself, I can let them in again," said James.

Uncle Lot looked at him with an odd sort of twinkle in the corner of his eye.

---

1. John Bunyan (1628–1688), noncomformist En-   famous of which is *The Pilgrim's Progress from this*
glish preacher and author of many works, the most   *World to that which is to come* (1678).

" 'Spose I must ask you to walk in," said he.

"Much obliged," said James; "but I am in a great hurry." So saying, he started in very business-like fashion towards the gate.

"You'd better jest stop a minute."

"Can't stay a minute."

"I don't see what possesses you to be all the while in sich a hurry; a body would think you had all creation on your shoulders."

"Just my situation, Uncle Lot," said James, swinging open the gate.

"Well, at any rate, have a drink of cider, can't ye?" said Uncle Lot, who was now quite engaged to have his own way in the case.

James found it convenient to accept this invitation, and Uncle Lot was twice as good-natured as if he had stayed in the first of the matter.

Once fairly forced into the premises, James thought fit to forget his long walk and excess of business, especially as about that moment Aunt Sally and Miss Grace returned from an afternoon call. You may be sure that the last thing these respectable ladies looked for was to find Uncle Lot and Master James tête-à-tête,[2] over a pitcher of cider; and when, as they entered, our hero looked up with something of a mischievous air, Miss Grace in particular was so puzzled that it took her at least a quarter of an hour to untie her bonnet strings. But James stayed, and acted the agreeable to perfection. First, he must needs go down into the garden to look at Uncle Lot's wonderful cabbages, and then he promenaded all around the corn patch, stopping every few moments and looking up with an appearance of great gratification, as if he had never seen such corn in his life; and then he examined Uncle Lot's favorite apple-tree with an expression of wonderful interest.

"I never!" he broke forth, having stationed himself against the fence opposite to it; "what kind of an apple-tree is that?"

"It's a bellflower, or somethin' another," said Uncle Lot.

"Why, where did you get it? I never saw such apples!" said our hero, with his eyes still fixed on the tree.

Uncle Lot pulled up a stalk or two of weeds, and threw them over the fence, just to show that he did not care anything about the matter; and then he came up and stood by James.

"Nothin' so remarkable, as I know on," said he.

Just then Grace came to say that supper was ready. Once seated at table, it was astonishing to see the perfect and smiling assurance with which our hero continued his addresses to Uncle Lot. It sometimes goes a great way towards making people like us to take it for granted that they do already; and upon this principle James proceeded. He talked, laughed, told stories, and joked with the most fearless assurance, occasionally seconding his words by looking Uncle Lot in the face, with a countenance so full of good will as would have melted any snowdrift of prejudices in the world.

James also had one natural accomplishment, more courtier-like than

---

2. Literally, head to head; a private conversation between two people.

all the diplomacy in Europe, and that was the gift of feeling a *real* interest for anybody in five minutes; so that, if he began to please in jest, he generally ended in earnest. With great simplicity of mind, he had a natural tact for seeing into others, and watched their motions with the same delight with which a child gazes at the wheels and springs of a watch, to "see what it will do."

The rough exterior and latent kindness of Uncle Lot were quite a spirit-stirring study; and when tea was over, as he and Grace happened to be standing together in the front door, he broke forth,—

"I do really like your father, Grace!"

"Do you?" said Grace.

"Yes, I do. He has something in him, and I like him all the better for having to fish it out."

"Well, I hope you will make him like you," said Grace unconsciously; and then she stopped, and looked a little ashamed.

James was too well bred to see this, or look as if Grace meant any more than she said,—a kind of breeding not always attendant on more fashionable polish,—so he only answered,—

"I think I shall, Grace, though I doubt whether I can get him to own it."

"He is the kindest man that ever was," said Grace; "and he always acts as if he was ashamed of it."

James turned a little away, and looked at the bright evening sky, which was glowing like a calm, golden sea; and over it was the silver new moon, with one little star to hold the candle for her. He shook some bright drops off from a rosebush near by, and watched to see them shine as they fell, while Grace stood very quietly waiting for him to speak again.

"Grace," said he at last, "I am going to college this fall."

"So you told me yesterday," said Grace.

James stooped down over Grace's geranium, and began to busy himself with pulling off all the dead leaves, remarking in the meanwhile,—

"And if I do get him to like me, Grace, will you like me too?"

"I like you now very well," said Grace.

"Come, Grace, you know what I mean," said James, looking steadfastly at the top of the apple-tree.

"Well, I wish, then, you would understand what I mean without my saying any more about it," said Grace.

"Oh, to be sure I will!" said our hero, looking up with a very intelligent air; and so, as Aunt Sally would say, the matter was settled, with "no words about it."

Now shall we narrate how our hero, as he saw Uncle Lot approaching the door, had the impudence to take out his flute, and put the parts together, arranging and adjusting the stops with great composure?

"Uncle Lot," said he, looking up, "this is the best flute that ever I saw."

"I hate them tooting critturs," said Uncle Lot snappishly.

"I declare! I wonder how you can," said James; "for I do think they exceed"—

So saying, he put the flute to his mouth, and ran up and down a long flourish.

"There! what do you think of that?" said he, looking in Uncle Lot's face with much delight.

Uncle Lot turned and marched into the house, but soon faced to the right-about, and came out again, for James was fingering "Yankee Doodle"—that appropriate national air for the descendants of the Puritans.

Uncle Lot's patriotism began to bestir itself; and now, if it had been anything, as he said, but "that 'ere flute"—As it was, he looked more than once at James's fingers.

"How under the sun could you learn to do that?" said he.

"Oh, it's easy enough," said James, proceeding with another tune; and, having played it through, he stopped a moment to examine the joints of his flute, and in the meantime addressed Uncle Lot: "You can't think how grand this is for pitching tunes[3] —I always pitch the tunes on Sunday with it."

"Yes; but I don't think it's a right and fit instrument for the Lord's house," said Uncle Lot.

"Why not? It is only a kind of a long pitchpipe, you see," said James; "and, seeing the old one is broken, and this will answer, I don't see why it is not better than nothing."

"Why, yes, it may be better than nothing," said Uncle Lot; "but, as I always tell Grace and my wife, it ain't the right kind of instrument, after all; it ain't solemn."

"Solemn!" said James; "that is according as you work it: see here, now."

So saying, he struck up Old Hundred,[4] and proceeded through it with great perseverance.

"There, now!" said he.

"Well, well, I don't know but it is," said Uncle Lot; "but as I said at first, I don't like the look of it in meetin'."

"But yet you really think it is better than nothing," said James, "for you see I couldn't pitch my tunes without it."

"Maybe 't is," said Uncle Lot; "but that isn't sayin' much."

This, however, was enough for Master James, who soon after departed, with his flute in his pocket, and Grace's last words in his heart; soliloquizing as he shut the gate, "There, now, I hope Aunt Sally won't go to praising me; for, just so sure as she does, I shall have it all to do over again."

---

3. Setting the musical pitch by which the congregation could then attempt to keep in tune when singing hymns.

4. Tune set to the old version (1562) of Psalm 100, "Make a joyful noise unto the Lord."

James was right in his apprehension. Uncle Lot could be privately converted, but not brought to open confession; and when, the next morning, Aunt Sally remarked, in the kindness of her heart,—

"Well, I always knew you would come to like James," Uncle Lot only responded, "Who said I did like him?"

"But I'm sure you seemed to like him last night."

"Why, I couldn't turn him out o' doors, could I? I don't think nothin' of him but what I always did."

But it was to be remarked that Uncle Lot contented himself at this time with the mere general avowal, without running it into particulars, as was formerly his wont. It was evident that the ice had begun to melt, but it might have been a long time in dissolving, had not collateral incidents assisted.

It so happened that about this time George Griswold, the only son before referred to, returned to his native village, after having completed his theological studies at a neighboring institution. It is interesting to mark the gradual development of mind and heart, from the time that the white-headed, bashful boy quits the country village for college, to the period when he returns, a formed and matured man; to notice how gradually the rust of early prejudices begins to cleave from him—how his opinions, like his handwriting, pass from the cramped and limited forms of a country school into that confirmed and characteristic style which is to mark the man for life. In George this change was remarkably striking. He was endowed by nature with uncommon acuteness of feeling and fondness for reflection—qualities as likely as any to render a child backward and uninteresting in early life.

When he left Newbury for college, he was a taciturn and apparently phlegmatic boy, only evincing sensibility by blushing and looking particularly stupefied whenever anybody spoke to him. Vacation after vacation passed, and he returned more and more an altered being; and he who once shrank from the eye of the deacon, and was ready to sink if he met the minister, now moved about among the dignitaries of the place with all the composure of a superior being.

It was only to be regretted that, while the mind improved, the physical energies declined, and that every visit to his home found him paler, thinner, and less prepared in body for the sacred profession to which he had devoted himself. But now he was returned, a minister—a real minister, with a right to stand in the pulpit and preach; and what a joy and glory to Aunt Sally—and to Uncle Lot, if he were not ashamed to own it!

The first Sunday after he came, it was known far and near that George Griswold was to preach; and never was a more ready and expectant audience.

As the time for reading the first psalm approached, you might see the white-headed men turning their faces attentively towards the pulpit; the anxious and expectant old women, with their little black bonnets, bent forward to see him rise. There were the children looking, because everybody else looked; there was Uncle Lot in the front pew, his face considerably adjusted; there was Aunt Sally, seeming as pleased as a mother could seem; and Miss Grace, lifting her sweet face to her brother, like a flower to the sun; there was our friend James in the front gallery, his joyous countenance a little touched with sobriety and expectation; in short, a more embarrassingly attentive audience never greeted the first effort of a young minister. Under these circumstances there was something touching in the fervent self-forgetfulness which characterized the first exercises of the morning—something which moved every one in the house.

The devout poetry of his prayer, rich with the Orientalism of Scripture, and eloquent with the expression of strong yet chastened emotion, breathed over his audience like music, hushing every one to silence, and beguiling everyone to feeling. In the sermon, there was the strong intellectual nerve, the constant occurrence of argument and statement, which distinguishes a New England discourse; but it was touched with life by the intense, yet half-subdued, feeling with which he seemed to utter it. Like the rays of the sun, it enlightened and melted at the same moment.

The strong peculiarities of New England doctrine, involving, as they do, all the hidden machinery of mind, all the mystery of its divine relations and future progression, and all the tremendous uncertainties of its eternal good or ill, seemed to have dwelt in his mind, to have burned in his thoughts, to have wrestled with his powers, and they gave to his manner the fervency almost of another world; while the exceeding paleness of his countenance, and a tremulousness of voice that seemed to spring from bodily weakness, touched the strong workings of his mind with a pathetic interest, as if the being so early absorbed in another world could not be long for this.

When the services were over, the congregation dispersed with the air of people who had felt rather than heard; and all the criticism that followed was similar to that of old Deacon Hart,—an upright, shrewd man,—who, as he lingered a moment at the church door, turned and gazed with unwonted feeling at the young preacher.

"He's a blessed cre'tur!" said he, the tears actually making their way to his eyes; "I hain't been so near heaven this many a day. He's a blessed cre'tur of the Lord; that's my mind about him!"

As for our friend James, he was at first sobered, then deeply moved, and at last wholly absorbed by the discourse; and it was only when meeting was over that he began to think where he really was.

With all his versatile activity, James had a greater depth of mental capacity than he was himself aware of, and he began to feel a sort of electric affinity for the mind that had touched him in a way so new; and when he saw the mild minister standing at the foot of the pulpit stairs, he made directly towards him.

"I do want to hear more from you," said he, with a face full of earnestness; "may I walk home with you?"

"It is a long and warm walk," said George, smiling.

"Oh, I don't care for that, if it does not trouble *you*," said James; and leave being gained, you might have seen them slowly passing along under the trees, James pouring forth all the floods of inquiry which the sudden impulse of his mind had brought out, and supplying his guide with more questions and problems for solution than he could have gone through with in a month.

"I cannot answer all your questions now," said he, as they stopped at Uncle Lot's gate.

"Well, then, when will you?" said James eagerly. "Let me come home with you to-night?"

The minister smiled assent, and James departed, so full of new thoughts that he passed Grace without even seeing her. From that time a friendship commenced between the two which was a beautiful illustration of the affinities of opposites. It was like a friendship between morning and evening—all freshness and sunshine on one side, and all gentleness and peace on the other.

The young minister, worn by long-continued ill health, by the fervency of his own feelings, and the gravity of his own reasonings, found pleasure in the healthful buoyancy of a youthful, unexhausted mind, while James felt himself sobered and made better by the moonlight tranquillity of his friend. It is one mark of a superior mind to understand and be influenced by the superiority of others; and this was the case with James. The ascendancy which his new friend acquired over him was unlimited, and did more in a month towards consolidating and developing his character than all the four years' course of a college. Our religious habits are likely always to retain the impression of the first seal which stamped them, and in this case it was a peculiarly happy one. The calmness, the settled purpose, the mild devotion of his friend, formed a just alloy to the energetic and reckless buoyancy of James's character, and awakened in him a set of feelings without which the most vigorous mind must be incomplete.

The effect of the ministrations of the young pastor, in awakening attention to the subjects of his calling in the village, was marked, and of a kind which brought pleasure to his own heart. But, like all other excitement, it tends to exhaustion, and it was not long before he sensibly felt the decline of the powers of life. To the best regulated mind there is something bitter in the relinquishment of projects for which we have been long and laboriously preparing, and there is something far more bitter in crossing the long-cherished expectations of friends. All this George felt. He could not bear to look on his mother, hanging on his words and following his steps with eyes of almost childish delight— on his singular father, whose whole earthly ambition was bound up in his success, and think how soon the "candle of their old age" must be put out. When he returned from a successful effort, it was painful to see the old man, so evidently delighted, and so anxious to conceal his triumph, as he would seat himself in his chair, and begin with,

"George, that 'ere doctrine is rather of a puzzler; but you seem to think you've got the run on't. I should re'ly like to know what business you have to think you know better than other folks about it;" and, though he would cavil most courageously at all George's explanations, yet you might perceive, through all, that he was inly uplifted to hear how his boy could talk.

If George was engaged in argument with anyone else, he would sit by, with his head bowed down, looking out from under his shaggy eyebrows with a shamefaced satisfaction very unusual with him. Expressions of affection from the naturally gentle are not half so touching as those which are forced out from the hard-favored and severe; and George was affected, even to pain, by the evident pride and regard of his father.

"He never said so much to anybody before," thought he, "and what will he do if I die?"

In such thoughts as these Grace found her brother engaged one still autumn morning, as he stood leaning against the garden fence.

"What are you solemnizing here for, this bright day, brother George?" said she, as she bounded down the alley.

The young man turned, and looked on her happy face with a sort of twilight smile.

"How happy you are, Grace!" said he.

"To be sure I am; and you ought to be too, because you are better."

"I am happy, Grace—that is, I hope I shall be."

"You are sick, I know you are," said Grace; "you look worn out. Oh, I wish your heart could *spring* once, as mine does."

"I am not well, dear Grace, and I fear I never shall be," said he, turning away, and fixing his eyes on the fading trees opposite.

"Oh George! dear George, don't, don't say *that*, you'll break all our hearts," said Grace, with tears in her own eyes.

"Yes, but it is *true*, sister: I do not feel it on my own account so much as— However," he added, "it will all be the same in heaven."

It was but a week after this that a violent cold hastened the progress of debility into a confirmed malady. He sunk very fast. Aunt Sally, with the self-deceit of a fond and cheerful heart, thought every day that "he *would* be better," and Uncle Lot resisted conviction with all the obstinate pertinacity of his character, while the sick man felt that he had not the heart to undeceive them.

James was now at the house every day, exhausting all his energy and invention in the case of his friend; and anyone who had seen him in his hours of recklessness and glee, could scarcely recognize him as the being whose step was so careful, whose eye so watchful, whose voice and touch were so gentle, as he moved around the sick-bed. But the same quickness which makes a mind buoyant in gladness often makes it gentlest and most sympathetic in sorrow.

It was now nearly morning in the sick-room. George had been restless and feverish all night; but towards day he fell into a slight slumber, and James sat by his side, almost holding his breath lest he should waken him. It was yet dusk, but the sky was brightening with a solemn glow, and the stars were beginning to disappear; all, save the bright and morning one, which, standing alone in the east, looked tenderly through the casement, like the eye of our Heavenly Father, watching over us when all earthly friendships are fading.

George awoke with a placid expression of countenance, and fixing his eyes on the brightening sky, murmured faintly,—

> "The sweet, immortal morning sheds
> Its blushes round the spheres."[5]

A moment after, a shade passed over his face; he pressed his fingers over his eyes, and the tears dropped silently on his pillow.

"George! *dear* George!" said James, bending over him.

"It's my friends—it's my father—my mother," said he faintly.

"Jesus Christ will watch over them," said James soothingly.

"Oh, yes, I know He will; for *He* loved his own which were in the world; He loved them unto the end. But I am dying—and before I have done any good."

"Oh, do not say so," said James; "think, think what you have done, if only for *me*. God bless you for it! God *will* bless you for it; it will follow you to heaven; it will bring me there. Yes, I will do as you have taught me. I will give my life, my soul, my whole strength to it; and then you will not have lived in vain."

George smiled, and looked upward; "his face was as that of an angel;"[6] and James, in his warmth, continued,—

"It is not I alone who can say this; we all bless you; every one in his place blesses you; you will be had in everlasting remembrance by some hearts here, I know."

"Bless God!" said George.

"We do," said James. "I bless him that I ever knew you; we all bless him, and we love you, and shall forever."

The glow that had kindled over the pale face of the invalid again faded as he said,—

"But, James, I must—I ought to—tell my father and mother; I ought to, and how can I?"

At that moment the door opened, and Uncle Lot made his appearance. He seemed struck with the paleness of George's face; and coming to the side of the bed, he felt his pulse, and laid his hand anxiously on his forehead, and, clearing his voice several times, inquired "if he didn't feel a little better."

"No, father," said George; then taking his hand, he looked anxiously in his face, and seemed to hesitate a moment. "Father," he began, "you know that we ought to submit to God."

There was something in his expression at this moment which flashed

---

5. Most likely, lines from a familiar hymn.   6. See Acts 6.15.

the truth into the old man's mind. He dropped his son's hand with an exclamation of agony, and, turning quickly, left the room.

"Father! father!" said Grace, trying to rouse him, as he stood with his arms folded by the kitchen window.

"Get away, child!" said he roughly.

"Father, mother says breakfast is ready."

"I don't want any breakfast," said he, turning short about. "Sally, what are you fixing in that 'ere porringer?"

"Oh, it's only a little tea for George; 't will comfort him up, and make him feel better, poor fellow."

"You won't make him feel better—he's gone," said Uncle Lot hoarsely.

"Oh, dear heart, no!" said Aunt Sally.

"Be still a-contradicting me; I won't be contradicted all the time by nobody. The short of the case is, that George is goin' to die just as we've got him ready to be a minister and all; and I wish to pity I was in my grave myself, and so"—said Uncle Lot, as he plunged out of the door, and shut it after him.

It is well for a man that there is one Being who sees the suffering heart as it is, and not as it manifests itself through the repellances of outward infirmity, and who, perhaps, feels more for the stern and wayward than for those whose gentler feelings win for them human sympathy. With all his singularities, there was in the heart of Uncle Lot a depth of religious sincerity; but there are few characters where religion does anything more than struggle with natural defect, and modify what would else be far worse.

In this hour of trial, all the native obstinacy and pertinacity of the old man's character rose, and while he felt the necessity of submission, it seemed impossible to submit; and thus reproaching himself, struggling in vain to repress the murmurs of nature, repulsing from him all external sympathy, his mind was "tempest-tossed, and not comforted."[7]

It was on the still afternoon of the following Sabbath that he was sent for, in haste, to the chamber of his son. He entered, and saw that the hour was come. The family were all there. Grace and James, side by side, bent over the dying one, and his mother sat afar off, with her face hid in her apron, "that she might not see the death of the child."[8] The aged minister was there, and the Bible lay open before him. The father walked to the side of the bed. He stood still, and gazed on the face now brightening with "life and immortality." The son lifted up his eyes; he saw his father, smiled, and put out his hand.

"I am glad you are come," said he.

"O George, to the pity, don't! don't smile on me so! I know what is coming; I have tried, and tried, and I can't, I can't have it so;" and his frame shook, and he sobbed audibly. The room was still as death; there

7. See Isaiah 54.11.　　　　8. See Genesis 21:16.

was none that seemed able to comfort him. At last the son repeated, in a sweet, but interrupted voice, those words of man's best Friend: "Let not your heart be troubled; in my Father's house are many mansions."[9]

"Yes; but I can't help being troubled; I suppose the Lord's will must be done, but it'll kill me."

"O father, don't, don't break my heart," said the son, much agitated. "I shall see you again in heaven, and you shall see me again; and then 'your heart shall rejoice, and your joy no man taketh from you.' "[1]

"I never shall get to heaven if I feel as I do now," said the old man. "I cannot have it so."

The mild face of the sufferer was overcast. "I wish he saw all that I do," said he, in a low voice. Then looking towards the minister, he articulated, "Pray for us."

They knelt in prayer. It was soothing, as real prayer always must be; and when they rose, everyone seemed more calm. But the sufferer was exhausted; his countenance changed; he looked on his friends; there was a faint whisper, "Peace I leave with you"—and he was in heaven.

We need not dwell on what followed. The seed sown by the righteous often blossoms over their grave; and so was it with this good man. The words of peace which he spoke unto his friends while he was yet with them came into remembrance after he was gone; and though he was laid in the grave with many tears, yet it was with softened and submissive hearts.

"The Lord bless him," said Uncle Lot, as he and James were standing, last of all, over the grave. "I believe my heart is gone to heaven with him; and I think the Lord really did know what was best after all."

Our friend James seemed now to become the support of the family; and the bereaved old man unconsciously began to transfer to him the affections that had been left vacant.

"James," said he to him one day, "I suppose you know that you are about the same to me as a son."

"I hope so," said James kindly.

"Well, well, you'll go to college next week, and none o' y'r keepin' school to get along. I've got enough to bring you safe out—that is, if you'll be car'ful and stiddy."[2]

James knew the heart too well to refuse a favor in which the poor old man's mind was comforting itself. He had the self-command to abstain from any extraordinary expressions of gratitude, but took it kindly, as a matter of course.

"Dear Grace," said he to her, the last evening before he left home, "I am changed; we both are altered since we first knew each other; and now I am going to be gone a long time, but I am sure"—

9. See John 14.2.   2. I.e., steady.
1. See John 16.22.

He stopped to arrange his thoughts.

"Yes, you may be sure of all those things that you wish to say, and cannot," said Grace.

"Thank you," said James; then, looking thoughtfully, he added, "God help me. I believe I have mind enough to be what I mean to; but whatever I am or have shall be given to God and my fellow men; and then, Grace, your brother in heaven will rejoice over me."

"I believe he does now," said Grace. "God bless you, James; I don't know what would have become of us if you had not been here.

"Yes, you will live to be like him, and to do even more good," she added, her face brightening as she spoke, till James thought she really must be right.

* * *

It was five years after this that James was spoken of as an eloquent and successful minister in the state of C., and was settled in one of its most thriving villages. Late one autumn evening, a tall, bony, hard-favored man was observed making his way into the outskirts of the place.

"Hallo, there!" he called to a man over the other side of a fence; "what town is these 'ere?"

"It's Farmington, sir."

"Well, I want to know if you know anything of a boy of mine that lives here?"

"A boy of yours? Who?"

"Why, I've got a boy here, that's livin' on the town,[3] and I thought I'd jest look him up."

"I don't know any boy that is living on the town. What's his name?"

"Why," said the old man, pushing his hat off from his forehead, "I believe they call him James Benton."

"James Benton! Why, that is our minister's name!"

"Oh, wal, I believe he is the minister, come to think on't. He's a boy o' mine, though. Where does he live?"

"In that white house that you see set back from the road there, with all those trees round it."

At this instant a tall, manly-looking person approached from behind. Have we not seen that face before? It is a touch graver than of old, and its lines have a more thoughtful significance; but all the vivacity of James Benton sparkles in that quick smile as his eye falls on the old man.

"I thought you could not keep away from us long," said he with the prompt cheerfulness of his boyhood, and laying hold of both of Uncle Lot's hard hands.

They approached the gate; a bright face glances past the window, and in a moment Grace is at the door.

---

3. "Going on the town" meant having to take charity from the townspeople; before the institution of social welfare, the way a rural community collectively supported its poor and indigent citizens.

"Father! dear father!"

"You'd better make believe be so glad," said Uncle Lot, his eyes glistening as he spoke.

"Come, come, father, I have authority in these days," said Grace, drawing him towards the house; "so no disrespectful speeches; away with your hat and coat, and sit down in this great chair."

"So, ho! Miss Grace," said Uncle Lot, "you are at your old tricks, ordering round as usual. Well, if I must, I must;" so down he sat.

"Father," said Grace, as he was leaving them, after a few days' stay, "it's Thanksgiving Day next month, and you and mother must come and stay with us."

Accordingly, the following month found Aunt Sally and Uncle Lot by the minister's fireside, delighted witnesses of the Thanksgiving presents which a willing people were pouring in;[4] and the next day they had once more the pleasure of seeing a son of theirs in the sacred desk, and hearing a sermon that everybody said was "the best that he ever preached;" and it is to be remarked, that this was the standing commentary on all James's discourses, so that it was evident he was going on unto perfection.

"There's a great deal that's worth having in this 'ere life after all," said Uncle Lot, as he sat by the coals of the bright evening fire of that day; "that is, if we'd only take it when the Lord lays it in our way."

"Yes," said James; "and let us only take it as we should and this life will be cheerfulness, and the next fullness of joy."

Western Monthly Magazine, April 1834; *The Mayflower,* 1843

From The Pearl of Orr's Island

Chapter IV

The sea lay like an unbroken mirror all around the pine-girt, lonely shores of Orr's Island. Tall, kingly spruces wore their regal crowns of cones high in air, sparkling with diamonds of clear exuded gum; vast old hemlocks of primeval growth stood darkling in their forest shadows, their branches hung with long hoary moss; while feathery larches, turned to brilliant gold by autumn frosts, lighted up the darker shadows of the evergreens. It was one of those hazy, calm, dissolving days of Indian summer, when everything is so quiet that the faintest kiss of the wave on the beach can be heard, and white clouds seem to faint into the blue of the sky, and soft swathing bands of violet vapor make all earth look dreamy, and give to the sharp, clear-cut outlines of the northern landscape all those mysteries of light and shade which impart such tenderness to Italian scenery.

---

4. Ministers depended for their subsistence on the supplementary gifts of food and fuel parishioners provided before the onset of winter.

The funeral was over,—the tread of many feet, bearing the heavy burden of two broken lives, had been to the lonely graveyard, and had come back again,—each footstep lighter and more unconstrained as each one went his way from the great old tragedy of Death to the common cheerful walks of Life.

The solemn black clock stood swaying with its eternal "tick-tock, tick-tock," in the kitchen of the brown house on Orr's Island. There was there that sense of a stillness that can be felt,—such as settles down on a dwelling when any of its inmates have passed through its doors for the last time, to go whence they shall not return. The best room was shut up and darkened, with only so much light as could fall through a little heart-shaped hole in the window-shutter,—for except on solemn visits, or prayer-meetings, or weddings, or funerals, that room formed no part of the daily family scenery.

The kitchen was clean and ample, with a great open fire-place and wide stone hearth, and oven on one side, and rows of old-fashioned splint-bottomed chairs against the wall. A table scoured to snowy whiteness, and a little work-stand whereon lay the Bible, the *Missionary Herald,* and the *Weekly Christian Mirror,* before named, formed the principal furniture. One feature, however, must not be forgotten,—a great sea-chest, which had been the companion of Zephaniah through all the countries of the earth. Old, and battered, and unsightly it looked, yet report said that there was good store within of that which men for the most part respect more than anything else; and, indeed, it proved often when a deed of grace was to be done,—when a woman was suddenly made a widow in a coast gale, or a fishing-smack was run down in the fogs off the banks, leaving in some neighboring cottage a family of orphans,—in all such cases, the opening of this sea-chest was an event of good omen to the bereaved; for Zephaniah had a large heart and a large hand, and was apt to take it out full of silver dollars when once it went in. So the ark of the covenant[1] could not have been looked on with more reverence than the neighbors usually showed to Captain Pennel's sea-chest.

The afternoon sun is shining in a square of light through the open kitchen-door, whence one dreamily disposed might look far out to sea, and behold ships coming and going in every variety of shape and size.

But Aunt Roxy and Aunt Ruey, who for the present were sole occupants of the premises, were not people of the dreamy kind, and consequently were not gazing off to sea, but attending to very terrestrial matters that in all cases somebody must attend to. The afternoon was warm and balmy, but a few smouldering sticks were kept in the great chimney, and thrust deep into the embers was a mongrel species of snub-nosed tea-pot, which fumed strongly of catnip-tea, a little of which gracious beverage Miss Roxy was preparing in an old-fashioned

---

1. The oblong box made of acacia wood which contained the two tablets of stone on which were engraved the covenant between Jehovah and Israel; when the Ark rests in a place, it symbolizes the immediate presence of God in that place.

cracked India china tea-cup, tasting it as she did so with the air of a connoisseur.

Apparently this was for the benefit of a small something in long white clothes, that lay face downward under a little blanket of very blue new flannel, and which something Aunt Roxy, when not otherwise engaged, constantly patted with a gentle tattoo, in tune to the steady trot of her knee.

All babies knew Miss Roxy's tattoo on their backs, and never thought of taking it in ill part. On the contrary, it had a vital and mesmeric effect of sovereign force against colic, and all other disturbers of the nursery; and never was infant known so pressed with those internal troubles which infants cry about, as not speedily to give over and sink to slumber at this soothing appliance.

At a little distance sat Aunt Ruey, with a quantity of black crape strewed on two chairs about her, very busily employed in getting up a mourning-bonnet, at which she snipped, and clipped, and worked, zealously singing, in a high cracked voice, from time to time, certain verses of a funeral psalm.

Miss Roxy and Miss Ruey Toothacre were two brisk old bodies of the feminine gender and singular number, well known in all the region of Harpswell Neck and Middle Bay, and such was their fame that it had even reached the town of Brunswick, eighteen miles away.

They were of that class of females who might be denominated, in the Old Testament language, "cunning women,"[2] —that is, gifted with an infinite diversity of practical "faculty," which made them an essential requisite in every family for miles and miles around.

It was impossible to say what they could not do: they could make dresses, and make shirts and vests and pantaloons, and cut out boys' jackets, and braid straw, and bleach and trim bonnets, and cook and wash, and iron and mend, could upholster and quilt, could nurse all kinds of sicknesses, and in default of a doctor, who was often miles away, were supposed to be infallible medical oracles.

Many a human being had been ushered into life under their auspices,—trotted, chirruped in babyhood on their knees, clothed by their handiwork in garments gradually enlarging from year to year, watched by them in the last sickness, and finally arrayed for the long repose by their hands.

These universally useful persons receive among us the title of "aunt" by a sort of general consent, showing the strong ties of relationship which bind them to the whole human family. They are nobody's aunts in particular, but aunts to human nature generally. The idea of restricting their usefulness to any one family, would strike dismay through a whole community.

Nobody would be so unprincipled as to think of such a thing as having their services more than a week or two at most. Your country factotum knows better than anybody else how absurd it would be

2. See Jeremiah 9.17.

"To give to a part what was meant for mankind."

Nobody knew very well the ages of these useful sisters. In that cold, clear, severe climate of the North the roots of human existence are hard to strike; but, if once people do take to living, they come in time to a place where they seem never to grow any older, but can always be found, like last year's mullein stalks, upright, dry, and seedy, warranted to last for any length of time.

Miss Roxy Toothacre, who sits trotting the baby, is a tall, thin, angular woman, with sharp black eyes, and hair once black, but now well streaked with gray. These ravages of time, however, were concealed by an ample mohair frisette[3] of glossy blackness woven on each side into a heap of stiff little curls, which pushed up her cap border in rather a bristling and decisive way.

In all her movements and personal habits, even to her tone of voice and manner of speaking, Miss Roxy was vigorous, spicy, and decided. Her mind on all subjects was made up, and she spoke generally as one having authority; and *who should*, if she should not? Was she not a sort of priestess and sibyl[4] in all the most awful straits and mysteries of life? How many births, and weddings, and deaths had come and gone under her jurisdiction? And amid weeping or rejoicing, was not Miss Roxy still the master-spirit,—consulted, referred to by all?—was not her word law and precedent? Her younger sister, Miss Ruey, a pliant, cosey, easy-to-be-entreated personage, plump and cushiony, revolved around her as a humble satellite. Miss Roxy looked on Miss Ruey as quite a frisky young thing, though under her ample frisette of carroty hair her head might be seen white with the same snow that had powdered that of her sister. Aunt Ruey had a face much resembling the kind of one you may see, reader, by looking at yourself in the convex side of a silver milk-pitcher. If you try the experiment, this description will need no further amplification.

The two almost always went together, for the variety of talent comprised in their stock could always find employment in the varying wants of a family. While one nursed the sick, the other made clothes for the well; and thus they were always chippering and chatting to each other, like a pair of antiquated house-sparrows, retailing over harmless gossips, and moralizing in that gentle jog-trot which befits serious old women. In fact, they had talked over everything in Nature, and said everything they could think of to each other so often, that the opinions of one were as like those of the other as two sides of a pea-pod. But as often happens in cases of the sort, this was not because the two *were* in all respects exactly alike, but because the stronger one had mesmerized the weaker into consent.

Miss Roxy was the master-spirit of the two, and, like the great coining machine of a mint, came down with her own sharp, heavy stamp on every opinion her sister put out. She was matter-of-fact,

3. A curled fringe of hair, here made of goat hair, usually worn on a woman's forehead.   4. A woman regarded as an oracle or prophetess by the ancient Greeks and Romans.

positive, and declarative to the highest degree, while her sister was naturally inclined to the elegiac and the pathetic, indulging herself in sentimental poetry, and keeping a store thereof in her thread-case, which she had cut from the *Christian Mirror*. Miss Roxy sometimes, in her brusque way, popped out observations on life and things, with a droll, hard quaintness that took one's breath a little, yet never failed to have a sharp crystallization of truth,—frosty though it were. She was one of those sensible, practical creatures who tear every veil, and lay their fingers on every spot in pure business-like good-will; and if we shiver at them at times, as at the first plunge of a cold bath, we confess to an invigorating power in them after all.

"Well, now," said Miss Roxy, giving a decisive push to the tea-pot, which buried it yet deeper in the embers, "a'n't it all a strange kind o' providence that this 'ere little thing is left behind so; and then their callin' on her by such a strange, mournful kind of name,—Mara.[5] I thought sure as could be 't was Mary, till the minister read the passage from Scriptur'.[6] Seems to me it's kind o' odd. I'd call it Maria, or I'd put an Ann on to it. Mara-ann, now, wouldn't sound so strange."

"It's a Scriptur' name, sister," said Aunt Ruey, "and that ought to be enough for us."

"Well, I don't know," said Aunt Roxy. "Now there was Miss Jones down on Mure P'int called her twins Tiglath-Pileser and Shalman-eser,[7] —Scriptur' names both, but I never liked 'em. The boys used to call 'em Tiggy and Shally, so no mortal could guess they was Scriptur'."

"Well," said Aunt Ruey, drawing a sigh which caused her plump proportions to be agitated in gentle waves, " 't a'n't much matter, after all, *what* they call the little thing, for 't a'n't 't all likely it's goin' to live,—cried and worried all night, and kep' a-suckin' my cheek and my night-gown, poor little thing! This 'ere's a baby that won't get along without its mother. What Mis' Pennel's a-goin' to do with it when we is gone, I'm sure I don't know. It comes kind o' hard on old people to be broke o' their rest. If it's going' to be called home, it's a pity, as I said, it didn't go with its mother"—

"And save the expense of another funeral," said Aunt Roxy. "Now when Mis' Pennel's sister asked her what she was going to do with Naomi's clothes, I couldn't help wonderin' when she said she should keep 'em for the child."

"She had a sight of things, Naomi did," said Aunt Ruey. "Nothin' was never too much for her. I don't believe that Cap'n Pennel ever went to Bath or Portland without havin' it in his mind to bring Naomi somethin'."

"Yes, and she had a faculty of puttin' of 'em on," said Miss Roxy, with a decisive shake of the head. "Naomi was a still girl, but her

5. See Ruth 1.20.
6. The Bible.
7. The name of several kings of ancient Assyria mentioned in the Bible; Tiglath-Peleser III ruled

Assyria 745–727 B.C.; see 2 Kings 15–17. Shalman-eser IV succeeded Tiglath-Pileser III as king of Assyria; see 2 Kings 17.3 and 18.9.

faculty[8] was uncommon; and I tell you, Ruey, 't a'n't everybody hes *faculty* as hes things."

"The poor Cap'n," said Miss Ruey, "he seemed greatly supported at the funeral, but he's dreadful broke down since. I went into Naomi's room this morning, and there the old man was a-sittin' by her bed, and he had a pair of her shoes in his hand,—you know what a leetle bit of a foot she had. I never saw nothin' look so kind o' solitary as that poor old man did!"

"Well," said Miss Roxy, "she was a master-hand for keepin' things, Naomi was; her drawers is just a sight; she's got all the little presents and things they ever give her since she was a baby, in one drawer. There's a little pair of red shoes there that she had when she wa'n't more 'n five year old. You 'member, Ruey, the Cap'n brought 'm over from Portland when we was to the house a-makin' Mis' Pennel's figured black silk that he brought from Calcutty. You 'member they cost just five and sixpence; but, law! the Cap'n he never grudged the money when 't was for Naomi. And so she's got all her husband's keepsakes and things, just as nice as when he giv' 'em to her."

"It's real affectin'," said Miss Ruey, "I can't all the while help a-thinkin' of the Psalm,[9] —

'So fades the lovely blooming flower,—
Frail, smiling solace of an hour;
So quick our transient comforts fly,
And pleasure only blooms to die.' "[1]

"Yes," said Miss Roxy; "and, Ruey, I was a-thinkin' whether or no it wa'n't best to pack away them things, 'cause Naomi hadn't fixed no baby drawers, and we seem to want some."

"I was kind o' hintin' that to Mis' Pennel this morning," said Ruey, "but she can't seem to want to have 'em touched."

"Well we may just as well come to such things first as last," said Aunt Roxy; "'cause if the Lord takes our friends, he does take 'em; and we can't lose 'em and have 'em too, and we may as well give right up at first, and done with it, that they are gone, and we 'v' got to do without 'em, and not to be hangin' on to keep things just as they was."

"So I was a-tellin' Mis' Pennel," said Miss Ruey, "but she'll come to it by and by. I wish the baby might live, and kind o' grow up into her mother's place."

"Well," said Miss Roxy, "I wish it might, but there'd be a sight o' trouble fetchin' on it up. Folks can do pretty well with children when they're young and spry, if they do get 'em up nights; but come to grandchildren, it's pretty tough."

"I'm a-thinkin', sister," said Miss Ruey, taking off her spectacles and rubbing her nose thoughtfully, "whether or no cow's milk a'n't goin' to

---

8. Great skill in a variety of household arts and occupations.

9. Here psalm means hymn.

1. Hymn written by Anne Steele (1716–1786).

be too hearty for it, it's such a pindlin'[2] little thing. Now, Mis' Badger she brought up a seven-months' child, and she told me she gave it nothin' but these 'ere little seed cookies, wet in water, and it throve nicely,—and the seed is good for wind."

"Oh, don't tell me none of Mis' Badger's stories," said Miss Roxy, "I don't believe in 'em. Cows is the Lord's ordinances for bringing up babies that's lost their mothers; it stands to reason they should be,— and babies that can't eat milk, why they can't be fetched up; but babies can eat milk, and this un will if it lives, and if it can't it won't live." So saying, Miss Roxy drummed away on the little back of the party in question, authoritatively, as if to pound in a wholesome conviction at the outset.

"I hope," said Miss Ruey, holding up a strip of black crape, and looking through it from end to end so as to test its capabilities, "I hope the Cap'n and Mis' Pennel 'll get some support at the prayer-meetin' this afternoon."

"It's the right place to go to," said Miss Roxy, with decision.

"Mis' Pennel said this mornin' that she was just beat out tryin' to submit; and the more she said, 'Thy will be done,' the more she didn't seem to feel it."

"Them's common feelin's among mourners, Ruey. These 'ere forty years that I've been round nussin', and layin'-out, and tendin' funerals, I've watched people's exercises.[3] People's sometimes supported wonderfully just at the time, and maybe at the funeral; but the three or four weeks after, most everybody, if they's to say what they feel, is unreconciled."

"The Cap'n, he don't say nothing'," said Miss Ruey.

"No, he don't, but he *looks* it in his eyes," said Miss Roxy; "he's one of the kind o' mourners as takes it deep; that kind don't cry; it's a kind o' dry, deep pain; them's the worst to get over it,—sometimes they just says nothin', and in about six months they send for you to nuss 'em in consumption or somethin'. Now, Mis' Pennel, she can cry and she can talk,—well, she'll get over it; but *he* won't get no support unless the Lord reaches right down and lifts him up over the world. I've seen that happen sometimes, and I tell you, Ruey, that sort makes powerful Christians."

At that moment the old pair entered the door.

Zephaniah Pennel came and stood quietly by the pillow where the little form was laid, and lifted a corner of the blanket. The tiny head was turned to one side, showing the soft, warm cheek, and the little hand was holding tightly a morsel of the flannel blanket. He stood swallowing hard for a few moments. At last he said, with deep humility, to the wise and mighty woman who held her, "I'll tell you what it is, Miss Roxy, I'll give all there is in my old chest yonder if you'll only make her—live."

---

2. Spindly. of weak growth.
3. Efforts to accept death as God's will in order to stop questioning God or experiencing anger at God.

Chapter V

It did live. The little life, so frail, so unprofitable in every mere material view, so precious in the eyes of love, expanded and flowered at last into fair childhood. Not without much watching and weariness. Many a night the old fisherman walked the floor with the little thing in his arms, talking to it that jargon of tender nonsense which fairies bring as love-gifts to all who tend a cradle. Many a day the good little old grandmother called the aid of gossips[4] about her, trying various experiments of catnip, and sweet fern, and bayberry, and other teas of rustic reputation for baby frailties.

At the end of three years, the two graves in the lonely graveyard were sodded and cemented down by smooth velvet turf, and playing round the door of the brown house was a slender child, with ways and manners so still and singular as often to remind the neighbors that she was not like other children,—a bud of hope and joy,—but the outcome of a great sorrow,—a pearl washed ashore by a mighty, uprooting tempest. They that looked at her remembered that her father's eye had never beheld her, and her baptismal cup had rested on her mother's coffin.

She was small of stature, beyond the wont of children of her age, and moulded with a fine waxen delicacy that won admiration from all eyes. Her hair was curly and golden, but her eyes were dark like her mother's, and the lids drooped over them in that manner which gives a peculiar expression of dreamy wistfulness.

Every one of us must remember eyes that have a strange, peculiar expression of pathos and desire, as if the spirit that looked out of them were pressed with vague remembrances of a past, or but dimly comprehended the mystery of its present life. Even when the baby lay in its cradle, and its dark, inquiring eyes would follow now one object and now another, the gossips would say the child was longing for something, and Miss Roxy would still further venture to predict that that child always would long and never would know exactly what she was after.

That dignitary sits at this minute enthroned in the kitchen corner, looking majestically over the press-board on her knee, where she is pressing the next year's Sunday vest of Zephaniah Pennel. As she makes her heavy tailor's goose[5] squeak on the work, her eyes follow the little delicate fairy form which trips about the kitchen, busily and silently arranging a little grotto of gold and silver shells and sea-weed. The child sings to herself as she works in a low chant, like the prattle of a brook, but ever and anon she rests her little arms on a chair and looks through the open kitchen-door far, far off where the horizon line of the blue sea dissolves in the blue sky.

"See that child now, Roxy," said Miss Ruey, who sat stitching beside her; "do look at her eyes. She's as handsome as a pictur', but 'ta'n't an

4. Close friends or companions, usually female; possibly neighbors who served as godparents for the orphaned baby.

5. A tailor's pressing iron with a long curved handle.

ordinary look she has neither; she seems a contented little thing; but what makes her eyes always look so kind o' wishful?"

"Wa'n't her mother always a-longin' and a-lookin' to sea, and watchin' the ships, afore she was born?" said Miss Roxy; "and didn't her heart break afore she was born? Babies like that is marked always. They don't know what ails 'em, nor nobody."

"It's her mother she's after?" said Miss Ruey.

"The Lord only knows," said Miss Roxy; "but them kind o' children always seem homesick to go back where they come from. They're mostly grave and old-fashioned like this 'un. If they gets past seven years, why they live; but it's always in 'em to *long;* they don't seem to be really unhappy neither, but if anything's ever the matter with 'em, it seems a great deal easier for 'em to die than to live. Some say it's the mothers longin' after 'em makes 'em feel so, and some say it's them longin' after their mothers; but dear knows, Ruey, what anything is or what makes anything. Children's mysterious, that's my mind."

"Mara, dear," said Miss Ruey, interrupting the child's steady lookout, "what you thinking of?"

"Me want somefin'," said the little one.

"That's what she's always sayin'," said Miss Roxy.

"Me want somebody to pay wis'," continued the little one.

"Want somebody to play with," said old Dame Pennel, as she came in from the back-room with her hands yet floury with kneading bread; "sure enough, she does. Our house stands in such a lonesome place, and there a'n't any children. But I never saw such a quiet little thing—always still and always busy."

"I'll take her down with me to Cap'n Kittridge's," said Miss Roxy, "and let her play with their little girl; she'll *chirk*[6] her up, I'll warrant. She's a regular little witch, Sally is, but she'll *chirk* her up. It a'n't good for children to be so still and old-fashioned; children ought to be children. Sally takes to Mara just 'cause she's so different."

"Well, now, you may," said Dame Pennel; "to be sure, *he* can't bear her out of his sight a minute after he comes in; but after all, old folks can't be company for children."

Accordingly, that afternoon, the little Mara was arrayed in a little blue flounced dress, which stood out like a balloon, made by Miss Roxy in first-rate style, from a French fashion-plate; her golden hair was twined in manifold curls by Dame Pennel, who, restricted in her ideas of ornamentation, spared, nevertheless, neither time nor money to enhance the charms of this single ornament to her dwelling. Mara was her picture-gallery, who gave her in the twenty-four hours as many Murillos or Greuzes[7] as a lover of art could desire; and as she tied over the child's golden curls a little flat hat, and saw her go dancing off along

6. Cheer.
7. Bartolome Esteban Murillo (1617–1682) was a Spanish painter, chiefly of religious subjects. Jean Baptiste Greuze (1725–1805): French genre and portrait painter, best known for his paintings of moralistic subjects.

the sea-sands, holding to Miss Roxy's bony finger, she felt she had in her what galleries of pictures could not buy.

It was a good mile to the one story, gambrel-roofed[8] cottage where lived Captain Kittridge,—the long, lean, brown man, with his good wife of the great Leghorn bonnet,[9] round, black bead eyes, and psalm-book, whom we told you of at the funeral.

The Captain, too, had followed the sea in his early life, but being not, as he expressed it, "very rugged," in time changed his ship for a tight little cottage on the sea-shore, and devoted himself to boat-building, which he found sufficiently lucrative to furnish his brown cottage with all that his wife's heart desired, besides extra money for knick-knacks when she chose to go up to Brunswick or over to Portland to shop.

The Captain himself was a welcome guest at all the fire-sides round, being a chatty body, and disposed to make the most of his foreign experiences, in which he took the usual advantages of a traveller. In fact, it was said, whether slanderously or not, that the Captain's yarns were spun to order; and as, when pressed to relate his foreign adventures, he always responded with, "What would you like to hear?" it was thought that he fabricated his article to suit his market. In short, there was no species of experience, finny, fishy, or aquatic,—no legend of strange and unaccountable incident of fire or flood,—no romance of foreign scenery and productions, to which his tongue was not competent, when he had once seated himself in a double bow-knot at a neighbor's evening fireside.

His good wife, a sharp-eyed, literal body, and a vigorous church-member, felt some concern of conscience on the score of these narrations; for, being their constant auditor, she, better than any one else, could perceive the variations and discrepancies of text which showed their mythical character, and oftentimes her black eyes would snap and her knitting-needles rattle with an admonitory vigor as he went on, and sometimes she would unmercifully come in at the end of a narrative with,—

"Well, now, the Cap'n's told them ar stories till he begins to b'lieve 'em himself, *I think.*"

But works of fiction, as we all know, if only well gotten up, have always their advantages in the hearts of listeners over plain, homely truth; and so Captain Kittridge's yarns were marketable fireside commodities still, despite the scepticisms which attended them.

The afternoon sunbeams at this moment are painting the gambrel-roof with a golden brown. It is September again, as it was three years ago when our story commenced, and the sea and sky are purple and amethystine with its Italian haziness of atmosphere.

The brown house stands on a little knoll, about a hundred yards from

8. A ridged roof having two slopes on each side, the lower slopes having the steeper pitch.

9. A hat made from braided straw derived from wheat exported from Leghorn (Livorno), Italy.

the open ocean. Behind it rises a ledge of rocks, where cedars and hemlocks make deep shadows into which the sun shoots golden shafts of light, illuminating the scarlet feathers of the sumach, which threw themselves jauntily forth from the crevices; while down below, in deep, damp, mossy recesses, rose ferns which autumn had just begun to tinge with yellow and brown. The little knoll where the cottage stood, had on its right hand a tiny bay, where the ocean water made up amid picturesque rocks—shaggy and solemn. Here trees of the primeval forest, grand and lordly, looked down silently into the waters which ebbed and flowed daily into this little pool. Every variety of those beautiful evergreens which feather the coast of Maine, and dip their wings in the very spray of its ocean foam, found here a representative. There were aspiring black spruces, crowned on the very top with heavy coronets of cones; there were balsamic firs, whose young buds breathe the scent of strawberries; there were cedars, black as midnight clouds, and white pines with their swaying plumage of needle-like leaves, strewing the ground beneath with a golden, fragrant matting; and there were the gigantic, wide-winged hemlocks, hundreds of years old, and with long, swaying, gray beards of moss, looking white and ghostly under the deep shadows of their boughs. And beneath, creeping round trunk and matting over stones, were many and many of those wild, beautiful things which embellish the shadows of these northern forests. Long, feathery wreaths of what are called ground-pines, ran here and there in little ruffles of green, and the prince's pine raised its oriental feather, with a mimic cone on the top, as if it conceived itself to be a grown-up tree. Whole patches of partridge-berry wove their evergreen matting, dotted plentifully with brilliant scarlet berries. Here and there, the rocks were covered with a curiously inwoven tapestry of moss, overshot with the exquisite vine of the Linnea borealis, which in early spring rings its two fairy bells on the end of every spray; while elsewhere the wrinkled leaves of the mayflower wove themselves through and through deep beds of moss, meditating silently thoughts of the thousand little cups of pink shell which they had it in hand to make when the time of miracles should come round next spring.

Nothing, in short, could be more quaintly fresh, wild, and beautiful than the surroundings of this little cove which Captain Kittridge had thought fit to dedicate to his boat-building operations,—where he had set up his tar-kettle between two great rocks above the highest tide-mark, and where, at the present moment, he had a boat upon the stocks.

Mrs. Kittridge, at this hour, was sitting in her clean kitchen, very busily engaged in ripping up a silk dress, which Miss Roxy had engaged to come and make into a new one; and, as she ripped, she cast now and then an eye at the face of a tall, black clock, whose solemn tick-tock was the only sound that could be heard in the kitchen.

By her side, on a low stool, sat a vigorous, healthy girl of six years, whose employment evidently did not please her, for her well-marked black eyebrows were bent in a frown, and her large black eyes looked surly and wrathful, and one versed in children's grievances could easily see what the matter was,—she was turning a sheet! Perhaps, happy young female reader, you don't know what that is,—most likely not; for in these degenerate days the strait and narrow ways of self-denial, formerly thought so wholesome for little feet, are quite grass-grown with neglect. Childhood nowadays is unceasingly fêted and caressed, the principal difficulty of the grown people seeming to be to discover what the little dears want,—a thing not always clear to the little dears themselves. But in old times, turning sheets was thought a most espe-cial and wholesome discipline for young girls; in the first place, be-cause it took off the hands of their betters a very uninteresting and monotonous labor; and in the second place, because it was such a long, straight, unending turnpike, that the youthful travellers, once started thereupon, could go on indefinitely, without requiring guidance and direction of their elders. For these reasons, also, the task was held in special detestation by children in direct proportion to their amount of life, and their ingenuity and love of variety. A dull child took it tolera-bly well; but to a lively, energetic one, it was a perfect torture.

"I don't see the use of sewing up sheets one side, and ripping up the other," at last said Sally, breaking the monotonous tick-tock of the clock by an observation which has probably occurred to every child in similar circumstances.

"Sally Kittridge, if you say another word about that ar sheet, I'll whip you," was the very explicit rejoinder; and there was a snap of Mrs. Kittridge's black eyes, that seemed to make it likely that she would keep her word. It was answered by another snap from the six-year-old eyes, as Sally comforted herself with thinking that when she was a woman she'd speak her mind out in pay for all this.

At this moment a burst of silvery child-laughter rang out, and there appeared in the door-way, illuminated by the afternoon sunbeams, the vision of Miss Roxy's tall, lank figure, with the little golden-haired, blue-robed fairy, hanging like a gay butterfly upon the tip of a thorn-bush. Sally dropped the sheet and clapped her hands, unnoticed by her mother, who rose to pay her respects to the "cunning woman" of the neighborhood.

"Well, now, Miss Roxy, I was 'mazin' afraid you wer'n't a-comin'. I'd just been an' got my silk ripped up, and didn't know how to get a step farther without you."

"Well, I was finishin' up Cap'n Pennel's best pantaloons," said Miss Roxy; "and I've got 'em along so, Ruey can go on with 'em; and I told Mis' Pennel I must come to you, if 't was only for a day; and I fetched the little girl down, 'cause the little thing's so kind o' lonesome like. I thought Sally could play with her, and chirk her up a little."

"Well, Sally," said Mrs. Kittridge, "stick in your needle, fold up your sheet, put your thimble in your work-pocket, and then you may take the little Mara down to the cove to play; but be sure you don't let her go near the tar, nor wet her shoes. D'ye hear?"

"Yes, ma'am," said Sally, who had sprung up in light and radiance, like a translated creature, at this unexpected turn of fortune, and performed the welcome orders with a celerity which showed how agreeable they were; and then, stooping and catching the little one in her arms, disappeared through the door, with the golden curls fluttering over her own crow-black hair.

The fact was, that Sally, at that moment, was as happy as human creature could be, with a keenness of happiness that children who have never been made to turn sheets of a bright afternoon can never realize.

The sun was yet an hour high, as she saw, by the flash of her shrewd, time-keeping eye, and she could bear her little prize down to the cove, and collect unknown quantities of gold and silver shells, and star-fish, and salad-dish shells, and white pebbles for her, besides quantities of well-turned shavings, brown and white, from the pile which constantly was falling under her father's joiner's bench,[1] and with which she would make long extemporaneous tresses, so that they might play at being mermaids, like those that she had heard her father tell about in some of his sea-stories.

"Now, railly, Sally, what you got there?" said Captain Kittridge, as he stood in his shirt-sleeves peering over his joiner's bench, to watch the little one whom Sally had dumped down into a nest of clean white shavings. "Wal', wal', I should think you'd a-stolen the big doll I see in a shop-window the last time I was to Portland. So this is Pennel's little girl?—poor child!"

"Yes, father, and we want some nice shavings."

"Stay a bit, I'll make ye a few a-purpose," said the old man, reaching his long, bony arm, with the greatest ease, to the farther part of his bench, and bringing up a board, from which he proceeded to roll off shavings in fine satin rings, which perfectly delighted the hearts of the children, and made them dance with glee; and, truth to say, reader, there are coarser and homelier things in the world than a well-turned shaving.

"There, go now," he said, when both of them stood with both hands full; "go now and play; and mind you don't let the baby wet her feet, Sally; them shoes o' hern must have cost five-and-sixpence at the very least."

That sunny hour before sundown seemed as long to Sally as the whole seam of the sheet; for childhood's joys are all pure gold; and as she ran up and down the white sands, shouting at every shell she found, or darted up into the overhanging forest for checkerberries and ground-pine, all the sorrows of the morning came no more into her remembrance.

The little Mara had one of those sensitive, excitable natures, on which every external influence acts with immediate power. Stimulated

---

1. Joiner is a British term for carpenter or cabinetmaker; hence, a carpenter's bench.

by the society of her energetic, buoyant little neighbor, she no longer seemed wishful or pensive, but kindled into a perfect flame of wild delight, and gambolled about the shore like a blue and gold-winged fly; while her bursts of laughter made the squirrels and blue jays look out inquisitively from their fastnesses in the old evergreens. Gradually the sunbeams faded from the pines, and the waves of the tide in the little cove came in, solemnly tinted with purple, flaked with orange and crimson, borne in from a great rippling sea of fire, into which the sun had just sunk.

"Mercy on us—them children!" said Miss Roxy.

"*He's* bringin' 'em along," said Mrs. Kittridge, as she looked out of the window and saw the tall, lank form of the Captain, with one child seated on either shoulder, and holding on by his head.

The two children were both in the highest state of excitement, but never was there a more marked contrast of nature. The one seemed a perfect type of well-developed childish health and vigor, good solid flesh and bones, with glowing skin, brilliant eyes, shining teeth, well-knit, supple limbs,—vigorously and healthily beautiful; while the other appeared one of those aerial mixtures of cloud and fire, whose radiance seems scarcely earthly. A physiologist, looking at the child, would shake his head, seeing one of those perilous organizations, all nerve and brain, which come to life under the clear stimulating skies of America, and, burning with the intensity of lighted phosphorous, waste themselves too early.

The little Mara seemed like a fairy sprite, possessed with a wild spirit of glee. She laughed and clapped her hands incessantly, and when set down on the kitchen-floor spun round like a little elf; and that night it was late and long before her wide, wakeful eyes could be veiled in sleep.

"Company jist sets this 'ere child crazy," said Miss Roxy; "it's jist her lonely way of livin'; a pity Mis' Pennel hadn't another child to keep company along with her."

"Mis' Pennel oughter be trainin' of her up to work," said Mrs. Kittridge. "Sally could oversew and hem when she wa'n't more 'n three years old; nothin' straightens out children like work. Miss' Pennel she jist keeps that ar child to look at."

"All children a'n't alike, Mis' Kittridge," said Miss Roxy, sententiously. "This 'un a'n't like your Sally. 'A hen and a bumble-bee can't be fetched up alike, fix it how you will!' "

The Independent, January 1861; 1862

Preface to *Oldtown Folks*

Gentle reader,—It is customary to omit prefaces. I beg you to make an exception in my particular case; I have something I really want to say. I have an object in this book, more than the mere telling of a story, and you can always judge of a book better if you compare it with the author's object. My object is to interpret to the world the New England life and character in that particular time of its history which may be called the seminal period. I would endeavor to show you New England in its *seed-bed*, before the hot suns of modern progress had developed its sprouting germs into the great trees of today.

New England has been to these United States what the Dorian hive was to Greece.[1] It has always been a capital country to emigrate from, and North, South, East, and West have been populated largely from New England, so that the seed-bed of New England was the seed-bed of this great American Republic, and of all that is likely to come of it.

New England people cannot be thus interpreted without calling into view many grave considerations and necessitating some serious thinking.

In doing this work, I have tried to make my mind as still and passive as a looking-glass, or a mountain lake, and then to give you merely the images reflected there. I desire that you should see the characteristic persons of those times, and hear them talk; and sometimes I have taken an author's liberty of explaining their characters to you, and telling you why they talked and lived as they did.

My studies for this object have been Pre-Raphaelite,[2] —taken from real characters, real scenes, and real incidents. And some of those things in the story which may appear most romantic and like fiction are simple renderings and applications of facts.

Anyone who may be curious enough to consult Rev. Elias Nason's book, called "Sir Charles Henry Frankland, or Boston in the Colonial Times," will there see a full description of the old manor-house which in this story is called the Dench House. It was by that name I always heard it spoken of in my boyhood.

In portraying the various characters which I have introduced, I have tried to maintain the part simply of a sympathetic spectator. I propose neither to teach nor preach through them, any farther than any spectator of life is preached to by what he sees of the workings of human nature around him.

Though Calvinist, Arminian, High-Church Episcopalian,[3] sceptic, and simple believer all speak in their turn, I merely listen, and endeavor to understand and faithfully represent the inner life of each. I myself am but the observer and reporter, seeing much, doubting much, questioning much, and believing with all my heart in only a very few things.

And so I take my leave of you.

Horace Holyoke 1869

---

1. The Dorians, a people of classical Greece, occupied southern and eastern Greece and were characterized by a marked dialect.

2. The name given to a group of English painters (1848–54) interested in pre-industrial and frequently religious subjects, direct observation of nature, and precisely realistic technique, characteristics they associated with Italian painters before Raphael (1483–1520).

3. All religious sects represented in 19th-century New England that differed in their fundamental beliefs; thus Horace Holyoke is claiming to be able to represent widely different characters in his narrative.

From OLDTOWN FOLKS

The Village Do-Nothing

"Wal naow, Horace, don't ye cry so. Why, I'm railly concerned for ye. Why, don't you s'pose your daddy's better off? Why, sartin *I* do. Don't cry, there's a good boy, now. I'll give ye my jack-knife now."

This was addressed to me the day after my father's death while the preparations for the funeral hung like a pall over the house, and the terror of the last cold mystery, the tears of my mother, and a sort of bustling dreariness on the part of my aunts and grandmother, all conspired to bear down on my childish nerves with fearful power. It was a doctrine of those good old times, no less than of many in our present days, that a house invaded by death should be made as forlorn as hands could make it. It should be rendered as cold and stiff, as unnatural, as dead and corpse-like as possible, by closed shutters, looking-glasses pinned up in white sheets, and the locking up and hiding out of sight of any pleasant little familiar object which would be thought out of place in a sepulchre. This work had been driven through with unsparing vigor by Aunt Lois, who looked like one of the Fates[1] as she remorselessly cleared away every little familiar object belonging to my father, and reduced every room to the shrouded stillness of a well-kept tomb.

Of course no one thought of looking after me. It was not the fashion of those days to think of children, if only they would take themselves off out of the way of the movements of the grown people; and so I had run out into the orchard back of the house, and, throwing myself down on my face under an apple-tree in the tall clover, I gave myself up to despair, and was sobbing aloud in a nervous paroxysm of agony, when these words were addressed to me. The speaker was a tall, shambling, loose-jointed man, with a long, thin visage, prominent watery blue eyes, very fluttering and seedy habiliments, who occupied the responsible position of first do-nothing-in-ordinary in our village of Oldtown, and as such I must introduce him to my readers' notice.

Every New England village, if you only think of it, must have its do-nothing as regularly as it has its school-house or meeting-house. Nature is always wide awake in the matter of compensation. Work, thrift, and industry are such an incessant steam-power in Yankee life, that society would burn itself out with intense friction were there not interposed here and there the lubricating power of a decided do-nothing,—a man who won't be hurried, and won't work, and will take his ease in his own way, in spite of the whole protest of his neighborhood to the contrary. And there is on the face of the whole earth no do-nothing whose softness, idleness, general inaptitude to labor, and everlasting, universal shiftlessness can compare with that of this worthy, as found in a brisk Yankee village.

---

1. From Greek and Roman mythology, the three goddesses who govern human destiny.

Sam Lawson filled this post with ample honor in Oldtown. He was a fellow dear to the souls of all "us boys" in the village, because, from the special nature of his position, he never had anything more pressing to do than croon and gossip with us. He was ready to spend hours in tinkering a boy's jack-knife, or mending his skate, or start at the smallest notice to watch at a woodchuck's hole, or give incessant service in tending a dog's sprained paw. He was always on hand to go fishing with us on Saturday afternoons; and I have known him to sit hour after hour on the bank, surrounded by a troop of boys, baiting our hooks and taking off our fish. He was a soft-hearted old body, and the wrigglings and contortions of our prey used to disturb his repose so that it was a regular part of his work to kill the fish by breaking their necks when he took them from the hook.

"Why, lordy massy, boys," he would say, "I can't bear to see no kind o' critter in torment. These 'ere pouts ain't to blame for bein' fish, and ye ought to put 'em out of their misery. Fish hes their rights as well as any on us."

Nobody but Sam would have thought of poking through the high grass and clover on our back lot to look me up, as I lay sobbing under the old apple-tree, the most insignificant little atom of misery that ever bewailed the inevitable.

Sam was of respectable family, and not destitute of education. He was an expert in at least five or six different kinds of handicraft, in all of which he had been pronounced by the knowing ones to be a capable workman, "if only he would stick to it." He had a blacksmith's shop, where, when the fit was on him, he would shoe a horse better than any man in the county. No one could supply a missing screw, or apply a timely brace, with more adroitness. He could mend cracked china so as to be almost as good as new; he could use carpenter's tools as well as a born carpenter, and would doctor a rheumatic door or a shaky window better than half the professional artisans in wood. No man could put a refractory clock to rights with more ingenuity than Sam,—that is, if you would give him his time to be about it.

I shall never forget the wrath and dismay which he roused in my Aunt Lois's mind by the leisurely way in which, after having taken our own venerable kitchen clock to pieces, and strewn the fragments all over the kitchen, he would roost over it in endless incubation, telling stories, entering into long-winded theological discussions, smoking pipes, and giving histories of all the other clocks in Oldtown, with occasional memoirs of those in Needmore, the North Parish, and Podunk, as placidly indifferent to all her volleys of sarcasm and contempt, her stinging expostulations and philippics,[2] as the sailing old moon is to the frisky, animated barking of some puppy dog of earth.

2. Verbal denunciations.

"Why, ye see, Miss Lois," he would say, "clocks can't be druv; that's jest what they can't. Some things can be druv, and then again some things can't, and clocks is that kind. They's jest got to be humored. Now this 'ere's a 'mazin' good clock; give me my time on it, and I'll have it so 't will keep straight on to the Millennium."[3]

"Millennium!" says Aunt Lois, with a snort of infinite contempt.

"Yes, the Millennium," says Sam, letting fall his work in a contemplative manner. "That 'ere 's an interestin' topic now. Parson Lothrop, he don't think the Millennium will last a thousand years. What's your 'pinion on that pint, Miss Lois?"

"My opinion is," said Aunt Lois, in her most nipping tones, "that if folks don't mind their own business, and do with their might what their hands finds to do, the Millennium won't come at all."

"Wal, you see, Miss Lois, it's just here,—one day is with the Lord as a thousand years, and a thousand years as one day."

"I should think you thought a day was a thousand years, the way you work," said Aunt Lois.

"Wal," says Sam, sitting down with his back to his desperate litter of wheels, weights, and pendulums, and meditatively caressing his knee as he watched the sailing clouds in abstract meditation, "ye see, ef a thing 's ordained, why it's got to be, ef you don't lift a finger. That 'ere 's so now, ain't it?"

"Sam Lawson, you are about the most aggravating creature I ever had to do with. Here you've got our clock all to pieces, and have been keeping up a perfect hurrah's nest[4] in our kitchen for three days, and there you sit maundering and talking with your back to your work, fussin' about the Millenium, which is none of your business, or mine, as I know of! Do either put that clock together or let it alone!"

"Don't you be a grain uneasy, Miss Lois. Why, I'll have your clock all right in the end, but I can't be druv. Wal, I guess I'll take another spell on 't tomorrow or Friday."

Poor Aunt Lois, horror-stricken, but seeing herself actually in the hands of the imperturbable enemy, now essayed the tack of conciliation. "Now do, Lawson, just finish up this job, and I'll pay you down, right on the spot; and you need the money."

"I'd like to 'blige ye, Miss Lois; but ye see money ain't everything in this world. Ef I work tew long on one thing, my mind kind o' gives out, ye see; and besides, I've got some 'sponsibilities to 'tend to. There's Mrs. Captain Brown, she made me promise to come today and look at the nose o' that 'ere silver teapot o'hern; it's kind o' sprung a leak. And then I 'greed to split a little oven-wood for the Widdah Pedee, that lives up on the Shelburn road. Must visit the widdahs in their affliction, Scriptur' says.[5] And then there's Hepsy: she's allers a

3. A thousand-year period of holiness during which Christ is to rule on earth; see Revelation 20.1–5.
4. A place of disorder and confusion; derived in various regional dialects from a wild, tangled, mat- ted common shrub, or from the enthusiasm created by a crowd's "hurrahs."
5. See James 1.27.

castin' it up at me that I don't do nothing for her and the chil'en; but then, lordy massy, Hepsy hain't no sort o' patience. Why jest this mornin' I was a tellin' her to count up her marcies, and I 'clare for 't if I didn't think she'd a throwed the tongs at me. That 'ere woman's temper railly makes me consarned. Wal, good day, Miss Lois. I'll be along again tomorrow or Friday, or the first o' next week." And away he went with long, loose strides down the village street, while the leisurely wail of an old fuguing tune[6] floated back after him,—

> "Thy years are an
> Etarnal day,
> Thy years are an
> Etarnal day."

"An eternal torment," said Aunt Lois, with a snap. "I'm sure, if there's a mortal creature on this earth that I pity, it's Hepsy Lawson. Folks talk about her scolding,—that Sam Lawson is enough to make the saints in Heaven fall from grace. And you can't *do* anything with him: it's like charging bayonet into a woolsack."

Now, the Hepsy thus spoken of was the luckless woman whom Sam's easy temper, and a certain youthful reputation for being a capable fellow, had led years before into the snares of matrimony with him, in consequence of which she was encumbered with the bringing up of six children on very short rations. She was a gnarly, compact, efficient little pepper-box of a woman, with snapping black eyes, pale cheeks, and a mouth always at half-cock, ready to go off with some sharp crack of reproof at the shoreless, bottomless, and tideless inefficiency of her husband. It seemed to be one of those facts of existence that she could not get used to, nor find anywhere in her brisk, fiery little body a grain of cool resignation for. Day after day she fought it with as bitter and intense a vigor, and with as much freshness of objurgation, as if it had come upon her for the first time,—just as a sharp, wiry little terrier will bark and bark from day to day, with never-ceasing pertinacity, into an empty squirrel-hole. She seemed to have no power within her to receive and assimilate the great truth that her husband was essentially, and was to be and always would be, only a do-nothing.

Poor Hepsy was herself quite as essentially a do-something,—an early-rising, bustling, driving, neat, efficient, capable little body,—who contrived, by going out to day's works,—washing, scrubbing, cleaning,—by making vests for the tailor, or closing and binding shoes for the shoemaker, by hoeing corn and potatoes in the garden at most unseasonable hours, actually to find bread to put into the mouths of the six young ravens aforesaid, and to clothe them decently. This might all do very well; but when Sam—who believed with all his heart in the modern doctrines of woman's rights so far as to have no sort of objection to Hepsy's sawing wood or hoeing potatoes if she chose—would

6. A tune composed in the form of a fugue.

make the small degree of decency and prosperity the family had attained by these means a text on which to preach resignation, cheerfulness, and submission, then Hepsy's last cobweb of patience gave out, and she often became, for the moment, really dangerous, so that Sam would be obliged to plunge hastily out of doors to avoid a strictly personal encounter.

It was not to be denied that poor Hepsy really was a scold, in the strong old Saxon acceptation of the word. She had fought life single-handed, tooth and nail, with all the ferocity of outraged sensibilities, and had come out of the fight scratched and dishevelled, with few womanly graces. The good wives of the village, versed in the outs and ins of their neighbors' affairs, while they admitted that Sam was not all he should be, would sometimes roll up the whites of their eyes mysteriously, and say, "But then, poor man, what could you expect when he hasn't a happy home? Hepsy's temper is, you know," etc., etc.

The fact is, that Sam's softly easy temper and habits of miscellaneous handiness caused him to have a warm corner in most of the households. No mothers ever are very hard on a man who always pleases the children; and everyone knows the welcome of a universal gossip, who carries round a district a wallet of choice bits of neighborhood information.

Now Sam knew everything about everybody. He could tell Mrs. Major Broad just what Lady Lothrop gave for her best parlor carpet, that was brought over from England, and just on what occasions she used the big silver tankard, and on what they were content with the little one, and how many pairs of long silk stockings the minister had, and how many rows of stitching there were on the shoulders of his Sunday shirts. He knew just all that was in Deacon Badger's best room, and how many silver table-spoons and teaspoons graced the beaufet[7] in the corner; and when each of his daughters was born, and just how Miss Susy came to marry as she did, and who wanted to marry her and couldn't. He knew just the cost of Major Broad's scarlet cloak and shoe-buckles, and how Mrs. Major had a real *Ingy* shawl up in her "camphire" trunk,[8] that cost nigh as much as Lady Lothrop's. Nobody had made love,[9] or married, or had children born, or been buried, since Sam was able to perambulate the country, without his informing himself minutely of every available particular; and his unfathomable knowledge on these subjects was an unfailing source of popularity.

Besides this, Sam was endowed with no end of idle accomplishments. His indolence was precisely of a turn that enjoyed the excitement of an occasional odd bit of work with which he had clearly no concern, and which had no sort of tendency toward his own support or that of his family. Something so far out of the line of practical utility as

7. Buffet.
8. Camphor is a crystalline compound obtained from camphor-tree wood and used as an insect repellent; placing camphor in a trunk of clothes was thought to repel moths and other insects. Ingy shawl: shawl from India.
9. In the 19th century, this meant to woo or to court someone.

to be in a manner an artistic labor would awaken all the energies of his soul. His shop was a perfect infirmary for decayed articles of *virtu*[1] from all the houses for miles around. Cracked china, lame tea-pots, broken shoe-buckles, rickety tongs, and decrepit fire-irons, all stood in melancholy proximity, awaiting Sam's happy hours of inspiration; and he was always happy to sit down and have a long, strictly confidential conversation concerning any of these with the owner, especially if Hepsy were gone out washing, or on any other work which kept her at a safe distance.

Sam could shave and cut hair as neatly as any barber, and was always in demand up and down the country to render these offices to the sick. He was ready to go for miles to watch with invalids, and a very acceptable watcher he made, beguiling the night hours with endless stories and legends. He was also an expert in psalmody, having in his youth been the pride of the village singing-school. In those days he could perform reputably on the bass-viol in the choir of a Sunday with a dolefulness and solemnity of demeanor in the highest degree edifying,—though he was equally ready of a week-evening in scraping on a brisk little fiddle, if any of the thoughtless ones wanted a performer at a husking or a quilting frolic. Sam's obligingness was many-sided, and he was equally prepared at any moment to raise a funeral psalm or whistle the time of a double-shuffle.

But the more particular delight of Sam's heart was in funerals. He would walk miles on hearing the news of a dangerous illness, and sit roosting on the fence of the premises, delighted to gossip over the particulars, but ready to come down at any moment to do any of the odd turns which sickness in a family makes necessary; and when the last earthly scene was over, Sam was more than ready to render those final offices from which the more nervous and fastidious shrink, but in which he took almost a professional pride.

The business of an undertaker is a refinement of modern civilization. In simple old days neighbors fell into one another's hands for all the last wants of our poor mortality; and there were men and women of note who took a particular and solemn pride in these mournful offices. Sam had in fact been up all night in our house, and having set me up in the clover, and comforted me with a jack-knife, he proceeded to inform me of the particulars.

"Why, ye see, Horace, I ben up with 'em pretty much all night; and I laid yer father out myself, and I never see a better-lookin' corpse. It's a 'mazin' pity your daddy hed such feelin's 'bout havin' people come to look at him, 'cause he does look beautiful, and it's been a long time since we've hed a funeral, anyway, and everybody was expectin' to come to his 'n, and they'll all be dissipinted if the corpse ain't show'd;

---

1. Italian for taste; thus, an article that is beautiful, rare, or otherwise interesting to a collector of fine arts.

but then, lordy massy, folks oughtn't to think hard on't ef folks hes their own way 'bout their own funeral. That 'ere's what I've been a tellin' on 'em all, over to the tavern and round to the store. Why, you never see such a talk as there was about it. There was Aunt Sally Morse, and Betsey and Patsy Sawin, and Mis' Zeruiah Bacon, come over early to look at the corpse, and when they was n't let in, you never heerd sich a jawin'. Betsey and Patsy Sawin said that they allers suspected your father was an infidel, or some sich, and now they was clear; and Aunt Sally, she asked who made his shroud, and when she heerd there wasn't to be none, he was laid out in his clothes, she said she never heerd such unchristian doin's,—that she always had heerd he had strange opinions, but she never thought it would come to that."

"My father isn't an infidel, and I wish I could kill 'em for talking so," said I, clenching my jack-knife in my small fist, and feeling myself shake with passion.

"Wal, wal, I kind o' spoke up to 'em about it. I wasn't a-goin' to hear no sich jaw; and says I, 'I think ef there is any body that knows what's what about funerals I'm the man, fur I don't s'pose there's a man in the county that's laid out more folks, and set up with more corpses, and ben sent for fur and near, than I have, and my opinion is that mourners must always follow the last directions gi'n to 'em by the person. Ef a man hasn't a right to have the say about his own body, what hes he a right to?' Wal, they said that it was putty well of me to talk so, when I had the privilege of sittin' up with him, and seein' all that was to be seen. 'Lordy massy,' says I, 'I don't see why ye need envi me; 't ain't my fault that folks thinks it's agreeable to have me round. As to bein' buried in his clothes, why, lordy massy, 't ain't nothin' so extraordinary. In the old country great folks is very often laid out in their clothes. 'Member, when I was a boy, old Mr. Sanger, the minister in Deerbrook, was laid out in his gown and bands, with a Bible in his hands, and he looked as nateral as a pictur. I was at Parson Rider's funeral, down to Wrentham. He was laid out in white flannel. But then there was old Captain Bigelow, down to the Pint there, he was laid out regular in his rigimentals, jest as he wore 'em in the war, epaulets and all.' Wal now, Horace, your daddy looks jest as peaceful as a psalmtune. Now, you don't know,—jest as nateral as if he'd only jest gone to sleep. So ye may set your heart at rest 'bout him."

It was one of those beautiful serene days of October, when the earth lies as bright and still as anything one can dream of in the New Jerusalem,[2] and Sam's homely expressions of sympathy had quieted me somewhat. Sam, tired of his discourse, lay back in the clover, with his hands under his head, and went on with his moralizing.

"Lordy massy, Horace, to think on 't,—it's so kind o' solemnizin'! It's

2. The Book of Revelation prophesies the recreation of the world with a new heaven, a new earth, and a heavenly Jerusalem; this is related to the establishment of a Millennium, which Stowe mentions earlier in this sketch.

one's turn today, and another's tomorrow. We never know when our turn'll come." And Sam raised a favorite stave,—

> "And must these active limbs of mine
> Lie moulderin' in the clay?"[3]

"Active limbs! I guess so!" said a sharp voice, which came through the clover-heads like the crack of a rifle. "Well, I've found you at last. Here you be, Sam Lawson, lyin' flat on your back at eleven o'clock in the morning, and not a potato dug, and not a stick of wood cut to get dinner with; and I won't cut no more if we never have dinner. It's no use a humorin' you,—doin' your work for you. The more I do, the more I may do; so come home, won't you?"

"Lordy massy, Hepsy," said Sam, slowly erecting himself out of the grass, and staring at her with white eyes, "you don't ought to talk so. I ain't to blame. I had to sit up with Mr. Holyoke all night, and help 'em lay him out at four o'clock this mornin'."

"You're always everywhere but where you've business to be," said Hepsy; "and helpin' and doin' for everybody but your own. For my part, I think charity ought to begin at home. You're everywhere, up and down and round,—over to Shelbun, down to Podunk, up to North Parish; and here Abram and Kiah Stebbins have been waitin' all the morning with a horse they brought all the way from Boston to get you to shoe."

"Wal now, that 'ere shows they know what's what. I told Kiah that ef they'd bring that 'ere hoss to me I'd 'tend to his huffs."

"And be off lying in the mowing, like a partridge, when they come after ye. That's one way to do business," said Hepsy.

"Hepsy, I was just a miditatin'. Ef we don't miditate sometimes on all these 'ere things, it'll be wus for us by and by."

"Meditate! I'll help your meditations in a way you won't like, if you don't look out. So now you come home, and stop your meditatin', and go to doin' something'. I told 'em to come back this afternoon, and I'd have you on the spot if 't was a possible thing," said the very practical Hepsy, laying firm hold of Sam's unresisting arm, and leading him away captive.

I stole into the darkened, silent room where my father had lain so long. Its desolate neatness struck a chill to my heart. Not even a bottle remained of the many familiar ones that used to cover the stand and the mantel-piece; but he, lying in his threadbare Sunday coat, looked to me as I had often seen him in later days, when he had come from school exhausted, and fallen asleep on the bed. I crept to his side and nestled down on the floor as quietly as a dog lies down by the side of his master.

Oldtown Folks, 1869

---

3. Most likely, lines from a familiar hymn.

The Minister's Housekeeper

Scene.—The shady side of a blueberry-pasture.—Sam Lawson with the
boys, picking blueberries.—Sam, *loq.*[1]

Wal, you see, boys, 'twas just here,—Parson Carryl's wife, she died
along in the forepart o' March: my cousin Huldy,[2] she undertook to
keep house for him. The way on't was, that Huldy, she went to take
care o' Mis' Carryl in the fust on't, when she fust took sick. Huldy was
a tailoress by trade; but then she was one o' these 'ere facultised
persons[3] that has a gift for most anything, and that was how Mis'
Carryl come to set sech store by her, that, when she was sick, nothin'
would do for her but she must have Huldy round all the time: and the
minister, he said he'd make it good to her all the same, and she
shouldn't lose nothin' by it. And so Huldy, she staid with Mis' Carryl
full three months afore she died, and got to seein' to everything pretty
much round the place.

"Wal, arter Mis' Carryl died, Parson Carryl, he'd got so kind o' used
to hevin' on her 'round, takin' care o' things, that he wanted her to stay
along a spell; and so Huldy, she staid along a spell, and poured out his
tea, and mended his close, and made pies and cakes, and cooked and
washed and ironed, and kep' every thing as neat as a pin. Huldy was
a dreffel chipper sort o' gal; and work sort o' rolled off from her like
water off a duck's back. There warn't no gal in Sherburne that could
put sich a sight o' work through as Huldy; and yet, Sunday mornin', she
always come out in the singers' seat like one o' these 'ere June roses,
lookin' so fresh and smilin', and her voice was jest as clear and sweet
as a meadow lark's—Lordy massy! I 'member how she used to sing
some o' them 'are places where the treble and counter used to go
together: her voice kind o' trembled a little, and it sort o' went thro'
and thro' a feller! tuck him right where he lived!"

Here Sam leaned contemplatively back with his head in a clump of
sweet fern, and refreshed himself with a chew of young wintergreen.
"This 'ere young wintergreen, boys, is jest like a feller's thoughts o'
things that happened when he was young: it comes up jest so fresh and
tender every year, the longest time you hev to live; and you can't help
chawin' on't tho' 'tis sort o' stingin'. I don't never get over likin' young
wintergreen."

"But about Huldah, Sam?"

"Oh, yes! about Huldy. Lordy massy! when a feller is Indianin'
round,[4] these 'ere pleasant summer days, a feller's thoughts gits like a
flock o' young partridges: they's up and down and everywhere; 'cause
one place is jest about as good as another, when they's all so kind o'

---

1. Abbreviation for Latin *loquitur,* "begins to
speak," often used as a stage direction.
2. Short for Huldah, a biblical name; an Old Testament prophetess: see 2 Kings 22.14.
3. I.e., persons who possess faculty, great skill in a

variety of household arts and occupations.
4. "To Indian 'round" was an expression colonists
used; it expressed their view that Indians moved
about stealthily.

comfortable and nice. Wal, about Huldy,—as I was a sayin'. She was jest as handsome a gal to look at as a feller could have; and I think a nice, well-behaved young gal in the singers' seat of a Sunday is a means o' grace: it's sort o' drawin' to the unregenerate, you know. Why, boys, in them days, I've walked ten miles over to Sherburne of a Sunday mornin', jest to play the bass-viol in the same singers' seat with Huldy. She was very much respected, Huldy was; and, when she went out to tailorin', she was allers bespoke[5] six months ahead, and sent for in waggins up and down for ten miles round; for the young fellers was allers 'mazin' anxious to be sent after Huldy, and was quite free to offer to go for her. Wal, after Mis' Carryl died, Huldy got to be sort o' housekeeper at the minister's, and saw to everything, and did everything: so that there warn't a pin out o' the way.

"But you know how 'tis in parishes: there allers is women that thinks the minister's affairs belongs to them, and they ought to have the rulin' and guidin' of 'em; and, if a minister's wife dies, there's folks that allers has their eyes open on providences,—lookin' out who's to be the next one.

"Now, there was Mis' Amaziah Pipperidge, a widder with snappin' black eyes, and a hook nose,—kind o' like a hawk; and she was one o' them up-and-down commandin' sort o' women, that feel that they have a call to be seein' to everything that goes on in the parish, and 'specially to the minister.

"Folks did say that Mis' Pipperidge sort o' sot her eye on the parson for herself: wal, now that 'are might a been, or it might not. Some folks thought it was a very suitable connection. You see she hed a good property of her own, right nigh to the minister's lot, and was allers kind o' active and busy; so, takin' one thing with another, I shouldn't wonder if Mis' Pipperidge should a thought that Providence p'inted that way. At any rate, she went up to Deakin[6] Blodgett's wife, and they two sort o' put their heads together a mournin' and condolin' about the way things was likely to go on at the minister's now Mis' Carryl was dead. Ye see, the parson's wife, she was one of them women who hed their eyes everywhere and on everything. She was a little thin woman, but tough as Inger rubber,[7] and smart as a steel trap; and there warn't a hen laid an egg, or cackled, but Mis' Carryl was right there to see about it; and she hed the garden made in the spring, and the medders mowed in summer, and the cider made, and the corn husked, and the apples got in the fall; and the doctor, he hedn't nothin' to do but jest sit stock still a meditatin' on Jerusalem and Jericho and them things that ministers think about. But Lordy massy! he didn't know nothin' about where anything he eat or drunk or wore come from or went to: his wife jest led him 'round in temporal things and took care on him like a baby.

---

5. I.e., she was always engaged, claimed, or reserved six months in advance.
6. Deacon.
7. Natural rubber from the tropical rubber tree, and the basis for the earliest manufactured rubber products; it was known for its durability and sometimes referred to as "India rubber."

"Wal, to be sure, Mis' Carryl looked up to him in spirituals, and thought all the world on him; for there warn't a smarter minister nowhere 'round. Why, when he preached on decrees and election,[8] they used to come clear over from South Parish, and West Sherburne, and Old Town to hear him; and there was sich a row o' waggins tied along by the meetin'-house that the stables was all full, and all the hitchin'-posts was full clean up to the tavern, so that folks said the doctor made the town look like a gineral trainin'-day[9] a Sunday.

"He was great on texts, the doctor was. When he hed a p'int to prove, he'd jest go thro' the Bible, and drive all the texts ahead o' him like a flock o' sheep; and then, if there was a text that seemed agin him, why, he'd come out with his Greek and Hebrew, and kind o' chase it 'round a spell, jest as ye see a fellar chase a contrary bell-wether,[1] and make him jump the fence arter the rest. I tell you, there wa'n't no text in the Bible that could stand agin the doctor when his blood was up. The year arter the doctor was app'inted to preach the 'lection sermon[2] in Boston, he made such a figger that the Brattle-street Church sent a committee right down to see if they couldn't get him to Boston; and then the Sherburne folks, they up and raised his salary; ye see, there ain't nothin' wakes folks up like somebody else's wantin' what you've got. Wal, that fall they made him a Doctor o' Divinity at Cambridge College,[3] and so they sot more by him than ever. Wal, you see, the doctor, of course he felt kind o' lonesome and afflicted when Mis' Carryl was gone; but railly and truly, Huldy was so up to everything about house, that the doctor didn't miss nothin' in a temporal way. His shirt-bosoms was pleated finer than they ever was, and them ruffles 'round his wrists was kep' like the driven snow; and there warn't a brack in his silk stockin's, and his shoe buckles was kep' polished up, and his coats brushed; and then there warn't no bread and biscuit like Huldy's; and her butter was like solid lumps o' gold; and there wern't no pies to equal hers; and so the doctor never felt the loss o' Miss Carryl at table. Then there was Huldy allers oppisite to him, with her blue eyes and her cheeks like two fresh peaches. She was kind o' pleasant to look at; and the more the doctor looked at her the better he liked her; and so things seemed to be goin' on quite quiet and comfortable ef it hadn't been that Mis' Pipperidge and Mis' Deakin Blodgett and Mis' Sawin got their heads together a talkin' about things.

" 'Poor man,' says Mis' Pipperidge, 'what can that child that he's got there do towards takin' the care of all that place? It takes a mature woman,' she says, 'to tread in Mis' Carryl's shoes.'

---

8. The Calvinist doctrine of predestined salvation for members of God's "elect."
9. The day on which military drill was required of civilians or the muster for such drill took place; it became an occasion for games, fireworks, and a public festival.
1. A male sheep, usually castrated, with a bell hung from its neck, supposed to serve as a lead sheep to keep the herd together.
2. The kind of sermon preached on election day in New England small towns, a jeremiad in which the sins of New England were tabulated over and over again, urging listeners to restore holiness to their society.
3. Harvard College in Cambridge, Mass.; Harvard established a divinity school in 1816.

" 'That it does,' said Mis' Blodgett; 'and, when things once get to runnin' down hill, there ain't no stoppin' on 'em,' says she.

"Then Mis' Sawin she took it up. (Ye see, Mis' Sawin used to go out to dress-makin', and was sort o' jealous, 'cause folks sot more by Huldy than they did by her.) 'Well,' says she, 'Huldy Peters is well enough at her trade. I never denied that, though I do say I never did believe in her way o' makin' button-holes; and I must say, if 'twas the dearest friend I hed, that I thought Huldy tryin' to fit Mis' Kittridge's plumb-colored silk was a clear piece o' presumption; the silk was jist spiled, so 'twarn't fit to come into the meetin'-house. I must say, Huldy's a gal that's always too ventersome about takin' 'sponsibilities she don't know nothin' about.'

" 'Of course she don't,' said Mis' Deakin Blodgett. 'What does she know about all the lookin' and seein' to that there ought to be in guidin' the minister's house. Huldy's well meanin', and she's good at her work, and good in the singers' seat; but Lordy massy! she hain't got no experience. Parson Carryl ought to have an experienced woman to keep house for him. There's the spring house-cleanin' and the fall house-cleanin' to be seen to, and the things to be put away from the moths; and then the gettin' ready for the association[4] and all the ministers' meetin's; and the makin' the soap and the candles, and settin' the hens and turkeys, watchin' the calves, and seein' after the hired men and the garden; and there that 'are blessed man jist sets there at home as serene, and has nobody 'round but that 'are gal, and don't even know how things must be a runnin' to waste!'

"Wal, the upshot on't was, they fussed and fuzzled and wuzzled[5] till they'd drinked up all the tea in the tea-pot; and then they went down and called on the parson, and wuzzled him all up talkin' about this, that, and t'other that wanted lookin' to, and that it was no way to leave everything to a young chit[6] like Huldy, and that he ought to be lookin' about for an experienced woman. The parson he thanked 'em kindly, and said he believed their motives was good, but he didn't go no further. He didn't ask Mis' Pipperidge to come and stay there and help him, nor nothin' o' that kind; but he said he'd attend to matters himself. The fact was, the parson had got such a likin' for havin' Huldy 'round, that he couldn't think o' such a thing as swappin' her off for the Widder Pipperidge.

"But he thought to himself, 'Huldy is a good girl; but I oughtn't to be a leavin' everything to her,—it's too hard on her. I ought to be instructin' and guidin' and helpin' of her; 'cause 'tain't everybody could be expected to know and do what Mis' Carryl did;' and so at it he went; and Lordy massy! didn't Huldy hev a time on't when the minister began to come out of his study, and want to tew 'round[7] and

---

4. Annual meeting of the society of the clergymen of a neighborhood.
5. Mixed up, jumbled.

6. A child, especially a young girl.
7. Worry, fret, fuss.

see to things? Huldy, you see, thought all the world of the minister, and she was 'most afraid to laugh; but she told me she couldn't, for the life of her, help it when his back was turned, for he wuzzled things up in the most singular way. But Huldy she'd jest say 'Yes, sir,' and get him off into his study, and go on her own way.

" 'Huldy,' says the minister one day, 'you ain't experienced out-doors; and, when you want to know anything, you must come to me.'

" 'Yes, sir,' says Huldy.

" 'Now, Huldy,' says the parson, 'you must be sure to save the turkey-eggs, so that we can have a lot of turkeys for Thanksgiving.'

" 'Yes, sir,' says Huldy; and she opened the pantry-door, and showed him a nice dishful she'd been a savin' up. Wal, the very next day the parson's hen-turkey was found killed up to old Jim Scroggs's barn. Folks said Scroggs killed it; though Scroggs, he stood to it he didn't: at any rate, the Scroggses, they made a meal on't, and Huldy, she felt bad about it 'cause she'd set her heart on raisin' the turkeys; and says she, 'Oh, dear! I don't know what I shall do. I was just ready to set her.'

" 'Do, Huldy?' says the parson: 'why, there's the other turkey, out there by the door; and a fine bird, too, he is.'

Sure enough, there was the old tom-turkey a struttin' and a sidlin' and a quitterin,' and a floutin' his tail-feathers in the sun, like a lively young widower, all ready to begin life over agin.

" 'But,' says Huldy, 'you know *he* can't set on eggs.'

" 'He can't? I'd like to know why,' says the parson. 'He *shall* set on eggs, and hatch 'em too.'

" 'O doctor!' says Huldy, all in a tremble; 'cause, you know, she didn't want to contradict the minister, and she was afraid she should laugh,—'I never heard that a tom-turkey would set on eggs.'

" 'Why, they ought to,' said the parson, getting quite 'arnest: 'what else be they good for? you just bring out the eggs, now, and put 'em in the nest, and I'll make him set on 'em.'

"So Huldy she thought there wern't no way to convince him but to let him try: so she took the eggs out, and fixed 'em all nice in the nest; and then she come back and found old Tom a skirmishin' with the parson pretty lively, I tell ye. Ye see, old Tom he didn't take the idee at all; and he flopped and gobbled, and fit the parson; and the parson's wig got 'round so that his cue[8] stuck straight out over his ear, but he'd got his blood up. Ye see, the old doctor was used to carryin' his p'ints o' doctrine; and he hadn't fit the Arminians and Socinians[9] to be beat by a tom-turkey; so finally he made a dive, and ketched him by the neck in spite o' his floppin', and stroked him down, and put Huldy's apron 'round him.

8. From *queue*; the braid or "tail" of the wig.
9. Christian sects that rejected fundamental beliefs of Calvinism; Arminians opposed the doctrine of absolute predestination and Socinians denied the divinity of Jesus.

" 'There, Huldy,' he says, quite red in the face, 'we've got him now;' and he travelled off to the barn with him as lively as a cricket.

"Huldy came behind jist chokin' with laugh, and afraid the minister would look 'round and see her.

" 'Now, Huldy, we'll crook his legs, and set him down,' says the parson, when they got him to the nest: 'you see he is getting quiet, and he'll set there all right.'

"And the parson, he sot him down; and old Tom he sot there solemn enough, and held his head down all droopin', lookin' like a rail pious old cock, as long as the parson sot by him.

" 'There: you see how still he sets,' says the parson to Huldy.

"Huldy was 'most dyin' for fear she should laugh. 'I'm afraid he'll get up,' says she, 'when you do.'

" 'Oh, no, he won't!' says the parson, quite confident. 'There, there,' says he, layin' his hands on him, as if pronouncin' a blessin'. But when the parson riz up, old Tom he riz up too, and began to march over the eggs.

" 'Stop, now!' says the parson. 'I'll make him get down agin: hand me that corn-basket; we'll put that over him.'

"So he crooked old Tom's legs, and got him down agin; and they put the corn-basket over him, and then they both stood and waited.

" 'That'll do the thing, Huldy,' said the parson.

" 'I don't know about it,' says Huldy.

" 'Oh, yes, it will, child! I understand,' says he.

"Just as he spoke, the basket riz right up and stood, and they could see old Tom's long legs.

" 'I'll make him stay down, confound him,' says the parson; for, ye see, parsons is men, like the rest on us, and the doctor had got his spunk up.

" 'You jist hold him a minute, and I'll get something that'll make him stay, I guess;' and out he went to the fence, and brought in a long, thin, flat stone, and laid it on old Tom's back.

"Old Tom he wilted down considerable under this, and looked railly as if he was goin' to give in. He staid still there a good long spell, and the minister and Huldy left him there and come up to the house; but they hadn't more than got in the door before they see old Tom a hippin' along, as high-steppin' as ever, sayin' 'Talk! talk! and quitter! quitter!' and struttin' and gobblin' as if he'd come through the Red Sea,[1] and got the victory.

" 'Oh, my eggs!' says Huldy. 'I'm afraid he's smashed 'em!'

"And sure enough, there they was, smashed flat enough under the stone.

---

1. The gulf between Egypt and Arabia, and the site where Moses stretched out his hand while the God of the Israelites parted the waters, allowing Moses to lead the Israelites out of Egypt and into the Promised Land; see Exodus 10–15.

" 'I'll have him killed,' said the parson: 'we won't have such a critter 'round.'

"But the parson, he slep' on't, and then didn't do it: he only come out next Sunday with a tip-top sermon on the ' 'Riginal Cuss'[2] that was pronounced on things in gineral, when Adam fell, and showed how everything was allowed to go contrary ever since. There was pig-weed, and pusley, and Canady thistles, cut-worms, and bag-worms, and can-ker-worms, to say nothin' of rattlesnakes. The doctor made it very impressive and sort o' improvin'; but Huldy, she told me, goin' home, that she hardly could keep from laughin' two or three times in the sermon when she thought of old Tom a standin' up with the corn-basket on his back.

"Wal, next week Huldy she jist borrowed the minister's horse and side-saddle, and rode over to South Parish to her Aunt Bascome's,— Widder Bascome's, you know, that lives there by the trout-brook,— and got a lot o' turkey-eggs o' her, and come back and set a hen on 'em, and said nothin'; and in good time there was as nice a lot o' turkey-chicks as ever ye see.

"Huldy never said a word to the minister about his experiment, and he never said a word to her; but he sort o' kep' more to his books, and didn't take it on him to advise so much.

"But not long arter he took it into his head that Huldy ought to have a pig to be a fattin' with the buttermilk. Mis' Pipperidge set him up to it; and jist then old Tim Bigelow, out to Juniper Hill, told him if he'd call over he'd give him a little pig.

"So he sent for a man, and told him to build a pig-pen right out by the well, and have it all ready when he came home with his pig.

"Huldy she said she wished he might put a curb round the well out there, because in the dark, sometimes, a body might stumble into it; and the parson, he told him he might do that.

"Wal, old Aikin, the carpenter, he didn't come till most the middle of the arternoon; and then he sort o' idled, so that he didn't get up the well-curb till sun-down; and then he went off and said he'd come and do the pig-pen next day.

"Wal, arter dark, Parson Carryl he driv into the yard, full chizel,[3] with his pig. He'd tied up his mouth to keep him from squeelin'; and he see what he thought was the pig-pen,—he was rather near-sight-ed,—and so he ran and threw piggy over; and down he dropped into the water, and the minister put out his horse and pranced off into the house quite delighted.

" 'There, Huldy, I've got you a nice little pig.'

" 'Dear me!' says Huldy: 'where have you put him?'

---

2. The Calvinists believed that when Adam and Eve disobeyed God—the original sin recounted in Genesis—human infants thereafter were born sin-ners and could only be saved by the redemption of Christ.

3. Full speed.

" 'Why, out there in the pig-pen, to be sure.'

" 'Oh, dear me!' says Huldy: 'that's the well-curb; there ain't no pig-pen built,' says she.

" 'Lordy massy!' says the parson: 'then I've thrown the pig in the well!'

"Wal, Huldy she worked and worked, and finally she fished piggy out in the bucket, but he was dead as a door-nail; and she got him out o' the way quietly, and didn't say much; and the parson, he took to a great Hebrew book in his study; and says he, 'Huldy, I ain't much in temporals,' says he. Huldy says she kind o' felt her heart go out to him, he was so sort o' meek and helpless and larned; and says she, 'Wal, Parson Carryl, don't trouble your head no more about it; I'll see to things;' and sure enough, a week arter there was a nice pen, all ship-shape, and two little white pigs that Huldy bought with the money for the butter she sold at the store.

" 'Wal, Huldy,' said the parson, 'you are a most amazin' child: you don't say nothin', but you do more than most folks.'

"Arter that the parson set sich store by Huldy that he come to her and asked her about everything, and it was amazin' how everything she put her hand to prospered. Huldy planted marigolds and larkspurs, pinks and carnations, all up and down the path to the front door, and trained up mornin' glories and scarlet-runners round the windows. And she was always a gettin' a root here, and a sprig there, and a seed from somebody else: for Huldy was one o' them that has the gift, so that ef you jist give 'em the leastest sprig of anything they make a great bush out of it right away; so that in six months Huldy had roses and geraniums and lilies, sich as it would a took a gardener to raise. The parson, he took no notice at fust; but when the yard was all ablaze with flowers he used to come and stand in a kind o' maze[4] at the front door, and say, 'Beautiful, beautiful: why, Huldy, I never see anything like it.' And then when her work was done arternoons, Huldy would sit with her sewin' in the porch, and sing and trill away till she'd draw the meadow-larks and the bobolinks, and the orioles to answer her, and the great big elm-tree overhead would get perfectly rackety with the birds; and the parson, settin' there in his study, would git to kind o' dreamin' about the angels, and golden harps, and the New Jerusalem; but he wouldn't speak a word, 'cause Huldy she was jist like them wood-thrushes, she never could sing so well when she thought folks was hearin'. Folks noticed, about this time, that the parson's sermons got to be like Aaron's rod, that budded and blossomed:[5] there was things in 'em about flowers and birds, and more 'special about the music o' heaven. And Huldy she noticed, that ef there was a hymn run

---

4. Amazement, as in the sense of being dazed, bewildered, or stupefied.
5. One of the ways God revealed his power to the Israelites; Aaron, Moses' older brother, stretched out his staff to produce several miracles intended to convince the Egyptians that the Israelites were God's chosen people; see Exodus 7–8.

in her head while she was 'round a workin' the minister was sure to give it out next Sunday. You see, Huldy was jist like a bee: she always sung when she was workin', and you could hear her trillin', now down in the corn-patch, while she was pickin' the corn; and now in the buttery, while she was workin' the butter; and now she'd go singin' down cellar, and then she'd be singin' up overhead, so that she seemed to fill a house chock full o' music.

"Huldy was so sort o' chipper and fair spoken, that she got the hired men all under her thumb: they come to her and took her orders jist as meek as so many calves; and she traded at the store, and kep' the accounts, and she hed her eyes everywhere, and tied up all the ends so tight that there want no gettin' 'round her. She wouldn't let nobody put nothin' off[6] on Parson Carryl, 'cause he was a minister. Huldy was allers up to anybody that wanted to make a hard bargain; and, afore he knew jist what he was about, she'd got the best end of it, and everybody said that Huldy was the most capable gal that they'd ever traded with.

"Wal, come to the meetin' of the Association, Mis' Deakin Blodgett and Mis' Pipperidge come callin' up to the parson's, all in a stew, and offerin' their services to get the house ready; but the doctor, he jist thanked 'em quite quiet, and turned 'em over to Huldy; and Huldy she told 'em that she'd got everything ready, and showed 'em her pantries, and her cakes and her pies and her puddin's, and took 'em all over the house; and they went peeking' and pokin', openin' cupboard-doors, and lookin' into drawers; and they couldn't find so much as a thread out o' the way, from garret to cellar, and so they went off quite discontented. Arter that the women set a new trouble a brewin'. Then they begun to talk that it was a year now since Mis' Carryl died; and it r'ally wasn't proper such a young gal to be stayin' there, who everybody could see was a settin' her cap for the minister.

"Mis' Pipperidge said, that, so long as she looked on Huldy as the hired gal, she hadn't thought much about it; but Huldy was railly takin' on airs as an equal, and appearin' as mistress o' the house in a way that would make talk if it went on. And Mis' Pipperidge she driv 'round up to Deakin Abner Snow's, and down to Mis' 'Lijah Perry's, and asked them if they wasn't afraid that the way the parson and Huldy was a goin' on might make talk. And they said they hadn't thought on't before, but now, come to think on't, they was sure it would; and they all went and talked with somebody else, and asked them if they didn't think it would make talk. So come Sunday, between meetin's there warn't nothin' else talked about; and Huldy saw folks a noddin' and a winkin', and a lookin' arter her, and she begun to feel dreffial sort o' disagreeable. Finally Mis' Sawin she says to her, 'My dear, didn't you never think folk would talk about you and the minister?'

6. I.e., cheat.

" 'No: why should they?' says Huldy, quite innocent.

"'Wal, dear,' says she, 'I think it's a shame; but they say you're tryin' to catch him, and that it's so bold and improper for you to be courtin' of him right in his own house,—you know folks will talk,—I thought I'd tell you 'cause I think so much of you,' says she.

"Huldy was a gal of spirit, and she despised the talk, but it made her dreful uncomfortable; and when she got home at night she sat down in the mornin'-glory porch, quite quiet, and didn't sing a word.

"The minister he had heard the same thing from one of his deakins that day; and, when he saw Huldy so kind o' silent, he says to her, 'Why don't you sing, my child?'

"He hed a pleasant sort o' way with him, the minister had, and Huldy had got to likin' to be with him; and it all come over her that perhaps she ought to go away; and her throat kind o' filled up so she couldn't hardly speak; and, says she, 'I can't sing to-night.'

"Says he, 'You don't know how much good your singin' has done me, nor how much good *you* have done me in all ways, Huldy. I wish I knew how to show my gratitude.'

" 'O sir!' says Huldy, *'is* it improper for me to be here?'

" 'No, dear,' says the minister, 'but ill-natured folks will talk; but there is one way we can stop it, Huldy—if you will marry me. You'll make me very happy, and I'll do all I can to make you happy. Will you?'

"Wal, Huldy never told me jist what she said to the minister,—gals never does give you the particulars of them 'are things jist as you'd like 'em,—only I know the upshot and the hull on't was, that Huldy she did a consid'able lot o' clear starchin' and ironin' the next two days; and the Friday o' next week the minister and she rode over together to Dr. Lothrop's in Old Town; and the doctor, he jist made 'em man and wife, 'spite of envy of the Jews,' as the hymn says. Wal, you'd better believe there was a starin' and a wonderin' next Sunday mornin' when the second bell was a tollin', and the minister walked up the broad aisle with Huldy, all in white, arm in arm with him, and he opened the minister's pew, and handed her in as if she was a princess; for, you see, Parson Carryl come of a good family, and was a born gentleman, and had a sort o' grand way o' bein' polite to women-folks. Wal, I guess there was a rus'lin' among the bunnets. Mis' Pipperidge gin a great bounce, like corn poppin' on a shovel, and her eyes glared through her glasses at Huldy as if they'd a sot her afire; and everybody in the meetin' house was a starin', I tell *yew*. But they couldn't none of 'em say nothin' agin Huldy's looks; for there wa'n't a crimp nor a frill about her that wa'n't jis' *so;* and her frock was white as the driven snow, and she had her bunnet all trimmed up with white ribbins; and all the fellows said the old doctor had stole a march, and got the handsomest gal in the parish.

"Wal, arter meetin' they all come 'round the parson and Huldy at the door, shakin' hands and laughin'; for by that time they was about agreed that they'd got to let putty well alone.

" 'Why, Parson Carryl,' says Mis' Deakin Blodgett, 'how you've come it over us.'[7]

" 'Yes,' says the parson, with a kind o' twinkle in his eye. 'I thought,' says he, 'as folks wanted to talk about Huldy and me, I'd give 'em somethin' wuth talkin' about.' "

Oldtown Fireside Stories, 1872

7. Put one over on us.

ALICE CARY
1820–1871

The legend that surrounded Alice Cary's life and became even more pronounced after her death portrayed her as an original genius who developed in isolation. While many of the details of her life support this legend, the larger literary context within which Cary grew up almost certainly would have influenced her development as a writer. Though no direct evidence exists to indicate that Alice Cary met Harriet Beecher Stowe during the period when the one resided near and the other in Cincinnati, or that the adolescent Cary read the sketch Stowe published in the *Western Monthly Magazine* in April 1834, one can surmise that Cary knew of her literary predecessor. Cary probably made her earliest contacts in the world of Cincinnati publishing through an older cousin, William D. Gallagher, who as poet and editor of various periodicals knew James Hall, editor of the *Western Monthly Magazine*. In 1834 Gallagher noted the publication of the prize-winning story, " 'A New England Sketch' by Miss Beecher, of this city" (Venable, 444). Cousin Gallagher also used his influence to help Cary become acquainted with Gamaliel Bailey, who would later edit the abolitionist weekly *The National Era* and publish concurrently *Uncle Tom's Cabin* and Cary's fiction. Moreover, Cincinnati in the 1830s and 1840s was no frontier town but rather a city with aspirations that included becoming the literary center of the West. Even though she lived outside the geographical perimeter of Cincinnati, Alice Cary must have responded to the city's literary aspirations with her own early attempts to write.

Alice Cary was born on April 26, 1820, on a farm in Hamilton County, Ohio, eight miles north of Cincinnati. The village built at the crossroads nearest this farm was called Mount Healthy; this village, with its surrounding farms and houses, became the Clovernook of her fiction. Death and deprivation marked Cary's early years. Her beloved older sister Rhoda, who on the way to and from school told Alice stories and who encouraged her first attempts at poetry, died in 1833, as did another favorite younger sister. Two years later her mother died. Robert Cary remarried in 1837, and his new wife apparently cared more for housework than for literature, forcing Cary and her younger sister Phoebe to compose at night and hide their manuscripts in a secret closet under the stairs. Cary's formal schooling was brief and her parents, whether from lack of interest or money or both, did not provide the resources that would have enabled her to continue her education informally.

Cary began her literary career as a poet, publishing her first poem in 1838. In 1848 Rufus Griswold included her work, and Phoebe's, in *The Female Poets of America*, and in 1849 he arranged for the publication of *Poems of Alice and Phoebe Cary*. She published her first short fiction in 1847 in *The National Era*, thus gaining the attention of contributing editor John Greenleaf Whittier. Recognition beyond the region opened doors for Cary, who with Phoebe moved to New York City in 1850. There she made her permanent home, buying in 1855 a house on East Twentieth Street. The household Cary established included both Phoebe and another younger sister, Elmina, and two servants who were also sisters. Although marriage was apparently a possibility, Cary chose to make sisterhood her primary bond, living out her life with her surviving sisters while never ceasing to mourn those she lost in 1833. Privately nourishing, the bond between sisters became a public force as well. For fifteen years, the Cary sisters hosted a reception on Sunday evening to which came such figures as Horace Greeley, J. G. Whittier, James and Annie Fields, Gail Hamilton, and William Lloyd Garrison.

During the last eighteen months of her life Cary was paralyzed and bedridden. She died on February 12, 1871, at age fifty and was buried in Brooklyn's Greenwood Cemetery. Phoebe survived her by only five months.

o   o   o

Moving east, Cary recollected "Clovernook," perhaps as Stowe, after moving west, found it possible to define the New Englandness of New England. Although she had published short fiction prior to her move, it was with the publication in 1852 of *Clovernook: or Sketches of Our Neighborhood in the West* and its sequel, *Clovernook, Second Series* (1853), that Cary reached the high point of her career as a writer of sketches. These sketches are the first pieces of regional fiction that realize the possibilities of the genre. Although some extraordinary sketches appear in the later collection, *Pictures of Country Life* (1859), such as "Passages from the Married Life of Eleanor Homes," included here, the collection as a whole presents diminished formal and thematic possibilities; *Pictures of Country Life* lacks the connecting device of Clovernook, and in many of the stories in this volume Cary relies on the "miraculous" ending to solve her formal and thematic problems.

Responding, like many of her contemporaries, to the call for a specifically *American* literature, Alice Cary, as she explains in her Preface to *Clovernook*, chose to explore rural life from the perspective of one who had lived it and could therefore paint "true" pictures. Later, local-color writers would go into rural areas and describe peculiarities of mannerism, dialect, and folkways for urban readers from a perspective clearly different from that of the region. From her earliest fiction, Alice Cary rejects a literature of place that would view a region's inhabitants as objects; instead she creates a literature that locates narrative subjectivity in the region. Moreover, Cary typically identifies the regional subject as female. In so doing she revises the connection between region and masculine values and perspective established by Stowe in "Uncle Lot." And, in contrast to Caroline Kirkland, who in *A New Home—Who'll Follow?* (1839) described the experience of encountering region as an adult leaving home to follow her husband's adventure, Cary, in recollecting Clovernook, was returning to the source of her identity and so recovering home. In Cary's story of how she "came up to womanhood," region provides the impetus to consciousness.

In the Preface to *Clovernook*, Cary establishes her commitment to recording accurately those "little histories every day revealed" that interest us in "humanity." When the subjects of such histories are women—or the perceptions of "shadows and sunbeams that fell about me as I came up to womanhood"— such accuracy may require a new form. Cary explicitly states that she had no "thought of making a book" as she began to accumulate the record of her memories, and she concludes her Preface by describing her work as a series of "sketches." Indeed, when Cary did set out to write books—by which she may

mean novels—she followed conventional plotlines and told stories about
women seduced and abandoned, as in *Hagar, A Story of Today* (1852). Yet in
her regional sketches, she found a way to tell a different story, possibly by
providing a form that could reflect the nature of lives frequently experienced
merely as "shadows and sunbeams." For Cary, the act of telling stories is a
means of development for women, who, through the telling, discover, understand, and record their experiences. In an early sketch, "Dreams and Tokens"
(1847), she notes explicitly that "the process of spinning two kinds of yarns
commenced at once." In contrast to Stowe's position in "Uncle Lot" and later
in the Sam Lawson stories, where Stowe associates storytelling with men,
Cary, harking back to older traditions, suggests that, as the spinners of yarn,
women were also the spinners of yarns. Thus, in "Uncle Christopher's," the
narrator's ability to tell her story is implicitly enhanced by the seven women
who sit knitting throughout the tale, their presence revealing their own "little
histories." For Cary, the regional sketch very much resembles the spinning—
and knitting—of the yarn of women's experience.

Preface to *Clovernook*

The pastoral life of our country has not been a favorite subject of
illustration by painters, poets, or writers of romance. Perhaps it has
been regarded as wanting in the elements of beauty; perhaps it has
been thought too passionless and even; or it may have been deemed
too immediate and familiar. I have had little opportunity for its observation in the eastern and northern states, and in the south there is no
such life, and in the far west where pioneers are still busy with felling
the opposing trees, it is not yet time for the reed's music;[1] but in the
interior of my native state, which was a wilderness when first my
father went to it, and is now crowned with a dense and prosperous
population, there is surely as much in the simple manners, and the little
histories every day revealed, to interest us in humanity, as there *can*
be in those old empires where the press of tyrannous laws and the
deadening influence of hereditary acquiescence necessarily destroy the
best life of society.

Without a thought of making a book, I began to recall some shadows
and sunbeams that fell about me as I came up to womanhood, incidents
for the most part of so little apparent moment or significance that they
who live in what is called the world would scarcely have marked them
had they been detained with me while they were passing, and before
I was aware, the record of my memories grew to all I now have printed.

Looking over the proof sheets, as from day to day they have come
from my publisher, the thought has frequently been suggested that
such experiences as I have endeavored to describe will fail to interest
the inhabitants of cities, where, however much there may be of pity
there is surely little of sympathy for the poor and humble, and perhaps

---

1. A reference to the shepherd's earliest flute and to classical Greek pastoral poetry.

still less of faith in their capacity for those finer feelings which are too often deemed the blossoms of a high and fashionable culture. The masters of literature who at any time have attempted the exhibition of rural life, have, with few exceptions, known scarcely anything of it from participation, and however brilliant may have been their pictures, therefore, they have seldom been true. Perhaps in their extravagance has been their greatest charm. For myself, I confess I have no invention, and I am altogether too poor an artist to dream of any success which may not be won by the simplest fidelity. I believe that for these sketches I may challenge of competent witnesses at least this testimony, that the circumstances have a natural and probable air which should induce their reception as honest relations unless there is conclusive evidence against them. Having this merit, they may perhaps interest if they do not instruct readers who have regarded the farming class as essentially different and inferior, and entitled only to that peculiar praise they are accustomed to receive in the resolutions of political conventions.

1852

From CLOVERNOOK

Uncle Christopher's

I

The night was intensely cold, but not dismal, for all the hills and meadows, all the steep roofs of the farm-houses, and the black roofs of the barns, were white as snow could make them. The haystacks looked like high, smooth heaps of snow, and the fences, in their zigzag course across the fields, seemed made of snow too, and half the trees had their limbs encrusted with the pure white.

Through the middle of the road, and between banks out of which it seemed to have been cut, ran a path, hard and blue and icy, and so narrow that only two horses could move in it abreast; and almost all the while I could hear the merry music of bells, or the clear and joyous voices of sleigh riders, exultant in the frosty and sparkling air.

With his head pushed under the curtain of the window next the road, so that his face touched the glass, stood my father, watching with as much interest, the things without, as I the pictures in the fire. His hands were thrust deep in his pockets; both his vest and coat hung loosely open; and so for a half hour he had stood, dividing my musings with joyous exclamations as the gay riders went by, singly, or in companies. Now it was a sled running over with children that he told me of;

now an old man and woman wrapt in a coverlid[1] and driving one poor horse; and now a bright sleigh with fine horses, jingling bells, and a troop of merry young folks. Then again he called out, "There goes a spider-legged thing that I wouldn't ride in," and this remark I knew referred to one of those contrivances which are gotten up on the spur of a moment, and generally after the snow begins to fall, consisting of two limber saplings on which a seat is fixed, and which serve for runners, fills, and all.

It was not often we had such a deep snow as this, and it carried the thoughts of my father away back to his boyhood, for he had lived among the mountains then, and been used to the hardy winters which keep their empire nearly half the year. Turning from the window, he remarked, at length, "This is a nice time to go to Uncle Christopher's, or somewhere."

"Yes," I said, "it would be a nice time"; but I did not think so, all the while, for the snow and I were never good friends. I knew, however, that my father would like above all things to visit Uncle Christopher, and that, better still, though he did not like to own it, he would enjoy the sleighing.

"I want to see Uncle Christopher directly," he continued, "about getting some spring wheat to sow."

"It is very cold," I said, "isn't it?" I really couldn't help the question.

"Just comfortably so," he answered, moving back from the fire.

Two or three times I tried to say, "Suppose we go," but the words were difficult, and not till he had said, "Nobody ever wants to go with me to Uncle Christopher's, nor anywhere," did I respond, heartily, "Oh, yes, father, I want to go."

In a minute afterwards, I heard him giving directions about the sleigh and horses.

"I am afraid, sir, you'll find it pretty cold," replied Billy, as he rose to obey.

"I don't care about going myself," continued my father, apologetically, "but my daughter has taken a fancy to a ride, and so I must oblige her."

A few minutes, and a pair of handsome, well-kept horses were champing the bit, and pawing the snow at the door, while shawls, mittens, etc., were warmed at the fire. It was hard to see the bright coals smothered under the ashes, and the chairs set away; but I forced a smile to my lips, and as my father said, "Ready?" I answered "Ready," and the door closed on the genial atmosphere—the horses stepped forward and backward, flung their heads up and down, curved their necks to the tightening rein, and we were off. The fates be praised, it is not to do again. All the shawls and muffs in Christendom could not avail against such a night—so still, clear, and intensely cold. The very stars seemed sharpened against the ice, and the white moon-

---

1. Coverlet or quilt.

beams slanted earthward, and pierced our faces like thorns—I think they had substance that night, and were stiff; and the thickest veil, doubled twice or thrice, was less than gossamer, and yet the wind did not blow, even so much as to stir one flake of snow from the bent boughs.

At first we talked with some attempts at mirth, but sobered presently and said little, as we glided almost noiselessly along the hard and smooth road. We had gone, perhaps, five miles to the northward, when we turned from the paved and level way into a narrow lane, or neighborhood road, as it was called, seeming to me hilly and winding and wild, for I had never been there before. The track was not so well worn, but my father pronounced it better than that we had left, and among the stumps and logs, and between hills and over hills, now through thick woods, and now through openings, we went crushing along. We passed a few cabins and old-fashioned houses, but not many, and the distances between them grew greater and greater, and there were many fields and many dark patches of woods between the lights. Every successive habitation I hoped would terminate our journey—our pleasure, I should have said—yet still we went on, and on.

"Is it much farther?" I asked, at length.

"Oh, no—only four or five miles," replied my father; and he added, "Why, are you getting cold?"

"Not much," I said, putting my hand to my face to ascertain that it was not frozen.

At last we turned into a lane, narrower, darker, and more lonesome still—edged with woods on either side, and leading up and up farther than I could see. No path had been previously broken, and the horses sunk knee deep at every step, their harness tightening as they strained forward, and their steamy breath drifting back, and freezing stiff my veil. At the summit the way was interrupted by a cross fence, and a gate was to be opened—a heavy thing, painted red, and fastened with a chain. It had been well secured, for after half an hour's attempts to open it, we found ourselves defied.

"I guess we'll have to leave the horses and walk to the house," said my father; "it's only a little step."

I felt terrible misgivings; the gate opened into an orchard; I could see no house, and the deep snow lay all unbroken; but there was no help; I must go forward as best I could, or remain and freeze. It was difficult to choose, but I decided to go on. In some places the snow was blown aside, and we walked a few steps on ground almost bare, but in the end high drifts met us, through which we could scarcely press our way. In a little while we began to descend, and soon, abruptly, in a nook sheltered by trees, and higher hills, I saw a curious combination of houses—brick, wood, and stone—and a great gray barn, looking desolate enough in the moonlight, though about it stood half a dozen of inferior size. But another and a more cheerful indication of humanity attracted me. On the brink of the hill stood two persons with a small hand-sled between them, which they seemed to have just drawn up; in the imperfect light, they appeared to be mere youths, the youngest not more than ten or twelve years of age. Their laughter rang on the cold air, and our approach, instead of checking, seemed to increase their mirth.

"Laugh, Mark, laugh," said the taller of the two, as we drew near, "so they will see our path—they're going right through the deep snow."

But instead, the little fellow stepped manfully forward, and directed us into the track broken by their sleds.

At the foot of the hill we came upon the medley of buildings, so incongruous that they might have been blown together by chance. Light appeared in the windows of that portion which was built of stone, but we heard no sound, and the snow about the door had not been disturbed since its fall. "And this," said I, "is where Uncle Christopher lives?"

A black dog, with yellow spots under his eyes, stood suddenly before us, and growled so forbiddingly that we drew back.

"He will not bite," said the little boy; for the merrymakers had landed on their sled at the foot of the hill, and followed us to the door; and in a moment the larger youth dashed past us, seized the dog by the fore paws, and dragged him violently aside, snarling and whimpering all the time. "Haven't you got no more sense," he exclaimed, "than to bark so at a gentleman and ladies?"

II

In answer to our quick rap, the door opened at once, and the circle about the great blazing log fire was broken by a general rising. The group consisted of eight persons—one man and seven women; the women so closely resembling each other, that one could not tell them apart; not even the mother from the daughters—for she appeared as young as the oldest of them—except by her cap and spectacles. All the seven were very slender, very straight, and very tall; all had dark complexions, black eyes, low foreheads, straight noses, and projecting teeth; and all were dressed precisely alike, in gowns of brown flannel, and coarse leather boots, with blue woollen stockings, and small capes, of red and yellow calico. The six daughters were all marriageable; at least the youngest of them was. They had staid, almost severe, expressions of countenances, and scarcely spoke during the evening. By one corner of the great fireplace they huddled together, each busy with knitting, and all occupied with long blue stockings, advanced in nearly similar degrees toward completion. Now and then they said "Yes, ma'am," or "no ma'am," when I spoke to them, but never or very rarely anything more. As I said, Mrs. Wright differed from her daughters in appearance, only in that she wore a cap and spectacles; but she was neither silent nor ill at ease as they were; on the contrary, she industriously filled up all the little spaces unoccupied by her good man in the conversation; she set off his excellencies, as a frame does a picture; and before we were even seated, she expressed her delight that we had come when "Christopher" was at home, as, owing to his *gift*, he was much abroad.

Uncle Christopher was a tall muscular man of sixty or thereabouts, dressed in what might be termed stylish homespun coat, trousers and waistcoat, of snuff-colored cloth. His cravat was of red-and-white-checked gingham, but it was quite hidden under his long grizzly beard, which he wore in full, this peculiarity being a part of his religion. His hair was of the same color, combed straight from his forehead, and turned over in one even curl on the back of the neck. Heavy gray eyebrows met over a hooked nose, and deep in his head twinkled two little blue eyes, which seemed to say, "I am delighted with myself, and, of course, you are with me." Between his knees he held a stout hickory stick, on which, occasionally, when he had settled something beyond the shadow of doubt, he rested his chin for a moment, and enjoyed the triumph. He rose on our entrance, for he had been seated beside a small table, where he monopolized a good portion of the light, and all the warmth, and having shaken hands with my father and welcomed him in a long and pompous speech, during which the good wife bowed her head, and listened as to an oracle, he greeted me in the same way, saying, "This, I suppose, is the virgin who abideth still in the house with you. She is not given, I hope, to gadding over much, nor to vain and foolish decorations of her person with ear-rings and finger-rings, and crisping-pins:[2] for such are unprofitable, yea, abominable. My daughter, consider it well, and look upon it, and receive instruction." I was about replying, I don't know what, when he checked me by saying, "Much speech in a woman is as the crackling of thorns under a pot. Open rebuke," he continued, "is better than secret love." Then pointing with his cane in the direction of the six girls, he said, "Rise, maidens, and salute your kinswoman"; and as they stood up, pointing to each with his stick, he called their names, beginning with Abigail, oldest of the daughters of Rachael Wright and Christopher Wright, and ending with Lucinda, youngest born of Rachael Wright and Christopher Wright. Each, as she was referred to, made a quick ungraceful curtsy, and resumed her seat and her knitting.

A half hour afterward, seeing that we remained silent, the father said, by way of a gracious permission of conversation, I suppose, "A little talk of flax and wool, and of household diligence, would not ill become the daughters of our house." Upon hearing this, Lucinda, who, her mother remarked, had the "liveliest turn" of any of the girls, asked me if I liked to knit; to which I answered, "Yes," and added, "is it a favorite occupation with you?" She replied, "Yes ma'am," and after a long silence, inquired how many cows we milked, and at the end of

2. Iron instruments used to curl or wave hair.

another pause, whether we had colored our flannel brown or blue; if we had gathered many hickory nuts; if our apples were keeping well, etc.

The room in which we sat was large, with a low ceiling, and bare floor, and so open about the windows and doors, that the slightest movement of the air without would keep the candle flame in motion, and chill those who were not sitting nearest the fire, which blazed and crackled and roared in the chimney. Uncle Christopher, as my father had always called him (though he was uncle so many degrees removed that I never exactly knew the relationship), laid aside the old volume from which he had been reading, removed the two pairs of spectacles he had previously worn, and hung them, by leather strings connecting their bows, on a nail in the stone jamb by which he sat, and talked, and talked, and talked, and I soon discovered by his conversation, aided by the occasional explanatory whispers of his wife, that he was one of those infatuated men who fancy themselves "called" to be teachers of religion, though he had neither talents, education, nor anything else to warrant such a notion, except a faculty for joining pompous and half scriptural phrases, from January to December.

That inward purity must be manifested by a public washing of the feet, that it was a sin to shave the beard, and an abomination for a man to be hired to preach, were his doctrines, I believe, and much time and some money he spent in their vindication. From neighborhood to neighborhood he traveled, now entering a blacksmith's shop and delivering a homily,[3] now debating with the boys in the cornfield, and now obtruding into some church, where peaceable worshippers were assembled, with intimations that they had "broken teeth, and feet out of joint," that they were "like cold and snow in the time of harvest, yea worse, even as pot-sheds covered with silver dross."[4] And such exhortations he often concluded by quoting the passage: "Though thou shouldst bray a fool in a mortar among wheat, with a postle, yet will not his foolishness depart from him."[5]

More than half an hour elapsed before the youths whose sliding down the hill had been interrupted by us, entered the house. Their hands and faces were red and stiffened with the cold, yet they kept shyly away from the fire, and no one noticed or made room for them. Both interested me at once, and partly, perhaps, that they seemed to interest nobody else. The taller was not so young as I at first imagined; he was ungraceful, shambling, awkward, and possessed one of those clean, pinky complexions which look so youthful; his hair was yellow, his eyes small and blue, with an unquiet expression, and his hands and feet inordinately large; and when he spoke, it was to the boy who sat

---

3. A moral lecture or admonition.
4. See Proverbs 26.23: "Pot-sheds" are potshards, or fragments of broken pottery; "silver dross" refers to something that has the appearance of silver but is really worthless.

5. See Proverbs 27.22: "Bray" means to crush and pound, as if with a mortar and pestle; "postle" means a pestle, a hand tool for grinding and mashing; Cary is also making a verbal pun on "apostle."

on a low stool beside him, in a whisper, which he evidently meant to
be inaudible to others, but which was, nevertheless, quite distinct to
me. He seemed to exercise a kind of brotherly care over the boy, but
he did not speak, nor move, nor look up, nor look down, nor turn aside,
nor sit still, without an air of the most wretched embarrassment. I
should not have written "sit still," for he changed his position continually, and each time his face grew crimson, and, to cover his confusion,
as it were, he drew from his pocket a large silk handkerchief, rubbed
his lips, and replaced it, at the same time moving and screwing and
twisting the toe of his boot in every direction.

I felt glad of his attention to the boy, for he seemed silent and
thoughtful beyond his years; perhaps he was lonesome, I thought;
certainly he was not happy, for he leaned his chin on his hand, which
was cracked and bleeding, and now and then when his companion
ceased to speak, the tears gathered to his eyes; but he seemed willing
to be pleased, and brushed the tears off his face and smiled, when the
young man laid his great hand on his head, and, shaking it roughly,
said, "Mark, Mark, Marky!"

"I can't help thinking about the money," said the boy, at last, "and
how many new things it would have bought: just think of it, Andrew!"

"How Towser did bark at them people, didn't he, Mark?" said
Andrew, not heeding what had been said to him.

"All new things!" murmured the boy, sorrowfully, glancing at his
patched trousers and ragged shoes.

"In three days it will be New Year's; and then, Mark, won't we have
fun!" and Andrew rubbed his huge hands together, in glee, at the
prospect.

"It won't be no fun as I know of," replied the boy.

"May be the girls will bake some cakes," said Andrew, turning red,
and looking sideways at the young women.

Mark laughed, and, looking up, he recognized the interested look
with which I regarded him, and from that moment we were friends.

At the sound of laughter, Uncle Christopher struck his cane on the
floor, and looking sternly toward the offenders, said, "A whip for the
horse, a bridle for the ass, and a rod for the fool's back!" leaving to
them the application, which they made, I suppose, for they became
silent—the younger dropping his chin in his hands again, and the elder
twisting the toe of his boot, and using his handkerchief very freely.

I thought we should never go home, for I soon tired of Uncle Christopher's conversation, and of Aunt Rachael's continual allusions to his
"gift;" he was evidently regarded by her as not only the man of the
house, but also as the man of all the world. The six young women had
knitted their six blue stockings from the heel to the toe, and had begun
precisely at the same time to taper them off, with six little white balls
of yarn.

The clock struck eleven, and I ventured, timidly, to suggest my wish
to return home. Mark, who sat drowsily in his chair, looked at me

beseechingly, and when Aunt Rachael said, "Tut, tut! you are not going home tonight!" he laughed again, despite the late admonition. All the six young women also said, "You can stay just as well as not"; and I felt as if I were to be imprisoned, and began urging the impossibility of doing so, when Uncle Christopher put an end to remonstrance by exclaiming, "It is better to dwell in the corner of the housetop, than with a brawling woman, and in a wide house." It was soon determined that I should remain, not only for the night, but till the weather grew warmer; and I can feel now something of the pang I experienced when I heard the horses snorting on their homeward way, after the door had closed upon me.

"I am glad you didn't get to go!" whispered Mark, close to me, favored by a slight confusion induced by the climbing of the six young ladies upon six chairs, to hang over six lines, attached to the rafters, the six stockings.

There was no variableness in the order of things at Uncle Christopher's, but all went regularly forward without even a casual observation, and to see one day, was to see the entire experience in the family.

"He has a great gift in prayer," said Aunt Rachael, pulling my sleeve, as the hour for worship arrived.

I did not then, nor can I to this day, agree with her. I would not treat such matters with levity, and will not repeat the formula which this "gifted man" went over morning and evening, but he did not fail on each occasion to make known to the All-Wise the condition in which matters stood, and to assure him, that he himself was doing a great deal for their better management in the future. It was not so much a prayer as an announcement of the latest intelligence, even to "the visit of his kinswoman who was still detained by the severity of the elements."

It was through the exercise of his wonderful gift, that I first learned the histories of Andrew and Mark; that the former was a relation from the interior of Indiana, who, for feeding and milking Uncle Christopher's cows morning and evening, and the general oversight of affairs, when the great man was abroad, enjoyed the privilege of attending the district school in the neighborhood; and that the latter was the "son of his son," a "wicked and troublesome boy, for the present subjected to the chastening influences of a righteous discipline."

As a mere matter of form, Uncle Christopher always said, I will do so or so, "Providence permitting"; but he felt competent to do anything and everything on his own account, to "the drawing out of the Leviathan[6] with an hook, or his tongue with a cord—to the putting a hook into his nose, or the boring his jaw through with a thorn."

"I believe it's getting colder," said Andrew, as he opened the door of the stairway, darkly winding over the great oven, to a low chamber; and, chuckling, he disappeared. He was pleased, as a child would be,

---

6. A mythological sea creature believed in biblical times to cause eclipses of the sun and moon by swallowing them.

with the novelty of a visitor, and perhaps half believed it was colder, because he hoped it was so. Mark gave me a smile as he sidled past his grandfather, and disappeared within the smoky avenue. We had scarcely spoken together, but somehow he had recognized the kindly disposition I felt toward him.

As I lay awake, among bags of meal and flour, boxes of hickory nuts and apples, with heaps of seed, wheat, oats, and barley, that filled the chamber into which I had been shown—cold, despite the twenty coverlids heaped over me—I kept thinking of little Mark, and wondering what was the story of the money he had referred to. I could not reconcile myself to the assumption of Uncle Christopher that he was a wicked boy; and, falling asleep at last, I dreamed the hard old man was beating him with his walking-stick, because the child was not big enough to fill his own snuff-colored coat and trousers. And certainly this would have been little more absurd than his real effort to change the boy into a man.

There was yet no sign of daylight, when the stir of the family awoke me, and, knowing they would think very badly of me should I further indulge my disposition for sleep, I began to feel in the darkness for the various articles of my dress. At length, half awake, I made my way through and over the obstructions in the chamber, to the room below, which the blazing logs filled with light. The table was spread, and in the genial warmth sat Uncle Christopher, doing nothing. He turned his blue eyes upon me as I entered, and said, "Let a bear robbed of her whelps meet a man, rather than she who crieth, A little more sleep, and a little more slumber."

"Did he say anything to you?" asked Aunt Rachael, as I entered the kitchen in search of a wash-bowl. "It must have been just to the purpose," she continued; "Christopher always says something to the purpose."

There was no bowl, no accommodations, for one's toilet: Uncle Christopher did not approve of useless expenditures. I was advised to make an application of snow to my hands and face, and while I was doing so, I saw a light moving about the stables, and heard Andrew say, in a chuckling, pleased tone, "B'lieve it's colder, Mark— she can't go home today; and if she is only here till New-Years, maybe they will kill the big turkey." I felt, while melting on my cheeks the snow, that it was no warmer, and, perhaps, a little flattered with the evident liking of the young man and the boy, I resolved to make the best of my detention. I could see nothing to do, for seven women were already moving about by the light of a single tallow candle; the pork was frying, and the coffee boiling; the bread and butter were on the table, and there was nothing more, apparently, to be accomplished. I dared not sit down, however, and so remained in the comfortless kitchen, as some atonement for my involuntary idleness. At length the tin-horn was sounded, and shortly after Andrew and Mark came in, and breakfast was announced; in

other words, Aunt Rachael placed her hand on her good man's
chair, and said, "Come."

To the coarse fare before us we all helped ourselves in silence,
except of the bread, and that was placed under the management of
Uncle Christopher, and with the same knife he used in eating, slices
were cut as they were required. The little courage I summoned while
alone in the snow—thinking I might make myself useful, and do something to occupy my time, and oblige the family—flagged and failed
during that comfortless meal. My poor attempts at cheerfulness fell
like moonbeams on ice, except, indeed, that Andrew and Mark looked
grateful.

Several times, before we left the table, I noticed the cry of a kitten,
seeming to come from the kitchen, and that when Uncle Christopher
turned his ear in that direction, Mark looked at Andrew, who rubbed
his lips more earnestly than I had seen him before.

When the breakfast, at last, was ended, the old man proceeded to
search out the harmless offender, with the instincts of some animal
hungry for blood. I knew its doom, when it was discovered, clinging so
tightly to the old hat, in which Mark had hidden it, dry and warm, by
the kitchen fire; it had been better left in the cold snow, for I saw that
the sharp little eyes which looked on it grew hard as stone.

"Mark," said Uncle Christopher, "into your hands I deliver this
unclean beast: there is an old well digged by my father, and which lieth
easterly a rod or more from the great barn—uncover the mouth
thereof, and when you have borne the creature thither, cast it down!"

Mark looked as if he were suffering torture, and when, with the
victim, he had reached the door, he turned, as if constrained by pity,
and said, "Can't it stay in the barn?"

"No," answered Uncle Christopher, bringing down his great stick on
the floor; "but you can stay in the barn, till you learn better than to
gainsay my judgment." Rising, he pointed in the direction of the well,
and followed, as I inferred, to see that his order was executed, deigning
to offer neither reason nor explanation.

Andrew looked wistfully after, but dared not follow, and, taking
from the mantle-shelf Walker's Dictionary, he began to study a column
of definitions, in a whisper sufficiently loud for everyone in the house
to hear.

I inquired if that were one of his studies at school; but so painful was
the embarrassment occasioned by the question, though he simply answered, "B'lieve it is," that I repented, and perhaps the more, as it
failed of its purpose of inducing a somewhat lower whisper, in his
mechanical repetitions of the words, which he resumed with the same
annoying distinctness.

With the first appearance of daylight the single candle was snuffed
out, and it now stood filling the room with smoke from its long limber
wick, while the seven women removed the dishes, and I changed from
place to place that I might seem to have some employment; and

Andrew, his head and face heated in the blaze from the fireplace, studied the Dictionary. In half an hour Uncle Christopher returned, with stern satisfaction depicted in his face: the kitten was in the well, and Mark was in the barn; I felt that, and was miserable.

I asked for something to do, as the old man, resuming his seat, and folding his hands over his staff, began a homily on the beauty of industry, and was given some patch-work; "There are fifty blocks in the quilt," said Aunt Rachel, "and each of them contains three hundred pieces."

I wrought diligently all the day, though I failed to see the use or beauty of the work on which I was engaged.

At last Andrew, putting his Dictionary in his pocket, saying, "I b'lieve I have my lesson by heart," and, a piece of bread and butter in the top of his hat, tucked the ends of his green woolen trousers in his cowhide boots, and, without a word of kindness or encouragement, left the house for the school.

By this time the seven women had untwisted seven skeins of blue yarn, which they wound into seven blue balls, and each at the same time began the knitting of seven blue stockings.

That was a very long day to me, and as the hours went by I grew restless, and then wretched. Was little Mark all this time in the cold barn? Scratching the frost from the window pane, I looked in the direction from which I expected him to come, but he was nowhere to be seen.

The quick clicking of the knitting-needles grew hateful, the shut mouths and narrow foreheads of the seven women grew hateful, and hatefulest of all grew the small blue shining eyes of Uncle Christopher, as they bent on the yellow worm-eaten page of the old book he read. He was warm and comfortable, and had forgotten the existence of the little boy he had driven out into the cold.

I put down my work at last, and cold as it was, ventured out. There were narrow paths leading to the many barns and cribs, and entering one after another, I called to Mark, but in vain. Calves started up, and, placing their fore feet in the troughs from which they usually fed, looked at me, half in wonder and half in fear; the horses—and there seemed to be dozens of them—stamped, and whinnied, and, thrusting their noses through their mangers, pressed them into a thousand wrinkles, snuffing the air instead of expected oats. It was so intensely cold I began to fear the boy was dead, and turned over bundles of hay and straw, half expecting to find his stiffened corpse beneath them, but I did not, and was about leaving the green walls of hay that rose smoothly on each side of me, the great dusty beams and black cobwebs swaying here and there in the wind, when a thought struck me: the well—he might have fallen in! Having gone "a rod or more, easterly from the barn," directed by great footprints and little footprints, I discovered the place, and to my joy, the boy also. There was no curb about the well, and, with his hands resting on a decayed strip of plank that lay across its mouth, the boy was kneeling beside it, and looking in. He had not heard my approach, and, stooping, I drew him carefully back, showed him how the plank was decayed, and warned him against such fearful hazards.

"But," he said, half laughing, and half crying, "just see!" and he pulled me toward the well. The opening was small and dark, and seemed very deep, and as I looked more intently my vision gradually penetrated to the bottom; I could see the still pool there, and a little above it, crouching on a loose stone or other projection of the wall, the kitten, turning her shining eyes upward now and then, and mewing piteously.

"Do you think she will get any of it?" said Mark, the tears coming into his eyes; "and if she does, how long will she live there?" The kind-hearted child had been dropping down bits of bread for the prisoner.

He was afraid to go to the house, but when I told him Uncle Christopher might scold me if he scolded any one, and that I would tell him so, he was prevailed upon to accompany me. The hard man was evidently ashamed when he saw the child hiding behind my skirts for fear, and at first said nothing. But directly Mark began to cry—there was such an aching and stinging in his fingers and toes, he could not help it.

"Boo, hoo, hoo!" said the old man, making three times as much noise as the boy—"what's the matter now?"

"I suppose his hands and feet are frozen," said I, as though I knew it, and would maintain it in spite of him, and I confess I felt a secret satisfaction in showing him his cruelty.

"Oh, I guess not," Aunt Rachel said, quickly, alarmed for my cool assertion as well as for the child: "Only a leetle frosted, I reckon. Where-abouts does it hurt you, my son?" she continued, stooping over him with a human sympathy and fondness I had not previously seen in any of the family.

"Frosted a leetle—that's all, Christopher," she said, by way of soothing her lord's compunction, and, at the same time, taking in her hands the feet of the boy, which he flung about for pain, crying bitterly. "Hush, little honey," she said, kissing him, and afraid the good man would be vexed at the crying; and as she sat there holding his feet, and tenderly soothing him, I at first could not believe she was the same dark and sedate matron who had been knitting the blue stocking.

"Woman, fret not thy gizzard!" said Christopher, slapping his book on the table, and hanging his spectacles on the jamb. The transient beauty all dropt away, the old expression of obsequious servility was back, and she resumed her seat and her knitting.

"There, let me doctor you," he continued, drawing the child's stocking off. The feet were covered with blisters, and presented the appearance of having been scalded. "Why, boy alive," said he, as he saw the blisters, "these are nothing—they will make you grow." He was forgetting his old pomposity, and, as if aware of it, resumed, "Thou hast been chastised according to thy deserts—go forth in the face of the wind, even the north wind, and, as the ox treadeth the mortar, tread thou the snow."

"You see, Markey," interposed Mrs. Wright, whose heart was really kind,—"you see your feet are a leetle frosted, and that will make them well."

The little fellow wiped his tears with his hand, which was cracked and bleeding from the cold; and, between laughing and crying, ran manfully out into the snow.

It was almost night, and the red clouds about the sunset began to cast their shadows along the hills. The seven women went into the kitchen for the preparation of dinner (we ate but two meals in the day), and I went to the window to watch Mark as he trod the snow "even as an ox treadeth the mortar." There he was, running hither and thither, and up and down, but, to my surprise, not alone. Andrew, who had returned from school, and found his little friend in such a sorry plight, had, for the sake of giving him courage, bared his own feet, and was chasing after him in generously well-feigned enjoyment. Towser, too, had come forth from his kennel of straw, and a gay frolic they made of it, all together.

I need not describe the dinner—it differed only from the breakfast, in that it had potatoes added to the bread and pork.

I remember never days so long, before nor since; and that night, as the women resumed their knitting, and Uncle Christopher his old book, I could hardly keep from crying like a child, I was so lonesome and home-sick. The wind roared in the neighboring woods, the frozen branches rattled against the stone wall, and sometimes the blaze was blown quite out of the fireplace. I could not see to make my patch-work, for Uncle Christopher monopolized the one candle, and no one questioned his right to do so; and, at last, conscious of the displeasure that would follow me, I put by the patches, and joined Mark and Andrew, who were shelling corn in the kitchen. They were not permitted to burn a candle, but the great fireplace was full of blazing logs, and, on seeing me, their faces kindled into smiles, which helped to light the room, I thought. The floor was covered with red and white cobs, and there were sacks of ripe corn, and tubs of shelled corn, about the floor, and, taking a stool, I joined them at their work. At first, Andrew was so much confused, and rubbed his mouth so much with his hand-kerchief, that he shelled but little; gradually, however, he overcame his diffidence, and seemed to enjoy the privilege of conversation, which he did not often have, poor fellow. Little Mark made slow progress; his tender hands shrank from contact with the rough ears, and when I took his place, and asked him where he lived, and how old he was, his heart was quite won, and he found delight in communicating to me his little joys and sorrows. He was not pretty, certainly—his eyes were gray and large, his hair red, his expression surly, his voice querulous, and his manner unamiable, except, indeed, when talking with Andrew or my-self.

I have been mistaken, I thought; he is really amiable and sweet-tempered; and, as I observed him very closely, his more habitual expression came to his face, and he said, abruptly, "I don't like grand-father!" "Why?" I said, smoothing back his hair, for I liked him the better for saying so. "Because," he replied, "he don't like me"; and, in a moment, he continued, while his eyes moistened, "nobody likes me—everybody says I'm bad and ugly." "Oh, Mark!" exclaimed An-drew, "I like you, but I know somebody I don't like—somebody that wears spectaclesses, and a long beard—I don't say it's Uncle Christo-pher, and I don't say it ain't." Mark laughed, partly at the peculiar manner in which Andrew expressed himself; and when I told him I liked him too, and didn't think him either bad or ugly, he pulled at the hem of my apron as he remarked, that he should like to live with Andrew and me, always.

I answered that I would very gladly take him with me when I went home, and his face shone with pleasure, as he told me he had never yet ridden in a sleigh. But the pleasure lasted only a moment, and, with an altered and pained expression, he said, "I can't go—these things are all I have got," and he pointed to his homely and ill-conditioned clothes.

"Never mind, I will mend them," I said; and, wiping his eyes, he told me that once he had enough money to buy ever so many clothes, that he earned it by doing errands, sawing wood, and other services, for the man who lived next door to his father in the city, and that one Saturday night, when he had done something that pleased his em-ployer, he paid him all he owed, and a little more, for being a good boy. "As I was running home," said he, "I met two boys that I knew; so I stopped to show them how much money I had, and when they told me to put it on the pavement in three little heaps, so we could see how much it made, I did so, and they, each one of them, seized a heap and ran away, and that," said Mark, "is just the truth."

"And what did you do then?" I asked.

"I told father," he answered, "and he said I was a simpleton, and it was good enough for me—that he would send me out here, and grand-father would straighten me."

"Never mind, Markey," said Andrew, "it will be New Year's, day after tomorrow."

And so, sitting in the light of the cob-fire, and guessing what they would get in their stockings, I left them for the night.

I did not dampen their expectations of a good time, but I saw little cause to believe any pleasant dreams of theirs would be realized, as I had seen no indications of preparation for the holidays, even to the degree of a plumb cake, or mince-pie. But I was certain of one thing—whatever Mark was, they would not make him any better. As he said, nobody loved him, nobody spoke to him, from morning till night, unless to correct or order him, in some way; and so, perhaps, he sometimes did things he ought not to do, merely to amuse his idleness. In all ways he was expected to have the wisdom of a man—to rise as early, and sit up as late, endure the heat and cold as well, and perform nearly as much labor. So, to say the truth, he was, for the most part, sulky and sullen, and did reluctantly that which he had to do, and no more, except, indeed, at the suggestion of Andrew, or while I was at the house, because it was at my request, and then work seemed only play to him.

The following morning was precisely like the morning that preceded it; the family rose before the daylight, and moved about by the tallow candle, and prepared breakfast, while Uncle Christopher sat in the great armchair, and Mark and Andrew fed the cattle by the light of a lantern.

"Tomorrow will be New Year's," said Mark, when breakfast was concluded, and Andrew took down the old Dictionary. No one noticed him, and he presently repeated it.

"Well, and what of it?" replied the old man, giving him a severe look.

"Nothing of it, as I know of," said the boy; "only I thought, maybe we would have something nice."

"Something nice!" echoed the grandfather; "don't we have something nice every day?"

"Well, but I want to do something," urged Mark, sure that he wished to have the dull routine broken in some way.

"Boys will be boys," said Aunt Rachael, in her most conciliatory tone, and addressing nobody in particular; and presently she asked Mark what had become of the potatoes he gleaned. He replied that they were in a barrel in the cellar.

"Eaten up by the rats," added Uncle Christopher.

"No, sir," said Mark, "they are as good as ever—may I sell them?"

"It's a great wonder you didn't let the rats eat them; but, I suppose, it's from no oversight of yours," Uncle Christopher said.

"Yes, sir, I covered them," replied the boy; "and now, may I sell them?—you said I might."

"Sell them—yes, you may sell them," replied the grandfather, in a mocking tone; "why don't you run along and sell them?"

Of course, the boy did not feel that he could sell his little crop, nor did the grandfather intend to grant any such permission.

"Uncle Christopher," said Andrew, looking up from his Dictionary, "do them ere potatoes belong to you, or do they belong to Markey?"

The old man did not reply directly, but said something about busybodies and meddlers, which caused Andrew to study very earnestly, while Mark withdrew to the kitchen and cried, alone. Toward noon, however, his grandfather asked him if he could ride the old sorrel horse to the blacksmith's, three miles away, and get new shoes set on him, "because," said he, "if you can, you can carry a bag of the potatoes, and sell them."

Mark forgot how cold it was, forgot his ragged trousers, forgot everything, except that the next day was New Year's, and that he should have some money; and, mounting the old horse, with a bag of potatoes for a saddle, he was soon facing the north wind. He had no warm cap to turn against his ears, and no mittens for his hands, but he had something pleasant to think about, and so did not feel the cold so much.

When Andrew came from school, and found that Mark was gone to sell his potatoes, he was greatly pleased, and went out early to feed the cattle, first carrying the bundles of oats over the hill to the sheep—a portion of the work belonging to Mark; and he also made a blazing fire, and watched his coming at the window; but no one else seemed to think of him—the supper was served and removed, and not even the tea was kept by the fire for him. It was long after dark when he came, cold and hungry—but nobody made room at the hearth, and nobody inquired the result of his speculation, or what he had seen or heard during the day.

"You will find bread and butter in the cupboard," said Aunt Rachael, after a while, and that was all.

But he had received a dollar for the potatoes; that was fortune enough for one day, and he was careless and thoughtless of their indifference.

There was no light for my patch-work, and Aunt Rachael gave me instead a fine linen sheet to hem. "Isn't it fine and pretty?" said Mark, coming close to me before he went to bed; "I wish I could have it over me."

"Thoughtless child," said the grandfather, "you will have it over you soon enough, and nothing else about you, but your coffin-boards." And, with this benediction, he was dismissed for the night.

I awoke in the morning early, and heard the laughter of Andrew and Mark—it was New Year's—and, in defiance of the gloomy prospect, they were merry; but when I descended the grandson looked grave— he had found nothing in his stockings.

"Put your feet in them," said Uncle Christopher, "and that will be something."

Fresh snow had fallen in the night, and the weather was milder than it had been, but within the house, the day began as usual.

"Grandfather," said Mark, "shall we not have the fat turkey-hen for dinner, today? I could run her down in the snow so easy!"

"So could I run you down in the snow, if I tried," he responded, with a surly quickness.

"New Year's day," said Aunt Rachael, "is no better than any other, that I know of; and if you get very hungry, you can eat good bread and milk."

So, as in other mornings, Andrew whispered over the Dictionary, the old man sat in the corner, and the seven women began to knit.

Toward the noon, a happy thought came into the mind of Uncle

Christopher: there would be wine-bibbers and mirth-makers at the village, three miles away—he would ride thither, and discourse to them of righteousness, temperance, and judgment to come. Mark was directed to bring his horse to the door, and, having combed his long beard with great care, and slipped over his head a knitted woollen cap, he departed on his errand, but not without having taken from little Mark the dollar he had received for his potatoes. "It may save a soul," he said, "and shall a wayward boy have his will, and a soul be lost?"

The child, however, was not likely in this way to be infused with religious feeling, whatever Uncle Christopher might think of the subject, and it was easy to see that a sense of the injustice he suffered had induced a change in his heart that no good angel would have joy to see. I tried to appease his anger, but he recounted, with the exactest particularity, all the history of the wrong he had suffered, and would not believe there was the slightest justification possible for robbing him of what was his own, instead of making him, as his grandfather should have done, a handsome present. About the middle of the afternoon Andrew came home from school, having been dismissed at so early an hour because it was a holiday, and to prepare for a spelling match to be held at the schoolhouse in the evening. The chores were done long before sundown, and Andrew was in high spirits, partly in anticipation of the night's triumphs, and partly at the prospect of bringing some happiness to the heart of Mark, with whom he several times read over the lesson, impressing on his memory with all the skill he had the harder words which might come to him. Andrew went early, having in charge the schoolhouse fire, and Mark did not accompany him, but I supposed he would follow presently, and so was not uneasy about him.

As the twilight darkened, Uncle Christopher came in, and, recounting his pious labors, with a conceited cant that was now become disgusting to me, he inquired for Mark, that the "brand" might hear and rejoice at the good accomplished with the money thus applied for the regeneration of the gentiles; but Mark was not to be found, and Aunt Rachael meekly hinted that from what she had overheard, she suspected he had gone with Andrew to the spelling match.

"Gone to the spelling match—and without asking me!" said the good man; "the rod has been spared too long." And taking from his pocket his knife, he opened it with deliberate satisfaction, and left the house.

I thought of the words of Mark, "I don't like my grandfather"; and I felt that he was not to blame. All the long evening the lithe sapling lay over the mantel, while Uncle Christopher knitted his brows, and the seven women knitted their seven stockings. I could not use my needle, nor think of what was being done about me; all the family practiced their monotonous tasks in gloomy silence; the wind shrieked in the trees, whose branches were flung violently sometimes against the windows; Towser came scratching and whining at the door, without attracting the notice of anyone; and Uncle Christopher sat in his easy-chair, in the most comfortable corner, seeming almost as if he were in an ecstasy with intense self-satisfaction, or, once in a while, looking joyously grim and stern as his eye rested on the instrument of torture he had prepared for poor Mark, for whose protection I found myself praying silently, as I half dreamed that he was in the hands of a pitiless monster.

The old clock struck eleven, from a distant part of the house, and we all counted the strokes, it was so still; the sheet I had finished lay on the settee beneath the window, where the rose-vine creaked, and the mice peered out of the gnawed holes, and the rats ran through the mouldy cellar. There was a stamping at the door, in the moist snow; I listened, but could hear no voices; the door opened, and Andrew came in alone.

"Where is Mark?" asked the stern voice of the disciplinarian.

"I don't know," replied Andrew; "isn't he here?"

"No," said Aunt Rachael, throwing down her knitting, "nor hasn't been these many hours. Mercy on us, where can he be?"

"Fallen asleep somewhere about the house, likely," replied the old man; and taking up the candle, he began the search.

"And he hasn't been with you, Andrew?" asked Aunt Rachael again, in the faint hope that he would contradict his previous assertion.

"No ma'am, as true as I live and breathe," he replied, with childish simplicity and earnestness.

"Mercy on us!" she exclaimed again.

We could hear doors opening and shutting, and floors creaking in distant parts of the house; but nothing more.

"It's very strange," said the old man. "Don't be afraid, girls"; but he was evidently alarmed, and his hand shook as he lighted the lantern, saying, "He must be in the barn!"

Aunt Rachael would go, and I would go, too—I could not stay away. Andrew climbed along the scaffolds, stooping and reaching the lantern before him, and now and then we called to know if he had found him, as if he would not tell it when he did. So all the places we could think of had been searched, and we had begun to call and listen, and call again.

"Hark," said Andrew, "I heard something."

We were all so still that it seemed as if we might hear the falling of flakes of snow.

"Only the howl of a dog," said Uncle Christopher.

"It's Towser's," suggested Andrew, fearfully; and with an anxious look he lowered the lantern to see what indications were in the way. Going toward the well were seen small footprints, and there were none returning. Even Uncle Christopher was evidently disturbed. Seeing the light, the dog began to yelp and whine, looking earnestly at us, and then suddenly down in the well, and when we came to the place everyone felt a sinking of the heart, and no one dared to speak. The plank, on which I had seen him resting, was broken, and a part of it had fallen in. Towser whined, and his eyes shone as if he were in agony for words, and trying to throw all his intelligence into each piteous look he gave us.

"Get a rope, and lower the light," said one of the sisters; but the loose stones of the well were already rattling to the touch of Andrew, who, planting hands and feet on either side, was rapidly but cautiously descending. In a moment he was out of sight, but still we heard him, and soon there was a pause, then the sound of a hand, plashing the water, then a groan, sounding hollow and awful through the damp, dark opening, and a dragging, soughing movement, as if something were drawn up from the water. Presently we heard hands and feet once more against the sides of the well, and then, shining through the blackness into the light, two fiery eyes, and quickly after, as the bent head and shoulders of Andrew came nearer the surface, the kitten leaped from them, and dashed blindly past the old man, who was kneeling and looking down, pale with remorseful fear. Approaching the top, Andrew said, "I've got him!" and the grandfather reached down and lifted the lifeless form of the boy into his arms, where he had never reposed before. He was laid on the settee, by the window; the fine white sheet that I had hemmed was placed over him; the stern and hard master walked backward and forward in the room, softened and contrite, though silent, except when occasional irrepressible groans disclosed the terrible action of his conscience; and Towser, who had been Mark's dearest playmate, nearly all the while kept his face, from without, against the window pane.

"Oh, if it were yesterday!" murmured Uncle Christopher, when the morning came; "Andrew," he said, and his voice faltered, as the young man took from the mantel the long, limber rod, and measured the shrouded form from the head to the feet, "get the coffin as good as you can—I don't care what it costs—get the best."

The Dictionary was not opened that day; Andrew was digging through the snow, on a lonesome hillside, pausing now and then to wipe his eyes on his sleeve. Upright on the grave's edge, his only companion, sat the black dog.

Poor little Mark!—we dressed him very carefully, more prettily, too, than he had ever been in his life, and as he lay on the white pillow, all who saw him said, "How beautiful he is!" The day after the funeral, I saw Andrew, previously to his setting out for school, cutting from the sweetbrier such of the limbs as were reddest with berries, and he placed them over the heaped earth, as the best offering he could bring to beautify the last home of his companion. In the afternoon I went home, and have never seen him since, but, ignorant and graceless as he was, he had a heart full of sympathy and love, and Mark had owed to him the happiest hours of his life.

Perhaps, meditating of the injustice he himself was suffering, the unhappy boy, whose terrible death had brought sadness and perhaps repentance to the house of Uncle Christopher, had thought of the

victim consigned by the same harsh master to the well, and determined, before starting for the schoolhouse, to go out and drop some
food for it over the decayed plank on which I had seen him resting, and
by its breaking had been precipitated down its uneven sides to the
bottom, and so killed. But whether the result was by such accident, or
by voluntary violence, his story is equally instructive to those straight
and ungenial natures which see no beauty in childhood, and would
drive before its time all childishness from life.

Clovernook, Second Series, 1853

Passages from the Married Life of Eleanor Homes

A good many years ago I fell in love and was married.

"How did it happen?"

Why, how does it ever happen? "I doubt if the sagest philosopher of
them all could explain how the like happened unto him, and therefore
it were presumptuous to expect a woman to make luminous so great a
mystery."

"You think a woman might understand her own heart, even though
a philosopher might fail to?"

"Audacious! Don't you know that women shine faintly at best, and
by reflection?"

"Really, I don't know. I never thought about it."

"Many women never do, and pass through life without ever being
sufficiently grateful for the blessings they are permitted to enjoy. However, I believe the minds of the sexes are wholly dissimilar, even when
of an equal power. Women *know* more, but *acquire* less than men;
they do not investigate and analyze, and infer and conclude—their
inferences and conclusions are independent of any process of reasoning. Since the beginning of time nature has said of every one of them—

> "This child I to myself will take;
> She shall be mine, and I will make
> A lady of my own."[1]

And if each were permitted to follow her instincts, and rely upon her
intuitions, there would not be among us so many miserable bewailings.
All women have more or less genius—which, after all, is simply power
of suspending the reasoning and reflecting faculties, and suffering the
light which, whatever it be, is neither external nor secondary, to flow
in. But I proposed to tell a story, and repeat, I fell in love, and was
married.

"Did I really love?"

I suppose so; indeed I am quite certain, from intimations now and

---

1. William Wordsworth, "Three Years She Grew."

then received, that it was one phase of that capability which lives under wrinkles and grey hairs, in all the freshness of youth. But it is difficult to define the exact limit of positive love—it shades itself by such fine gradations into pity and passion, friendship and frenzy. The state of feeling I fell into was none of these latter, I am quite sure, and yet I should be loth to affirm it was that condition of self-abnegation which admits of no consideration aside from the happiness of the object beloved; for, if I remember rightly, there came to me at rare intervals some visions of my own personal interests and pleasures. And yet I had no hesitancy in pledging myself to love, honor, and obey, because I had no idea that these pledges conflicted with the widest liberty. Was not he to whom I should make these pledges a most excellent and honorable gentleman, who would have no requirement to prefer at variance with my wishes? To be sure he was. Did he not always prefer my pleasure to his own, or rather have no pleasure but mine? So he was pleased to say, and for my part, I never doubted it.

We took long moonlight walks together—talked sentiment, of course—read poetry, and now and then quarrelled prettily about the shade of a rose, or the pencilling of a tulip, and interspersed our discourse with allusions to our cottage that was to be. Should it be smothered in trees or open to the sun?

"Just as you prefer, my dear."

"Oh, no, darling! it shall all be just as you say."

Could I have a pot of geraniums and a canary bird to brighten my cottage window?

"A thousand of them," if I chose; but my own self would be the grace that graced all other graces—the beautifier of every beauty beside.

What should our recreations be? That was an absurd question, and soon dismissed. The introduction of a foreign element would never be necessary into society so perfect as we two should compose.

So we were married—never having exchanged a single thought concerning the great duties and responsibilities of life—I, for my part, having no slightest conception of the homely cares and ingenious planning; of the fearing and hoping, patience, forbearance, and endurance, that must needs make a part of life's drama, wherever enacted.

The bridal veil was never looked through after the bridal day; consequently the world took another coloring before very long. I must be allowed to say I was not yet twenty, as some extenuation of the follies I should have been ashamed of, even then, and must also relate some little incidents and particulars of my married life that gave ineffaceable colors to my maturer mind and character.

My husband's name was Henry Doughty—Harry, I used to call him, partly because the designation pleased him, and partly because I entertained a special dislike for the name of Doughty. I gave a much better one away for it, however.

My maiden name was Homes—Eleanor Homes—Nellie, they called

me among my friends, before I was married; afterward, when the
novelty of calling me *Mrs.* Doughty was over, they said *poor* Nell.

We had not been an hour from church—my bridesmaids were about
me, among them my haughty sister Katharine, who had not very
cordially received her new relative. Someone rallied me on my promise
to obey, and asked Mr. Doughty how he proposed to enforce my
obligation.

"Oh, after this sort," he replied gaily, brandishing the little switch-
cane he was playing with about my shoulder. I turned carelessly, and
the point of it struck my eye.

"It was your own fault!" was his first exclamation. The pain of the
wound was intense, but it was the harsh words that made the tears
come. I was frightened when I saw them, for I felt that it was an awful
impropriety to cry then and there, and putting by all proffered remedies as though the little accident were quite unworthy of attention, I
smiled, nay, even affected to laugh, and said it was solely and entirely
my own foolish fault, and moreover, that I always cried on like occasions—not, of course, on account of any suffering, but owing to a
nervous susceptibility I could not overcome.

Katharine, meantime, to augment the criminality of the offense, was
proffering various medicines; among them, she brought me at this
juncture, a towel, wet with I know not what.

"Take it away again," said Mr. Doughty; "nothing I so much dislike
as nervous susceptibility—pray don't encourage it."

Katharine would not speak, but she replied by a very significant
look, and, to conciliate both, I accepted the towel, but did not apply it
to the wounded eye—swollen and red by this time to an unsightly
degree; in truth, I was afraid to do so. My sensations were certainly
new, as I thus trifled with my afflictions, forcing myself even to make
pitiable advances toward my offender, in the hope of winning him to
some little display of tenderness, for the sake of appearances wholly,
for I was not in the mood to receive them appreciatively just then. I
was singularly unfortunate, however, and might have spared myself
the humiliation.

I had succeeded, in some sort, in reviving my spirits, for it is hard to
dampen the ardor of a young woman on her wedding-day, when my
enthusiasm received another check. I was sitting at the window, that
I might find some excuse for my occasional abstraction in observation,
and also to keep the wounded eye away from the company. Happening
once to change my position, my husband said to me: "Keep your face
to the window, my dear madam; your ridiculous applications have
made your eye really shocking!"

"Why, Harry!" I said—if I had taken time to think, I would not have
said anything; but the unkindness was so obvious it induced the involuntary exclamation, and everybody saw that I felt myself injured.

By some sisterly subterfuge, Kate decoyed me into her own room,
where my husband did not take occasion to seek me very soon. When

he did so, he patted my cheek and said half-playfully, "I have come to scold you, Nell."

My heart beat fast. He had felt my absence, then, and was come with some tender reproach. I began to excuse myself, when he interrupted me with an exclamation of impatience. He was sorry to find me so impetuous and *womanish*—exhibitions of any emotion, but more especially of tender emotion, were in bad taste. I must manage in some way to control my impulses, and also to discriminate—he was always pleased to be called Harry, when we were alone, but in miscellaneous company a little more formality was usual!

"Your name is not so beautiful," I replied, angrily, "that you should want to hear it unnecessarily."

He elevated his eyebrows a little, and smiled one of his peculiar smiles, never too sweet to be scornful.

I hid my face in my sister's pillow, and almost wished I might never lift it up.

Seeing me shaken with suppressed sobs, he bent over me and kissed my forehead, much as we give a child a sugar-plum after having whipped it, and left me with the hope that I would compose myself, and not wrong my beauty by such ill-timed tears!

Excellent advice, but not very well calculated to aid me in its execution. Many times after that I wronged such poor beauty as I brought to him, by my ill-timed tears.

The story of the accident, and of my crying on my wedding-day, went abroad with many exaggerations, and my husband gave me to understand, without any direct reference to anything that had taken place, that I had unnecessarily brought reproach upon him. It had been arranged that we were to live at home a year; my parents—foolish old folks! could not bear the thought of giving me up at once—as if the hope to make all things as they were, were not utterly useless, after I had once given myself up.

The experiment proved a delusion—empty of comfort to all parties concerned; and here let me say, that if two persons, when they are once married, cannot find happiness with each other, no third party can in any wise mend the matter.

I think now if there had been no one to strengthen my obstinacy, and hinder such little conciliations as, unobserved, I might have proffered, our early differences might have been healed over without any permanent alienation.

However well two persons may have known each other before marriage, the new relation develops new characteristics, and necessitates a process of assimilation, difficult under the most genial circumstances.

Of course my family took my part, whether or not I was in the right, and thus sustained I took larger liberties, sometimes, than it was wise to take—trifled and played with all my husband's predilections—called them whimsies, if I noticed them, but for the most part affected an unconsciousness of their existence. For instance, I had a foolish habit of turning through books and papers in a noisy way, which I persevered in rather in consequence of his admonitions than in spite of them.

One night he did not come home at the usual time. I grew impatient, uneasy, and at last, in spite of Kate's sneer, took my station at the window to watch for him: in a minute or two thereafter he came up the walk. I opened the door and my arms at the same time, crying, "How glad I am!"

"What for?" he said, gliding past me in his quiet way.

"Are you not glad?" I inquired, determined not to be put out of humor for once; my best feelings had been really stirred.

"Certainly," he answered, seating himself in the corner opposite to me, and opening the evening paper. "I am glad to get home. I am very tired."

He did not once look at me as he said this, and Kate completed my discomfort by saying—

"Well, I suppose Nell is blessed enough to be permitted to look upon you, even in the distance. She used to have a little spirit, but I believe marriage has crushed even that out of her."

"Humph!" said my husband.

"What do you find interesting in the paper tonight?" I said, determined to enforce some attention by way of triumph over Kate. He made a motion which deprecated interruption, and taking a new novel from his pocket, threw it into my lap.

"Milk for babes!" said Kate, sarcastically. I said nothing, and she went on provokingly: "Take your plaything away, child, and don't make a bit of noise with it."

Here was a happy suggestion. I had failed in my effort to be agreeable. I would be disagreeable now to my heart's content. I was at some pains to find an old pair of jagged scissors, and having found them, I seated myself at my husband's elbow, and began to saw open the leaves of my book,[2] with the double purpose of annoying him and convincing Kate that I had some spirit left yet.

Now and then I glanced towards him to see if his brows were not knitting, and the angry spot rising in his cheek, but to my surprise and vexation I saw no manifestation of annoyance—he read on apparently completely absorbed, and wearing a smile on his face—a little too fixed, perhaps, to be quite spontaneous.

So I went on to the last leaf, cutting and ruffling as noisily as I could, but I had only my trouble for my pains—he did not lift his eyes towards me for an instant.

When Kate left us alone, I felt exceedingly uncomfortable—for I had felt my behavior countenanced by her presence. After all, I thought, presently, my husband is perhaps quite unconscious of any effort on my part to annoy him; but whether he were so or not, my best course, I

---

2. Before reading a new book, 19th-century readers first had to cut open the pages where they had been folded during binding.

concluded, would be to affect unconsciousness of it myself. Thus resolved, I yawned, naturally, I thought, and, as if impulsively, threw down the book—took the paper from his hand with a wifely privilege, and seated myself on his knee. He suffered me to sit there, but neither smiled nor spoke.

"Why don't you say something to me?" I was reduced to ask at length.

"What shall I say?"

"Why, something sweet, to be sure."

"Well, sugar-candy—is that sweet enough?"

"What a provoking wretch you are!" I cried, flying out of the room in hot haste.

I hoped he would forbid my going, or call me back, but he did neither.

After some tears and a confidential interview with Kate, that made me more angry with her and with myself than with my husband, I returned, and found him quietly lolling in the easy-chair, and eating an apple!

As time went by, Kate's arrogance and insolence towards Mr. Doughty became insupportable—twenty times I quarrelled with her, taking his part stoutly against her accusations. One evening, after one of these accustomed disputations, my husband said to me—

"Nell, we must take a house of our own; I can't live in this atmosphere any longer."

"Why can't you?" I knew why, well enough.

"I don't like your sister Kate."

"Does she poison the atmosphere, my dainty sir?"

"Yes."

Of course I flew into a rage and defended Kate with all my powers. She was my own good sister then, and had done everything to make the house pleasant which it was possible for her to do—I would like to know who would please him.

"You, my dear," he replied.

The end of the matter was, I refused to go away from my father's house with him; said I would not be deprived of the little comfort I now had in the sympathy of, and association with, my family; he had agreed, I reminded him, before our marriage, to my remaining at home one year at least—his promises might pass for nothing with himself, they would not with me; if he chose to take a house he might do so, but his housekeeping would be done independently of me; if my wishes were never to be consulted by him, I should have to consult them myself—that was all.

I never gave him greater pleasure, he replied provokingly, than when I consulted my own wishes; for his part, he could have none in which I did not heartily concur.

He admitted that he had cordially agreed to my remaining at home a year after marriage, but that late experience had slightly modified his views; he was not infallible, however, and probably erred in judgment—indeed, he was quite sure he did, since I differed from him; he hoped I would pardon his unkind suggestion, and believe him what he really was, the most faithful and devoted of husbands.

Amongst my weaknesses was a passion for emeralds. Mr. Doughty had heard me express my admiration for them many a time. The day following our little rencounter he came home an hour earlier than usual, seated himself on the sofa beside me, and taking two little parcels from his pocket and concealing them beneath his hand, said playfully—

"Which one will you have, Nell?"

"The best one!" I replied, reaching out my hand.

"The better one," he rejoined quickly; "the best of the two is not elegant—at least it was not till you made it so."

I withdrew my hand and averted my face. If he and I had been alone, I might have taken the reproof more kindly; but Kate heard it all, as it seemed to me she always did everything that was disagreeable. I might have made some angry retort, but a visitor was just then announced—an old classmate of Mr. Doughty's, whom I had never seen.

"He is come specially to pay his respects to you," my husband said as he rose to join him. "You will see him, of course."

"If it is my lord's pleasure," I replied; "bring him to me when it suits you."

Involuntarily he put his hand on my hair, and smoothed it away, glancing over me at the same time from head to foot. The motion and the glance implied a doubt of my observance of external proprieties, and also, I felt at the moment, personal dissatisfaction with myself. The interview was embarrassed and restrained; I was self-conscious every moment, and crippled completely by the knowledge that in my husband's eyes I was appearing very badly.

I misquoted a familiar line from Shakespeare; expressed admiration for a popular author, and when asked which of his works I read with most delight, could not remember the name of anything I had read.

My discomfiture was completed when my husband said apologetically, "I dare say that wiser heads than my little Nellie's have been confused by similar questions—in truth, she is not quite well to-day."

The old classmate related some very amusing blunders of his own, calculated to soothe, but rasping my wounded feelings only into deeper soreness, and presently the conversation fell into the hands of the gentlemen altogether; and I am sure it was felt to be a relief, by all parties, when our guest announced the expiration of the time to which he was *unfortunately* limited. My husband walked down street with him, and during his brief absence I wrought myself into a state of unwomanly ugliness, including dissatisfaction with everything and everybody.

The words "my little Nellie," which my husband had used, rung

offensively in my ears. *My* little Nellie, indeed! What implied owner-
ship and what tender disparagement!

When my husband returned he took no notice of my ill-humor, but
proceeded to his reading as usual. It was never his habit to read aloud;
on this occasion I chose to fancy he had, in his own estimation, selected
a work above my appreciation.

"There, Nell, I forgot!" he exclaimed after a few moments of silent
reading, and he threw into my lap the little box which I had declined
to receive. I did not open it immediately, and when I did so I expressed
neither surprise nor pleasure, though it contained what I had so much
desired to possess—a pin set with emeralds.

"Very pretty," I said carelessly, "for those who can wear such ornaments; as for myself it would only make my plainness seem the plainer
by contrast." And before the eyes of my husband, who had thought to
make everything right by its purchase, I transferred it to my sister
Kate. From that time forth it glittered in the faces of both of us daily,
but we neither of us ever mentioned it.

It was not many days after this occurrence that Mr. Doughty informed me that he was called suddenly, by matters of some importance
to him, to a neighboring state. He did not say *us,* but limited the
interest entirely to himself—nor did he intimate by word or act that the
necessity of absence involved any regret. I inquired how long he proposed to remain away—not when should *I* expect him.

He was not definitely advised—from one to three months. We
parted without any awakening of tender emotion. Our letters were
brief and formal—containing no hints, on either side, of a vacuum in
life which nothing but the presence of the other could supply.

I was informed from time to time that affairs protracted themselves
beyond his expectation, but the nature of the affairs I was left in
ignorance of. The prospect of staying at home a year added nothing to
my happiness. Kate and I agreed no better now that we were alone
than before. I secretly blamed her for my unfortunate alienation from
my husband: it was not the importunate nature of his business that
detained him, I was quite sure. I grew uneasy, and irritable, wished to
have him back, not for any need my nature had, that he alone could
answer. I wanted him to want to come back—that was all.

Kate accused me of unfilial and unsisterly preference for a vulgar
and heartless man, to my own family.

"The dear old Nell was completely merged in the selfish Doughty,"
she said, "and she might just as well have no sister for all the comfort
I was to her."

So we kept apart a good deal, and by keeping apart, soon grew apart
pretty thoroughly. In truth our natures had never been cast in the same
mould, and it was impossible that they should more than touch at some
single point now and then.

At the end of six months a portion of my fret and worry had worked
itself into my face. My hair had fallen off and was beginning to have

a faded and neglected look. I was careless about dress, and suffered my whole outer and inner person to fall into ruins. By fits I resolved to project my general discontent into some one of the reforms, I hardly knew which, when after a day of unusual irksomeness and personal neglect, my husband unexpectedly returned.

He was in perfect health, and rejoiced in the possession of affluent beard and spirits—he was really quite handsome. I looked at him with wonder, admiration, and some pride—kissed him and said I was very glad; but there was no thrill in my heart—no tremor in my voice—the old fires of anger had left the best part of my nature in ashes, I found. He was sorry to find me looking so badly—I must go with him on his next adventure and get back my beauty again! If I could only see his smiling, blushing cousin Jane, it would shame my melancholy and sallow face into some bloom! And by the way, I must know her—he was sure I would love her just as he did—she had done so much to make his banishment from me delightful—no, not delightful—but bearable. He would defy anyone to be very miserable where she was. She kept about her under all circumstances such an atmosphere of cheerfulness and comfort; was so self-sustained and womanly, and yet as capable of receiving pleasure as a child; as an example of a beautiful and childlike trait in her disposition, he told with what almost pious care she preserved every little trinket he ever gave her. She would clap her hands and laugh like a very baby over the least trifle bestowed upon her.

I thought of the emerald pin, and of (as doubtless he did) the contrast my whole character presented to his charming wonder.

"Ah, me!" he concluded, and fell into a fit of musing. I did not interrupt him by any poor attempt at cheerfulness I did not feel.

Before long I succeeded in coaxing upon myself a headache—slighted the advice proposed, and at nightfall had my pillows brought to the sofa, and gave up altogether.

I was almost glad to be sick—it would revive in my husband some of the old tenderness perhaps; but what was my disappointment when he took up his hat to leave the house.

"What, you are not going out tonight?" I inquired in surprise.

"Why, yes, my dear, why not?"

"If you ask why not, I suppose there is no reason."

"Is there anything I can do, or shall I send the doctor?"

"No, there is nothing special I need, but I thought you would stay at home tonight—I am unhappy every way."

"I am very sorry, but my engagement tonight is imperative—I promised Jenny I would immediately see some friends of hers, here."

I hid my face in my pillows and cried, and I confess there was some method in my tears—I did not think he would leave me under such circumstances. I was mistaken—he did.

"Have you seen any house that you thought would suit us?" I ventured to ask him before long.

"No, I have not been looking for a house."

He did not follow up my suggestion, and I added, as if I had but to intimate my wishes to have them carried out, though the hollowness of the sham was appalling—"I really wish you would look." He still was silent, and I continued—"Won't you?"

He replied, evidently without the slightest interest in the matter, "Why, yes, when I have time." He paid no further attention to my request, however, and when I reminded him of it again, he said he had forgotten it.

It seemed to me I could not live from one day to another—change would be a relief, at any rate, and my husband's indifference to my wishes made me importunate; but from week to week he put me off with promises and excuses, both of which I felt were alike false.

He could not see any places. "Inquire of your friends." He had, and could not hear of any.

"Why, I saw plenty of houses to let, and was sure I could secure one any day—would he go with me some time?"

"Yes, certainly at his earliest convenience."

I awaited his convenience, but it did not come. In very desperation, I set out myself; but searching without having fixed upon any locality, size of house, or price to be paid, was only a waste of time, I felt, and accordingly I wandered about the streets, looking at the outsides of houses, and now and then inquiring the terms at the door, but declining in all instances to examine the premises, or take the slightest step towards the securing of a house.

"Had you not better consider it a little?" Mr. Doughty said at length, as if I had not been considering it for six months!

He feared I would find it lonesome—he might be from home a good deal, such was the unfortunate nature of his prospects. Where was he going and what for?

He was not going at all that he positively knew of, but his affairs were in such a state that contingencies might arise at any time, that would demand his absence for a few weeks or months.

"A happy state of affairs!" I said with womanish spite; "I suppose one of the contingencies is your charming cousin Jenny!"

He would only reply to my foolish accusation by saying it was quite unworthy of my generous nature—I wronged myself and him, and also the sweetest and most innocent little creature in the world.

For some days nothing was said about the house; but I was a woman, and could not maintain silence on a disagreeable subject, so I renewed it with the importunate demand to know, once for all, whether or not we were ever to keep house. Thus urged, he consented to go with me in search of a house.

The air was biting on the day we set out—the streets slippery with ice, and gusts of sharp snow now and then caused women to walk backward, and bury their faces in their muffs.

We turned into streets and out of streets, just as it happened—Mr.

Doughty did not care where he looked—anywhere I chose;—sometimes we passed whole blocks of houses that seemed eligible, without
once ringing a bell: he did not suggest looking here or there, made no
objection to terms, and suggested no proposals. Now we turned into a
by-street and examined some dilapidated tenement, and now sought a
fashionable quarter, and went over some grand mansion to be let for
six months only, and furnished!—an exorbitant rent demanded, of
course.

The whole thing was so evidently a sham, that I at last burst into
tears and proposed to go home. Mr. Doughty assented, and with my
face swollen and shining with the cold, my hands aching and my feet
numb, I arrived there in a condition of outraged and indignant feeling
that could go no further.

I comforted myself as I best could, for nobody comforted me, and my
husband, monopolizing the easy-chair and a great part of the fire,
opened the letters that awaited him.

When he had concluded the reading of the first one—addressed, as
I observed, in a woman's hand—he said suddenly, "Come here, Nell,
and sit on my knee."

I did so.

"What should you think of taking the house in ——— street?"

"I should like it very well."

"I think that would suit us—room for ourselves, and a visitor now
and then, perhaps."

I did not sit on his knee any longer; I felt instinctively that the letter
he had just read was from the charming cousin, and that the prospect
of having her for a guest had changed the aspect of affairs.

The house was taken at once, and Mr. Doughty informed me before
long that I had a great happiness in prospect—that of knowing the little
cousin I had heard him speak of.

She came almost before we were settled; impossible, thought I, that
I should be jealous; the idea of affinity between her and Mr. Doughty
was so ridiculous. She was white, short, and fat as a worm in a chestnut, and almost as incapable of thought. The flax-like hair was so thin
you could see her head beneath it all the time; her cheeks and chin
trembled with fatness; her eyes were of the faintest blue, and cloudy
with vague apprehension; her arms hung stiff and round as two rolling
pins, and her pink and blue silk dresses were pinned up and fringed
out, and greasy: but she was amiable—too simple-hearted and indolent to be otherwise, indeed.

"She is a child, you see," said my husband, "and I bespeak for her
childish indulgences; you must not be surprised to find her arms
around my neck any time—playful little kitten, that she is."

I was not so much surprised to find her big arms around his neck, as
by the fact which gradually broke in upon me, that they had power to
detain him from the most important duties.

Towards her he was gentle and indulgent to the tenderest degree—
towards me exacting, severe, and unyielding.

If I fretted, he was surprised that I could do so with so patient an example before me; if I forbore complaint, he gave me no praise; I had done nothing more than I ought to do. If I slighted or blamed Jenny, as I was sometimes driven to do, he was surprised and indignant that I, a reasonable woman, should treat a mere child, quite incapable of defense or retaliation, so cruelly.

By turns, I resorted to every device: grave and reserved dignity, playful badinage, affected indifference, rivalry in dress and manner, pouting, positive anger, threats of divorce and separate maintenance—all would not do. I ruined thereby the slender stock of amiability and fair looks I began with, and gained nothing. Now I went home for a few days, and now I affected illness; but I gained nothing, for of all lost things most difficult to be regained, lost affection is the most hopeless.

This state of feeling could not last always; the nerves of sensibility could not be laid bare and left bare without becoming indurated,[3] and by degrees I became incapable of receiving or of giving enjoyment. In our treatment of one another, my husband and I fell into a kind of civility which was the result of indifference. Before folks we said "my dear"; and when we were alone—but we never were alone—we had ceased to have any of those momentous nothings to communicate which require to be done without observation. I had no longer any motive in life—duty was tiresome, and pleasure a mask that smothered me; love was a fable, and religion, I knew not what—nothing that comforted me, for it can only enter the heart that is open to the sweet influences of love.

In a fit of the most abject depression I swallowed poison, and lying down on my sofa awaited death with more interest in the process of its approaches than I had felt for months. The pain and the burning were easier to bear than I had borne many and many a time; gradually the world receded; my eyes closed, and a struggle shook my whole frame—death had indeed got hold of me. A terrible noise filled my ears; my dead and stiffening body seemed to drop away; I sat upright and saw about me all familiar and household things. On the floor beside me lay the picture of Mr. Doughty which I had been holding in my hand when I fell asleep—the noise of its falling had waked me.

"Then it had been only a dream, after all?"

"Why, to be sure; did you not see all along that such things could not have really happened?"

The Home, January 1859; *Pictures of Country Life*, 1859

---

3. Hardened, unfeeling.

ROSE TERRY COOKE
1827–1892

Rose Terry Cooke, born February 17, 1827, on a farm six miles west of Hartford, would spend most of her life in the New England region that she documents in her fiction. She was the descendant of two old Connecticut families. From her father, Henry Wadsworth Terry, a landscape gardener, Cooke learned a love of nature; from her mother, Ann Wright Hurlbut, she received her early education, one that both inspired and disciplined her interest in writing. During childhood her mother required her to learn a page of the dictionary every day and to record the events of her life in a copybook. Later, signing her earliest poetry with her mother's initials, "A.W.H.," Cooke showed her deep feeling for her mother, whom she credited for her literary accomplishments. Cooke's friend and contemporary author, Harriet Prescott Spofford, wrote that "one of the strongest feelings Rose had was her love of her mother" (155). And a year before her death Cooke told Spofford, " 'My mother was nursed by a gypsy, and in her were the oddest streaks. Severer in her Puritanism than ever I was, there was a favorable wildness about her, a passion for getting out of doors, and in just as little covering as possible' " (155).

Cooke graduated at the age of sixteen from the Hartford Female Seminary. At the same time that she ended her formal schooling she joined the Congregational Church, and although she remained a committed Christian throughout her life, she was to have—at least in her fiction—an ongoing argument with the church as an institution. After graduation Cooke worked for almost four years as a teacher and governess in New Jersey before returning to live with her family in Hartford. An inheritance from her grand-uncle Daniel in 1848, when she was twenty-one, enabled her to give up teaching and devote herself to writing.

Cooke did not marry until relatively late in life. In 1873, the year following her mother's death, she married a widower, Rollin T. Cooke, a man sixteen years her junior. As a consequence of this marriage, Cooke lost her financial independence. Her husband, who worked infrequently, never managed to contribute substantially to their household, and her father-in-law used Cooke's money unwisely in his business ventures. As the result of her attempt to make ends meet, much of Cooke's writing after her marriage consisted of short stories for children's magazines and potboilers for religious weeklies. After 1887 Cooke lived in Pittsfield, Massachusetts, where she died July 18, 1892, at the age of sixty-five.

As was the case with Alice Cary, Cooke's first love as a writer was poetry, and it was as a poet that she wished to make her mark on American literature. But, like Cary, and perhaps for many of the same reasons, Cooke also wrote fiction. After publishing poetry and short fiction in various magazines, includ-

92

ing several stories in *Putnam's* between 1855 and 1857, Cooke was invited to contribute to the first issue of the *Atlantic Monthly* (November 1857), where she published "Sally Parsons's Duty." Four years later, the *Atlantic* publication of "Miss Lucinda" (August 1861) established Cooke as a gifted writer of specifically regional fiction. During the course of her career, she would eventually publish over a hundred stories, twenty-one of which appeared in the prestigious *Atlantic* and almost thirty in the only slightly less prestigious *Harper's*. Her best stories were collected in *Somebody's Neighbors* (1881), *The Sphinx's Children and Other People's* (1886), and *Huckleberries Gathered from New England Hills* (1891).

o   o   o

Cooke's fiction reflects a self-conscious use of regional materials. In each of the stories included here she turns New England imagery into metaphors for character. Aunt Huldah is a prickly "chestnut burr," and Jack is a "veritable little pickle"; Lowly is a sun-loving vine trying to find a footing in the granite of her husband's nature. And although the use of vernacular language by early nineteenth-century humorists, from the dramatist Royall Tyler to the Yankee dialect writers among whom James Russell Lowell figured most prominently, had become a commonplace in popular magazine literature by mid-century, Rose Terry Cooke became the first to make it an integral part of serious American fiction. Cooke used dialect as early as the 1850s and 1860s to establish vernacular speech as one of the identifying features of regionalism. Moreover, she used dialect to direct her readers' attention to regional values, which she associated with women's experience of language and culture, as well as to identify conflict between women's and men's values as a major theme of her fiction. For dialect, appearing in opposition to the standard English of her expository passages, calls attention to the opposition her regional speakers see between the interests of men and the interests of women.

Freedom Wheeler asserts his view of women's subordinate place in the world when he says, after his daughter Marah is born, " "Tain't nothin' to me what ye call her: gals ain't worth namin' anyhow!' " Yet by making them the primary focus of her fiction Cooke rescues women from this derivative or "offspring" position. Thus, although at first glance "Freedom Wheeler's Controversy with Providence" seems to pit man against God, the real controversy in the story results from conflict between men and women over the nature of providence. Although outwardly shocked, Aunt Huldah and Aunt Hannah are not finally surprised when Marah refuses to say the Lord's Prayer, which requires her to begin, "Our Father, who art in heaven." In this story Cooke redefines providence as mother-love and substitutes mother on earth for father in heaven. Although Stowe's Mara in *The Pearl of Orr's Island* can reveal the secret that "God has always been to me not so much like a father as like a dear and tender mother," she can only reach mother and heaven through death. In Cooke's fiction, however, women achieve "heaven" when they receive their rewards within their own lifetimes.

In "Miss Beulah's Bonnet" and "How Celia Changed Her Mind" Cooke depicts women who do receive such rewards. When Beulah Larkin chooses to have her mother's "weddin' bunnit" made over by a country shop in order to save money and when she holds her ground against the deacons who find themselves confronted by a "truly feminine tangle" in the circumstances of that bonnet's demise, she proves herself to be a " 'real home-made kind of a saint.' " The source of the "tangle" is Jack, the boy who hides the bonnet under the seat cushion where it can be sat on by the minister's wife; thus, Beulah seems justified in asserting " 'I'm free to say I never did like boys.' " She endures the loss of her bonnet—which she feels must also keep her home from church—in order to keep her promise to her niece's daughter, thereby earning "sainthood" in Cooke's terms.

Cooke defends women fiercely, and even, in "How Celia Changed Her Mind," takes up the case of the "despised class" of unmarried women. When Celia hosts her Thanksgiving dinner for all the old maids in Basset and makes her vow to raise dead Rosabel Stearn's two orphaned children " 'and fetch 'em up to be dyed-in-the-wool old maids,' " she acknowledges the sweetness of freedom for women who have never married, or who, like herself, decide to try marriage and then to "change their minds." Cooke places controversy with what the American republic has provided for women at the center of her own fiction. By insisting that mother-love is closer to providence than the "dreadful" word "father," Cooke offers both her characters and her readers an alternative vision, capable of providing women with the "food" of self-love and self-respect.

Freedom Wheeler's Controversy with Providence[1]

A Story of Old New England

I

Aunt Huldy and Aunt Hannah[2] sat in the kitchen,—Aunt Huldah[3] bolt upright in a straight-backed wooden chair, big silver-bowed spectacles astride her high nose, sewing carpet-rags with such energy that her eyes snapped, and her brown, wrinkled fingers flew back and forth like the spokes of a rapid wheel; Aunt Hannah in a low, creaky old rocker, knitting diligently but placidly, and rocking gently. You could almost hear her purr, and you wanted to stroke her; but Aunt Huldah!—an electric machine could not be less desirable to handle than she, or a chestnut-burr pricklier.

The back-log simmered and sputtered; the hickory-sticks in front shot up bright, soft flames; and through the two low, green-paned windows the pallid sun of February sent in a pleasant shining on to the clean kitchen-floor. Cooking-stoves were not made then, nor Merrimac calicoes. The two old women had stuff petticoats and homespun short-gowns, clean mob-caps[4] over their decent gray hair, and big blue-check aprons: hair-dye, wigs, flowered chintz, and other fineries had not

---

1. The title is an allusion to Michael Wigglesworth's 1662 poem, "God's Controversy with New England," which sketched out the pattern of the jeremiad, a form of Puritan sermon that exhorted the listeners to enumerate their sins.
2. A biblical name; the mother of Samuel, the prophet: see 1 Samuel 1–2.
3. A biblical name; an Old Testament prophetess;

see 2 Kings 22.14.
4. Large, high caps trimmed with frills and ribbons. Calico: lightweight cotton fabric, originally from Calicut, India, popular for its bright colors and attractive designs; the Merrimac is a river in New Hampshire and Massachusetts noted for the mill towns erected on its banks. Stuff: woven material such as wool.

reached the lonely farms of Dorset in those days. "Spinsters" was not
a mere name. The big wool wheel stood in one corner of the kitchen,
and a little flax-wheel by the window. In summer both would be moved
to the great garret, where it was cool and out of the way.

"Curus, ain't it?" said Aunt Huldah. "Freedom never come home
before, later'n nine-o'clock bell, and he was mortal mighty then; kep'
his tongue between his teeth same way he did to breakfast this mornin'. There's suthin' a-goin' on, Hanner, you may depend on't."

"Mabbe he needs some wormwood-tea," said Aunt Hannah, who,
like Miss Hannah More, thought the only two evils in the world were
sin and bile, and charitably preferred to lay things first to the physical
disorder.

"I du b'lieve, Hanner, you think 'riginal sin is nothin' but a bad
stomick."

"Ef 'tain't 'riginal sin, it's actual transgression pretty often, Huldy,"
returned the placid old lady with a gentle cackle. The Assembly's
Catechism had been ground into them both, as any old-fashioned New
Englander will observe, and they quoted its forms of speech, as Boston
people do Emerson's Essays, by "an automatic action of the unconscious nervous centres."[5]

The door opened, and Freedom walked in, scraping his boots upon
the husk-mat, as a man will who has lived all his days with two old
maids, but nevertheless spreading abroad in that clean kitchen an odor
of the barn that spoke of "chores," yet did not disturb the accustomed
nostrils of his aunts. He was a middle-sized, rather "stocky" man, with
a round head well covered with tight-curling short hair, that revenged
itself for being cut too short to curl by standing on end toward every
point of the compass. You could not call him a common-looking man:
something in his keen blue eye, abrupt nose, steady mouth, and square
chin always made a stranger look at him twice. Rugged sense, but more
rugged obstinacy, shrewdness, keen perception, tempered somewhat
by a certain kindliness that he himself felt to be his weak spot,—all
these were to be read in Freedom Wheeler's well-bronzed face, sturdy
figure, positive speech, and blunt manner.

He strode up to the fireplace, sat down in an armchair rudely shaped
out of wood by his own hands, and plunged, after his fashion, at once
into the middle of things.

"Aunt Huldy and Aunt Hanner, I'm a-goin' to git married." The
domestic bombshell burst in silence. Aunt Hannah dropped a stitch,
and couldn't see to pick it up for at least a minute. Aunt Huldah's
scissors snipped at the rags with a vicious snap, as if they were responsible agents, and she would end their proceedings then and there:
presently she said, "Well, I *am* beat!" To which rather doubtful utterance Freedom made no reply, and the scissors snipped harder yet.

---

5. Ralph Waldo Emerson, 19th-century American poet, philosopher, and clergyman, who collected his work
in two series of *Essays* (1841 and 1844).

Aunt Hannah recovered herself first. "Well, I'm real glad on't," purred she. It was her part to do the few amenities of the family.

"I dono whether I be or not, till I hear who 'tis," dryly answered Aunt Huldah, who was obviously near akin to Freedom.

"It's Lowly Mallory," said the short-spoken nephew, who by this time was whittling busily at a peg for his ox-yoke.

"Du tell!" said Aunt Hannah in her lingering, deliberate tones, the words running into each other as she spoke. "She's jest's clever's the day is long. You've done a good thing, Freedom, 's sure's you live."

"He might ha' done wuss: that's a fact." And with this approval Freedom seemed satisfied; for he brushed his chips into the fire, ran his fingers through his already upright hair, eyed his peg with the keen aspect of a critic in pegs, and went off to the barn. He knew instinctively that his aunts must have a chance to talk the matter over.

"This is the beateree!"[6] exclaimed Aunt Huldah as the door shut after him. "Lowly Mallory, of all creturs! Freedom's as masterful as though he was the Lord above, by natur; and ef he gets a leetle softly cretur like that, without no more grit'n a November chicken, he'll ride right over everything, and she won't darst to peep nor mutter a mite. Good land!"

"Well, well," murmured Aunt Hannah, "she is a kind o' feeble piece, but she's real clever; an' I dono but what it's as good as he could do. Ef she was like to him, hard-headed, 'n' sot in her way, I tell ye, Huldy, the fur'd fly mightily; and it's putty bad to have fight to home when there's a fam'ly to fetch up."

"Well, you be forecastin', I must say, Hanner; but mabbe you're abaout right. Besides, I've obsarved that folks will marry to suit themselves, not other people. An' mabbe it's the best way, seein' it's their own loss or likin' more'n anybody else's."

"But, Huldy, 'pears as if you'd forgot one thing: I expect we'd better be a-movin' out into the old house, ef there's goin' to be more folks here."

"Well, I declare! I never thought on't. 'Tis best, I guess. I wonder ef Freedom's got the idee."

"I dono. But that hadn't oughter make no difference. There never was a house big enough for two families; an', ef we go before we're obleeged to, it's a sight better'n stayin' till we be."

"That's so, Hanner: you allers was a master-hand for takin' things right end foremost. I'll sort out our linen right off, 'nd set by our furnitoor into the back-chamber. I guess the old house'll want a leetle paintin' an' scrapin'. It's dreadful lucky Amasy Flint's folks moved to Noppit last week: seems as though there was a Providence about it."

"I shouldn't wonder ef Freedom had give 'em a sort o' hint to go, Huldy."

"Well, you do beat all! I presume likely he did."

---

6. The thing that beats all, that surpasses all expectations.

And Aunt Huldah picked up the rags at her feet, piled them into a splint basket, hung the shears on a steel chain by her side, and lifting her tall, gaunt figure from the chair, betook herself up stairs. But Aunt Hannah kept on knitting. She was the thinker, and Huldah the doer, of the family. Now her thoughts ran before her to the coming change, and she sighed; for she knew her nephew thoroughly, and she pitied the gentle, sweet nature that was to come in contact with his.

Dear Aunt Hannah! She had never had any romance in her own life: she did not know anything about love, except as the placid and quite clear-eyed affection she felt for Freedom, who was her only near relation, and she saw little Lowly Mallory's future on its hardest side. But she could not help it; and her nature was one that never frets against a difficulty, any more than the green turf beats against the rock to whose edge it clings.

So the slow, sad New England spring, with storm and tempest, drifting snows, and beating rains, worked its reluctant way into May. And when the lilacs were full of purple and white plumes, delicate as cut coral sprays, and luscious with satiating odor, and the heavy-headed daffodils thrust golden locks upward from the sward, Aunt Huldah and Aunt Hannah moved their wool-wheel and their flax-wheel, the four stiff-backed chairs, the settle and big red chest, the high four-post bedstead, and the two rush-bottomed rockers that had been Grandsir Wheeler's, back into the small red house, for which these furnishings had been purchased sixty years before, laid the rag-carpet, that Aunt Huldah had sewed and dyed and woven, on the "settin'-room" floor, and with a barrel of potatoes and a keg of salt pork, went to housekeeping.

There was some home-made linen belonging to them, and a few cups and dishes, also a feather-bed, and a pair of blankets. Freedom kept them supplied with what necessaries they wanted, and, though he was called "dreadful near"[7] in the town, he was not an unjust man. His two aunts had taken him in charge, an orphan at six, and been faithful and kind to him all his days, and he could do no less than care for them now. Beside, they owned half the farm, and though one was fifty-six, and the other fifty-eight, there was much hard work left in them yet. Aunt Huldah was a skilful tailoress, in demand for miles about; and Aunt Hannah was the best sick-nurse in the county. They would not suffer: and, truth to tell, they rather enjoyed the independence of their own house; for Freedom and Aunt Huldah were chips of the same block, and only Aunt Hannah's constant, quiet restraint and peace-making kept the family tolerably harmonious. And in the farmhouse a new reign began,—the reign of Queen Log.[8]

Lowly Mallory was a fragile, slender, delicate girl, with sweet gray

---

7. Stingy, parsimonious.
8. The log which Jupiter in the fable made ruler over the frogs; often a reference to inertness on the part of rulers, as contrasted with the excess of activity typified by Queen Stork (later referred to in this story).

eyes and plenty of brown hair; pale as a spring anemone, with just such faint pinkness in her lips and on her high cheek-bones as tints that pensile, egg-shaped bud, when its

> "Small flower layeth
> Its fairy gem beneath some giant tree"

on the first warm days of May. She had already the line of care that marks New-England women across the forehead, like a mark of Cain,[9] —the signal of a life in which work has murdered health and joy and freedom; for Lowly was the oldest of ten children, and her mother was bed-ridden. Lovina was eighteen now, and could take her place; and Lowly loved Freedom with the reticent, undemonstrative affection of her race and land: moreover, she was glad of change, of rest. Rest!— much of that awaited her! Freedom's first step after the decorous wedding and home-coming was to buy ten cows—he had two already—and two dozen new milk-pans.

"I calkerlate we can sell a good lot of butter 'n' cheese down to Dartford, Lowly," he said, on introducing her to the new dairy he had fitted up at one end of the woodshed; and, if the gentle creature's heart sank within her at the prospect, she did not say so, and Freedom never asked how she liked it. He was "masterful" indeed; and having picked out Lowly from all the other Dorset girls, because she was a still and hard-working maiden, and would neither rebel against nor criticise his edicts, he took it for granted things would go on as he wished.

Poor little Lowly! Her simple, tender heart went out to her husband like a vine feeling after a trellis; and, even when she found it was only a boulder that chilled and repelled her slight ardors and timid caresses, she did still what the vine does,—flung herself across and along the granite faces of the rock, and turned her trembling blossoms sunward, where life and light were free and sure.

Aunt Huldah and Aunt Hannah soon grew to be her ministering angels; and if they differed from the gold-haired, pink-enamelled, straight-nosed creations of Fra Angelico, and would have figured ill,— in their short-gowns and mob-caps,—bowing before an ideal Madonna,[1] Lowly wanted no better tendance and providing than they gave her, when in due season there appeared in the farmhouse a red and roaring baby, evidently patterned after his father, morally as well as physically; the white down on his raw pink head twisting into tight kinks, and his stubby fists set in as firm a grasp as ever Freedom's big brown paws were. Lowly was a happy little woman: she had loved children always, and here was one all her own. Two weeks were dreamed away in rest and rapture; then Freedom began to bustle and

9. The eldest son of Adam and Eve, who killed his brother Abel because of jealous rivalry. Afterwards God placed a mark upon Cain so that no one would kill him; Cain's punishment was to live in full consciousness of his act; see Genesis 4.1–16.

1. Mary, the mother of Jesus; frequently the subject of idealized portraits by painters such as Fra Angelico. Fra Angelico: Italian religious painter (1400– 1455); he was also an ordained priest.

fret, and growl about the neglected dairy, and the rusty pork, and the hens that wanted care.

"Don't ye s'pose she'll git 'raound next week, Aunt Huldy? Things is gittin' dredful behind-hand!" Freedom had left the bedroom-door open on purpose. Aunt Huldah got up, and shut it with a slam, while he went on: "Them hens had oughter be set,[2] 'n' I never git time to be a half a day prowlin' araound after 'em: they've stole their nests, I expect, the hull tribe; 'nd Hepsy don't make butter to compare along-side o' Lowly's; then there's that 'ere pork a-gittin' rusty, 'n' Aunt Hanner, she's over to Mallory's nussin Loviny, so's't I can't call on you; 'n' it doos seem's though two weeks was a plenty for well folks to lie in bed."

Here Aunt Huldah exploded: "Freedom Wheeler, you hain't got a mite o' compassion into ye! Lowly ain't over 'n' above powerful, any-way: she'll break clear down ef she ain't real keerful; mabbe I ain't"—

The shutting of the back-door stopped her tirade. While she hunted in a table-drawer for her thimble, Freedom had coolly walked off: he did not choose to argue the subject. But next day Lowly got up, and was dressed. There were two lines across the sad, low forehead now, but she went about her work in silence. There is a type of feminine character that can endure to the edge of death, and endure silently, and that character was eminently hers.

"Good little feller, so he was, as ever was; there, there, there! should be cuddled up good 'n' warm, so he should," Aunt Hannah purred to the small boy a month after, seeing him for the first time, as she had been taking care of Lovina Mallory through a low fever, when he was born.

"What be ye a-going' to call him, Freedom?"

"I calkerlate he'll be baptized Shearjashub.[3] There's allus ben a Shearjashub 'nd a Freedom amongst our folks. I've heered Grandsir Wheeler tell on't more'n forty times, how the' was them two names away back as fur as there's gravestones to tell on't down to Litchfield meetin'-house, 'nd back o' that in the old graveyard to Har'ford. I expect this here feller'll be called Shearjashub, 'nd the next one Free-dom: that's the way they've allus run."

"For the land's sakes!" sputtered Aunt Huldah. "I was in hopes you hadn't got that notion inter your head. Why can't ye call the child some kind o' pootty Scripter[4] name, like David, or Samwell, or Eber, 'nd not set him a-goin' with a kite's tail like that tied on to him?"

"I guess what's ben good 'nough for our folks time out o' mind'll be good 'nough for him," stiffly answered Freedom. And Aunt Huldah, with inward rage, accepted the situation, and went out to the barn to help Lowly set some refractory hens, where she found the poor little

---

2. A little further along in the story, Cooke explains to the reader the process of "setting a hen" as Aunt Huldah does it.

3. A biblical name; a son of the prophet Isaiah; see Isaiah 7.3.

4. I.e., Scripture, the Bible.

woman, with suspiciously red eyes, counting eggs on a corner of the hay-mow.

"Hanner's come, Lowly," said she, "so she's got baby, 'nd I come out to give ye a lift about them hens. I've ben a-dealin' with Freedom about that there child's name; but you might jest as well talk to White Rock: I will say for't he's the sottest man I ever see. I b'lieve he'd set to to fight his own way out with the Lord above, if he hed to."

Lowly gave a little plaintive smile, but, after the manner of her sex, took her husband's part. "Well, you see, Aunt Huldy, it's kind o' nateral he should want to foller his folks's ways. I don't say but what I did want to call baby Eddard, for my little brother that died. I set great story by Eddy,"—here Lowly's checked apron wiped a certain mist from her patient eyes,—"and 'twould ha' been my mind to call him for Eddy; but Freedom don't feel to, and you know Scripter says wives must be subject to husbands."[5]

"Hm!" sniffed Aunt Huldah, who was lost to the strong-minded party of her sex by being born before its creation,—"Scripter has a good deal to answer for!" with which enigmatical and shocking remark, she turned, and pounced upon the nearest hen. Poor old hen! She evidently represented a suffering and abject sex to Aunt Huldah, and exasperated her accordingly. Do I not know? Have not I, weakly and meekly protesting against their ways and works, also been hustled and bustled by the Rights Women?[6] —even as this squawking, crawking, yellow biddy was fluffed and cuffed and shaken up by Aunt Huldah, and plunged at last, in spite of nips and peeks and screaks, into the depths of a barrel, the head wedged on above her, and the unwilling matron condemned to solitary confinement, with hard labor, on thirteen eggs!

So Freedom had his way, of course; and Lowly went on, with the addition of a big naughty baby to take care of, waking before light to get her "chores" out of the way, prepare breakfast, skim cream, strain new milk and set it, scald pans, churn, work and put down butter, feed pigs and hens, bake, wash, iron, scrub, mend, make, nurse baby, fetch wood from the shed, and water from the well,—a delicate, bending, youthful figure, with hands already knotted, and shoulders bowed by hard work; her sole variety of a week-day being when one kind of pie gave place to another, or when the long winter evenings, with dim light of tallow candles, made her spinning shorter, and her sewing longer.

For Sundays were scarce a rest: breakfast was as early, milk as abundant, on that day as on any other and then there was a five-mile ride to meeting, for which ample lunch must be prepared, since they stayed at noon; there was baby to dress, and her own Sunday clothes to put on, in which stiff and unaccustomed finery she sat four mortal

---

5. The legal domination of husbands over wives is frequently interpreted as beginning with the laws of God to Moses; see Exodus 20.17, and in the New Testament see Ephesians 5.22 and Colossians 3.18.

6. Women such as Elizabeth Cady Stanton and Susan B. Anthony who advocated women's rights and women's suffrage.

hours, with but the brief interval of nooning, on a hard and comfortless seat, and then home again to get the real dinner of the day, to feed her pigs and hens, to get the clamorous baby quiet: this was hardly rest. And summer—that brings to overstrained nerves and exhausted muscles the healing of sun, sweet winds, fresh air, and the literal "balm of a thousand flowers"—only heralded to her the advent of six strong hungry men at haying, shearing, and reaping time, with extra meals, increased washing, and, of course, double fatigue. Yet this is the life that was once the doom of all New England farmers' wives; the life that sent them to early graves, to mad-houses, to suicide; the life that is so beautiful in the poet's numbers,[7] so terrible in its stony, bloomless, oppressive reality. It would have been hard to tell if Lowly was glad or sorry, when, on a soft day in June, Aunt Hannah, this time at home, was hurriedly called from the red house to officiate as doctor and nurse both at the arrival of another baby. This time, Freedom growled and scowled by himself in the kitchen, instead of condescending to look at and approve the child; for it was a girl.

Aunt Hannah chuckled in her sleeve. Freedom had intimated quite frankly that this child was to be called after himself, nothing doubting but that another boy was at hand; and great was his silent rage at the disappointment.

"Imperdent, ain't it?" queried Aunt Huldah, who sat by the kitchen-fire stirring a mess of Indian-meal porridge. "To think it darst to be a girl when ye was so sot on its turnin' out a boy! Seems as though Providence got the upper hand on ye, Freedom, after all!"

But Freedom never gave retort to Aunt Huldah. He had been brought up in certain superstitions, quite obsolete now, about respecting his elders; and, though the spirit was wanting sometimes, the letter of the law had observance. He could rage at Aunt Huldah privately, but before her he held his tongue. It was his wife who suffered as the sinner should for disturbing his plans in this manner. He snubbed her, he despised the baby, and forthwith bought two more cows, with the grim remark, "Ef I've got to fetch up a pack o' girls, I guess I'd better scratch around 'n' make a leetle more money."

But, if the new baby was an eyesore to Freedom, she was a delight to Lowly. All the more because her father ignored and seemed to dislike her, the affluent mother-heart flowed out upon her. She was a cooing, clinging, lovely little creature; and when, worn out with her day's work, Lowly had at last coaxed her cross, teething boy to sleep, and she sat down in the old creaky rocker to nurse and tend her baby, the purest joy that earth knows stole over her like the tranquil breath of heaven. The touch of tiny fingers on her breast; the warm shining head against her heart; the vague baby-smile and wandering eyes that neither the wistfulness of doubt, the darkness of grief, nor the fire of passion clouded as yet; the inarticulate murmurs of satisfaction; the

7. Metrical feet in poetry.

pressure of the little helpless form upon her lap; the silent, ardent tenderness that awoke and burned in her own heart for this precious creature,—all made for the weary woman a daily oasis of peace and beauty that perhaps saved her brain from that common insanity we call nervousness, and her body from utter exhaustion; for happiness is a medicine of God's own sending: no quack has ever pretended to dispense its potent and beneficent cordial; and the true, honest physician, he whose very profession is the nearest approach to that of the Saviour and Healer of men, knows well that one drop of the only elixir he cannot bring outweighs all he can. Shearjashub grew up to the height of three years, and the baby toddled about, and chattered like a merry chipping-bird, when, one Fast Day[8] morning, Lowly stayed at home from meeting with a sinking heart, and Aunt Hannah was sent for again. Freedom went off to hear the usual sermon, on a pretence of taking Shearjashub out of the way; he being irrepressible except by his father, whom alone he feared. Mother and aunts the youngster manfully defied and scorned; but the very sound of his father's steps reduced him to silence. Shingles were not out of fashion then as a means of discipline; and the hot tingle of the application dwelt vividly in the boy's mind ever since he had been "tuned mightily," as his father phrased it, for disobedience and obstinacy; Aunt Huldah's comment at the first punishment being, "Hemlock all three on 'em,—man an' boy an' shingle: it's tough to tell which'll beat."[9]

Little Love stayed at home with old Hepsy, and prattled all day long in the kitchen. Lowly could not spare the sweet voice from her hearing, and she had need of all its comfort: for, when Freedom came home from Dorset Centre, a great girl-baby lay by Lowly in the bed; and if its welcome from the mother had been bitter tears, whose traces still shone on her wan face, from the father came far bitterer words,—curses in all but the wording; for Freedom was a "professor,"[1] and profanity was a sin. Mint and anise and cumin he tithed scrupulously; but mercy and judgment fled from him, and hid their shamefaced heads.[2] Aunt Huldah and Aunt Hannah made their tansy-pudding that day, after the custom of their forefathers, and ate it with unflinching countenances; but Lowly fasted in her secret soul; and since her husband grimly remarked, "'Tain't nothin' to me what ye call her: gals ain't worth namin' anyhow!" the new baby was baptized Marah,[3] and behaved herself neither with the uproarious misconduct of Shearjashub, nor the gentle sweetness of Love, but, quite in defiance of her name, was the merriest, maddest little grig[4] that could be, afraid of

---

8. A day reserved by church authorities for the entire congregation to fast; special sermons arraigning the sins of the society and exhorting the people to repentance were preached on Fast Days.
9. Reference to the hemlock, a common eastern conifer, known for the stonelike hardness of its knots, which are capable of chipping steel blades; thus, Aunt Huldah is making a comment on the hardness of both Freedom and Shearjashub.
1. One who professed to be a member of God's

"elect," thereby to be among God's "saved."
2. Freedom is scrupulous in providing for the household (measuring out herbs and spices) but he doesn't provide the equivalent spiritual nourishment (mercy and judgment).
3. The biblical Naomi asks to be called "Mara" because it means "bitter"; see Ruth 1.20.
4. A bright, lively person; possibly derived from "cricket."

nothing and nobody, but as submissive to Lovey as a lamb could be, and full of fight when Shearjashub intruded himself on her domains. For this baby was a sturdy, rosy girl of three, before the fourth appeared. Lowly by this time had fallen into a listless carelessness toward her husband, that was simply the want of all spring in a long downtrodden heart. Lovey alone could stir her to tears or smiles. Marah tired and tormented her with her restless and overflowing vitality, though she loved her dearly; and her boy was big enough now to cling a little to "mother," and reward her for her faithful patience and care: but Lovey was the darling of her secret heart; and, being now five years old, the little maid waited on mother like a cherub on a saint, ran of errands, wound yarn, and did many a slight task in the kitchen that saved Lowly's bent and weary fingers.

It was with an impotent rage beyond speech that Freedom took the birth of another daughter,—a frail, tiny creature, trembling and weak as a new-born lamb in a snow-drift, but for that very reason rousing afresh in Lowly's breast the eternal floods of mother-love, the only love that never fails among all earthly passions, the only patience that is never weary, the sole true and abiding trust for the helpless creatures who come into life as waifs from the great misty ocean to find a shelter or a grave. Lowly was not only a mother according to the flesh,—for there are those whose maternity goes no further, and there are childless women who have the motherliness that could suffice for a countless brood,—but she had, too, the real heart: she clung to her weakling with a fervor and assertion that disgusted Freedom, and astounded Aunt Huldah, who, like the old Scotch woman, sniffed at the idea of children in heaven: "No, no! a hantle o' weans there! an' me that could never abide bairns onywhere! I'll no believe it."

"It does beat all, Hanner, to see her take to that skinny, miser'ble little crittur! The others was kind o' likely, all on 'em; but this is the dreadfulest weakly, peeked thing I ever see. I should think she'd be sick on't."[5]

"I expect mothers—anyway them that's real motherly, Huldy— thinks the most of them that needs it the most. I've seen women with children quite a spell now, bein' out nussin' 'round, an' I allers notice that the sickly ones gets the most lovin' an' cuddlin'. I s'pose it's the same kind o' feeling' the Lord hez for sinners: they want him a sight more'n the righteous do."

"Why, Hanner Wheeler, what be you a-thinkin of! Where's your Catechis'? Ain't all men by nater under the wrath an' cuss o' God 'cause they be fallen sinners? And here you be a-makin' out he likes 'em better'n good folks."

"Well, Huldy, I warn't a-thinkin' of Catechism: I was a-thinkin' about what it sez in the Bible."

Here the new baby cried; and Aunt Huldah, confounded but uncon-

5. Peaked; sickly, pale, or emaciated in appearance.

vinced, gave a loud sniff, and carried off Shearjashub and Marah to the red house, where their fights and roars and general insubordination soon restored her faith in the Catechism.[6]

Lowly got up very slowly from little Phoebe's birth; and Freedom grumbled loud and long over the expense of keeping Hepsy a month in the kitchen. But his wife did not care now: a dumb and sudden endurance possessed her. She prayed night and morning, with a certain monomaniac persistence, that she and Lovey and the baby might die; but she did her work just as faithfully and silently as ever, and stole away at night to lie down on the little cot-bed in the back-chamber by Lovey and Marah, her hot cheek against the cool, soft face of her darling, and the little hand hid deep in her bosom, for an hour of rest and sad peace.

Freedom, meanwhile, worked all day on the farm, and carried Shearjashub, whose oppressive name had lapsed into Bub, into wood and field with him; taught him to drive the oxen, to hunt hens' nests in the barn on the highest mow, to climb trees, in short to risk his neck however he could "to make a man of him"; and the boy learned, among other manly ways, a sublime contempt for "gals," and a use of all the forcible words permitted to masculine tongues. But Shear-jashub's sceptre was about to tremble. Little Phoebe had lingered in this world through a year of fluttering life, when another baby was announced; but this time it was a boy!—small even to Phoebe's first size, pallid, lifeless almost, but still a boy.

"By Jinks!" exclaimed Freedom, his hard face glowing with pleasure. "I told ye so, Aunt Huldy! There's bound to be a Freedom Wheeler in this house, whether or no."

"Hm!" said Aunt Huldah. "You call to mind old Hepsy Tinker, don't ye?—she that was a-going' to Har'ford a Tuesday, Providence permittin', an' Wednesday whether or no. Mabbe ye'll live to wish ye hadn't fit with the Lord's will the way ye hev."

"I've got a boy, anyhow," was the grim exultant answer. "And he'll be Freedom Wheeler afore night; for I'm a-goin' to fetch the parson right off."

Strenuously did Parson Pitcher object to private baptism[7] : but he was an old man now; and Freedom threatened that he would go to Hartford and fetch the Episcopal minister, if Parson Pitcher refused, and the old doctor knew he was quite sure to keep to his word: so, with a groan at the stiff-necked brother, he got out his cloak and hat, and rode home with victorious Freedom to the farmhouse. Here the punch-bowl was made ready on a stand in the parlor, and a fire kindled on the hearth, for it was a chilly April day; and from the open door into Lowly's bedroom the wailing day-old baby was brought, and given into its father's arms. a mere scrid[8] and atom of humanity, but a boy.

---

6. When the children fight, it restores Aunt Huldah's belief in the Catechism because it seems to be evidence that children are born sinners and must be redeemed by God's grace, which is what Calvinists believed the Bible teaches.

7. Calvinist doctrine holds that baptism must take place in public among the community of believers.

8. Slice or shred; from Dutch *schrood*.

The rite was over, the long prayer said, and Freedom strode into the chamber to lay his namesake beside its mother; but, as he stopped, the child quivered suddenly all over, gasped, opened its half-shut eyes glazed with a fatal film, and then closed the pallid, violet-shadowed lids forever.

The next entry in the family Bible was,—

"Freedom. Born April 11; died same day."

"Well, he hain't got nobody but the Lord to querrel with this 'bout!" snapped Aunt Huldah. "He's had his way, 'nd now see what come on't!"

Lowly got up again, after the fashion of her kind, without a murmur. She felt her baby's death, she mourned her loss, she was sorry for Freedom. She had loved him once dearly; and, if she had known it, Freedom loved her as much as he could anything but himself: but it was not his way to show affection, even to his boy; as much of it as ever came to the surface was a rough caress offered now and then to Lowly,—a usage that had died out, and died with no mourning on either side. But as there is a brief sweet season often-times in our bitter climate, that comes upon the sour and angry November weather like a respite of execution, a few soft, misty, pensively sweet days, when the sun is red and warm in the heavens, the dead leaves give out their tender and melancholy odor, and the lingering birds twitter in the pine-boughs as if they remembered spring, so there came to Lowly a late and last gleam of tranquil pleasure.

Aunt Huldah brought it about, for her tongue never failed her for fear. She caught Freedom by himself one day, looking like an ill-used bull-dog, all alone in the barn, setting some new rake-teeth.

"I've hed it on my mind quite a spell, Freedom," began the valorous old woman, "to tell ye, that, ef ye expect Lowly is ever a-goin' to hev a rousin' hearty child ag'in, you'll hev to cosset[9] her up some. She ain't like our folks."

"That's pretty trew, Aunt Huldy," was the bitter interruption.

"She ain't a nether millstone,[1] thet's a fact," answered Aunt Huldah with vigor; "nor she ain't band leather, by a good sight: she's one o' the weakly, meekly sort; 'nd you can't make a whistle out o' a pig's tail, I've heerd father say, 'nd you no need to try: no more can ye make a stubbid,[2] gritty cretur out o' Lowly. She's good as gold: but she's one o' them that hankers arter pleasantness, an' lovin', an' sich; they're vittles an' drink to her, I tell ye. You an' I can live on pork an' cabbage, and sass each other continooal, without turnin' a hair; but Lowly won't stan' it; 'nd, ef ye expect this next baby to git along, I tell ye it's got to be easy goin' with her. You want to keep your fight with the Lord up, I s'pose: you're sot on hevin' another Freedom Wheeler?"

"I be," was the curt response. But though Aunt Huldah turned her back upon him without further encouragement, and marched through

---

9. Pamper, fondle.
1. The lower and harder of a pair of stones used in   a mill for grinding grain.
2. I.e., stupid.

the ranks of "garden-sass" back to the house, her apron over her head, and her nose high in air, like one who snuffeth the battle from afar,[3] her pungent words fell not to the ground. Freedom perceived the truth of what she said, and his uneasy conscience goaded him considerably as to past opportunities; but he was an honest man, and, when he saw a thing was to be done, he did it. Next day he brought Lowly a new rocking-chair from the Centre. He modified his manners daily. He helped her lift the heavy milk-pails, he kept her wood-pile by the shed-door well heaped, and was even known to swing the great dinner-pot off the crane, if it was full and weighty.

"For the land sakes!" exclaimed Aunt Hannah, "what's a-comin' to Freedom? He does act halfway decent, Huldah."

Aunt Huldah shook her cap-ruffle up and down, and looked sagacious as an ancient owl. "That's me! I gin it to him, I tell ye, Hanner! Lowly wants cossetin', 'nd handlin' tender-like, or we'll be havin' more dyin' babies 'round. I up an' told him so Wednesday mornin' out in the barn, 's true's I'm alive."

"I'm glad on't! I'm real glad on't!" exclaimed Aunt Hannah. "You done right, Huldy. But, massy[4] to me! how darst ye?"

"Ho!" sniffed Aunt Huldah. "Ef you think I'm afeard o' Freedom. you're clean mistook. I've spanked him too often, 'n' I wish to goodness I'd ha' spanked him a heap more: he'd ha' ben a heap the better for't. You reklect I had the tunin' of him, Hanner? You was allus a-nussin' mother: Freedom come to us jest as she got bedrid. Land! what a besom[5] he was! His folks never tuned him, nor never took him to do, a mite. I hed it all to do, 'nd my mind misgives me now I didn't half do it. 'Jest as the twig is bent the tree's inclined,' ye know it says in the Speller."[6]

"But, Huldy, 'tain't so easy bending a white-oak staddle;[7] 'specially ef it's got a six-years' growth."

"Well, I got the hang of him, anyhow; 'nd he'll hear to me most allus, whether he performs accordin', or not."

"Mabbe it's too late, though, now, Huldy."

"Law, don't ye croak, Hanner. The little cretur'l hev a pleasant spell anyhow, for a while."

And so she did. Lowly's ready heart responded to sunshine as a rain-drenched bird will, preening its feathers, shaking its weary wings, welcoming the warm gladness with faint chirps and tiny brightening eyes, and then—taking flight.

A long and peaceful winter passed away, and in early May another boy was born: alas, it was another waxen, delicate creature. The old parson was brought in haste to baptize it. The pallid mother grew more white all through the ceremony, but nobody noticed her. She took the

3. See Job 39.25.
4. Mercy.
5. An old English word meaning broom; often used in the phrase "a besom of destruction"; see Isaiah

14.23.
6. Spelling book; a book that frequently combined moral instruction with instruction in letters.
7. A young tree or sapling.

child in her arms with a wan smile, and tried to call it by name: "Free," was all she said. Her arms closed about it with a quick shudder and stringent grasp; her lips parted wide. Lowly and her baby were both "free," for its last breath fluttered upward with its mother's; and in the family Bible there was another record:—

"Lowly Wheeler. Died May 3."

"Freedom Wheeler. Born May 3, died same day."

"Well," said Aunt Huldah, as they came back to the ghastly quiet of the shut and silent house, after laying Lowly and her boy under the ragged turf of Dorset graveyard, "I guess Freedom'll give up his wrastle with Providence now, sence the Lord's took wife, 'nd baby, 'nd all."

"I don't feel sure of that," answered Aunt Hannah, for once sarcastic.

II

Aunt Huldah and Aunt Hannah took Love and Phoebe over to the red house to live with them; for they found a little note in Lowly's Bible requesting them to take charge of these two, and their father did not object. Phoebe was a baby still, hopelessly feeble: she could not stand alone, though she was more than two years old; and Love was devoted to her. Bub and Marah could "fend for themselves"; and the old woman, who came as usual in Lowly's frequent absences from the kitchen, had promised to stay all summer. But, before the summer was over, Phoebe faded away like a tiny snow-wreath in the sun, and made a third little grave at her mother's feet; and Lovey grieved for her so bitterly that Aunt Hannah insisted she should stay with them still, and made her father promise she should be their little girl always; certain forebodings of their own as to the future prompting them to secure her a peaceful home while they lived.

As for Freedom, if he mourned Lowly, it was with no soft or sentimental grief, but with a certain resentful aching in his heart, and a defiant aspect of soul toward the divine will that had overset his intentions and desires,—a feeling that deepened into savage determination; for this man was made of no yielding stuff. Obstinacy stood him in stead of patience, an active instead of a passive trait; and in less than six months after Lowly's death he was "published," according to the custom of those days; the first intimation his aunts or his children had of the impending crisis being this announcement from the pulpit by Parson Pitcher, that "Freedom Wheeler of this town, and Melinda Bassett of Hartland, intend marriage."

Aunt Huldah looked at Aunt Hannah from under her poke-bonnet with the look of an enraged hen; her cap-frill trembled with indignation: and Lovey shrank up closer to Aunt Hannah than before; for she saw two tears rise to her kind old eyes as they met Huldah's, and she loved Aunt Hannah with all her gentle little soul. As for Freedom, he sat bolt upright, and perfectly unmoved.

"Set his face as a flint!" raged Aunt Huldah as soon as she got out of church, and went to take her "noon-spell" in the graveyard, where the basket of doughnuts, cheese, pie, cake, and early apples was usually unpacked on the stone wall on pleasant Sundays, and the aunts sitting on a tombstone, and the children on the grass, ate their lunch. Today Lovey and Marah were left on the stone to eat their fill. Bub had gone to the spring for water, and Freedom nobody knew where; while the aunts withdrew to "talk it over."

"Yis," repeated Aunt Huldah, "set his face like a flint. I tell ye he hain't got no more feelin' than a cherub on a tombstone, Hanner! She ain't cold in her grave afore he's off to Hartland, buyin' calves. Calves! I guess likely, comin' home jest as plausible as a passnip: 'I sha'n't make no butter this year: so I bought a lot o' calves to raise.' Ho! heifer-calves every one on 'em, mind ye. Ef we hadn't ha' ben a pair o' fools, we should ha' mistrusted suthin'. Ef that gal's Abigail Bassett's darter, things'll fly, I tell ye." And here Aunt Huldah blew a long breath out, as if her steam was at high pressure, and could not help opening a valve for relief; and wise Aunt Hannah seized the chance to speak.

"Well, Huldy, I declare I'm beat myself; but we can't help it. I must say I looked forrard to the time when he would do it; but I didn't reelly expect it jest yet. We've got Lovey anyway; and, if Melindy ain' a pootty capable woman, she'll hev her hands full with Bub and Marah."

"Thet's a fact," returned Aunt Huldah, whose inmost soul rejoiced at the prospect of Bub's contumaciousness under new rule; for he was not a small boy any more, and shingles were in vain, though he still made a certain outward show of obedience. Marah, too, was well calculated to be a thorn in the flesh of any meek step-mother, with her high spirits, untamed temper, and utter wilfulness; and Aunt Huldah, whose soul was sore,—not because of Freedom's marriage, for she recognized its necessity, but because of its indecent haste, which not only seemed an insult to gentle Lowly, whom Aunt Huldah had loved dearly, but a matter of talk to all the town where the Wheelers had been respected for many a long year,—Aunt Huldah rejoiced in that exasperated soul of hers at a prospect of torment to the woman who stepped into Lowly's place quite unconscious of any evil design or desire on the part of her new relatives.

But it was no meek step-mother whom Freedom brought home from a very informal wedding, in his old wagon, some three weeks after. Melinda Bassett was quite capable of holding her own, even with Aunt Huldah,—a strapping, buxom, rosy-faced girl, with abundant rough dark hair, and a pair of bright, quick, dark eyes, an arm of might in the dairy, and a power of work and management that would have furnished forth at least five feeble pieces like Lowly. Freedom soon found he had inaugurated Queen Stork.[8] Bub was set to rights as to his

---

8. Reference to the fable of the frogs who chose a stork for their ruler; associated with an excess of activity, in contrast to Queen Log (referred to earlier in the story), associated with inertness.

clothes, and "pitched into," as he sulkily expressed it, in a way that gave him a new and unwilling respect for the other sex; and Marah entered at once into an alliance, offensive and defensive, with the new "mammy"; for Melinda was pleasant and cheerful when things went right, and generally meant they should go right. She was fond of children, too, when they were "pretty behaved"; and Marah was bright enough to find out, with the rapid perception of a keen-witted child, that it was much better for her to *be* pretty behaved than otherwise.

But Freedom—it was new times to him to have his orders unheeded, and his ways derided. He had been lord and master in his house a long time; but here was a capable, plucky, courageous, and cheery creature, who made no bones of turning him out of her dominions when he interfered, or ordering her own ways without his help at all.

"Land of Goshen!" said Melinda to the wondering Aunt Hannah, "do you s'pose I'm goin' to hev a man tewin' round[9] in my way all the time, jest cos he's my husband? I guess not. I know how to 'tend to my business, and I expect to 'tend right up to it: moreover I expect he'll tend to his'n. When I get a-holt of his plough, or fodder his team, or do his choppin', 'll be time enough for him to tell me how to work butter, 'n' scald pans. I ain't nobody's fool, I tell ye, Aunt Hanner."

"I'm glad on't, I'm glad on't!" growled Aunt Huldah, when she heard of this manifesto.

"That's the talk: she'll straighten him out, I'll bet ye! Ef poor Lowly'd had that spunk she might ha' been livin' today. But I guess she's better off," suddenly wound up Aunt Huldah, remembering her Catechism, no doubt, as she walked off muttering, "Are at their death made perfect in holiness, and do immediately pass into glory,"—an assurance that has upheld many a tried and weary soul more conversant with the language of the Assembly of Divines[1] than that of their Lord and Head; for in those old days this formula of the faith was ground into every infant memory, though the tender gospel words were comparatively unknown.

So the first year of the new reign passed on; and in the next February Freedom was mastered by a more stringent power than Melinda, for he fell ill of old-fashioned typhus-fever, a malign evil that lights down here and there in lonely New England farmhouses, utterly regardless of time or place; and in a week this strong man was helpless, muttering delirious speech, struggling for life with the fire that filled his veins and consumed his flesh. Aunt Hannah came to his aid, and the scarce neighbors did what they could for him. Brother-farmers snored away the night in a chair beside his bed, and said that they had "sot up with Freedom Wheeler last night,"—ministrations worse than useless, but

9. "Tew round" means to worry, fret, fuss.
1. In 1643, the Westminster Assembly of Divines in England created the Presbyterian Catechism, which continued to serve as the theological foundation for New England Congregationalists.

yet repeated as a sort of needful observance. And at the end of the first week Aunt Hannah was called away to the "up-chamber" room, where Melinda slept now, and a big boy was introduced into the Wheeler family; while Moll Thunder, an old woman skilled in "yarbs,"[2] as most of her race are,—for she was a half-breed Indian,— was sent for from Wingfield, and took command of the fever-patient, who raged and raved at his will, dosed with all manner of teas, choked with lukewarm porridge, smothered in blankets, bled twice a week, and kept as hot, as feeble, and as dirty as the old practice of medicine required, till disease became a mere question of "the survival of the fittest."[3] Our grandfathers and grandmothers are vaunted to this day as a healthy, hard-working race, because the weakly share of each generation was neatly eliminated according to law.

But, if Freedom was helpless and wandering, Melinda was not. A week was all she spared to the rites and rights of the occasion; and when she first appeared in the kitchen, defying and horrifying Aunt Huldah, there ensued a brief and spicy conversation between the three women concerning this new baby, who lay sucking his fist in the old wooden cradle, looking round, hard, and red as a Baldwin apple, and quite unconscious what a firebrand he was about to be.

"It's real bad, ain't it?" purred Aunt Hannah, "to think Freedom shouldn't know nothin' about the baby? He'd be jest as tickled!"

"I don' know what for," snapped Melinda. "I should think there was young uns enough round now to suit him."

"But they wasn't boys," answered Aunt Hannah. "Freedom is sot on havin' a boy to be called for him. There's allus ben a Freedom Wheeler amongst our folks, as well as a Shearjashub, and I never see him more pestered by a little thing than when them two babies died, both on 'em bein' baptized Freedom; and he's had a real controversy with Providence, Parson Pitcher sez, his mind's so sot on this business."

"Well, this little feller isn't a-goin' to be called Freedom, now, I tell ye," uttered Melinda, with a look of positiveness that chilled Aunt Hannah to the heart. "He's jest as much my baby's he is his pa's, and a good sight more, I b'lieve. Sha'n't I hev all the trouble on him? an' jest as quick as he's big enough to help, instead o' hinder, won't he be snaked off inter the lots to work? I've seen men-folks afore; and I tell ye, Aunt Hanner, you give 'em an inch, 'n' they take a harf a yard certain."

"Well, Melindy," interfered Aunt Huldah, for once in her life essaying to make peace, "Freedom's dreadful sick now: reelly he's dangerous." (This is New-England vernacular for in danger.) "What ef he should up 'n' die? Wouldn't ye feel kind o' took aback to think on't?"

"Things is right 'n' wrong jest the same ef everybody dies: everybody doos, sooner or later. I don't see what odds that makes, Aunt Huldy. I ain't a-going' to make no fuss about it. Fust Sunday in March is sacrament day, and children is allers presented for baptism then. I'll jest fix it right; and, ef his pa gits well, why, there 'tis, 'nd he'll hev to git used to't; and, ef he don't, it ain't no matter, he won't never know. I guess I've got folks as well as you, and names too. There's old Grandsir Bassett: he sot a sight by me, 'nd he was ninety years old 'n' up'ards when he died. Why, he fit the British out to Ticonderogy long o' Ethan Allen![4] He was a dreadful spry man, and had a kind o' pootty name too, smart-soundin'; and I'm a-going' to call the boy for him. Freedom! Land o' Goshen! 'tain't a half a name anyhow; sounds like Fourth o' July oh-rations, 'nd Hail Columby, 'nd fire-crackers, 'nd root-beer, 'nd Yankee Doodle thrown in! Now Grandsir Bassett's name was Tyagustus.[5] That sounds well, I tell ye!—kinder mighty an pompous, 's though it come out o' them columns o' long proper names to the end of the Speller."

Here Melinda got out of breath; and dismayed Aunt Huldah followed Aunt Hannah, who had stolen off to Freedom's room with a certain instinct of protecting him, as a hen who sees the circling wings of a hawk in the high blue heaven runs to brood her chicks.

Moll Thunder was smoking a clay pipe up the wide chimney; and Freedom lay on the bed with half-shut eyes, drawn and red visage, parched lips, and restless, tossing head, murmuring wild words,—here and there calls for Lowly, a tender word for Love (whom he scarce ever noticed in health), or a muttered profanity at some balky horse or stupid ox-team.

"Kinder pootty sick," grunted Moll Thunder, nodding to the visitants. "Plenty much tea-drink drown him ole debbil fever clear out 'fore long. He, he, he! Moll knows: squaw-vine, pep'mint, cohosh, fever-wort; pootty good steep."[6] And from a pitcher of steaming herbs, rank of taste and evil of smell, she proceeded to dose her patient, a heroic remedy that might have killed or cured, but that now Aunt Hannah was no more needed upstairs, and could resume her place by Freedom. And Moll was sent home to Wingfield with a piece of pork, a bag of meal, and a jug of cider-brandy,—a professional fee she much preferred to money.

But even Aunt Hannah could not arrest the fever: it had its sixty days of fight and fire. While yet it raged in Freedom's gaunt frame with unrelenting fierceness, Melinda carried out her programme, and had her baby baptized Tyagustus Bassett. Parson Pitcher came now and then to visit the sick man; but, even when recovery had proceeded so far that the reverend divine thought fit to exhort and catechise his

---

4. While the Second Continental Congress was assembled in Philadelphia during the late spring of 1775 to decide whether to declare independence from Great Britain, Ethan Allen led his Green Mountain Boys in an attack against the British at Fort Ticonderoga, New York.
5. Not a biblical name, but perhaps made up to sound like a biblical name.
6. Tea.

weak brother in reference to his religious experience, the old gentleman shook his head, and took numerous pinches of snuff at the result.

"There seems to be a root of bitterness,—a root of bitterness remaining, Huldy. His speritooal frame is cold and hard. There is a want of
tenderness,—a want of tenderness."

"He didn't never have no great," dryly remarked Aunt Huldah.

"Grace has considerable of a struggle, no doubt, with the nateral
man; it is so with all of us: but after such a dispensation, an amazing
dispensation,—brought into the jaws of death,—Huldy, where death
got hold of him, and destruction made him afraid, in the words of
Scripter, I should expect, I did expect, to find him in a tender frame.
But he seems to kick against the pricks,—to kick against the pricks."[7]

"Well, Parson Pitcher, folks don't allus do jest as ye calc'late to have
'em here below; and grace doos have a pootty hard clinch on't with
Freedom, I'm free to confess. He's dreadful sot,[8] dreadful; and I don't
mind tellin' ye, seein' we're on the subject, that he's ben kinder
thwarted in suthin' whilst he was sick, and' he hain't but jest found it
out, and it doos rile him peskily: he dono how on airth to put up
with't."

"Indeed, indeed! Well, Huldy, the heart knoweth its own bitterness.
I guess I will pray with the family now, and set my face homeward
without dealing with Freedom further today."

"I guess I would," frankly replied Aunt Huldah. "A little hullsome
lettin' alone's good for grown folks as 'tis for children; and after a spell
he'll kinder simmer down: as Hanner sez, when ye can't fix a thing
your way, you've got to swaller it some other way; but it doos choke
ye awful sometimes."

There is no doubt that "Tyagustus" did choke Freedom, when he
found that sonorous name tacked irremediably on to the great hearty
boy he had hoped for so long, but never seen till it was six weeks' old,
and solemnly christened after Grandsir Basset. A crosser and a more
disagreeable man than this convalescent never made a house miserable. The aunts went delicately, in bitterness of soul, after Agag's fashion;[9] Bub fled from before the paternal countenance, and almost lived
in the barn; Marah had been for two months tyrannizing over Lovey
at the Red House, as happy and as saucy as a bobolink on a fence-post;
while Melinda, quite undaunted by the humors of her lord and master,
went about her work with her usual zeal and energy, scolding Bub,
working the hired man up to his extremest capacity, scrubbing, chattering, and cheery, now and then stopping to feed and hug the great

7. Jesus asked Saul (before he saw the light on the
road to Damascus and was converted) why he continued to resist the evidence of Jesus' divinity (the
"pricks" were Christ's wounds); here, Parson
Pitcher is commenting on Freedom's resistance to
giving up his own will and accepting the will of God;
see Acts 26.14.

8. Set; fixed, rigid, unyielding.

9. As king of a tribe that Samuel commissioned Saul
to exterminate because of their history of hostility to
Israel, Agag himself was initially spared. However,
his biblical "cheerfulness" must have changed to
bitterness when Samuel, after announcing the sentence to Agag, hewed him in pieces as a sacrifice to
God; see 1 Samuel 15.

good-tempered baby, or fetching some savory mess to Freedom, whose growls and groans disturbed her no more than the scrawks and croaks of the gossiping old hens about the doorstep.

By June he was about again, and things had found their level. If this were not a substantially true story, I should like to branch off here from the beaten track, and reform my hero,—make the gnarly oak into a fluent and facile willow-tree, and create a millennial peace and harmony in the old farmhouse, just to make things pleasant for dear Aunt Hannah and gentle little Lovey: but facts are stubborn things; and, if circumstances and the grace of God modify character, they do not change it. Peter and Paul were Paul and Peter still, though the end and aim of life were changed for them after conversion.[1]

So Freedom Wheeler returned to his active life unchastened, indeed rather exasperated, by his illness. The nervous irritation and general unhinging of mind and body that follow a severe fever added, of course, to his disgust and rebellion against the state of things about him. His heart's desire had been refused him over and over; but it grew up again like a pruned shrub, the stronger and sturdier for every close cutting; and, grinding his teeth against fate,—he dared not say against God,—he went his bitter way.

Melinda never feared him, but he was a terror to the children; and, had there been any keen observer at hand, it would have been painful to see how "father" was a dreadful word, instead of a synonym for loving protection and wise guidance. Aunt Hannah was shocked when Marah refused to say the Lord's Prayer[2] one night. "Me won't! Me don't want Father in heaven: fathers is awful cross. Me won't say it, aunty."

"Now, you jest clap down 'nd say, 'Now I lay me' quick as a wink!" interposed Aunt Huldah. "Hanner, don't ye let that child talk so to ye. I'd tune her, afore I would, I tell ye."

But, in the secrecy of her own apartment, Aunt Huldah explained, "You see, Hanner, I've took the measure of that young un's foot. She's pa all over,—no more like Lowly'n chalk is like cheese. Ef you'd ha' battled it out with her, she'd ha' got the better of ye, 'nd more'n likely gone home an' told the hull story; and then Freedom would nigh about ha' slartered[3] her; 'nd I don't want the leetle cretur's sperit broke. Fact is, I feel jes' so myself. He is so all-fired ugly, seems as though I should bust sometimes. Moreover, 'nd above all, 'tain't never best to let children git the better of ye. They don't never go back on their tracks ef they do. I put in my finger that time so's't she shouldn't querrel with you, 'nd she said t'other thing jest like a cosset lamb: she was sort o' surprised into't, ye see."

"I presume likely, I presume likely, Huldy. She's a masterful piece,

---

1. Peter, one of Christ's twelve apostles, and Paul, a later convert.
2. The title traditionally given to the prayer that Jesus taught his disciples; beginning with the words, "Our father, who art in heaven," the prayer includes the petitions "Hallowed be thy name" and "thy will be done, on earth as it is in heaven."
3. Slaughtered.

Marah is. I'm afeard she'll taste trouble afore she dies. Sech as she has
to have a lot of discipline to fetch 'em into the kingdom."

"Don't seem to be no use to Freedom, 'flictions don't, Hanner.
Sometimes, I declare for't, I have my doubts ef he ever got religion,
anyhow."

"Why, Huldy Wheeler!" Aunt Hannah's eyes glowed with mild
wrath,—" 'nd he's ben a professor nigh on to thirty year. How can ye
talk so? I'm clean overcome."

"Well, I can't help it. There's some things stand to reason, ef they
be speritooal things; 'nd one on 'em is, that, ef a man's born again, he's
a new cretur. You're paowerful on Bible-texts; so I won't sling no
Catechism at ye this time: but there's suthin', somewhere 'long in
some o' the 'Pistles,[4] about 'love, joy, peace, gentleness, goodness,
meekness,' 'nd so on, for quite a spell: and, if that cap fits Freedom,
why, I'm free to say I don't see it."

"Well, Huldy, we must make allowances: ye see, he's dreadful
disapp'inted."

"That's so. You'd better believe *he* don't say the Lord's Prayer no
more'n Marah; or, ef he doos, it goes, 'My will be done': he hain't
learnt how to spell it t'other way." Aunt Hannah sighed. She was
getting old now; and Freedom was as dear to her as an only child,
wayward and wilful though it be, to a loving mother; but she rested her
heart on its lifelong comfort,—a merciful presence that was her daily
strength,—and hoped for the best, for some future time, even if she did
not live to see it, when this stubborn heart of her boy's should become
flesh, and his soul accept a divine Master, with strong and submissive
faith.

Poor Aunt Hannah! She had shed countless tears, and uttered countless prayers, to this end, but as yet in vain. Next year only brought fresh
exasperation to Freedom in the birth of a daughter, as cross, noisy, and
disagreeable as she was unwelcome. He flung out of the house, and
went to ploughing the ten-acre lot, though the frost was only out of the
surface: he broke his share, goaded his oxen till even those patient
beasts rebelled, and at last left the plough in the furrow, and took a last
year's colt out to train. Melinda escaped a great deal through that poor
colt; for what he dared not pour on her offending head in the way of
reviling, he safely hurled at the wild creature he found so restive in
harness; and many a kick and blow taught the brute how superior a
being man is—particularly when he is out of temper.

"Keep that brat out o' my sight, Aunt Hanner," was his first greeting
to the child. "Don't fetch it 'round here: it's nothin' but a noosance."

Aunt Hannah retreated in dismay; but she dared not tell Melinda,
whose passion for fine-sounding names was mightily gratified at the
opportunity to select a girl's appellation. Before she issued from her

---

4. Epistles, or letters; the literary form of the greater portion of New Testament writings.

sick-room she made up her mind to call this child Chimera Una Vilda.[5]

Dear reader, give me no credit for imagination here. These are actual names, registered on church records and tombstones, with sundry others of the like sort, such as Secretia, Luelle, Lorilla Allaroila, Lue, Plumy, Antha, Loruhama, Lophelia, Bethursda, and a host more. But it mattered little to Freedom: the child might have any name, or no name, as far as he cared. It was a naughty baby, and rent the air with cries of temper in a manner that was truly hereditary.

"I never see such a piece in all my days!" sighed Aunt Hannah, whose belief in total depravity became an active principle under this dispensation. "I declare for't, Huldy, you can hear her scream way over here."

"Well, I b'lieve you, Hanner: the winders is wide open, and we ain't but jest acrost the road. I guess you could hear her a good mile. An' she keeps it up the hull endurin' time. Makes me think o' them cherubims[6] the Rev'lations tells about, that continooally do cry: only she ain't cryin' for praise."

"I expect she'd cry for suthin' besides crossness ef she knew how her pa feels about her. It's awful, Huldy, it is awful, to see him look at the child once in a while."

"She knows it in her bones, I tell ye. Talk about 'riginal sin! I guess she won't want no sin more 'riginal than what's come down pootty straight from him. She's jest another of 'em, now I tell ye."

But Melinda was equal to the situation, whether she picked up the last maple-twig Marah brought in from driving the cows, or pulled the stiff wooden busk from her maternal bosom, or "ketched[7] off her shoe," or even descended upon that chubby form with her own hard hand, and pungently "reversed the magnetic currents," as they say in Boston. Those currents were reversed so often, it might have been matter of doubt which way they originally ran after a year or two. But the old Adam[8] was strong; and when Chimera—no chimera to them, but a dreadful reality—was sent over to stay a while at the red house, the aunts were at their wits' ends, and Lovey both tired and tormented.

This time, for Chimera's visit to the aunts was occasioned by the immediate prospect of another baby, Aunt Hannah was not able to take care of Melindy. The dear old woman was getting old: a "shock-anum palsy," as Aunt Huldah called a slight paralytic stroke, had given her warning; her head shook perpetually, and her hands trembled. She

5. Chimera was a fire-breathing monster from Greek mythology represented with the head of a lion, the body of a goat, and the tail of a serpent; Una is Spenser's pure heroine from his epic poem *The Faerie Queen;* the source of Vilda is unclear. 6. One of the highest classes of angels, in the Book of Revelation; they are full of eyes in front and behind, "all round and within"; they sing praises to God constantly, night and day; see Revelation 4.8. 7. Kicked. 8. I.e., the old sinner; a reference to Chimera's mischief and the apparent lack of effect Melinda's various forms of corrections have on her.

could still do a little work about the house; but her whole failing body was weary with the perpetual motion, and she knew life was near its end for her. So they sent to Dorset Centre for the village nurse,—a fat, good-natured creature; and one morning, early, a boy—a rosy, sturdy, big boy—appeared on the stage.

Now Freedom exulted: he strode over to the red house to tell the news. "Fact, Aunt Hannah! I've got him now,—a real stunner too. You won't see no tricks played now, I tell ye! By jingo! I'm goin' off for Parson Pitcher quicker'n lightnin'. I'll bet ye Melindy won't git ahead o' me this time. That leetle feller'll be Freedom Wheeler in two hours' time, sure's ye live."

"Providence permitting," put in Aunt Hannah softly, as if to avert the omen of this loud and presumptuous rejoicing. But, soft as the prayer was, Freedom heard it, and, as he opened the door, turned on his heel, and answered, "Whether or no, this time."

Aunt Hannah lay back in her chair, utterly shocked. This was rank blasphemy in her ears: she did not remember the illustrative story Aunt Huldah told Freedom, on a time long past, about a certain old woman's intention to go to Hartford, or she might, perhaps, have been less horrified. Still it was bad enough; for, if the words were lightly spoken, the spirit within the man accorded fully with his tone, and never was keener triumph rampant in any conqueror's heart than in this rough, self-willed farmer's as he drove his horse, full tilt, down the long hills, and up the sharp ascents, that lay between him and the parsonage. But Parson Pitcher had been called up higher than Freedom Wheeler's. That very morning he had fallen asleep in his bed, weak and wasted with a long influenza; and, being almost ninety years old, the sleep of weakness had slipped quietly into the deeper calm of death.

He had for a year past been obliged to have a colleague: so Freedom hunted the young man up at his boarding-place, and took him instead,—a little aggrieved, indeed, for long custom made Parson Pitcher seem the only valid authority for religious observances of this kind; and, years after he ceased to preach, the little children were always brought to him for baptism.

"But I s'pose one on 'em's reelly as good as t'other for this puppus," hilariously remarked Freedom to the old lady who lodged the colleague, receiving a grim stare of disapproval for his answer, as he deserved. However, there was one advantage in having Mr. Brooks instead of the parson. Freedom was but slightly acquainted with the new-comer: so he poured out all his troubles, his losses, and his present rejoicing, all the way home, with a frankness and fluency strange enough; for New Englanders as a race are reticent both of their affairs and their feelings, and Freedom Wheeler was more so by nature than by race. This exultation seemed to have fused his whole character for the time into glowing, outpouring fervor: a deep and ardent excitement fired his eye, and loosed his tongue; and Mr. Brooks, who had a tinge of the metaphysical and inquisitive about him, was mightily interested in the man; and being, as he phrased it, a "student of character,"—which is, being interpreted, an impertinent soul who makes puppets of his fellows to see how their wires work, and discover the thoughts of their hearts for his own theories and speculations,—he gently drew out this intoxicated man, "drunken, but not with wine," as he was, with judicious suggestions and inquiries, till he knew him to the core; a knowledge of use to neither party, and to the young clergyman only another apple off the tree from which Eve plucked sin and misery, and a sour one at that.

Once more the old china punch-bowl that had been a relic in the Wheeler family beyond their record, and would have crazed a china-fancier with the lust of the eye, was filled from the spring, and set on the claw-footed round table in the parlor, the door left open into Melinda's room so she could see all the ceremony, the aunts and nurse assembled in solemn array (all the children being sent over to Lovey's care at the red house); and with due propriety the new baby, squirming and kicking with great vigor in his father's arms, was baptized Freedom Wheeler.

Why is it that "the curse of a granted prayer" comes sometimes immediately? Why do we pant and thirst, and find the draught poisonous? or, after long exile, come home, only to find home gone? Alas! these are the conditions of humanity, the questions we all ask, the thwarting and despair we all endure, and also the mystery and incompleteness which tell us in hourly admonition that this life is a fragment and a beginning, and that its ends are not peace and rapture, but discipline and education. Freedom Wheeler was no apt pupil, but his sharpest lesson came today.

Full of exultation over fate, Melinda, and the aunts, chuckling to himself with savage satisfaction at the conscious feeling that it was no use for anybody—even the indefinite influence he dared not call God—to try to get the better of him, he strode across the room to give his boy back to Melinda, stumbled over a little stool that intruded from below the sofa, fell full-length on the floor, with the child under him; and when he rose to his feet, dazed with the jar of the fall, it was but just in time to see those baby eyelids quiver once, and close forever. The child was dead.

Melinda rose up in the bed with a dreadful face: shriek on shriek burst from her lips. The women crowded about Freedom, and took the limp little body from his arms. He leaned against the door-way like a man in a dream. The torrents of reproach and agony that burst from Melinda's lips seemed not to enter his ears: "Now, you've done it! you've killed him! you have! you have!" But why repeat the wild and bitter words of a mother bereft of her child in the first hours of its fresh, strong life? Melinda was not a cruel or ungenerous woman naturally; but now she was weak and nervous, and the shock was too much for her brain.

In this sudden stress Mr. Brooks forgot his metaphysics, and fell back on the old formulas, which, after all, do seem to wear better than metaphysics in any real woe or want. He drew near to Freedom, and put his hand on the wretched man's shoulder. "My brother," said he gently, "this evil is from the hand of the Lord: bear it like a Christian."

"He ain't no Christian!" shouted Melinda, with accents of concentrated bitterness. "Christians ain't that sort, growlin' and scoldin', and fightin' with the Lord that made him, cos he couldn't hev his own way, and uplifted sky-high when he got it: 'nd now look to where 'tis! The hypocrite's hope is cut off, cut off! Oh, my baby, my baby, my baby!" Here she fell into piteous wailing and fainting; and Mr. Brooks led the passive, stricken man away; while Aunt Huldah dispatched Reuben Stark for the doctor, and Aunt Hannah and the nurse tried to calm and restore Melinda.

But it was idle to try to draw Freedom from his silent gloom. He would neither speak nor hear, apparently; and Mr. Brooks, seeing Reuben hitching the horse to the wagon, took his hat to leave. Aunt Huldah followed him to the door for politeness.

"Send for me when you are ready for the funeral, Miss Huldah," said he in taking leave. "I feel deeply for you all, especially for brother Wheeler. The Lord seems to have a controversy with him indeed."

"That's so," curtly replied Aunt Huldah; "an' I don't see but what he's kep' up his end on't pootty well. But I guess he's got to let go. This makes three on 'em; and it's an old saying', 'three times an' out.'"

A suddenly subdued smile curled the corners of Mr. Brooks's mouth for a second. Poor man, he had a keen sense of the ludicrous, and was minister in a country parish.

"Good-day," nodded Aunt Huldah, quite unaware that she had said anything peculiar; and then she returned to Freedom. But he had gone out of the kitchen; nor did anyone know where he was, till the horn called to supper, when he came in, swallowed a cup of tea, and went speechless to bed, not even asking about Melinda, whom the doctor found in the first stage of fever, and pronounced "dangerous."

But Melinda was strong, and could bear a great deal yet. She was comparatively a young woman; and, after a month's severe illness, she began to improve daily, and in another month was like her old self again,—perhaps a trifle less cheery, but still busy, vivacious, and unsparing of herself or others. But Freedom was a changed man. The scornful and bitter words Melinda had uttered in her frantic passion burnt deep into his soul, though he gave no sign even of hearing them.

Kingsley speaks of "the still, deep-hearted Northern, whose pride breaks slowly and silently, but breaks once for all; who tells to God what he never will tell to man, and, having told it, is a new creature from that day forth forever";[9] and something after this fashion was

---

9. Charles Kingsley (1819–1875); British poet, novelist, historian, minister, and sermon-writer; professor of modern history at Cambridge University 1860–69. "The still, deep-hearted . . . : probably from a course of lectures entitled *The Roman and the Teuton* (1864).

Freedom Wheeler shaped. He had been brought up in the strictest Calvinism, had his "experience" in due form, and then united with the church. But Parson Pitcher never preached to anybody but unconverted sinners: hell-fire drove him on to save from the consequences of sin. Its conditions, people who were once converted must look out for themselves. And Freedom's strong will, sullen temper, and undisciplined character grew up like the thorns in the parable,[1] and choked the struggling blades of grain that never reached an ear. Melinda's accusations were the first sermon that ever awoke his consciousness. He had always prided himself on his honesty, and here he saw that he had been an utter hypocrite.

With all his faults, he had a simple faith in the truths of the Bible, and a conscientious respect for ordinances; and now there fell upon him a deep conviction of heinous sin, a gloom, a despair, that amounted almost to insanity. But he asked no counsel, he implored no divine aid: with the peculiar sophistry of religious melancholy, he considered that his prayers would be an abomination to the Lord. So he kept silence, poring more and more over his Bible, appropriating its dreadful texts all to himself, and turning his eyes away from every gracious and tender promise, as one unworthy to read them.

He worked more faithfully than ever,—worked from day's first dawn into the edge of darkness, as if the suffering of a worn-out body had a certain counter-irritation for the tortured mind. There are many rods of stone wall on that old farm today, laid up of such great stones, made so wide and strong and close, that the passer-by looks at it with wonder, little knowing that the dreadful struggles of a wandering and thwarted soul mark the layers of massive granite, and record the exhaustion of flesh mastered by strong and strenuous spirit.

When Melinda was herself again, it was yet sometime before she noticed the change in Freedom. There was a certain simple selfishness about her that made her own grief hide every other, and impelled her to try with all her might to forget her trouble, to get rid of the sharp memory that irked her soul like a rankling thorn. She hid all her baby-clothes away in the garret; she sent the cradle out to the shed-loft, and never opened her lips about that lost boy, whose name Aunt Huldah had recorded in the same record with the two who had preceded him, and whose little body lay under the mulleins and golden-rods, beside the others, at Lowly's feet.

But, as time wore on, Melinda began to see that some change had passed over her husband. She had quite forgotten her own mad words, spoken in the first delirium of her anguish, and followed by the severe fever that had almost swept away life as well as memory. No remorse, therefore, softened her heart; but it was not needed. Though Melinda was an incisive, stirring, resolute woman, with her warm temper she had also a warm heart: she could not live in the

---

1. Here Cooke refers to the parable of the sower; what is sown among thorns does not prosper; see Matthew 13.18–23.

house with a dog or a cat without feeling a certain kindly affection for the creature. Her step-children never suffered at her hands, but shared in all the care she gave her own, and loved her as well as shy, careless children of a healthy sort love anybody. She loved her husband truly. Her quick, stormy words meant no more than the scolding of a wren: in her heart she held Freedom dear and honored, only he did not know it.

But she began now, in her anxiety about his sad and gloomy ways, to soften her manner toward him daily. She remembered the things he liked to eat, and prepared them for the table; she made him a set of new shirts, and set the stitches in them with scrupulous neatness; she kept the house in trim and pleasant order, and sat up at night to mend his working-clothes, so that they were always whole,—homely services and demonstrations, no doubt, but having as much fitness to place and person as the scenic passion of a novel in high life, or a moral drama where the repentant wife throws herself into a stern husband's arms, and, with flying tresses and flowing tears, vows never to vex or misunderstand his noble soul again.

Freedom's conscious controversy with his Maker still went on within him, and raged between doubt and despair; but he was human, and the gentle ray of affection that stole from Melinda's "little candle" did its work in his "naughty world." He felt a certain comfort pervading home when he came in at night sad and weary: the children's faces were clean, the hearth washed, the fire bright; warmth and peace brooded over the old kitchen, crackled softly from the back-log, purred in the cat, sang from the kettle-nose; Melinda's shining hair was smooth, her look quiet and wistful; the table was neatly spread,—little things, surely; but life is made up of them, and hope and happiness and success.

The dark cloud in this man's soul began to lift imperceptibly; and he was called out of himself presently to stand by Aunt Hannah's bed and see her die. A second shock of paralysis suddenly prostrated her, and she was laid on the pillows speechless and senseless. Twenty-four hours of anxiety and tears passed, and then she seemed to revive: she stirred her hand, her face relaxed, her eyes opened; but the exhaustion was great, and she was unable to speak. Conscious and patient, she endured through a few days more, and then the final message came. Another paralysis, a longer silence, and those grouped about her bed in the old red house, thinking every moment to see the shadow of death fall over those beloved features, beheld with surprise the soft brown eyes open, and fix upon Freedom such a look of longing, tender, piteous affection as might have broken the heart of a stone; a long, long gaze, a very passion of love, pity, and yearning, and then those eyes turned heavenward, grew glorious with light and peace, and closed slowly,— closed forever.

Freedom went out and wept bitterly: he had denied his Lord too; and it was a look that smote him to the heart, as that divine glance did

Peter.[2] But no man knew or saw it. Hidden in the barn, a dim and fragrant oratory that has seen more than one struggle of soul in the past and unknown records of New England, Freedom "gave up," and gave up finally.

He was no longer a young man, and he was not the stuff that saints are made of; but he had a stern honesty, an inward uprightness, that held him to his new resolve like hooks of steel. If his temper softened a little, his obstinacy yielded here and there, his manner gave out now and then some scanty spark of affection and consideration, these were the outward signs of a mighty change within; for an old and weather-beaten tree does not bloom in its spring resurrection with the flowers and promise of a young and vigorous growth: it is much if the gnarled boughs put out their scanty share of verdure, if there is a blossom on a few branches, and shelter enough for a small bird's nest from sun or rain. Lovey, grown by this time a tall and helpful girl, with her mother's delicate sweetness in face and figure, was first perhaps to feel this vital change in her father. Aunt Hannah's death was a woful loss to her tender, clinging nature; and she turned to him with the instinct of a child, and found a shy and silent sympathy from him that was strangely dear and sweet, and bound them together as never before. Aunt Huldah, too, noticed it. "Dear me!" said she to herself, as she sat alone by the fire, knitting red stockings for Chimera, who had begun to mend her ways a little under the steady birch-and-shingle disci-pline,—"dear me, I'm real afraid Freedom ain't long for this world. He is kinder mellerin', like a stone-apple in June: it's onnateral. I expect he's struck with death, Hanner, don't you? Oh, my land, what a old fool I be! Hanner's gone, 'nd here I be a-talking' to her jest as though"— Aunt Huldah wiped her dimmed eyes with a red silk handkerchief, and rubbed her misty glasses before she went on, still leaving the sentence unfinished. "Mabbe it's a triumph o' grace. I s'pose grace can get the better o' Freedom: seems kinder doubtful, I must confess; but I don't see nothin' else that could fetch him, and he is a-growin' soft, sure as ye live."

But Melinda, less sensitive or perceptive, perceived only that her efforts had "kinder sorter slicked him down," as she said.

It was reserved for the birth of another child to demonstrate how Freedom had laid down his arms, and gone over to the king at last. Yes, two years after Aunt Hannah's death, another fine and hearty boy entered the family, but not this time with such acclaim and welcome as the last. Melinda, weak and happy, grew gentler than ever before, between present bliss and future fear: and Freedom, hiding his face in his hard brown hands, thanked God with shame and trembling for this undeserved mercy; and even while he shuddered, naturally enough, at

2. Jesus' disciple Peter, overcome with cowardice and fearing the consequences for himself, denied that he knew Jesus; see Matthew 26.69–75; Mark 14.66–72; Luke 22.56–62; John 18.16–18, 25–27. As that divine glance . . . : Jesus looked at Peter after Peter denied him (Luke 22.61).

the possibilities the past recalled, he could say humbly and fervently, "Thy will be done."

Nobody spoke of sending for the minister now, nor was even a name for baby suggested till two months after, when Melinda said to Freedom one night, when the children were all in bed, and they sat alone by the fire, waiting for the last brand to fall in two before it could be raked up, "Next Sunday but one is sacrament Sunday, Freedom. It's good weather now: hadn't the little feller better be presented fur baptism?"

"I guess so," answered he.

"What do ye calkerlate to call him?" asked Melinda shyly, after a pause.

"Thet's for you to say, Melinda: I wish ye to do jest as ye're a mind to," he said gently, with a stifled sigh.

"That's easy settled then," she replied, a pretty smile about her red lips, and laying her hand on her husband's knee: "I don't want to call him nothin' more nor less than Freedom."

He put his hand on hers for a moment, looked the other way, and then got up and went out silently.

So one bright June day baby was taken to the meeting-house, and received his name, and was duly recorded in the family Bible, but with no ominous monosyllable added to his birth-date: and Aunt Huldah, as she went out of church, said to Mr. Brooks, by no means inaudibly, "I guess Freedom's gin up his controversy finally. He did keep up his end on't quite a spell; but he's gin up for good now, I expect."

"Yes," answered the young parson, with a smile of mingled feeling and reverence. "The Lord was in the still small voice."[3]

Atlantic Monthly, July 1877; *Somebody's Neighbors,* 1881

Miss Beulah's Bonnet

"I don't want to be too fine, ye know, Mary Jane,—somethin' tasty and kind of suitable. It's an old bunnit; but my! them Leghorns[1] 'll last a generation if you favor 'em. That was mother's weddin' bunnit."

"You don't say so! Well, it has kept remarkable well; but a good Leghorn will last, that's a fact, though they get real brittle after a spell: and you'll have to be awful careful of this, Miss Beulah; it's brittle now, I see."

"Yes, I expect it is; but it'll carry me through this summer, I guess. But I want you to make it real tasty, Mary Jane; for my niece Miss Smith, she that was 'Liza Barber, is coming to stay a while to our house this summer, and she lives in the city, you know."

" 'Liza Barber! Do tell! Why, I haven't seen her sence she was knee-high to a hop-toad, as you may say. He ain't livin', is he?"

3. See 1 Kings 19.12.
1. A hat made from braided straw derived from wheat exported from Leghorn (Livorno), Italy.

"No: he died two years ago, leavin' her with three children. Sarah is a grown girl; and then there's Jack, he's eight, and Janey, she's three. There was four died between Jack and Sarah. I guess she's full eighteen."

"Mercy to me! time flies, don't it? But about the bunnit: what should you say to this lavender ribbin?"

"Ain't I kind of dark for lavender? I had an idee to have brown, or mabbe dark green."

"Land! for spring? Why, that ain't the right thing. This lavender is real han'some; and I'll set it off with a little black lace, and put a bow on't in the front. It'll be real dressy and seemly for you."

"Well, you can try it, Mary Jane; but I give you fair warnin', if I think it's too dressy, you'll have to take it all off."

"I'm willin'," laughed Miss Mary Jane Beers, a good old soul, and a contemporary of her customer, Miss Beulah Larkin, who was an old maid living in Dorset on a small amount of money carefully invested, and owning the great red house which her grandfather had built for a large family on one corner of his farm. Farm and family were both gone now, save and except Miss Beulah and her niece; but the old lady and a little maid she had taken to bring up dwelt in one end of the wide house, and contrived to draw more than half their subsistence from the garden and orchard attached to it. Here they spun out an innocent existence, whose chief dissipations were evening meetings, sewing-societies, funerals, and the regular Sunday services, to which all the village faithfully repaired, and any absence from which was commented on, investigated, and reprobated, if without good excuse, in the most unsparing manner. Miss Beulah Larkin was tall, gaunt, hard-featured, and good. Everybody respected her, some feared, and a few loved her: but she was not that sort of soul which thirsts to be loved; her whole desire and design was to do her duty and be respectable. Into this latter clause came the matter of a bonnet, over which she had held such anxious discourse. If she had any feminine vanity,—and she was a woman,—it took this virtuous aspect of a desire to be "respectit like the lave,"[2] for decency of dress as well as demeanor. This spring she had received a letter from her niece, the widowed Mrs. Smith, asking if she could come to visit her; and, sending back a pleased assent, Miss Beulah and her little handmaid Nanny Starks bestirred themselves to sweep and garnish the house, already fresh and spotless from its recent annual cleaning. Windows were opened, beds put out to sun, blankets aired, spreads unfolded, sheets taken from the old chests, and long-disused dimity curtains washed, ironed, and tacked up against the small-paned sashes, and tied back with scraps of flowered ribbon, exhumed from hidden shelves, that might well have trimmed that Leghorn bonnet in its first youth.

Mrs. Eliza Smith was a poor woman, but a woman of resource. Her visit was not purely of affection, or of family respect. Her daughter

2. Laver, a large basin used in ancient Judaism by the priest before making a sacrificial offering.

Sarah—a pretty, slight, graceful girl, with gold-brown hair, dark straight brows above a pair of limpid gray eyes, red lips, and a clear pale skin—had been intended by her mother to blossom into beauty in due season, and "marry well," as the phrase goes; but Sarah and a certain Fred Wilson, telegraph-operator in Dartford, had set all the thrifty mother's plans at defiance, and fallen head over heels in love, regardless of Mrs. Smith or anybody else. Sarah's brows were not black and straight, or her chin firm and cleft with a dimple, for nothing: she meant to marry Fred Wilson as soon as was convenient; and Mrs. Smith, having unusual common sense, as well as previous experience of Sarah's capacity of resistance, ceased to oppose that young lady's resolute intention. Master Wilson had already gone West, to a more lucrative situation than Dartford afforded; and Sarah was only waiting to get ready as to her outfit, and amass enough money for the cost of travelling, to follow him, since he was unable to return for her, both from lack of money and time. In this condition of things it occurred to Mrs. Smith that it would save a good deal of money if she could spend the summer with Aunt Beulah, and so be spared the expense of board and lodging for her family. Accordingly she looked about for a tenant for her little house; and, finding one ready to come in sooner than she had anticipated, she answered aunt Beulah's friendly letter of invitation with an immediate acceptance, and followed her own epistle at once, arriving just as the last towel had been hung on the various wash-stands, and while yet the great batch of sweet home-made bread was hot from the oven, and, alas for Miss Beulah! before that Leghorn bonnet had come home from Miss Beers's front-parlor, in which she carried on her flourishing millinery business.

Miss Larkin was unfeignedly glad to see Eliza again, though her eyes grew a little dim, perceiving how time had transformed the fresh, gay girl she remembered into this sad and sallow woman; but she said nothing of these changes, and, giving the rest an equal welcome, established them in the clean, large, cool chambers that were such a contrast to the hot rooms, small and dingy, of their city home.

Jack was a veritable little pickle, tall of his age, and light of foot and hand; nature had framed him in body and mind for mischief: while Sarah was a pleasant, handy young girl, as long as nothing opposed her; and Janey a round and rosy poppet, who adored Jack, and rebelled against her mother and Sarah hourly. Jack was a born nuisance: Miss Beulah could hardly endure him, he did so controvert all the orders and manners of her neat house. He hunted the hens to the brink of distraction, and broke up their nests till eggs were scarce to find,—a state of things never before known in that old barn, where the hens had dwelt and done their duty, till that duty had consigned them to the stew-pan, for years and years. He made the cat's life a burden to her in a hundred ways; and poor Nanny Starks had never any rest or peace till her tormentor was safe in bed.

Mrs. Smith began to fear her visit would be prematurely shortened on Jack's account: and Sarah, who had wisely confided her love-affair to Aunt Beulah, and stirred that hardened heart to its core by her pathetic tale of poverty and separation, began to dread the failure of her hopes also; for her aunt had more than hinted that she would give something toward that travelling money which was now the girl's great object in life, since by diligent sewing she had almost finished her bridal outfit. As for Janey, she was already, in spite of her naughtiness, mistress of Aunt Beulah's very soul. Round, fat, rosy, bewitching as a child and only a child can be, the poor spinster's repressed affection, her denied maternity, her love of beauty,—a secret to herself,—and her protecting instinct, all blossomed for this baby, who stormed or smiled at her according to the caprice of the hour, but was equally lovely in the old lady's eyes whether she smiled or stormed. If Janey said, "Tum!" in her imperative way, Miss Beulah came, whether her hands were in the wash-tub or the bread-tray. Janey ran riot over her most cherished customs; and, while she did not hesitate to scold or even slap Jack harshly for his derelictions, she had an excuse always ready for Janey's worst sins, and a kiss instead of a blow for her wildest exploits of mischief. Jack hated the old aunty as much as he feared her tongue and hand: and this only made matters worse; for he felt a certain right to torment her that would not have been considered a right, had he felt instead any shame for abusing her kindness. But a soft answer from her never turned away his wrath, or this tale of woe about her bonnet had never been told.

There had been long delay concerning that article. The bleacher had been slow, and the presser impracticable: it had been sent back once to be reshaped, and then the lavender ribbon had proved of scant measure, and had to be matched. But at last, one hot day in May, Nanny brought the queer old bandbox home from Miss Beers's, and Aunt Beulah held up her head-gear to be commented on. It was really a very good-looking bonnet. The firm satin ribbon was a pleasant tint, and contrasted well with the pale color of the Leghorn; and a judicious use of black lace gave it an air of sobriety and elegance combined, which pleased Miss Beulah's eye, and even moved Mrs. Smith to express approbation.

"Well, I'm free to own it suits me," said the old lady, eying the glass with her head a little on one side, as a bird eyes a worm. "It's neat, and it's becomin', as fur as a bunnit can be said to be becomin' to an old woman, though I ain't really to call old. Mary Jane Beers is older than me; and she ain't but seventy-three,—jest as spry as a lark too. Yes, I like the bunnit; but it doos—sort of—seem—as though that there bow wa'n't really in the middle of it. What do you think, 'Lizy?"

"I don't see but what it's straight, Aunt Beulah."

" 'Tain't," said the spinster firmly. "Sary, you look at it."

Sarah's eye was truer than her mother's. " 'Tis a mite too far to the left, Aunt Beulah; but I guess I can fix it."

"You let her take it," said Mrs. Smith. "She's a real good hand at millinery: she made her own hat, and Janey's too. I should hate to have her put her hand to that bunnit if she wa'n't; for it's real pretty—'specially for a place like Dorset to get up."

"Lay it off on the table, Aunt Beulah. I'm going upstairs to make my bed, and I'll fetch my work-basket down, and fix that bow straight in a jiffy."

"Well, I must go up too," said Mrs. Smith, and followed Sarah out of the room; but Miss Beulah, though duty called her too, in the imperative shape of a batch of bread waiting to be moulded up, lingered a little longer, poising the bonnet on her hand, holding it off to get a distant view, turning it from side to side, and, in short, behaving exactly as younger and prettier women do over a new hat, even when it is a miracle of art from Paris, instead of a revamped Leghorn from a country shop.

She laid it down with a long breath of content, for taste and economy had done their best for her; and then she, too, left the room, never perceiving that Jack and Janey had been all the time deeply engaged under the great old-fashioned breakfast-table, silently ripping up a new doll to see what was inside it,—silently, because they had an inward consciousness that it was mischief they were about; and Jack, at least, did not want to be interrupted till he was through. But he had not been too busy to hear and understand that Aunt Beulah was pleased; and, still smarting from the switch with which she had whipped his shoulders that very morning for putting the cat into the cistern, he saw an opportunity for revenge before his eyes: he would hide this precious bonnet so aunt Beulah could never find it again. How to do this, and not be found out, was a problem to be considered; but mischief is quick-witted. There stood in the window a large rocking-chair, well stuffed under its chintz cover, and holding a plump soft feather cushion so big it fairly overflowed the seat. Under this cushion he was sure nobody would think of looking; and, to save himself from consequences, he resolved to make Janey a cat's-paw: so he led her up to the table, made her lift the precious hat and deposit it under the cushion, which he raised for the purpose; then, carefully dropping the frill, he tugged Janey, unwilling but scared and silent, out into the yard, and, impressing on her infant mind with wild threats of bears and guns that she must never tell where the bonnet was, he contrived to interest her in a new play so intensely, that the bonnet went utterly into oblivion, as far as she was concerned; and when they were called in to dinner, and she had taken her daily nap, Janey had become as innocent of her mischief in her own memory as the dolly who lay all disemboweled and forlorn under the table.

When Sarah came down and did not find the bonnet, she concluded Aunt Beulah had put it away in her own room, for fear a sacrilegious fly or heedless speck of dust might do it harm: so she took up a bit of lace she was knitting, and went out into the porch, glad to get into a cool place, the day was so warm.

And when the bread was moulded up, Aunt Beulah came back, and, not seeing her bonnet, supposed Sarah had taken it upstairs to change the bow. She was not an impatient woman, and the matter was not pressing: so she said nothing about the bonnet at dinner, but hurried over that meal in order to finish her baking. Mrs. Smith had not come down again, for a morning headache had so increased upon her, she had lain down: so that no one disturbed the rocking-chair in which that bonnet lay hid till Mrs. Blake, the minister's wife, came in to make a call about four o'clock. She was a stout woman, and the walk had tired her. Aunt Beulah's hospitable instincts were roused by that red, weary face.

"You're dreadful warm, ain't you, Miss Blake?" said she. "It's an amazin' warm day for this time of year, and it's consider'ble more'n a hen-hop from your house up here. Lay your bunnit off, do, and set down in the rocker. I'll tell Nanny to fetch some shrub[3] and water. Our ras'berry shrub is good, if I do say it; and it's kep' over as good as new."

So Mrs. Blake removed her bonnet, and sank down on that inviting cushion with all her weight, glad enough to rest, and ignorant of the momentous consequences. Her call was somewhat protracted. Had there been any pins in that flattened Leghorn beneath her, she might have shortened her stay. But Miss Mary Jane Beers was conscientiously opposed to pins; and every lavender bow was sewed on with silk to match, and scrupulous care. After the whole village news had been discussed, the state of religion lamented, and the short-comings of certain sisters who failed in attending prayer-meetings talked over,—with the charitable admission, to be sure, that one had a young baby, and another a sprained ankle,—Mrs. Blake rose to go, tied on her bonnet, and said good-by all round, quite as ignorant as her hosts of the remediless ruin she had done.

It was tea-time now; and, as they sat about the table, Sarah said, "I guess I'll fix your bonnet after tea, Aunty: 'twon't take but a minute, and I'd rather do it while I recollect just where that bow goes."

"Why, I thought you had fixed it!" returned Miss Beulah.

"Well, I came right back to; but it wa'n't here. I thought you'd took it into your bedroom."

"I hain't touched it sence it lay right here on the table."

"I'll run up and ask ma: maybe she laid it by."

But Mrs. Smith had not been downstairs since she left aunt Beulah with the bonnet in her hands. And now the old lady turned on Jack. "Have you ben and carried off my bunnit, you little besom?"[4]

"I hain't touched your old bonnet!" retorted Jack with grand scorn.

"I don't believe he has," said Sarah; "for, when I come down stairs and found it wa'n't here, I went out and set on the bench to the

3. Beverage made from fruit juice, sugar, and a liquor such as rum or brandy.
4. An old English word meaning broom; often used

in the phrase "a besom of destruction," from Isaiah
14.23.

front-door, and I heard him and Janey away off the other side of the yard, playin'; and you know they wa'n't in here when the bonnet come."

"Well, of course Janey hasn't seen it, if Jack hasn't; and, if she had, the blessed child wouldn't have touched old aunty's bonnet for a dollar—would she, precious lamb?" And Aunt Beulah stroked the bright curls of her darling, who looked up into her face, and laughed; while Jack grinned broadly between his bites of bread and butter, master of the situation, and full of sweet revenge. "And Nanny hain't seen it, I know," went on aunt Beulah; "for she was along of me the whole enduring time. She set right to a-parin' them Roxbury russets[5] the minnit she fetched home the bunnit; and I kep' her on the tight jump ever sence, because it's bakin'-day, and there was a sight to do. But I'll ask her: 'tain't lost breath to ask, my mother used to say, and mabbe it's a gain."

The old lady strode out into the kitchen with knit brows, but came back without any increased knowledge. "She hain't ben in here once sence she set down the bandbox; and, come to think on't, I know she hain't, for I cleared the table myself today, and, besides, the bunnit wa'n't here at dinner-time. Now let's hunt for it. Things don't gener'lly vanish away without hands; but, if we can't find no hands, why, it's as good as the next thing to look for the bunnit."

So they went to work and searched the house, as they thought, most thoroughly. No nook or corner but was investigated, if it was large enough to hold that bonnet; but nobody once thought of looking under the chair-cushion. If it had been as plump and fluffy as when Jack first had Janey put the lost structure under it, there might have been a suspicion of its hiding-place; but Mrs. Blake's two hundred pounds of solid flesh had reduced bonnet and cushion alike to unusual flatness. Or, if it had been any other day but Saturday, the chair might have been dusted and shaken up, and revealed its mystery; but early that very morning the house below stairs had been swept, and the furniture dusted, the cushions shaken out, the brasses polished, and all the weekly order and purity restored everywhere. The bonnet was evidently lost; and Jack, who had followed the domestic detectives up stairs and down, retired behind the wood-pile, and executed a joyful dance to relieve his suppressed feelings, snapping his fingers, and slapping his knees, and shouting scraps of all the expletives he knew, in the joy of his heart. How tragic would this mirth have seemed to a spectator aware of its cause, contrasted with the portentous gloom on Aunt Beulah's forehead, and the abstracted glare of her eye! For several days this deluded spinster mused and mazed over her bonnet, going to church on Sunday in her shabby old velvet hat, which had scarcely been respectable before, but now, in the glare of a hot May sun, not only showed all its rubbed and worn places, its shiny streaks

5. Apples from Roxbury; winter apples with a rough, reddish-brown skin.

and traces of eaves-drops in the depressed and tangled nap, but also made her head so hot that she fairly went to bed at last with sick-headache, unable to attend evening service,—a most unheard-of thing for her.

Before the week was half done, she had settled into a profound belief that some tramp had passed while they were all out of the room, and, charmed by that lavender satin ribbon and black lace, stolen the bonnet, and carried it off to sell; and many a time did Miss Beulah sit rocking to and fro on top of her precious Leghorn, wondering and bemoaning at its loss. But murder will out—sometimes, and would certainly have come out in the weekly cleaning the next Saturday, if, on the Friday morning, Miss Beulah had not set down a pitcher of milk, just brought in by a neighbor, on the end of the table nearest to that rocking-chair—set it down only for a moment, to get the neighbor a recipe for sugar gingerbread peculiar to the Larkin family. Janey happened to be thirsty, and reached after the pitcher, but was just tall enough to grasp the handle so low down, that when she pulled at it, steadying herself against the chair, it tipped sideways, and poured a copious stream of fresh milk on the cushion. The chintz was old, and had lost its glaze, and the feathers were light: so the rich fluid soaked in at once; and before the two women, recalled from the cupboard by Janey's scream, could reach the pitcher, there was only a very soppy and wet cushion in the chair.

"For mercy's sakes!" said the neighbor. But Miss Beulah, with great presence of mind, snatched up the dripping mass and flung it out of the open window, lest her carpet should suffer. She reverted to the chair in a second, and stood transfixed.

"What under the everlastin' canopy!"[6] broke from her dismayed lips; for there, flattened out almost beyond recognition, and broken wherever it was bent, its lavender ribbons soaked with milk, the cheap lace limp and draggled, lay the remains of the Leghorn bonnet.

"Of all things!" exclaimed the neighbor; but there was an echo of irrepressible amusement in her tones. Aunt Beulah glared at her, and lifted the damp bonnet as tenderly as if it had been Janey's curls, regarding it with an expression pen or pencil fails to depict,—a mixture of grief, pity, indignation, and amazement, that, together with the curious look of the bonnet, was too much for the neighbor; and, to use her own after-expression in describing the scene, she "snickered right out."

"Laugh, do," said Aunt Beulah witheringly,—"do laugh! I guess, if your best bunnit had ben set on and drownded, you'd laugh the other side of your mouth, Miss Jackson. This is too much."

"Well, I be sorry," said the placable female; "but it does look so dreadful ridiculous like, I couldn't noways help myself. But how on earth did it git there, I admire to know?"

6. The sky or heavens.

"I dono myself as I know; but I hain't a doubt in my own mind it was that besom of a Jack. He is *the* fullest of 'riginal sin and actual transgression of any boy I ever see. He did say, now I call to mind, that he hadn't never touched it; but I mistrust he did. He beats all for mischief that ever I see. I'm free to say I never did like boys. I suppose divine Providence ordained 'em to some good end; but it takes a sight o' grace to believe it: and, of all the boys that ever was sent into this world for any purpose, I do believe he is the hatefulest. I'd jest got my bunnit to my mind, calc'latin' to wear it all summer; and I am a mite pernickity, I'll allow that, about my bunnits. Well, 'tain't no use to cry over spilt milk."

"I'll fetch ye some more tomorrow," said the literal neighbor.

"You're real good, Miss Jackson; but I'm more exercised a lot about my bunnit than I be about the milk.—Sary, look a-here!"

Sarah, just coming in at the door, did look, and, like Mrs. Jackson, felt a strong desire to smile, but with native tact controlled it.

"Why, where on earth did you find it, Aunt Beulah?"

"Right under the rocker-cushion. It must have ben there when Miss Blake come in that day and set down there; for I remember thinkin' Nanny must ha' shook that cushion up more'n usual, it looked so comfortable and high."

"I don't wonder it's flat, if Miss Blake set on't," giggled Mrs. Jackson, at which Aunt Beulah's face darkened so perceptibly that the good neighbor took her leave. Comedy to her was tragedy to the unhappy owner of the bonnet; and she had the sense to know she was alien to the spirit of the hour, and go home.

"But how did it get there?" asked Sarah.

"You tell," replied Miss Beulah, "for I can't. I do mistrust Jack."

"Jack said he hadn't touched it, though; and it couldn't get there without hands."

"Well, mabbe Jack don't always say the thing that is. 'Foolishness is bound up in the heart of a child,'[7] Scriptur says; and I guess he hain't had enough of the rod o' correction to drive it out of him yet. He's the behavin'est youngster *I* ever see; and I'm quite along in years, if I be spry."

"I'll call him, Aunty, and see what he'll say this time."

" 'Twon't be no use: if he's lied once, he'll lie twice. Scriptur says the Devil was a liar from the beginnin';[8] and I expect that means that lyin' is ingrain. I never knowed it to be fairly knocked out of anybody yet, even when amazin' grace wrastled with it. There's Deacon Shubael Morse: why, he's as good as gold; but them Morses is a proverb, you may say, and always hes ben, time out o' mind,—born liars, so to speak. I've heerd Grandsir Larkin say, that, as fur back as he could call to mind, folks would say,—

7. Proverbs 22.15.
8. Satan is associated throughout the New Testament with falsehood; see, for example, Acts 5.3 and Revelation 12.9.

"Steal a horse,
An' b'lieve a Morse."

But the deacon he's a hero at prayer, and gives heaps to the s'cieties; but he ain't reely to be relied on. He's sharper'n a needle to bargain with; and, if his word ain't writ down in black and white, why, 'tain't nowhere. He don't read no novils, nor play no cards: he'd jest as lives swear outright as do one or t'other. But I do say for't, I'd ruther myself see him real honest than any o' them things. I don't believe in no sort o' professin' that falls short in practicin'; but I can't somehow feel so real spry to blame the deacon as though he wa'n't a Morse. But you call Jack anyhow."

So Jack was called.

He came in, with Janey, flushed, lovely, and dirty, trotting behind him, and was confronted with the bonnet.

"Jack, did you hide it?"

"I hain't touched your old bonnet. I said so before."

An idea struck Sarah.

"Janey," she said sharply, "did you put Aunty's bonnet under the cushion?"

"Janey don't 'member," said the child, smiling as innocently as the conventional cherub of art.

"Well, you must remember!" said Sarah, picking her up from the floor, and setting her down with emphasis on the table.

Janey began to cry.

"Naughty Salah hurt Janey!" and the piteous tears coursed down her rosy, dust-smeared cheeks from those big blue eyes that looked like dew-drowned forget-me-nots.

Aunt Beulah could not stand this. "You let that baby alone, Sarah! She don't know enough to be naughty, bless her dear little soul!— There, there, don't you cry a mite more, Janey. Aunty'll give you ginger-cooky this very minute!"

And Janey was comforted with kisses and smiles and gingerbread, her face washed, and her curls softly turned on tender fingers; while Jack, longing for gingerbread with the preternatural appetite of a growing boy, was sent off in disgrace.

"I make no doubt you done it, you little rascal, and lied it out too. But I don't b'lieve you no more for your lyin': so don't look for no extries from me. Fellers like you don't get gingerbread nor turnovers, now I tell you!"

How Jack hated her! How glad he was he had spoiled her bonnet! Shall I draw a moral here to adorn my tale? No, dear reader: this is not a treatise on education. Miss Beulah was a good woman; and if she made mistakes, like the rest of us, she took the consequences as the rest of us do; and the consequences of this spoiled bonnet were not yet ended.

She felt as if she must have a new one for Sunday. She really did not know how to afford it; for she had promised to help Sarah, and in her eyes a promise was as sacred as an oath. And, as for giving up her subscriptions to home missions,[9] that would be a wilful sin. But, without a bonnet, she could not go to meeting; and that was a sin too. So she put on her sun-bonnet; and taking the wreck of the Leghorn, carefully concealed in a paper, she set out after tea that same evening for a conference with Miss Beers, stopping at the post-office as she went along. She found one letter awaiting her, and knew by the superscription that it was from a second-cousin of hers in Dartford, who had charge of such money of hers as was not in the savings bank or Dartford and Oldbay Railroad stock—a road paying steady dividends. But, besides the three or four thousands in these safe investments that Miss Beulah owned, she had two shares in a manufacturing company, and one in Dartford Bridge stock, from which her cousin duly remitted the annual dividends: so, knowing what was in the letter, for the tool company's payment was just due, she did not open it till she sat down in Miss Beers's shop, and first opened the Leghorn to view.

"Of all things!" said Miss Beers, lifting up hands and eyes during Miss Beulah's explanations. "And you can't do nothing with it—never. Why, it's flatter'n a pancake. Well, you couldn't expect nothing else, with Miss Blake on top on't: she'd squash a baby out as thin as a tin plate if she happened to set on't, which I do hope she won't. See! the Leghorn's all broke up. I told you 'twas dreadful brittle. And the ribbin is spoiled entire. You can't never clean lavender, nor yet satin, it frays so. And the lace is all gum: anyway, that's gone. Might as well chuck the hull into the fire."

"So do, Mary Jane, so do. I never want to set eyes on't again. I haven't no patience with that boy now, and the bunnit riles me to look at. I do want to do right by the boy, but it goes against the grain dreadful. I mistrust I shall have to watch and pray real hard before I can anyway have patience with him. I tell you he's a cross to 'Liza as well as to me. But don't let's talk about him. What have you got that'll do for a bunnit for me?"

Then the merits of the various bonnets in Miss Beers's small stock were canvassed. A nice black chip suited Aunt Beulah well; and a gray corded ribbon, with a cluster of dark pansies, seemed just the thing for trimming. In fact, she liked it, and with good reason, better than the Leghorn; but it was expensive. All the materials, though simple, were good and rich. Try as she would, Miss Beers could not get it up for less than six dollars, and that only allowed twenty-five cents for her own work. The alternative was a heavy coarse straw, which she proposed to deck with a yellow-edged black ribbon, and put some gold-eyed black daisies inside. But Miss Beulah did want the chip.

"Let's see," said she. "Mabbe this year's dividend is seven per cent:

9. Individuals would pledge or contribute money to help the poor in their own parish or community rather than abroad.

'tis once in a while. I'll see what cousin Joseph says. If 'tain't more than usual, I must take the straw."

But cousin Joseph had to tell her, that owing to damage by flood and fire, as well as a general disturbance of business all over the country, the C. A. Company paid *no* dividend this year.

"Then I sha'n't have no bunnit," said Miss Larkin firmly.

"Why, you've got to have some kind of a bunnit," said the amazed Miss Beers.

"I hain't got to if I can't."

"But why can't ye, Beulah? All your money and all your dividends ain't in that comp'ny."

"Well, there's other uses for money this year besides bunnits."

"You can't go to meetin'."

"I can stay to home."

"Why, Beulah Larkin, I'll trust you, and welcome."

"But I won't be trusted. I never was, and I never will be. What if I should up and die?"

"I'd sue the estate," practically remarked Miss Beers.

"No: 'out of debt, out of danger,' mother always said, and I believe in't. I shall hate to stay to home Sundays, but I can go to prayer-meetin' in my slat bunnit[1] well enough."

"Why, the church'll deal with ye, Beulah, if ye neglect stated means of grace."[2]

"Let 'em deal," was the undaunted answer. Miss Beulah had faced the situation, arranged it logically, and accepted it. She had promised Sarah fifteen dollars in June. She had lost a dividend of twelve dollars on which she had reckoned with certainty; five dollars was due to home missions; and, with her increased family, there would be no margin for daily expenses. There were twenty dollars in the savings bank over and above the five hundred she had laid up for a rainy day, and left in her will, made and signed but last week, to little Janey. On this she would not trench, come what might, except in case of absolute distress; and the twenty dollars were sacred to Sarah and home missions. But this was her private affair: she would not make the poverty of her niece known abroad, or the nature of her will. If the church chose to deal with her, it might; but her lips should never open to explain,—a commonplace martyrdom enough, and less than saintly because so much of human pride and self-will mingled in its suffering; yet honesty and uprightness are so scarce in these days as to make even such a sturdy witness for them respectable, and many a woman who counts herself a model of sanctity might shrink from a like daily ordeal. But Aunt Beulah set her face as a flint, and pursued her way in silence. June came and went; and with it went Sarah to her expectant bride-

---

1. Slate-colored bonnet.
2. Calvinist theology stated that although grace (salvation) could not be earned, churchgoers were more likely than non-churchgoers to be members of God's elect.

groom in Chicago, from whence a paper with due notice of her marriage presently returned. Aunt Beulah strove hard to make both ends
meet in her housekeeping, and, being a close manager, succeeded.
There was no margin, not even twenty-five spare cents to take Janey
to the circus; though she cut Aunt Beulah's heart with entreaties to be
taken to see "lions an' el'phants," and said, "P'ease take Janey," in a
way to melt a stone. For to get food enough to satisfy Jack was in itself
a problem. Often and often the vexed spinster declared to Nanny, her
sympathizing handmaid,—

" 'Tain't no use a-tryin' to fill him. He's holler down to his boots, I
know. He eat six b'iled eggs for breakfast, and heaps of johnny-cake,
besides a pint o' milk, and was as sharp-set for dinner as though he'd
ben a-mowin' all the forenoon. 'Lizy says he's growing'. If he grows
anyways accordin' to what he eats, he'll be as big as Goliath of Gath,
as sure as you're born. I don't begrudge the boy reasonable vittles, but
I can't buy butcher's-meat enough to satisfy him noway. And as to
garden sass,[3] he won't eat none. That would be real fillin' if he would.
Thanks be to praise! he likes Indian. Pudding and johnny-cake do help
a sight."

But while Aunt Beulah toiled and moiled, and filled her wide measure of charity toward these widowed and fatherless with generous
hand, the church, mightily scandalized at her absence from its services,
was preparing to throw a shell into her premises. It was all very well
to say to Miss Beers that she was not afraid of such a visitation; but a
trouble at hand is of quite another aspect than a trouble afar off. Her
heart quailed and fluttered, when, one July afternoon, Nanny ushered
into the dark, cool parlor Deacon Morse and Deacon Flint, come to ask
her why she had not attended church since the middle of last May,
when she was in usual health and exercise of her faculties. Miss Beulah, however, was equal to the occasion. She faced the deacons sternly,
but calmly.

"It is so," she said, when they had finished their accusation. "I hain't
ben to meetin' for good cause. You can't say I've did any thing that's
give occasion to the enemy more'n this. I've attended reg'lar to prayer-
meeting's and sewin'-circle. I've give as usual to home missions. You
can't say I've made any scandal, or done nothin' out o' rule, save an'
except stayin' at home sabbath days; and my family has attended
punctooally."

But this did not satisfy the deacons: they pressed for a reason.

"If you would free your mind, sister Larkin, it would be for the good
of the church," said Deacon Morse.

"Mabbe 'twouldn't be altogether to your likin', deacon, if I did free
my mind. Seems as though stayin' at home from meetin' wa'n't no
worse'n sandin' sugar an' waterin' rum; and I never heerd you was
dealt with for them things."

---

3. Sauce; refers to vegetables, especially greens.

Deacon Morse was dumb, but Deacon Flint took up the discourse.

"Well, sister Larkin, we didn't know but what you was troubled in your mind."

"I ain't!" snapped Miss Beulah.

"Or perhaps was gettin' a mite doubtful about doctrines, or suthin'."

"No, I ain't. I go by the 'Sembly's Catechism,[4] and believe in every word on't, questions and all."

"Well, you seem to be a leetle contumacious, sister Larkin, so to speak: if you had a good reason, why, of course, you'd be willin' to tell it."

This little syllogism caught Miss Beulah.

"Well, if you must know, I hain't got no bunnit."

The deacons stared mutually; and Deacon Morse, forgetful of his defeat, and curious, as men naturally are, asked abruptly, "Why not?"

"Cause Miss Blake sot on it."

The two men looked at each other in blank amazement, and shook their heads. Here was a pitfall. Was it proper, dignified, possible, to investigate this truly feminine tangle? They were dying to enter into particulars, but ashamed to do so: nothing was left but retreat. Miss Beulah perceived the emergency, and chuckled grimly. This was the last straw. The deacons rose as one man, and said, "Good-day," with an accent of reprobation, going their ways in deep doubt as to what they should report to the church, which certainly would not receive with proper gravity the announcement that Miss Beulah Larkin could not come to church because the minister's wife had sat on her Sunday bonnet. The strife of tongues, however, did not spare Aunt Beulah, if the deacons did; and for a long time Miss Beers, who had the key to the situation, did not hear any of the gossip, partly because she had been ill of low fever, and then gone to her sister's in Dartford for change of air, and partly, that, during July and August, the sewing-circle was temporarily suspended. But it renewed its sessions in September; and Miss Beers was an active member, sure to be at the first meeting. It was then and there she heard the scorn and jeers and unfounded stories come on like a tidal wave to overwhelm her friend's character. She listened a few minutes in silence, growing more and more indignant. Then, for she was a little woman as far as stature went, she mounted into a chair, and demanded the floor in her own fashion.

"Look a-here!" said she, her shrill voice soaring above the busy clapper of tongues below. "It's a burnin' shame to say a hard word about Beulah Larkin. She's as good a woman as breathes the breath of life, and I know the hull why and wherefore she hain't ben to meetin'. She hain't had no bunnit. I made her as tasty a bunnit as ever you see last spring; and that jackanapes of a boy he chucked it under the

4. In 1643, the Westminster Assembly of Divines in England created the Presbyterian Catechism, which continued to serve as the theological foundation for New England Congregationalists.

rocker-cushion jest to plague her, and Miss Blake she come in and sot right down on it, not knowin', of course, that 'twas there; and, as if that wa'n't enough to spile it" (an involuntary titter seemed to express the sense of the audience that it was), "that other sprig, she took and upsot a pitcher of milk onto the cushion, and you'd better believe that bunnit was a sight!"

"Why didn't she get another?" severely asked Deacon Morse's wife.

"Why? Why, becos she's a-most a saint. Her dividends some on 'em didn't come in, and she'd promised that biggest girl fifteen dollars to help her get out to her feller at Chicago, for Sary told me on't herself; and then she gives five dollars to hum missions every year, and she done it this year jest the same; and she's took that widder and them orphans home all summer, and nigh about worked her head off for 'em, and never charged a cent o' board; and therefor and thereby she hain't had no money to buy no bunnit, and goes to prayer-meetin' in her calico slat."

A rustle of wonder and respect went through the room as the women moved uneasily in their chairs, exchanged glances, and said, "My!" which inspired Miss Beers to go on.

"And here everybody's ben a-talkin' bad about her, while she's ben a real home-made kind of a saint. I know she don't look it; but she doos it, and that's a sight better. I don't b'lieve there's one woman in forty could ha' had the grit and the perseverance to do what she done, and hold her tongue about it too. I know I couldn't for one."

"She shouldn't ha' let her good be evil spoken of," said Mrs. Morse with an air of authority.

"I dono as anybody had oughter have spoken evil of her good," was Miss Beers's dry answer; and Mrs. Morse said no more.

But such a warm and generous vindication touched many a feminine heart, which could appreciate Miss Beulah's self-sacrifice better than the deacons could. There was an immediate clustering and chattering among the good women, who, if they did love a bit of gossip, were none the less kindly and well-meaning; and presently a spokeswoman approached Miss Beers with the proposition, that, if she would make Miss Beulah a handsome bonnet, a dozen or more had volunteered to buy the materials.

"Well," said Miss Mary Jane, wiping her spectacles, "this is real kind; and I make no doubt but what Beulah'd think the same, though she's a master-hand to be independent, and some folks say proud. Mabbe she is; but I know she couldn't but take it kind of friends and neighbors to feel for her. However, there ain't no need on't. It seems that Sary's husband ain't very forehanded, and she's got a dreadful taste for the millinery business: so she's gone to work in one of the fust shops there, and is gettin' great wages, for her; and only yesterday there come a box by *ex*press for Miss Beulah, with the tastiest bunnit in it I ever see in my life,—good black velvet, with black satin kinder puffed into the brim, and a dark-green wing to one side of the band,

and a big bow in under a jet buckle behind. I tell *you* it was everlastin' pretty. Sary she sent a note to say she hoped aunt Beulah'd give her the pleasure to accept it; for she'd knowed all along how that she was the cause of her goin' without a bunnit all summer (I expect her ma had writ to her), and she felt real bad about it. You'd better b'lieve Beulah was pleased."

And Miss Beulah was pleased again when the women from the village began to call on her even more frequently than before, and express cordial and friendly interest in a way that surprised her, all unaware as she was of Miss Beers's enthusiastic vindication of her character before the sewing-circle. Yet, poor, dear, silly old woman,— only a woman, after all,—nothing so thrilled and touched her late-awakened heart as little Janey's soft caresses and dimpled patting hands on that sallow old face, when she climbed into her lap the next Sunday, and, surveying Miss Beulah's new bonnet exclaimed, with her silvery baby voice, "Pitty, pitty bonnet!"

Jack did not say anything about it, nor did the congregation, though on more than one female face beamed a furtive congratulatory smile; and Deacon Flint looked at Deacon Morse across the aisle.

If there is any moral to this story, as no doubt there should be, it lies in the fact that Mrs. Blake never again sat down in a chair without first lifting the cushion.

Harper's, March 1880; *Somebody's Neighbors*, 1881

How Celia Changed Her Mind

"If there's anything on the face of the earth I *do* hate, it's an old maid!"

Mrs. Stearns looked up from her sewing in astonishment.

"Why, Miss Celia!"

"Oh, yes! I know it. I'm one myself, but all the same, I hate 'em worse than p'ison. They ain't nothing nor nobody; they're cumberers of the ground."[1] And Celia Barnes laid down her scissors with a bang, as if she might be Atropos[2] herself, ready to cut the thread of life for all the despised class of which she was a notable member.

The minister's wife was genuinely surprised at this outburst; she herself had been well along in life before she married, and though she had been fairly happy in the uncertain relationship to which she had attained, she was, on the whole, inclined to agree with St. Paul, that the woman who did not marry "doeth better."[3] "I don't agree with you, Miss Celia," she said gently. "Many, indeed, most of my best friends are maiden ladies, and I respect and love them just as much as if they were married women."

1. See Luke 13.7.
2. From Greek mythology, the eldest of the three goddesses (Fates, Moirae) who presided over birth, life, and death; she cut the thread of human life with her shears.
3. See 1 Corinthians 7.8.

"Well, I don't. A woman that's married is somebody; she's got a place in the world; she ain't everybody's tag; folks don't say, 'Oh, it's nobody but that old maid Celye Barnes'; it's 'Mis' Price,' and 'Mis' Simms,' or 'Thomas Smith's wife,' as though you was somebody. I don't know how 't is elsewheres, but here in Bassett you might as well be a dog as an old maid. I allow it might be better if they all had means or eddication: money's 'a dreadful good thing to have in the house,' as I see in a book once, and learning is sort of comp'ny to you if you're lonesome; but then lonesome you be, and you've got to be, if you're an old maid, and it can't be helped noway."

Mrs. Stearns smiled a little sadly, thinking that even married life had its own loneliness when your husband was shut up in his study, or gone off on a long drive to see some sick parishioner or conduct a neighbor-hood prayer-meeting, or even when he was the other side of the fireplace absorbed in a religious paper or a New York daily, or meditating on his next sermon, while the silent wife sat unnoticed at her mending or knitting. "But married women have more troubles and responsibilities than the unmarried, Miss Celia," she said. "You have no children to bring up and be anxious about, no daily dread of not doing your duty by the family whom you preside over, and no fear of the supplies giving out that are really needed. Nobody but your own self to look out for."

"That's jest it," snapped Celia, laying down the boy's coat she was sewing with a vicious jerk of her thread. "There 'tis! Nobody to home to care if you live or die; nobody to peek out of the winder to see if you're comin', or to make a mess of gruel or a cup of tea for you, or to throw ye a feelin' word if you're sick nigh unto death. And old maids is just as li'ble to up and die as them that's married. And as to responsi-bility, I ain't afraid to tackle that. Never! I don't hold with them that cringe and crawl and are skeert at a shadder, and won't do a living thing that they had ought to do because they're 'afraid to take the responsibility.' Why, there's Mrs. Deacon Trimble, she durstn't so much as set up a prayer-meetin' for missions or the temp'rance cause, because 'twas 'sech a reesponsibility to take the lead in them matters.' I suppose it's somethin' of a responsible chore to preach the gospel to the heathen, or grab a drinkin' feller by the scruff of his neck and haul him out of the horrible pit anyway, but if it's dooty it's got to be done, whether or no; and I ain't afraid of pitchin' into anything the Lord sets me to do!"

"Except being an old maid," said Mrs. Stearns.

Celia darted a sharp glance at her over her silver-rimmed spectacles, and pulled her needle through and through the seams of Willy's jacket with fresh vigor, while a thoughtful shadow came across her fine old face. Celia was a candid woman, for all her prejudices, a combination peculiarly characteristic of New England, for she was a typical Yankee. Presently she said abruptly, "I had n't thought on 't in that light." But then the minister opened the door, and the conversation stopped.

Parson Stearns was tired and hungry and cross, and his wife knew all that as soon as she saw his face. She had learned long ago that ministers, however good they may be, are still men; so today she had kept her husband's dinner warm in the under-oven, and had the kettle boiling to make him a cup of tea on the spot to assuage his irritation in the shortest and surest way; but though the odor of a savory stew and the cheerful warmth of the cooking-stove greeted him as he preceded her through the door into the kitchen, he snapped out, sharply enough for Celia to hear him through the half-closed door, "What do you have that old maid here for so often?"

"There!" said Celia to herself,—"there 'tis! *He* don't look upon't as a dispensation, if she doos. Men-folks run the world, and they know it. There ain't one of the hull caboodle but what despises an onmarried woman! Well, 't ain't altogether my fault. I wouldn't marry them that I could; I couldn't—not and be honest; and them that I would hev had didn't ask me. I don't know as I'm to blame, after all, when you look into 't."

And she went on sewing Willy's jacket, contrived with pains and skill out of an old coat of his father's, while Mrs. Stearns poured out her husband's tea in the kitchen, replenished his plate with stew, and cut for him more than one segment of the crisp, fresh apple-pie, and urged upon him the squares of new cheese that legitimately accompany this deleterious viand of the race and country, the sempiternal, insistent, flagrant, and alas! also fragrant pie.

Celia Barnes was the tailoress of the little scattered country town of Bassett. Early left an orphan, without near relatives or money, she had received the scantiest measure of education that our town authorities deal to the pauper children of such organizations. She was ten years old when her mother, a widow for almost all those ten years, left her to the tender mercies of the selectmen of Bassett. The selectmen of our country towns are almost irresponsible governors of their petty spheres, and gratify the instinct of oligarchy peculiar to, and conservative of, the human race. Men must be governed and tyrannized over,— it is an inborn necessity of their nature; and while a republic is a beautiful theory, eminently fitted for a race who are "non Angli, sed Angeli,"[4] it has in practice the effect of producing more than Russian tyranny, but on smaller scales and in far and scattered localities. Nowhere are there more despots than among village selectmen in New England. Those who have wrestled with their absolute monarchism in behalf of some charity that might abstract a few of the almighty dollars made out of poverty and distress from their official pockets know how positive and dogmatic is their use of power—*experto crede*.[5] The Bassett "first selectman" promptly bound out little Celia Barnes to a hard,

---

4. When the Romans conquered part of Britain, they were reported to have said that the Anglo-Saxons they encountered (with their fair skins and blue eyes) were not Angles but angels.
5. Believe one who has experienced or tried; i.e., believe me, I know.

imperious woman, who made a white slave[6] of the child, and only dealt out to her the smallest measure of schooling demanded by law, because the good old minister, Father Perkins, interfered in the child's behalf.

As she was strong and hardy and resolute, Celia lived through her bondage, and at the "free" age of eighteen apprenticed herself to old Miss Polly Mariner, the Bassett tailoress, and being deft with her fingers and quick of brain, soon outran her teacher, and when Polly died, succeeded to her business.

She was a bright girl, not particularly noticeable among others, for she had none of that delicate flower-like New England beauty which is so peculiar, so charming, and so evanescent; her features were tolerably regular, her forehead broad and calm, her gray eyes keen and perceptive, and she had abundant hair of an uncertain brown; but forty other girls in Bassett might have been described in the same way; Celia's face was one to improve with age; its strong sense, capacity for humor, fine outlines of a rugged sort, were always more the style of fifty than fifteen, and what she said of herself was true.

She had been asked to marry an old farmer with five uproarious boys, a man notorious in East Bassett for his stinginess and bad temper, and she had promptly declined the offer. Once more fate had given her a chance. A young fellow of no character, poor, "shiftless," and given to cider as a beverage, had considered it a good idea to marry someone who would make a home for him and earn his living. Looking about him for a proper person to fill this pleasant situation, he pounced on Celia—and she returned the attention!

"Marry *you?* I wonder you've got the sass to ask any decent girl to marry ye, Alfred Hatch! What be you good for, anyway? I don't know what under the canopy[7] the Lord spares you for,—only He doos let the tares grow amongst the wheat, Scripter says,[8] and I'm free to suppose He knows why, but I don't. No, *sir!* Ef you was the last man in the livin' universe I would n't tech ye with the tongs. If you'd got a speck of grit into you, you'd be ashamed to ask a woman to take ye in and support ye, for that's what it comes to. You go 'long! I can make my hands save my head so long as I hev the use of 'em, and I haven't no call to set up a private poor-house!"

So Alfred Hatch sneaked off, much like a cur that has sought to share the kennel of a mastiff, and been shortly and sharply convinced of his presumption.

Here ended Celia's "chances," as she phrased it. Young men were few in Bassett; the West had drawn them away with its subtle attraction of unknown possibilities, just as it does today, and Celia grew old in the service of those established matrons who always want clothes cut over for their children, carpet rags sewed, quilts quilted, and comforta-

---

6. Although this term more often refers to a woman held unwillingly for purposes of prostitution, Cooke most likely means to invoke the condition of American slavery and to suggest that Celia Barnes was placed in the care of a woman who treated her like a slave.

7. Sky, heavens.

8. See Matthew 13.24–30.

bles[9] tacked. She was industrious and frugal, and in time laid up some money in the Dartford Savings' Bank; but she did not, like many spinsters, invest her hard-earned dollars in a small house. Often she was urged to do so, but her reasons were good for refusing.

"I should be so independent? Well, I'm as independent now as the law allows. I've got two good rooms to myself, south winders, stairs of my own and outside door, and some privileges. If I had a house there'd be taxes, and insurance, and cleanin' off snow come winter-time, and hoein' paths; and likely enough I should be so fur left to myself that I should set up a garden, and make my succotash cost a dollar a pint a-hirin' of a man to dig it up and hoe it down. Like enough, too, I should be gettin' flower seeds and things; I'm kinder fond of blows[1] in the time of 'em. My old fish-geran'um is a sight of comfort to me as 'tis, and there would be a bill of expense again. Then you can't noway build a house with only two rooms in 't, it would be all outside; and you might as well try to heat the universe with a cookin'-stove as such a house. Besides, how lonesome I should be! It's forlorn enough to be an old maid anyway, but to have it sort of ground into you, as you may say, by livin' all alone in a hull house, that ain't necessary nor agreeable. Now, if I'm sick or sorry, I can just step downstairs and have Aunt Nabby to help or hearten me. Deacon Everts he did set to work one time to persuade me to buy a house; he said 'twas a good thing to be able to give somebody shelter 't was poorer 'n I was. Says I, 'Deacon, I've worked for my livin' ever sence I remember, and I know there's no use in anybody bein' poorer than I be. I haven't no call to take any sech in and do for 'em. I give what I can to missions,—home ones,[2] —and I'm willin', cheerfully willin', to do a day's work now and again for somebody that is strivin' with too heavy burdens; but as for keepin' free lodgin' and board, I sha'n't do it.' 'Well, well, well,' says he, kinder as if I was a fractious young one, and a-sawin' his fat hand up and down in the air till I wanted to slap him, 'just as you'd ruther, Celye,—just as you'd ruther. I don't mean to drive ye a mite, only, as Scripter says, "Provoke one another to love and good works." '[3]

"That did rile me! Says I: 'Well, you've provoked me full enough, though I don't know as you've done it in the Scripter sense; and mabbe I shouldn't have got so fur provoked if I hadn't have known that little red house your grandsir' lived and died in was throwed back on your hands just now, and advertised for sellin'. I see the "Mounting County Herald," Deacon Everts.' He shut up, I tell ye. But I sha'n't never buy no house so long as Aunt Nabby lets me have her two south chambers, and use the back stairway and the north door continual."

So Miss Celia had kept on in her way till now she was fifty, and today making over old clothes at the minister's. The minister's wife

9. Comforters or quilts.
1. A mass of blossoms, or flowers that bloom in a profuse way.

2. Help for the poor in one's own parish or community rather than abroad.
3. Hebrews 10.24.

had, as we have seen, little romance or wild happiness in her life; it is not often the portion of country ministers' wives; and, moreover, she had two step-daughters who were girls of sixteen and twelve when she married their father. Katy was married herself now, this ten years, and doing her hard duty by an annual baby and a struggling parish in Dakota; but Rosabel, whose fine name had been the only legacy her dying mother left the day-old child she had scarce had time to kiss and christen before she went to take her own "new name" above, was now a girl of twenty-two, pretty, headstrong, and rebellious. Nature had endowed her with keen dark eyes, crisp dark curls, a long chin, and a very obstinate mouth, which only her red lips and white even teeth redeemed from ugliness; her bright color and her sense of fun made her attractive to young men wherever she encountered one of that rare species. Just now she was engaged in a serious flirtation with the station-master at Bassett Centre,—an impecunious youth of no special interest to other people and quite unable to maintain a wife. But out of the "strong necessity of loving," as it is called, and the want of young society or settled occupation, Rosa Stearns chose to fall in love with Amos Barker, and her father considered it a "fall" indeed. So, with the natural clumsiness of a man and a father, Parson Stearns set himself to prevent the matter, and began by forbidding Rosabel to see or speak or write to the youth in question, and thereby inspired in her mind a burning desire to do all three. Up to this time she had rather languidly amused herself by mild and gentle flirtations with him, such as looking at him sidewise in church on Sunday, meeting him accidentally on his way to and from the station, for she spent at least half her time at her aunt's in Bassett Centre, and had even taught the small school there during the last six months. She had also sent him her tintype,[4] and his own was secreted in her bureau drawer. He had invited her to go with him to two sleigh-rides and one sugaring-off,[5] and always came home with her from prayer-meeting and singing-school; but like a wise youth he had never yet proposed to marry her in due form, not so much because he was wise as because he was thoughtless and lazy; and while he enjoyed the society of a bright girl, and liked to dangle after the prettiest one in Bassett, and the minister's daughter too, he did not love work well enough to shoulder the responsibility of providing for another those material but necessary supplies that imply labor of an incessant sort.

Rosabel, in her first inconsiderate anger at her father's command, sat down and wrote a note to Amos, eminently calculated to call out his sympathy with her own wrath, and promptly mailed it as soon as it was written. It ran as follows:—

4. An early photographic process in which a positive image was made directly on an iron plate varnished with a thin sensitized film.

5. The process of boiling down maple sap to yield maple syrup and maple sugar; often the basis for a social gathering at which the guests assist with this process.

Dear Friend,—Pa has forbidden me to speak to you any more, or to correspond with you. I suppose I must submit so far; but he did not say I must return your picture [the parson had not an idea that she possessed that precious thing], so I shall keep it to remind me of the pleasant hours we have passed together.

> "Fare thee well, and if forever,
> Still forever fare thee well!"[6]

Your true friend,

Rosabel Stearns.

P.S.—I think pa is *horrid!*

So did Amos as he read this heart-rending missive, in which the postscript, according to the established sneer at woman's postscripts, carried the whole force of the epistle.

Now Amos had made a friend of Miss Celia by once telegraphing for her trunk, which she had lost on her way home from the only journey of her life, a trip to Boston, whither she had gone, on the strength of the one share of B. & A. R. R. stock she held, to spend the allotted three days granted to stockholders on their annual excursions, presumably to attend the annual meeting. Amos had put himself to the immense trouble of sending two messages for Miss Celia, and asked her nothing for the civility, so that ever after, in the fashion of solitary women, she held herself deeply in his debt. He knew that she was at work for Mrs. Stearns when he received Rosa's epistle, for he had just been over to Bassett on the train—there was but a mile to traverse—to get her to repair his Sunday coat, and not found her at home, but had no time to look her up at the parson's, as he must walk back to his station. Now he resolved to take his answer to Rosa to Miss Celia in the evening, and so be sure that his abused sweetheart received it, for he had read too many dime novels[7] to doubt that her tyrannic father would intercept their letters, and drive them both to madness and despair. That well-meaning but rather dull divine never would have thought of such a thing; he was a puffy, absent-minded, fat little man, with a weak, squeaky voice, and a sudden temper that blazed up like a bunch of dry weeds at a passing spark, and went out at once in flattest ashes. It had been Mrs. Stearns's step-motherly interference that drove him into his harshness to Rosa. She meant well and he meant well, but we all know what good intentions with no further sequel of act are good for, and nobody did more of that "paving"[8] than these two excellent but futile people.

Miss Celia was ready to do anything for Amos Barker, and she

6. George Gordon, Lord Byron, "Fare Thee Well."
7. Romance or adventure stories cheaply produced in book form to sell for ten cents.

8. A reference to the common proverb, "The road to hell is paved with good intentions."

considered it little less than a mortal sin to stand in the way of any marriage that was really desired by two parties. That Amos was poor did not daunt her at all; she had the curious faith that possesses some women, that any man can be prosperous if he has the will so to be; and she had a high opinion of this youth, based on his civility to her. It may be said of men, as of elephants, that it is lucky they do not know their own power; for how many more women would become their worshipers and slaves than are so today if they knew the abject gratitude the average woman feels for the least attention, the smallest kindness, the faintest expression of affection or good will. We are all, like the Syrophenician woman,[9] glad and ready to eat of the crumbs which fall from the children's table, so great is our faith—in men.

Miss Celia took the note in her big basket over to the minister's the very next day after that on which we introduced her to our readers. She was perhaps more rejoiced to contravene that reverend gentleman's orders than if she had not heard his querulous and contemptuous remark about her through the crack of the door on the previous afternoon; and it was with a sense of joy that, after all, an old maid could do something, that she slipped the envelope into Rosa's hands, and told her to put it quickly into her pocket, the very first moment she found herself alone with that young woman.

Many a hasty word had Parson Stearns spoken in the suddenness of his petulant temper, but never one that bore direr fruit than that when he called Celia Barnes "that old maid."

For of course Amos and Rosabel found in her an ardent friend. They had the instinct of distressed lovers to cajole her with all their confidences, caresses, and eager gratitude, and for once she felt herself dear and of importance. Amos consulted her on his plans for the future, which of course pointed westward, where he had a brother editing and owning a newspaper. This brother had before offered him a place in his office, but Amos had liked better the easy work of a station-master in a tiny village. Now his ambition was aroused, for the time at least. He wanted to make a home for Rosabel, but, alack! he had not one cent to pay their united expenses to Peoria, and a lion stood in the way. Here again Celia stepped in: she had some money laid up; she would lend it to them.

I do not say that at this stage she had no misgivings, but even these were set at rest by a conversation she had with Mrs. Stearns some six weeks after the day on which Celia had so fully expressed her scorn of spinsters. She was there again to tack a comfortable for Rosabel's bed, and bethought herself that it was a good time to feel her way a little concerning Mrs. Stearns's opinion of things.

"They do say," she remarked, stopping to snip off her thread and twist the end of it through her needle's eye, "that your Rosy don't go with Amos Barker no more. Is that so?"

---

9. The woman who asks Jesus to cast the devil out of her daughter and who asserts her humility by her willingness to eat of the Lord's "crumbs"; see Mark 7.25–30.

"Yes," said Mrs. Stearns, with a half sigh. "Husband was rather prompt about it; he don't think Amos Barker ever'll amount to much, and he thinks his people are not just what they should be. You know his father never was very much of a man, and his grandfather is a real old reprobate. Husband says he never knew anything but crows come out of a crow's nest, and so he told Rosa to break acquaintance with him."

"Who does he like to hev come to see her?" asked Celia, with a grim set of her lips, stabbing her needle fiercely through the unoffending calico.

Mrs. Stearns laughed rather feebly. "I don't think he has anybody on his mind, Miss Celia. I don't think there are any young men in Bassett. I dare say Rosa will never marry. I wish she would, for she isn't happy here, and I can't do much to help it, with all my cares."

"And you can't feel for her as though she was your own, if you try ever so," confidently asserted Celia.

"No, I suppose not. I try to do my duty by her, and I am sorry for her; but I know all the time an own mother would understand her better and make it easier for her. Mr. Stearns is peculiar, and men don't know just how to manage girls."

It was a cautious admission, but Miss Celia had sharp eyes, and knew very well that Rosabel neither loved nor respected her father, and that they were now on terms of real if unavowed hostility.

"Well," said she, "I don't know but you will have to have one of them onpleasant creturs, an old maid, in your fam'ly. I declare for 't, I'd hold a Thanksgiving Day all to myself ef I'd escaped that marcy."

"You may not always think so, Celia."

"I don't know what'll change me. 'Twill be something I don't look forrard to now," answered Celia obstinately.

Mrs. Stearns sighed. "I hope Rosa will do nothing worse than to live unmarried," she said; but she could not help wishing silently that some worthy man would carry the perverse and annoying girl out of the parsonage for good.

After this Celia felt a certain freedom to help Rosabel; she encouraged the lovers to meet at her house, helped plan their elopement, sewed for the girl, and at last went with them as far as Brimfield when they stole away one evening, saw them safely married at the Methodist parsonage there, and bidding them good-speed, returned to Bassett Centre on the midnight train, and walked over to her own dwelling in the full moonshine of the October night, quite fearless and entirely exultant.

But she was not to come off unscathed. There was a scene of wild commotion at the parsonage next day, when Rosa's letter, modeled on that of the last novel heroine she had become acquainted with, was found on her bureau, as per novel aforesaid.

With her natural thoughtlessness she assured her parents that she "fled not uncompanioned," that her "kind and all but maternal friend, Miss Celia Barnes, would accompany her to the altar, and give her support and her countenance to the solemn ceremony that should make Rosabel Stearns the blessed wife of Amos Barker!"

It was all the minister could do not to swear as he read this astounding letter. His flabby face grew purple; his fat, sallow hands shook with rage; he dared not speak, he only sputtered, for he knew that profane and unbecoming words would surely leap from his tongue if he set it free; but he must—he really must—do or say something! So he clapped on his old hat, and with coat tails flying in the breeze, and rage in every step, set out to find Celia Barnes; and find her he did.

It would be unpleasant, and it is needless, to depict this encounter; language both unjust and unsavory smote the air and reverberated along the highway, for he met the spinster on her road to an engagement at Deacon Stiles's. Suffice it to say that both freed their minds with great enlargement of opinion, and the parson wound up with,—

"And I never want to see you again inside of my house, you confounded old maid!"

"There! that's it!" retorted Celia. "Ef I wasn't an old maid, you would n't no more have darst to 'a' talked to me this way than nothin'. Ef I'd had a man to stand up to ye you 'd have been dumber 'n Balaam's ass a great sight,—afore it seen the angel, I mean.[1] I swow to man, I b'lieve I'd marry a hitchin'-post if 't was big enough to trounce ye. You great lummox, if I could knock ye over you wouldn't peep nor mutter agin, if I be a woman!"

And with a burst of furious tears that asserted her womanhood Miss Celia went her way. Her hands were clinched under her blanket-shawl, her eyes red with angry rain, and as she walked on she soliloquized aloud:—

"I declare for 't, I b'lieve I'd marry the Old Boy[2] himself if he'd ask me. I'm sicker 'n ever of bein' an old maid!"

"Be ye?" queried a voice at her elbow. "P'r'aps, then, you might hear to me if I was to speak my mind, Celye."

Celia jumped. As she said afterward, "I vum I thought 'twas the Enemy, for certain; and to think 't was only Deacon Everts!"

"Mercy me!" she said now; "is 't you, deacon?"

"Yes, it's me; and I think 'tis a real providence I come up behind ye just in the nick of time. I've sold my farm only last week, and I've come to live on the street in that old red house of grandsir's, that you mistrusted once I wanted you to buy. I'm real lonesome sence I lost my partner" (he meant his wife), "and I've been a-hangin' on by the edges the past two year; hired help is worse than nothing onto a farm, and hard to get at that; so I sold out, and I'm a-movin' yet, but the old house looks forlorn enough, and I was intendin' to look about for a second; so if you'll have me, Celye, here I be."

Celia looked at him sharply; he was an apple-faced little man, with shrewd, twinkling eyes, a hard, dull red still lingering on his round

---

1. See Numbers 22.21–35.   2. Satan.

cheeks in spite of the deep wrinkles about his pursed-up lips and around his eyelids; his mouth gave him a consequential and self-important air, to which the short stubbly hair, brushed up "like a blaze" above his forehead, added; and his old blue coat with brass buttons, his homespun trousers, the old-fashioned aspect of his un-bleached cotton shirt, all attested his frugality. Indeed, everybody knew that Deacon Everts was "near,"[3] and also that he had plenty of money, that is to say, far more than he could spend. He had no children, no near relations; his first wife had died two years since, after long invalidism, and all her relations had moved far west. All this Celia knew and now recalled; her wrath against Parson Stearns was yet fresh and vivid; she remembered that Simeon Everts was senior dea-con of the church, and had it in his power to make the minister extremely uncomfortable if he chose. I have never said Celia was a very good woman; her religion was of the dormant type not uncommon nowadays; she kept up its observances properly, and said her prayers every day, bestowed a part of her savings on each church collection, and was rated as a church-member "in good and regular standing"; but the vital transforming power of that Christianity which means to "love the Lord thy God with all thy heart, and mind, and soul, and strength, and thy neighbor as thyself"[4] had no more entered into her soul than it had into Deacon Everts's; and while she would have honestly admitted that revenge was a very wrong sentiment, and entirely improper for any other person to cherish, she felt that she did well to be angry with Parson Stearns, and had a perfect right to "pay him off" in any way she could.

Now here was her opportunity. If she said "Yes" to Deacon Everts, he would no doubt take her part. Her objections to housekeeping were set aside by the fact that the house-owner himself would have to do those heavy labors about the house which she must otherwise have hired a man to do; and the cooking and the indoor work for two people could not be so hard as to sew from house to house for her daily bread. In short, her mind was slowly turning favorably toward this sudden project, but she did not want this wooer to be too sure; so she said: "W-e-ll, 'tis a life sentence, as you may say, deacon, and I want to think on 't a spell. Let's see,—today's Tuesday; I'll let yet know Thursday night, after prayer-meetin'."

"Well," answered the deacon.

Blessed Yankee monosyllable that means so much and so little; that has such shades of phrase and intention in its myriad inflections; that is "yes," or "no," or "perhaps," just as you accent it; that is at once preface and peroration, evasion and definition! What would all New England speech be without "well"? Even as salt without any savor, or pepper with no pungency.

Now it meant to Miss Celia assent to her proposition; and in accord-

<hr>

3. Strictly economical; stingy, parsimonious.   4. See Luke 10.27.

ance the deacon escorted her home from meeting Thursday night, and received for reward a consenting answer. This was no love affair, but a matter of mere business. Deacon Everts needed a housekeeper, and did not want to pay out wages for one; and Miss Celia's position she expressed herself as she put out her tallow candle on that memorable night, and breathed out on the darkness the audible aspiration, "Thank goodness, I sha'n't hev to die an old maid!"

There was no touch of sanctifying love or consoling affection, or even friendly comradeship, in this arrangement; it was as truly a *marriage de convenance*[5] as was ever contracted in Paris itself, and when the wedding day came, a short month afterward, the sourest aspect of November skies threatening a drenching pour, the dead and sodden leaves that strewed the earth, the wailing northeast wind, even the draggled and bony old horse behind which they jogged over to Bassett Centre, seemed fit accompaniments to the degraded ceremony performed by a justice of the peace, who concluded this merely legal compact, for Miss Celia stoutly refused to be married by Parson Stearns; she would not be accessory to putting one dollar in his pocket, even as her own wedding fee. So she went home to the little red house on Bassett Street, and begun her married life by scrubbing the dust and dirt of years from the kitchen table, making biscuit for tea, washing up the dishes, and at last falling asleep during the deacon's long nasal prayer, wherein he wandered to the ends of the earth, and prayed fervently for the heathen, piteously unconscious that he was little better than a heathen himself.

It did not take many weeks to discover to Celia what is meant by "the curse of a granted prayer." She could not at first accept the situation at all; she was accustomed to enough food, if it was plain and simple, when she herself provided it; but now it was hard to get such viands as would satisfy a healthy appetite.

"You've used a sight of pork, Celye," the deacon would remonstrate. "My first never cooked half what you do. We shall come to want certain, if you're so free-handed."

"Well, Mr. Everts, there wasn't a mite left to set by. We eat it all, and I didn't have no more 'n I wanted, if you did."

"We must mortify the flesh, Celye. It's hullsome to get up from your victuals hungry. Ye know what Scripter says, 'Jeshurun waxed fat an' kicked.' "[6]

"Well, I ain't Jeshurun, but I expect I shall be more likely to kick if I don't have enough to eat, when it's only pork 'n' potatoes."

"My first used to say them was the best, for steady victuals, of anything, and she never used but two codfish and two quarts of m'lasses the year round; and as for butter, she was real sparin'; she'd fry our bread along with the salt pork, and 'twas just as good."

"Look here!" snapped Celia. "I don't want to hear no more about your 'first.' I'm ready to say I wish 't she 'd ha' been your last too."

---

5. Marriage of convenience.   6. See Deuteronomy 32.15.

"Well, well, well! this is onseemly contention, Celye," sputtered the alarmed deacon. "Le' 's dwell together in unity so fur as we can, Mis' Everts. I haven't no intention to starve ye, none whatever. I only want to be keerful, so as we sha'n't have to fetch up in the poor-us."

"No need to have a poor-house to home," muttered Celia.

But this is only a mild specimen of poor Celia's life as a married woman. She did not find the honor and glory of "Mrs." before her name a compensation for the thousand evils that she "knew not of"[7] when she fled to them as a desirable change from her single blessedness. Deacon Everts entirely refused to enter into any of her devices against Parson Stearns; he did not care a penny about Celia's wrongs, and he knew very well that no other man than dreamy, unpractical Mr. Stearns, who eked out his minute pittance by writing school-books of a primary sort, would put up with four hundred dollars a year from his parish; yet that was all Bassett people would pay. If they must have the gospel, they must have it at the lowest living rates, and everybody would not assent to that.

So Celia found her revenge no more feasible after her marriage than before, and, gradually absorbed in her own wrongs and sufferings, her desire to reward Mr. Stearns in kind for his treatment of her vanished; she thought less of his futile wrath and more of her present distresses every day.

For Celia, like everybody who profanes the sacrament of marriage, was beginning to suffer the consequences of her misstep. As her husband's mean, querulous, loveless character unveiled itself in the terrible intimacy of constant and inevitable companionship, she began to look woefully back to the freedom and peace of her maiden days. She learned that a husband is by no means his wife's defender always, not even against reviling tongues. It did not suit Deacon Everts to quarrel with anyone, whatever they said to him, or of him and his; he "didn't want no enemies," and Celia bitterly felt that she must fight her own battles; she had not even an ally in her husband. She became not only defiant, but also depressed; the consciousness of a vital and life-long mistake is not productive of cheer or content; and now, admitted into the free-masonry of married women, she discovered how few among them were more than household drudges, the servants of their families, worked to the verge of exhaustion, and neither thanked nor rewarded for their pains. She saw here a woman whose children were careless of, and ungrateful to her, and her husband coldly indifferent; there was one on whom the man she had married wreaked all his fiendish temper in daily small injuries, little vexatious acts, petty tyrannies, a "street-angel, house-devil" of a man, of all sorts the most hateful. There were many whose lives had no other outlook than hard work until the end should come, who rose up to labor and lay down in sleepless exhaustion, and some whose days were a constant terror to them from the intemperate brutes to

7. See *Hamlet* 3.1.81.

whom they had intrusted their happiness, and indeed their whole existence.

It was no worse with Celia than with most of her sex in Bassett; here and there, there were of course exceptions, but so rare as to be shining examples and objects of envy. Then, too, after two years, there came forlorn accounts of poor Rosabel's situation at the west. Amos Barker had done his best at first to make his wife comfortable, but change of place or new motives do not at once, if ever, transform an indolent man into an active and efficient one. He found work in his brother's office, but it was the hard work of collecting bills all about the country; the roads were bad, the weather as fluctuating as weather always is, the climate did not agree with him, and he got woefully tired of driving about from dawn till after dark, to dun unwilling debtors. Rosa had chills and fever and babies with persistent alacrity; she had indeed enough to eat, with no appetite, and a house, with no strength to keep it. She grew untidy, listless, hysterical; and her father, getting worried by her despondent and infrequent letters, actually so far roused himself as to sell his horse, and with this sacrificial money betook himself to Mound Village, where he found Rosabel with two babies in her arms, dust an inch deep on all her possessions, nothing but pork, potatoes, and corn bread in the pantry, and a slatternly Negress washing some clothes in a kitchen that made the parson shudder.

The little man's heart was bigger than his soul. He put his arms about Rosa and the dingy babies, and forgave her all; but he had to say, even while he held them closely and fondly to his breast, "Oh, Rosy, I told you what would happen if you married that fellow."

Of course Rosa resented the speech, for, after all, she had loved Amos; perhaps could love him still if the poverty and malaria and babies could have all been eliminated from her daily life.

Fortunately the parson's horse had sold well, for it was strong and young, and the rack of venerable bones with which he replaced it was bought very cheap at a farmer's auction, so he had money enough to carry Rosa and the two children home to Bassett, where two months after she added another feeble, howling cipher to the miserable sum of humanity.

Miss—no, Mrs.—Celia's conscience stung her to the quick when she encountered this ghastly wreck of pretty Rosabel Stearns, now called Mrs. Barker. She remembered with deep regret how she had given aid and comfort to the girl who had defied and disobeyed parental counsel and authority, and so brought on herself all this misery. She fancied that Parson Stearns glared at her with eyes of bitter accusation and reproach, and not improbably he did, for beside his pity and affection for his daughter, it was no slight burden to take into his house a feeble woman with two children helpless as babies, and to look forward to the expense and anxiety of another soon to come. And Mrs. Stearns had never loved Rosa well enough to be complacent at this addition to her family cares. She gave the parson no sympathy. It would have been her way to let Rosabel lie on the bed she had made, and die there if need be. But the poor worn-out creature died at home, after all, and the third baby lay on its mother's breast in her coffin: they had gone together.

Celia felt almost like a murderess when she heard that Rosabel Barker was dead. She did not reflect that in all human probability the girl would have married Amos if she, Celia, had refused to help or encourage her. It began to be an importunate question in our friend's mind whether she herself had not made a mistake too; whether the phrase "single blessedness" was not an expression of a vital truth rather than a scoff. Celia was changing her mind no doubt, surely if slowly.

Meantime Deacon Everts did not find all the satisfaction with his "second" that he had anticipated. Celia had a will of her own, quite undisciplined, and it was too often asserted to suit her lord and master. Secretly he planned devices to circumvent her purposes, and sometimes succeeded. In prayer-meeting and in Sunday-school the idea haunted him; his malice lay down and rose up with him. Even when he propounded to his Bible class the important question, "How fur be the heathen *ree*-sponsible for what they dun know?" and asked them "to ponder on 't through the comin' week," he chuckled inwardly at the thought that Celia could not evade *her* responsibility; she knew enough, and would be judged accordingly: the deacon was not a merciful man.

At last he hit upon that great legal engine whereby men do inflict the last deadly kick upon their wives: he would remodel his will. Yes, he would leave those gathered thousands to foreign missions; he would leave behind him the indisputable testimony and taunt that he considered the wife of his bosom less than the savages and heathen afar off. He forgot conveniently that the man "who provideth not for his own household hath denied the faith, and is worse than an infidel."[8] And in his delight of revenge he also forgot that the law of the land provides for a man's wife and children in spite of his wicked will. Nor did he remember that his life-insurance policy for five thousand dollars was made out in his wife's name, simply as his wife, her own name not being specified. He had paid the premium always from his "first's" small annual income, and agreed that it should be written for her benefit, but he supposed that at her death it had reverted to him. He forgot that he still had a wife when he mentioned that policy in his assets recorded in the will, and to save money he drew that evil document up himself, and had it signed down at "the store" by three witnesses.

Celia had borne her self-imposed yoke for four years, when it was suddenly broken. A late crop of grass was to be mowed in mid-July on the meadow which appertained to the old house, and the deacon, now

8. See 1 Timothy 5.8.

some seventy years old, to save hiring help, determined to do it by himself. The grass was heavy and over-ripe, the day extremely hot and breathless, and the grim Mower of Man trod side by side with Simeon Everts, and laid him too, all along by the rough heads of timothy and the purpled feather-tops of the blue-grass. He did not come home at noon or at night, and when Celia went down to the lot to call him he heard no summons of hers; he had answered a call far more imperative and final.

After the funeral Celia found his will pushed back in the deep drawer of an old secretary, where he kept his one quill pen, a bottle of dried ink, a lump of chalk, some rat-poison, and various other odds and ends.

She was indignant enough at its tenor; but it was easily broken, and she not only had her "thirds," but the life policy reverted to her also, as it was made out to Simeon Everts's wife, and surely she had occupied that position for four wretched years. Then, also, she had a right to her support for one year out of the estate, and the use of the house for that time.

Oh, how sweet was her freedom! With her characteristic honesty she refused to put on mourning, and even went to the funeral in her usual gray Sunday gown and bonnet. "I won't lie, anyhow!" she answered to Mrs. Stiles's remonstrance. "I ain't a mite sorry nor mournful. I could ha' wished he'd had time to repent of his sins, but sence the Lord saw fit to cut him short, I don't feel to rebel ag'inst it. I wish 't I'd never married him, that's all!"

"But, Celye, you got a good livin'."

"I earned it."

"And he's left ye with means too."

"He done his best not to. I don't owe him nothing for that; and I earned that too,—the hull on 't. It's poor pay for what I've lived through; and I'm a'most a mind to call it the wages of sin, for I done wrong, ondeniably wrong, in marryin' of him; but the Lord knows I've repented, and said my lesson, if I did get it by the hardest."

Yet all Bassett opened eyes and mouth both when on the next Thanksgiving Day Celia invited every old maid in town—seven all told—to take dinner with her. Never before had she celebrated this old New England day of solemn revel. A woman living in two small rooms could not "keep the feast," and rarely had she been asked to any family conclave. We Yankees are conservative at Thanksgiving if nowhere else, and like to gather our own people only about the family hearth; so Celia had but once or twice shared the turkeys of her more fortunate neighbors.

Now she called in Nabby Hyde and Sarah Gillett, Ann Smith, Celestia Potter, Delia Hills, Sophronia Ann Jenkins and her sister Delia Ann, ancient twins, who lived together on next to nothing, and were happy.

Celia bloomed at the head of the board, not with beauty, but with gratification. "Well," she said, as soon as they were seated, "I sent for ye all to come because I wanted to have a good time, for one thing, and because it seems as though I'd ought to take back all the sassy and disagreeable things I used to be forever flingin' at old maids. 'I spoke in my haste,' as Scripter says,[9] and also in my ignorance, I'm free to confess. I feel as though I could keep Thanksgivin' today with my hull soul. I'm so thankful to be an old maid ag'in!'"

"I thought you was a widder," snapped Sally Gillett.

Celia flung a glance of wrath at her, but scorned to reply.

"And I'm thankful too that I'm spared to help ondo somethin' done in that ignorance. I've got means, and, as I've said before, I earned 'em. I don't feel noway obleeged to him for 'em; he did n't mean it. But now I can I'm goin' to adopt Rosy Barker's two children, and fetch 'em up to be dyed-in-the-wool old maids; and every year, so long as I live, I'm goin' to keep an old maids' Thanksgivin' for a kind of a burnt-offering,[1] sech as the Bible tells about, for I've changed my mind clear down to the bottom, and I go the hull figure with the 'postle Paul when he speaks about the onmarried, 'It is better if she so abide.'[2] Now let's go to work at the victuals."

No magazine publication; *Huckleberries*, 1891

9. See Psalms 31 and 116.

1. A ceremony of animal sacrifice, frequent to the Old Testament, expressing adoration and thanksgiving.

2. See 1 Corinthians 7.8.

CELIA THAXTER
1835–1894

"Landing for the first time, the stranger is struck only by the sadness of the place,—the vast loneliness; for there are not even trees to whisper with familiar voices,—nothing but sky and sea and rocks." In this way Celia Thaxter would later describe the outsider's view of the cluster of islands nine miles off the New Hampshire coast that was her home from early childhood. But for Thaxter as both child and adult, sea and rocks became familiar voices, while loneliness and sadness were feelings she connected with being away from the islands. In *Among the Isles of Shoals,* Thaxter offers her readers the chance to experience such a shift in perspective, such a change of mind, and to become like herself an insider, not a stranger, to the islands.

Born June 29, 1835, in Portsmouth, New Hampshire, Thaxter first landed on the Isles of Shoals at the age of four. Her father, Thomas B. Laighton, purchased four of the nine islands in 1839 and moved his wife Eliza and their three children to White Island, a few acres of rock in the northern Atlantic, where he was to be the keeper of the lighthouse. Since during the winter months the Laighton family was not only island-bound but house-bound for weeks at a time, one can understand why her mother's strength as a homemaker emerged as Thaxter's earliest and most significant influence. Thaxter's granddaughter Rosamond writes in *Sandpiper* that Eliza was "almost worshipped by her daughter" (10).

In 1847 Laighton began to build the Appledore Hotel on Hog Island (which he renamed Appledore) and entered into partnership with Harvard-educated Levi Lincoln Thaxter. Although he soon bought out Levi's interest, he hired the scholarly man to tutor his daughter and two younger sons. Except for one term at Mt. Washington Female Seminary in Boston, Thaxter had no other formal education. Eighteen forty-seven is also the effective date of Thaxter's betrothal, for, like Shakespeare's Miranda (Hawthorne made the analogy in the *American Notebooks* after he visited the islands in 1852 and Stowe extended it in using Thaxter as a model for Mara in *The Pearl of Orr's Island*), Thaxter fell in love with the first male "creature" other than her father and the Shoalers who ever entered her "brave new world." In 1851, at the age of sixteen, she married her tutor, eleven years her senior.

By all accounts the marriage was unsuccessful. Levi served one year as preacher on Star Island and twenty years later he would become for a season a professional reader of Browning's poetry; otherwise, he never worked regularly and appears to have lived on his family's money. However, the Thaxter money did not help Celia, for Levi did not contribute substantially to her support after the publication of her first volume, *Poems,* in 1872. He refused to hire a housekeeper and turned over to her the care of the eldest of their three sons, Karl, who was born emotionally and mentally impaired. Thaxter therefore had to struggle throughout her life to make a living, first by her writing, and during the 1880s by her china painting, an art form in which she was totally self-taught but very successful. A family photograph depicts Levi and his son Roland carrying guns, for Levi shot and stuffed birds as a hobby. Thaxter, known to her friends as "Sandpiper," loved birds (she believed she had begun conscious life as a bird in another age) and became an active member of the Audubon Society. In a March 14, 1876, letter to "sweet Saint" Annie Fields (who, with John Greenleaf Whittier, became one of Thaxter's confidantes), she writes, "Oh Annie, if it were only possible to go back and pick up the thread of one's life anew.—Could I be 10 years old again—I would climb to my lighthouse top and set at defiance anything in the shape of man" (quoted in Thaxter, *Sandpiper*, 115). A decade later, Sarah Orne Jewett, Thaxter's friend and Fields's life companion, would immortalize in her story, "A White Heron" (1886), the life of that child who "sets at defiance" a young ornithologist.

Even after her marriage Thaxter spent most of her summers on Appledore, helping first her father and later her brothers to manage what she calls, in *Among the Isles of Shoals*, the "house of entertainment." In the parlor of her cottage there she was host to most of the literary and artistic figures of her day: Fields and Jewett, Whittier, William Morris Hunt, and Childe Hassam. At one time or another, Emerson, Hawthorne, Lowell, Holmes, Longfellow, and Clemens would all visit Appledore, the first summer resort hotel on the New England coast. During the period of her mother's declining health in the 1870s, Thaxter became estranged from her husband, who after a boating accident in 1855 refused to visit the islands, and spent winters as well as summers on Appledore. When she herself died, of cerebral hemorrhage on August 25, 1894, her son Karl, in reporting her death to the rest of the family, said, "Her mother came in the night and took her away" (Fields, *Authors and Friends*, 232). In addition to *Among the Isles of Shoals*, Thaxter published another prose work, *An Island Garden* (1894). She also published several volumes of poetry and a collection of stories and poems for children.

o o o

Although Thaxter was best known in her own time as a poet, *Among the Isles of Shoals*, first published as a series of essays in the *Atlantic Monthly* in 1869–70, received critical acclaim and is a significant text in the regional tradition. Except for the sections of autobiography in that narrative (added when she collected the essays in book form) and some anecdotes about the inhabitants of the fishing village of Gosport (no longer in existence) on Star Island, *Among the Isles of Shoals* primarily describes the topography, geology, and history of the islands; their relation to weather, the ocean, and the constellations; the line of land in the west and the unbroken line of sea on the eastern horizon; and the sea-fowl and other birds, the flowers, insects, and bats who served as "friends" and "neighbors" to the small child growing up on White Island.

To Thaxter, the islands, initially so forbidding, proved a natural world of the size that one woman could know intimately. Like Thoreau, who declared himself to have traveled a good deal in Concord, Thaxter experienced the "great world" from her island perspective, rarely traveling beyond Boston and Portsmouth. She sought instead to know one place in detail and to create familiarity out of strangeness. Every natural form and inhabitant on the islands possesses individuality for Thaxter; she learns the value of single, original things and prizes "one single root of fern, the only one within the circle of my little world." In this world of single things, she becomes the center and the landscape enhances her own sense of uniqueness. When allowed as a child to kindle the lamps herself, she marvels that "so little a creature as I might do that much for the great world." On the island rock, the lighthouse emerges as an emblem for Thaxter herself.

She writes of the sea that it appeared like "a vast, round mirror." The landscape of the islands is "the world" for Thaxter, and that world, despite the perils of winter storms, becomes "a basket," the sky "the golden handle." In these and many other passages, *Among the Isles of Shoals* reveals Thaxter's intimate association of islanded nature with the mirroring and holding a mother gives her child; and she offers landscape as a sensual, spiritual, and permanent resource that continues to mother the adult. A wife at sixteen with a child at seventeen, Thaxter early encountered the realities of being a mother. Unlike husband and child, the islands for Thaxter give rather than take emotional and spiritual sustenance. The mirroring and mothering that men and children expect to receive from women Thaxter finds as an adult in the landscape and in her imaginative recreation of place.

In writing of the landscape she knew intimately, Thaxter easily found her own voice. Later, having difficulty with *An Island Garden,* she wrote Jewett, who had apparently made some suggestions about the new manuscript, "I was so happy when I wrote the Shoals book—it wrote itself" (Thaxter, *Letters,* 199). One passage from her "Shoals book" clearly locates the source of her literary authority in the island landscape. After seeing the rainbow that followed a storm at the islands, she writes, "I hid my face from the glory,—it was too much to bear. Ever I longed to *speak* these things that made life so sweet, to speak the wind, the cloud, the bird's flight, the sea's murmur." Islanded nature inspires the longing to speak, and, finding herself in the landscape, Thaxter develops her passion "until it was impossible to be silent any longer."

From Among the Isles of Shoals

In a series of papers published not many years ago, Herman Melville made the world acquainted with the "Encantadas," or Enchanted Islands, which he describes as lying directly under the equator, off the coast of South America, and of which he says: "It is to be doubted whether any spot of earth can, in desolateness, furnish a parallel to this group." But their dark volcanic crags and melancholy beaches can hardly seem more desolate than do the low bleached rocks of the Isles of Shoals to eyes that behold them for the first time. Very sad they look, stern, bleak, and unpromising, yet are they enchanted islands in a better sense of the word than are the great Gallipagos of which Mr. Melville discourses so delightfully.

There is a strange charm about them, an indescribable influence in their atmosphere, hardly to be explained, but universally acknowledged. People forget the hurry and worry and fret of life after living

there awhile, and, to an imaginative mind, all things become dreamy
as they were to the lotus-eaters,[1] to whom

> "The gushing of the wave
> Far, far away did seem to mourn and rave
> On alien shores."[2]

The eternal sound of the sea on every side has a tendency to wear
away the edge of human thought and perception; sharp outlines
become blurred and softened like a sketch in charcoal; nothing appeals
to the mind with the same distinctness as on the mainland, amid the
rush and stir of people and things, and the excitements of social life.
This was strikingly illustrated during the late war,[3] which, while it
wrung the heart of the whole country, and stirred the blood of every
man, woman, and child on the continent, left the handful of human
beings upon these lonely rocks almost untouched. The echoes of woe
and terror were so faint and far they seemed to lose their significance
among the many-voiced waters they crossed, and reached at last the
indifferent ears they sought with no more force than a spent wave.

Nine miles of the Atlantic Ocean intervene between these islands
and the nearest point of the coast of New Hampshire; but from this
nearest point the coast-line recedes gradually, in dim and dimmer
distance, to Cape Ann, in Massachusetts, twenty-one miles away at the
southwest, and to Cape Neddick, in Maine, sixteen miles distant in the
northeast (in clear weather another cape is faintly distinguishable
beyond this), and about one third of the great horizon is filled by this
beautiful, undulating line of land, which, under the touch of atmospheric change, is almost as plastic[4] as the clouds, and wears a new
aspect with every turn of wind and weather.

Sailing out from Portsmouth Harbor with a fair wind from the northwest, the Isles of Shoals lie straight before you, nine miles away,—ill-
defined and cloudy shapes, faintly discernible in the distance. A word
about the origin of this name, "Isles of Shoals." They are supposed to
have been so called, not because the ragged reefs run out beneath the
water in all directions, ready to wreck and destroy, but because of the
"shoaling," or "schooling," of fish about them, which, in the mackerel
and herring seasons, is remarkable. As you approach they separate,
and show each its own peculiar characteristics, and you perceive that
there are six islands if the tide is low; but if it is high, there are eight,
and would be nine, but that a breakwater connects two of them.
Appledore, called for many years Hog Island, from its rude resemblance to a hog's back rising from the water, when seen from out at sea,
is the largest and most regular in shape. From afar, it looks smoothly
rounded, like a gradually sloping elevation, the greatest height of

---

1. The North African people described in Homer's
Odyssey who lived on the lotus plant in a drugged,
indolent state.

2. Alfred, Lord Tennyson, "The Lotos-Eaters."
3. The American Civil War, 1861–65.
4. Capable of being shaped, formed.

which is only seventy-five feet above high-water mark. A little valley in which are situated the buildings belonging to the house of entertainment, which is the only habitation, divides its four hundred acres into two unequal portions. Next, almost within a stone's throw, is Haley's Island, or "Smutty-nose," so christened by passing sailors, with a grim sense of humor, from a long black point of rock stretching out to the southeast, upon which many a ship has laid her bones. This island is low and flat, and contains a greater depth of soil than the others. At low tide, Cedar and Malaga are both connected with it,—the latter permanently by a breakwater,—the whole comprising about one hundred acres. Star Island contains one hundred and fifty acres, and lies a quarter of a mile southwest of Smutty-nose. Toward its northern end are clustered the houses of the little village of Gosport, with a tiny church crowning the highest rock. Not quite a mile southwest from Star, White Island lifts a lighthouse for a warning. This is the most picturesque of the group, and forms, with Seavey's Island, at low water, a double island, with an area of some twenty acres. Most westerly lies Londoner's, an irregular rock with a bit of beach, upon which all the shells about the cluster seem to be thrown. Two miles northeast from Appledore, Duck Island thrusts out its lurking ledges on all sides beneath the water, one of them running half a mile to the northwest. This is the most dangerous of the islands, and, being the most remote, is the only one visited to any great degree by the shy sea-fowl that are nearly banished by civilization. Yet even now, at low tide, those long black ledges are often whitened by the dazzling plumage of gulls whose exquisite and stainless purity rivals the new-fallen snow. The ledges run toward the west and north; but at the east and south the shore is bolder, and Shag and Mingo Rocks, where, during or after storms, the sea breaks with magnificent effect, lie isolated by a narrow channel from the main granite fragment. A very round rock west of Londoner's, perversely called "Square," and Anderson's Rock, off the southeast end of Smutty-nose, complete the catalogue.

Smutty-nose and Appledore are almost united by a reef, bare at low tide, though a large vessel can pass between them even then. Off the landing at White Island the Devil's Rock rolls an incessant breaker, and makes an attempt to reach the shore perilous in any but the serenest weather. Between Londoner's and Star is another, hardly bare at low tide; a perpetual danger, for it lies directly in the path of most of the sailing vessels, and many a schooner has been "brought up all standing" by this unexpected obstacle. Another rock, about four miles east of Appledore, rejoices in the significant title of the "Old Harry." Old Harry is deeply sunk beneath the surface, and never betrays himself except in great storms, when an awful white spray rises afar off, and the Shoalers know how tremendous are the breakers that send it skyward.

The names of the towns, Appledore, Gosport, and, along the coast, Portsmouth, Newcastle, Rye, Ipswich, Portland, Bangor, Newbury,

Amesbury, Salisbury, and many more, are all borrowed from towns on, or not far from, the coasts of England and Wales, as may be seen from the maps of those countries. Salisbury Beach fronts our islands. Amesbury lies farther inland, but the gentle outline of Po Hill, in that town, is the last eminence of any importance on the southern end of the coast line.

The dividing line between Maine and New Hampshire passes through the group, giving Appledore, Smutty-nose, and Duck Islands to Maine, and the rest to New Hampshire; but their allegiance to either is a matter of small importance, the few inhabitants troubling themselves but little about what State they belong to. Till within a few years no taxes were required of them, and they enjoyed immunity from this and various other earthly ills as completely as the gulls and loons that shared their dwelling-place.

Swept by every wind that blows, and beaten by the bitter brine for unknown ages, well may the Isles of Shoals be barren, bleak, and bare. At first sight nothing can be more rough and inhospitable than they appear. The incessant influences of wind and sun, rain, snow, frost, and spray, have so bleached the tops of the rocks, that they look hoary as if with age, though in the summer-time a gracious greenness of vegetation breaks here and there the stern outlines, and softens somewhat their rugged aspect. Yet so forbidding are their shores, it seems scarcely worth while to land upon them,—mere heaps of tumbling granite in the wide and lonely sea,—when all the smiling, "sapphire-spangled marriage-ring of the land"[5] lies ready to woo the voyager back again, and welcome his returning prow with pleasant sights and sounds and scents that the wild wastes of water never know. But to the human creature who has eyes that will see and ears that will hear, nature appeals with such a novel charm, that the luxurious beauty of the land is half forgotten before one is aware. Its sweet gardens, full of color and perfume, its rich woods and softly swelling hills, its placid waters, and fields and flowery meadows, are no longer dear and desirable; for the wonderful sound of the sea dulls the memory of all past impressions, and seems to fulfil and satisfy all present needs. Landing for the first time, the stranger is struck only by the sadness of the place,—the vast loneliness; for there are not even trees to whisper with familiar voices,—nothing but sky and sea and rocks. But the very wildness and desolation reveal a strange beauty to him. Let him wait till evening comes,

"With sunset purple soothing all the waste,"

and he will find himself slowly succumbing to the subtile charm of that sea atmosphere. He sleeps with all the waves of the Atlantic murmuring in his ears, and wakes to the freshness of a summer morning; and it seems as if morning were made for the first time. For the world is like

5. Tennyson, "Maud."

a new-blown[6] rose, and in the heart of it he stands, with only the
caressing music of the water to break the utter silence, unless, perhaps,
a song-sparrow pours out its blissful warble like an embodied joy. The
sea is rosy, and the sky; the line of land is radiant; the scattered sails
glow with the delicious color that touches so tenderly the bare, bleak
rocks. These are lovelier than sky or sea or distant sails, or graceful
gulls' wings reddened with the dawn; nothing takes color so beautifully as the bleached granite; the shadows are delicate, and the fine,
hard outlines are glorified and softened beneath the fresh first blush of
sunrise. All things are speckless and spotless; there is no dust, no noise,
nothing but peace in the sweet air and on the quiet sea. The day goes
on; the rose changes to mellow gold, the gold to clear, white daylight,
and the sea is sparkling again. A breeze ripples the surface, and wherever it touches the color deepens. A seine-boat[7] passes, with the tawny
net heaped in the stern, and the scarlet shirts of the rowers brilliant
against the blue. Pleasantly their voices come across the water, breaking the stillness. The fishing-boats steal to and fro, silent, with glittering sails; the gulls wheel lazily; the far-off coasters glide rapidly along
the horizon; the mirage steals down the coast-line, and seems to remove it leagues away. And what if it were to slip down the slope of the
world and disappear entirely? You think, in a half-dream, you would
not care. Many troubles, cares, perplexities, vexations, lurk behind that
far, faint line for you. Why should you be bothered any more?

> "Let us alone. Time driveth onward fast,
> And in a little while our lips are dumb."[8]

And so the waves, with their lulling murmur, do their work, and you
are soothed into repose and transient forgetfulness.

The natives, or persons who have been brought up here, find it
almost as difficult to tear themselves away from the islands as do the
Swiss to leave their mountains. From a civilized race's point of view,
this is a curious instance of human perversity, since it is not good for
men to live their whole lives through in such remote and solitary
places. Nobody hears of people dying of home-sickness for New York,
or Albany, or Maine, or California, or any place on the broad continent; but to wild and lonely spots like these isles humanity clings with
an intense and abiding affection. No other place is able to furnish the
inhabitants of the Shoals with sufficient air for their capacious lungs;
there is never scope enough elsewhere, there is no horizon; they must
have sea-room. On shore it is to them as if all the trees and houses
crowded against the windows to suffocation; and I know a youth who,
when at the age of thirteen he made his first visit to the mainland,
descended to the cellar of the house in which he found himself, in the
not over-populous city of Portsmouth, and spent the few hours of his
stay sitting dejectedly upon a wood-pile, in mute protest against the

---

6. Newly and completely opened.   the water with weights and floats.
7. A boat with a large fishing net hung vertically in   8. Tennyson, "The Lotos-Eaters."

condition of things in general, and the pressure of human society in particular.

Each island has its peculiar characteristics, as I said before, and no two are alike, though all are of the same coarse granite, mixed with masses and seams of quartz and felspar and gneiss and mica-slate, and interspersed with dikes of trap[9] running in all directions. Upon Appledore, for the most part, the trap runs from north to south, while the veins of quartz and felspar run from east to west. Sometimes the narrow white quartz veins intersect the dark trap, in parallel lines, now wavering, and now perfectly straight, and showing a surface like that of some vast piece of inlaid work. Each island presents its boldest shore to the east, to breast the whole force of the great Atlantic, which every year assails the iron cliffs and headlands with the same ponderous fury, yet leaves upon them so little trace of its immense power,—though at White Island, on the top of a precipitous rock called "The Head," which is nearly fifty feet high, lies a boulder weighing fifteen tons, tossed there from below by the breakers. The shores are seldom very bold, but on the east they are often very striking with their rifts and chasms, and roughly piled gorges, and square quarries of stone, and stairways cut as if by human hands. The trap rock, softer than the granite, is worn away in many places, leaving bare perpendicular walls fifteen or twenty feet high. The largest trap dike upon Appledore runs across the island from northeast to southwest, disappears in the sea, and reappears upon Smutty-nose, a quarter of a mile distant in a straight line. In some places, the geologist will tell you, certain deep scratches in the solid rock mean that here the glacier ground its way across in the world's earlier ages. Frequently the trap rock is honeycombed in a curious fashion,—filled with small holes on the surface, as if drops of water falling for years in the same spots had worn these smooth round hollows. This always happens close to the water, and only in the trap rock, and looks as if it might be the result of the flying spray which, in winter and toward spring, when the northwest gales blow sometimes for three weeks steadily day and night, beats continually upon the shore.

The coast-line varies, of course, with high or low tide. At low water the shores are much more forbidding than at high tide, for a broad band of dark sea-weed girdles each island, and gives a sullen aspect to the whole group. But in calm days, when the moon is full and the tides are so low that it sometimes seems as if the sea were being drained away on purpose to show to eager eyes what lies beneath the lowest ebb, banks of golden-green and brown moss thickly clustered on the moist ledges are exposed, and the water is cut by the ruffled edges of the kelps[1] that grow in brown and shining forests on every side. At sunrise or sunset the effect of the long rays slanting across these masses of rich color is very beautiful. But at high tide the shores are most charming; every little cove and inlet is filled with the music of the

9. A steplike configuration in igneous rocks.   1. Large brown seaweeds.

waves, and their life, light, color, and sparkle. Who shall describe that wonderful noise of the sea among the rocks, to me the most suggestive of all the sounds in nature? Each island, every isolated rock, has its own peculiar rote, and ears made delicate by listening, in great and frequent peril, can distinguish the bearings of each in a dense fog. The threatening speech of Duck Island's ledges, the swing of the wave over Halfway Rock, the touch of the ripples on the beach at Londoner's, the long and lazy breaker that is forever rolling below the lighthouse at White Island,—all are familiar and distinct, and indicate to the islander his whereabouts almost as clearly as if the sun shone brightly and no shrouding mist were striving to mock and to mislead him.

*   *   *

Within the lovely limits of summer it is beautiful to live almost anywhere; most beautiful where the ocean meets the land; and here particularly, where all the varying splendor of the sea encompasses the place, and the ceaseless changing of the tides brings continual refreshment into the life of every day. But summer is late and slow to come; and long after the mainland has begun to bloom and smile beneath the influence of spring, the bitter northwest winds still sweep the cold, green water about these rocks, and tear its surface into long and glittering waves from morning till night, and from night till morning, through many weeks. No leaf breaks the frozen soil, and no bud swells on the shaggy bushes that clothe the slopes. But if summer is a laggard in her coming, she makes up for it by the loveliness of her lingering into autumn; for when the pride of trees and flowers is despoiled by frost on shore, the little gardens here are glowing at their brightest, and day after day of mellow splendor drops like a benediction from the hand of God. In the early mornings in September the mists draw away from the depths of inland valleys, and rise into the lucid western sky,—tall columns and towers of cloud, solid, compact, superb; their pure, white, shining heads uplifted into the ether, solemn, stately, and still, till some wandering breeze disturbs their perfect outline, and they melt about the heavens in scattered fragments as the day goes on. Then there are mornings when "all in the blue, unclouded weather"[2] the coast-line comes out so distinctly that houses, trees, bits of white beach, are clearly visible, and with a glass, moving forms of carriages and cattle are distinguishable nine miles away. In the transparent air the peaks of Mounts Madison, Washington, and Jefferson are seen distinctly at a distance of one hundred miles. In the early light even the green color of the trees is perceptible on the Rye shore. All through these quiet days the air is full of wandering thistle-down, the inland golden-rod waves its plumes, and close by the water's edge, in rocky clefts, its seaside sister blossoms in gorgeous color; the rose-haws redden, the iris unlocks its shining caskets, and casts its closely packed seeds about, gray berries cluster on the bayberry-bushes, the sweet life-everlasting sends out its wonderful, delicious fragrance, and the pale asters spread

2. Tennyson, "The Lady of Shalott."

their flowers in many-tinted sprays. Through October and into November the fair, mild weather lasts. At the first breath of October, the hillside at Appledore fires up with the living crimson of the huckleberry-bushes, as if a blazing torch had been applied to it; the slanting light at sunrise and sunset makes a wonderful glory across it. The sky deepens its blue; beneath it the brilliant sea glows into violet, and flashes into splendid purple where the "tide-rip," or eddying winds, make long streaks across its surface (poets are not wrong who talk of "purple seas,") the air is clear and sparkling, the lovely summer haze withdraws, all things take a crisp and tender outline, and the cry of the curlew and the plover is doubly sweet through the pure, cool air. Then sunsets burn in clear and tranquil skies, or flame in piled magnificence of clouds. Some night a long bar lies, like a smouldering brand, along the horizon, deep carmine where the sun has touched it; and out of that bar breaks a sudden gale before morning, and a fine fury and tumult begins to rage. Then comes the fitful weather,—wild winds and hurrying waves, low, scudding clouds, tremendous rains that shut out everything; and the rocks lie weltering between the sea and sky, with the brief fire of the leaves quenched and swept away on the hillside,— only rushing wind and streaming water everywhere, as if a second deluge were flooding the world.[3]

After such a rain comes a gale from the south-east to sweep the sky clear,—a gale so furious that it blows the sails straight out of the bolt-ropes, if any vessel is so unfortunate as to be caught in it with a rag of canvas aloft; and the coast is strewn with the wrecks of such craft as happen to be caught on the lee shore, for

"Anchors drag, and topmasts lap,"

and nothing can hold against this terrible, blind fury. It is appalling to listen to the shriek of such a wind, even though one is safe upon a rock that cannot move; and more dreadful is it to see the destruction one cannot lift a finger to avert.

As the air grows colder, curious atmospheric effects become visible. At the first biting cold the distant mainland has the appearance of being taken off its feet, as it were,—the line shrunken and distorted, detached from the water at both ends: it is as if one looked under it and saw the sky beyond. Then, on bright mornings with a brisk wind, little wafts of mist rise between the quick, short waves, and melt away before noon. At some periods of intense cold these mists, which are never in banks like fog, rise in irregular, whirling columns reaching to the clouds,—shadowy phantoms, torn and wild, that stalk past like Ossian's ghosts,[4] solemnly and noiselessly throughout the bitter day. When the sun drops down behind these weird processions, with a

3. A reference to the first flood, the biblical story of Noah, and the destruction of the world in very early times; see Genesis 6–9.
4. Ossian was a legendary Irish warrior and poet said to have lived in the third century A.D., whose adventures are recounted in the Ossianic cycle of tales. In the 1760s the Scottish poet James MacPherson published epic poems which he falsely attributed to Ossian.

dark-red, lurid light, it is like a vast conflagration, wonderful and terrible to see. The columns, that strike and fall athwart the island, sweep against the windows with a sound like sand, and lie on the ground in ridges, like fine, sharp hail; yet the heavens are clear, the heavily rolling sea dark-green and white, and, between the breaking crests, the misty columns stream toward the sky.

Sometimes a totally different vapor, like cold, black smoke, rolls out from the land, and flows over the sea to an unknown distance, swallowing up the islands on its way. Its approach is hideous to witness. "It's all thick o' black vapor," some islander announces, coming in from out of doors; just as they say, "It's all thick o' white foam," when the sudden squall tears the sea into fringes of spray.

In December the colors seem to fade out of the world, and utter ungraciousness prevails. The great, cool, whispering, delicious sea, that encircled us with a thousand caresses the beautiful summer through, turns slowly our sullen and inveterate enemy; leaden it lies beneath a sky like tin, and rolls its "white, cold, heavy-plunging foam"[5] against a shore of iron. Each island wears its chalk-white girdle of ice between the rising and falling tides (edged with black at low-water, where the lowest-growing seaweed is exposed), making the stern bare rocks above more forbidding by their contrast with its stark whiteness,—and the whiteness of salt-water ice is ghastly. Nothing stirs abroad, except perhaps

"A lonely sea-bird crosses,
With one waft of wing,"[6]

your view, as you gaze from some spray-in-crusted window; or you behold the weather-beaten schooners creeping along the blurred coast-line from Cape Elizabeth and the northern ports of Maine towards Cape Ann, laden with lumber or lime, and sometimes, rarely, with hay or provisions.

After winter has fairly set in, the lonely dwellers at the Isles of Shoals find life quite as much as they can manage, being so entirely thrown upon their own resources that it requires all the philosophy at their disposal to answer the demand. In the village, where several families make a little community, there should be various human interests outside each separate fireside; but of their mode of life I know little. Upon three of the islands live isolated families, cut off by the "always wind-obeying deep" from each other and from the mainland, sometimes for weeks together, when the gales are fiercest, with no letters nor intercourse with any living thing. Some sullen day in December the snow begins to fall, and the last touch of desolation is laid upon the scene; there is nothing any more but white snow and dark water, hemmed in by a murky horizon; and nothing moves or sounds within its circle but the sea harshly assailing the shore, and

5. Tennyson, "A Dream of Fair Women."   6. Tennyson, "The Captain."

the chill wind that sweeps across. Toward night the wind begins to rise, the snow whirls and drifts, and clings wherever it can find a resting-place; and though so much is blown away, yet there is enough left to smother up the rock and make it almost impossible to move about on it. The drifts sometimes are very deep in the hollows; one winter, sixteen sheep were buried in a drift, in which they remained a week, and, strange to say, only one was dead when they were discovered. One goes to sleep in the muffled roar of the storm, and wakes to find it still raging with senseless fury; all day it continues; towards night the curtain of falling flakes withdraws, a faint light shows westward; slowly the clouds roll together, the lift grows bright with pale, clear blue over the land, the wind has hauled to the northwest, and the storm is at an end. When the clouds are swept away by the besom[7] of the pitiless northwest, how the stars glitter in the frosty sky! What wondrous streamers of northern lights flare through the winter darkness! I have seen the sky at midnight crimson and emerald and orange and blue in palpitating sheets along the whole northern half of the heavens, or rosy to the zenith, or belted with a bar of solid yellow light from east to west, as if the world were a basket, and it the golden handle thereto. The weather becomes of the first importance to the dwellers on the rock; the changes of the sky and sea, the flitting of the coasters to and fro, the visits of the sea-fowl, sunrise and sunset, the changing moon, the northern lights, the constellations that wheel in splendor through the winter night,— all are noted with a love and careful scrutiny that is seldom given by people living in populous places. One grows accustomed to the aspect of the constellations, and they seem like the faces of old friends looking down out of the awful blackness; and when in summer the great Orion disappears, how it is missed out of the sky! I remember the delight with which we caught a glimpse of the planet Mercury, in March, 1868, following close at the heels of the sinking sun, redly shining in the reddened horizon,—a stranger mysterious and utterly unknown before.

For these things make our world: there are no lectures, operas, concerts, theatres, no music of any kind, except what the waves may whisper in rarely gentle moods; no galleries of wonders like the Natural History rooms, in which it is so fascinating to wander; no streets, shops, carriages, no postman, no neighbors, not a door-bell within the compass of the place! Never was life so exempt from interruptions. The eight or ten small schooners that carry on winter fishing, flying to and fro through foam and squall to set and haul in their trawls, at rare intervals bring a mail,—an accumulation of letters, magazines, and newspapers that it requires a long time to plod through. This is the greatest excitement of the long winters; and no one can truly appreci-

---

7. An old English word meaning broom; often used in the phrase "a besom of destruction." See Isaiah 14.23.

ate the delight of letters till he has lived where he can hear from his
friends only once in a month.

But the best balanced human mind is prone to lose its elasticity, and
stagnate, in this isolation. One learns immediately the value of work to
keep one's wits clear, cheerful, and steady; just as much real work of
the body as it can bear without weariness being always beneficent, but
here indispensable. And in this matter women have the advantage of
men, who are condemned to fold their hands when their tasks are
done. No woman need ever have a vacant minute,—there are so many
pleasant, useful things which she may, and had better do. Blessed be
the man who invented knitting! (I never heard that a woman invented
this or any other art.) It is the most charming and picturesque of quiet
occupations, leaving the knitter free to read aloud, or talk, or think,
while steadily and surely beneath the flying fingers the comfortable
stocking grows.

No one can dream what a charm there is in taking care of pets,
singing-birds, plants, etc., with such advantages of solitude; how every
leaf and bud and flower is pored over, and admired, and loved! A
whole conservatory, flushed with azaleas, and brilliant with forests of
camellias and every precious exotic that blooms, could not impart so
much delight as I have known a single rose to give, unfolding in the
bleak bitterness of a day in February, when this side of the planet
seemed to have arrived at its culmination of hopelessness, with the
Isles of Shoals the most hopeless speck upon its surface. One gets close
to the heart of these things; they are almost as precious as Picciola to
the prisoner,[8] and yield a fresh and constant joy, such as the pleasure-
seeking inhabitants of cities could not find in their whole round of
shifting diversions. With a bright and cheerful interior, open fires,
books, and pictures, windows full of thrifty blossoming plants and
climbing vines, a family of singing-birds, plenty of work, and a clear
head and quiet conscience, it would go hard if one could not be happy
even in such loneliness. Books, of course, are inestimable. Nowhere
does one follow a play of Shakespeare's with greater zest, for it brings
the whole world, which you need, about you; doubly precious the deep
thoughts wise men have given to help us,—doubly sweet the songs of
all the poets; for nothing comes between to distract you.

One realizes how hard it was for Robinson Crusoe to keep the record
of his lonely days; for even in a family of eight or nine the succession
is kept with difficulty. I recollect that, after an unusually busy Saturday, when household work was done, and lessons said, and the family
were looking forward to Sunday and merited leisure, at sunset came a
young Star-Islander on some errand to our door. One said to him,
"Well, Jud, how many fish have they caught today at Star?" Jud looked
askance and answered, like one who did not wish to be trifled with,

8. "Picciola," a story written by Joseph Xavier Boniface (1797–1864) about a prisoner who found consolation
cultivating a flower.

"We don't go a-fishing Sundays!" So we had lost our Sunday, thinking it was Saturday; and next day began the usual business, with no break of refreshing rest between.

Though the thermometer says that here it is twelve degrees warmer in winter than on the mainland, the difference is hardly perceptible,— the situation is so bleak, while the winds of the north and west bite like demons, with all the bitter breath of the snowy continent condensed in their deadly chill. Easterly and southerly gales are milder; we have no east winds such as sadden humanity on shore; they are tempered to gentleness by some mysterious means. Sometimes there are periods of cold which, though not intense (the mercury seldom falling lower than 11° above zero), are of such long duration that the fish are killed in the sea. This happens frequently with perch, the dead bodies of which strew the shores and float on the water in masses. Sometimes ice forms in the mouth of the Piscataqua River, which, continually broken into unequal blocks by the rushing tide and the immense pressure of the outer ocean, fills the space between the islands and the shore, so that it is very difficult to force a boat through. The few schooners moored about the islands become so loaded with ice that sometimes they sink; every plunge into the assailing waves adds a fresh crust, infinitely thin; but in twenty-four hours enough accumulates to sink the vessel; and it is part of the day's work in the coldest weather to beat off the ice,—and hard work it is. Every time the bowsprit dips under, the man who sits astride it is immersed to his waist in the freezing water, as he beats at the bow to free the laboring craft. I cannot imagine a harder life than the sailors lead in winter in the coasting-vessels that stream in endless processions to and fro along the shore; and they seem to be the hardest set of people under the sun,—so rough and reckless that they are not pleasant even at a distance. Sometimes they land here. A crew of thirteen or fourteen came on shore last winter; they might have been the ghosts of the men who manned the picaroons[9] that used to swarm in these seas. A more piratical-looking set could not well be imagined. They roamed about, and glared in at the windows with weather-beaten, brutal faces, and eyes that showed traces of whiskey, ugly and unmistakable.

No other visitors break the solitude of Appledore, except neighbors from Star once in a while; if any one is sick, they send, perhaps, for medicine or milk; or they bring some rare fish; or if any one dies, and they cannot reach the mainland, they come to get a coffin made. I never shall forget one long, dreary, drizzly northeast storm, when two men rowed across from Star to Appledore on this errand. A little child had died, and they could not sail to the mainland, and had no means to construct a coffin among themselves. All day I watched the making of that little chrysalis; and at night the last nail was driven in, and it lay across a bench in the midst of the litter of the workshop, and a

9. Pirate ships.

curious stillness seemed to emanate from the senseless boards. I went back to the house and gathered a handful of scarlet geranium, and returned with it through the rain. The brilliant blossoms were sprinkled with glittering drops. I laid them in the little coffin, while the wind wailed so sorrowfully outside, and the rain poured against the windows. Two men came through the mist and storm, and one swung the light little shell to his shoulder, and they carried it away, and the gathering darkness shut down and hid them as they tossed among the waves. I never saw the little girl, but where they buried her I know: the lighthouse shines close by, and every night the quiet, constant ray steals to her grave and softly touches it, as if to say, with a caress, "Sleep well! Be thankful you are spared so much that I see humanity endure, fixed here forever where I stand!"

It is exhilarating, spite of the intense cold, to wake to the brightness the northwest gale always brings, after the hopeless smother of a prolonged snow-storm. The sea is deep indigo, whitened with flashing waves all over the surface; the sky is speckless; no cloud passes across it the whole day long; and the sun sets red and clear, without any abatement of the wind. The spray flying on the western shore for a moment is rosy as the sinking sun shines through, but for a moment only,—and again there is nothing but the ghastly whiteness of the salt-water ice, the cold, gray rock, the sullen, foaming brine, the unrelenting heavens, and the sharp wind cutting like a knife. All night long it roars beneath the hollow sky,—roars still at sunrise. Again the day passes precisely like the one gone before; the sun lies in a glare of quicksilver on the western water, sinks again in the red west to rise on just such another day; and thus goes on, for weeks sometimes, with an exasperating pertinacity that would try the most philosophical patience. There comes a time when just that glare of quicksilver on the water is not to be endured a minute longer. During this period no boat goes to or comes from the mainland, and the prisoners on the rock are cut off from all intercourse with their kind. Abroad, only the cattle move, crowding into the sunniest corners, and stupidly chewing the cud; and the hens and ducks, that chatter and cackle and cheerfully crow in spite of fate and the northwest gale. The dauntless and graceful gulls soar on their strong pinions over the drift cast up about the coves. Sometimes flocks of snow-buntings wheel about the house and pierce the loud breathing of the wind with sweet, wild cries. And often the spectral arctic owl may be seen on a height, sitting upright, like a column of snow, its large, round head slowly turning from left to right, ever on the alert, watching for the rats that plague the settlement almost as grievously as they did Hamelin town, in Brunswick, five hundred years ago.[1]

How the rats came here first is not known; probably some old ship

---

1. A reference to the German legend of the town of Hamelin cured of a rat infestation by the piping of the Pied Piper.

imported them. They live partly on mussels, the shells of which lie in heaps about their holes, as the violet-lined fresh-water shells lie about the nests of the muskrats on the mainland. They burrow among the rocks close to the shore, in favorable spots, and, somewhat like the moles, make subterranean galleries, whence they issue at low tide, and, stealing to the crevices of seaweed-curtained rocks, they fall upon and dislodge any unfortunate crabs they may find, and kill and devour them. Many a rat has caught a Tartar[2] in this perilous kind of hunting, has been dragged into the sea and killed,—drowned in the clutches of the crab he sought to devour; for the strength of these shell-fish is something astonishing.

Several snowy owls haunt the islands the whole winter long. I have never heard them cry like other owls; when disturbed or angry, they make a sound like a watchman's rattle, very loud and harsh, or they whistle with intense shrillness, like a human being. Their habitual silence adds to their ghostliness; and when at noonday they sit, high up, snow-white above the snow-drifts, blinking their pale yellow eyes in the sun, they are weird indeed. One night in March I saw one perched upon a rock between me and the "last remains of sunset dimly burning" in the west, his curious outline drawn black against the redness of the sky, his large head bent forward, and the whole aspect meditative and most human in its expression. I longed to go out and sit beside him and talk to him in the twilight, to ask of him the story of his life, or, if he would have permitted it, to watch him without a word. The plumage of this creature is wonderfully beautiful,—white, with scattered spots like little flecks of tawny cloud,—and his black beak and talons are powerful and sharp as iron; he might literally grapple his friend, or his enemy, with hooks of steel. As he is clothed in a mass of down, his outlines are so soft that he is like an enormous snowflake while flying; and he is a sight worth seeing when he stretches wide his broad wings, and sweeps down on his prey, silent and swift, with an unerring aim, and bears it off to the highest rock he can find, to devour it. In the summer one finds frequently upon the heights a little, solid ball of silvery fur and pure white bones, washed and bleached by the rain and sun; it is the rat's skin and skeleton in a compact bundle, which the owl rejects after having swallowed it.

Some quieter day, on the edge of a southerly wind, perhaps, boats go out over the gray, sad water after sea-fowl,—the murres that swim in little companies, keeping just out of reach of shot, and are so spiteful that they beat the boat with their beaks, when wounded, in impotent rage, till they are despatched with an oar or another shot; or kit-tiwakes,—exquisite creatures like living forms of snow and cloud in color, with beaks and feet of dull gold,—that come when you wave a white handkerchief, and flutter almost within reach of your hand; or oldwives, called by the natives *scoldenores*, with clean white caps; or

2. Grappled with an unexpectedly formidable opponent.

clumsy eider-ducks, or coots, or mergansers, or whatever they may find. Black ducks, of course, are often shot. Their jet-black, shining plumage is splendidly handsome, set off with the broad, flame-colored beak. Little auks, stormy-petrels, loons, grebes, lords-and-ladies, sea-pigeons, sea-parrots, various guillemots, and all sorts of gulls abound. Sometimes an eagle sweeps over; gannets pay occasional visits; the great blue heron is often seen in autumn and spring. One of the most striking birds is the cormorant, called here "shag"; from it the rock at Duck Island takes its name. It used to be an object of almost awful[3] interest to me when I beheld it perched upon White Island Head,—a solemn figure, high and dark against the clouds. Once, while living on that island, in the thickest of a great storm in autumn, when we seemed to be set between two contending armies, deafened by the continuous cannonading of breakers, and lashed and beaten by winds and waters till it was almost impossible to hear ourselves speak, we became aware of another sound, which pierced to our ears, bringing a sudden terror lest it should be the voices of human beings. Opening the window a little, what a wild combination of sounds came shrieking in! A large flock of wild geese had settled for safety upon the rock, and completely surrounded us,—agitated, clamorous, weary. We might have secured any number of them, but it would have been a shameful thing. We were glad, indeed, that they should share our little foothold in that chaos, and they flew away unhurt when the tempest lulled. I was a very young child when this happened, but I never can forget that autumn night,—it seemed so wonderful and pitiful that those storm-beaten birds should have come crying to our rock; and the strange, wild chorus that swept in when the window was pried open a little took so strong a hold upon my imagination that I shall hear it as long as I live. The lighthouse, so beneficent to mankind, is the destroyer of birds,—of land birds particularly, though in thick weather sea-birds are occasionally bewildered into breaking their heads against the glass, plunging forward headlong towards the light, just as the frail moth of summer evenings madly seeks its death in the candle's blaze. Some-times in autumn, always in spring, when birds are migrating, they are destroyed in such quantities by this means that it is painful to reflect upon. The keeper living at the island three years ago told me that he picked up three hundred and seventy-five in one morning at the foot of the lighthouse, all dead. They fly with such force against the glass that their beaks are often splintered. The keeper said he found the destruction greatest in hazy weather, and he thought "they struck a ray at a great distance and followed it up." Many a May morning have I wandered about the rock at the foot of the tower mourning over a little apron brimful of sparrows, swallows, thrushes, robins, fire-winged blackbirds, many-colored warblers and fly-catchers, beautifully clothed yellow-birds, nuthatches, cat-birds, even the purple finch and

---

3. Appalling, fearsome.

scarlet tanager and golden oriole, and many more beside,—enough to break the heart of a small child to think of! Once a great eagle flew against the lantern and shivered the glass. That was before I lived there; but after we came, two gulls cracked one of the large, clear panes, one stormy night.

The sea-birds are comparatively few and shy at this time; but I remember when they were plentiful enough, when on Duck Island in summer the "medrakes," or tern, made rude nests on the beach, and the little yellow gulls, just out of the eggs, ran tumbling about among the stones, hiding their foolish heads in every crack and cranny, and, like the ostrich, imagining themselves safe so long as they could not see the danger. And even now the sandpipers build in numbers on the islands, and the young birds, which look like tiny tufts of fog, run about among the bayberry-bushes, with sweet, scared piping. They are exquisitely beautiful and delicate, covered with a down just like gray mist, with brilliant black eyes, and slender, graceful legs that make one think of grass-stems. And here the loons congregate in spring and autumn. These birds seem to me the most human and at the same time the most demoniac of their kind. I learned to imitate their different cries; they are wonderful! At one time the loon language was so familiar that I could almost always summon a considerable flock by going down to the water and assuming the neighborly and conversational tone which they generally use: after calling a few minutes, first a far-off voice responded, then other voices answered him, and when this was kept up a while, half a dozen birds would come sailing in. It was the most delightful little party imaginable; so comical were they, so entertaining, that it was impossible not to laugh aloud,—and they could laugh too, in a way which chilled the marrow of one's bones. They always laugh, when shot at, if they are missed; as the Shoalers say, "They laugh like a warrior." But their long, wild, melancholy cry before a storm is the most awful note I ever heard from a bird. It is so sad, so hopeless,—a clear, high shriek, shaken, as it drops into silence, into broken notes that make you think of the fluttering of a pennon in the wind,—a shudder of sound. They invariably utter this cry before a storm.

Between the gales from all points of the compass, that

> " 'twixt the green sea and the azured vault
>   Set roaring war,"

some day there falls a dead calm; the whole expanse of the ocean is like a mirror; there's not a whisper of a wave, not a sigh from any wind about the world,—an awful, breathless pause prevails. Then if a loon swims into the motionless little bights[4] about the island, and raises his weird cry, the silent rocks re-echo the unearthly tone, and it seems as if the creature were in league with the mysterious forces that are so

---

4. A bend or curve in a shoreline.

soon to turn this deathly stillness into confusion and dismay. All through the day the ominous quiet lasts; in the afternoon, while yet the sea is glassy, a curious undertone of mournful sound can be perceived,—not fitful,—a steady moan such as the wind makes over the mouth of an empty jar. Then the islanders say, "Do you hear Hog Island crying? Now look out for a storm!" No one knows how that low moaning is produced, or why Appledore, of all the islands, should alone lament before the tempest. Through its gorges, perhaps, some current of wind sighs with that hollow cry. Yet the sea could hardly keep its unruffled surface were a wind abroad sufficient to draw out the boding sound. Such a calm preceded the storm which destroyed the Minot's Ledge Lighthouse in 1849. I never knew such silence. Though the sun blazed without a cloud, the sky and sea were utterly wan and colorless, and before sunset the mysterious tone began to vibrate in the breezeless air. "Hog Island's crying!" said the islanders. One could but think of the Ancient Mariner,[5] as the angry sun went down in a brassy glare, and still no ripple broke the calm. But with the twilight gathered the waiting wind, slowly and steadily; and before morning the shock of the breakers was like the incessant thundering of heavy guns; the solid rock perceptibly trembled; windows shook, and glass and china rattled in the house. It is impossible to describe the confusion, the tumult, the rush and roar and thunder of waves and wind overwhelming those rocks,—the whole Atlantic rushing headlong to cast itself upon them. It was very exciting: the most timid among us lost all sense of fear. Before the next night the sea had made a breach through the valley on Appledore, in which the houses stand,—a thing that never had happened within the memory of the oldest inhabitant. The waves piled in from the eastward (where Old Harry was tossing the breakers sky-high),—a maddened troop of giants, sweeping everything before them,—and followed one another, white as milk, through the valley from east to west, strewing the space with boulders from a solid wall six feet high and as many thick, which ran across the top of the beach, and which one tremendous wave toppled over like a child's fence of blocks. Kelp and seaweed were piled in banks high up along the shore, and strewed the doorsteps; and thousands of the hideous creatures known among the Shoalers as sea-mice, a holothurian (a livid, shapeless mass of torpid life), were scattered in all directions. While the storm was at its height, it was impossible to do anything but watch it through windows beaten by the blinding spray which burst in flying clouds all over the island, drenching every inch of the soil in foaming brine. In the coves the "yeasty surges"[6] were churned into yellow masses of foam, that blew across in trembling flakes, and clung wherever they lit, leaving a hoary scum of salt when dry, which remained till sweet, fair water dropped out of the clouds to wash it all away. It

---

5. Samuel Taylor Coleridge, "The Rime of the An-   6. Tennyson, "The Sailor Boy."
cient Mariner."

was long before the sea went down; and, days after the sun began to shine, the fringe of spray still leaped skyward from the eastern shore, and Shag and Mingo Rocks at Duck Island tossed their distant clouds of snow against the blue.

After the wind subsided, it was curious to examine the effects of the breakers on the eastern shore, where huge masses of rock were struck off from the cliffs, and flung among the wild heaps of scattered boulders, to add to the already hopeless confusion of the gorges. The eastern aspects of the islands change somewhat every year or two from this cause; and, indeed, over all their surfaces continual change goes on from the action of the weather. Under the hammer and chisel of frost and heat, masses of stone are detached and fall from the edges of cliffs, whole ledges become disintegrated, the rock cracks in smooth, thin sheets, and, once loosened, the whole mass can be pulled out, sheet by sheet. Twenty years ago those subtle, irresistible tools of the weather had cracked off a large mass of rock from a ledge on the slope of a gentle declivity. I could just lay my hand in the space then: now three men can walk abreast between the ledge and the detached mass; and nothing has touched it save heat and cold. The whole aspect of the rocks is infinitely aged. I never can see the beautiful salutation of sunrise upon their hoary fronts, without thinking how many millions of times they have answered to that delicate touch. On Boone Island,—a low, dangerous rock fifteen miles east of the Shoals,—the sea has even greater opportunities of destruction, the island is so low. Once, after a stormy night, the lighthouse-keeper told me the family found a great stone, weighing half a ton, in the back entry, which Father Neptune had deposited there,—his card, with his compliments!

Often tremendous breakers encompass the islands when the surface of the sea is perfectly calm and the weather serene and still,—the results of great storms far out at sea. A "long swell" swings indolently, and the ponderous waves roll in as if tired and half asleep, to burst into clouds of splendor against the cliffs. Very different is their hurried, eager breaking when the shoulder of a gale compels them. There is no sound more gentle, more slumberous, than the distant roll of these billows,—

"The rolling sea resounding soft,"[7]

as Spenser has it. The rush of a fully alive and closely pursued breaker is, at a distance, precisely like that which a rocket makes, sweeping headlong upward through the air; but the other is a long and peaceful sigh, a dreamy, lulling, beautiful sound, which produces a Lethean forgetfulness[8] of care and pain, makes all earthly ill seem unreal, and it is as if one wandered

7. Edmund Spenser, The Faerie Queene 2.12.33.
8. Lethe is the river of forgetfulness in Hades, the Greek underworld, according to Greek mythology.

"In dreamful wastes, where footless fancies dwell."[9]

It requires a strong effort to emerge from this lotus-eating state of mind. O, lovely it is, on sunny afternoons to sit high up in a crevice of the rock and look down on the living magnificence of breakers such as made music about us after the Minot's Ledge storm,—to watch them gather, one after another,

"Cliffs of emerald topped with snow,
That lift and lift, and then let go
A great white avalanche of thunder,"

which makes the solid earth tremble, and you, clinging to the moist rock, feel like a little cockle-shell! If you are out of the reach of the heavy fall of spray, the fine salt mist will still stream about you, and salute your cheek with the healthful freshness of the brine, make your hair damp, and encrust your eyebrows with salt. While you sit watching the shifting splendor, uprises at once a higher cloud than usual; and across it springs a sudden rainbow, like a beautiful thought beyond the reach of human expression. High over your head the white gulls soar, gathering the sunshine in the snowy hollows of their wings. As you look up to them floating in the fathomless blue, there is something awful in the purity of that arch beneath their wings, in light or shade, as the broad pinions move with stately grace. There is no bird so white,—nor swan, nor dove, nor mystic ibis: about the ocean-marges there is no dust to soil their perfect snow, and no stormy wind can ruffle their delicate plumes,—the beautiful, happy creatures! One never tires of watching them. Again and again appears the rainbow with lovely colors melting into each other and vanishing, to appear again at the next upspringing of the spray. On the horizon the white sails shine; and far and wide spreads the blue of the sea, with nothing between you and the eastern continent across its vast, calm plain.

I well remember my first sight of White Island, where we took up our abode on leaving the mainland. I was scarcely five years old; but from the upper windows of our dwelling in Portsmouth, I had been shown the clustered masts of ships lying at the wharves along the Piscataqua River, faintly outlined against the sky, and, baby as I was, even then I was drawn, with a vague longing, seaward. How delightful was that long, first sail to the Isles of Shoals! How pleasant the unaccustomed sound of the incessant ripple against the boat-side, the sight of the wide water and limitless sky, the warmth of the broad sunshine that made us blink like young sandpipers as we sat in triumph, perched among the household goods with which the little craft was laden! It was at sunset in autumn that we were set ashore on that loneliest, lovely rock, where the lighthouse looked down on us like some tall, black-capped giant, and filled me with awe and wonder. At its base a

9. Tennyson, "Maud."

few goats were grouped on the rock, standing out dark against the red sky as I looked up at them. The stars were beginning to twinkle; the wind blew cold, charged with the sea's sweetness; the sound of many waters half bewildered me. Someone began to light the lamps in the tower. Rich red and golden, they swung round in mid-air; everything was strange and fascinating and new. We entered the quaint little old stone cottage that was for six years our home. How curious it seemed, with its low, whitewashed ceiling and deep window-seats, showing the great thickness of the walls made to withstand the breakers, with whose force we soon grew acquainted! A blissful home the little house became to the children who entered it that quiet evening and slept for the first time lulled by the murmur of the encircling sea. I do not think a happier triad ever existed than we were, living in that profound isolation. It takes so little to make a healthy child happy; and we never wearied of our few resources. True, the winters seemed as long as a whole year to our little minds, but they were pleasant, nevertheless. Into the deep window-seats we climbed, and with pennies (for which we had no other use) made round holes in the thick frost, breathing on them till they were warm, and peeped out at the bright, fierce, windy weather, watching the vessels scudding over the intensely dark blue sea, all "feather-white" where the short waves broke hissing in the cold, and the sea-fowl soaring aloft or tossing on the water; or, in calmer days, we saw how the stealthy Star-Islander paddled among the ledges, or lay for hours stretched on the wet sea-weed, with his gun, watching for wild-fowl. Sometimes the round head of a seal moved about among the kelp-covered rocks. A few are seen every winter, and are occasionally shot; but they are shyer and more alert even than the birds.

We were forced to lay in stores of all sorts in the autumn, as if we were fitting out a ship for an Arctic expedition. The lower story of the lighthouse was hung with mutton and beef, and the store-room packed with provisions.

In the long, covered walk that bridged the gorge between the lighthouse and the house, we played in stormy days; and every evening it was a fresh excitement to watch the lighting of the lamps, and think how far the lighthouse sent its rays, and how many hearts it gladdened with assurance of safety. As I grew older I was allowed to kindle the lamps sometimes myself. That was indeed a pleasure. So little a creature as I might do that much for the great world! But by the fireside our best pleasure lay,—with plants and singing birds and books and playthings and loving care and kindness the cold and stormy season wore itself at last away, and died into the summer calm. We hardly saw a human face beside our own all winter; but with the spring came manifold life to our lonely dwelling,—human life among other forms. Our neighbors from Star rowed across; the pilot-boat from Portsmouth steered over, and brought us letters, newspapers, magazines, and told us the news of months. The faint echoes from the far-off world hardly touched us little ones. We listened to the talk of our elders. "Winfield Scott and Santa Anna!" "The war in Mexico!" "The famine in Ireland!"[1] It all meant nothing to us. We heard the reading aloud of details of the famine, and saw tears in the eyes of the reader, and were vaguely sorry; but the fate of Red Riding-Hood was much more near and dreadful to us. We waited for the spring with an eager longing; the advent of the growing grass, the birds and flowers and insect life, the soft skies and softer winds, the everlasting beauty of the thousand tender tints that clothed the world,—these things brought us unspeakable bliss. To the heart of Nature one must needs be drawn in such a life; and very soon I learned how richly she repays in deep refreshment the reverent love of her worshipper. With the first warm days we built our little mountains of wet gravel on the beach, and danced after the sandpipers at the edge of the foam, shouted to the gossiping kittiwakes that fluttered above, or watched the pranks of the burgomaster gull, or cried to the crying loons. The gannet's long, white wings stretched overhead, perhaps, or the dusky shag made a sudden shadow in mid-air, or we startled on some lonely ledge the great blue heron that flew off, trailing legs and wings, stork-like, against the clouds. Or, in the sunshine on the bare rocks, we cut from the broad, brown leaves of the slippery, varnished kelps, grotesque shapes of man and bird and beast that withered in the wind and blew away; or we fashioned rude boats from bits of driftwood, manned them with a weird crew of kelpies, and set them adrift on the great deep, to float we cared not whither.

We played with the empty limpet-shells; they were mottled gray and brown, like the song-sparrow's breast. We launched fleets of purple mussel-shells on the still pools in the rocks, left by the tide,—pools that were like bits of fallen rainbow with the wealth of the sea, with tints of delicate sea-weeds, crimson and green and ruddy brown and violet; where wandered the pearly eolis with rosy spines and fairy horns; and the large, round sea-urchins, like a boss upon a shield, were fastened here and there on the rock at the bottom, putting out from their green, prickly spikes transparent tentacles to seek their invisible food. Rosy and lilac star-fish clung to the sides; in some dark nook, perhaps, a holothure unfolded its perfect ferns, a lovely, warm buff color, delicate as frost-work; little forests of coralline moss grew up in stillness, gold-colored shells crept about, and now and then flashed the silver-darting fins of slender minnows. The dimmest recesses were haunts of sea-anemones that opened wide their starry flowers to the flowing tide, or drew themselves together, and hung in large, half-transparent drops, like clusters of some strange, amber-colored fruit, along the crevices as the water ebbed away. Sometimes we were cruel

---

1. During 1845–49, the potato blights produced the great famine, which resulted in extensive Irish migration to the United States. Winfield Scott and Antonio Lopez de Santa Anna: opposing generals from the United States and Mexico during the war with Mexico (1846–47). War in Mexico: ostensibly fought over the question of the boundary between Texas and Mexico; President James K. Polk used victory in this war to gain California from Mexico.

enough to capture a female lobster hiding in a deep cleft, with her millions of mottled eggs; or we laughed to see the hermit-crabs challenge each other, and come out and fight a deadly battle till the stronger overcame, and, turning the weaker topsy-turvy, possessed himself of his ampler cockle-shell, and scuttled off with it triumphant. Or, pulling all together, we dragged up the long kelps, or devil's-aprons; their roots were almost always fastened about large, living mussels; these we unclasped, carrying the mussels home to be cooked; fried in crumbs or batter, they were as good as oysters. We picked out from the kelp-roots a kind of star-fish which we called sea-spider; the moment we touched it an extraordinary process began. One by one it disjointed all its sections,—whether from fear or anger we knew not; but it threw itself away, bit by bit, until nothing was left of it save the little, round body whence the legs had sprung!

With crab and limpet, with grasshopper and cricket, we were friends and neighbors, and we were never tired of watching the land-spiders that possessed the place. Their webs covered every window-pane to the lighthouse top, and they rebuilt them as fast as they were swept down. One variety lived among the round gray stones on the beach, just above high-water mark, and spun no webs at all. Large and black, they speckled the light stones, swarming in the hot sun; at the first footfall they vanished beneath the pebbles.

All the cracks in the rocks were draped with swinging veils like the window-panes. How often have we marveled at them, after a fog or a heavy fall of dew, in the early morning, when every slender thread was strung with glittering drops,—the whole symmetrical web a wonder of shining jewels trembling in the breeze! Tennyson's lines,

> "The cobweb woven across the cannon's throat
> Shall shake its threaded tears in the wind no more,"[2]

always bring back to my mind the memory of those delicate, spangled draperies, more beautiful than any mortal loom could weave, that curtained the rocks at White Island and "shook their threaded tears" in every wind.

Sometimes we saw the bats wheel through the summer dusk, and in profoundly silent evenings heard, from the lighthouse top, their shrill, small cries, their voices sharper and finer than needle-points. One day I found one clinging to the under side of a shutter,—a soft, dun-colored, downy lump. I took it in my hand, and in an instant it changed to a hideous little demon, and its fierce white teeth met in the palm of my hand. So much fury in so small a beast I never encountered, and I was glad enough to give him his liberty without more ado.

A kind of sandhopper about an inch long, that infested the beach, was a great source of amusement. Lifting the stranded sea-weed that marked the high-water line, we always startled a gray and brown cloud

---

2. Tennyson, "Maud."

of them from beneath it, leaping away, like tiny kangaroos, out of sight. In storms these were driven into the house, forcing their way through every crack and cranny till they strewed the floors,—the sea so encircled us! Dying immediately upon leaving the water from which they fled, they turned from a clear brown, or what Mr. Kingsley[3] would call a "pellucid gray," to bright brick-color, like a boiled lobster, and many a time I have swept them up in ruddy heaps; they looked like bits of coral.

I remember in the spring kneeling on the ground to seek the first blades of grass that pricked through the soil, and bringing them into the house to study and wonder over. Better than a shop full of toys they were to me! Whence came their color? How did they draw their sweet, refreshing tint from the brown earth, or the limpid air, or the white light? Chemistry was not at hand to answer me, and all her wisdom would not have dispelled the wonder. Later the little scarlet pimpernel charmed me. It seemed more than a flower; it was like a human thing. I knew it by its homely name of poor-man's weather-glass. It was so much wiser than I, for, when the sky was yet without a cloud, softly it clasped its small red petals together, folding its golden heart in safety from the shower that was sure to come! How could it know so much? Here is a question science cannot answer. The pimpernel grows everywhere about the islands, in every cleft and cranny where a suspicion of sustenance for its slender root can lodge; and it is one of the most exquisite of flowers, so rich in color, so quaint and dainty in its method of growth. I never knew its silent warning fail. I wondered much how every flower knew what to do and to be; why the morning-glory didn't forget sometimes, and bear a cluster of elder-bloom, or the elder hang out pennons of gold and purple like the iris, or the golden-rod suddenly blaze out a scarlet plume, the color of the pimpernel, was a mystery to my childish thought. And why did the sweet wild primrose wait till after sunset to unclose its pale yellow buds; why did it unlock its treasure of rich perfume to the night alone? Few flowers bloomed for me upon the lonesome rock; but I made the most of all I had, and neither knew of nor desired more. Ah, how beautiful they were! Tiny stars of crimson sorrel threaded on their long brown stems; the blackberry blossoms in bridal white; the surprise of the blue-eyed grass; the crowfoot flowers, like drops of yellow gold spilt about among the short grass and over the moss; the rich, blue-purple beach-pea, the sweet, spiked germander, and the homely, delightful yarrow that grows thickly on all the islands. Sometimes its broad clusters of dull white bloom are stained a lovely reddish-purple, as if with the light of sunset. I never saw it colored so elsewhere. Quantities of slender, widespreading mustard-bushes grew about the house; their delicate flowers were like fragrant golden clouds. Dandelions, buttercups, and clover

---

3. Charles Kingsley (1819–1875), British poet, novelist, historian, minister, and sermon-writer; profes- sor of modern history at Cambridge University 1860–69.

were not denied to us; though we had no daisies nor violets nor wild roses, no asters, but gorgeous spikes of golden-rod, and wonderful wild morning-glories, whose long, pale, ivory buds I used to find in the twilight, glimmering among the dark leaves, waiting for the touch of dawn to unfold and become each an exquisite incarnate blush,—the perfect color of a South Sea shell. They ran wild, knotting and twisting about the rocks, and smothering the loose boulders in the gorges with lush green leaves and pink blossoms.

Many a summer morning have I crept out of the still house before any one was awake, and, wrapping myself closely from the chill wind of dawn, climbed to the top of the high cliff called the Head to watch the sunrise. Pale grew the lighthouse flame before the broadening day as, nestled in a crevice at the cliff's edge, I watched the shadows draw away and morning break. Facing the east and south, with all the Atlantic before me, what happiness was mine as the deepening rose-color flushed the delicate cloudflocks that dappled the sky, where the gulls soared, rosy too, while the calm sea blushed beneath. Or perhaps it was a cloudless sunrise with a sky of orange-red, and the sea-line silver-blue against it, peaceful as heaven. Infinite variety of beauty always awaited me, and filled me with an absorbing, unreasoning joy such as makes the song-sparrow sing,—a sense of perfect bliss. Coming back in the sunshine, the morning-glories would lift up their faces, all awake, to my adoring gaze. Like countless rosy trumpets sometimes I thought they were, tossed everywhere about the rocks, turned up to the sky, or drooping toward the ground, or looking east, west, north, south, in silent loveliness. It seemed as if they had gathered the peace of the golden morning in their still depths even as my heart had gathered it.

In some of those matchless summer mornings when I went out to milk the little dun cow, it was hardly possible to go farther than the doorstep, for pure wonder, as I looked abroad at the sea lying still, like a vast, round mirror, the tide drawn away from the rich brown rocks, a sail or two asleep in the calm, not a sound abroad except a few bird voices; dew lying like jewel-dust sifted over everything,—diamond and ruby, sapphire, topaz, and amethyst, flashing out of the emerald deeps of the tufted grass or from the bending tops. Looking over to the mainland, I could dimly discern in the level sunshine the depths of glowing green woods faintly revealed in the distance, fold beyond fold of hill and valley thickly clothed with the summer's splendor. But my handful of grass was more precious to me than miles of green fields, and I was led to consider every blade where there were so few. Not long ago I had watched them piercing the ground toward the light; now, how strong in their slender grace were these stems, how perfect the poise of the heavy heads that waved with such harmony of movement in the faintest breeze! And I noticed at mid-day when the dew was dry, where the tall, blossoming spears stood in graceful companies, that, before they grew purple, brown, and ripe, when they began to blossom, they put out first a downy ring of pollen in tiny, yellow rays, held by an almost invisible thread, which stood out like an aureole from each slow-waving head,—a fairy-like effect. On Seavey's Island (united to ours by a narrow beach covered at high tide with contending waves) grew one single root of fern, the only one within the circle of my little world. It was safe in a deep cleft, but I was in perpetual anxiety lest my little cow, going there daily to pasture, should leave her cropping of the grass and eat it up some day. Poor little cow! One night she did not come home to be milked as usual, and on going to seek her we found she had caught one foot in a crevice and twisted her hoof entirely off! That was a calamity; for we were forced to summon our neighbors and have her killed on the spot.

I had a scrap of garden, literally not more than a yard square, wherein grew only African marigolds, rich in color as barbaric gold. I knew nothing of John Keats at that time,—poor Keats, "who told Severn that he thought his intensest pleasure in life had been to watch the growth of flowers,"—but I am sure he never felt their beauty more devoutly than the little, half-savage being who knelt, like a fire-worshipper, to watch the unfolding of those golden disks. When, later, the "brave new world" of poets was opened to me, with what power those glowing lines of his went straight to my heart,

> "Open afresh your rounds of starry folds,
> Ye ardent marigolds!"[4]

All flowers had for me such human interest, they were so dear and precious, I hardly liked to gather them, and when they were withered, I carried them all to one place and laid them tenderly together, and never liked to pass the spot where they were hidden.

Once or twice every year came the black, lumbering old "oil-schooner" that brought supplies for the lighthouse, and the inspector, who gravely examined everything, to see if all was in order. He left stacks of clear red and white glass chimneys for the lamps, and several doe-skins for polishing the great, silver-lined copper reflectors, large bundles of wicks, and various pairs of scissors for trimming them, heavy black casks of ill-perfumed whale-oil, and other things, which were all stowed in the round, dimly lighted rooms of the tower. Very awe-struck, we children always crept into corners, and whispered and watched the intruders till they embarked in their ancient, clumsy vessel, and, hoisting their dark, weather-stained sails, bore slowly away again. About ten years ago that old white lighthouse was taken away, and a new, perpendicular brick tower built in its place. The lantern, with its fifteen lamps, ten golden and five red, gave place to Fresnel's powerful single burner,[5] or, rather, three burners in one, enclosed in its case of prisms. The old lighthouse was by far the most

4. John Keats, "I Stood Tip-toe upon a Little Hill."
5. The French physicist Augustin Jean Fresnel (1788–1827), known for his experimentation with diffraction of light, pioneered in the use of compound lenses for lighthouses; the Fresnel lens, first used in the U.S. in 1841, revolutionized lighthouse construction.

picturesque; but perhaps the new one is more effective, the light being, undoubtedly, more powerful.

Often, in pleasant days, the head of the family sailed away to visit the other islands, sometimes taking the children with him, oftener going alone, frequently not returning till after dark. The landing at White Island is so dangerous that the greatest care is requisite, if there is any sea running, to get ashore in safety. Two long and very solid timbers about three feet apart are laid from the boat-house to low-water mark, and between those timbers the boat's bow must be accurately steered; if she goes to the right or the left, woe to her crew unless the sea is calm! Safely lodged in the slip, as it is called, she is drawn up into the boat-house by a capstan, and fastened securely. The light-house gave no ray to the dark rock below it; sending its beams far out to sea, it left us at its foot in greater darkness for its lofty light. So when the boat was out late, in soft, moonless summer nights, I used to light a lantern, and, going down to the water's edge, take my station between the timbers of the slip, and, with the lantern at my feet, sit waiting in the darkness, quite content, knowing my little star was watched for, and that the safety of the boat depended in a great measure upon it. How sweet the summer wind blew, how softly plashed the water round me, how refreshing was the odor of the sparkling brine! High above, the lighthouse rays streamed out into the humid dark, and the cottage windows were ruddy from the glow within. I felt so much a part of the Lord's universe, I was no more afraid of the dark than the waves or winds; but I was glad to hear at last the creaking of the mast and the rattling of the row-locks as the boat approached; and, while yet she was far off, the lighthouse touched her one large sail into sight, so that I knew she was nearing me, and shouted, listening for the reply that came so blithely back to me over the water.

Unafraid, too, we watched the summer tempests, and listened to the deep, melodious thunder rolling away over the rain-calmed ocean. The lightning played over the iron rods that ran from the lighthouse-top down into the sea. Where it lay on the sharp ridgepole of the long, covered walk that spanned the gorge, the strange fire ran up the spikes that were set at equal distances, and burnt like pale flame from their tips. It was fine indeed from the lighthouse itself to watch the storm come rushing over the sea and ingulf us in our helplessness. How the rain weltered down over the great panes of plate glass,—floods of sweet, fresh water that poured off the rocks and mingled with the bitter brine. I wondered why the fresh floods never made the salt sea any sweeter. Those pale flames that we beheld burning from the spikes of the lightning-rod, I suppose were identical with the St. Elmo's fire[6] that I have since seen described as haunting the spars of ships in

6. The bluish glow sometimes seen at the tips of trees or other tall objects in a thunderstrom; derived from the name of a fourth-century saint, Erasmus, whom sailors took as their patron, and who associated the glow with his protection.

thunder-storms. And here I am reminded of a story told by some gentlemen visiting Appledore sixteen or eighteen years ago. They started from Portsmouth for the Shoals in a whaleboat, one evening in summer, with a native Star-Islander, Richard Randall by name, to manage the boat. They had sailed about half the distance, when they were surprised at seeing a large ball of fire, like a rising moon, rolling toward them over the sea from the south. They watched it eagerly as it bore down upon them, and, veering off, went east of them at some little distance, and then passed astern, and there, of course, they expected to lose sight of it; but while they were marveling and speculating, it altered its course, and suddenly began to near them, coming back upon its track against the wind and steadily following in their wake. This was too much for the native Shoaler. He took off his jacket and turned it inside out to exorcise the fiend, and lo, the apparition most certainly disappeared! We heard the excited account of the strange gentlemen and witnessed the holy horror of the boatman on the occasion; but no one could imagine what had set the globe of fire rolling across the sea. Someone suggested that it might be an exhalation, a phosphorescent light, from the decaying body of some dead fish; but in that case it must have been taken in tow by some living finny creature, else how could it have sailed straight "into the teeth of the wind"? It was never satisfactorily accounted for, and must remain a mystery.

One autumn at White Island our little boat had been to Portsmouth for provisions, etc. With the spy-glass we watched her returning, beating against the head wind. The day was bright, but there had been a storm at sea, and the breakers rolled and roared about us. The process of "beating" is so tedious that, though the boat had started in the morning, the sun was sending long yellow light from the west before it reached the island. There was no cessation in those resistless billows that rolled from the Devil's Rock upon the slip; but still the little craft sailed on, striving to reach the landing. The hand at the tiller was firm, but a huge wave swept suddenly in, swerving the boat to the left of the slip, and in a moment she was overturned and flung upon the rocks, and her only occupant tossed high upon the beach, safe except for a few bruises; but what a moment of terror it was for us all, who saw and could not save! All the freight was lost except a roll of iron wire and a barrel of walnuts. These were spread on the floor of an unoccupied eastern chamber in the cottage to dry. And they did dry; but before they were gathered up came a terrible storm from the southeast. It raved and tore at lighthouse and cottage; the sea broke into the windows of that eastern chamber where the walnuts lay, and washed them out till they came dancing down the stairs in briny foam! The sea broke the windows of the house several times during our stay at the lighthouse. Everything shook so violently from the concussion of the breakers, that dishes on the closet shelves fell to the floor, and one member of the family was at first always made sea-sick in storms, by the tremor and deafening confusion. One night when, from the southeast, the very soul of chaos seemed to have been let loose upon the world, the whole ponderous "walk" (the covered bridge that connected the house and lighthouse) was carried thundering down the gorge and dragged out into the raging sea.

It was a distressing situation for us,—cut off from the precious light that must be kept alive; for the breakers were tearing through the gorge so that no living thing could climb across. But the tide could not resist the mighty impulse that drew it down; it was forced to obey the still voice that bade it ebb; all swollen and raging and towering as it was, slowly and surely, at the appointed time, it sank away from our rock, so that, between the billows that still strove to clutch at the white, silent, golden-crowned tower, one could creep across, and scale the height, and wind up the machinery that kept the great clustered light revolving till the gray daylight broke to extinguish it.

I often wondered how it was possible for the sea-birds to live through such storms as these. But, when one could see at all, the gulls were always soaring, in the wildest tumult, and the stormy petrels half flying, half swimming in the hollows of the waves.

Would it were possible to describe the beauty of the calm that followed such tempests! The long lines of silver foam that streaked the tranquil blue, the "tender-curving lines of creamy spray"[7] along the shore, the clear-washed sky, the peaceful yellow light, the mellow breakers murmuring slumberously!

Of all the storms our childish eyes watched with delighted awe, one thunder-storm remains fixed in my memory. Late in an August afternoon it rolled its awful clouds to the zenith, and, after the tumult had subsided, spread its lightened vapors in an under-roof of gray over all the sky. Presently this solemn gray lid was lifted at its western edge, and an insufferable splendor streamed across the world from the sinking sun. The whole heaven was in a blaze of scarlet, across which sprang a rainbow unbroken to the topmost clouds, "with its seven perfect colors chorded in a triumph" against the flaming background; the sea answered the sky's rich blush, and the gray rocks lay drowned in melancholy purple. I hid my face from the glory,—it was too much to bear. Ever I longed to *speak* these things that made life so sweet, to speak the wind, the cloud, the bird's flight, the sea's murmur. A vain longing! I might as well have sighed for the mighty pencil of Michael Angelo[8] to wield in my impotent child's hand. Better to "hush and bless one's self with silence"; but ever the wish grew. Facing the July sunsets, deep red and golden through and through, or watching the summer northern lights,—battalions of brilliant streamers advancing and retreating, shooting upward to the zenith, and glowing like fiery veils before the stars; or when the fog-bow spanned the silver mist of

7. Tennyson, "The Lotos-Eaters."
8. Michaelangelo Buonarroti (1475–1564), Italian sculptor, painter, architect, and poet of the European Renaissance.

morning, or the earth and sea lay shimmering in a golden haze of noon; in storm or calm, by day or night, the manifold aspects of Nature held me and swayed all my thoughts until it was impossible to be silent any longer, and I was fain to mingle my voice with her myriad voices, only aspiring to be in accord with the Infinite harmony, however feeble and broken the notes might be.

*   *   *

Atlantic Monthly, August 1869, February 1870, May 1873; 1873

SARAH ORNE JEWETT
1849–1909

"Born within the scent of the sea but not within sight of it, in a beautiful old house full of strange and lovely things brought home from all over the globe by seafaring ancestors, she spent much of her childhood driving about the country with her doctor father on his professional rounds among the farms" (Cather 16). With these words, Willa Cather introduced her own readers in 1925 to Sarah Orne Jewett—a friend and mentor since 1908—and to the Maine landscape that served as Jewett's subject and inspiration.

Sarah Orne Jewett was born September 3, 1849, in South Berwick, Maine, the second of three sisters. As a child she moved into the eighteenth-century house of her paternal grandfather, Captain Theodore F. Jewett, and she inhabited this house until her death. Jewett received very little formal education as a child but rather studied with her father, Theodore Herman Jewett, whose combination of practical knowledge and wide reading proved invaluable to his writer daughter. Jewett's relationship with her mother, Caroline Frances Perry Jewett, may be inferred from her fiction, which often explores the bonds between daughters and their mothers or older women, and from Jewett's and her sister Mary's devotion to their mother during her invalidism late in life.

Jewett published her first sketch, "Mr. Bruce," in the *Atlantic Monthly*. "The Shore House," her first significant regional publication, appeared in the *Atlantic* in 1873. This sketch and others would comprise *Deephaven* (1877), in whose preface Jewett acknowledges her literary debt to Harriet Beecher Stowe and to *The Pearl of Orr's Island* (1862), which Jewett first read when she was about fourteen. From the time of the publication of *Deephaven*, Jewett's writing career, her interest in regional fiction, and her developing circle of friends became intertwined. It was during this period that she met Annie Adams Fields, then wife of Boston publisher James T. Fields, and many years her husband's junior. And it was during the winter of 1881, following James T. Fields's death (and after Jewett had experienced the death of her father in 1878), that Sarah Jewett and Annie Fields became friends. Extant correspondence from Jewett to Fields during this period records the intense and loving bond that the two women formed. Thereafter, Jewett lived part of each year with Annie Fields at her home at 148 Charles Street in Boston or at her summer cottage in Manchester-by-the-Sea, and part of the year with her mother or sister in South Berwick. As companions in what the late nineteenth century recognized as a stable and primary union between women, referred to as a "Boston marriage," Jewett and Fields maintained a wide circle of friends, which included John Greenleaf Whittier, Thomas Bailey Aldrich, and Celia Thaxter. Together they met, visited, or corresponded with many of the writers in this volume: Rose Terry Cooke, Stowe, Thaxter, Mary Noialles Murfree, Mary Wilkins Freeman, and Cather.

Jewett published numerous collections of regional sketches, including *A White Heron and Other Stories* (1886) and *The Queen's Twin and Other Stories* (1899), as well as *The Country of the Pointed Firs* (1896). On her fifty-third birthday, in 1902, Jewett was seriously injured in a fall from her carriage from which she never fully recovered. She spent the last years of her life keeping in touch with friends and died June 24, 1909, at her home in South Berwick, three months after suffering a cerebral hemorrhage.

○ ○ ○

Visits provide the fictional occasion and developing friendship the unfolding narrative in many of Jewett's sketches because, for Jewett, friendship provided the means for continuing growth and development. In her own life, it is impossible to distinguish between personal and literary friendship; most of her friends were also writers or artists, and most of the prominent writers of her day valued her friendship.

After *Deephaven,* which presents a model of female development based primarily on friendship with a peer, Jewett connects female development with the friendship of mother and daughter, and asserts that, through generations of mothers or mother-figures, an American daughter, or even, as Sarah Way Sherman terms Jewett in her critical study, "An American Persephone," may retain her connection or become reconnected with spiritual as well as cultural roots. By taking Stowe as her model, Jewett began her career as a writer already recognizing the need to "return" to her literary mothers. The literary mode Stowe initiated allowed Jewett to develop her vision; by the time she began to write regional fiction, the work of Stowe, Cary, Cooke, and Thaxter had already created a form in which the stories of regional women and the experiences of their daily lives could be told.

In most of her work, and in each of the sketches included in this volume, Jewett demonstrates the importance of empathy to the development of the regional character and perspective. In "The Circus at Denby," Helen, Kate, and Mrs. Kew enter the circus tent intending to look at the Kentucky giantess, but end by listening to her tell her story, thereby demonstrating their empathy for her. "A White Heron" reflects Jewett's further exploration of the process and power of empathy. The hunter resembles the typical onlookers at the circus sideshow. If he can persuade Sylvy to tell the secret she discovers about the bird's nest, he will be able to find, shoot, and stuff the bird. But Sylvy does not share the bird's secret, much as she would like to please the hunter; she refuses to speak unless she can speak without destroying. Sylvy's dilemma is Jewett's own, evident in the tensions of "The Circus at Denby": how can she portray the lives of regional people without betraying them? How can she create the conditions necessary for silent persons to speak their secrets without writing fiction that will "stuff" her characters and put them in a sideshow for gawkers to mock?

Jewett solves this narrative problem by focusing on the transformation of her narrator over the span of her life's work. She shifts her own focus, and the function of telling the regional tale, from the stories her characters have to tell to the process of eliciting their voices. Helen Denis is the narrator of *Deephaven,* but it is Mrs. Kew, not Helen, whose presence empowers Marilly to speak. The narrator of "A White Heron" stands entirely outside the sketch, reflecting on but not participating in the listening process. However, in *The Country of the Pointed Firs*, Jewett transforms the narrator herself into a character capable of empathy. The process by which the narrator makes such a transformation in *Pointed Firs*, visible in the excerpts we have included here, equates growth and development with the ability to listen empathically.

"The Return"—the opening sketch or "chapter" in *The Country of the Pointed Firs*—introduces the reader to Jewett's unnamed narrator, who has come to Dunnet Landing to write in solitude, and who initially believes that she can't afford "the pleasure of what we called 'seein' folks.'" But Mrs. Todd, the herbalist and healer, begins to "teach" the narrator that to be a writer is to be a listener; the narrator's ability to write must be matched and transformed by her ability to listen. By drawing the narrator out of her solitude and by giving her the opportunity to hear the stories of the inhabitants of Dunnet Landing—as the chapters "The Outer Island," "Green Island," and "The Old Singers" demonstrate—Mrs. Todd enables the narrator to grow as a listener. Jewett identifies this nurturing relationship between speaker and listener with the relationship between mother and daughter, a tie most clearly drawn in "Green Island" where the narrator meets Mrs. Todd's mother and is able to "hear" her story at first hand. Throughout *Pointed Firs*, Jewett's imagery of visits to the inner islands suggests a journey of initiation. However, unlike Sylvy, Jewett's narrator has a guide who willingly shares the "secret" of the inner islands, trusting her not to "kill" the secret when she, in turn, shares it through writing about it.

Two later Dunnet Landing stories are included here; both were published after *The Country of the Pointed Firs*, although "The Queen's Twin" appeared in the 1925 edition, for which Willa Cather wrote the introduction. "The Foreigner" and "The Queen's Twin" continue Jewett's portrayal of the development of empathy in her own narrator. In "The Foreigner" Jewett's narrator plays the role of listener to Mrs. Todd, who has herself offered the comfort of listening to others, thereby enabling Mrs. Todd to tell a story that comforts her during an evening when she is worried about her mother's safety, out on Green Island, during a storm. And in "The Queen's Twin," she helps Abby Martin tell the story which most comforts her by joining, with Mrs. Todd, in an act of empathic listening.

From DEEPHAVEN

The Circus at Denby

Kate and I looked forward to a certain Saturday with as much eagerness as if we had been little school-boys, for on that day we were to go to a circus at Denby, a town perhaps eight miles inland. There had not been a circus so near Deephaven for a long time, and nobody had dared to believe the first rumor of it, until two dashing young men had deigned to come themselves to put up the big posters on the end of 'Bijah Mauley's barn. All the boys in town came as soon as possible to see these amazing pictures, and some were wretched in their secret hearts at the thought that they might not see the show itself. Tommy

Dockum was more interested than any one else, and mentioned the subject so frequently one day when he went blackberrying with us, that we grew enthusiastic, and told each other what fun it would be to go, for everybody would be there, and it would be the greatest loss to us if we were absent. I thought I had lost my childish fondness for circuses, but it came back redoubled; and Kate may contradict me if she chooses, but I am sure she never looked forward to the Easter Oratorio[1] with half the pleasure she did to this "caravan," as most of the people called it.

We felt that it was a great pity that any of the boys and girls should be left lamenting at home, and finding that there were some of our acquaintances and Tommy's who saw no chance of going, we engaged Jo Sands and Leander Dockum to carry them to Denby in two fish-wagons, with boards laid across for the extra seats. We saw them join the straggling train of carriages which had begun to go through the village from all along shore, soon after daylight, and they started on their journey shouting and carousing, with their pockets crammed with early apples and other provisions. We thought it would have been fun enough to see the people go by, for we had had no idea until then how many inhabitants that country held.

We had asked Mrs. Kew to go with us; but she was half an hour later than she had promised, for, since there was no wind, she could not come ashore in the sail-boat, and Mr. Kew had had to row her in in the dory.[2] We saw the boat at last nearly in shore, and drove down to meet it: even the horse seemed to realize what a great day it was, and showed a disposition to friskiness, evidently as surprising to himself as to us.

Mrs. Kew was funnier that day than we had ever known her, which is saying a great deal, and we should not have had half so good a time if she had not been with us; although she lived in the light-house, and had no chance to "see passing," which a woman prizes so highly in the country, she had a wonderful memory for faces, and could tell us the names of all Deephaveners and of most of the people we met outside its limits. She looked impressed and solemn as she hurried up from the water's edge, giving Mr. Kew some parting charges over her shoulder as he pushed off the boat to go back; but after we had convinced her that the delay had not troubled us, she seemed more cheerful. It was evident that she felt the importance of the occasion, and that she was pleased at our having chosen her for company. She threw back her veil entirely, sat very straight, and took immense pains to bow to every acquaintance whom she met. She wore her best Sunday clothes, and her manner was formal for the

---

1. An oratorio is a musical composition, for voices and orchestra, telling a sacred story, such as Handel's *Messiah* (1742); the reference here may also be to the *Easter Oratorio* of J.S. Bach.
2. A small, narrow, flat-bottomed fishing boat with high sides and a sharp prow.

first few minutes; it was evident that she felt we were meeting under
unusual circumstances, and that, although we had often met before
on the friendliest terms, our having asked her to make this excursion
in public required a different sort of behavior at her hands, and a due
amount of ceremony and propriety. But this state of things did not
last long, as she soon made a remark at which Kate and I laughed so
heartily in lighthouse-acquaintance fashion, that she unbent, and
gave her whole mind to enjoying herself.

When we came by the store where the post-office was kept we saw
a small knot of people gathered round the door, and stopped to see
what had happened. There was a forlorn horse standing near, with his
harness tied up with fuzzy ends of rope, and the wagon was cobbled
together with pieces of board; the whole craft looked as if it might be
wrecked with the least jar. In the wagon were four or five stupid-
looking boys and girls, one of whom was crying softly. Their father was
sick, some one told us. "He was took faint, but he is coming to all right;
they have give him something to take: their name is Craper, and they
live way over beyond the Ridge, on Stone Hill. They were goin' over
to Denby to the circus, and the man was calc'lating to get doctored, but
I d' know's he can get so fur; he's powerful slim-looking to me." Kate
and I went to see if we could be of any use, and when we went into
the store we saw the man leaning back in his chair, looking ghastly
pale, and as if he were far gone in consumption. Kate spoke to him, and
he said he was better; he had felt bad all the way along, but he hadn't
given up. He was pitiful, poor fellow, with his evident attempt at
dressing up. He had the bushiest, dustiest red hair and whiskers, which
made the pallor of his face still more striking, and his illness had
thinned and paled his rough, clumsy hands. I thought what a hard
piece of work it must have been for him to start for the circus that
morning, and how kind-hearted he must be to have made such an effort
for his children's pleasure. As we went out they stared at us gloomily.
The shadow of their disappointment touched and chilled our pleasure.

Somebody had turned the horse so that he was heading toward
home, and by his actions he showed that he was the only one of the
party who was glad. We were so sorry for the children; perhaps it had
promised to be the happiest day of their lives, and now they must go
back to their uninteresting home without having seen the great show.

"I am so sorry you are disappointed," said Kate, as we were wondering how the man who had followed us could ever climb into the wagon.

"Heh?" said he, blankly, as if he did not know what her words
meant. "What fool has been a turning o' this horse?" he asked a man
who was looking on.

"Why, which way be ye goin'?"

"To the circus," said Mr. Craper, with decision, "where d' ye
s'pose? That's where I started for, anyways." And he climbed in and
glanced round to count the children, struck the horse with the willow

switch, and they started off briskly, while everybody laughed. Kate and I joined Mrs. Kew, who had enjoyed the scene.

"Well, there!" said she, "I wonder the folks in the old North burying-ground ain't a-rising up to go to Denby to that caravan!"

We reached Denby at noon; it was an uninteresting town which had grown up around some mills. There was a great commotion in the streets, and it was evident that we had lost much in not having seen the procession. There was a great deal of business going on in the shops, and there were two or three hand-organs at large, near one of which we stopped awhile to listen, just after we had met Leander and given the horse into his charge. Mrs. Kew finished her shopping as soon as possible, and we hurried toward the great tents, where all the flags were flying. I think I have not told you that we were to have the benefit of seeing a menagerie in addition to the circus, and you may be sure we went faithfully round to see everything that the cages held.

I cannot truthfully say that it was a good show; it was somewhat dreary, now that I think of it quietly and without excitement. The creatures looked tired, and as if they had been on the road for a great many years. The animals were all old, and there was a shabby great elephant whose look of general discouragement went to my heart, for it seemed as if he were miserably conscious of a misspent life. He stood dejected and motionless at one side of the tent, and it was hard to believe that there was a spark of vitality left in him. A great number of the people had never seen an elephant before, and we heard a thin little old man, who stood near us, say delightedly, "There's the old creatur', and no mistake, Ann 'Liza. I wanted to see him most of anything. My sakes alive, ain't he big!"

And Ann 'Liza, who was stout and sleepy-looking, droned out, "Ye-es, there's consider'ble of him; but he looks as if he ain't got no animation."

Kate and I turned away and laughed, while Mrs. Kew said confidentially, as the couple moved away, "*She* needn't be a reflectin' on the poor beast. That's Mis Seth Tanner, and there isn't a woman in Deephaven nor East Parish to be named the same day with her for laziness. I'm glad she didn't catch sight of me; she'd have talked about nothing for a fortnight."

There was a picture of a huge snake in Deephaven, and I was just wondering where he could be, or if there ever had been one, when we heard a boy ask the same question of the man whose thankless task it was to stir up the lions with a stick to make them roar. "The snake's dead," he answered good-naturedly. "Didn't you have to dig an awful long grave for him?" asked the boy; but the man said he reckoned they curled him up some, and smiled as he turned to his lions, who looked as if they needed a tonic.[3] Everybody lingered longest before the monkeys, who seemed to be the only lively creatures in the whole

3. Anything that invigorates, refreshes, or restores; may be a medicinal or herbal preparation.

collection; and finally we made our way into the other tent, and perched ourselves on a high seat, from whence we had a capital view of the audience and the ring, and could see the people come in. Mrs. Kew was on the lookout for acquaintances, and her spirits as well as our own seemed to rise higher and higher. She was on the alert, moving her head this way and that to catch sight of people, giving us a running commentary in the meantime. It was very pleasant to see a person so happy as Mrs. Kew was that day, and I dare say in speaking of the occasion she would say the same thing of Kate and me,—for it was such a good time! We bought some peanuts, without which no circus seems complete, and we listened to the conversations which were being carried on around us while we were waiting for the performance to begin. There were two old farmers whom we had noticed occasionally in Deephaven; one was telling the other, with great confusion of pronouns, about a big pig which had lately been killed. "John did feel dreadful disappointed at having to kill now," we heard him say, "bein' as he had calc'lated to kill along near Thanksgivin' time; there was goin' to be a new moon then, and he expected to get seventy-five or a hundred pound more on to him. But he didn't seem to gain, and me and 'Bijah both told him he'd be better to kill now, while everything was favor'ble, and if he set out to wait something might happen to him, and then I've always held that you can't get no hog only just so fur, and for my part I don't like these great overgrown creatur's. I like well enough to see a hog that'll weigh six hunderd, just for the beauty on 't, but for my eatin' give me one that'll just rise three. 'Bijah's accurate, and he says he is goin' to weigh risin' five hundred and fifty. I shall stop, as I go home, to John's wife's brother's and see if they've got the particulars yet; John was goin' to get the scales this morning. I guess likely consider'ble many'll gather there tomorrow after meeting. John didn't calc'late to cut up till Monday."

"I guess likely I'll stop in tomorrow," said the other man; "I like to see a han'some hog. Chester White, you said? Consider them best, don't ye?" But this question never was answered, for the greater part of the circus company in gorgeous trappings came parading in.

The circus was like all other circuses, except that it was shabbier than most, and the performers seemed to have less heart in it than usual. They did their best, and went through with their parts conscientiously, but they looked as if they never had had a good time in their lives. The audience was hilarious, and cheered and laughed at the tired clown until he looked as if he thought his speeches might possibly be funny, after all. We were so glad we had pleased the poor thing; and when he sang a song our satisfaction was still greater, and so he sang it all over again. Perhaps he had been associating with people who were used to circuses. The afternoon was hot, and the boys with Japanese fans and trays of lemonade did a remarkable business for so late in the season; the brass band on the other side of the tent shrieked its very best, and all the young men of the region had brought their

girls, and some of these countless pairs of country lovers we watched
a great deal, as they "kept company" with more or less depth of
satisfaction in each other. We had a grand chance to see the fashions,
and there were many old people and a great number of little children,
and some families had evidently locked their house door behind them,
since they had brought both the dog and the baby.

"Doesn't it seem as if you were a child again?" Kate asked me. "I
am sure this is just the same as the first circus I ever saw. It grows more
and more familiar, and it puzzles me to think they should not have
altered in the least while I have changed so much, and have even had
time to grow up. You don't know how it is making me remember other
things of which I have not thought for years. I was seven years old
when I went that first time. Uncle Jack invited me. I had a new parasol,
and he laughed because I would hold it over my shoulder when the sun
was in my face. He took me into the side-shows and bought me everything I asked for, on the way home, and we did not get home until
twilight. The rest of the family had dined at four o'clock and gone out
for a long drive, and it was such fun to have our dinner by ourselves.
I sat at the head of the table in mamma's place, and when Bridget
came down and insisted that I must go to bed, Uncle Jack came softly
upstairs and sat by the window, smoking and telling me stories. He ran
and hid in the closet when we heard mamma coming up, and when she
found him out by the cigar-smoke, and made believe scold him, I
thought she was in earnest, and begged him off. Yes; and I remember
that Bridget sat in the next room, making her new dress so she could
wear it to church next day. I thought it was a beautiful dress, and
besought mamma to have one like it. It was bright green with yellow
spots all over it," said Kate. "Ah, poor Uncle Jack! he was so good to
me! We were always telling stories of what we would do when I was
grown up. He died in Canton the next year, and I cried myself ill; but
for a long time I thought he might not be dead, after all, and might
come home any day. He used to seem so old to me, and he really was
just out of college and not so old as I am now. That day at the circus
he had a pink rosebud in his buttonhole, and—ah! when have I ever
thought of this before!—a woman sat before us who had a stiff little
cape on her bonnet like a shelf, and I carefully put peanuts round the
edge of it, and when she moved her head they would fall. I thought it
was the best fun in the world, and I wished Uncle Jack to ride the
donkey; I was sure he could keep on, because his horse had capered
about with him one day on Beacon Street, and I thought him a perfect
rider, since nothing had happened to him then."

"I remember," said Mrs. Kew, presently, "that just before I was
married 'he' took me over to Wareham Corners to a caravan. My sister
Hannah and the young man who was keeping company with her went
too. I haven't been to one since till today, and it does carry me back
same's it does you, Miss Kate. It doesn't seem more than five years ago,
and what would I have thought if I had known 'he' and I were going

to keep a lighthouse and be contented there, what's more, and sometimes not get ashore for a fortnight; settled, gray-headed old folks! We
were gay enough in those days. I know old Miss Sabrina Smith warned
me that I'd better think twice before I took up with Tom Kew, for he
was a light-minded young man. I speak o' that to him in the winter-
time, when he sets reading the almanac half asleep and I'm knitting,
and the wind's a'howling and the waves coming ashore on those rocks
as if they wished they could put out the light and blow down the
lighthouse. We were reflected on a good deal for going to that caravan;
some of the old folks didn't think it was improvin'—Well, I should think
that man was a trying to break his neck!''

Coming out of the great tent was disagreeable enough, and we
seemed to have chosen the worst time, for the crowd pushed fiercely,
though I suppose nobody was in the least hurry, and we were all
severely jammed, while from somewhere underneath came the wails
of a deserted dog. We had not meant to see the side-shows, and went
carelessly past two or three tents; but when we came in sight of the
picture of the Kentucky giantess, we noticed that Mrs. Kew looked at
it wistfully, and we immediately asked if she cared anything about
going to see the wonder, whereupon she confessed that she never
heard of such a thing as a woman's weighing six hundred and fifty
pounds, so we all three went in. There were only two or three persons
inside the tent, beside a little boy who played the hand-organ.

The Kentucky giantess sat in two chairs on a platform, and there was
a large cage of monkeys just beyond, toward which Kate and I went at
once. "Why, she isn't more than two-thirds as big as the picture," said
Mrs. Kew, in a regretful whisper; "but I guess she's big enough;
doesn't she look discouraged, poor creatur'?" Kate and I felt ashamed
of ourselves for being there. No matter if she had consented to be
carried round for a show, it must have been horrible to be stared at and
joked about day after day; and we gravely looked at the monkeys, and
in a few minutes turned to see if Mrs. Kew were not ready to come
away, when to our surprise we saw that she was talking to the giantess
with great interest, and we went nearer.

"I thought your face looked natural the minute I set foot inside the
door," said Mrs. Kew; "but you've—altered some since I saw you, and
I couldn't place you till I heard you speak. Why, you used to be spare;
I am amazed, Marilly! Where are your folks?"

"I don't wonder you are surprised," said the giantess. "I was a good
ways from this when you knew me, wasn't I? But father he run through
with every cent he had before he died, and 'he' took to drink and it
killed him after a while, and then I begun to grow worse and worse,
till I couldn't do nothing to earn a dollar, and everybody was a coming
to see me, till at last I used to ask 'em ten cents a piece, and I scratched
along somehow till this man came round and heard of me, and he
offered me my keep and good pay to go along with him. He had
another giantess before me, but she had begun to fall away consider'-

ble, so he paid her off and let her go. This other giantess was an awful expense to him, she was such an eater; now I don't have no great of an appetite,"—this was said plaintively,—"and he's raised my pay since I've been with him because we did so well. I took up with his offer because I was nothing but a drag and never will be. I'm as comfortable as I can be, but it's a pretty hard business. My oldest boy is able to do for himself, but he's married this last year, and his wife don't want me. I don't know's I blame her either. It would be something like if I had a daughter now; but there, I'm getting to like travelling first-rate; it gives anybody a good deal to think of."

"I was asking the folks about you when I was up home the early part of the summer," said Mrs. Kew, "but all they knew was that you were living out in New York State. Have you been living in Kentucky long? I saw it on the picture outside."

"No," said the giantess, "that was a picture the man bought cheap from another show that broke up last year. It says six hundred and fifty pounds, but I don't weigh more than four hundred. I haven't been weighed for some time past. Between you and me I don't weigh so much as that, but you mustn't mention it, for it would spoil my reputa-tion, and might hender my getting another engagement." And then the poor giantess lost her professional look and tone as she said, "I believe I'd rather die than grow any bigger. I do lose heart sometimes, and wish I was a smart woman and could keep house. I'd be smarter than ever I was when I had the chance; I tell you that! Is Tom along with you?"

"No. I came with these young ladies, Miss Lancaster and Miss Denis, who are stopping over to Deephaven for the summer." Kate and I turned as we heard this introduction; we were standing close by, and I am proud to say that I never saw Kate treat anyone more politely than she did that absurd, pitiful creature with the gilt crown and many bracelets. It was not that she said much, but there was such an exquis-ite courtesy in her manner, and an apparent unconsciousness of there being anything in the least surprising or uncommon about the giantess.

Just then a party of people came in, and Mrs. Kew said good by reluctantly. "It has done me sights of good to see you," said our new acquaintance; "I was feeling down-hearted just before you came in. I'm pleased to see somebody that remembers me as I used to be." And they shook hands in a way that meant a great deal, and when Kate and I said good afternoon the giantess looked at us gratefully, and said, "I'm very much obliged to you for coming in, young ladies."

"Walk in! walk in!" the man was shouting as we came away. "Walk in and see the wonder of the world, ladies and gentlemen,—the largest woman ever seen in America,—the great Kentucky giantess!"

"Wouldn't you have liked to stay longer?" Kate asked Mrs. Kew as we came down the street. But she answered that it would be no satisfaction; the people were coming in, and she would have no chance to talk. "I never knew her very well; she is younger than I, and she

used to go to meeting where I did, but she lived five or six miles from
our house. She's had a hard time of it, according to her account," said
Mrs. Kew. "She used to be a dreadful flighty, high-tempered girl, but
she's lost that now, I can see by her eyes. I was running over in my
mind to see if there was anything I could do for her, but I don't know
as there is. She said the man who hired her was kind. I guess your
treating her so polite did her as much good as anything. She used to be
real ambitious. I had it on my tongue's end to ask her if she couldn't
get a few days' leave and come out to stop with me, but I thought just
in time that she'd sink the dory in a minute. There! seeing her has took
away all the fun," said Mrs. Kew ruefully; and we were all dismal for
a while, but at last, after we were fairly started for home, we began to
be merry again.

We passed the Craper family whom we had seen at the store in the
morning; the children looked as stupid as ever, but the father, I am
sorry to say, had been tempted to drink more whiskey than was good
for him. He had a bright flush on his cheeks, and he was flourishing his
whip, and hoarsely singing some meaningless tune. "Poor creature!"
said I, "I should think this day's pleasuring would kill him." "Now,
wouldn't you think so?" said Mrs. Kew, sympathizingly; "but the truth
is, you couldn't kill one of those Crapers if you pounded him in a
mortar."

We had a pleasant drive home, and we kept Mrs. Kew to supper,
and afterward went down to the shore to see her set sail for home. Mr.
Kew had come in some time before, and had been waiting for the moon
to rise. Mrs. Kew told us that she should have enough to think of for
a year, she had enjoyed the day so much; and we stood on the pebbles
watching the boat out of the harbor, and wishing ourselves on board,
it was such a beautiful evening.

° ° °

We went to another show that summer, the memory of which will
never fade. It is somewhat impertinent to call it a show, and "public
entertainment" is equally inappropriate, though we certainly were
entertained. It had been raining for two or three days; the Deephave-
nites spoke of it as "a spell of weather." Just after tea, one Thursday
evening, Kate and I went down to the post-office. When we opened the
great hall door, the salt air was delicious, but we found the town
apparently wet through and discouraged; and though it had almost
stopped raining just then, there was a Scotch mist, like a snow-storm
with the chill taken off, and the Chantrey elms dripped hurriedly, and
creaked occasionally in the east-wind.

"There will not be a cap'n on the wharves for a week after this," said
I to Kate; "only think of the cases of rheumatism!"

We stopped for a few minutes at the Carews', who were as much
surprised to see us as if we had been mermaids out of the sea, and
begged us to give ourselves something warm to drink, and to change
our boots the moment we got home. Then we went on to the post-

office. Kate went in, but stopped, as she came out with our letters, to read a written notice securely fastened to the grocery door by four large carpet-tacks with wide leathers round their necks.

"Dear," said she, exultantly, "there's going to be a lecture tonight in the church,—a free lecture on the Elements of True Manhood. Wouldn't you like to go?" And we went.

We were fifteen minutes later than the time appointed, and were sorry to find that the audience was almost imperceptible. The dampness had affected the antiquated lamps so that those on the walls and on the front of the gallery were the dimmest lights I ever saw, and sent their feeble rays through a small space the edges of which were clearly defined. There were two rather more energetic lights on the table near the pulpit, where the lecturer sat, and as we were in the rear of the church, we could see the yellow fog between ourselves and him. There were fourteen persons in the audience, and we were all huddled together in a cowardly way in the pews nearest the door: three old men, four women, and four children, besides ourselves and the sexton, a deaf little old man with a wooden leg.

The children whispered noisily, and soon, to our surprise, the lecturer rose and began. He bowed, and treated us with beautiful deference, and read his dreary lecture with enthusiasm. I wish I could say, for his sake, that it was interesting; but I cannot tell a lie, and it was so long! He went on and on, until it seemed as if I had been there ever since I was a little girl. Kate and I did not dare to look at each other, and in my desperation at feeling her quiver with laughter, I moved to the other end of the pew, knocking over a big hymn-book on the way, which attracted so much attention that I have seldom felt more embarrassed in my life. Kate's great dog rose several times to shake himself and yawn loudly, and then lie down again despairingly.

You would have thought the man was addressing an enthusiastic Young Men's Christian Association. He exhorted with fervor upon our duties as citizens and as voters, and told us a great deal about George Washington and Benjamin Franklin, whom he urged us to choose as our examples. He waited for applause after each of his outbursts of eloquence, and presently went on again, in no wise disconcerted at the silence, and as if he were sure that he would fetch us next time. The rain began to fall again heavily, and the wind wailed around the meeting-house. If the lecture had been upon any other subject it would not have been so hard for Kate and me to keep sober faces; but it was directed entirely toward young men, and there was not a young man there.

The children in front of us mildly scuffled with each other at one time, until the one at the end of the pew dropped a marble, which struck the floor and rolled with a frightful noise down the edge of the aisle where there was no carpet. The congregation instinctively started up to look after it, but we recollected ourselves and leaned back again in our places, while the awed children, after keeping unnaturally quiet, fell asleep, and tumbled against each other helplessly. After a time the man sat down and wiped his forehead, looking well satisfied; and when we were wondering whether we might with propriety come away, he rose again, and said it was a free lecture, and he thanked us for our kind patronage on that inclement night; but in other places which he had visited there had been a contribution taken up for the cause. It would, perhaps, do no harm—would the sexton—

But the sexton could not have heard the sound of a cannon at that distance, and slumbered on. Neither Kate nor I had any money, except a twenty-dollar bill in my purse, and some coppers in the pocket of her water-proof cloak which she assured me she was prepared to give; but we saw no signs of the sexton's waking, and as one of the women kindly went forward to wake the children, we all rose and came away.

After we had made as much fun and laughed as long as we pleased that night, we became suddenly conscious of the pitiful side of it all; and being anxious that everyone should have the highest opinion of Deephaven, we sent Tom Dockum early in the morning with an anonymous note to the lecturer, whom he found without much trouble; but afterward we were disturbed at hearing that he was going to repeat his lecture that evening,—the wind having gone round to the northwest,— and I have no doubt there were a good many women able to be out, and that he harvested enough ten-cent pieces to pay his expenses without our help; though he had particularly told us it was for "the cause," the evening before, and that ought to have been a consolation.

No magazine publication; 1877

A White Heron

I

The woods were already filled with shadows one June evening, just before eight o' clock, though a bright sunset still glimmered faintly among the trunks of the trees. A little girl was driving home her cow, a plodding, dilatory, provoking creature in her behavior, but a valued companion for all that. They were going away from the western light, and striking deep into the dark woods, but their feet were familiar with the path, and it was no matter whether their eyes could see it or not.

There was hardly a night the summer through when the old cow could be found waiting at the pasture bars; on the contrary, it was her greatest pleasure to hide herself away among the high huckleberry bushes, and though she wore a loud bell she had made the discovery that if one stood perfectly still it would not ring. So Sylvia had to hunt for her until she found her, and call Co'! Co'! with never an answering Moo, until her childish patience was quite spent. If the creature had not given good milk and plenty of it, the case would have seemed very different to her owners. Besides, Sylvia had all the time there was, and very little use to make of it. Sometimes in pleasant weather it was a consolation to look upon the cow's pranks as an intelligent attempt to play hide and seek, and as the child had no playmates she lent herself to this amusement with a good deal of zest. Though this chase had been so long that the wary animal herself had given an unusual signal of her whereabouts, Sylvia had only laughed when she came upon Mistress Moolly at the swamp-side, and urged her affectionately homeward with a twig of birch leaves. The old cow was not inclined to wander farther, she even turned in the right direction for once as they left the pasture, and stepped along the road at a good pace. She was quite ready to be milked now, and seldom stopped to browse. Sylvia wondered what her grandmother would say because they were so late. It was a great while since she had left home at half past five o'clock, but everybody knew the difficulty of making this errand a short one. Mrs. Tilley had chased the hornéd torment too many summer evenings herself to blame anyone else for lingering, and was only thankful as she waited that she had Sylvia, nowadays, to give such valuable assistance. The good woman suspected that Sylvia loitered occasionally on her own account; there never was such a child for straying out-of-doors since the world was made! Everybody said that it was a good change for a little maid who had tried to grow for eight years in a crowded manufacturing town, but, as for Sylvia herself, it seemed as if she never had been alive at all before she came to live at the farm. She thought often with wistful compassion of a wretched dry geranium that belonged to a town neighbor.

" 'Afraid of folks,' " old Mrs. Tilley said to herself, with a smile, after she had made the unlikely choice of Sylvia from her daughter's houseful of children, and was returning to the farm. " 'Afraid of folks,' they said! I guess she won't be troubled no great with 'em up to the old place!" When they reached the door of the lonely house and stopped to unlock it, and the cat came to purr loudly, and rub against them, a deserted pussy, indeed, but fat with young robins, Sylvia whispered that this was a beautiful place to live in, and she never should wish to go home.

* * *

The companions followed the shady woodroad, the cow taking slow steps, and the child very fast ones. The cows stopped long at the brook to drink, as if the pasture were not half a swamp, and Sylvia stood still and waited, letting her bare feet cool themselves in the shoal water, while the great twilight moths struck softly against her. She waded on through the brook as the cow moved away, and listened to the thrushes with a heart that beat fast with pleasure. There was a stirring in the great boughs overhead. They were full of little birds and beasts that seemed to be wide-awake, and going about their world, or else saying good-night to each other in sleepy twitters. Sylvia herself felt sleepy as she walked along. However, it was not much farther to the house, and the air was soft and sweet. She was not often in the woods so late as this, and it made her feel as if she were a part of the gray shadows and the moving leaves. She was just thinking how long it seemed since she first came to the farm a year ago, and wondering if everything went on in the noisy town just the same as when she was there; the thought of the great red-faced boy who used to chase and frighten her made her hurry along the path to escape from the shadow of the trees.

Suddenly this little woods-girl is horror-stricken to hear a clear whistle not very far away. Not a bird's whistle, which would have a sort of friendliness, but a boy's whistle, determined, and somewhat aggressive. Sylvia left the cow to whatever sad fate might await her, and stepped discreetly aside into the bushes, but she was just too late. The enemy had discovered her, and called out in a very cheerful and persuasive tone, "Halloa, little girl, how far is it to the road?" and trembling Sylvia answered almost inaudibly, "A good ways."

She did not dare to look boldly at the tall young man, who carried a gun over his shoulder, but she came out of her bush and again followed the cow, while he walked alongside.

"I have been hunting for some birds," the stranger said kindly, "and I have lost my way, and need a friend very much. Don't be afraid," he added gallantly. "Speak up and tell me what your name is, and whether you think I can spend the night at your house, and go out gunning early in the morning."

Sylvia was more alarmed than before. Would not her grandmother consider her much to blame? But who could have foreseen such an accident as this? It did not appear to be her fault, and she hung her head as if the stem of it were broken, but managed to answer "Sylvy," with much effort when her companion again asked her name.

Mrs. Tilley was standing in the doorway when the trio came into view. The cow gave a loud moo by way of explanation.

"Yes, you'd better speak up for yourself, you old trial! Where'd she tuck herself away this time, Sylvy?" Sylvia kept an awed silence; she knew by instinct that her grandmother did not comprehend the gravity of the situation. She must be mistaking the stranger for one of the farmer-lads of the region.

The young man stood his gun beside the door, and dropped a heavy game-bag beside it; then he bade Mrs. Tilley good-evening, and repeated his wayfarer's story, and asked if he could have a night's lodging.

"Put me anywhere you like," he said. "I must be off early in the morning, before day; but I am very hungry, indeed. You can give me some milk at any rate, that's plain."

"Dear sakes, yes," responded the hostess, whose long slumbering hospitality seemed to be easily awakened. "You might fare better if you went out on the main road a mile or so, but you're welcome to what we've got. I'll milk right off, and you make yourself at home. You can sleep on husks or feathers," she proffered graciously. "I raised them all myself. There's good pasturing for geese just below here towards the ma'sh. Now step round and set a plate for the gentleman, Sylvy!" and Sylvia promptly stepped. She was glad to have something to do, and she was hungry herself.

It was a surprise to find so clean and comfortable a little dwelling in this New England wilderness. The young man had known the horrors of its most primitive housekeeping, and the dreary squalor of that level of society which does not rebel at the companionship of hens. This was the best thrift of an old-fashioned farmstead, though on such a small scale it seemed like a hermitage. He listened eagerly to the old woman's quaint talk, he watched Sylvia's pale face and shining gray eyes with ever growing enthusiasm, and insisted that this was the best supper he had eaten for a month; then, afterward, the new-made friends sat down in the doorway together while the moon came up.

Soon it would be berry-time, and Sylvia was a great help at picking. The cow was a good milker, though a plaguy thing to keep track of, the hostess gossiped frankly, adding presently that she had buried four children, so that Sylvia's mother, and a son (who might be dead) in California were all the children she had left. "Dan, my boy, was a great hand to go gunning," she explained sadly. "I never wanted for pa'-tridges or gray squer'ls while he was to home. He's been a great wand'rer, I expect, and he's no hand to write letters. There, I don't blame him, I'd ha' seen the world myself if it had been so I could.

"Sylvia takes after him," the grandmother continued affectionately, after a minute's pause. "There ain't a foot o' ground she don't know her way over, and the wild creatur's counts her one o' themselves. Squer'ls she'll tame to come an' feed right out o' her hands, and all sorts o' birds. Last winter she got the jay-birds to bangeing[1] here, and I believe she'd 'a' scanted herself of her own meals to have plenty to throw out amongst 'em, if I hadn't kep' watch. Anything but crows, I tell her, I'm willin' to help support,—though Dan he went an' tamed one o' them that did seem to have reason same as folks. It was round here a good spell after he went away. Dan an' his father they didn't hitch,—but he never held up his head ag'in after Dan had dared him an' gone off."

The guest did not notice this hint of family sorrows in his eager interest in something else.

"So Sylvy knows all about birds, does she?" he exclaimed, as he looked round at the little girl who sat, very demure but increasingly sleepy, in the moonlight. "I am making a collection of birds myself. I have been at it ever since I was a boy." (Mrs. Tilley smiled.) "There are two or three very rare ones I have been hunting for these five years. I mean to get them on my own ground if they can be found."

"Do you cage 'em up?" asked Mrs. Tilley doubtfully, in response to this enthusiastic announcement.

---

1. "Bange" means to frequent a place without definite purpose; to idle about.

"Oh, no, they're stuffed and preserved, dozens and dozens of them," said the ornithologist, "and I have shot or snared every one myself. I caught a glimpse of a white heron three miles from here on Saturday, and I have followed it in this direction. They have never been found in this district at all. The little white heron, it is," and he turned again to look at Sylvia with the hope of discovering that the rare bird was one of her acquaintances.

But Sylvia was watching a hop-toad in the narrow footpath.

"You would know the heron if you saw it," the stranger continued eagerly. "A queer tall white bird with soft feathers and long thin legs. And it would have a nest perhaps in the top of a high tree, made of sticks, something like a hawk's nest."

Sylvia's heart gave a wild beat; she knew that strange white bird, and had once stolen softly near where it stood in some bright green swamp grass, away over at the other side of the woods. There was an open place where the sunshine always seemed strangely yellow and hot, where tall, nodding rushes grew, and her grandmother had warned her that she might sink in the soft black mud underneath and never be heard of more. Not far beyond were the salt marshes and beyond those was the sea, the sea which Sylvia wondered and dreamed about, but never had looked upon, though its great voice could often be heard above the noise of the woods on stormy nights.

"I can't think of anything I should like so much as to find that heron's nest," the handsome stranger was saying. "I would give ten dollars to anybody who could show it to me," he added desperately, "and I mean to spend my whole vacation hunting for it if need be. Perhaps it was only migrating, or had been chased out of its own region by some bird of prey."

Mrs. Tilley gave amazed attention to all this, but Sylvia still watched the toad, not divining, as she might have done at some calmer time, that the creature wished to get to its hole under the doorstep, and was much hindered by the unusual spectators at that hour of the evening. No amount of thought, that night, could decide how many wished-for treasures the ten dollars, so lightly spoken of, would buy.

The next day the young sportsman hovered about the woods, and Sylvia kept him company, having lost her first fear of the friendly lad, who proved to be most kind and sympathetic. He told her many things about the birds and what they knew and where they lived and what they did with themselves. And he gave her a jack-knife, which she thought as great a treasure as if she were a desert-islander. All day long he did not once make her troubled or afraid except when he brought down some unsuspecting singing creature from its bough. Sylvia would have liked him vastly better without his gun; she could not understand why he killed the very birds he seemed to like so much. But as the day waned, Sylvia still watched the young man with loving admiration. She had never seen anybody so charming and delightful; the woman's heart, asleep in the child, was vaguely thrilled by a dream of love. Some premonition of that great power stirred and swayed these young foresters who traversed the solemn woodlands with soft-footed silent care. They stopped to listen to a bird's song; they pressed forward again eagerly, parting the branches,—speaking to each other rarely and in whispers; the young man going first and Sylvia following, fascinated, a few steps behind, with her gray eyes dark with excitement.

She grieved because the longed-for white heron was elusive, but she did not lead the guest, she only followed, and there was no such thing as speaking first. The sound of her own unquestioned voice would have terrified her,—it was hard enough to answer yes or no when there was need of that. At last evening began to fall, and they drove the cow home together, and Sylvia smiled with pleasure when they came to the place where she heard the whistle and was afraid only the night before.

II

Half a mile from home, at the farther edge of the woods, where the land was highest, a great pine-tree stood, the last of its generation. Whether it was left for a boundary mark, or for what reason, no one could say; the woodchoppers who had felled its mates were dead and gone long ago, and a whole forest of sturdy trees, pines and oaks and maples, had grown again. But the stately head of this old pine towered above them all and made a landmark for sea and shore miles and miles away. Sylvia knew it well. She had always believed that whoever climbed to the top of it could see the ocean; and the little girl had often laid her hand on the great rough trunk and looked up wistfully at those dark boughs that the wind always stirred, no matter how hot and still the air might be below. Now she thought of the tree with a new excitement, for why, if one climbed it at break of day, could not one see all the world, and easily discover whence the white heron flew, and mark the place, and find the hidden nest?

What a spirit of adventure, what wild ambition! What fancied triumph and delight and glory for the later morning when she could make known the secret! It was almost too real and too great for the childish heart to bear.

All night the door of the little house stood open, and the whippoorwills came and sang upon the very step. The young sportsman and his old hostess were sound asleep, but Sylvia's great design kept her broad awake and watching. She forgot to think of sleep. The short summer night seemed as long as the winter darkness, and at last when the whippoorwills ceased, and she was afraid the morning would after all come too soon, she stole out of the house and followed the pasture path through the woods, hastening toward the open ground beyond, listening with a sense of comfort and companionship to the drowsy twitter of a half-awakened bird, whose perch she had jarred in passing. Alas, if the great wave of human interest which flooded for the first time this dull little life should sweep away the satisfaction of an existence heart to heart with nature and the dumb life of the forest!

There was the huge tree asleep yet in the paling moonlight, and small and hopeful Sylvia began with utmost bravery to mount to the top of it, with tingling, eager blood coursing the channels of her whole frame, with her bare feet and fingers, that pinched and held like bird's claws to the monstrous ladder reaching up, up, almost to the sky itself. First she must mount the white oak tree that grew alongside, where she was almost lost among the dark branches and the green leaves heavy and wet with dew; a bird fluttered off its nest, and a red squirrel ran to and fro and scolded pettishly at the harmless housebreaker. Sylvia felt her way easily. She had often climbed there, and knew that higher still one of the oak's upper branches chafed against the pine trunk, just where its lower boughs were set close together. There, when she made the dangerous pass from one tree to the other, the great enterprise would really begin.

She crept out along the swaying oak limb at last, and took the daring step across into the old pine-tree. The way was harder than she thought; she must reach far and hold fast, the sharp dry twigs caught and held her and scratched her like angry talons, the pitch made her thin little fingers clumsy and stiff as she went round and round the tree's great stem, higher and higher upward. The sparrows and robins in the woods below were beginning to wake and twitter to the dawn, yet it seemed much lighter there aloft in the pine-tree, and the child knew that she must hurry if her project were to be of any use.

The tree seemed to lengthen itself out as she went up, and to reach farther and farther upward. It was like a great main-mast to the voyaging earth; it must truly have been amazed that morning through all its ponderous frame as it felt this determined spark of human spirit creeping and climbing from higher branch to branch. Who knows how steadily the least twigs held themselves to advantage this light, weak creature on her way! The old pine must have loved his new dependent. More than all the hawks, and bats, and moths, and even the sweet-voiced thrushes, was the brave, beating heart of the solitary gray-eyed child. And the tree stood still and held away the winds that June morning while the dawn grew bright in the east.

Sylvia's face was like a pale star, if one had seen it from the ground, when the last thorny bough was past, and she stood trembling and tired but wholly triumphant, high in the tree-top. Yes, there was the sea with the dawning sun making a golden dazzle over it, and toward that glorious east flew two hawks with slow-moving pinions. How low they looked in the air from that height when before one had only seen them far up, and dark against the blue sky. Their gay feathers were as soft as moths; they seemed only a little way from the tree, and Sylvia felt as if she too could go flying away among the clouds. Westward, the woodlands and farms reached miles and miles into the distance; here and there were church steeples, and white villages; truly it was a vast and awesome world.

The birds sang louder and louder. At last the sun came up bewilderingly bright. Sylvia could see the white sails of ships out at sea, and the clouds that were purple and rose-colored and yellow at first began to fade away. Where was the white heron's nest in the sea of green branches, and was this wonderful sight and pageant of the world the only reward for having climbed to such a giddy height? Now look down again, Sylvia, where the green marsh is set among the shining birches and dark hemlocks; there where you saw the white heron once you will see him again; look, look! a white spot of him like a single floating feather comes up from the dead hemlock and grows larger, and rises, and comes close at last, and goes by the landmark pine with steady sweep of wing and outstretched slender neck and crested head. And wait! wait! do not move a foot or a finger, little girl, do not send an arrow of light and consciousness from your two eager eyes, for the heron has perched on a pine bough not far beyond yours, and cries back to his mate on the nest, and plumes his feathers for the new day!

The child gives a long sigh a minute later when a company of shouting cat-birds comes also to the tree, and vexed by their fluttering and lawlessness the solemn heron goes away. She knows his secret now, the wild, light, slender bird that floats and wavers, and goes back like an arrow presently to his home in the green world beneath. Then Sylvia, well satisfied, makes her perilous way down again, not daring to look far below the branch she stands on, ready to cry sometimes because her fingers ache and her lamed feet slip. Wondering over and over again what the stranger would say to her, and what he would think when she told him how to find his way straight to the heron's nest.

○ ○ ○

"Sylvy, Sylvy!" called the busy old grandmother again and again, but nobody answered, and the small husk bed was empty, and Sylvia had disappeared.

The guest waked from a dream, and remembering his day's pleasure hurried to dress himself that it might sooner begin. He was sure from the way the shy little girl looked once or twice yesterday that she had at least seen the white heron, and now she must really be persuaded to tell. Here she comes now, paler than ever, and her worn old frock is torn and tattered, and smeared with pine pitch. The grandmother and the sportsman stand in the door together and question her, and the splendid moment has come to speak of the dead hemlock-tree by the green marsh.

But Sylvia does not speak after all, though the old grandmother fretfully rebukes her, and the young man's kind appealing eyes are looking straight into her own. He can make them rich with money; he has promised it, and they are poor now. He is so well worth making happy, and he waits to hear the story she can tell.

No, she must keep her silence! What is it that suddenly forbids her and makes her dumb? Has she been nine years growing, and now, when the great world for the first time puts out a hand to her, must she thrust it aside for a bird's sake? The murmur of the pine's green branches is in her ears, she remembers how the white heron came flying through the golden air and how they watched the sea and the morning together, and Sylvia cannot speak; she cannot tell the heron's secret and give its life away.

o   o   o

Dear loyalty, that suffered a sharp pang as the guest went away disappointed later in the day, that could have served and followed him and loved him as a dog loves! Many a night Sylvia heard the echo of his whistle haunting the pasture path as she came home with the loitering cow. She forgot even her sorrow at the sharp report of his gun and the piteous sight of thrushes and sparrows dropping silent to the ground, their songs hushed and their pretty feathers stained and wet with blood. Were the birds better friends than their hunter might have been,—who can tell? Whatever treasures were lost to her, woodlands and summer-time, remember! Bring your gifts and graces and tell your secrets to this lonely country child!

No magazine publication; A White Heron, 1886

From The Country of the Pointed Firs

I. The Return

There was something about the coast town of Dunnet which made it seem more attractive than other maritime villages of eastern Maine. Perhaps it was the simple fact of acquaintance with that neighborhood which made it so attaching, and gave such interest to the rocky shore and dark woods, and the few houses which seemed to be securely wedged and tree-nailed in among the ledges by the Landing. These houses made the most of their seaward view, and there was a gaiety and determined floweriness in their bits of garden ground; the small-paned high windows in the peaks of their steep gables were like knowing eyes that watched the harbor and the far sea-line beyond, or looked northward all along the shore and its background of spruces and balsam firs. When one really knows a village like this and its surroundings, it is like becoming acquainted with a single person. The process of falling in love at first sight is as final as it is swift in such a case, but the growth of true friendship may be a lifelong affair.

After a brief visit made two or three summers before in the course of a yachting cruise, a lover of Dunnet Landing returned to find the unchanged shores of the pointed firs, the same quaintness of the village with its elaborate conventionalities; all that mixture of remoteness, and childish certainty of being the center of civilization of which her affectionate dreams had told. One evening in June, a single passenger landed upon the steam-boat wharf. The tide was high, there was a fine

crowd of spectators, and the younger portion of the company followed
her with subdued excitement up the narrow street of the salt-aired,
white-clapboarded little town.

II. Mrs. Todd

Later, there was only one fault to find with this choice of a summer
lodging-place, and that was its complete lack of seclusion. At first the
tiny house of Mrs. Almira Todd, which stood with its end to the street,
appeared to be retired and sheltered enough from the busy world,
behind its bushy bit of a green garden, in which all the blooming things,
two or three gay hollyhocks and some London-pride, were pushed back
against the gray-shingled wall. It was a queer little garden and puzzling to a stranger, the few flowers being put at a disadvantage by so
much greenery; but the discovery was soon made that Mrs. Todd was
an ardent lover of herbs, both wild and tame, and the sea-breezes blew
into the low end-window of the house laden with not only sweet-brier
and sweet-mary, but balm and sage and borage and mint, wormwood
and southernwood. If Mrs. Todd had occasion to step into the far
corner of her herb plot, she trod heavily upon thyme, and made its
fragrant presence known with all the rest. Being a very large person,
her full skirts brushed and bent almost every slender stalk that her feet
missed. You could always tell when she was stepping about there, even
when you were half awake in the morning, and learned to know, in the
course of a few weeks' experience, in exactly which corner of the
garden she might be.

At one side of this herb plot were other growths of a rustic phar-
macopoeia, great treasures and rarities among the commoner herbs.
There were some strange and pungent odors that roused a dim sense
and remembrance of something in the forgotten past. Some of these
might once have belonged to sacred and mystic rites, and have had
some occult knowledge handed with them down the centuries; but
now they pertained only to humble compounds brewed at intervals
with molasses or vinegar or spirits in a small caldron on Mrs. Todd's
kitchen stove. They were dispensed to suffering neighbors, who usually came at night as if by stealth, bringing their own ancient-looking
vials to be filled. One nostrum was called the Indian remedy, and its
price was but fifteen cents; the whispered directions could be heard
as customers passed the windows. With most remedies the purchaser
was allowed to depart unadmonished from the kitchen, Mrs. Todd
being a wise saver of steps; but with certain vials she gave cautions,
standing in the doorway, and there were other doses which had to be
accompanied on their healing way as far as the gate, while she muttered long chapters of directions, and kept up an air of secrecy and
importance to the last. It may not have been only the common ails of
humanity with which she tried to cope; it seemed sometimes as if
love and hate and jealousy and adverse winds at sea might also find

their proper remedies among the curious wild-looking plants in Mrs. Todd's garden.

The village doctor and this learned herbalist were upon the best of terms. The good man may have counted upon the unfavorable effect of certain potions which he should find his opportunity in counteracting; at any rate, he now and then stopped and exchanged greetings with Mrs. Todd over the picket fence. The conversation became at once professional after the briefest preliminaries, and he would stand twirling a sweet-scented sprig in his fingers, and make suggestive jokes, perhaps about her faith in a too persistent course of thorough-wort elixir, in which my landlady professed such firm belief as sometimes to endanger the life and usefulness of worthy neighbors.

To arrive at this quietest of seaside villages late in June, when the busy herb-gathering season was just beginning, was also to arrive in the early prime of Mrs. Todd's activity in the brewing of old-fashioned spruce beer. This cooling and refreshing drink had been brought to wonderful perfection through a long series of experiments; it had won immense local fame, and the supplies for its manufacture were always giving out and having to be replenished. For various reasons, the seclusion and uninterrupted days which had been looked forward to proved to be very rare in this otherwise delightful corner of the world. My hostess and I had made our shrewd business agreement on the basis of a simple cold luncheon at noon, and liberal restitution in the matter of hot suppers, to provide for which the lodger might sometimes be seen hurrying down the road, late in the day, with cunner line[1] in hand. It was soon found that this arrangement made large allowance for Mrs. Todd's slow herb-gathering progresses through woods and pastures. The spruce-beer customers were pretty steady in hot weather, and there were many demands for different soothing syrups and elixirs with which the unwise curiosity of my early residence had made me acquainted. Knowing Mrs. Todd to be a widow, who had little beside this slender business and the income from one hungry lodger to maintain her, one's energies and even interest were quickly bestowed, until it became a matter of course that she should go afield every pleasant day, and that the lodger should answer all peremptory knocks at the side door.

In taking an occasional wisdom-giving stroll in Mrs. Todd's company, and in acting as business partner during her frequent absences, I found the July days fly fast, and it was not until I felt myself confronted with too great pride and pleasure in the display, one night, of two dollars and twenty-seven cents which I had taken in during the day, that I remembered a long piece of writing, sadly belated now, which I was bound to do. To have been patted kindly on the shoulder and called "darlin'," to have been offered a surprise of early mushrooms for supper, to have had all the glory of making two dollars and

---

1. Fishing line; the cunner is a fish common to the North American Atlantic.

twenty-seven cents in a single day, and then to renounce it all and
withdraw from these pleasant successes, needed much resolution. Literary employments are so vexed with uncertainties at best, and it was
not until the voice of conscience sounded louder in my ears than the sea
on the nearest pebble beach that I said unkind words of withdrawal to
Mrs. Todd. She only became more wistfully affectionate than ever in
her expressions, and looked as disappointed as I expected when I
frankly told her that I could no longer enjoy the pleasure of what we
called "seein' folks." I felt that I was cruel to a whole neighborhood in
curtailing her liberty in this most important season for harvesting the
different wild herbs that were so much counted upon to ease their
winter ails.

"Well, dear," she said sorrowfully, "I've took great advantage o'
your bein' here. I ain't had such a season for years, but I have never
had nobody I could so trust. All you lack is a few qualities, but with
time you'd gain judgment an' experience, an' be very able in the
business. I'd stand right here an' say it to anybody."

                              *   *   *

Mrs. Todd and I were not separated or estranged by the change in
our business relations; on the contrary, a deeper intimacy seemed to
begin. I do not know what herb of the night it was that used sometimes to send out a penetrating odor late in the evening, after the
dew had fallen, and the moon was high, and the cool air came up
from the sea. Then Mrs. Todd would feel that she must talk to somebody, and I was only too glad to listen. We both fell under the spell,
and she either stood outside the window, or made an errand to my
sitting-room, and told, it might be very commonplace news of the
day, or, as happened one misty summer night, all that lay deepest in
her heart. It was in this way that I came to know that she had loved
one who was far above her.

"No, dear, him I speak of could never think of me," she said. "When
we was young together his mother didn't favor the match, an' done
everything she could to part us; and folks thought we both married
well, but't wa'n't what either one of us wanted most; an' now we're
left alone again, an' might have had each other all the time. He was
above bein' a seafarin' man, an' prospered more than most; he come
of a high family, an' my lot was plain an' hard-workin'. I ain't seen him
for some years; he's forgot our youthful feelin's, I expect, but a
woman's heart is different; them feelin's comes back when you think
you've done with 'em, as sure as spring comes with the year. An' I've
always had ways of hearin' about him."

She stood in the center of a braided rug, and its rings of black and
gray seemed to circle about her feet in the dim light. Her height and
massiveness in the low room gave her the look of a huge sibyl,[2] while
the strange fragrance of the mysterious herb blew in from the little
garden.

2. A woman regarded as an oracle or prophetess by the ancient Greeks and Romans.

VII. The Outer Island

Gaffett with his good bunk and the bird-skins, the story of the wreck of the Minerva, the human-shaped creatures of fog and cobweb, the great words of Milton with which he described their onslaught upon the crew, all this moving tale had such an air of truth that I could not argue with Captain Littlepage. The old man looked away from the map as if it had vaguely troubled him, and regarded me appealingly.

"We were just speaking of"—and he stopped. I saw that he had suddenly forgotten his subject.

"There were a great many persons at the funeral," I hastened to say.

"Oh yes," the captain answered, with satisfaction. "All showed respect who could. The sad circumstances had for a moment slipped my mind. Yes, Mrs. Begg will be very much missed. She was a capital manager for her husband when he was at sea. Oh yes, shipping is a very great loss." And he sighed heavily. "There was hardly a man of any standing who didn't interest himself in some way in navigation. It always gave credit to a town. I call it low-water mark now here in Dunnet."

He rose with dignity to take leave, and asked me to stop at his house some day, when he would show me some outlandish things that he had brought home from sea. I was familiar with the subject of the decadence of shipping interests in all its affecting branches, having been already some time in Dunnet, and I felt sure that Captain Littlepage's mind had now returned to a safe level.

As we came down the hill toward the village our ways divided, and when I had seen the old captain well started on a smooth piece of sidewalk which would lead him to his own door, we parted, the best of friends. "Step in some afternoon," he said, as affectionately as if I were a fellow-shipmaster wrecked on the lee shore of age like himself. I turned toward home, and presently met Mrs. Todd coming toward me with an anxious expression.

"I see you sleevin'[3] the old gentleman down the hill," she suggested.

"Yes. I've had a very interesting afternoon with him," I answered; and her face brightened.

"Oh, then he's all right. I was afraid 'twas one o' his flighty spells, an' Mari' Harris wouldn't"—

"Yes," I returned, smiling, "he has been telling me some old stories, but we talked about Mrs. Begg and the funeral beside, and Paradise Lost."

"I expect he got tellin' of you some o' his great narratives," she answered, looking at me shrewdly. "Funerals always sets him goin'. Some o' them tales hangs together toler'ble well," she added, with a sharper look than before. "An' he's been a great reader all his seafarin' days. Some thinks he overdid, and affected his head, but for a man o'

3. "Sleeve" means to take a person by the sleeve.

his years he's amazin' now when he's at his best. Oh, he used to be a beautiful man!"

* * *

We were standing where there was a fine view of the harbor and its long stretches of shore all covered by the great army of the pointed firs, darkly cloaked and standing as if they waited to embark. As we looked far seaward among the outer islands, the trees seemed to march seaward still, going steadily over the heights and down to the water's edge.

It had been growing gray and cloudy, like the first evening of autumn, and a shadow had fallen on the darkening shore. Suddenly, as we looked, a gleam of golden sunshine struck the outer islands, and one of them shone out clear in the light, and revealed itself in a compelling way to our eyes. Mrs. Todd was looking off across the bay with a face full of affection and interest. The sunburst upon that outermost island made it seem like a sudden revelation of the world beyond this which some believe to be so near.

"That's where mother lives," said Mrs. Todd. "Can't we see it plain? I was brought up out there on Green Island. I know every rock an' bush on it."

"Your mother!" I exclaimed, with great interest.

"Yes, dear, cert'in; I've got her yet, old's I be. She's one of them spry, light-footed little women; always was, an' light-hearted, too," answered Mrs. Todd, with satisfaction. "She's seen all the trouble folks can see, without it's her last sickness; an' she's got a word of courage for everybody. Life ain't spoilt her a mite. She's eighty-six an' I'm sixty-seven, and I've seen the time I've felt a good sight the oldest. 'Land sakes alive!' says she, last time I was out to see her. 'How you do lurch about steppin' into a bo't?' I laughed so I liked to have gone right over into the water; an' we pushed off, an' left her laughin' there on the shore."

The light had faded as we watched. Mrs. Todd had mounted a gray rock, and stood there grand and architectural, like a caryatide.[4] Presently she stepped down, and we continued our way homeward.

"You an' me, we'll take a bo't an' go out some day and see mother," she promised me. " 'Twould please her very much, an' there's one or two sca'ce herbs grows better on the island than anywheres else. I ain't seen their like nowheres here on the main."

"Now I'm goin' right down to get us each a mug o' my beer," she announced as we entered the house, "an' I believe I'll sneak in a little mite o' camomile. Goin' to the funeral an' all, I feel to have had a very wearin' afternoon."

I heard her going down into the cool little cellar; and then there was considerable delay. When she returned, mug in hand, I noticed the taste of camomile, in spite of my protest; but its flavor was disguised

---

4. A supporting column sculptured in the form of a woman.

by some other herb that I did not know, and she stood over me until I drank it all and said that I liked it.

"I don't give that to everybody," said Mrs. Todd kindly; and I felt for a moment as if it were part of a spell and incantation, and as if my enchantress would now begin to look like the cobweb shapes of the arctic town. Nothing happened but a quiet evening and some delightful plans that we made about going to Green Island, and on the morrow there was the clear sunshine and blue sky of another day.

VIII. Green Island

One morning, very early, I heard Mrs. Todd in the garden outside my window. By the unusual loudness of her remarks to a passer-by, and the notes of a familiar hymn which she sang as she worked among the herbs, and which came as if directed purposely to the sleepy ears of my consciousness, I knew that she wished I would wake up and come and speak to her.

In a few minutes she responded to a morning voice from behind the blinds. "I expect you're goin' up to your schoolhouse to pass all this pleasant day; yes, I expect you're goin' to be dreadful busy," she said despairingly.

"Perhaps not," said I. "Why, what's going to be the matter with you, Mrs. Todd?" For I supposed that she was tempted by the fine weather to take one of her favorite expeditions along the shore pastures to gather herbs and simples,[5] and would like to have me keep the house.

"No, I don't want to go nowhere by land," she answered gaily,— "no, not by land; but I don't know's we shall have a better day all the rest of the summer to go out to Green Island an' see mother. I waked up early thinkin' of her. The wind's light northeast,—'twill take us right straight out; an' this time o' year it's liable to change round southwest an' fetch us home pretty, 'long late in the afternoon. Yes, it's goin' to be a good day."

"Speak to the captain and the Bowden boy, if you see anybody going by toward the landing," said I. "We'll take the big boat."

"Oh, my sakes! now you let me do things my way," said Mrs. Todd scornfully. "No, dear, we won't take no big bo't. I'll just git a handy dory,[6] an' Johnny Bowden an' me, we'll man her ourselves. I don't want no abler bo't than a good dory, an' a nice light breeze ain't goin' to make no sea; an' Johnny's my cousin's son,—mother'll like to have him come; an' he'll be down to the herrin' weirs all the time we're there, anyway; we don't want to carry no men folks havin' to be considered every minute an' takin' up all our time. No, you let me do; we'll just slip out an' see mother by ourselves. I guess what breakfast you'll want's about ready now."

5. Medicinal plants or the medicines obtained from them.

6. A small, narrow, flat-bottomed fishing boat with high sides and sharp prow.

I had become well acquainted with Mrs. Todd as landlady, herb-gatherer, and rustic philosopher; we had been discreet fellow-passengers once or twice when I had sailed up the coast to a larger town than Dunnet Landing to do some shopping; but I was yet to become acquainted with her as a mariner. An hour later we pushed off from the landing in the desired dory. The tide was just on the turn, beginning to fall, and several friends and acquaintances stood along the side of the dilapidated wharf and cheered us by their words and evident interest. Johnny Bowden and I were both rowing in haste to get out where we could catch the breeze and put up the small sail which lay clumsily furled along the gunwale. Mrs. Todd sat aft, a stern and unbending lawgiver.

"You better let her drift; we'll get there 'bout as quick; the tide'll take her right out from under these old buildin's; there's plenty wind outside."

"Your bo't ain't trimmed proper, Mis' Todd!" exclaimed a voice from shore. "You're loaded so the bo't'll drag; you can't git her before the wind, ma'am. You set 'midships, Mis' Todd, an' let the boy hold the sheet 'n' steer after he gits the sail up; you won't never git out to Green Island that way. She's lo'ded bad, your bo't is,—she's heavy behind's she is now!"

Mrs. Todd turned with some difficulty and regarded the anxious adviser, my right oar flew out of water, and we seemed about to capsize. "That you, Asa? Good-mornin'," she said politely. "I al'ays liked the starn seat best. When'd you git back from up country?"[7]

This allusion to Asa's origin was not lost upon the rest of the company. We were some little distance from shore, but we could hear a chuckle of laughter, and Asa, a person who was too ready with his criticism and advice on every possible subject, turned and walked indignantly away.

When we caught the wind we were soon on our seaward course, and only stopped to underrun a trawl, for the floats of which Mrs. Todd looked earnestly, explaining that her mother might not be prepared for three extra to dinner; it was her brother's trawl, and she meant to just run her eye along for the right sort of a little haddock. I leaned over the boat's side with great interest and excitement, while she skillfully handled the long line of hooks, and made scornful remarks upon worthless, bait-consuming creatures of the sea as she reviewed them and left them on the trawl or shook them off into the waves. At last we came to what she pronounced a proper haddock, and having taken him on board and ended his life resolutely, we went our way.

As we sailed along I listened to an increasingly delightful commentary upon the islands, some of them barren rocks, or at best giving sparse pasturage for sheep in the early summer. On one of these an eager little flock ran to the water's edge and bleated at us so affectingly

---

7. The inland or interior region of a country, or, here, of Maine.

that I would willingly have stopped; but Mrs. Todd steered away from the rocks, and scolded at the sheep's mean owner, an acquaintance of hers, who grudged the little salt and still less care which the patient creatures needed. The hot midsummer sun makes prisons of these small islands that are a paradise in early June, with their cool springs and short thick-growing grass. On a larger island, farther out to sea, my entertaining companion showed me with glee the small houses of two farmers who shared the island between them, and declared that for three generations the people had not spoken to each other even in times of sickness or death or birth. "When the news come that the war was over, one of 'em knew it a week, and never stepped across his wall to tell the other," she said. "There, they enjoy it; they've got to have somethin' to interest 'em in such a place; 'tis a good deal more tryin' to be tied to folks you don't like than 'tis to be alone. Each of 'em tell the neighbors their wrongs; plenty likes to hear and tell again; them as fetch a bone'll carry one, an' so they keep the fight a-goin'. I must say I like variety myself; some folks washes Monday an' irons Tuesday the whole year round, even if the circus is goin' by!"

A long time before we landed at Green Island we could see the small white house, standing high like a beacon, where Mrs. Todd was born and where her mother lived, on a green slope above the water, with dark spruce woods still higher. There were crops in the fields, which we presently distinguished from one another. Mrs. Todd examined them while we were still far at sea. "Mother's late potatoes looks backward; ain't had rain enough so far," she pronounced her opinion. "They look weedier than what they call Front Street down to Cowper Centre. I expect brother William is so occupied with his herrin' weirs[8] an' servin' out bait to the schooners that he don't think once a day of the land."

"What's the flag for, up above the spruces there behind the house?" I inquired, with eagerness.

"Oh, that's the sign for herrin'," she explained kindly, while Johnny Bowden regarded me with contemptuous surprise. "When they get enough for schooners they raise that flag; an' when 'tis a poor catch in the weir pocket they just fly a little signal down by the shore, an' then the small bo'ts comes and get enough an' over for their trawls. There, look! there she is: mother sees us; she's wavin' somethin' out o' the fore door! She'll be to the ladin'-place quick's we are."

I looked, and could see a tiny flutter in the doorway, but a quicker signal had made its way from the heart on shore to the heart on the sea.

"How do you suppose she knows it is me?" said Mrs. Todd, with a tender smile on her broad face. "There, you never get over bein' a child long's you have a mother to go to. Look at the chimeny, now; she's gone right in an' brightened up the fire. Well, there, I'm glad mother's well; you'll enjoy seein' her very much."

---

8. Fences placed across a body of water to catch or hold fish.

Mrs. Todd leaned back into her proper position, and the boat trimmed again. She took a firmer grasp of the sheet, and gave an impatient look up at the gaff and the leech of the little sail, and twitched the sheet as if she urged the wind like a horse. There came at once a fresh gust, and we seemed to have doubled our speed. Soon we were near enough to see a tiny figure with handkerchiefed head come down across the field and stand waiting for us at the cove above a curve of pebble beach.

Presently the dory grated on the pebbles, and Johnny Bowden, who had been kept in abeyance during the voyage, sprang out and used manful exertions to haul us up with the next wave, so that Mrs. Todd could make a dry landing.

"You done that very well," she said, mounting to her feet, and coming ashore somewhat stiffly, but with great dignity, refusing our outstretched hands, and returning to possess herself of a bag which had lain at her feet.

"Well, mother, here I be!" she announced with indifference; but they stood and beamed in each other's faces.

"Lookin' pretty well for an old lady, ain't she?" said Mrs. Todd's mother, turning away from her daughter to speak to me. She was a delightful little person herself, with bright eyes and an affectionate air of expectation like a child on a holiday. You felt as if Mrs. Blackett were an old and dear friend before you let go her cordial hand. We all started together up the hill.

"Now don't you haste too fast, mother," said Mrs. Todd warningly; " 'tis a far reach o' risin' ground to the fore door, and you won't set an' get your breath when you're once there, but go trotting about. Now don't you go a mite faster than we proceed with this bag an' basket. Johnny, there, 'll fetch up the haddock. I just made one stop to under-run William's trawl till I come to jes' such a fish's I thought you'd want to make one o' your nice chowders of. I've brought an onion with me that was layin' about on the window-sill at home."

"That's just what I was wantin'," said the hostess. "I give a sigh when you spoke o' chowder, knowin' my onions was out. William forgot to replenish us last time he was to the Landin'. Don't you haste so yourself, Almiry, up this risin' ground. I hear you commencin' to wheeze a'ready."

This mild revenge seemed to afford great pleasure to both giver and receiver. They laughed a little, and looked at each other affectionately, and then at me. Mrs. Todd considerately paused, and faced about to regard the wide sea view. I was glad to stop, being more out of breath than either of my companions, and I prolonged the halt by asking the names of the neighboring islands. There was a fine breeze blowing, which we felt more there on the high land than when we were running before it in the dory.

"Why, this ain't that kitten I saw when I was out last, the one that I said didn't appear likely?" exclaimed Mrs. Todd as we went our way.

"That's the one, Almiry," said her mother. "She always had a likely look to me, an' she's right after business. I never see such a mouser for one of her age. If 't wan't for William, I never should have housed that other dronin' old thing so long; but he sets by her on account of her havin' a bob tail. I don't deem it advisable to maintain cats just on account of their havin' bob tails; they're like all other curiosities, good for them that wants to see 'm twice. This kitten catches mice for both, an' keeps me respectable as I ain't been for a year. She's a real understandin' little help, this kitten is. I picked her from among five Miss Augusta Pennell had over to Burnt Island," said the old woman, trudging along with the kitten close at her skirts. "Augusta, she says to me, 'Why, Mis' Blackett, you've took the homeliest'; and says I, 'I've got the smartest; I'm satisfied.' "

"I'd trust nobody sooner'n you to pick out a kitten, mother," said the daughter handsomely, and we went on in peace and harmony.

The house was just before us now, on a green level that looked as if a huge hand had scooped it out of the long green field we had been ascending. A little way above, the dark, spruce woods began to climb the top of the hill and cover the seaward slopes of the island. There was just room for the small farm and the forest; we looked down at the fish-house and its rough sheds, and the weirs stretching far out into the water. As we looked upward, the tops of the firs came sharp against the blue sky. There was a great stretch of rough pasture-land round the shoulder of the island to the eastward, and here were all the thick-scattered gray rocks that kept their places, and the gray backs of many sheep that forever wandered and fed on the thin sweet pasturage that fringed the ledges and made soft hollows and strips of green turf like growing velvet. I could see the rich green of bayberry bushes here and there, where the rocks made room. The air was very sweet; one could not help wishing to be a citizen of such a complete and tiny continent and home of fisherfolk.

The house was broad and clean, with a roof that looked heavy on its low walls. It was one of the houses that seem firm-rooted in the ground, as if they were two-thirds below the surface, like icebergs. The front door stood hospitably open in expectation of company, and an orderly vine grew at each side; but our path led to the kitchen door at the house-end, and there grew a mass of gay flowers and greenery, as if they had been swept together by some diligent garden broom into a tangled heap: there were portulacas all along under the lower step and straggling off into the grass, and clustering mallows that crept as near as they dared, like poor relations. I saw the bright eyes and brainless little heads of two half-grown chickens who were snuggled down among the mallows as if they had been chased away from the door more than once, and expected to be again.

"It seems kind o' formal comin' in this way," said Mrs. Todd impulsively, as we passed the flowers and came to the front door-step; but

she was mindful of the proprieties, and walked before us into the best
room on the left.

"Why, mother, if you haven't gone an' turned the carpet!" she
exclaimed, with something in her voice that spoke of awe and admiration. "When'd you get to it? I s'pose Mis' Addicks come over an' helped
you, from White Island Landing?"

"No, she didn't," answered the old woman, standing proudly erect,
and making the most of a great moment. "I done it all myself with
William's help. He had a spare day, an' took right holt with me; an'
'twas all well beat on the grass, an' turned, an' put down again afore
we went to bed. I ripped an' sewed over two o' them long breadths.
I ain't had such a good night's sleep for two years."

"There, what do you think o' havin' such a mother as that for
eighty-six year old?" said Mrs. Todd, standing before us like a large
figure of Victory.

As for the mother, she took on a sudden look of youth; you felt as if
she promised a great future, and was beginning, not ending, her summers and their happy toils.

"My, my!" exclaimed Mrs. Todd. "I couldn't ha' done it myself, I've
got to own it."

"I was much pleased to have it off my mind," said Mrs. Blackett,
humbly; "the more so because along at the first of the next week I
wasn't very well. I suppose it may have been the change of weather."

Mrs. Todd could not resist a significant glance at me, but, with
charming sympathy, she forbore to point the lesson or to connect this
illness with its apparent cause. She loomed larger than ever in the little
old-fashioned best room, with its few pieces of good furniture and
pictures of national interest. The green paper curtains were stamped
with conventional landscapes of a foreign order,—castles on inaccessi-
ble crags, and lovely lakes with steep wooded shores; under-foot the
treasured carpet was covered thick with home-made rugs. There were
empty glass lamps and crystallized bouquets of grass and some fine
shells on the narrow mantelpiece.

"I was married in this room," said Mrs. Todd unexpectedly; and I
heard her give a sigh after she had spoken, as if she could not help the
touch of regret that would forever come with all her thoughts of
happiness.

"We stood right there between the windows," she added, "and the
minister stood here. William wouldn't come in. He was always odd
about seein' folks, just's he is now. I run to meet 'em from a child, an'
William, he'd take an' run away."

"I've been the gainer," said the old mother cheerfully. "William has
been son an' daughter both since you was married off the island. He's
been 'most too satisfied to stop at home 'long o' his old mother, but I
always tell 'em I'm the gainer."

We were all moving toward the kitchen as if by common instinct.

The best room was too suggestive of serious occasions, and the shades were all pulled down to shut out the summer light and air. It was indeed a tribute to Society to find a room set apart for her behests out there on so apparently neighborless and remote an island. Afternoon visits and evening festivals must be few in such a bleak situation at certain seasons of the year, but Mrs. Blackett was of those who do not live to themselves, and who have long since passed the line that divides mere self-concern from a valued share in whatever Society can give and take. There were those of her neighbors who never had taken the trouble to furnish a best room, but Mrs. Blackett was one who knew the uses of a parlor.

"Yes, do come right out into the old kitchen; I shan't make any stranger of you," she invited us pleasantly, after we had been properly received in the room appointed to formality. "I expect Almiry, here, 'll be driftin' out 'mongst the pasture-weeds quick's she can find a good excuse. 'Tis hot now. You'd better content yourselves till you get nice an' rested, an' 'long after dinner the sea-breeze 'll spring up, an' then you can take your walks, an' go up an' see the prospect from the big ledge. Almiry'll want to show off everything there is. Then I'll get you a good cup o' tea before you start to go home. The days are plenty long now."

While we were talking in the best room the selected fish had been mysteriously brought up from the shore, and lay all cleaned and ready in an earthen crock on the table.

"I think William might have just stopped an' said a word," remarked Mrs. Todd, pouting with high affront as she caught sight of it. "He's friendly enough when he comes ashore, an' was remarkable social the last time, for him."

"He ain't disposed to be very social with the ladies," explained William's mother, with a delightful glance at me, as if she counted upon my friendship and tolerance. "He's very particular, and he's all in his old fishin'-clothes today. He'll want me to tell him everything you said and done, after you've gone. William has very deep affections. He'll want to see you, Almiry. Yes, I guess he'll be in by an' by."

"I'll search for him by 'n' by, if he don't," proclaimed Mrs. Todd, with an air of unalterable resolution. "I know all of his burrows down 'long the shore. I'll catch him by hand 'fore he knows it. I've got some business with William, anyway. I brought forty-two cents with me that was due him for them last lobsters he brought in."

"You can leave it with me," suggested the little old mother, who was already stepping about among her pots and pans in the pantry, and preparing to make the chowder.

I became possessed of a sudden unwonted curiosity in regard to William, and felt that half the pleasure of my visit would be lost if I could not make his interesting acquaintance.

XI. The Old Singers

William was sitting on the side door step, and the old mother was busy making her tea; she gave into my hand an old flowered-glass tea-caddy.

"William thought you'd like to see this, when he was settin' the table. My father brought it to my mother from the island of Tobago; an' here's a pair of beautiful mugs that came with it." She opened the glass door of a little cupboard beside the chimney. "These I call my best things, dear," she said. "You'd laugh to see how we enjoy 'em Sunday nights in winter: we have a real company tea 'stead o' livin' right along just the same, an' I make somethin' good for a s'prise an' put on some o' my preserves, an' we get a-talkin' together an' have real pleasant times."

Mrs. Todd laughed indulgently, and looked to see what I thought of such childishness.

"I wish I could be here some Sunday evening," said I.

"William an' me'll be talkin' about you an' thinking' o' this nice day," said Mrs. Blackett affectionately, and she glanced at William, and he looked up bravely and nodded. I began to discover that he and his sister could not speak their deeper feelings before each other.

"Now I want you an' mother to sing," said Mrs. Todd abruptly, with an air of command, and I gave William much sympathy in his evident distress.

"After I've had my cup o' tea, dear," answered the old hostess cheerfully; and so we sat down and took our cups and made merry while they lasted. It was impossible not to wish to stay on forever at Green Island, and I could not help saying so.

"I'm very happy here, both winter an' summer," said old Mrs. Blackett. "William an' I never wish for any other home, do we, William? I'm glad you find it pleasant; I wish you'd come an' stay, dear, whenever you feel inclined. But here's Almiry; I always think Providence was kind to plot an' have her husband leave her a good house where she really belonged. She'd been very restless if she'd had to continue here on Green Island. You wanted more scope, didn't you, Almiry, an' to live in a large place where more things grew? Sometimes folks wonders that we don't live together; perhaps we shall some time," and a shadow of sadness and apprehension flitted across her face. "The time o' sickness an' failin' has got to come to all. But Almiry's got an herb that's good for everything." She smiled as she spoke, and looked bright again.

"There's some herb that's good for everybody, except for them that thinks they're sick when they ain't," announced Mrs. Todd, with a truly professional air of finality. "Come, William, let's have Sweet Home, an' then mother'll sing Cupid an' the Bee for us."

Then followed a most charming surprise. William mastered his timidity and began to sing. His voice was a little faint and frail, like the family daguerreotypes, but it was a tenor voice, and perfectly true and sweet. I have never heard Home, Sweet Home sung as touchingly and seriously as he sang it; he seemed to make it quite new; and when he paused for a moment at the end of the first line and began the next, the old mother joined him and they sang together, she missing only the higher notes, where he seemed to lend his voice to hers for the moment and carry on her very note and air. It was the silent man's real and only means of expression, and one could have listened forever, and have asked for more and more songs of old Scotch and English inheritance and the best that have lived from the ballad music of the war. Mrs. Todd kept time visibly, and sometimes audibly, with her ample foot. I saw the tears in her eyes sometimes, when I could see beyond the tears in mine. But at last the songs ended and the time came to say good-by; it was the end of a great pleasure.

Mrs. Blackett, the dear old lady, opened the door of her bedroom while Mrs. Todd was tying up the herb bag, and William had gone down to get the boat ready and to blow the horn for Johnny Bowden, who had joined a roving boat party who were off the shore lobstering.

I went to the door of the bedroom, and thought how pleasant it looked, with its pink-and-white patchwork quilt and the brown un-painted paneling of its woodwork.

"Come right in, dear," she said. "I want you to set down in my old quilted rockin'-chair there by the window; you'll say it's the prettiest view in the house. I set there a good deal to rest me and when I want to read."

There was a worn red Bible on the nightstand, and Mrs. Blackett's heavy silver-bowed glasses; her thimble was on the narrow window-ledge, and folded carefully on the table was a thick striped-cotton shirt that she was making for her son. Those dear old fingers and their loving stitches, that heart which had made the most of everything that needed love! Here was the real home, the heart of the old house on Green Island! I sat in the rocking-chair, and felt that it was a place of peace, the little brown bedroom, and the quiet outlook upon field and sea and sky.

I looked up, and we understood each other without speaking. "I shall like to think o' your settin' here today," said Mrs. Blackett. "I want you to come again. It has been so pleasant for William."

The wind served us all the way home, and did not fall or let the sail slacken until we were close to the shore. We had a generous freight of lobsters in the boat, and new potatoes which William had put aboard, and what Mrs. Todd proudly called a full "kag"[9] of prime number one salted mackerel; and when we landed we had to make business arrangements to have these conveyed to her house in a wheelbarrow.

I never shall forget the day at Green Island. The town of Dunnet Landing seemed large and noisy and oppressive as we came ashore.

9. Keg.

Such is the power of contrast; for the village was so still that I could hear the shy whipporwills singing that night as I lay awake in my downstairs bedroom, and the scent of Mrs. Todd's herb garden under the window blew in again and again with every gentle rising of the seabreeze.

1896

The Queen's Twin

I

The coast of Maine was in former years brought so near to foreign shores by its busy fleet of ships that among the older men and women one still finds a surprising proportion of travelers. Each seaward-stretching headland with its high-set houses, each island of a single farm, has sent its spies to view many a Land of Eshcol;[1] one may see plain, contented old faces at the windows, whose eyes have looked at far-away ports and known the splendors of the Eastern world. They shame the easy voyager of the North Atlantic and the Mediterranean; they have rounded the Cape of Good Hope and braved the angry seas of Cape Horn in small wooden ships; they have brought up their hardy boys and girls on narrow decks; they were among the last of the Northmen's children to go adventuring to unknown shores. More than this one cannot give to a young State for its enlightenment; the sea captains and the captains' wives of Maine knew something of the wide world, and never mistook their native parishes for the whole instead of a part thereof; they knew not only Thomaston and Castine and Portland, but London and Bristol and Bordeaux, and the strange-mannered harbors of the China Sea.

One September day, when I was nearly at the end of a summer spent in a village called Dunnet Landing, on the Maine coast, my friend Mrs. Todd, in whose house I lived, came home from a long, solitary stroll in the wild pastures, with an eager look as if she were just starting on a hopeful quest instead of returning. She brought a little basket with blackberries enough for supper, and held it towards me so that I could see that there were also some late and surprising raspberries sprinkled on top, but she made no comment upon her wayfaring. I could tell plainly that she had something very important to say.

"You haven't brought home a leaf of anything," I ventured to this practiced herb-gatherer. "You were saying yesterday that the witch hazel might be in bloom."

1. Moses sent men to "spy out" the land of Canaan; when they returned from the Valley of Eschol, they brought back grapes, pomegranates, and figs, calling it "the land of milk and honey"; see Numbers 13:- 21–27.

"I dare say, dear," she answered in a lofty manner; "I ain't goin' to say it wasn't; I ain't much concerned either way 'bout the facts o' witch hazel. Truth is, I've been off visitin'; there's an old Indian footpath leadin' over towards the Back Shore through the great heron swamp that anybody can't travel over all summer. You have to seize your time some day just now, while the low ground's summer-dried as it is today, and before the fall rains set in. I never thought of it till I was out o' sight o' home, and I says to myself, 'Today's the day, certain!' and stepped along smart as I could. Yes, I've been visitin'. I did get into one spot that was wet underfoot before I noticed; you wait till I get me a pair o' dry woolen stockings, in case of cold, and I'll come an' tell ye."

Mrs. Todd disappeared. I could see that something had deeply interested her. She might have fallen in with either the sea-serpent or the lost tribes of Israel,[2] such was her air of mystery and satisfaction. She had been away since just before mid-morning, and as I sat waiting by my window I saw the last red glow of autumn sunshine flare along the gray rocks of the shore and leave them cold again, and touch the far sails of some coast-wise schooners so that they stood like golden houses on the sea.

o   o   o

I was left to wonder longer than I liked. Mrs. Todd was making an evening fire and putting things in train for supper; presently she returned, still looking warm and cheerful after her long walk.

"There's a beautiful view from a hill over where I've been," she told me; "yes, there's a beautiful prospect of land and sea. You wouldn't discern the hill from any distance, but 'tis the pretty situation of it that counts. I sat there a long spell, and I did wish for you. No, I didn't know a word about goin' when I set out this morning" (as if I had openly reproached her!); "I only felt one o' them travelin' fits comin' on, an' I ketched up my little basket; I didn't know but I might turn and come back time for dinner. I thought it wise to set out your luncheon for you in case I didn't. Hope you had all you wanted; yes, I hope you had enough."

"Oh, yes, indeed," said I. My landlady was always peculiarly bountiful in her supplies when she left me to fare for myself, as if she made a sort of peace-offering or affectionate apology.

"You know that hill with the old house right on top, over beyond the heron swamp? You'll excuse me for explainin'," Mrs. Todd began, "but you ain't so apt to strike inland as you be to go right along shore. You know that hill; there's a path leadin' right over to it that you have to look sharp to find nowadays; it belonged to the up-country Indians when they had to make a carry to the landing here to get to the out' islands. I've heard the old folks say that there used to be a place across

2. Ten tribes of Israel conquered by the Assyrians in 721 B.C.; after this time they disappear from Hebrew records. Among speculations as to their fate, one theory proposed that they migrated to America and were the ancestors of the Native Americans.

a ledge where they'd worn a deep track with their moccasin feet, but I never could find it. 'Tis so overgrown in some places that you keep losin' the path in the bushes and findin' it as you can; but it runs pretty straight considerin' the lay o' the land, and I keep my eye on the sun and the moss that grows one side o' the tree trunks. Some brook's been choked up and the swamp's bigger than it used to be. Yes; I did get in deep enough, one place!"

I showed the solicitude that I felt. Mrs. Todd was no longer young, and in spite of her strong, great frame and spirited behavior, I knew that certain ills were apt to seize upon her, and would end some day by leaving her lame and ailing.

"Don't you go worryin' about me," she insisted, "settin' still's the only way the Evil One'll ever get the upper hand o' me. Keep me movin' enough, an' I'm twenty year old summer an' winter both. I don't know why 'tis, but I've never happened to mention the one I've been to see. I don't know why I never happened to speak the name of Abby Martin, for I often give her a thought, but 'tis a dreadful out-o-the-way place where she lives, and I haven't seen her myself for three or four years. She's a real good interesting woman, and we're well acquainted; she's nigher mother's age than mine, but she's very young feeling. She made me a nice cup o' tea, and I don't know but I should have stopped all night if I could have got word to you not to worry."

Then there was a serious silence before Mrs. Todd spoke again to make a formal announcement.

"She is the Queen's Twin," and Mrs. Todd looked steadily to see how I might bear the great surprise.

"The Queen's Twin?" I repeated.

"Yes, she's come to feel a real interest in the Queen, and anybody can see how natural 'tis. They were born the very same day, and you would be astonished to see what a number o' other things have corresponded. She was speaking o' some o' the facts to me today, an' you'd think she'd never done nothing but read history. I see how earnest she was about it as I never did before. I've often and often heard her allude to the facts, but now she's got to be old and the hurry's over with her work, she's come to live a good deal in her thoughts, as folks often do, and I tell you 'tis a sight o' company for her. If you want to hear about Queen Victoria, why Mis' Abby Martin'll tell you everything. And the prospect from that hill I spoke of is as beautiful as anything in this world; 'tis worth while your goin' over to see her just for that."

"When can you go again?" I demanded eagerly.

"I should say tomorrow," answered Mrs. Todd; "yes, I should say tomorrow; but I expect 'twould be better to take one day to rest, in between. I considered that question as I was comin' home, but I hurried so that there wa'n't much time to think. It's a dreadful long way to go with a horse; you have to go 'most as far as the old Bowden place an' turn off to the left, a master[3] long, rough road, and

---

3. A superlative; here it means the road is exceedingly rough and long.

then you have to turn right round as soon as you get there if you
mean to get home before nine o'clock at night. But to strike across
country from here, there's plenty o' time in the shortest day, and you
can have a good hour or two's visit beside; 'tain't but a very few
miles, and it's pretty all the way along. There used to be a few good
families over there, but they've died and scattered, so now she's far
from neighbors. There, she really cried, she was so glad to see anybody comin'. You'll be amused to hear her talk about the Queen, but
I thought twice or three times as I set there 'twas about all the company she'd got."

"Could we go day after tomorrow?" I asked eagerly.

" 'Twould suit me exactly," said Mrs. Todd.

II

One can never be so certain of good New England weather as in the
days when a long easterly storm has blown away the warm late-
summer mists, and cooled the air so that however bright the sunshine
is by day, the nights come nearer and nearer to frostiness. There was
a cold freshness in the morning air when Mrs. Todd and I locked the
house-door behind us; we took the key of the fields into our own hands
that day, and put out across country as one puts out to sea. When we
reached the top of the ridge behind the town it seemed as if we had
anxiously passed the harbor bar and were comfortably in open sea at
last.

"There, now!" proclaimed Mrs. Todd, taking a long breath, "now I
do feel safe. It's just the weather that's liable to bring somebody to
spend the day; I've had a feeling of Mis' Elder Caplin from North Point
bein' close upon me ever since I waked up this mornin', an' I didn't
want to be hampered with our present plans. She's a great hand to
visit; she'll be spendin' the day somewhere from now till Thanksgivin',
but there's plenty o' places at the Landin' where she goes, an' if I ain't
there she'll just select another. I thought mother might be in, too, 'tis
so pleasant; but I run up the road to look off this mornin' before you
was awake, and there was no sign of the boat. If they hadn't started
by that time they wouldn't start, just as the tide is now; besides, I see
a lot o' mackerel-men headin' Green Island way, and they'll detain
William. No, we're safe now, an' if mother should be comin' in tomorrow we'll have this to tell her. She an' Mis' Abby Martin's very old
friends."

We were walking down the long pasture slopes towards the dark
woods and thickets of the low ground. They stretched away northward like an unbroken wilderness; the early mists still dulled much
of the color and made the uplands beyond look like a very far-off
country.

"It ain't so far as it looks from here," said my companion reassuringly, "but we've got no time to spare either," and she hurried on,
leading the way with a fine sort of spirit in her step; and presently we

struck into the old Indian footpath, which could be plainly seen across the long-unploughed turf of the pastures, and followed it among the thick, low-growing spruces. There the ground was smooth and brown under foot, and the thin-stemmed trees held a dark and shadowy roof overhead. We walked a long way without speaking; sometimes we had to push aside the branches, and sometimes we walked in a broad aisle where the trees were larger. It was a solitary wood, birdless and beastless; there was not even a rabbit to be seen, or a crow high in air to break the silence.

"I don't believe the Queen ever saw such a lonesome trail as this," said Mrs. Todd, as if she followed the thoughts that were in my mind. Our visit to Mrs. Abby Martin seemed in some strange way to concern the high affairs of royalty. I had just been thinking of English landscapes, and of the solemn hills of Scotland with their lonely cottages and stone-walled sheepfolds, and the wandering flocks on high cloudy pastures. I had often been struck by the quick interest and familiar allusion to certain members of the royal house which one found in distant neighborhoods of New England; whether some old instincts of personal loyalty have survived all changes of time and national vicissitudes, or whether it is only that the Queen's own character and disposition have won friends for her so far away, it is impossible to tell. But to hear of a twin sister was the most surprising proof of intimacy of all, and I must confess that there was something remarkably exciting to the imagination in my morning walk. To think of being presented at Court in the usual way was for the moment quite commonplace.

III

Mrs. Todd was swinging her basket to and fro like a schoolgirl as she walked, and at this moment it slipped from her hand and rolled lightly along the ground as if there were nothing in it. I picked it up and gave it to her, whereupon she lifted the cover and looked in with anxiety.

" 'Tis only a few little things, but I don't want to lose 'em," she explained humbly. " 'Twas lucky you took the other basket if I was goin' to roll it round. Mis' Abby Martin complained o' lacking some pretty pink silk to finish one o' her little frames, an' I thought I'd carry her some, and I had a bunch o' gold thread that had been in a box o' mine this twenty year. I never was one to do much fancy work, but we're all liable to be swept away by fashion. And then there's a small packet o' very choice herbs that I gave a good deal of attention to; they'll smarten her up and give her the best of appetites, come spring. She was tellin' me that spring weather is very wiltin' an' tryin' to her, and she was beginnin' to dread it already. Mother's just the same way; if I could prevail on mother to take some o' these remedies in good season 'twould make a world o' difference, but she gets all down hill before I have a chance to hear of it, and then William comes in to tell

THE QUEEN'S TWIN   225

me, sighin' and bewailin', how feeble mother is. 'Why can't you remember 'bout them good herbs that I never let her be without?' I say
to him—he does provoke me so; and then off he goes, sulky enough,
down to his boat. Next thing I know, she comes in to go to meetin',
wantin' to speak to everybody and feelin' like a girl. Mis' Martin's case
is very much the same; but she's nobody to watch her. William's kind
o' slow-moulded;[4] but there, any William's better than none when you
get to be Mis' Martin's age."

"Hadn't she any children?" I asked.

"Quite a number," replied Mrs. Todd grandly, "but some are gone
and the rest are married and settled. She never was a great hand to go
about visitin'. I don't know but Mis' Martin might be called a little
peculiar. Even her own folks has to make company of her; she never
slips in and lives right along with the rest as if 'twas at home, even in
her own children's houses. I heard one o' her sons' wives say once she'd
much rather have the Queen to spend the day if she could choose
between the two, but I never thought Abby was so difficult as that. I
used to love to have her come; she may have been sort o' ceremonious,
but very pleasant and sprightly if you had sense enough to treat her her
own way. I always think she'd know just how to live with great folks,
and feel easier 'long of them an' their ways. Her son's wife's a great
driver with farm-work, boards a great tableful o' men in hayin' time,
an' feels right in her element. I don't say but she's a good woman an'
smart, but sort o' rough. Anybody that's gentle-mannered an' precise
like Mis' Martin would be a sort o' restraint.

"There's all sorts o' folks in the country, same's there is in the city,"
concluded Mrs. Todd gravely, and I as gravely agreed. The thick
woods were behind us now, and the sun was shining clear overhead,
the morning mists were gone, and a faint blue haze softened the
distance; as we climbed the hill where we were to see the view, it
seemed like a summer day. There was an old house on the height,
facing southward,—a mere forsaken shell of an old house, with empty
windows that looked like blind eyes. The frost-bitten grass grew close
about it like brown fur, and there was a single crooked bough of lilac
holding its green leaves close by the door.

"We'll just have a good piece of bread-an'-butter now," said the
commander of the expedition, "and then we'll hang up the basket on
some peg inside the house out o' the way o' the sheep, and have a
han'some entertainment as we're comin' back. She'll be all through her
little dinner when we get there, Mis' Martin will; but she'll want to
make us some tea, an' we must have our visit an' be starting back
pretty soon after two. I don't want to cross all that low ground again
after it's begun to grow chilly. An' it looks to me as if the clouds might
begin to gather late in the afternoon."

Before us lay a splendid world of sea and shore. The autumn colors

---

4. Somewhat "slow" or mentally dull by birth.

already brightened the landscape; and here and there at the edge of a dark tract of pointed firs stood a row of bright swamp-maples like scarlet flowers. The blue sea and the great tide inlets were untroubled by the lightest winds.

"Poor land, this is!" sighed Mrs. Todd as we sat down to rest on the worn doorstep. "I've known three good hard-workin' families that come here full o' hope an' pride and tried to make something o' this farm, but it beat 'em all. There's one small field that's excellent for potatoes if you let half of it rest every year; but the land's always hungry. Now, you see them little peakéd-topped spruces an' fir balsams comin' up over the hill all green an' hearty; they've got it all their own way! Seems sometimes as if wild Natur' got jealous over a certain spot, and wanted to do just as she'd a mind to. You'll see here; she'll do her own ploughin' an' harrowin' with frost an' wet, an' plant just what she wants and wait for her own crops. Man can't do nothin' with it, try as he may. I tell you those little trees mean business!"

I looked down the slope, and felt as if we ourselves were likely to be surrounded and overcome if we lingered too long. There was a vigor of growth, a persistence and savagery about the sturdy little trees that put weak human nature at complete defiance. One felt a sudden pity for the men and women who had been worsted after a long fight in that lonely place; one felt a sudden fear of the unconquerable, immediate forces of Nature, as in the irresistible moment of a thunderstorm.

"I can recollect the time when folks were shy o' these woods we just come through," said Mrs. Todd seriously. "The men-folks themselves never'd venture into 'em alone; if their cattle got strayed they'd collect whoever they could get, and start off all together. They said a person was liable to get bewildered in there alone, and in old times folks had been lost. I expect there was considerable fear left over from the old Indian times, and the poor days o' witchcraft; anyway, I've seen bold men act kind o' timid. Some women o' the Asa Bowden family went out one afternoon berryin' when I was a girl, and got lost and was out all night; they found 'em middle o' the mornin' next day, not half a mile from home, scared most to death, an' saying' they'd heard wolves and other beasts sufficient for a caravan. Poor creatur's! they'd strayed at last into a kind of low place amongst some alders, an' one of 'em was so overset[5] she never got over it, an' went off in a sort o' slow decline. 'Twas like them victims that drowns in a foot o' water; but their minds did suffer dreadful. Some folks is born afraid of the woods and all wild places, but I must say they've always been like home to me."

I glanced at the resolute, confident face of my companion. Life was very strong in her, as if some force of Nature were personified in this simple-hearted woman and gave her cousinship to the ancient deities. She might have walked the primeval fields of Sicily; her strong gingham skirts might at that very moment bend the slender stalks of aspho-

5. Upset.

del and be fragrant with trodden thyme, instead of the brown wind-brushed grass of New England and frost-bitten goldenrod. She was a great soul, was Mrs. Todd, and I her humble follower, as we went our way to visit the Queen's Twin, leaving the bright view of the sea behind us, and descending to a lower countryside through the dry pastures and fields.

The farms all wore a look of gathering age, though the settlement was, after all, so young. The fences were already fragile, and it seemed as if the first impulse of agriculture had soon spent itself without hope of renewal. The better houses were always those that had some hold upon the riches of the sea; a house that could not harbor a fishing-boat in some neighboring inlet was far from being sure of everyday comforts. The land alone was not enough to live upon in that stony region; it belonged by right to the forest, and to the forest it fast returned. From the top of the hill where we had been sitting we had seen prosperity in the dim distance, where the land was good and the sun shone upon fat barns, and where warm-looking houses with three or four chimneys apiece stood high on their solid ridge above the bay.

As we drew nearer to Mrs. Martin's it was sad to see what poor bushy fields, what thin and empty dwelling-places had been left by those who had chosen this disappointing part of the northern country for their home. We crossed the last field and came into a narrow rain-washed road, and Mrs. Todd looked eager and expectant and said that we were almost at our journey's end. "I do hope Mis' Martin'll ask you into her best room where she keeps all the Queen's pictures. Yes, I think likely she will ask you; but 'tain't everybody she deems worthy to visit 'em, I can tell you!" said Mrs. Todd warningly. "She's been collectin' 'em an' cuttin' 'em out o' newspapers an' magazines time out o' mind, and if she heard of anybody sailin' for an English port she'd contrive to get a little money to 'em and ask to have the last likeness there was. She's most covered her best-room wall now; she keeps that room shut up sacred as a meetin'-house! 'I won't say but I have my favorites amongst 'em,' she told me t'other day, 'but they're all beauti-ful to me as they can be!' And she's made some kind o' pretty little frames for 'em all—you know there's always a new fashion o' frames comin' round; first 'twas shell-work, and then 'twas pine-cones, and bead-work's had its day, and now she's much concerned with perfora-ted cardboard worked with silk. I tell you that best room's a sight to see! But you mustn't look for anything elegant," continued Mrs. Todd, after a moment's reflection. "Mis' Martin's always been in very poor, strugglin' circumstances. She had ambition for her children, though they took right after their father an' had little for themselves; she wa'n't over an' above well married, however kind she may see fit to speak. She's been patient an' hardworkin' all her life, and always high above makin' mean complaints of other folks. I expect all this business about the Queen has buoyed her over many a shoal place in life. Yes, you might say that Abby'd been a slave, but there ain't any slave but has some freedom."

IV

Presently I saw a low gray house standing on a grassy bank close to the road. The door was at the side, facing us, and a tangle of snowberry bushes and cinnamon roses grew to the level of the window-sills. On the doorstep stood a bent-shouldered, little old woman; there was an air of welcome and of unmistakable dignity about her.

"She sees us coming," exclaimed Mrs. Todd in an excited whisper. "There, I told her I might be over this way again if the weather held good, and if I came I'd bring you. She said right off she'd take great pleasure in havin' a visit from you; I was surprised, she's usually so retirin'."

Even this reassurance did not quell a faint apprehension on our part; there was something distinctly formal in the occasion, and one felt that consciousness of inadequacy which is never easy for the humblest pride to bear. On the way I had torn my dress in an unexpected encounter with a little thornbush, and I could now imagine how it felt to be going to Court and forgetting one's feathers or her Court train.

The Queen's Twin was oblivious of such trifles; she stood waiting with a calm look until we came near enough to take her kind hand. She was a beautiful old woman, with clear eyes and a lovely quietness and genuineness of manner; there was not a trace of anything pretentious about her, or high-flown, as Mrs. Todd would say comprehensively. Beauty in age is rare enough in women who have spent their lives in the hard work of a farm-house; but autumnlike and withered as this woman may have looked, her features had kept, or rather gained, a great refinement. She led us into her old kitchen and gave us seats, and took one of the little straight-backed chairs herself and sat a short distance away, as if she were giving audience to an ambassador. It seemed as if we should all be standing; you could not help feeling that the habits of her life were more ceremonious, but that for the moment she assumed the simplicities of the occasion.

Mrs. Todd was always Mrs. Todd, too great and self-possessed a soul for any occasion to ruffle. I admired her calmness, and presently the slow current of neighborhood talk carried one easily along; we spoke of the weather and the small adventures of the way, and then, as if I were after all not a stranger, our hostess turned almost affectionately to speak to me.

"The weather will be growing dark in London now. I expect that you've been in London, dear?" she said.

"Oh, yes," I answered. "Only last year."

"It is a great many years since I was there, along in the forties," said Mrs. Martin. " 'Twas the only voyage I ever made; most of my neighbors have been great travelers. My brother was master of a vessel, and his wife usually sailed with him; but that year she had a young child more frail than the others, and she dreaded the care of it at sea. It happened that my brother got a chance for my husband to go as super-cargo,[6] being a good accountant, and came one day to urge him to take it; he was very ill-disposed to the sea, but he had met with losses, and I saw my own opportunity and persuaded them both to let me go too. In those days they didn't object to a woman's being aboard to wash and mend, the voyages were sometimes very long. And that was the way I come to see the Queen."

Mrs. Martin was looking straight in my eyes to see if I showed any genuine interest in the most interesting person in the world.

"Oh, I am very glad you saw the Queen," I hastened to say. "Mrs. Todd has told me that you and she were born the very same day."

"We were indeed, dear!" said Mrs. Martin, and she leaned back comfortably and smiled as she had not smiled before. Mrs. Todd gave a satisfied nod and glance, as if to say that things were going on as well as possible in this anxious moment.

"Yes," said Mrs. Martin again, drawing her chair a little nearer, "'twas a very remarkable thing; we were born the same day, and exactly at the same hour, after you allowed for all the difference in time. My father figures it out sea-fashion. Her Royal Majesty and I opened our eyes upon this world together; say what you may, 'tis a bond between us."

Mrs. Todd assented with an air of triumph and untied her hatstrings and threw them back over her shoulders with a gallant air.

"And I married a man by the name of Albert, just the same as she did, and all by chance, for I didn't get the news that she had an Albert[7] too till a fortnight afterward; news was slower coming then than it is now. My first baby was a girl, and I called her Victoria after my mate; but the next one was a boy, and my husband wanted the right to name him, and took his own name and his brother Edward's, and pretty soon I saw in the paper that the little Prince o' Wales had been christened just the same. After that I made excuse to wait till I knew what she'd name her children. I didn't want to break the chain, so I had an Alfred, and my darling Alice that I lost long before she lost hers, and there I stopped. If I'd only had a dear daughter to stay at home with me, same's her youngest one, I should have been so thankful! But if only one of us could have a little Beatrice,[8] I'm glad 'twas the Queen; we've both seen trouble, but she's had the most care."

I asked Mrs. Martin if she lived alone all the year, and was told that she did except for a visit now and then from one of her grandchildren, "the only one that really likes to come an' stay quiet 'long o' grandma. She always says quick as she's through her schoolin' she's goin' to live

6. An officer on board a merchant ship who has charge of the cargo and its sale and purchase.
7. Prince consort, i.e. husband, of Queen Victoria.
8. The youngest of the children born to Queen Victoria and Prince Albert.

with me all the time, but she's very pretty an' has taking ways," said Mrs. Martin, looking both proud and wistful, "so I can tell nothing at all about it! Yes, I've been alone most o' the time since my Albert was taken away, and that's a great many years; he had a long time o' failing and sickness first." (Mrs. Todd's foot gave an impatient scuff on the floor.) "An' I've always lived right here. I ain't like the Queen's Majesty, for this is the only palace I've got," said the dear old thing, smiling again. "I'm glad of it too. I don't like changing about, an' our stations in life are set very different. I don't require what the Queen does, but sometimes I've thought 'twas left to me to do the plain things she don't have time for. I expect she's a beautiful housekeeper, nobody couldn't have done better in her high place, and she's been as good a mother as she's been a queen."

"I guess she has, Abby," agreed Mrs. Todd instantly. "How was it you happened to get such a good look at her? I meant to ask you again when I was here t'other day."

"Our ship was layin' in the Thames, right there above Wapping. We was dischargin' cargo, and under orders to clear as quick as we could for Bordeaux to take on an excellent freight o' French goods," explained Mrs. Martin eagerly. "I heard that the Queen was goin' to a great review of her army, and would drive out o' her Buckin'ham Palace about ten o'clock in the mornin', and I run aft to Albert, my husband, and brother Horace where they was standin' together by the hatchway, and told 'em they must one of 'em take me. They laughed, I was in such a hurry, and said they couldn't go; and I found they meant it and got sort of impatient when I began to talk, and I was 'most broken-hearted; 'twas all the reason I had for makin' that hard voyage. Albert couldn't help often reproachin' me, for he did so resent the sea, an' I'd known how 'twould be before we sailed; but I'd minded nothing all the way till then, and I just crep' back to my cabin an' begun to cry. They was disappointed about their ship's cook, an' I'd cooked for fo'c's'le an' cabin[9] myself all the way over; 'twas dreadful hard work, specially in rough weather; we'd had head winds an' a six weeks' voyage. They'd acted sort of ashamed o' me when I pled so to go ashore, an' that hurt my feelin's most of all. But Albert come below pretty soon; I'd never given way so in my life, an' he begun to act frightened, and treated me gentle just as he did when we was goin' to be married, an' when I got over sobbin' he went on deck and saw Horace an' talked it over what they could do; they really had their duty to the vessel, and couldn't be spared that day. Horace was real good when he understood everything, and he come an' told me I'd more than worked my passage an' was goin' to do just as I liked now we was in port. He'd engaged a cook, too, that was comin' aboard that mornin', and he was goin' to send the ship's carpenter with me—a nice fellow from up Thomaston way; he'd gone to put on his ashore clothes as

9. Metonyms for the ship's crew and its officers; the forecastle is the superstructure at the bow of a merchant ship, where the crew is housed.

quick's he could. So then I got ready, and we started off in the small boat and rowed up river. I was afraid we were too late, but the tide was setting up very strong, and we landed an' left the boat to a keeper, and I run all the way up those great streets and across a park. 'Twas a great day, with sights o' folks everywhere, but 'twas just as if they was nothin' but wax images to me. I kep' askin' my way an' runnin' on, with the carpenter comin' after as best he could, and just as I worked to the front o' the crowd by the palace, the gates was flung open and out she came; all prancin' horses and shinin' gold, and in the beautiful carriage there she sat; 'twas a moment o' heaven to me. I saw her plain, and she looked right at me so pleasant and happy, just as if she knew there was somethin' different between us from other folks."

There was a moment when the Queen's Twin could not go on and neither of her listeners could ask a question.

"Prince Albert was sitting right beside her in the carriage," she continued. "Oh, he was a beautiful man! Yes, dear, I saw 'em both together just as I see you now, and then she was gone out o' sight in another minute, and the common crowd was all spread over the place pushin' an' cheerin'. 'Twas some kind o' holiday, an' the carpenter and I got separated, an' then I found him again after I didn't think I should, an' he was all for makin' a day of it, and goin' to show me all the sights; he'd been in London before but I didn't want nothin' else, an' we went back through the streets down to the waterside an' took the boat. I remember I mended an old coat o' my Albert's as good as I could, sittin' on the quarter-deck in the sun all that afternoon, and 'twas all as if I was livin' in a lovely dream. I don't know how to explain it, but there hasn't been no friend I've felt so near to me ever since."

One could not say much—only listen. Mrs. Todd put in a discerning question now and then, and Mrs. Martin's eyes shone brighter and brighter as she talked. What a lovely gift of imagination and true affection was in this fond old heart! I looked about the plain New England kitchen, with its wood-smoked walls and homely braided rugs on the worn floor, and all its simple furnishings. The loud-ticking clock seemed to encourage us to speak; at the other side of the room was an early newspaper portrait of Her Majesty the Queen of Great Britain and Ireland. On a shelf below were some flowers in a little glass dish, as if they were put before a shrine.

"If I could have had more to read, I should have known 'most everything about her," said Mrs. Martin wistfully. "I've made the most of what I did have, and thought it over and over till it came clear. I sometimes seem to have her all my own, as if we'd lived right together. I've often walked out into the woods alone and told her what my troubles was, and it always seemed as if she told me 'twas all right, an' we must have patience. I've got her beautiful book about the Highlands;[1] 'twas dear Mis' Todd here that found out about her print-

1. *Leaves from a Journal of Our Life in the High-lands* 1848–61; Queen Victoria's journal, published in 1868, of the royal family's years living in Balmoral House in Scotland.

ing it and got a copy for me, and it's been a treasure to my heart, just as if 'twas written right to me. I always read it Sundays now, for my Sunday treat. Before that I used to have to imagine a good deal, but when I come to read her book, I knew what I expected was all true. We do think alike about so many things," said the Queen's Twin with affectionate certainty. "You see, there is something between us, being born just at the same time; 'tis what they call a birthright. She's had great tasks put upon her, being the Queen, an' mine has been the humble lot; but she's done the best she could, nobody could say to the contrary, and there's something between us; she's been the great lesson I've had to live by. She's been everything to me. An' when she had her Jubilee, oh, how my heart was with her!"

"There, 'twouldn't play the part in her life it has in mine," said Mrs. Martin generously, in answer to something one of her listeners had said. "Sometimes I think now she's older, she might like to know about us. When I think how few old friends anybody has left at our age, I suppose it may be just the same with her as it is with me; perhaps she would like to know how we came into life together. But I've had a great advantage in seeing her, an' I can always fancy her goin' on, while she don't know nothin' yet about me, except she may feel my love stayin' her heart sometimes an' not know just where it comes from. An' I dream about our being together out in some pretty fields, young as ever we was, and holdin' hands as we walk along. I'd like to know if she ever has that dream too. I used to have days when I made believe she did know, an' was comin' to see me," confessed the speaker shyly, with a little flush on her cheeks; "and I'd plan what I could have nice for supper, and I wasn't goin' to let anybody know she was here havin' a good rest, except I'd wish you, Almira Todd, or dear Mis' Blackett would happen in, for you'd know just how to talk with her. You see, she likes to be up in Scotland, right out in the wild country, better than she does anywhere else."

"I'd really love to take her out to see mother at Green Island," said Mrs. Todd with a sudden impulse.

"Oh, yes! I should love to have you," exclaimed Mrs. Martin, and then she began to speak in a lower tone. "One day I got thinkin' so about my dear Queen," she said, "an' livin' so in my thoughts, that I went to work an' got all ready for her, just as if she was really comin'. I never told this to a livin' soul before, but I feel you'll understand. I put my best fine sheets and blankets I spun an' wove myself on the bed, and I picked some pretty flowers and put 'em all round the house, an' I worked as hard an' happy as I could all day, and had as nice a supper ready as I could get, sort of telling myself a story all the time. She was comin' an' I was goin' to get to see her again, an' I kep' it up until nightfall; an' when I see the dark an' it come to me I was all alone, the dream left me, an' I sat down on the doorstep an' felt all foolish an' tired. An' if you'll believe it, I heard steps comin', an' an old cousin o' mine come wanderin' along, one I was apt to be shy of. She wasn't all there, as folks used to say, but harmless enough and a kind of poor old talking body. And I went right to meet her when I first heard her call, 'stead o' hidin' as I sometimes did, an' she come in dreadful willin', an' we sat down to supper together; 'twas a supper I should have had no heart to eat alone."

"I don't believe she ever had such a splendid time in her life as she did then. I heard her tell all about it afterwards," exclaimed Mrs. Todd compassionately. "There, now I hear all this it seems just as if the Queen might have known and couldn't come herself, so she sent that poor old creatur' that was always in need!"

Mrs. Martin looked timidly at Mrs. Todd and then at me. " 'Twas childish o' me to go an' get supper," she confessed.

"I guess you wa'n't the first one to do that," said Mrs. Todd. "No, I guess you wa'n't the first one who's got supper that way, Abby," and then for a moment she could say no more.

Mrs. Todd and Mrs. Martin had moved their chairs a little so that they faced each other, and I, at one side, could see them both.

"No, you never told me o' that before, Abby," said Mrs. Todd gently. "Don't it show that for folks that have any fancy in 'em, such beautiful dreams is the real part o' life? But to most folks the common things that happens outside 'em is all in all."

Mrs. Martin did not appear to understand at first, strange to say, when the secret of her heart was put into words; then a glow of pleasure and comprehension shone upon her face. "Why, I believe you're right, Almira!" she said, and turned to me.

"Wouldn't you like to look at my pictures of the Queen?" she asked, and we rose and went into the best room.

v

The mid-day visit seemed very short; September hours are brief to match the shortening days. The great subject was dismissed for a while after our visit to the Queen's pictures, and my companions spoke much of lesser persons until we drank the cup of tea which Mrs. Todd had foreseen. I happily remembered that the Queen herself is said to like a proper cup of tea, and this at once seemed to make her Majesty kindly join so remote and reverent a company. Mrs. Martin's thin cheeks took on a pretty color like a girl's. "Somehow I always have thought of her when I made it extra good," she said. "I've got a real china cup that belonged to my grandmother, and I believe I shall call it hers now."

"Why don't you?" responded Mrs. Todd warmly, with a delightful smile.

Later they spoke of a promised visit which was to be made in the Indian summer to the Landing and Green Island, but I observed that Mrs. Todd presented the little parcel of dried herbs, with full directions, for a cure-all in the spring, as if there were no real chance of their meeting again first. As we looked back from the turn of the road the Queen's Twin was still standing on the doorstep watching us away, and Mrs. Todd stopped, and stood still for a moment before she waved her hand again.

"There's one thing certain, dear," she said to me with great discernment; "it ain't as if we left her all alone!"

Then we set out upon our long way home over the hill, where we lingered in the afternoon sunshine, and through the dark woods across the heron-swamp.

Atlantic Monthly, February 1899;
Cornhill Magazine, February 1899; *The Queen's Twin*, 1899.

The Foreigner

I

One evening, at the end of August, in Dunnet Landing, I heard Mrs. Todd's firm footstep crossing the small front entry outside my door, and her conventional cough which served as a herald's trumpet, or a plain New England knock, in the harmony of our fellowship.

"Oh, please come in!" I cried, for it had been so still in the house that I supposed my friend and hostess had gone to see one of her neighbors. The first cold northeasterly storm of the season was blowing hard outside. Now and then there was a dash of great raindrops and a flick of wet lilac leaves against the window, but I could hear that the sea was already stirred to its dark depths, and the great rollers were coming in heavily against the shore. One might well believe that Summer was coming to a sad end that night, in the darkness and rain and sudden access of autumnal cold. It seemed as if there must be danger offshore among the outer islands.

"Oh, there!" exclaimed Mrs. Todd, as she entered. "I know nothing ain't ever happened out to Green Island since the world began, but I always do worry about mother in these great gales. You know those tidal waves occur sometimes down to the West Indies, and I get dwellin' on 'em so I can't set still in my chair, nor knit a common row to a stocking. William might get mooning, out in his small bo't, and not observe how the sea was making, an' meet with some accident. Yes, I thought I'd come in and set with you if you wa'n't busy. No, I never feel any concern about 'em in winter 'cause then they're prepared, and all ashore and everything snug. William ought to keep help, as I tell him; yes, he ought to keep help."

I hastened to reassure my anxious guest by saying that Elijah Tilley had told me in the afternoon, when I came along the shore past the fish houses, that Johnny Bowden and the Captain were out at Green Island; he had seen them beating up the bay, and thought they must have put into Burnt Island cove, but one of the lobstermen brought word later that he saw them hauling out at Green Island as he came by, and Captain Bowden pointed ashore and shook his head to say that he did not mean to try to get in. "The old Miranda just managed it, but she will have to stay at home a day or two and put new patches in her sail," I ended, not without pride in so much circumstantial evidence.

Mrs. Todd was alert in a moment. "Then they'll all have a very pleasant evening," she assured me, apparently dismissing all fears of tidal waves and other sea-going disasters. "I was urging Alick Bowden to go ashore some day and see mother before cold weather. He's her own nephew; she sets a great deal by him. And Johnny's a great chum o' William's; don't you know the first day we had Johnny out 'long of us, he took an' give William his money to keep for him that he'd been a-savin', and William showed it to me an' was so affected I thought he was goin' to shed tears? 'Twas a dollar an' eighty cents; yes, they'll have a beautiful evenin' all together, and like's not the sea'll be flat as a doorstep come morning."

I had drawn a large wooden rocking-chair before the fire, and Mrs. Todd was sitting there jogging herself[1] a little, knitting fast, and wonderfully placid of countenance. There came a fresh gust of wind and rain, and we could feel the small wooden house rock and hear it creak as if it were a ship at sea.

"Lord, hear the great breakers!" exclaimed Mrs. Todd. "How they pound!—there, there! I always run of an idea that the sea knows anger these nights and gets full o' fight. I can hear the rote[2] o' them old black ledges way down the thoroughfare. Calls up all those stormy verses in the Book o' Psalms; David he knew how the old sea-goin' folks have to quake at the heart."[3]

I thought as I had never thought before of such anxieties. The families of sailors and coastwise adventurers by sea must always be worrying about somebody, this side of the world or the other. There was hardly one of Mrs. Todd's elder acquaintances, men or women, who had not at some time or other made a sea voyage, and there was often no news until the voyagers themselves came back to bring it.

"There's a roaring high overhead, and a roaring in the deep sea," said Mrs. Todd solemnly, "and they battle together nights like this. No, I couldn't sleep; some women folks always goes right to bed an' to sleep, so's to forget, but 'tain't my way. Well, it's a blessin' we don't all feel alike; there's hardly any of our folks at sea to worry about, nowadays, but I can't help my feelin's, an' I got thinking of mother all alone, if William had happened to be out lobsterin' an' couldn't make the cove gettin' back."

1. Rocking by giving herself a slight push.
2. The noise the sea makes among the rocks.
3. The biblical David is considered to be the author of the poetry of the Psalms, many of which make references to storms at sea.

"They will have a pleasant evening," I repeated. "Captain Bowden is the best of good company."

"Mother'll make him some pancakes for his supper, like's not," said Mrs. Todd, clicking her knitting needles and giving a pull at her yarn. Just then the old cat pushed open the latched door and came straight toward her mistress's lap. She was regarded severely as she stepped about and turned on the broad expanse, and then made herself into a round cushion of fur, but was not openly admonished. There was another great blast of wind overhead, and a puff of smoke came down the chimney.

"This makes me think o' the night Mis' Cap'n Tolland died," said Mrs. Todd, half to herself. "Folks used to say these gales only blew when somebody's a-dyin', or the devil was a-comin' for his own, but the worst man I ever knew died a real pretty mornin' in June."

"You have never told me any ghost stories," said I; and such was the gloomy weather and the influence of the night that I was instantly filled with reluctance to have this suggestion followed. I had not chosen the best of moments; just before I spoke we had begun to feel as cheerful as possible. Mrs. Todd glanced doubtfully at the cat and then at me, with a strange absent look, and I was really afraid that she was going to tell me something that would haunt my thoughts on every dark stormy night as long as I lived.

"Never mind now; tell me tomorrow by daylight, Mrs. Todd," I hastened to say, but she still looked at me full of doubt and deliberation.

"Ghost stories!" she answered. "Yes, I don't know but I've heard a plenty of 'em first an' last. I was just sayin' to myself that this is like the night Mis' Cap'n Tolland died. 'Twas the great line storm in September all of thirty, or maybe forty, year ago. I ain't one that keeps much account o' time."

"Tolland? That's a name I have never heard in Dunnet," I said.

"Then you haven't looked well about the old part o' the buryin' ground, no'theast corner," replied Mrs. Todd. "All their women folks lies there; the sea's got most o' the men. They were a known family o' shipmasters in early times. Mother had a mate, Ellen Tolland, that she mourns to this day; died right in her bloom with quick consumption, but the rest o' that family was all boys but one, and older than she, an' they lived hard seafarin' lives an' all died hard. They were called very smart seamen. I've heard that when the youngest went into one o' the old shippin' houses in Boston, the head o' the firm called out to him: 'Did you say Tolland from Dunnet? That's recommendation enough for any vessel!' There was some o' them old shipmasters as tough as iron, an' they had the name o' usin' their crews very severe, but there wa'n't a man that wouldn't rather sign with 'em an' take his chances, than with the slack ones that didn't know how to meet accidents."

II

There was so long a pause, and Mrs. Todd still looked so absent-minded, that I was afraid she and the cat were growing drowsy together before the fire, and I should have no reminiscences at all. The wind struck the house again, so that we both started in our chairs and Mrs. Todd gave a curious, startled look at me. The cat lifted her head and listened too, in the silence that followed, while after the wind sank we were more conscious than ever of the awful roar of the sea. The house jarred now and then, in a strange, disturbing way.

"Yes, they'll have a beautiful evening out to the island," said Mrs. Todd again; but she did not say it gaily. I had not seen her before in her weaker moments.

"Who was Mrs. Captain Tolland?" I asked eagerly, to change the current of our thoughts.

"I never knew her maiden name; if I ever heard it, I've gone an' forgot; 'twould mean nothing to me," answered Mrs. Todd.

"She was a foreigner, an' he met with her out in the island o' Jamaica. They said she'd been left a widow with property. Land knows what become of it; she was French born, an' her first husband was a Portugee, or somethin'."

I kept silence now, a poor and insufficient question being worse than none.

"Cap'n John Tolland was the least smartest of any of 'em, but he was full smart enough, an' commanded a good brig[4] at the time, in the sugar trade; he'd taken out a cargo o' pine lumber to the islands from somewheres up the river, an' had been loadin' for home in the port o' Kingston, an' had gone ashore that afternoon for his papers, an' remained afterwards 'long of three friends o' his, all shipmasters. They was havin' their suppers together in a tavern; 'twas late in the evenin' an' they was more lively than usual, an' felt boyish; and over opposite was another house full o' company, real bright and pleasant lookin', with a lot o' lights, an' they heard somebody singin' very pretty to a guitar. They wa'n't in no go-to-meetin' condition, an' one of 'em, he slapped the table an' said, 'Le's go over an' hear that lady sing!' an' over they all went, good honest sailors, but three sheets in the wind,[5] and stepped in as if they was invited, an' made their bows inside the door an' asked if they could hear the music; they were all respectable well-dressed men. They saw the woman that had the guitar, an' there was a company a-listin', regular highbinders[6] all of 'em; an' there was a long table all spread out with big candlesticks like little trees of light, and a sight o' glass an' silver ware; an' part o' the men was young officers in uniform, an' the colored folks was steppin' round servin' 'em, an' they had the lady singin'. 'Twas a wasteful scene, an' a loud talkin' company, an' though they was three sheets in the wind themselves

4. A two-masted sailing ship.   6. Riotous fellows. A-listin': i.e., listening.
5. I.e., drunk.

there wa'n't one o' them cap'ns but had sense to perceive it. The others
had pushed back their chairs, an' their decanters an' glasses was standin' thick about, an' they was teasin' the one that was singin' as if
they'd just got her in to amuse 'em. But they quieted down; one o' the
young officers had beautiful manners, an' invited the four cap'ns to join
'em, very polite; 'twas a kind of public house, and after they'd all heard
another song, he come to consult with 'em whether they wouldn't git
up and dance a hornpipe or somethin' to the lady's music.

"They was all elderly men an' shipmasters, and owned property;
two of 'em was church members in good standin'," continued Mrs.
Todd loftily, "an' they wouldn't lend theirselves to no such kick-shows
as that, an' spite o' bein' three sheets in the wind, as I have once
observed; they waved aside the tumblers of wine the young officer was
pourin' out for 'em so freehanded, and said they should rather be
excused. An' when they all rose, still very dignified, as I've been well
informed, and made their partin' bows and was goin' out, them young
sports got round 'em an' tried to prevent 'em, and they had to push an'
strive considerable, but out they come. There was this Cap'n Tolland,
and two Cap'n Bowdens, and the fourth was my own father." (Mrs.
Todd spoke slowly, as if to impress the value of her authority.) "Two
of them was very religious, upright men, but they would have their
night off sometimes, all o' them old-fashioned cap'ns, when they was
free of business and ready to leave port.

"An' they went back to their tavern an' got their bills paid, an' set
down kind o' mad with everybody by the front windows, mistrusting
some o' their tavern charges, like's not, by that time, an' when they got
tempered down, they watched the house over across, where the party
was.

"There was a kind of a grove o' trees between the house an' the
road, an' they heard the guitar a-goin' an' a-stoppin' short by turns,
and pretty soon somebody began to screech, an' they saw a white dress
come runnin' out through the bushes, an' tumbled over each other in
their haste to offer help; an' out she come, with the guitar, cryin' into
the street, and they just walked off four square with her amongst 'em,
down toward the wharves where they felt more to home. They
couldn't make out at first what 'twas she spoke,—Cap'n Lorenzo
Bowden was well acquainted in Havre an' Bordeaux,[7] an' spoke a poor
quality o' French, an' she knew a little mite o' English, but not much;
and they come somehow or other to discern that she was in real
distress. Her husband and her children had died o' yellow fever; they'd
all come up to Kingston from one o' the far Wind'ard Islands to get
passage on a steamer to France, an' a Negro had stole their money off
her husband while he lay sick o' the fever, an' she had been befriended
some, but the folks that knew about her had died too; it had been a
dreadful run o' the fever that season, an' she fell at last to playin' an'

7. French seaports.

singin' for hire, and for what money they'd throw to her round them harbor houses.

" 'Twas a real hard case, an' when them cap'ns made out about it, there wa'n't one that meant to take leave without helpin' of her. They was pretty mellow, an' whatever they might lack o' prudence they more'n made up with charity: they didn't want to see nobody abused, an' she was sort of a pretty woman, an' they stopped in the street then an' there an' drew lots who should take her aboard, bein' all bound home. An' the lot fell to Cap'n Jonathan Bowden who did act discouraged; his vessel had but small accommodations, though he could stow a big freight, an' she was a dreadful slow sailer through bein' square as a box, an' his first wife, that was livin' then, was a dreadful jealous woman. He threw himself right onto the mercy o' Cap'n Tolland."

Mrs. Todd indulged herself for a short time in a season of calm reflection.

"I always thought they'd have done better, and more reasonable, to give her some money to pay her passage home to France, or wherever she may have wanted to go," she continued.

I nodded and looked for the rest of the story.

"Father told mother," said Mrs. Todd confidentially, "that Cap'n Jonathan Bowden an' Cap'n John Tolland had both taken a little more than usual; I wouldn't have you think, either, that they both wasn't the best o' men, an' they was solemn as owls, and argued the matter between 'em, an' waved aside the other two when they tried to put their oars in. An' spite o' Cap'n Tolland's bein' a settled old bachelor they fixed it that he was to take the prize on his brig; she was a fast sailer, and there was a good spare cabin or two where he'd sometimes carried passengers, but he'd filled 'em with bags o' sugar on his own account an' was loaded very heavy beside. He said he'd shift the sugar an' get along somehow, an' the last the other three cap'ns saw of the party was Cap'n John handing the lady into his bo't, guitar and all, an' off they all set tow'ds their ships with their men rowin' 'em in the bright moonlight down to Port Royal where the anchorage was, an' where they all lay, goin' out with the tide an' mornin' wind at break o' day. An' the others thought they heard music of the guitar, two o' the bo'ts kept well together, but it may have come from another source."

"Well; and then?" I asked eagerly after a pause. Mrs. Todd was almost laughing aloud over her knitting and nodding emphatically. We had forgotten all about the noise of the wind and sea.

"Lord bless you! he come sailing into Portland with his sugar, all in good time, an' they stepped right afore a justice o' the peace, and Cap'n John Tolland came paradin' home to Dunnet Landin' a married man. He owned one o' them thin, narrow-lookin' houses with one room each side o' the front door, and two slim black spruces spindlin' up against the front windows to make it gloomy inside. There was no horse nor cattle of course, though he owned pasture land, an' you could see rifts o' light right through the barn as you drove by. And there was a good excellent kitchen, but his sister reigned over that; she had a right to two rooms, and took the kitchen an' a bedroom that led out of it; an' bein' given no rights in the kitchen had angered the cap'n so they weren't on no kind of speakin' terms. He preferred his old brig for comfort, but now and then, between voyages, he'd come home for a few days, just to show he was master over his part o' the house, and show Eliza she couldn't commit no trespass.

"They stayed a little while; 'twas pretty spring weather, an' I used to see Cap'n John rollin' by with his arms full o' bundles from the store, lookin' as pleased and important as a boy; an' then they went right off to sea again, an' was gone a good many months. Next time he left her to live there alone, after they'd stopped at home together some weeks, an' they said she suffered from bein' at sea, but some said that the owners wouldn't have a woman aboard. 'Twas before father was lost on that last voyage of his, an' he and mother went up once or twice to see them. Father said there wa'n't a mite o' harm in her, but somehow or other a sight o' prejudice arose; it may have been caused by the remarks of Eliza an' her feelin's tow'ds her brother. Even my mother had no regard for Eliza Tolland. But mother asked the cap'n's wife to come with her one evenin' to a social circle that was down to the meetin'-house vestry, so she'd get acquainted a little, an' she appeared very pretty until they started to have some singin' to the melodeon.[8] Mari' Harris an' one o' the younger Caplin girls undertook to sing a duet, an' they sort o' flatted, an' she put her hands right up to her ears, and give a little squeal, an' went quick as could be an' give 'em the right notes, for she could read the music like plain print an' made 'em try it over again. She was real willin' an' pleasant, but that didn't suit, an' she made faces when they got it wrong. An' then there fell a dead calm, an' we was all settin' round prim as dishes, an' my mother, that never expects ill feelin', asked her if she wouldn't sing somethin', an' up she got,—poor creatur', it all seems so different to me now,—an' sung a lovely little song standin' in the floor; it seemed to have something gay about it that kept a-repeatin', an' nobody could help keepin' time, an' all of a sudden she looked round at the tables and caught up a tin plate that somebody'd fetched a Washin'ton pie in, an' she begun to drum on it with her fingers like one o' them tambourines, an' went right on singin' faster an' faster, and next minute she begun to dance a little pretty dance between the verses, just as light and pleasant as a child. You couldn't help seein' how pretty 'twas; we all got to trottin' a foot, an' some o' the men clapped their hands quite loud, a-keepin' time, 'twas so catchin', an' seemed so natural to her. There wa'n't one of 'em but enjoyed it; she just tried to do her part, and some urged her on, till she stopped with a little twirl of her skirts an' went to her place

8. A small reed organ.

again by mother. And I can see mother now, reachin' over an' smilin' an' pattin' her hand.

"But next day there was an awful scandal goin' in the parish, an' Mari' Harris reproached my mother to her face, an' I never wanted to see her since, but I've had to a good many times. I said Mis' Tolland didn't intend no impropriety,—I reminded her of David's dancin' before the Lord;[9] but she said such a man as David would never have thought o' dancin' right there in the Orthodox vestry, and she felt I spoke with irreverence.

"And next Sunday Mis' Tolland came walkin' into our meeting, but I must say she acted like a cat in a strange garret, and went right out down the aisle with her head in air, from the pew Deacon Caplin had showed her into. 'Twas just in the beginning of the long prayer. I wish she'd stayed through, whatever her reasons were. Whether she'd expected somethin' different, or misunderstood some o' the pastor's remarks, or what 'twas, I don't really feel able to explain, but she kind o' declared war, at least folks thought so, an' war 'twas from that time. I see she was cryin', or had been, as she passed by me; perhaps bein' in meetin' was what had power to make her feel homesick and strange.

"Cap'n John Tolland was away fittin' out; that next week he come home to see her and say farewell. He was lost with his ship in the Straits of Malacca, and she lived there alone in the old house a few months longer till she died. He left her well off; 'twas said he hid his money about the house and she knew where 'twas. Oh, I expect you've heard that story told over an' over twenty times, since you've been here at the Landin'?"

"Never one word," I insisted.

"It was a good while ago," explained Mrs. Todd with reassurance. "Yes, it all happened a great while ago."

III

At this moment, with a sudden flaw of the wind, some wet twigs outside blew against the window panes and made a noise like a distressed creature trying to get in. I started with sudden fear, and so did the cat, but Mrs. Todd knitted away and did not even look over her shoulder.

"She was a good-looking woman; yes, I always thought Mis' Tolland was good-looking, though she had, as was reasonable, a sort of foreign cast, and she spoke very broken English, no better than a child. She was always at work about her house, or settin' at a front window with her sewing; she was a beautiful hand to embroider. Sometimes, summer evenings, when the windows was open she'd set an' drum on her guitar, but I don't know as I ever heard her sing but once after the cap'n went away. She appeared very happy about havin' him, and took

9. See 2 Samuel 6.25.

on dreadful at partin' when he was down here on the wharf, going back
to Portland by boat to take ship for that last v'y'ge. He acted kind of
ashamed, Cap'n John did; folks about here ain't so much accustomed
to show their feelings. The whistle had blown an' they was waitin' for
him to get aboard, an' he was put to it to know what to do and treated
her very affectionate in spite of all impatience; but mother happened
to be there and she went an' spoke, and I remember what a comfort
she seemed to be. Mis' Tolland clung to her then, and she wouldn't
give a glance after the boat when it had started, though the captain was
very eager a-wavin' to her. She wanted mother to come home with her
and wouldn't let go her hand, and mother had just come in to stop all
night with me an' had plenty o' time ashore, which didn't always
happen, so they walked off together, an' 'twas some considerable time
before she got back.

" 'I want you to neighbor with that poor lonesome creatur',' says
mother to me, lookin' reproachful. 'She's a stranger in a strange land,'
says mother. 'I want you to make her have a sense that somebody feels
kind to her.'

" 'Why, since that time she flaunted out o' meetin', folks have felt
she liked other ways better'n our'n,' says I. I was provoked because I'd
had a nice supper ready, an' mother'd let it wait so long 'twas spoiled.
'I hope you'll like your supper!' I told her. I was dreadful ashamed
afterward of speakin' so to mother.

" 'What consequence is my supper?' says she to me; mother can be
very stern,—'or your comfort or mine, beside letting a foreign person
an' a stranger feel so desolate; she's done the best a woman could do
in her lonesome place, and she asks nothing of anybody except a little
common kindness. Think if 'twas you in a foreign land!'

"And mother set down to drink her tea, an' I set down humbled
enough over by the wall to wait till she finished. An' I did think it all
over, an' next day I never said nothin', but I put on my bonnet, and
went to see Mis' Cap'n Tolland, if 'twas only for mother's sake. 'Twas
about three quarters of a mile up the road here, beyond the schoolhouse. I forgot to tell you that the cap'n had bought out his sister's right
at three or four times what 'twas worth, to save trouble, so they'd got
clear o' her, an' I went round into the side yard sort o' friendly an'
sociable, rather than stop an' deal with the knocker an' the front door.
It looked so pleasant an' pretty I was glad I come; she had set a little
table for supper, though 'twas still early, with a white cloth on it, right
out under an old apple tree close by the house. I noticed 'twas same
as with me at home, there was only one plate. She was just coming out
with a dish; you couldn't see the door nor the table from the road.

"In the few weeks she'd been there she'd got some bloomin' pinks an'
other flowers next the doorstep. Somehow it looked as if she'd known
how to make it homelike for the cap'n. She asked me to set down; she was
very polite, but she looked very mournful, and I spoke of mother, an' she
put down her dish and caught holt o' me with both hands an' said my

mother was an angel. When I see the tears in her eyes 'twas all right between us, and we were always friendly after that, and mother had us come out and make a little visit that summer; but she come a foreigner and she went a foreigner, and never was anything but a stranger among our folks. She taught me a sight o' things about herbs I never knew before nor since; she was well acquainted with the virtues o' plants. She'd act awful secret about some things too, an' used to work charms for herself sometimes, an' some o' the neighbors told to an' fro after she died that they knew enough not to provoke her, but 'twas all nonsense; 'tis the believin' in such things that causes 'em to be any harm, an' so I told 'em," confided Mrs. Todd contemptuously. "That first night I stopped to tea with her she'd cooked some eggs with some herb or other sprinkled all through, and 'twas she that first led me to discern mushrooms; an' she went right down on her knees in my garden here when she saw I had my different officious herbs. Yes, 'twas she that learned me the proper use o' parsley too; she was a beautiful cook."

Mrs. Todd stopped talking, and rose, putting the cat gently in the chair, while she went away to get another stick of apple-tree wood. It was not an evening when one wished to let the fire go down, and we had a splendid bank of bright coals. I had always wondered where Mrs. Todd had got such an unusual knowledge of cookery, of the varieties of mushrooms, and the use of sorrel as a vegetable, and other blessings of that sort. I had long ago learned that she could vary her omelettes like a child of France, which was indeed a surprise in Dunnet Landing.

IV

All these revelations were of the deepest interest, and I was ready with a question as soon as Mrs. Todd came in and had well settled the fire and herself and the cat again.

"I wonder why she never went back to France, after she was left alone?"

"She come here from the French islands," explained Mrs. Todd. "I asked her once about her folks, an' she said they were all dead; 'twas the fever took 'em. She made this her home, lonesome as 'twas; she told me she hadn't been in France since she was 'so small,' and measured me off a child o' six. She'd lived right out in the country before, so that part wa'n't unusual to her. Oh yes, there was something very strange about her, and she hadn't been brought up in high circles nor nothing o' that kind. I think she'd been really pleased to have the cap'n marry her an' give her a good home, after all she'd passed through, and leave her free with his money an' all that. An' she got over bein' so strange-looking to me after a while, but 'twas a very singular expression: she wore a fixed smile that wa'n't a smile; there wa'n't no light behind it, same's a lamp can't shine if it ain't lit. I don't know just how to express it, 'twas a sort of made countenance."

One could not help thinking of Sir Philip Sidney's phrase, "A made countenance, between simpering and smiling."[1]

"She took it hard, havin' the captain go off on that last voyage," Mrs. Todd went on. "She said somethin' told her when they was partin' that he would never come back. He was lucky to speak a home-bound ship this side o' the Cape o' Good Hope, an' got a chance to send her a letter, an' that cheered her up. You often felt as if you was dealin' with a child's mind, for all she had so much information that other folks hadn't. I was a sight younger than I be now, and she made me imagine new things, and I got interested watchin' her an' findin' out what she had to say, but you couldn't get to no affectionateness with her. I used to blame me sometimes; we used to be real good comrades goin' off for an afternoon, but I never give her a kiss till the day she laid in her coffin and it come to my heart there wa'n't no one else to do it."

"And Captain Tolland died," I suggested after a while.

"Yes, the cap'n was lost," said Mrs. Todd, "and of course word didn't come for a good while after it happened. The letter come from the owners to my uncle, Cap'n Lorenzo Bowden, who was in charge of Cap'n Tolland's affairs at home, and he come right up for me an' said I must go with him to the house. I had known what it was to be a widow, myself, for near a year, an' there was plenty o' widow women along this coast that the sea had made desolate, but I never saw a heart break as I did then.

" 'Twas this way: we walked together along the road, me an' uncle Lorenzo. You know how it leads straight from just above the school-house to the brook bridge, and their house was just this side o' the brook bridge on the left hand; the cellar's there now, and a couple or three good-sized gray birches growin' in it. And when we come near enough I saw that the best room, this way, where she most never set, was all lighted up, and the curtains up so that the light shone bright down the road, and as we walked, those lights would dazzle and dazzle in my eyes, and I could hear the guitar a-goin', an' she was singin'. She heard our steps with her quick ears and come running to the door with her eyes a-shinin', an' all that set look gone out of her face, an' begun to talk French, gay as a bird, an' shook hands and behaved very pretty an' girlish, sayin' 'twas her fête day.[2] I didn't know what she meant then. And she had gone an' put a wreath of flowers on her hair an' wore a handsome gold chain that the cap'n had given her; an' there she was poor creatur', makin' believe have a party all alone in her best room; 'twas prim enough to discourage a person, with too many chairs set close to the walls, just as the cap'n's mother had left it, but she had put sort o' long garlands on the walls, droopin' very graceful, and a sight of green boughs in the corners, till it looked lovely, and all lit up with a lot o' candles."

1. Sir Philip Sidney (1554–1587), English courtier, soldier, poet, and essayist; the quote no doubt refers to the passage from The Countess of Pembroke's Arcadia (The New Arcadia) (1590), Book I: "mad countenance about her mouth between simpering and smiling."
2. Her saint's day or birthday.

"Oh dear!" I sighed. "Oh, Mrs. Todd, what did you do?"

"She beheld our countenances," answered Mrs. Todd solemnly. "I expect they was telling everything plain enough, but Cap'n Lorenzo spoke the sad words to her as if he had been her father; and she wavered a minute and then over she went on the floor before we could catch hold of her, and then we tried to bring her to herself and failed, and at last we carried her upstairs, an' I told uncle to run down and put out the lights, and then go fast as he could for Mrs. Begg, being very experienced in sickness, an' he so did. I got off her clothes and her poor wreath, and I cried as I done it. We both stayed there that night, and the doctor said 'twas a shock when he come in the morning; he'd been over to Black Island an' had to stay all night with a very sick child."

"You said that she lived alone some time after the news came," I reminded Mrs. Todd then.

"Oh yes, dear," answered my friend sadly, "but it wa'n't what you'd call livin'; no, it was only dyin', though at a snail's pace. She never went out again those few months, but for a while she could manage to get about the house a little, and do what was needed, an' I never let two days go by without seein' her or hearin' from her. She never took much notice as I came an' went except to answer if I asked her anything. Mother was the one who gave her the only comfort."

"What was that?" I asked softly.

"She said that anybody in such trouble ought to see their minister, mother did, and one day she spoke to Mis' Tolland, and found that the poor soul had been believin' all the time that there weren't any priests here. We'd come to know she was a Catholic by her beads and all, and that had set some narrow minds against her. And mother explained it just as she would to a child; and uncle Lorenzo sent word right off somewheres up river by a packet that was bound up the bay, and the first o' the week a priest come by the boat, an' uncle Lorenzo was on the wharf 'tendin' to some business; so they just come up for me, and I walked with him to show him the house. He was a kind-hearted old man; he looked so benevolent an' fatherly I could ha' stopped an' told him my own troubles; yes, I was satisfied when I first saw his face, an' when poor Mis' Tolland beheld him enter the room, she went right down on her knees and clasped her hands together to him as if he'd come to save her life, and he lifted her up and blessed her, an' I left 'em together, and slipped out into the open field and walked there in sight so if they needed to call me, and I had my own thoughts. At last I saw him at the door; he had to catch the return boat. I meant to walk back with him and offer him some supper, but he said no, and said he was comin' again if needed, and signed me to go into the house to her, and shook his head in a way that meant he understood everything. I can see him now; he walked with a cane, rather tired and feeble; I wished somebody would come along, so's to carry him down to the shore.

"Mis' Tolland looked up at me with a new look when I went in, an' she even took hold o' my hand and kept it. He had put some oil on her forehead, but nothing anybody could do would keep her alive very long; 'twas his medicine for the soul rather'n the body. I helped her to bed, and next morning she couldn't get up to dress her, and that was Monday, and she began to fail, and 'twas Friday night she died." (Mrs. Todd spoke with unusual haste and lack of detail.) "Mrs. Begg and I watched with her, and made everything nice and proper, and after all the ill will there was a good number gathered to the funeral. 'Twas in Reverend Mr. Bascom's day, and he done very well in his prayer, considering he couldn't fill in with mentioning all the near connections by name as was his habit. He spoke very feeling about her being a stranger and twice widowed, and all he said about her being reared among the heathen was to observe that there might be roads leadin' up to the New Jerusalem[3] from various points. I says to myself that I guessed quite a number must ha' reached there that wa'n't able to set out from Dunnet Landin'!"

Mrs. Todd gave an odd little laugh as she bent toward the firelight to pick up a dropped stitch in her knitting, and then I heard a heartfelt sigh.

" 'Twas most forty years ago," she said; "most everybody's gone a'ready that was there that day."

V

Suddenly Mrs. Todd gave an energetic shrug of her shoulders, and a quick look at me, and I saw that the sails of her narrative were filled with a fresh breeze.

"Uncle Lorenzo, Cap'n Bowden that I have referred to"—

"Certainly!" I agreed with eager expectation.

"He was the one that had been left in charge of Cap'n John Tolland's affairs, and had now come to be of unforeseen importance.

"Mrs. Begg an' I had stayed in the house both before an' after Mis' Tolland's decease, and she was now in haste to be gone, having affairs to call her home; but uncle come to me as the exercises[4] was beginning, and said he thought I'd better remain at the house while they went to the buryin' ground. I couldn't understand his reasons, an' I felt disappointed, bein' as near to her as most anybody; 'twas rough weather, so mother couldn't get in, and didn't even hear Mis' Tolland was gone till next day. I just nodded to satisfy him, 'twa'n't no time to discuss anything. Uncle seemed flustered; he'd gone out deep-sea fishin' the day she died, and the storm I told you of rose very sudden, so they got blown off way down the coast beyond Monhegan, and he'd just got back in time to dress himself and come.

"I set there in the house after I'd watched her away down the

3. The Book of Revelation predicts the end of the world followed by the creation of a new heaven, a new earth, and a heavenly Jerusalem.

4. Religious ceremonies, here associated with a funeral.

straight road far's I could see from the door; 'twas a little short walkin'
funeral[5] an' a cloudy sky, so everything looked dull an' gray, an' it
crawled along all in one piece, same's walking funerals do, an' I wondered how it ever come to the Lord's mind to let her begin down
among them gay islands all heat and sun, and end up here among the
rocks with a north wind blowin'. 'Twas a gale that begun the afternoon
before she died, and had kept blowin' off an' on ever since. I'd thought
more than once how glad I should be to get home an' out o' sound o'
them black spruces a-beatin' an' scratchin' at the front windows.

"I set to work pretty soon to put the chairs back, an' set outdoors
some that was borrowed, an' I went out in the kitchen, an' I made up
a good fire in case somebody come an' wanted a cup o' tea; but I didn't
expect anyone to travel way back to the house unless 'twas uncle
Lorenzo. 'Twas growin' so chilly that I fetched some kindlin' wood and
made fires in both the fore rooms. Then I set down an' begun to feel
as usual, and I got my knittin' out of a drawer. You can't be sorry for
a poor creature that's come to the end o' all her troubles; my only
discomfort was I thought I'd ought to feel worse at losin' her than I did;
I was younger then than I be now. And as I set there, I begun to hear
some long notes o' dronin' music from upstairs that chilled me to the
bone."

Mrs. Todd gave a hasty glance at me.

"Quick's I could gather me, I went right upstairs to see what 'twas,"
she added eagerly, "an' 'twas just what I might ha' known. She'd
always kept her guitar hangin' right against the wall in her room; 'twas
tied by a blue ribbon, and there was a window left wide open; the wind
was veerin' a good deal, an' it slanted in and searched the room. The
strings was jarrin' yet.

" 'Twas growin' pretty late in the afternoon, an' I begun to feel
lonesome as I shouldn't now, and I was disappointed at having to stay
there, the more I thought it over, but after a while I saw Cap'n Lorenzo
polin'[6] back up the road all alone, and when he come nearer I could see
he had a bundle under his arm and had shifted his best black clothes
for his everyday ones. I run out and put some tea into the teapot and
set it back on the stove to draw, an' when he come in I reached down
a little jug o' spirits—Cap'n Tolland had left his house well provisioned
as if his wife was goin' to put to sea same's himself, an' there she'd
gone an' left it. There was some cake that Mis' Begg an' I had made
the day before. I thought that uncle an' me had a good right to the
funeral supper, even if there wasn't anyone to join us. I was lookin'
forward to my cup o' tea; 'twas beautiful tea out of a green lacquered
chest that I've got now."

"You must have felt very tired," said I, eagerly listening.

"I was 'most beat out, with watchin' an' tendin' and all," answered

5. In rural New England, funeral ceremonies included the mourners walking with the body to the
cemetery.
6. Go slouching along slowly.

Mrs. Todd, with as much sympathy in her voice as if she were speaking of another person. "But I called out to uncle as he came in, 'Well, I expect it's all over now, an' we've all done what we could. I thought we'd better have some tea or somethin' before we go home. Come right out in the kitchen, sir,' say I, never thinking but we only had to let the fires out and lock up everything safe an' eat our refreshment, an' go home.

" 'I want both of us to stop here tonight,' says uncle, looking at me very important.

" 'Oh, what for?' says I, kind of fretful.

" 'I've got proper reasons,' says uncle. 'I'll see you well satisfied, Almira. Your tongue ain't so easy-goin' as some o' the women folks, an' there's property here to take charge of that you don't know nothin' at all about.'

" 'What do you mean?' says I.

" 'Cap'n Tolland acquainted me with his affairs; he hadn't no sort o' confidence in nobody but me an' his wife, after he was tricked into signin' that Portland note, an' lost money. An' she didn't know nothin' about business; but what he didn't take to sea to be sunk with him he's hid somewhere in this house. I expect Mis' Tolland may have told you where she kept things?' said uncle.

"I see he was dependin' a good deal on my answer," said Mrs. Todd, "but I had to disappoint him; no, she had never said nothin' to me.

" 'Well, then, we've got to make a search,' says he, with considerable relish; but he was all tired and worked up, and we set down to the table, an' he had somethin', an' I took my desired cup o' tea, and then I begun to feel more interested.

" 'Where you goin' to look first?' says I, but he give me a short look an' made no answer, and begun to mix me a very small portion out of the jug, in another glass. I took it to please him; he said I looked tired, speakin' real fatherly, and I did feel better for it, and we set talkin' a few minutes, an' then he started for the cellar, carrying an old ship' lantern he fetched out o' the stairway an' lit.

" 'What are you lookin' for, some kind of a chist?'[7] I inquired, and he said yes. All of a sudden it come to me to ask who was the heirs; Eliza Tolland, Cap'n John's own sister, had never demeaned herself to come near the funeral, and uncle Lorenzo faced right about and begun to laugh, sort o' pleased. I thought queer of it; 'twa'n't what he'd taken, which would be nothin' to an old weathered sailor like him.

" 'Who's the heir?' said I the second time.

" 'Why, it's you, Almiry,' says he; and I was so took aback I set right down on the turn o' the cellar stairs.

" 'Yes 'tis,' said uncle Lorenzo. 'I'm glad of it too. Some thought she didn't have no sense but foreign sense, an' a poor stock o' that, but she

---

7. I.e., sea chest.

said you was friendly to her, an' one day after she got news of Tolland's death, an' I had fetched up his will that left everything to her, she said she was goin' to make a writin', so's you could have things after she was gone, an' she give five hundred to me for bein' executor. Square[8] Pease fixed up the paper, an' she signed it; it's all accordin' to law.' There, I begun to cry," said Mrs. Todd; "I couldn't help it. I wished I had her back again to do somethin' for, an' to make her know I felt sisterly to her more'n I'd ever showed, an' it come over me 'twas all too late, an' I cried the more, till uncle showed impatience, an' I got up an' stumbled along down cellar with my apern to my eyes the greater part of the time.

" 'I'm goin' to have a clean search,' says he; 'you hold the light.' An' I held it, and he rummaged in the arches an' under the stairs, an' over in some old closet where he reached out bottles an' stone jugs an' canted some kags[9] an' one or two casks, an' chuckled well when he heard there was somethin' inside,—but there wa'n't nothin' to find but things usual in a cellar, an' then the old lantern was givin' out an' we come away.

" 'He spoke to me of a chist, Cap'n Tolland did,' says uncle in a whisper. 'He said a good sound chist was as safe a bank as there was, an' I beat him out of such nonsense, 'count o' fire an' other risks.' 'There's no chist in the rooms above,' says I; 'no, uncle, there ain't no sea-chist, for I've been here long enough to see what there was to be seen.' Yet he couldn't feel contented till he'd mounted up into the top loft; 'twas one o' them single, hip-roofed houses that don't give proper accommodation for a real garret, like Cap'n Littlepage's down here at the Landin'. There was broken furniture and rubbish, an' he let down a terrible sign o' dust into the front entry, but sure enough there wasn't no chist. I had it all to sweep up next day.

" 'He must have took it away to sea,' says I to the cap'n, an' even then he didn't want to agree, but we was both beat out. I told him where I'd always seen Mis' Tolland get her money from, and we found much as a hundred dollars there in an old red morocco wallet. Cap'n John had been gone a good while a'ready, and she had spent what she needed. 'Twas in an old desk o' his in the settin' room that we found the wallet."

"At the last minute he may have taken his money to sea," I suggested.

"Oh, yes," agreed Mrs. Todd. "He did take considerable to make his venture to bring home, as was customary, an' that was drowned with him as uncle agreed; but he had other property in shipping, and a thousand dollars invested in Portland in a cordage shop, but 'twas about the time shipping begun to decay, and the cordage shop failed, and in the end I wa'n't so rich as I thought I was goin' to be for those

---

8. I.e., Squire.   9. Decanted some kegs.

few minutes on the cellar stairs. There was an auction that accumulated something. Old Mis' Tolland, the cap'n's mother, had
heired some good furniture from a sister: there was above thirty chairs
in all, and they're apt to sell well. I got over a thousand dollars when
we come to settle up, and I made uncle take his five hundred; he was
getting along in years and had met with losses in navigation, and he left
it back to me when he died, so I had a real good lift. It all lays in the
bank over to Rockland, and I draw my interest fall an' spring, with the
little Mr. Todd was able to leave me; but that's kind o' sacred money;
'twas earnt and saved with the hope o' youth, an' I'm very particular
what I spend it for. Oh yes, what with ownin' my house, I've been
enabled to get along very well, with prudence!" said Mrs. Todd contentedly.

"But there was the house and land," I asked,—"What became of
that part of the property?"

Mrs. Todd looked into the fire, and a shadow of disapproval flitted
over her face.

"Poor old uncle!" she said, "he got childish about the matter. I was
hoping to sell at first, and I had an offer, but he always run of an idea
that there was more money hid away, and kept wanting me to delay;
an' he used to go up there all alone and search, and dig in the cellar,
empty an' bleak as 'twas in winter weather or any time. An' he'd come
and tell me he'd dreamed he found gold behind a stone in the cellar
wall, or somethin'. And one night we all see the light o' fire up that
way, an' the whole Landin' took the road, and run to look, and the
Tolland property was all in a light blaze. I expect the old gentleman
had dropped the fire about; he said he'd been up there to see if
everything was safe in the afternoon. As for the land, 'twas so poor that
everybody used to have a joke that the Tolland boys preferred to farm
the sea instead. It's 'most all grown up to bushes now, where it ain't
poor water grass in the low places. There's some upland that has a
pretty view, after you cross the brook bridge. Years an' years after she
died, there was some o' her flowers used to come up an' bloom in the
door garden. I brought two or three that was unusual down here; they
always come up and remind me of her, constant as the spring. But I
never did want to fetch home that guitar, some way or 'nother; I
wouldn't let it go at the auction, either. It was hangin' right there in the
house when the fire took place. I've got some o' her other little things
scattered about the house: that picture on the mantelpiece belonged to
her."

I had often wondered where such a picture had come from, and why
Mrs. Todd had chosen it; it was a French print of the statue of the
Empress Josephine in the Savane at old Fort Royal, in Martinique.[1]

---

1. Martinique is an island in the French West In- Napoleon I; savane: a savannah is a flat, treeless
dies; Josephine de Beauharnais, who was born on grassland.
Martinique, was Empress of the French as wife of

VI

Mrs. Todd drew her chair closer to mine; she held the cat and her knitting with one hand as she moved, but the cat was so warm and so sound asleep that she only stretched a lazy paw in spite of what must have felt like a slight earthquake. Mrs. Todd began to speak almost in a whisper.

"I ain't told you all," she continued; "no, I haven't spoken of all to but very few. The way it came was this," she said solemnly, and then stopped to listen to the wind, and sat for a moment in deferential silence, as if she waited for the wind, to speak first. The cat suddenly lifted her head with quick excitement and gleaming eyes, and her mistress was leaning forward toward the fire with an arm laid on either knee, as if they were consulting the glowing coals for some augury. Mrs. Todd looked like an old prophetess as she sat there with the firelight shining on her strong face; she was posed for some great painter. The woman with the cat was as unconscious and as mysterious as any sibyl of the Sistine Chapel.[2]

"There, that's the last struggle o' the gale," said Mrs. Todd, nodding her head with impressive certainty and still looking into the bright embers of the fire. "You'll see!" She gave me another quick glance, and spoke in a low tone as if we might be overheard.

" 'Twas such a gale as this the night Mis' Tolland died. She appeared more comfortable the first o' the evenin'; and Mrs. Begg was more spent than I, bein' older, and a beautiful nurse that was the first to see and think of everything, but perfectly quiet an' never asked a useless question. You remember her funeral when you first come to the Landing? And she consented to goin' an' havin' a good sleep while she could, and left me one o' those good little pewter lamps that burnt whale oil an' made plenty o' light in the room, but not too bright to be disturbin'.

"Poor Mis' Tolland had been distressed the night before, an' all that day, but as night come on she grew more and more easy, an' was layin' there asleep; 'twas like settin' by any sleepin' person, and I had none but usual thoughts. When the wind lulled and the rain, I could hear the seas, though more distant than this, and I don' know's I observed any other sound than what the weather made; 'twas a very solemn feelin' night. I set close by the bed; there was times she looked to find somebody when she was awake. The light was on her face, so I could see her plain; there was always times when she wore a look that made her seem a stranger you'd never set eyes on before. I did think what a world it was that her an' me should have come together so, and she have nobody but Dunnet Landin' folks about her in her extremity. 'You're one o' the stray ones, poor creatur',' I said. I remember those very words passin' through my mind, but I saw reason to be glad she had some comforts, and didn't lack friends at the last, though she'd

2. A chapel built during the late 15th century in the Vatican, best known for the frescoes painted by Michaelangelo on the ceiling and over the altar.

seen misery an' pain. I was glad she was quiet; all day she'd been restless, and we couldn't understand what she wanted from her French speech. We had the window open to give her air, an' now an' then a gust would strike that guitar that was on the wall and set it swinging by the blue ribbon, and soundin' as if somebody begun to play it. I come near takin' it down, but you never know what'll fret a sick person an' put 'em on the rack, an' that guitar was one o' the few things she'd brought with her."

I nodded assent, and Mrs. Todd spoke still lower.

"I set there close by the bed; I'd been through a good deal for some days back, and I thought I might's well be droppin' asleep too, bein' a quick person to wake. She looked to me as if she might last a day longer, certain, now she'd got more comfortable, but I was real tired, an' sort o' cramped as watchers will get, an' a fretful feeling begun to creep over me such as they often do have. If you give way, there ain't no support for the sick person; they can't count on no composure o' their own. Mis' Tolland moved then; a little restless, an' I forgot me quick enough, an' begun to hum out a little part of a hymn tune just to make her feel everything was as usual an' not wake up into a poor uncertainty. All of a sudden she set right up in bed with her eyes wide open, an' I stood an' put my arm behind her; she hadn't moved like that for days. And she reached out both her arms toward the door, an' I looked the way she was lookin', an' I see someone was standin' there against the dark. No, 'twa'n't Mis' Begg; 'twas somebody a good deal shorter than Mis' Begg. The lamplight struck across the room between us. I couldn't tell the shape, but 'twas a woman's dark face lookin' right at us; 'twa'n't but an instant I could see. I felt dreadful cold, and my head begun to swim; I thought the light went out; 'twa'n't but an instant, as I say, an' when my sight come back I couldn't see nothing there. I was one that didn't know what it was to faint away, no matter what happened; time was I felt above it in others, but 'twas somethin' that made poor human natur' quail. I saw very plain while I could see; 'twas a pleasant enough face, shaped somethin' like Mis' Tolland's, and a kind of expectin' look."

"No, I don't expect I was asleep," Mrs. Todd assured me quietly, after a moment's pause, though I had not spoken. She gave a heavy sigh before she went on. I could see that the recollection moved her in the deepest way.

"I suppose if I hadn't been so spent an' quavery with long watchin', I might have kept my head an' observed much better," she added humbly; "but I see all I could bear. I did try to act calm, an' I laid Mis' Tolland down on her pillow, an' I was a-shakin' as I done it. All she did was look up to me so satisfied and sort o' questioning, an' I looked back to her.

" 'You saw her, didn't you?' she says to me, speakin' perfectly reasonable. ' 'Tis my mother,' she says again, very feeble, but lookin' straight up at me, kind of surprised with the pleasure, and smiling as if she saw I was overcome, an' would have said more if she could, but we had hold of hands. I see then her change was comin', but I didn't call Mis' Begg, nor make no uproar. I felt calm then, an' lifted to somethin' different as I never was since. She opened her eyes just as she was goin'—

" 'You saw her, didn't you?' she said the second time, an' I says, '*Yes, dear, I did; you ain't never goin' to feel strange an' lonesome no more.*' An' then in a few quiet minutes 'twas all over. I felt they'd gone away together. No, I wa'n't alarmed afterward; 'twas just that one moment I couldn't live under, but I never called it beyond reason I should see the other watcher. I saw plain enough there was somebody there with me in the room.

VII

" 'Twas just such a night as this Mis' Tolland died," repeated Mrs. Todd, returning to her usual tone and leaning back comfortably in her chair as she took up her knitting. " 'Twas just such a night as this. I've told the circumstances to but very few; but I don't call it beyond reason. When folks is goin' 'tis all natural, and only common things can jar upon the mind. You know plain enough there's somethin' beyond this world; the doors stand wide open. 'There's somethin' of us that must still live on; we've got to join both worlds together an' live in one but for the other.' The doctor said that to me one day, an' I never could forget it; he said 'twas in one o' his old doctor's books."

❋   ❋   ❋

We sat together in silence in the warm little room; the rain dropped heavily from the eaves, and the sea still roared, but the high wind had done blowing. We heard the far complaining fog horn of a steamer up the Bay.

"There goes the Boston boat out, pretty near on time," said Mrs. Todd with satisfaction. "Sometimes these late August storms'll sound a good deal worse than they really be. I do hate to hear the poor steamers callin' when they're bewildered in thick nights in winter, comin' on the coast. Yes, there goes the boat; they'll find it rough at sea, but the storm's all over."

Atlantic Monthly, August 1900;
The World of Dunnet Landing, 1962

MARY NOIALLES MURFREE
1850-1922

When Mary Noialles Murfree was four years old, she suffered an illness that left her permanently lame. In his biography Edd Parks notes that Murfree's lameness "entitled her to special consideration from the mountaineers, who . . . regarded the cripple . . . with peculiar veneration" (130). Murfree's lameness did not keep her from being active and curious; she was at the center of family life during the family's summers at Beersheba Springs in the Cumberland Mountains. Often her mother would play the piano for hours and Murfree would sing to the mountaineers, and she and her older sister Fanny—her closest companion throughout her life—would ride their horses into mountain communities in search of butter and eggs. However, while Murfree could walk and ride without difficulty, she could not or would not be part of conventional social life, where her inability to dance or even stand for long led her to stay on the sidelines observing.

Mary Noailles Murfree lived most of her life in Tennessee. She was born January 24, 1850, the second of three children, on the family's Grantland Plantation near Murfreesboro. Her father William Law Murfree, a lawyer, and her mother Fanny Priscilla Dickinson owned cotton plantations in Mississippi as well as Tennessee. Initially tutored at home, Mary and Fanny attended Nashville Female Academy from 1857 until the outbreak of the Civil War in 1861. During the war, while the Murfrees lived in garrisoned Nashville, William tutored his own children, then sent Mary and Fanny to Chegaray Institute, a boarding school in Philadelphia. After he lost his Mississippi plantations in 1869 and returned to the practice of law, he continued to spend much time with his daughters, telling them Irish, mountain, and Negro dialect tales that he encouraged Mary to preserve.

Murfree began to write with her father's encouragement, and her first published essay, "Flirts and Their Ways" (*Lippincott's*, May 1874), resulted from their collaboration. Parks notes, however, that Murfree could not use her father's material in her fiction, and that she preferred to write about the mountaineers she knew from her summers at Beersheba Springs. Murfree sent "The Dancin' Party at Harrison's Cove," her first significant regional work and written as the first chapter of a planned novel about mountain life, to William Dean Howells. Howells immediately accepted it for publication in the *Atlantic Monthly*, where it appeared under the name "Charles Egbert Craddock" in May 1878. Murfree retained her pseudonym and her male identity (signing her letters "M. N. Murfree") until the spring of 1885, after publishing *In the Tennessee Mountains* to wide acclaim the previous year. When Murfree revealed her identity to Thomas Bailey Aldrich in the offices of the *Atlantic Monthly*, the event created national publicity; journalists reported that everyone had considered her style to be "masculine."

As a result of her trip to Boston, Murfree met Annie Fields, Sarah Orne Jewett, and Celia Thaxter, and she and Fanny paid a visit to Thaxter at the Isles of Shoals. Parks notes that Thaxter and Jewett " 'sought to reclaim this almost lost member of their sex' "—"almost lost" because they had thought she was male,—suggesting that they saw affinities between their own work and the stories collected in *In the Tennessee Mountains* (127). Although Murfree published successfully throughout most of her life, writing twenty-five books before her death on July 31, 1922, and although she supported herself by her writing and contributed to her family's support after her father went blind in 1889, she never equaled the literary quality of the mountain fiction she had published as "Charles Egbert Craddock."

o   o   o

In publishing the stories later collected in *In the Tennessee Mountains* (1884), Mary Noialles Murfree became the first southern writer whose works demonstrate the features of regionalism; however, as the anthologized stories illustrate, regionalism is shown in a different light in Murfree's writing than in the works of her New England predecessors and contemporaries. When Sarah Orne Jewett shifts the center of perception in "The Circus at Denby" from the outsiders looking at the Kentucky giantess to the giantess herself, she reaffirms a central assumption of New England regionalism—that character and narrator are more alike than different, and that regional narratives can be based on empathy. As a southern woman born near a small Tennessee city that already bore her family name (Murfreesboro), and as a woman who enjoyed the class privileges of plantation life and education at a Philadelphia boarding school, Murfree did not assume that all Tennesseans or all southerners were potentially alike. Rather, she perceived the mountaineers she came to know during summers in the Cumberland Mountains as different from her even while she developed sympathies for what she described, in an 1884 letter to Aldrich, as "their primitive customs, dialect, and peculiar view of life" (quoted in Parks, 119).

Murfree honors difference at the same time as she reduces hierarchies of class, language, and regional identity. In her fiction, outsiders look at and describe mountaineers in genteel and "literary" language; the mountaineers, with a voice new to American literature in the 1880s, look back at outsiders, and speak in dialect that, though difficult to decipher, is faithful to the phonetic and stylistic features of Southern Appalachian English. Neither Murfree's outsiders nor her mountaineers control the center of perception. In "The Star in the Valley," despite the fact that her own narrative language is often indistinguishable from his, Murfree undermines Chevis's credibility as an interpreter of mountains and mountaineers. While Chevis watches Celia Shaw, she watches him back; two perspectives clearly exist in this story. Indeed, in exaggerating the stylistic features of her own and Chevis's voice, Murfree implies that this "literary" language is itself merely a dialect and simply reflects another way of speaking. Similarly, "Over on the T'other Mounting" balances narration in "literary" dialect with narration by mountaineers in their own dialect, the "range" of one language facing the "range" of "t'other." In both stories, Murfree uses this contrast in perspective to question the dominance simply assumed by characters like Chevis.

In "The 'Harnt' That Walks Chilhowee," Murfree perhaps achieves her most effective combination of mountain dialect and the "t'other" dialect of "literary" language. And in "The 'Harnt,' " she grants Clarsie Giles a voice to speak out—"ter jaw"—in defense of herself, the "harnt," and the principle of feeding those who are hungry, thus expressing many of the values we associate with the female characters created by the New England regionalists. Moreover, in the figure of Reuben Crabb, whose starving pitiful face is drawn with a descriptive power rare in Murfree's work, Murfree gives her reader a portrait that perhaps expresses her own relation to the world of the mountains, a world that, in her fiction, at least accommodates the starving cripple. In her writing of that world we can speculate that she fed some deeply personal hunger. Still, *In the Tennessee Mountains* retains the distance of difference rather than the empathic fusion of narrator and regional character. Murfree can write about the mountaineers without the condescension of the local colorist, but without, either, claiming to be a mountaineer herself.

The Star in the Valley

He first saw it in the twilight of a clear October evening. As the earliest planet sprang into the sky, an answering gleam shone red amid the glooms in the valley. A star too it seemed. And later, when the myriads of the fairer, whiter lights of a moonless night were all athrob in the great concave vault bending to the hills, there was something very impressive in that solitary star of earth, changeless and motionless beneath the ever-changing skies.

Chevis never tired of looking at it. Somehow it broke the spell that draws all eyes heavenward on starry nights. He often strolled with his cigar at dusk down to the verge of the crag, and sat for hours gazing at it and vaguely speculating about it. That spark seemed to have kindled all the soul and imagination within him, although he knew well enough its prosaic source, for he had once questioned the gawky mountaineer whose services he had secured as guide through the forest solitudes during this hunting expedition.

"That thar spark in the valley?" Hi Bates had replied, removing the pipe from his lips and emitting a cloud of strong tobacco smoke. " 'Tain't nuthin' but the light in Jerry Shaw's house, 'bout haffen mile from the foot of the mounting.[1] Ye pass that thar house when ye goes on the Christel road, what leads down the mounting off the Back-bone. That's Jerry Shaw's house,—that's what it is. He's a blacksmith, an' he kin shoe a horse toler'ble well when he ain't drunk, ez he mos'ly is."

"Perhaps that is the light from the forge," suggested Chevis.

"That thar forge ain't run more'n half the day, let 'lone o'nights. I hev never hearn tell on Jerry Shaw a-workin' o' nights,—nor in the daytime nuther, ef he kin git shet of it. No sech no 'count critter 'twixt hyar an' the Settlemint."[2]

So spake Chevis's astronomer. Seeing the star even through the prosaic lens of stern reality did not detract from its poetic aspect. Chevis never failed to watch for it. The first faint glinting in the azure evening sky sent his eyes to that red reflection suddenly aglow in the

---

1. Cumberland dialect for "mountain."   2. The nearest established community.

valley; even when the mists rose above it and hid it from him, he gazed at the spot where it had disappeared, feeling a calm satisfaction to know that it was still shining beneath the cloud-curtain. He encouraged himself in this bit of sentimentality. These unique eventide effects seemed a fitting sequel to the picturesque day, passed in hunting deer, with horn and hounds, through the gorgeous autumnal forest; or perchance in the more exciting sport in some rocky gorge with a bear at bay and the frenzied pack around him; or in the idyllic pleasures of bird-shooting with a thoroughly trained dog; and coming back in the crimson sunset to a well-appointed tent and a smoking supper of venison or wild turkey,—the trophies of his skill. The vague dreaminess of his cigar and the charm of that bright bit of color in the night-shrouded valley added a sort of romantic zest to these primitive enjoyments, and ministered to that keen susceptibility of impressions which Reginald Chevis considered eminently characteristic of a highly wrought mind and nature.

He said nothing of his fancies, however, to his fellow sportsman, Ned Varney, nor to the mountaineer. Infinite as was the difference between these two in mind and cultivation, his observation of both had convinced him that they were alike incapable of appreciating and comprehending his delicate and dainty musings. Varney was essentially a man of this world; his mental and moral conclusions had been adopted in a calm, mercantile spirit, as giving the best return for the outlay, and the market was not liable to fluctuations. And the mountaineer could go no further than the prosaic fact of the light in Jerry Shaw's house. Thus Reginald Chevis was wont to sit in contemplative silence on the crag until his cigar was burnt out, and afterward to lie awake deep in the night, listening to the majestic lyric welling up from the thousand nocturnal voices of these mountain wilds.

During the day, in place of the red light a gauzy little curl of smoke was barely visible, the only sign or suggestion of human habitation to be seen from the crag in all the many miles of long, narrow valley and parallel tiers of ranges. Sometimes Chevis and Varney caught sight of it from lower down on the mountain side, whence was faintly distinguishable the little log-house and certain vague lines marking a rectangular inclosure; near at hand, too, the forge, silent and smokeless. But it did not immediately occur to either of them to theorize concerning its inmates and their lives in this lonely place; for a time, not even to the speculative Chevis. As to Varney, he gave his whole mind to the matter in hand,—his gun, his dog, his game,—and his note-book was as systematic and as romantic as the ledger at home.

It might be accounted an event in the history of that log-hut when Reginald Chevis, after riding past it eighty yards or so, chanced one day to meet a country girl walking toward the house. She did not look up, and he caught only an indistinct glimpse of her face. She spoke to him, however, as she went by, which is the invariable custom with the inhabitants of the sequestered nooks among the encompassing mountains, whether meeting stranger or acquaintance. He lifted his hat in return, with that punctilious courtesy which he made a point of according to persons of low degree. In another moment she had passed down the narrow sandy road, overhung with gigantic trees, and, at a deft, even pace, hardly slackened as she traversed the great log extending across the rushing stream, she made her way up the opposite hill, and disappeared gradually over its brow.

The expression of her face, half-seen though it was, had attracted his attention. He rode slowly along, meditating. "Did she go into Shaw's house, just around the curve of the road?" he wondered. "Is she Shaw's daughter, or some visiting neighbor?"

That night he looked with a new interest at the red star, set like a jewel in the floating mists of the valley.

"Do you know," he asked of Hi Bates, when the three men were seated, after supper, around the camp-fire, which sent lurid tongues of flame and a thousand bright sparks leaping high in the darkness, and illumined the vistas of the woods on every side, save where the sudden crag jutted over the valley,—"Do you know whether Jerry Shaw has a daughter,—a young girl?"

"Ye-es," drawled Hi Bates, disparagingly, "he hev."

A pause ensued. The star in the valley was blotted from sight; the rising mists had crept to the verge of the crag; nay, in the undergrowth fringing the mountain's brink, there were softly clinging white wreaths.

"Is she pretty?" asked Chevis.

"Waal, no, she ain't," said Hi Bates, decisively. "She's a pore, no 'count critter." Then he added, as if he were afraid of being misapprehended, "Not ez thar is any harm in the gal, ye onderstand. She's a mighty good, saft-spoken, quiet sort o' gal, but she's a pore, white-faced, slim little critter. She looks like she hain't got no sort'n grit in her. She makes me think o' one o' them slim little slips o' willow every time nor I sees her. She hain't got long ter live, I reckon," he concluded, dismally.

Reginald Chevis asked him no more questions about Jerry Shaw's daughter.

Not long afterward, when Chevis was hunting through the deep woods about the base of the mountain near the Christel road, his horse happened to cast a shoe. He congratulated himself upon his proximity to the forge, for there was a possibility that the blacksmith might be at work; according to the account which Hi Bates had given of Jerry Shaw's habits, there were half a dozen chances against it. But the shop was at no great distance, and he set out to find his way back to the Christel road, guided by sundry well-known landmarks on the mountain side: certain great crags hanging above the tree-tops, showing in grander sublimity through the thinning foliage, or beetling[3] bare and

3. Jutting out or overhanging.

grim; a dismantled and deserted hovel, the red-berried vines twining amongst the rotting logs; the full flow of a tumultuous stream making its last leap down a precipice eighty feet high, with yeasty, maddening waves below and a rainbow-crowned crystal sheet above. And here again the curves of the woodland road. As the sound of the falling water grew softer and softer in the distance, till it was hardly more than a drowsy murmur, the faint vibrations of a far-off anvil rang upon the air. Welcome indeed to Chevis, for however enticing might be the long rambles through the redolent October woods with dog and gun, he had no mind to tramp up the mountain to his tent, five miles distant, leading the resisting horse all the way. The afternoon was so clear and so still that the metallic sound penetrated far through the quiet forest. At every curve of the road he expected to see the log-cabin with its rail fence, and beyond the low-hanging chestnut-tree, half its branches resting upon the roof of the little shanty of a blacksmith's shop. After many windings a sharp turn brought him full upon the humble dwelling, with its background of primeval woods and the purpling splendors of the western hills. The chickens were going to roost in a stunted cedar-tree just without the door; an incredibly old man, feeble and bent, sat dozing in the lingering sunshine on the porch; a girl, with a pail on her head, was crossing the road and going down a declivity toward a spring which bubbled up in a cleft of the gigantic rocks that were piled one above another, rising to a great height. A mingled breath of cool, dripping water, sweet-scented fern, and pungent mint greeted him as he passed it. He did not see the girl's face, for she had left the road before he went by, but he recognized the slight figure, with that graceful poise acquired by the prosaic habit of carrying weights upon the head, and its lithe, swaying beauty reminded him of the mountaineer's comparison,—a slip of willow.

And now, under the chestnut-tree, in anxious converse with Jerry Shaw, who came out hammer in hand from the anvil, concerning the shoe to be put on Strathspey's left fore-foot, and the problematic damage sustained since the accident. Chevis's own theory occupied some minutes in expounding, and so absorbed his attention that he did not observe, until the horse was fairly under the blacksmith's hands, that, despite Jerry Shaw's unaccustomed industry, this was by no means a red-letter day in his habitual dissipation. He trembled for Strathspey, but it was too late now to interfere. Jerry Shaw was in that stage of drunkenness which is greatly accented by an elaborate affectation of sobriety. His desire that Chevis should consider him perfectly sober was abundantly manifest in his rigidly steady gait, the preternatural gravity in his bloodshot eyes, his sparingness of speech, and the earnestness with which he enunciated the acquiescent formulæ which had constituted his share of the conversation. Now and then, controlling his faculties by a great effort, he looked hard at Chevis to discover what doubts might be expressed in his face concerning the genuineness of this staid deportment; and Chevis presently found it best to affect too. Believing that the blacksmith's histrionic attempts in the rôle of sober artisan were occupying his attention more than the paring of Strathspey's hoof, which he held between his knees on his leather apron, while the horse danced an animated measure on the other three feet, Chevis assumed an appearance of indifference, and strolled away into the shop. He looked about him, carelessly, at the horseshoes hanging on a rod in the rude aperture that served as window, at the wagon-tires, the plow-shares, the glowing fire of the forge. The air within was unpleasantly close, and he soon found himself again in the door-way.

"Can I get some water here?" he asked, as Jerry Shaw reëntered, and began hammering vigorously at the shoe destined for Strathspey.

The resonant music ceased for a moment. The solemn, drunken eyes were slowly turned upon the visitor, and the elaborate affectation of sobriety was again obtrusively apparent in the blacksmith's manner. He rolled up more closely the blue-checked homespun sleeve from his corded hammer-arm, twitched nervously at the single suspender that supported his copper-colored jeans trousers, readjusted his leather apron hanging about his neck, and, casting upon Chevis another glance, replete with a challenging gravity, fell to work upon the anvil, every heavy and well-directed blow telling with the precision of machinery.

The question had hardly been heard before forgotten. At the next interval, when he was going out to fit the horse, Chevis repeated his request.

"Water, did ye say?" asked Jerry Shaw, looking at him with narrowing eyelids, as if to shut out all other contemplation that he might grapple with this problem. "Thar 's no fraish water hyar, but ye kin go yander ter the house and ax fur some; or," he added, shading his eyes from the sunlight with his broad, blackened hand, and looking at the huge wall of stone beyond the road, "ye kin go down yander ter the spring, an' ax that thar gal fur a drink."

Chevis took his way, in the last rays of sunshine, across the road and down the declivity in the direction indicated by the blacksmith. A cool gray shadow fell upon him from the heights of the great rocks, as he neared them; the narrow path leading from the road grew dank and moist, and presently his feet were sunk in the still green and odorous water-loving weeds, the clumps of fern, and the pungent mint. He did not notice the soft verdure; he did not even see the beautiful vines that hung from earth-filled niches among the rocks, and lent to their forbidding aspect something of a smiling grace; their picturesque grouping, where they had fallen apart to show this sparkling fountain of bright up-springing water, was all lost upon his artistic perceptions. His eyes were fixed on the girl standing beside the spring, her pail filled, but waiting, with a calm, expectant look on her face, as she saw him approaching.

No creature could have been more coarsely habited: a green cotton dress, faded to the faintest hue; rough shoes, just visible beneath her skirts; a dappled gray and brown calico sun-bonnet, thrown aside on a moss-grown boulder near at hand. But it seemed as if the wild nature about her had been generous to this being toward whom life and fortune had played the niggard. There were opaline lights in her dreamy eyes which one sees nowhere save in sunset clouds that brood above dark hills; the golden sunbeams, all faded from the landscape, had left a perpetual reflection in her bronze hair; there was a subtle affinity between her and other pliant, swaying, graceful young things, waving in the mountain breezes, fed by the rain and the dew. She was hardly more human to Chevis than certain lissome little woodland flowers, the very names of which he did not know,—pure white, star-shaped, with a faint green line threading its way through each of the five delicate petals; he had seen them embellishing the banks of lonely pools, or growing in dank, marshy places in the middle of the unfrequented road, where perhaps it had been mended in a primitive way with a few rotting rails.

"May I trouble you to give me some water?" asked Chevis, prosaically enough. She neither smiled nor replied. She took the gourd from the pail, dipped it into the lucent depths of the spring, handed it to him, and stood awaiting its return when he should have finished. The cool, delicious water was drained, and he gave the gourd back. "I am much obliged," he said.

"Ye 're welcome," she replied, in a slow, singing monotone. Had the autumn winds taught her voice that melancholy cadence?

Chevis would have liked to hear her speak again, but the gulf between his station and hers—so undreamed of by her (for the differences of caste are absolutely unknown to the independent mountaineers), so patent to him—could be bridged by few ideas. They had so little in common that for a moment he could think of nothing to say. His cogitation suggested only the inquiry, "Do you live here?" indicating the little house on the other side of the road.

"Yes," she chanted in the same monotone, "I lives hyar."

She turned to lift the brimming pail. Chevis spoke again: "Do you always stay at home? Do you never go anywhere?"

Her eyes rested upon him, with a slight surprise looking out from among their changing lights. "No," she said, after a pause; "I hev no call to go nowhar ez I knows on."

She placed the pail on her head, took the dappled sun-bonnet in her hand, and went along the path with the assured, steady gait and the graceful backward poise of the figure that precluded the possibility of spilling a drop from the vessel.

He had been touched in a highly romantic way by the sweet beauty of this little woodland flower. It seemed hard that so perfect a thing of its kind should be wasted here, unseen by more appreciative eyes than those of bird, or rabbit, or the equally uncultured human beings about her; and it gave him a baffling sense of the mysterious injustice of life to reflect upon the difference in her lot and that of others of her age in higher spheres. He went thoughtfully through the closing shadows to the shop, mounted the re-shod Strathspey, and rode along the rugged ascent of the mountain, gravely pondering on worldly inequalities.

He saw her often afterward, although he spoke to her again but once. He sometimes stopped as he came and went on the Christel road, and sat chatting with the old man, her grandfather, on the porch, sunshiny days, or lounged in the barn-like door of Jerry Shaw's shop talking to the half-drunken blacksmith. He piqued himself on the readiness with which he became interested in these people, entered into their thoughts and feelings, obtained a comprehensive idea of the machinery of life in this wilderness,—more complicated than one could readily believe, looking upon the changeless face of the wide, un-populated expanse of mountain ranges stretching so far beneath that infinite sky. They appealed to him from the basis of their common humanity, he thought, and the pleasure of watching the development of the common human attributes in this peculiar and primitive state of society never palled upon him. He regarded with contempt Varney's frivolous displeasure and annoyance because of Hi Bates's utter insen-sibility to the difference in their social position, and the necessity of either acquiescing in the supposititious equality or dispensing with the invaluable services of the proud and independent mountaineer; be-cause of the *patois*[4] of the untutored people, to hear which, Varney was wont to declare, set his teeth on edge; because of their narrow preju-dices, their mental poverty, their idle shiftlessness, their uncouth dress and appearance. Chevis flattered himself that he entertained a broader view. He had not even a subacute idea that he looked upon these people and their inner life only as picturesque bits of the mental and moral landscape; that it was an æsthetic and theoretical pleasure their contemplation afforded him; that he was as far as ever from the basis of common humanity.

Sometimes while he talked to the old man on the sunlit porch, the "slip o' willow" sat in the door-way, listening too, but never speaking. Sometimes he would find her with her father at the forge, her fair, ethereal face illumined with an alien and fluctuating brilliancy, shining and fading as the breath of the fire rose and fell. He came to remember that face so well that in a sorry sketch-book, where nothing else was finished, there were several laborious pages lighted up with a faint reflection of its beauty. But he was as much interested perhaps, though less poetically, in that massive figure, the idle blacksmith. He looked at it all from an ideal point of view. The star in the valley was only a brilliant, set in the night landscape, and suggested a unique and pleas-ing experience.

How should he imagine what luminous and wistful eyes were turned upward to where another star burned,—the light of his camp-fire on

4. Any regional dialect.

the crag; what pathetic, beautiful eyes had learned to watch and wait for that red gleam high on the mountain's brow—hardly below the stars in heaven it seemed! How could he dream of the strange, vague, unreasoning trouble with which his idle comings and goings had clouded that young life, a trouble as strange, as vague, as vast, as the limitless sky above her.

She understood him as little. As she sat in the open door-way, with the flare of the fire behind her, and gazed at the red light shining on the crag, she had no idea of the heights of worldly differences that divided them, more insurmountable than precipices and flying chutes of mountain torrents, and chasms and fissures of the wild ravine: she knew nothing of the life he had left, and of its rigorous artificialities and gradations of wealth and estimation. And with a heart full of pitiable unrealities she looked up at the glittering simulacrum of a star on the crag, while he gazed down on the ideal star in the valley.

The weeks had worn deep into November. Chevis and Varney were thinking of going home; indeed, they talked of breaking camp day after tomorrow, and saying a long adieu to wood and mountain and stream. They had had an abundance of good sport and a surfeit of roughing it. They would go back to town and town avocations invigorated by their holiday, and taking with them a fresh and exhilarating recollection of the forest life left so far behind.

It was near dusk, on a dull, cold evening, when Chevis dismounted before the door of the blacksmith's little log-cabin. The chestnut-tree hung desolate and bare on the eaves of the forge; the stream rushed by in swift gray whirlpools under a sullen gray sky; the gigantic wall of broken rocks loomed gloomy and sinister on the opposite side of the road,—not so much as a withered leaf of all their vines clung to their rugged surfaces. The mountains had changed color: the nearest ranges were black with the myriads of the grim black branches of the denuded forest; far away they stretched in parallel lines, rising tier above tier, and showing numberless gradations of a dreary, neutral tint, which grew ever fainter in the distance, till merged in the uniform tone of the sombre sky.

Indoors it was certainly more cheerful. A hickory fire dispensed alike warmth and light. The musical whir of a spinning-wheel added its unique charm. From the rafters depended numberless strings of bright red pepper-pods and ears of pop-corn; hanks of woolen and cotton yarn; bunches of medicinal herbs; brown gourds and little bags of seeds. On rude shelves against the wall were ranged cooking utensils, drinking vessels, etc., all distinguished by that scrupulous cleanliness which is a marked feature of the poor hovels of these mountaineers, and in striking contrast to the poor hovels of lowlanders. The rush-bottomed chairs, drawn in a semicircle before the rough, ill-adjusted stones which did duty as hearth, were occupied by several men, who seemed to be making the blacksmith a prolonged visit; various members of the family were humbly seated on sundry inverted domestic articles, such as wash-tubs, and splint-baskets made of white oak. There was circulating among Jerry Shaw's friends a flat bottle, facetiously denominated "tickler," readily emptied, but as readily replenished from a keg in the corner. Like the widow's cruse of oil, that keg was miraculously never empty.[5] The fact of a still near by in the wild ravine might suggest a reason for its perennial flow. It was a good strong article of apple-brandy, and its effects were beginning to be distinctly visible.

Truly the ethereal woodland flower seemed strangely incongruous with these brutal and uncouth conditions of her life, as she stood at a little distance from this group, spinning at her wheel. Chevis felt a sudden sharp pang of pity for her when he glanced toward her; the next instant he had forgotten it in his interest in her work. It was altogether at variance with the ideas which he had hitherto entertained concerning that humble handicraft. There came across him a vague recollection from his city life that the peasant girls of art galleries and of the lyric stage were wont to sit at the wheel. "But perhaps they were spinning flax," he reflected. This spinning was a matter of walking back and forth with smooth, measured steps and graceful, undulatory motion; a matter, too, of much pretty gesticulation,—the thread in one hand, the other regulating the whirl of the wheel. He thought he had never seen attitudes so charming.

Jerry Shaw hastened to abdicate and offer one of the rush-bottomed chairs with the eager hospitality characteristic of these mountaineers,—a hospitality that meets a stranger on the threshold of every hut, presses upon him, ungrudgingly, its best, and follows him on his departure with protestations of regret out to the rickety fence. Chevis was more or less known to all of the visitors, and after a little, under the sense of familiarity and the impetus of the apple-brandy, the talk flowed on as freely as before his entrance. It was wilder and more antagonistic to his principles and prejudices than anything he had hitherto heard among these people, and he looked on and listened, interested in this new development of a phase of life which he had thought he had sounded from its lowest note to the top of its compass. He was glad to remain; the scene had impressed his cultivated perceptions as an interior by Teniers[6] might have done, and the vehemence and lawlessness of the conversation and the threats of violence had little reality for him; if he thought about the subject under discussion at all, it was with a reassuring conviction that before the plans could be carried out the already intoxicated mountaineers would he helplessly drunk. Nevertheless, he glanced ever and anon at the young girl, loath that she should hear it, lest its virulent, angry bitterness should startle her. She was evidently listening, too, but her fair face was as

5. By Old Testament law (see Deuteronomy 24.21), widows were to receive as charity the gleanings of the vineyard; thus their earthenware jar (cruse) of oil might never be empty.

6. A family of Flemish painters, including David the Elder (1582–1649) and David the Younger (1610–1690).

calm and untroubled as one of the pure white faces of those flower-stars of his early stay in the mountains.

"Them Peels oughtn't ter be let live!" exclaimed Elijah Burr, a gigantic fellow, arrayed in brown jeans, with the accompaniments of knife, powder-horn, etc., usual with the hunters of the range; his gun stood, with those of the other guests, against the wall in a corner of the room. "They oughtn't ter be let live, an' I'd top off all three of 'em fur the skin an' horns of a deer."

"That thar is a true word," assented Jerry Shaw. "They oughter be run down an' kilt,—all three o' them Peels."

Chevis could not forbear a question. Always on the alert to add to his stock of knowledge of men and minds, always analyzing his own inner life and the inner life of those about him, he said, turning to his intoxicated host, "Who are the Peels, Mr. Shaw,—if I may ask?"

"Who air the Peels?" repeated Jerry Shaw, making a point of seizing the question. "They air the meanest men in these hyar mountings. Ye might hunt from Copperhead Ridge ter Clinch River, an' the whole spread o' the valley, an' never hear tell o' no sech no 'count critters."

"They oughtn't ter be let live!" again urged Elijah Burr. "No man ez treats his wife like that dad-burned scoundrel Ike Peel do oughter be let live. That thar woman is my sister an' Jerry Shaw's cousin,—an' I shot him down in his own door year afore last'. I shot him ter kill; but somehow 'nother I war that shaky, an' the cussed gun hung fire a-fust, an' that thar pore wife o' his'n screamed an' hollered so, that I never done nuthin' arter all but lay him up for four month an' better for that thar pore critter ter nuss. He'll see a mighty differ[7] nex' time I gits my chance. An' 'tain't fur off," he added threateningly.

"Wouldn't it be better to persuade her to leave him?" suggested Chevis pacifically, without, however, any wild idea of playing peace-maker between fire and tow.

Burr growled a fierce oath, and then was silent.

A slow fellow on the opposite side of the fire-place explained: "Thar's whar all the trouble kem from. She wouldn't leave him, fur all he treated her awful. She said ez how he war mighty good ter her when he warn't drunk. So 'Lijah shot him."

This way of cutting the Gordian knot[8] of domestic difficulties might have proved efficacious but for the shakiness induced by the thrill of fraternal sentiment, the infusion of apple-brandy, the protest of the bone of contention, and the hanging fire of the treacherous gun. Elijah Burr could remember no other failure of aim for twenty years.

"He won't git shet of me that easy agin!" Burr declared, with another pull at the flat tickler. "But ef it hedn't hev been fur what happened las' week, I mought hev let him off fur awhile," he con-

---

7. Difference.
8. An intricate knot tied by King Gordius of Phrygia and cut by Alexander the Great with his sword after he heard an oracle promise that whoever could undo it would be the next ruler of Asia; thus, to solve a problem by resorting to prompt and bold measures.

tinued, evidently actuated by some curiously distorted sense of duty in the premises. "I oughter hev kilt him afore. But now the cussed critter is a gone coon. Dad-burn the whole tribe!"

Chevis was desirous of knowing what had happened last week. He did not, however, feel justified in asking more questions. But apple-brandy is a potent tongue-loosener, and the unwonted communicativeness of the stolid and silent mountaineers attested its strength in this regard. Jerry Shaw, without inquiry, enlightened him.

"Ye see," he said, turning to Chevis, " 'Lijah he thought ez how ef he could git that fool woman ter come ter his house, he could shoot Ike fur his meanness 'thout botherin' of her, an' things would all git easy agin. Waal, he went thar one day when all them Peels, the whole lay-out, war gone down ter the Settlemint ter hear the rider preach,[9] an' he jes' run away with two of the brats,—the littlest ones, ye onderstand,—a-thinkin' he mought tole[1] her off from Ike that thar way. We hearn ez how the pore critter war nigh on ter distracted 'bout 'em, but Ike never let her come arter 'em. Leastways, she never kem. Las' week Ike kem fur 'em hisself,—him an' them two cussed brothers o' his'n. All 'Lijah's folks war out 'n the way; him an' his boys war off a-huntin', an' his wife hed gone down ter the spring, a haffen mile an' better, a-washin' clothes; nobody war ter the house 'ceptin' them two chillen o' Ike's. An' Ike an' his brothers jes' tuk the chillen away, an' set fire ter the house; an' time 'Lijah's wife got thar, 'twar nuthin' but a pile o' ashes. So we've determinated ter go up yander ter Laurel Notch, twenty mile along the ridge of the mounting, ter-night, an' wipe out them Peels,—'kase they air a-goin' ter move away. That thar wife o' Ike's, what made all the trouble, hev fretted an' fretted at Ike till he hev determinated ter break up an' wagon across the range ter Kaintucky, whar his uncle lives in the hills thar. Ike hev gin his cornsent ter go jes' ter pleasure her, 'kase she air mos' crazed ter git Ike away whar 'Lijah can't kill him. Ike's brothers is a-goin', too. I hearn ez how they'll make a start at noon ter-morrer."

"They'll never start ter Kaintucky ter-morrer," said Burr, grimly. "They'll git off, afore that, fur hell, stiddier Kaintucky. I hev been a-tryin' ter make out ter shoot that thar man ever sence that thar gal war married ter him, seven year ago,—seven year an' better. But what with her a-foolin' round, an' a-talkin', an' a-goin' on like she war distracted—she run right 'twixt him an' the muzzle of my gun wunst, or I would hev hed him that time fur sure—an' somehow 'nother that critter makes me so shaky with her ways of goin' on that I feel like I hain't got good sense, an' can't git no good aim at nuthin'. Nex' time, though, thar'll be a differ. She ain't a-goin' ter Kaintucky along of him ter be beat fur nuthin' when he's drunk."

It was a pitiable picture presented to Chevis's open-eyed imagina-

---

9. The circuit rider was a minister who traveled from church to church in an era where not every congregation could afford a minister of its own.
1. "Tole off" means to entice or lure away.

tion,—this woman standing for years between the two men she loved: holding back her brother from his vengeance of her wrongs by that subtle influence that shook his aim; and going into exile with her brute of a husband when that influence had waned and failed, and her wrongs were supplemented by deep and irreparable injuries to her brother. And the curious moral attitude of the man: the strong fraternal feeling that alternately nerved and weakened his revengeful hand.

"We air goin' thar 'bout two o'clock ternight," said Jerry Shaw, "and wipe out all three o' them Peels,—Ike an' his two brothers."

"They ought n't ter be let live," reiterated Elijah Burr, moodily. Did he speak to his faintly stirring conscience, or to a woful premonition of his sister's grief?

"They'll all three be stiff an' stark afore daybreak," resumed Jerry Shaw. "We air all kin ter 'Lijah, an' we air goin' ter holp him top off them Peels. Thar's ten of us an' three o' them, an' we won't hev no trouble 'bout it. An' we'll bring that pore critter, Ike's wife, an' her chillen hyar ter stay. She's welcome ter live along of us till 'Lijah kin fix some sort'n place fur her an' the little chillen. Thar won't be no trouble a-gittin' rid of the men folks, ez thar is ten of us an' three o' them, an' we air goin' ter take 'em in the night."

There was a protest from an unexpected quarter. The whir of the spinning-wheel was abruptly silenced. "I don't see no sense," said Celia Shaw, her singing monotone vibrating in the sudden lull,—"I don't see no sense in shootin' folks down like they war nuthin' better nor bear, nor deer, nor suthin' wild. I don't see no sense in it. An' I never did see none."

There was an astonished pause.

"Shet up, Cely! Shet up!" exclaimed Jerry Shaw, in mingled anger and surprise. "Them folks ain't no better nor bear, nor sech. They hain't got no right ter live,—them Peels."

"No, that they hain't!" said Burr.

"They is powerful no 'count critters, I know," replied the little woodland flower, the firelight bright in her opaline eyes and on the flakes of burnished gold gleaming in the dark masses of her hair. "They is always a-hangin' round the still an' a-gittin' drunk; but I don't see no sense in a-huntin' 'em down an' a-killin' 'em off. 'Pears ter me like they air better nor the dumb ones. I don't see no sense in shootin' 'em."

"Shet up, Cely! Shet up!" reiterated Shaw.

Celia said no more. Reginald Chevis was pleased with this indication of her sensibility; the other women—her mother and grandmother— had heard the whole recital with the utmost indifference, as they sat by the fire monotonously carding cotton.[2] She was beyond her station in sentiment, he thought. However, he was disposed to recant this favorable estimate of her higher nature when, twice afterward, she stopped her work, and, filling the bottle from the keg, pressed it upon

2. Combing fibers of cotton with wire-toothed brushes prior to spinning.

her father, despite her unfavorable criticism of the hangers-on of stills. Nay, she insisted. "Drink some more," she said. "Ye hain't got half enough yit." Had the girl no pity for the already drunken creature? She seemed systematically trying to make him even more helpless than he was.

He had fallen into a deep sleep before Chevis left the house, and the bottle was circulating among the other men with a rapidity that boded little harm to the unconscious Ike Peel and his brothers at Laurel Notch, twenty miles away. As Chevis mounted Strathspey he saw the horses of Jerry Shaw's friends standing partly within and partly without the blacksmith's shop. They would stand there all night, he thought. It was darker when he commenced the ascent of the mountain than he had anticipated. And what was this driving against his face,— rain? No, it was snow. He had not started a moment too soon. But Strathspey, by reason of frequent travel, knew every foot of the way, and perhaps there would only be a flurry. And so he went on steadily up and up the wild, winding road among the great, bare, black trees and the grim heights and chasms. The snow fell fast,—so fast and so silently, before he was half-way to the summit he had lost the vague companionship of the sound of his horse's hoofs, now muffled in the thick carpet so suddenly flung upon the ground. Still the snow fell, and when he had reached the mountain's brow the ground was deeply covered, and the whole aspect of the scene was strange. But though obscured by the fast-flying flakes, he knew that down in the bosom of the white valley there glittered still that changeless star.

"Still spinning, I suppose," he said to himself, as he looked toward it and thought of the interior of the log-cabin below. And then he turned into the tent to enjoy his cigar, his æsthetic reveries, and a bottle of wine.

But the wheel was no longer awhirl. Both music and musician were gone. Toiling along the snow-filled mountain ways; struggling with the fierce gusts of wind as they buffeted and hindered her, and fluttered derisively among her thin, worn, old garments; shivering as the driving flakes came full into the pale, calm face, and fell in heavier and heavier wreaths upon the dappled calico sun-bonnet; threading her way through unfrequented woodland paths, that she might shorten the distance; now deftly on the verge of a precipice, whence a false step of those coarse, rough shoes would fling her into unimaginable abysses below; now on the sides of steep ravines, falling sometimes with the treacherous, sliding snow, but never faltering; tearing her hands on the shrubs and vines she clutched to help her forward, and bruised and bleeding, but still going on; trembling more than with the cold, but never turning back, when a sudden noise in the terrible loneliness of the sheeted woods suggested the close proximity of a wild beast, or perhaps, to her ignorant, superstitious mind, a supernatural presence,—thus she journeyed on her errand of deliverance.

Her fluttering breath came and went in quick gasps; her failing limbs wearily dragged through the deep drifts; the cruel winds untiringly lashed her; the snow soaked through the faded green cotton dress to the chilled white skin,—it seemed even to the dull blood coursing feebly through her freezing veins. But she had small thought for herself during those long, slow hours of endurance and painful effort. Her pale lips moved now and then with muttered speculations: how the time went by; whether they had discovered her absence at home; and whether the fleeter horsemen were even now ploughing their way through the longer, winding mountain road. Her only hope was to outstrip their speed. Her prayer—this untaught being!—she had no prayer, except perhaps her life, the life she was so ready to imperil. She had no high, cultured sensibilities to sustain her. There was no instinct stirring within her that might have nerved her to save her father's, or her brother's, or a benefactor's life. She held the creatures that she would have died to warn in low estimation, and spoke of them with reprobation and contempt. She had known no religious training, holding up forever the sublimest ideal. The measureless mountain wilds were not more infinite to her than that great mystery. Perhaps, without any philosophy, she stood upon the basis of a common humanity.

When the silent horsemen, sobered by the chill night air and the cold snow, made their cautious approach to the little porch of Ike Peel's log-hut at Laurel Notch, there was a thrill of dismayed surprise among them to discover the door standing half open, the house empty of its scanty furniture and goods, its owners fled, and the very dogs disappeared; only, on the rough stones before the dying fire, Celia Shaw, falling asleep and waking by fitful starts.

"Jerry Shaw swore ez how he would hev shot that thar gal o' his'n,—that thar Cely," Hi Bates said to Chevis and Varney the next day, when he recounted the incident, "only he didn't think she hed her right mind; a-walkin' through this hyar deep snow full fifteen mile,—it's fifteen mile by the short cut ter Laurel Notch,—ter git Ike Peel's folks off 'fore 'Lijah an' her dad could come up an' settle Ike an' his brothers. Leastways, 'Lijah an' the t'others, fur Jerry hed got so drunk he couldn't go; he war dead asleep till ter-day, when they kem back a-fotchin' the gal with 'em. That thar Cely Shaw never did look ter me like she hed good sense, nohow. Always looked like she war queer an' teched in the head."

There was a furtive gleam of speculation on the dull face of the mountaineer when his two listeners broke into enthusiastic commendation of the girl's high heroism and courage. The man of ledgers swore that he had never heard of anything so fine, and that he himself would walk through fifteen miles of snow and midnight wilderness for the honor of shaking hands with her. There was that keen thrill about their hearts sometimes felt in crowded theatres, responsive to the cleverly simulated heroism of the boards; or in listening to a poet's mid-air song; or in looking upon some grand and ennobling phase of life translated on a great painter's canvas.

Hi Bates thought that perhaps they too were a little "teched in the head."

There had fallen upon Chevis a sense of deep humiliation. Celia Shaw had heard no more of that momentous conversation than he; a wide contrast was suggested. He began to have a glimmering perception that despite all his culture, his sensibility, his yearnings toward humanity, he was not so high a thing in the scale of being; that he had placed a false estimate upon himself. He had looked down on her with a mingled pity for her dense ignorance, her coarse surroundings, her low station, and a dilettante's delight in picturesque effects, and with no recognition of the moral splendors of that star in the valley. A realization, too, was upon him that fine feelings are of most avail as the motive power of fine deeds.

He and his friend went down together to the little log-cabin. There had been only jeers and taunts and reproaches for Celia Shaw from her own people. These she had expected, and she had stolidly borne them. But she listened to the fine speeches of the city-bred men with a vague wonderment on her flower-like face,—whiter than ever today.

"It was a splendid—a noble thing to do," said Varney, warmly.

"I shall never forget it," said Chevis, "it will always be like a sermon to me."

There was something more that Reginald Chevis never forgot: the look on her face as he turned and left her forever; for he was on his way back to his former life, so far removed from her and all her ideas and imaginings. He pondered long upon that look in her inscrutable eyes,— was it suffering, some keen pang of despair?—as he rode down and down the valley, all unconscious of the heart-break he left behind him. He thought of it often afterward; he never penetrated its mystery.

He heard of her only once again. On the eve of a famous day, when visiting the outposts of a gallant corps, Reginald Chevis happened to recognize in one of the pickets the gawky mountaineer who had been his guide through those autumnal woods so far away. Hi Bates was afterward sought out and honored with an interview in the general's tent; for the accidental encounter had evoked many pleasant reminiscences in Chevis's mind, and among other questions he wished to ask was what had become of Jerry Shaw's daughter.

"She's dead,—long ago," answered Hi Bates. "She died afore the winter war over the year ez ye war a-huntin' thar. She never hed good sense ter my way o' thinkin', nohow, an' one night she run away, an' walked 'bout fifteen mile through a big snow-storm. Some say it settled on her chist. Anyhow, she jes' sorter fell away like afterward, an' never held up her head good no more. She always war a slim little critter, an' looked like she war teched in the head."

There are many things that suffer unheeded in those mountains: the birds that freeze on the trees; the wounded deer that leaves its cruel kind to die alone; the despairing, flying fox with its pursuing train of savage dogs and men. And the jutting crag whence had shone the camp-fire she had so often watched—her star, set forever—looked far over the valley beneath, where in one of those sad little rural grave-yards she had been laid so long ago.

But Reginald Chevis has never forgotten her. Whenever he sees the earliest star spring into the evening sky, he remembers the answering red gleam of that star in the valley.

Atlantic Monthly, November 1878;
In the Tennessee Mountains, 1884

Over on the T'other Mounting

Stretching out laterally from a long oblique line of the Southern Allegh-anies are two parallel ranges, following the same course through sev-eral leagues, and separated by a narrow strip of valley hardly half a mile in width. As they fare along arm in arm, so to speak, sundry differences between the close companions are distinctly apparent. One is much the higher, and leads the way; it strikes out all the bold curves and angles of the course, meekly attended by the lesser ridge; its shadowy coves and sharp ravines are repeated in miniature as its comrade falls into the line of march; it seems to have its companion in charge, and to conduct it away from the majestic procession of moun-tains that traverses the State.

But, despite its more imposing appearance, all the tangible advan-tages are possessed by its humble neighbor. When Old Rocky-Top, as the lower range is called, is fresh and green with the tender verdure of spring, the snow still lies on the summit of the T'other Mounting, and drifts deep into treacherous rifts and chasms, and muffles the voice of the singing pines; and all the crags are hung with gigantic glittering icicles, and the woods are gloomy and bleak. When the sun shines bright on Old Rocky-Top, clouds often hover about the loftier moun-tain, and storms brew in that higher atmosphere; the all-pervading winter winds surge wildly among the groaning forests, and wrench the limbs from the trees, and dash huge fragments of cliffs down deep gorges, and spend their fury before they reach the sheltered lower spur. When the kindly shades of evening slip softly down on drowsy Rocky-Top, and the work is laid by in the rough little houses, and the simple home-folks draw around the hearth, day still lingers in a weird, paralytic life among the tree-tops of the T'other Mounting; and the only remnant of the world visible is that stark black line of its summit, stiff and hard against the faint green and saffron tints of the sky. Before the birds are well awake on Old Rocky-Top, and while the shadows are still thick, the T'other Mounting has been called up to a new day. Lonely dawns these: the pale gleam strikes along the October woods, bringing first into uncertain twilight the dead yellow and red of the foliage, presently heightened into royal gold and crimson by the first ray of sunshine; it rouses the timid wild-fowl; it drives home the plundering fox; it meets, perhaps, some lumbering bear or skulking mountain wolf; it flecks with light and shade the deer, all gray and antlered; it falls upon no human habitation, for the few settlers of the region have a persistent predilection for Old Rocky-Top. Somehow, the T'other Mounting is vaguely in ill repute among its neighbors,—it has a bad name.

"It's the onluckiest place ennywhar nigh about," said Nathan White, as he sat one afternoon upon the porch of his log-cabin, on the summit of Old Rocky-Top, and gazed up at the heights of the T'other Mounting across the narrow valley. "I hev hearn tell all my days ez how, ef ye go up thar on the T'other Mounting, suthin' will happen ter ye afore ye kin git away. An' I knows myself ez how—'twar ten year ago an' better—I went up thar, one Jan'ry day, a-lookin' fur my cow, ez hed strayed off through not hevin' enny calf ter our house; an' I fund the cow, but jes' tuk an' slipped on a icy rock, an' bruk my ankle-bone. 'Twar sech a job a-gittin' off 'n that thar T'other Mounting an' back over hyar, it hev l'arned me ter stay away from thar."

"Thar war a man," piped out a shrill, quavering voice from within the door,—the voice of Nathan White's father, the oldest inhabitant of Rocky-Top,—"thar war a man hyar, nigh on ter fifty year ago,—he war mightily gin ter[1] thievin' horses; an' one time, while he war a-runnin' away with Pete Dilks's dapple-gray mare,—they called her Luce, five year old she war,—Pete, he war a-ridin' a-hint him on his old sorrel mare,—*her* name 'twar Jane, an'—the Jeemes boys, they war a-ridin' arter the horse-thief too. Thar, now! I clar forgits what horses them Jeemes boys war a-riding' of." He paused for an instant in anxious reflection. "Waal, sir! it do beat all that I can't remember them Jeemes boys' horses! Anyways, they got ter that thar tricky ford through Wild-Duck River, thar on the side o' the T'other Mounting, an' the horse-thief war ahead, an' he hed ter take it fust. An' that thar river,— it rises yander in them pines, nigh about," pointing with a shaking fore-finger,—"an' that thar river jes' spun him out 'n the saddle like a top, an' he war n't seen no more till he hed floated nigh ter Colbury, ez dead ez a door-nail, nor Pete's dapple-gray mare nuther; she bruk her knees agin them high stone banks. But he war a good swimmer, an' he war drowned. He war witched with the place, ez sure ez ye air born."

A long silence ensued. Then Nathan White raised his pondering eyes with a look of slow curiosity. "What did Tony Britt say he war a-doin' of, when ye kem on him suddint in the woods on the T'other Mounting?" he asked, addressing his son, a stalwart youth, who was sitting upon the step, his hat on the back of his head, and his hands in the pockets of his jeans trousers.

"He said he war a-huntin', but he hedn't hed no sort 'n luck. It 'pears

1. I.e., given to.

ter me ez all the game thar is witched somehow, an' ye can't git no good shot at nuthin'. Tony tole me today that he got up three deer, an' hed toler'ble aim; an' he missed two, an' the t'other jes' trotted off with a rifle-ball in his flank, ez onconsarned ez ef he hed hit him with an acorn."

"I hev always hearn ez everything that belongs on that thar T'other Mounting air witched, an' ef ye brings away so much ez a leaf, or a stone, or a stick, ye fotches a curse with it," chimed in the old man, " 'kase thar hev been sech a many folks killed on the T'other Mounting."

"I tole Tony Britt that thar word," said the young fellow, "an' 'lowed ter him ez how he hed tuck a mighty bad spot ter go a-huntin'."

"What did he say?" demanded Nathan White.

"He say he never knowed ez thar war murders commit on T'other Mounting, an' ef thar war he 'spects 'twar nuthin' but Injuns, long time ago. But he 'lowed the place war powerful onlucky, an' he believed the mounting war witched."

"Ef Tony Britt's arter enny harm," said the octogenarian, "he'll never come off 'n that thar T'other Mounting. It's a mighty place fur bad folks ter make thar eend. Thar's that thar horse thief I war a-tellin' 'bout, an' that dapple-gray mare,—her name 'twar Luce. An' folks ez is a-runnin' from the sheriff jes' takes ter the T'other Mounting ez nateral ez ef it war home; an' ef they don't git cotched, they is never hearn on no more." He paused impressively. "The rocks falls on 'em, an' kills 'em; an' I'll tell ye jes' how I knows," he resumed, oracularly. " 'Twar sixty year ago, nigh about, an' me an' them Jeemes boys war a-burnin' of lime[2] tergether over on the T'other Mounting. We hed a lime-kiln over thar, jes' under Piney Notch, an' never hed no luck, but jes' stuck ter it like fools, till Hiram Jeemes got one of his eyes put out. So we quit burnin' of lime on the T'other Mounting, 'count of the place bein' witched, an' kem over hyar ter Old Rocky-Top, an' got along toler'ble well, cornsiderin'. But one day, whilst we war a-workin' on the T'other Mounting, what d' ye think I fund in the rock? The print of a bare foot in the solid stone, ez plain an' ez nateral ez ef the track hed been lef' in the clay yestiddy. Waal, I know it war the track o' Jeremiah Stubbs, what shot his step-brother, an' gin the sheriff the slip, an' war las' seen on the T'other Mounting, 'kase his old shoe jes' fit the track, fur we tried it. An' a good while arterward I fund on that same T'other Mounting—in the solid stone, mind ye—a fish, what he had done br'iled fur supper, jes' turned ter a stone."

"So thar's the Bible made true," said an elderly woman, who had come to the door to hear this reminiscence, and stood mechanically stirring a hoe-cake batter in a shallow wooden bowl. "Ax fur a fish, an' ye 'll git a stone."[3]

2. When limestone is heated, it decomposes to yield quicklime, a chemical important to agriculture, leather tanning, and the manufacture of cement.
3. See Matthew 7.10.

The secret history of the hills among which they lived was indeed as a sealed book to these simple mountaineers.

"The las' time I war ter Colbury," said Nathan White, "I hearn the sheriff a-talkin' 'bout how them evil-doers an' sech runs fur the T'other Mounting fust thing; though he 'lowed ez it war powerful foxy in 'em ter try ter hide thar, 'kase he said, ef they wunst reaches it, he mought ez well look fur a needle in a hay-stack. He 'lowed ef he hed a posse a thousand men strong he couldn't git 'em out."

"He can't find 'em, 'kase the rocks falls on 'em, or swallers 'em in," said the old man. "Ef Tony Britt is up ter mischief he'll never come back no more. He'll git into worser trouble than ever he see afore."

"He hev done seen a powerful lot of trouble, fust one way an' another, 'thout foolin' round the T'other Mounting," said Nathan White. "They tells me ez he got hisself indicted, I believes they calls it, or suthin', down yander ter the court at Colbury,—that war year afore las',—an' he hed ter pay twenty dollars fine; 'kase when he war overseer of the road he jes' war constant in lettin' his friends, an' folks ginerally, off 'thout hevin' 'em fined, when they didn't come an' work on the road,—though that air the way ez the overseers hev always done, without nobody a-tellin' on 'em an' sech. But them ez warn't Tony Britt's friends seen a mighty differ. He war dead sure ter fine Caleb Hoxie seventy-five cents, 'cordin' ter the law, fur every day that he war summonsed ter work an' never come; 'kase Tony an' Caleb hed some sort 'n grudge agin one another 'count of a spavined[4] horse what Caleb sold ter Tony, makin' him out to be a sound critter,—though Caleb swears he never knowed the horse war spavined when he sold him ter Tony, no more 'n nuthin'. Caleb war mightily worked up 'bout this hyar finin' business, an' him an' Tony hed a tussle 'bout it every time they kem tergether. But Caleb war always sure ter git the worst of it, 'kase Tony, though he air toler'ble spindling sort o' build, he air somehow or other sorter stringy an' tough, an' makes a right smart show in a reg'lar knock-down an' drag-out fight. So Caleb he war beat every time, an' fined too. An' he tried wunst ter shoot Tony Britt, but he missed his aim. An' when he war a-layin' off how ter fix Tony, fur treatin' him that way, he war a-stoppin', one day, at Jacob Green's blacksmith's shop, yander, a mile down the valley, an' he war a-talkin' 'bout it ter a passel[5] o' folks thar. An' Lawyer Rood from Colbury war thar, an' Jacob war a-shoein' of his mare; an' he hearn the tale, an' axed Caleb whyn't he report Tony ter the court, an' git him fined fur neglect of his duty, bein' overseer of the road. An' Caleb never knowed before that it war the law that everybody what war summonsed an' didn't come must be fined, or the overseer must be fined hisself; but he knowed that Tony hed been a-letting' of his friends off, an' folks

4. "Spavin" is a disease affecting horses that en-   5. I.e., parcel; a large quantity or number.
larges or stiffens their joints.

ginerally, an' he jes' 'greed fur Lawyer Rood ter stir up trouble fur Tony. An' he done it. An' the court fined Tony twenty dollars fur them ways o' his'n. An' it kept him so busy a-scufflin' ter raise the twenty dollars that he never hed a chance ter give Caleb Hoxie more 'n one or two beatin's the whole time he war a-scrapin' up the money."

This story was by no means unknown to the little circle, nor did its narrator labor under the delusion that he was telling a new thing. It was merely a verbal act of recollection, and an attentive silence reigned as he related the familiar facts. To people who live in lonely regions this habit of retrospection (especially noticeable in them) and an enduring interest in the past may be something of a compensation for the scanty happenings of the present. When the recital was concluded, the hush for a time was unbroken, save by the rush of the winds, bringing upon their breath the fragrant woodland odors of balsams and pungent herbs, and a fresh and exhilarating suggestion of sweeping over a volume of falling water. They stirred the fringed shadow of a great pine that stood, like a sentinel, before Nathan White's door and threw its colorless simulacrum, a boastful lie twice its size, far down the sunset road. Now and then the faint clangor of a cow-bell came from out the tangled woods about the little hut, and the low of homeward-bound cattle sounded upon the air, mellowed and softened by the distance. The haze that rested above the long, narrow valley was hardly visible, save in the illusive beauty with which it invested the scene,—the tender azure of the far-away ranges; the exquisite tones of the gray and purple shadows that hovered about the darkening coves and along the deep lines marking the gorges; the burnished brilliance of the sunlight, which, despite its splendor, seemed lonely enough, lying motionless upon the lonely landscape and on the still figures clustered about the porch. Their eyes were turned toward the opposite steeps, gorgeous with scarlet oak and sumac, all in autumnal array, and their thoughts were busy with the hunter on the T'other Mounting and vague speculations concerning his evil intent.

"It 'pears ter me powerful strange ez Tony goes a-foolin' round that thar T'other Mounting, cornsiderin' what happened yander in its shadow," said the woman, coming again to the door, and leaning idly against the frame; the bread was baking over the coals. "That thar wife o' his'n, afore she died, war always frettin' 'kase way down thar on the backbone, whar her house war, the shadow o' the T'other Mounting laid on it fur an hour an' better every day of the worl'. She 'lowed ez it always put her in mind o' the shadow o' death. An' I thought 'bout that thar sayin' o' hern the day when I see her a-lyin' stiff an' cold on the bed, an' the shadow of the T'other Mounting drapping in at the open door, an' a-creepin' an' a-creepin' over her face. An' I war plumb glad when they got that woman under ground, whar, ef the sunshine can't git ter her, neither kin the shadow. Ef ever thar war a murdered woman, she war one. Arter all that hed come an' gone with

Caleb Hoxie, fur Tony Britt ter go arter him, 'kase he war a yerb-doctor,[6] ter git him ter physic his wife, who war nigh about dead with the lung fever, an' gin up by old Dr. Marsh!—it looks ter me like he war plumb crazy,—though him an' Caleb hed sorter made friends 'bout the spavined horse an' sech afore then. Jes' ez soon ez she drunk the stuff that Caleb fixed fur her she laid her head back an' shet her eyes, an' never opened 'em no more in this worl'. She war a murdered woman, an' Caleb Hoxie done it through the yerbs he fixed fur her."

A subtile amethystine mist had gradually overlaid the slopes of the T'other Mounting, mellowing the brilliant tints of the variegated foliage to a delicious hazy sheen of mosaics; but about the base the air seemed dun-colored, though transparent; seen through it, even the red of the crowded trees was but a sombre sort of magnificence, and the great masses of gray rocks, jutting out among them here and there, wore a darkly frowning aspect. Along the summit there was a blaze of scarlet and gold in the full glory of the sunshine; the topmost cliffs caught its rays, and gave them back in unexpected gleams of green or grayish-yellow, as of mosses, or vines, or huckleberry bushes, nourished in the heart of the deep fissures.

"Waal," said Nathan White, "I never did believe ez Caleb gin her ennythink ter hurt,—though I knows thar is them ez does. Caleb is the bes' yerb-doctor I ever see. The rheumatiz would nigh on ter hev killed me, ef it warn't fur him, that spell I hed las' winter. An' Dr. Marsh, what they hed up afore the gran' jury, swore that the yerbs what Caleb gin her war nuthin' ter hurt; *he* said, though, they couldn't holp nor hender. An' but fur Dr. Marsh they would hev jailed Caleb ter stand his trial, like Tony wanted 'em ter do. But Dr. Marsh said she died with the consumption,[7] jes' the same, an' Caleb's yerbs war wholesome, though they warn't no 'count at all."

"I knows I ain't a-goin' never ter tech nuthin' he fixes fur me no more," said his wife, "an' I'll be bound nobody else in these hyar mountings will, nuther."

"Waal," drawled her son, "I knows fur true ez he air tendin' now on old Gideon Croft, what lives over yander in the valley on the t'other side of the T'other Mounting, an' is down with the fever. He went over thar yestiddy evening, late; I met him when he war goin', an' he tole me."

"He hed better look out how he comes across Tony Britt," said Nathan White; "fur I hearn, the las' time I war ter the Settlemint, how Tony hev swore ter kill him the nex' time he see him, fur a-givin' of pizenous yerbs ter his wife. Tony air mightily outdone 'kase the gran' jury let him off. Caleb hed better be sorter keerful how he goes a-foolin' round these hyar dark woods."

The sun had sunk, and the night, long held in abeyance, was coming

6. An herbalist, someone who grows, collects, or specializes in the use of herbs, especially medicinal herbs.
7. Tuberculosis.

fast. The glooms gathered in the valley; a soft gray shadow hung over
the landscape, making familiar things strange. The T'other Mounting
was all a dusky, sad purple under the faintly pulsating stars, save that
high along the horizontal line of its summit gleamed the strange red
radiance of the dead and gone sunset. The outline of the foliage was
clearly drawn against the pure lapis lazuli tint[8] of the sky behind it;
here and there the uncanny light streamed through the bare limbs of
an early leafless tree, which looked in the distance like some bony hand
beckoning, or warning, or raised in horror.

"*Anythink* mought[9] happen thar!" said the woman, as she stood on
night-wrapped Rocky-Top and gazed up at the alien light, so red in the
midst of the dark landscape. When she turned back to the door of the
little hut, the meagre comforts within seemed almost luxury, in their
cordial contrast to the desolate, dreary mountain yonder and the
thought of the forlorn, wandering hunter. A genial glow from the
hearth diffused itself over the puncheon floor;[1] the savory odor of
broiling venison filled the room as a tall, slim girl knelt before the fire
and placed the meat upon the gridiron, her pale cheeks flushing with
the heat; there was a happy suggestion of peace and unity when the
four generations trooped in to their supper, grandfather on his grandson's arm, and a sedate two-year-old bringing up the rear. Nathan
White's wife paused behind the others to bar the door, and once more,
as she looked up at the T'other Mounting, the thought of the lonely
wanderer smote her heart. The red sunset light had died out at last, but
a golden aureola heralded the moon-rise, and a gleaming thread edged
the masses of foliage; there was no faint suggestion now of mist in the
valley, and myriads of stars filled a cloudless sky. "He hev done gone
home by this time," she said to her daughter-in-law, as she closed the
door, "an' ef he ain't, he'll hev a moon ter light him."

"Air ye a-studyin' 'bout Tony Britt yit?" asked Nathan White. "He
hev done gone home a good hour by sun, I'll be bound. Jes' ketch Tony
Britt a-huntin' till sundown, will ye! He air a mighty pore hand ter
work. 'Stonishes me ter hear he air even a-huntin' on the T'other
Mounting."

"I don't believe he's up ter enny harm," said the woman; "he hev
jes' tuk ter the woods with grief."

" 'Pears ter me," said the daughter-in-law, rising from her kneeling
posture before the fire, and glancing reproachfully at her husband,—
" 'pears ter me ez ye mought hev brought him hyar ter eat his supper
along of we-uns, stiddier a-leavin' him a-grievin' over his dead wife in
them witched woods on the T'other Mounting."

The young fellow looked a trifle abashed at this suggestion. "I never
wunst thought of it," he said. "Tony never stopped ter talk more'n a
minit, nohow."

---

8. The deep-blue color of the gemstone of lazurite.   1. Floor made from broad, heavy, roughly finished
9. I.e., might.   timber.

The evening wore away; the octogenarian and the sedate two-year-old fell asleep in their chairs shortly after supper; Nathan White and his son smoked their cob-pipes, and talked fitfully of the few incidents of the day; the women sat in the firelight with their knitting, silent and absorbed, except that now and then the elder, breaking from her reverie, declared, "I can't git Tony Britt out'n my head nohow in the worl'.

The moon had come grandly up over the T'other Mounting, casting long silver lights and deep black shadows through all the tangled recesses and yawning chasms of the woods and rocks. In the vast wilderness the bright rays met only one human creature, the belated hunter making his way homeward through the dense forest with an experienced woodman's craft. For no evil intent had brought Tony Britt to the T'other Mounting; he had spent the day in hunting, urged by that strong necessity without which the mountaineer seldom makes any exertion. Dr. Marsh's unavailing skill had cost him dear; his only cow was sold to make up the twenty dollars fine which his revenge on Caleb Hoxie had entailed upon him; without even so much as a spavined horse tillage was impossible, and the bounteous harvest left him empty-handed, for he had no crops to gather. The hardships of extreme poverty had reinforced the sorrows that came upon him in battalions,[2] and had driven him far through long aisles of the woods, where the night fell upon him unaware. The foliage was all embossed with exquisite silver designs that seemed to stand out some little distance from the dark masses of leaves; now and then there came to his eyes that emerald gleam never seen upon verdure in the day-time,—only shown by some artificial light, or the moon's sweet uncertainty. The wind was strong and fresh, but not cold; here and there was a glimmer of dew. Once, and once only, he thought of the wild traditions which peopled the T'other Mounting with evil spirits. He paused with a sudden chill; he glanced nervously over his shoulder down the illimitable avenues of the lonely woods. The grape-vines, hanging in festoons from tree to tree, were slowly swinging back and forth, stirred by the wind. There was a dizzy dance of shadows whirling on every open space where the light lay on the ground. The roar and fret of Wild-Duck River, hidden there somewhere in the pines, came on the breeze like a strange, weird, fitful voice, crying out amid the haunted solitudes of the T'other Mounting. He turned abruptly, with his gun on his shoulder, and pursued his way through the trackless desert in the direction of his home. He had been absorbed in his quest and his gloomy thoughts, and did not realize the distance he had traversed until it lay before him to be retraced; but his superstitious terror urged him to renewed exertions. "Ef ever I gits off'n this hyar witched mounting," he said to himself, as he tore away the vines and brambles that beset his course, "I'll never come back agin while I lives." He grew calmer when he

2. See *Hamlet* 4.5.

paused on a huge projecting crag, and looked across the narrow valley at the great black mass opposite, which he knew was Old Rocky-Top; its very presence gave him a sense of companionship and blunted his fear, and he sat down to rest for a few minutes, gazing at the outline of the range he knew so well, so unfamiliar from a new stand-point. How low it seemed from the heights of the T'other Mounting! Could that faint gleam be the light in Nathan White's house? Tony Britt glanced further down the indistinct slope, where he knew his own desolate, deserted hut was crouched. "Jes' whar the shadow o' the T'other Mounting can reach it," he thought, with a new infusion of bitterness. He averted his eyes; he would look no longer; he threw himself at full length among the ragged clumps of grass and fragments of rock, and turned his face to the stars. It all came back to him then. Sometimes, in his sordid cares and struggles for his scanty existence, his past troubles were dwarfed by the present. But here on the lonely cliff, with the infinite spaces above him and the boundless forest below, he felt anew his isolation. No light on earth save the far gleam from another man's home, and in heaven only the drowning face of the moon, drifting slowly through the blue floods of the skies. He was only twenty-five; he had youth and health and strength, but he felt that he had lived his life; it seemed long, marked as it was by cares and privation and persistent failure. Little as he knew of life, he knew how hard his had been, even meted[3] by those of the poverty-stricken wretches among whom his lot was cast. "An' sech luck!" he said, as his sad eyes followed the drifting dead face of the moon. "Along o' that thar step-mother o' mine till I war growed; an' then when I war married, an' we hed got the house put up, an' war beginnin' ter git along like other folks kin, an' Car'line's mother gin her that thar calf what growed ter a cow, an' through pinchin' an' savin' we made out ter buy that thar horse from Caleb Hoxie, jes' ez we war a-startin' ter work a crap[4] he lays down an' dies; an' that cussed twenty dollars ez I hed ter pay ter the court; an' Car'line jes' a-gittin' sick, an' a-wastin' an' a-wastin' away, till I, like a fool, brung Caleb thar, an' he pizens her with his yerbs—God A'mighty! ef I could jes' lay my hands wunst on that scoundrel I wouldn't leave a mite of him, ef he war pertected by a hundred lyin', thievin' gran' juries! But he can't stay a-hidin' forevermo'. He's got ter 'count ter me, ef he ain't ter the law; an' he'll see a mighty differ atwixt us. I swear he'll never draw another breath!"

He rose with a set, stern face, and struck a huge boulder beside him with his hard clenched hand as he spoke. He had not even an ignorant idea of an impressive dramatic pose; but if the great gaunt cliff had been the stage of a theatre his attitude and manner at that instant would have won him applause. He was all alone with his poverty and his anguished memories, as men with such burdens are apt to be.

The boulder on which, in his rude fashion, he had registered his oath

---

3. Measured.   4. I.e., crop.

was harder than his hard hand, and the vehemence of the blow brought blood; but he had scarcely time to think of it. His absorbed reverie was broken by a rustling other than that of the eddying wind. He raised his head and looked about him, half expecting to see the antlers of a deer. Then there came to his ears the echo of the tread of man. His eyes mechanically followed the sound. Forty feet down the face of the crag a broad ledge jutted out, and upon it ran a narrow path, made by stray cattle, or the feet of their searching owners; it was visible from the summit for a distance of a hundred yards or so, and the white glamour of the moonbeams fell full upon it. Before a speculation had suggested itself, a man walked slowly into view along the path, and with starting eyes the hunter recognized his dearest foe. Britt's hand lay upon the boulder; his oath was in his mind; his unconscious enemy had come within his power. Swifter than a flash the temptation was presented. He remembered the warnings of his lawyer at Colbury last week, when the grand jury had failed to find a true bill against Caleb Hoxie,—that he was an innocent man, and must go unscathed, that any revenge for fancied wrongs would be dearly rued; he remembered, too, the mountain traditions of the falling rocks burying evil-doers in the heart of the hills. Here was his opportunity. He would have a life for a life, and there would be one more legend of the very stones conspiring to punish malefactors escaped from men added to the terrible "sayin's" of the T'other Mounting. A strong belief in the supernatural influences of the place was rife within him; he knew nothing of Gideon Croft's fever and the errand that had brought the herb-doctor through the "witched mounting;" had he not been transported thither by some invisible agency, that the rocks might fall upon him and crush him?

The temptation and the resolve were simultaneous. With his hand upon the boulder, his hot heart beating fast, his distended eyes burning upon the approaching figure, he waited for the moment to come. There lay the long, low, black mountain opposite, with only the moonbeams upon it, for the lights in Nathan White's house were extinguished; there was the deep, dark gulf of the valley; there, forty feet below him, was the narrow, moon-flooded path on the ledge, and the man advancing carelessly. The boulder fell with a frightful crash, the echoes rang with a scream of terror, and the two men—one fleeing from the dreadful danger he had barely escaped, the other from the hideous deed he thought he had done—ran wildly in opposite directions through the tangled autumnal woods.

Was every leaf of the forest endowed with a woful voice, that the echo of that shriek might never die from Tony Britt's ears? Did the storied, retributive rocks still vibrate with this new victim's frenzied cry? And what was this horror in his heart! Now,—so late,—was coming a terrible conviction of his enemy's innocence, and with it a fathomless remorse.

All through the interminable night he fled frantically along the mountain's summit, scarcely knowing whither, and caring for nothing except to multiply the miles between him and the frightful object that he believed lay under the boulder which he had dashed down the precipice. The moon sank beneath the horizon; the fantastic shadows were merged in the darkest hour of the night; the winds died, and there was no voice in all the woods, save the wail of Wild-Duck River and the forever-resounding screams in the flying wretch's ears. Sometimes he answered them in a wild, hoarse, inarticulate cry; sometimes he flung his hands above his head and wrung them in his agony; never once did he pause in his flight. Panting, breathless, exhausted, he eagerly sped through the darkness; tearing his face upon the brambles; plunging now and then into gullies and unseen quagmires; sometimes falling heavily, but recovering himself in an instant, and once more struggling on; striving to elude the pursuing voices, and to distance forever his conscience and his memory.

And then came that terrible early daylight that was wont to dawn upon the T'other Mounting when all the world besides was lost in slumber; the wan, melancholy light showed dimly the solemn trees and dense undergrowth; the precarious pitfalls about his path; the long deep gorges; the great crags and chasms; the cascades, steely gray, and white; the huge mass, all hung about with shadows, which he knew was Old Rocky-Top, rising from the impenetrably dark valley below. It seemed wonderful to him, somehow, that a new day should break at all. If, in a revulsion of nature, that utter blackness had continued forever and ever it would not have been strange, after what had happened. He could have borne it better than the sight of the familiar world gradually growing into day, all unconscious of his secret. He had begun the descent of the T'other Mounting, and he seemed to carry that pale dawn with him; day was breaking when he reached the foot of Old Rocky-Top, and as he climbed up to his own deserted, empty little shanty, it too stood plainly defined in the morning light. He dragged himself to the door, and impelled by some morbid fascination he glanced over his shoulder at the T'other Mounting. There it was, unchanged, with the golden largess of a gracious season blazing upon every autumnal leaf. He shuddered, and went into the fireless, comfortless house. And then he made an appalling discovery. As he mechanically divested himself of his shotpouch and powder-horn he was stricken by a sudden consciousness that he did not have his gun! One doubtful moment, and he remembered that he had laid it upon the crag when he had thrown himself down to rest. Beyond question, it was there yet. His conscience was still now,—his remorse had fled. It was only a matter of time when his crime would be known. He recollected his meeting with young White while he was hunting, and then Britt cursed the gun which he had left on the cliff. The discovery of the weapon there would be strong evidence against him, taken in connection with all the other circumstances. True, he could even yet go back and recover it, but he was mastered by the fear of meeting someone

on the unfrequented road, or even in the loneliness of the T'other
Mounting, and strengthening the chain of evidence against him by the
fact of being once more seen in the fateful neighborhood. He resolved
that he would wait until night-fall, and then he would retrace his way,
secure his gun, and all might yet be well with him. As to the boulder,—
were men never before buried under the falling rocks of the T'other
Mounting?

Without food, without rest, without sleep, his limbs rigid with the
strong tension of his nerves, his eyes bloodshot, haggard, and eager, his
brain on fire, he sat through the long morning hours absently gazing
across the narrow valley at the solemn, majestic mountain opposite,
and that sinister jutting crag with the indistinctly defined ledges of its
rugged surface.

After a time, the scene began to grow dim; the sun was still shining,
but through a haze becoming momently more dense. The brilliantly
tinted foliage upon the T'other Mounting was fading; the cliffs showed
strangely distorted faces through the semi-transparent blue vapor, and
presently they seemed to recede altogether; the valley disappeared,
and all the country was filled with the smoke of distant burning woods.
He was gasping when he first became sensible of the smoke-laden
haze, for he had seen nothing of the changing aspect of the landscape.
Before his vision was the changeless picture of a night of mingled
moonlight and shadow, the ill-defined black mass where Old Rocky-
Top rose into the air, the impenetrable gloom of the valley, the ledge
of the crag, and the unconscious figure slowly coming within the power
of his murderous hand. His eyes would look on no other scene, no other
face, so long as he should live.

He had a momentary sensation of stifling, and then a great weight
was lifted. For he had begun to doubt whether the unlucky locality
would account satisfactorily for the fall of that boulder and the horrible
object beneath it; a more reasonable conclusion might be deduced
from the fact that he had been seen in the neighborhood, and the
circumstance of the deadly feud. But what wonder would there be if
the dry leaves on the T'other Mounting should be ignited and the
woods burned! What explanations might not such a catastrophe suggest!—a frantic flight from the flames toward the cliff and an accidental fall. And so he waited throughout the long day, that was hardly day
at all, but an opaque twilight, through which could be discerned only
the stony path leading down the slope from his door, only the blurred
outlines of the bushes close at hand, only the great gaunt limbs of a
lightning-scathed tree, seeming entirely severed from the unseen
trunk, and swinging in the air sixty feet above the earth.

Toward night-fall the wind rose and the smoke-curtain lifted, once
more revealing to the settlers upon Old Rocky-Top the sombre T'other
Mounting, with the belated evening light still lurid upon the trees,—
only a strange, faint resemblance of the sunset radiance, rather the

ghost of a dead day. And presently this apparition was gone, and the deep purple line of the witched mountain's summit grew darker against the opaline skies, till it was merged in a dusky black, and the shades of the night fell thick on the landscape.

The scenic effects of the drama, that serve to widen the mental vision and cultivate the imagination of even the poor in cities, were denied these primitive, simple people; but that magnificent pageant of the four seasons, wherein was forever presented the imposing splendor of the T'other Mounting in an ever-changing grandeur of aspect, was a gracious recompense for the spectacular privileges of civilization. And this evening the humble family party on Nathan White's porch beheld a scene of unique impressiveness.

The moon had not yet risen; the winds were awhirl; the darkness draped the earth as with a pall. Out from the impenetrable gloom of the woods on the T'other Mounting there started, suddenly, a scarlet globe of fire; one long moment it was motionless, but near it the spectral outline of a hand appeared beckoning, or warning, or raised in horror,—only a leafless tree, catching in the distance a semblance of humanity. Then from the still ball of fire there streamed upward a long, slender plume of golden light, waving back and forth against the pale horizon. Across the dark slope of the mountain below, flashes of lightning were shooting in zigzag lines, and wherever they gleamed were seen those frantic skeleton hands raised and wrung in anguish. It was cruel sport for the cruel winds; they maddened over gorge and cliff and along the wooded steeps, carrying far upon their wings the sparks of desolation. From the summit, myriads of jets of flame reached up to the placid stars; about the base of the mountain lurked a lake of liquid fire, with wreaths of blue smoke hovering over it; ever and anon, athwart the slope darted the sudden lightning, widening into sheets of flame as it conquered new ground.

The astonishment on the faces grouped about Nathan White's door was succeeded by a startled anxiety. After the first incoherent exclamations of surprise came the pertinent inquiry from his wife, "Ef Old Rocky-Top war ter ketch too, whar would we-uns run ter?"

Nathan White's countenance had in its expression more of astounded excitement than of bodily fear. "Why, bless my soul!" he said at length, "the woods away over yander, what hev been burnin' all day, ain't nigh enough ter the T'other Mounting ter ketch it,—nuthin' like it."

"The T'other Mounting would burn, though, ef fire war put ter it," said his son. The two men exchanged a glance of deep significance.

"Do ye mean ter say," exclaimed Mrs. White, her fire-lit face agitated by a sudden superstitious terror, "that that thar T'other Mounting is fired by witches an' sech?"

"Don't talk so loud, Matildy," said her husband. "Them knows best ez done it."

"Thar's one thing sure," quavered the old man: "that thar fire will never tech a leaf on Old Rocky-Top. Thar's a church on this hyar mounting,—bless the Lord fur it!—an' we lives in the fear o' God."

There was a pause, all watching with distended eyes the progress of the flames.

"It looks like it mought hev been kindled in torment," said the young daughter-in-law.

"It looks down thar," said her husband, pointing to the lake of fire, "like the pit itself."[5]

The apathetic inhabitants of Old Rocky-Top were stirred into an activity very incongruous with their habits and the hour. During the conflagration they traversed long distances to reach each other's houses and confer concerning the danger and the questions of supernatural agency provoked by the mysterious firing of the woods. Nathan White had few neighbors, but above the crackling of the timber and the roar of the flames there rose the quick beat of running footsteps; the undergrowth of the forest near at hand was in strange commotion; and at last, the figure of a man burst forth, the light of the fire showing the startling pallor of his face as he staggered to the little porch and sank, exhausted, into a chair.

"Waal, Caleb Hoxie!" exclaimed Nathan White, in good-natured raillery; "ye're skeered, fur true! What ails ye, ter think Old Rocky-Top air a-goin' ter ketch too? 'Tain't nigh dry enough, I'm a-thinkin'."

"Fire kindled that thar way can't tech a leaf on Old Rocky-Top," sleepily piped out the old man, nodding in his chair, the glare of the flames which rioted over the T'other Mounting gilding his long white hair and peaceful, slumberous face. "Thar's a church on Old Rocky-Top,—bless the"—The sentence drifted away with his dreams.

"Does ye believe—them—them"—Caleb Hoxie's trembling white lips could not frame the word—"them—done it?"

"Like ez not," said Nathan White. "But that ain't a-troublin' of ye an' me. I ain't never hearn o' them witches a-tormentin' of honest folks what ain't done nuthin' hurtful ter nobody," he added, in cordial reassurance.

His son was half hidden behind one of the rough cedar posts, that his mirth at the guest's display of cowardice might not be observed. But the women, always quick to suspect, glanced meaningly at each other with widening eyes, as they stood together in the door-way.

"I dunno,—I dunno," Caleb Hoxie declared huskily. "I ain't never done nuthin' ter nobody, an' what do ye s'pose them witches an' sech done ter me las' night, on that T'other Mounting? I war a-goin' over yander to Gideon Croft's fur ter physic him, ez he air mortal low with the fever; an' ez I war a-comin' alongside o' that thar high bluff"—it was very distinct, with the flames wreathing fantastically about its gray, rigid features—"they throwed a boulder ez big ez this hyar porch

5. I.e., hell.

down on ter me. It jes' grazed me, an' knocked me down, an' kivered me with dirt. An' I run home a-hollerin'; an' it seemed ter me ter-day ez I war a-goin' ter screech an' screech all my life, like some onsettled crazy critter. It 'peared like 'twould take a bar'l o' hop tea[6] ter git me quiet. An' now look yander!" and he pointed tremulously to the blazing mountain.

There was an expression of conviction on the women's faces. All their lives afterward it was there whenever Caleb Hoxie's name was mentioned; no more to be moved or changed than the stern, set faces of the crags among the fiery woods.

"Thar's a church on this hyar mounting," said the old man feebly, waking for a moment, and falling asleep the next.

Nathan White was perplexed and doubtful, and a superstitious awe had checked the laughing youngster behind the cedar post.

A great cloud of flame came rolling through the sky toward them, golden, pellucid, spangled through and through with fiery red stars; poising itself for one moment high above the valley, then breaking into myriads of sparks, and showering down upon the dark abysses below.

"Look-a-hyar!" said the elder woman in a frightened under-tone to her daughter-in-law; "this hyar wicked critter air too onlucky ter be a-sittin' 'longside of us; we'll all be burnt up afore he gits hisself away from hyar. An' who is that a-comin' yander?" For from the encompassing woods another dark figure had emerged, and was slowly approaching the porch. The wary eyes near Caleb Hoxie saw that he fell to trembling, and that he clutched at a post for support. But the hand pointing at him was shaken as with a palsy, and the voice hardly seemed Tony Britt's as it cried out, in an agony of terror, "What air ye a-doin' hyar, a-sittin' 'longside o' livin' folks? Yer bones air under a boulder on the T'other Mounting, an' ye air a dead man!"

°   °   °

They said ever afterward that Tony Britt had lost his mind "through goin' a-huntin' jes' one time on the T'other Mounting. His spirit air all broke, an' he's a mighty tame critter nowadays." Through his persistent endeavor he and Caleb Hoxie became quite friendly, and he was even reported to " 'low that he war sati'fied that Caleb never gin his wife nuthin' ter hurt." "Though," said the gossips of Old Rocky-Top, "them women up ter White's will hev it no other way but that Caleb pizened her, an' they wouldn't take no yerbs from him no more 'n he war a rattlesnake. But Caleb always 'pears sorter skittish when he an' Tony air tergether, like he didn't know when Tony war a-goin' ter fotch him a lick. But law! Tony air that changed that ye can't make him mad 'thout ye mind him o' the time he called Caleb a ghost."

A dark, gloomy, deserted place was the charred T'other Mounting through all the long winter. And when spring came, and Old Rocky-Top was green with delicate fresh verdure, and melodious with singing

6. Beer.

birds and chorusing breezes, and bedecked as for some great festival with violets and azaleas and laurel-blooms, the T'other Mounting was stark and wintry and black with its desolate, leafless trees. But after a while the spring came for it, too: the buds swelled and burst; flowering vines festooned the grim gray crags; and the dainty freshness of the vernal season reigned upon its summit, while all the world below was growing into heat and dust. The circuit-rider[7] said it reminded him of a tardy change in a sinner's heart: though it come at the eleventh hour, the glorious summer is before it, and a full fruition; though it work but an hour in the Lord's vineyard, it receives the same reward as those who labored through all the day.

"An' it always did 'pear ter me ez thar war mighty little jestice in that," was Mrs. White's comment.

But at the meeting when that sermon was preached Tony Britt told his "experience." It seemed a confession, for according to the gossips he " 'lowed that he hed flung that boulder down on Caleb Hoxie,— what the witches flung, ye know,—'kase he believed then that Caleb hed killed his wife with pizenous yerbs; an' he went back the nex' night an' fired the woods, ter make folks think when they fund Caleb's bones that he war a-runnin' from the blaze an' fell off'n the bluff." And everybody on Old Rocky-Top said incredulously, "Pore Tony Britt! He hev los' his mind through goin' a-huntin' jes' one time on the T'other Mounting."

Atlantic Monthly, June 1881; *In the Tennessee Mountains*, 1884

The "Harnt"[1] That Walks Chilhowee

June had crossed the borders of Tennessee. Even on the summit of Chilhowee Mountain the apples in Peter Giles's orchard were beginning to redden, and his Indian corn, planted on so steep a declivity that the stalks seemed to have much ado to keep their footing, was crested with tassels and plumed with silk. Among the dense forests, seen by no man's eye, the elder was flying its creamy banners in honor of June's coming, and, heard by no man's ear, the pink and white bells of the azalea rang out melodies of welcome.

"An' it air a toler'ble for'ard season. Yer wheat looks likely; an' yer gyarden truck[2] air thrivin' powerful. Even that cold spell we-uns hed about the full o' the moon in May ain't done sot it back none, it 'pears like ter me. But, 'cording ter my way o' thinkin', ye hev got chickens enough hyar ter eat off every pea-bloom ez soon ez it opens." And Simon Burney glanced with a gardener's disapproval at the numerous fowls, lifting their red combs and tufted top-knots here and there among the thick clover under the apple-trees.

---

7. A minister who traveled from church to church in an era where not every congregation could afford a minister of its own.

1. Haunt, ghost, or supernatural being.
2. Produce.

"Them's Clarsie's chickens,—my darter, ye know," drawled Peter
Giles, a pale, listless, and lank mountaineer. "An' she hev been gin ter
onderstand ez they hev got ter be kep' out'n the gyarden; 'thout," he
added indulgently,—" 'thout I'm a-plowin', when I lets 'em foller in
the furrow ter pick up worms. But law! Clarsie is so spry that she don't
ax no better'n ter be let ter run them chickens off'n the peas."

Then the two men tilted their chairs against the posts of the little
porch in front of Peter Giles's log cabin, and puffed their pipes in
silence. The panorama spread out before them showed misty and
dreamy among the delicate spiral wreaths of smoke. But was that
gossamer-like illusion, lying upon the far horizon, the magic of nico-
tian,[3] or the vague presence of distant heights? As ridge after ridge
came down from the sky in ever-graduating shades of intenser blue,
Peter Giles might have told you that this parallel system of enchant-
ment was only "the mountings:" that here was Foxy, and there was
Big Injun, and still beyond was another, which he had "hearn tell ran
spang up into Virginny." The sky that bent to clasp this kindred blue
was of varying moods. Floods of sunshine submerged Chilhowee in
liquid gold, and revealed that dainty outline limned upon the northern
horizon; but over the Great Smoky mountains clouds had gathered,
and a gigantic rainbow bridged the valley.

Peter Giles's listless eyes were fixed upon a bit of red clay road,
which was visible through a gap in the foliage far below. Even a tiny
object, that ant-like crawled upon it, could be seen from the summit of
Chilhowee. "I reckon that's my brother's wagon an' team," he said, as
he watched the moving atom pass under the gorgeous triumphal arch.
"He 'lowed he war goin' ter the Cross-Roads ter-day."

Simon Burney did not speak for a moment. When he did, his words
seemed widely irrelevant. "That's a likely gal o' yourn," he drawled,
with an odd constraint in his voice,—"a likely gal, that Clarsie."

There was a quick flash of surprise in Peter Giles's dull eyes. He
covertly surveyed his guest, with an astounded curiosity rampant in his
slow brains. Simon Burney had changed color; an expression of embarrassment lurked in every line of his honest, florid, hard-featured face.
An alert imagination might have detected a deprecatory self-consciousness in every gray hair that striped the black beard raggedly fringing
his chin.

"Yes," Peter Giles at length replied, "Clarsie air a likely enough gal.
But she air mightily sot ter hevin' her own way. An' ef 'tain't give ter
her peaceable-like, she jes' takes it, whether or no."

This statement, made by one presumably fully informed on the
subject, might have damped the ardor of many a suitor,—for the
monstrous truth was dawning on Peter Giles's mind that suitor was the
position to which this slow, elderly widower aspired. But Simon Burney, with that odd, all-pervading constraint still prominently apparent,
mildly observed, "Waal, ez much ez I hev seen of her goin's-on, it

---

3. Nicotiana, the night-blooming, richly odorous tobacco plant.

'pears ter me ez her way air a mighty good way. An' it ain't comical that she likes it."

Urgent justice compelled Peter Giles to make some amends to the absent Clarissa. "That's a fac'," he admitted. "An' Clarsie ain't no hand ter jaw. She don't hev no words. But then," he qualified, truth and consistency alike constraining him, "she air a toler'ble hard-headed gal. That air a true word. Ye mought ez well try ter hender the sun from shining ez ter make that thar Clarsie Giles do what she don't want ter do."

To be sure, Peter Giles had a right to his opinion as to the hardness of his own daughter's head. The expression of his views, however, provoked Simon Burney to wrath; there was something astir within him that in a worthier subject might have been called a chivalric thrill, and it forbade him to hold his peace. He retorted: "Of course ye kin say that, ef so minded; but ennybody ez hev got eyes kin see the change ez hev been made in this hyar place sense that thar gal hev been growed. I ain't a-purtendin' ter know that thar Clarsie ez well ez you-uns knows her hyar at home, but I hev seen enough, an' a deal more 'n enough, of her goin's-on, ter know that what she does ain't done fur *herself*. An' ef she will hev her way, it air fur the good of the whole tribe of ye. It 'pears ter me ez thar ain't many gals like that thar Clarsie. An' she air a merciful critter. She air mighty savin' of the feelin's of everything, from the cow an' the mare down ter the dogs, an' pigs, an' chickens; always a-feedin' of 'em jes' ter the time, an' never draggin', an' clawin', an' beatin' of 'em. Why, that thar Clarsie can't put her foot out 'n the door, that every dumb beastis on this hyar place ain't a-runnin' ter git nigh her. I hev seen them pigs mos' climb the fence when she shows her face at the door. 'Pears ter me ez that thar Clarsie could tame a b'ar, ef she looked at him a time or two, she's so savin' o' the critter's feelin's! An' thar's that old yaller dog o' yourn," pointing to an ancient cur that was blinking in the sun, "he's older 'n Clarsie, an' no 'count in the worl'. I hev hearn ye say forty times that ye would kill him, 'ceptin' that Clarsie purtected him, an' hed sot her heart on his a-livin' along. An' all the home-folks, an' everybody that kems hyar to sot an' talk awhile, never misses a chance ter kick that thar old dog, or poke him with a stick, or cuss him. But Clarsie!—I hev seen that gal take the bread an' meat off'n her plate, an' give it ter that old dog, ez 'pears ter me ter be the worst dispositionest dog I ever see, an' no thanks lef' in him. He hain't hed the grace ter wag his tail fur twenty year. That thar Clarsie air surely a merciful critter, an' a mighty spry, likely young gal, besides."

Peter Giles sat in stunned astonishment during this speech, which was delivered in a slow, drawling monotone, with frequent meditative pauses, but nevertheless emphatically. He made no reply, and as they were once more silent there rose suddenly the sound of melody upon the air. It came from beyond that tumultuous stream that raced with the wind down the mountain's side; a great log thrown from bank to bank served as bridge. The song grew momentarily more distinct; among the leaves there were fugitive glimpses of blue and white, and at last Clarsie appeared, walking lightly along the log, clad in her checked homespun dress, and with a pail upon her head.

She was a tall, lithe girl, with that delicately transparent complexion often seen among the women of these mountains. Her lustreless black hair lay along her forehead without a ripple or wave; there was something in the expression of her large eyes that suggested those of a deer,—something free, untamable, and yet gentle. " 'Tain't no wonder ter me ez Clarsie is all tuk up with the wild things, an' critters giner-ally," her mother was wont to say. "She sorter looks like 'em, I'm a-thinkin'."

As she came in sight there was a renewal of that odd constraint in Simon Burney's face and manner, and he rose abruptly. "Wall," he said, hastily, going to his horse, a raw-boned sorrel, hitched to the fence, "it's about time I war a-startin' home, I reckons."

He nodded to his host, who silently nodded in return, and the old horse jogged off with him down the road, as Clarsie entered the house and placed the pail upon a shelf.

"Who d' ye think hev been hyar a-speakin' of compli*mints* on ye, Clarsie?" exclaimed Mrs. Giles, who had overheard through the open door every word of the loud, drawling voice on the porch.

Clarsie's liquid eyes widened with surprise, and a faint tinge of rose sprang into her pale face, as she looked an expectant inquiry at her mother.

Mrs. Giles was a slovenly, indolent woman, anxious, at the age of forty-five, to assume the prerogatives of advanced years. She had placed all her domestic cares upon the shapely shoulders of her willing daughter, and had betaken herself to the chimney-corner and a pipe.

"Yes, thar hev been somebody hyar a-speaking' of compli*mints* on ye, Clarsie," she reiterated, with chuckling amusement. "He war a mighty peart,[4] likely boy,—that he war!"

Clarsie's color deepened.

"Old Simon Burney!" exclaimed her mother, in great glee at the incongruity of the idea. "*Old Simon Burney!*—jes' a-sitting' out thar, a-wastin' the time, an' a-burnin' of daylight—jes' ez perlite an' smilin' ez a basket of chips[5]—a-speakin' of compli*mints* on ye!"

There was a flash of laughter among the sylvan suggestions of Clarsie's eyes,—a flash as of sudden sunlight upon water. But despite her mirth she seemed to be unaccountably disappointed. The change in her manner was not noticed by her mother, who continued banteringly,—

"Simon Burney air a mighty pore old man. Ye oughter be sorry fur him, Clarsie. Ye mustn't think less of folks than ye does of the dumb

---

4. High-spirited, vivacious.
5. "Chips" were pieces of dried animal dung used as fuel.

beastis,—that ain't religion. Ye knows ye air sorry fur mos' everything; why not fur this comical old consarn?[6] Ye oughter marry him ter take keer of him. He said ye war a merciful critter; now is yer chance ter show it! Why, air ye a-going' ter weavin', Clarsie, jes' when I wants ter talk ter ye 'bout 'n old Simon Burney? But law! I knows ye kerry him with ye in yer heart."

The girl summarily closed the conversation by seating herself before a great hand-loom; presently the persistent thump, thump, of the batten and the noisy creak of the treadle filled the room, and through all the long, hot afternoon her deft, practiced hands lightly tossed the shuttle[7] to and fro.

The breeze freshened, after the sun went down, and the hop and gourd vines were all astir as they clung about the little porch where Clarsie was sitting now, idle at last. The rain clouds had disappeared, and there bent over the dark, heavily wooded ridges a pale blue sky, with here and there the crystalline sparkle of a star. A halo was shimmering in the east, where the mists had gathered about the great white moon, hanging high above the mountains. Noiseless wings flitted through the dusk; now and then the bats swept by so close as to wave Clarsie's hair with the wind of their flight. What an airy, glittering, magical thing was that gigantic spider-web suspended between the silver moon and her shining eyes! Ever and anon there came from the woods a strange, weird, long-drawn sigh, unlike the stir of the wind in the trees, unlike the fret of the water on the rocks. Was it the voiceless sorrow of the sad earth? There were stars in the night besides those known to astronomers: the stellular fireflies gemmed the black shadows with a fluctuating brilliancy; they circled in and out of the porch, and touched the leaves above Clarsie's head with quivering points of light. A steadier and an intenser gleam was advancing along the road, and the sound of languid footsteps came with it; the aroma of tobacco graced the atmosphere, and a tall figure walked up to the gate.

"Come in, come in," said Peter Giles, rising, and tendering the guest a chair. "Ye air Tom Pratt, ez well ez I kin make out by this light. Waal, Tom, we hain't furgot ye sence ye done been hyar."

As Tom had been there on the previous evening, this might be considered a joke, or an equivocal compliment. The young fellow was restless and awkward under it, but Mrs. Giles chuckled with great merriment.

"An' how air ye a-coming' on, Mrs. Giles?" he asked propitiatorily.

"Jes' toler'ble, Tom. Air they all well ter yer house?"

"Yes, they're toler'ble well, too." He glanced at Clarsie, intending to address to her some polite greeting, but the expression of her shy, half-startled eyes, turned upon the far-away moon, warned him. "Thar

---

6. Article, contrivance.

7. Batten, treadle, shuttle: all terms from weaving; the batten is a narrow strip of wood that presses the loom threads together, the treadle is a foot pedal that lifts warp threads or yarns so as to pass the shuttle through; the shuttle carries the woof thread back and forth between the warp threads.

never war a gal so skittish," he thought. "She'd run a mile, skeered ter death, ef I said a word ter her."

And he was prudently silent.

"Waal," said Peter Giles, "what's the news out yer way, Tom? Ennything a-goin' on?"

"Thar war a shower yander on the Backbone; it rained toler'ble hard fur a while, an' sot up the corn wonderful. Did ye git enny hyar?"

"Not a drap."

" 'Pears ter me ez I kin see the clouds a-circlin' round Chilhowee, an' a-rainin' on everybody's corn-field 'ceptin' ourn," said Mrs. Giles. "Some folks is the favored of the Lord, an' t'others hev ter work fur everything an' git nuthin'. Waal, waal; we-uns will see our reward in the nex' worl'. Thar's a better worl' than this, Tom."

"That's a fac'," said Tom, in orthodox assent.

"An' when we leaves hyar once, we leaves all trouble an' care behind us, Tom; fur we don't come back no more." Mrs. Giles was drifting into one of her pious moods.

"I dunno," said Tom. "Thar hev been them ez hev."

"Hev what?" demanded Peter Giles, startled.

"Hev come back ter this hyar yearth. Thar's a harnt that walks Chilhowee every night o' the worl'. I know them ez hev seen him."

Clarsie's great dilated eyes were fastened on the speaker's face. There was a dead silence for a moment, more eloquent with these looks of amazement than any words could have been.

"I reckons ye remember a puny, shriveled little man, named Reuben Crabb, ez used ter live yander, eight mile along the ridge ter that thar big sulphur spring," Tom resumed, appealing to Peter Giles. "He war born with only one arm."

"I 'members him," interpolated Mrs. Giles, vivaciously. "He war a mighty porely, sickly little critter, all the days of his life. 'Twar a wonder he war ever raised ter be a man,—an' a pity, too. An' 'twar powerful comical, the way of his takin' off; a stunted, one-armed little critter a-ondertakin' ter fight folks an' shoot pistols. He hed the use o' his one arm, sure."

"Waal," said Tom, "his house ain't thar now, 'kase Sam Grim's brothers burned it ter the ground fur his a-killin' of Sam. That warn't all that war done ter Reuben fur killin' of Sam. The sheriff run Reuben Crabb down this hyar road 'bout a mile from hyar,—mebbe less,—an' shot him dead in the road, jes' whar it forks. Waal, Reuben war in company with another evil-doer,—he war from the Cross-Roads, an' I furgits what he hed done, but he war a-tryin' ter hide in the mountings, too; an' the sheriff lef' Reuben a-lying thar in the road, while he tries ter ketch up with the t'other; but his horse got a stone in his hoof, an' he los' time, an' hed ter gin it up. An' when he got back ter the forks o' the road whar he had lef' Reuben a-lyin' dead, thar war nuthin' thar 'ceptin' a pool o' blood. Waal, he went right on ter Reuben's house, an' them Grim boys hed burnt it ter the ground; but he seen Reuben's

brother Joel. An' Joel, he tole the sheriff that late that evenin' he hed
tuk Reuben's body out'n the road an' buried it, 'kase it hed been lyin'
thar in the road ever sence early in the mornin', an' he couldn't leave
it thar all night, an' he hedn't no shelter fur it, since the Grim boys hed
burnt down the house. So he war obleeged ter bury it. An' Joel showed
the sheriff a new-made grave, an' Reuben's coat whar the sheriff's
bullet hed gone in at the back an' kem out'n the breast. The sheriff
'lowed ez they'd fine Joel fifty dollars fur a-buryin' of Reuben afore the
cor'ner[8] kem; but they never done it, ez I knows on. The sheriff said
that when the cor'ner kem the body would be tuk up fur a 'quest.[9] But
thar hed been a powerful big frishet,[1] an' the river 'twixt the cor'ner's
house an' Chilhowee couldn't be forded fur three weeks. The cor'ner
never kem, an' so thar it all stayed. That war four year ago."

"Waal," said Peter Giles, dryly, "I ain't seen no harnt yit. I knowed
all that afore."

Clarsie's wondering eyes upon the young man's moonlit face had
elicited these facts, familiar to the elders, but strange, he knew, to her.

"I war jes' a-goin' on ter tell," said Tom, abashed. "Waal, ever sence
his brother Joel died, this spring, Reuben's harnt walks Chilhowee. He
war seen week afore las', 'bout daybreak, by Ephraim Blenkins, who
hed been a-fishin', an' war a-goin' home. Eph happened ter stop in the
laurel ter wind up his line, when all in a minit he seen the harnt go by,
his face white, an' his eye-balls like fire, an' puny an' one-armed, jes'
like he lived. Eph, he owed me a haffen day's work; I holped him ter
plow las' month, an' so he kem ter-day an' hoed along cornsider'ble ter
pay fur it. He say he believes the harnt never seen him, 'kase it went
right by. He 'lowed ef the harnt hed so much ez cut one o' them blazin'
eyes round at him he couldn't but hev drapped dead. Waal, this mornin', 'bout sunrise, my brother Bob's little gal, three year old, strayed
off from home while her mother war out milkin' the cow. An' we went
a-huntin' of her, mightily worked up, 'kase thar hev been a b'ar prowlin' round our cornfield twict this summer. An' I went to the right, an'
Bob went to the lef'. An' he say ez he war a-pushin' 'long through the
laurel, he seen the bushes ahead of him a-rustlin'. An' he jes' stood still
an' watched 'em. An' fur a while the bushes war still too; an' then they
moved jes' a little, fust this way an' then that, till all of a suddint the
leaves opened, like the mouth of hell mought hev done, an' thar he
seen Reuben Crabb's face. He say he never seen sech a face! Its mouth
war open, an' its eyes war a-startin' out 'n its head, an' its skin war
white till it war blue; an' ef the devil hed hed it a-hangin' over the coals
that minit it couldn't hev looked no more skeered. But that war all that
Bob seen, 'kase he jes' shet his eyes an' screeched an' screeched like
he war destracted. An' when he stopped a second ter ketch his breath
he hearn su'thin' a-answerin' him back, sorter weak-like, an' thar war
little Peggy a-pullin' through the laurel. Ye know she's too little ter talk

8. I.e., coroner.
9. Inquest.

1. Freshet; a sudden overflow of a stream resulting
from a heavy rain or thaw.

good, but the folks down ter our house believes she seen the harnt, too."

"My Lord!" exclaimed Peter Giles. "I 'low I couldn't live a minit ef I war ter see that thar harnt that walks Chilhowee!"

"I know *I* couldn't," said his wife.

"Nor me, nuther," murmured Clarsie.

"Waal," said Tom, resuming the thread of his narrative, "we hev all been a-talkin' down yander ter our house ter make out the reason why Reuben Crabb's harnt hev sot out ter walk *jes' sense his brother Joel died,*—'kase it war never seen afore then. An' ez nigh ez we kin make it out, the reason is 'kase thar 's nobody lef' in this hyar worl' what believes he warn't ter blame in that thar killin' o' Sam Grim. Joel always swore ez Reuben never killed him no more 'n nuthin'; that Sam's own pistol went off in his own hand, an' shot him through the heart jes' ez he war a-drawin' of it ter shoot Reuben Crabb. An' I hev hearn other men ez war a-standin' by say the same thing, though them Grims tells another tale; but ez Reuben never owned no pistol in his life, nor kerried one, it don't 'pear ter me ez what them Grims say air reasonable. Joel always swore ez Sam Grim war a mighty mean man,—a great big feller like him a-rockin' of a deformed little critter, an' a-mockin' of him, an' a hittin' of him. An' the day of the fight Sam jes' knocked him down fur nuthin' at all; an' afore ye could wink Reuben jumped up suddint, an' flew at him like an eagle, an' struck him in the face. An' then Sam drawed his pistol, an' it went off in his own hand, an' shot him through the heart, an' killed him dead. Joel said that ef he could hev kept that pore little critter Reuben still, an' let the sheriff arrest him peaceable-like, he war sure the jury would hev let him off; 'kase how war Reuben a-goin ter shoot ennybody when Sam Grim never left a-holt of the only pistol between 'em, in life, or in death? They tells me they hed ter bury Sam Grim with that thar pistol in his hand; his grip war too tight fur death to unloose it. But Joel said that Reuben war sartain they'd hang him. He hedn't never seen no jestice from enny one man, an' he couldn't look fur it from twelve men. So he jes' sot out ter run through the woods, like a painter[2] or a wolf, ter be hunted by the sheriff, an' he war run down an' kilt in the road. Joel said *he* kep' up arter the sheriff ez well ez he could on foot,—fur the Crabbs never hed no horse,—ter try ter beg fur Reuben, ef he war cotched, an' tell how little an' how weakly he war. I never seen a young man's head turn white like Joel's done; he said he reckoned it war his troubles. But ter the las' he stuck ter his rifle faithful. He war a powerful hunter; he war out rain or shine, hot or cold, in sech weather ez other folks would think thar warn't no use in tryin' ter do nuthin' in. I'm mightily afeard o' seein' Reuben, now, that 's a fac'," concluded Tom, frankly; " 'kase I hev hearn tell, an' I believes it, that ef a harnt speaks ter ye, it air sartain ye 're bound ter die right then."

" 'Pears ter me," said Mrs. Giles, "ez many mountings ez thar air

---

2. Panther, mountain lion.

round hyar, he mought hev tuk ter walkin' some o' them, stiddier[3] Chilhowee."

There was a sudden noise close at hand: a great inverted splint-basket, from which came a sound of flapping wings, began to move slightly back and forth. Mrs. Giles gasped out an ejaculation of terror, the two men sprang to their feet, and the coy Clarsie laughed aloud in an exuberance of delighted mirth, forgetful of her shyness. "I declar' ter goodness, you-uns air all skeered fur true! Did ye think it war the harnt that walks Chilhowee?"

"What's under that thar basket?" demanded Peter Giles, rather sheepishly, as he sat down again.

"Nuthin' but the duck-legged Dominicky,"[4] said Clarsie, "what air bein' broke up from settin'." The moonlight was full upon the dimpling merriment in her face, upon her shining eyes and parted red lips, and her gurgling laughter was pleasant to hear. Tom Pratt edged his chair a trifle nearer, as he, too, sat down.

"Ye oughtn't never ter break up a duck-legged hen, nor a Domi-nicky, nuther," he volunteered, " 'kase they air sech a good kind o' hen ter kerry chickens; but a hen that is duck-legged an' Dominicky too oughter be let ter set, whether or no."

Had he been warned in a dream, he could have found no more secure road to Clarsie's favor and interest than a discussion of the poultry. "I'm a-thinkin'," she said, "that it air too hot fur hens ter set now, an' 'twill be till the las' of August."

"It don't 'pear ter me ez it air hot much in June up hyar on Chil-howee,—thar's a differ,[5] I know, down in the valley; but till July, on Chilhowee, it don't 'pear ter me ez it air too hot ter set a hen. An' a duck-legged Dominicky air mighty hard ter break up."

"That's a fac'," Clarsie admitted; "but I'll hev ter do it, somehow, 'kase I ain't got no eggs fur her. All my hens air kerryin' of chickens."

"Waal!" exclaimed Tom, seizing his opportunity, "I'll bring ye some ter-morrer night, when I come agin. We-uns hev got eggs ter our house."

"Thanky," said Clarsie, shyly smiling.

This unique method of courtship would have progressed very pros-perously but for the interference of the elders, who are an element always more or less adverse to love-making. "Ye oughter turn out yer hen now, Clarsie," said Mrs. Giles, "ez Tom air a-goin' ter bring ye some eggs ter-morrer. I wonder ye don't think it's mean ter keep her up longer'n ye air obleeged ter. Ye oughter remember ye war called a merciful critter jes' ter-day."

Clarsie rose precipitately, raised the basket, and out flew the "duck-legged Dominicky," with a frantic flutter and hysterical cackling. But

---

3. Instead of.
4. Dominique is the name of an American breed of domestic fowl having gray, barred plumage, yellow legs, and a rose-colored comb.
5. Difference.

Mrs. Giles was not to be diverted from her purpose; her thoughts had recurred to the absurd episode of the afternoon, and with her relish of the incongruity of the joke she opened upon the subject at once.

"Waal, Tom," she said, "we'll be hevin' Clarsie married, afore long, I'm a-thinkin'." The young man sat bewildered. He, too, had entertained views concerning Clarsie's speedy marriage, but with a distinctly personal application; and this frank mention of the matter by Mrs. Giles had a sinister suggestion that perhaps her ideas might be antagonistic. "An' who d'ye think hev been hyar ter-day, a-speakin' of complimints on Clarsie?" He could not answer, but he turned his head with a look of inquiry, and Mrs. Giles continued, "He is a mighty peart, likely boy,—*he* is."

There was a growing anger in the dismay on Tom Pratt's face; he leaned forward to hear the name with a fiery eagerness, altogether incongruous with his usual lack-lustre manner.

"Old Simon Burney!" cried Mrs. Giles, with a burst of laughter. "*Old Simon Burney! Jes'* a-speakin' of complimints on Clarsie!"

The young fellow drew back with a look of disgust. "Why, he's a old man; he ain't no fit husband fur Clarsie."

"Don't ye be too sure ter count on that. I war jes' a-layin' off ter tell Clarsie that a gal oughter keep mighty clar o' widowers, 'thout she wants ter marry one. Fur I believes," said Mrs. Giles, with a wild flight of imagination, "ez them men hev got some sort'n trade with the Evil One, an' he gives 'em the power ter witch the gals, somehow, so 's ter git 'em ter marry; 'kase I don't think that any gal that's got good sense air a-goin' ter be a man's second ch'ice, an' the mother of a whole pack of step-chil'ren, 'thout she air under some sort 'n spell. But them men carries the day with the gals, ginerally, an' I'm a-thinkin' they 're banded with the devil. Ef I war a gal, an' a smart, peart boy like Simon Burney kem around a-speakin' of complimints, an' sayin' I war a merciful critter, I'd jes' give it up, an' marry him fur second ch'ice. Thar's one blessin'," she continued, contemplating the possibility in a cold-blooded fashion positively revolting to Tom Pratt: "he ain't got no tribe of chil'ren fur Clarsie ter look arter; nary chick nor child hev old Simon Burney got. He hed two, but they died."

The young man took leave presently, in great depression of spirit,— the idea that the widower was banded with the powers of evil was rather overwhelming to a man whose dependence was in merely mortal attractions; and after he had been gone a little while Clarsie ascended the ladder to a nook in the roof, which she called her room.

For the first time in her life her slumber was fitful and restless, long intervals of wakefulness alternating with snatches of fantastic dreams. At last she rose and sat by the rude window, looking out through the chestnut leaves at the great moon, which had begun to dip toward the dark uncertainty of the western ridges, and at the shimmering, translucent, pearly mists that filled the intermediate valleys. All the air was dew and incense; so subtle and penetrating an odor came from that fir-tree beyond the fence that it seemed as if some invigorating infusion were thrilling along her veins; there floated upward, too, the warm fragrance of the clover, and every breath of the gentle wind brought from over the stream a thousand blended, undistinguishable perfumes of the deep forests beyond. The moon's idealizing glamour had left no trace of the uncouthness of the place which the daylight revealed; the little log house, the great overhanging chestnut-oaks, the jagged precipice before the door, the vague outlines of the distant ranges, all suffused with a magic sheen, might have seemed a stupendous alto-rilievo in silver repoussé.[6] Still, there came here and there the sweep of the bat's dusky wings; even they were a part of the night's witchery. A tiny owl perched for a moment or two amid the dew-tipped chestnut-leaves, and gazed with great round eyes at Clarsie as solemnly as she gazed at him.

"I'm thankful enough that ye hed the grace not ter screech while ye war hyar," she said, after the bird had taken his flight. "I ain't ready ter die yit, an' a screech-ow*el* air the sure sign."

She felt now and then a great impatience with her wakeful mood. Once she took herself to task: "Jes' a-sittin' up hyar all night, the same ez ef I war a fox, or that thar harnt that walks Chilhowee!"

And then her mind reverted to Tom Pratt, to old Simon Burney, and to her mother's emphatic and oracular declaration that widowers are in league with Satan, and that the girls upon whom they cast the eye of supernatural fascination have no choice in the matter. "I wish I knowed ef that thar sayin' war true," she murmured, her face still turned to the western spurs, and the moon sinking so slowly toward them.

With a sudden resolution she rose to her feet. She knew a way of telling fortunes which was, according to tradition, infallible, and she determined to try it, and ease her mind as to her future. Now was the propitious moment. "I hev always hearn that it won't come true 'thout ye try it jes' before day break, an' a-kneelin' down at the forks of the road." She hesitated a moment and listened intently. "They'd never git done a-laffin' at me, ef they fund it out," she thought.

There was no sound in the house, and from the dark woods arose only those monotonous voices of the night, so familiar to her ears that she accounted their murmurous iteration as silence too. She leaned far out of the low window, caught the wide-spreading branches of the tree beside it, and swung herself noiselessly to the ground. The road before her was dark with the shadowy foliage and dank with the dew; but now and then, at long intervals, there lay athwart it a bright bar of light, where the moonshine fell through a gap in the trees. Once, as she went rapidly along her way, she saw speeding across the white radiance, lying just before her feet, the ill-omened shadow of a rabbit. She

---

6. A term from metalworking in which a design is hammered in relief. Alto-relievo: high relief, a term from sculpture, in which the modeled forms project from the background by at least half their depth.

paused, with a superstitious sinking of the heart, and she heard the animal's quick, leaping rush through the bushes near at hand; but she mustered her courage, and kept steadily on. " 'Tain't no use a-goin' back ter git shet o' bad luck," she argued. "Ef old Simon Burney air my fortune, he 'll come whether or no,—ef all they say air true."

The serpentine road curved to the mountain's brink before it forked, and there was again that familiar picture of precipice, and far-away ridges, and shining mist, and sinking moon, which was visibly turning from silver to gold. The changing lustre gilded the feathery ferns that grew in the marshy dip. Just at the angle of the divergent paths there rose into the air a great mass of indistinct white blossoms, which she knew were the exquisite mountain azaleas, and all the dark forest was starred with the blooms of the laurel.

She fixed her eyes upon the mystic sphere dropping down the sky, knelt among the azaleas at the forks of the road, and repeated the time-honored invocation:—

"Ef I'm a-goin' ter marry a young man, whistle, Bird, whistle. Ef I'm a-goin' ter marry an old man, low, Cow, low. Ef I ain't a-goin' ter marry nobody, knock, Death, knock."

There was a prolonged silence in the matutinal freshness and perfume of the woods. She raised her head, and listened attentively. No chirp of half-awakened bird, no tapping of woodpecker, or the mysterious death-watch; but from far along the dewy aisles of the forest, the ungrateful Spot, that Clarsie had fed more faithfully than herself, lifted up her voice, and set the echoes vibrating. Clarsie, however, had hardly time for a pang of disappointment. While she still knelt among the azaleas her large, deer-like eyes were suddenly dilated with terror. From around the curve of the road came the quick beat of hastening footsteps, the sobbing sound of panting breath, and between her and the sinking moon there passed an attenuated, one-armed figure, with a pallid, sharpened face, outlined for a moment on its brilliant disk, and dreadful starting eyes, and quivering open mouth. It disappeared in an instant among the shadows of the laurel, and Clarsie, with a horrible fear clutching at her heart, sprang to her feet.

Her flight was arrested by other sounds. Before her reeling senses could distinguish them, a party of horsemen plunged down the road. They reined in suddenly as their eyes fell upon her, and their leader, an eager, authoritative man, was asking her a question. Why could she not understand him? With her nerveless hands feebly catching at the shrubs for support, she listened vaguely to his impatient, meaningless words, and saw with helpless deprecation the rising anger in his face. But there was no time to be lost. With a curse upon the stupidity of the mountaineer, who couldn't speak when she was spoken to, the party sped on in a sweeping gallop, and the rocks and the steeps were hilarious with the sound.

When the last faint echo was hushed, Clarsie tremblingly made her way out into the road; not reassured, however, for she had a frightful

conviction that there was now and then a strange stir in the laurel, and
that she was stealthily watched. Her eyes were fixed upon the dense
growth with a morbid fascination, as she moved away; but she was
once more rooted to the spot when the leaves parted and in the golden
moonlight the ghost stood before her. She could not nerve herself to
run past him, and he was directly in her way homeward. His face was
white, and lined, and thin; that pitiful quiver was never still in the
parted lips; he looked at her with faltering, beseeching eyes. Clarsie's
merciful heart was stirred. "What ails ye, ter come back hyar, an' foller
me?" she cried out, abruptly. And then a great horror fell upon her.
Was not one to whom a ghost should speak doomed to death, sudden
and immediate?

The ghost replied in a broken, shivering voice, like a wail of pain, "I
war a-starvin',—I war a-starvin'," with despairing iteration.

It was all over, Clarsie thought. The ghost had spoken, and she was
a doomed creature. She wondered that she did not fall dead in the
road. But while those beseeching eyes were fastened in piteous appeal
on hers, she could not leave him. "I never hearn that 'bout ye," she
said, reflectively. "I knows ye hed awful troubles while ye war alive,
but I never knowed ez ye war starved."

Surely that was a gleam of sharp surprise in the ghost's prominent
eyes, succeeded by a sly intelligence.

"Day is nigh ter breakin'," Clarsie admonished him, as the lower rim
of the moon touched the silver mists of the west. "What air ye a-wan-
tin' of me?"

There was a short silence. Mind travels far in such intervals. Clarsie's thoughts had overtaken the scenes when she should have died
that sudden terrible death: when there would be no one left to feed the
chickens; when no one would care if the pigs cried with the pangs of
hunger, unless, indeed, it were time for them to be fattened before
killing. The mare,—how often would she be taken from the plow, and
shut up for the night in her shanty without a drop of water, after her
hard day's work! Who would churn, or spin, or weave? Clarsie could
not understand how the machinery of the universe could go on without
her. And Towse, poor Towse! He was a useless cumberer of the
ground,[7] and it was hardly to be supposed that after his protector was
gone he would be spared a blow or a bullet, to hasten his lagging death.
But Clarsie still stood in the road, and watched the face of the ghost,
as he, with his eager, starting eyes, scanned her open, ingenuous
countenance.

"Ye do ez ye air bid, or it 'll be the worse for ye," said the "harnt,"
in the same quivering, shrill tone. "Thar 's hunger in the nex' worl' ez
well ez in this, an' ye bring me some vittles hyar this time ter-morrer,
an' don't ye tell nobody ye hev seen me, nuther, or it'll be the worse
for ye."

7. See Luke 13-7.

There was a threat in his eyes as he disappeared in the laurel, and left the girl standing in the last rays of moonlight.

A curious doubt was stirring in Clarsie's mind when she reached home, in the early dawn, and heard her father talking about the sheriff and his posse, who had stopped at the house in the night, and roused its inmates, to know if they had seen a man pass that way.

"Clarsie never hearn none o' the noise, I'll be bound, 'kase she always sleeps like a log," said Mrs. Giles, as her daughter came in with the pail, after milking the cow. "Tell her 'bout'n it."

"They kem a-bustin' along hyar a while afore day-break, a-runnin' arter the man," drawled Mr. Giles, dramatically. "An' they knocked me up, ter know ef ennybody hed passed. An' one o' them men—I never seen none of 'em afore; they 's all valley folks, I'm a-thinkin'— an' one of 'em bruk his saddle-girt' a good piece down the road, an' he kem back ter borrer mine; an' ez we war a-fixin' of it, he tole me what they war all arter. He said that word war tuk ter the sheriff down yander in the valley—'pears ter me them town-folks don't think no-body in the mountings hev got good sense—word war tuk ter the sheriff 'bout this one-armed harnt that walks Chilhowee; an' he sot it down that Reuben Crabb war n't dead at all, an' Joel jes' purtended ter hev buried him, an' it air Reuben hisself that walks Chilhowee. An' thar air two hundred dollars blood-money reward fur ennybody ez kin ketch him. These hyar valley folks air powerful cur'ous critters,—two hundred dollars blood-money reward fur that thar harnt that walks Chilhowee! I jes' sot myself ter laffin' when that thar cuss told it so solemn. I jes' 'lowed ter him ez he couldn't shoot a harnt nor hang a harnt, an' Reuben Crabb hed about got done with his persecutions in this worl'. An' he said that by the time they hed scoured this mounting, like they hed laid off ter do, they would find that that thar puny little harnt war nuthin' but a mortal man, an' could be kep' in a jail ez handy ez enny other flesh an' blood. He said the sheriff 'lowed ez the reason Reuben hed jes' taken ter walk Chilhowee sence Joel died is 'kase thar air nobody ter feed him, like Joel done, mebbe, in the nights; an' Reuben always war a pore, one-armed, weakly critter, what can't even kerry a gun, an' he air driv by hunger out'n the hole whar he stays, ter prowl round the cornfields an' hen-coops ter steal suthin',—an' that's how he kem ter be seen frequent. The sheriff 'lowed that Reuben can't find enough roots an' yerbs ter keep him up; but law!—a harnt eatin'! It jes' sot me off ter laffin'. Reuben Crabb hev been too busy in torment fur the las' four year ter be a-studyin' 'bout eatin'; an' it air his harnt that walks Chilhowee."

The next morning, before the moon sank, Clarsie, with a tin pail in her hand, went to meet the ghost at the appointed place. She under-stood now why the terrible doom that falls upon those to whom a spirit may chance to speak had not descended upon her, and that fear was gone; but the secrecy of her errand weighed heavily. She had been scrupulously careful to put into the pail only such things as had fallen to her share at the table, and which she had saved from the meals of yesterday. "A gal that goes a-robbin' fur a hongry harnt," was her moral reflection, "oughter be throwed bodaciously[8] off'n the bluff."

She found no one at the forks of the road. In the marshy dip were only the myriads of mountain azaleas, only the masses of feathery ferns, only the constellated glories of the laurel blooms. A sea of shining white mist was in the valley, with glinting golden rays striking athwart it from the great cresset of the sinking moon; here and there the long, dark, horizontal line of a distant mountain's summit rose above the vaporous shimmer, like a dreary, sombre island in the midst of enchanted waters. Her large, dreamy eyes, so wild and yet so gentle, gazed out through the laurel leaves upon the floating gilded flakes of light, as in the deep coverts of the mountain, where the fulvous-tinted[9] deer were lying, other eyes, as wild and as gentle, dreamily watched the vanishing moon. Overhead, the filmy, lace-like clouds, fretting the blue heavens, were tinged with a faint rose. Through the trees she caught a glimpse of the red sky of dawn, and the glister of a great lucent, tremulous star. From the ground, misty blue exhalations were rising, alternating with the long lines of golden light yet drifting through the woods. It was all very still, very peaceful, almost holy. One could hardly believe that these consecrated solitudes had once reverberated with the echoes of man's death-dealing ingenuity, and that Reuben Crabb had fallen, shot through and through, amid that wealth of flowers at the forks of the road. She heard suddenly the far-away baying of a hound. Her great eyes dilated, and she lifted her head to listen. Only the solemn silence of the woods, the slow sinking of the noiseless moon, the voiceless splendor of that eloquent day-star.

Morning was close at hand, and she was beginning to wonder that the ghost did not appear, when the leaves fell into abrupt commotion, and he was standing in the road, beside her. He did not speak, but watched her with an eager, questioning intentness, as she placed the contents of the pail upon the moss at the roadside. "I'm a-coming' agin ter-morrer," she said, gently. He made no reply, quickly gathered the food from the ground, and disappeared in the deep shades of the woods.

She had not expected thanks, for she was accustomed only to the gratitude of dumb beasts; but she was vaguely conscious of something wanting, as she stood motionless for a moment, and watched the burnished rim of the moon slip down behind the western mountains. Then she slowly walked along her misty way in the dim light of the coming dawn. There was a footstep in the road behind her; she thought it was the ghost once more. She turned, and met Simon Burney, face to face. His rod was on his shoulder, and a string of fish was in his hand.

"Ye air a-doin' wrongful, Clarsie," he said, sternly. "It air agin the

---

8. Boldly, with daring.   9. Reddish, yellow.

law fur folks ter feed an' shelter them ez is a-runnin' from jestice. An' ye 'll git yerself inter trouble. Other folks will find ye out, besides me, an' then the sheriff'll be up hyar arter ye."

The tears rose to Clarsie's eyes. This prospect was infinitely more terrifying than the awful doom which follows the horror of a ghost's speech.

"I can't holp it," she said, however, doggedly swinging the pail back and forth. "I can't gin my consent ter starvin' of folks, even ef they air a-hidin' an' a-runnin' from jestice."

"They mought put ye in jail, too,—I dunno," suggested Simon Burney.

"I can't holp that, nuther," said Clarsie, the sobs rising, and the tears falling fast. "Ef they comes an' gits me, and puts me in the pen'tiary away down yander, somewhars in the valley, like they done Jane Simpkins, fur a-cuttin' of her step-mother's throat with a butcher-knife, while she war asleep,—though some said Jane war crazy,—I can't gin my consent ter starvin' of folks."

A recollection came over Simon Burney of the simile of "hendering the sun from shining."

"She hev done sot it down in her mind," he thought, as he walked on beside her and looked at her resolute face. Still he did not relinquish his effort.

"Doin' wrong, Clarsie, ter aid folks what air a-doin' wrong, an' mebbe *hev* done wrong, air powerful hurtful ter everybody, an' henders the law an' jestice."

"I can't holp it," said Clarsie.

"It 'pears toler'ble comical ter me," said Simon Burney, with a sudden perception of a curious fact which has proved a marvel to wiser men, "that no matter how good a woman is, she ain't got no respect fur the laws of the country, an' don't sot no store by jestice." After a momentary silence he appealed to her on another basis. "Somebody will ketch him arter a while, ez sure ez ye air born. The sheriff's a-sarchin' now, an' by the time that word gits around, all the mounting boys'll turn out, 'kase thar air two hundred dollars blood-money fur him. An' then he'll think, when they ketches him,—an' everybody 'll say so, too,—ez ye war constant in feedin' him jes' ter 'tice him ter comin' ter one place, so ez ye could tell somebody whar ter go ter ketch him, an' make them gin ye haffen the blood-money, mebbee. That's what the mounting will say, mos' likely."

"I can't holp it," said Clarsie, once more.

He left her walking on toward the rising sun, and retraced his way to the forks of the road. The jubilant morning was filled with the song of birds; the sunlight flashed on the dew; all the delicate enameled bells of the pink and white azaleas were swinging tremulously in the wind; the aroma of ferns and mint rose on the delicious fresh air. Presently he checked his pace, creeping stealthily on the moss and grass beside the road rather than in the beaten path. He pulled aside the leaves of the laurel with no more stir than the wind might have made, and stole cautiously through its dense growth, till he came suddenly upon the puny little ghost, lying in the sun at the foot of a tree. The frightened creature sprang to his feet with a wild cry of terror, but before he could move a step he was caught and held fast in the strong grip of the stalwart mountaineer beside him. "I hev kem hyar ter tell ye a word, Reuben Crabb," said Simon Burney. "I hev kem hyar ter tell ye that the whole mounting air a-goin' ter turn out ter sarch fur ye; the sheriff air a-ridin' now, an' ef ye don't come along with me they 'll hev ye afore night, 'kase thar air two hundred dollars reward fur ye."

What a piteous wail went up to the smiling blue sky, seen through the dappling leaves above them! What a horror, and despair, and prescient agony were in the hunted creature's face! The ghost struggled no longer; he slipped from his feet down upon the roots of the tree, and turned that woful face, with its starting eyes and drawn muscles and quivering parted lips, up toward the unseeing sky.

"God A'mighty, man!" exclaimed Simon Burney, moved to pity. "Whyn't ye quit this hyar way of livin' in the woods like ye war a wolf? Whyn't ye come back an' stand yer trial? From all I've hearn tell, it 'pears ter me ez the jury air obleeged ter let ye off, an' I'll take keer of ye agin them Grims."

"I hain't got no place ter live in," cried out the ghost, with a keen despair.

Simon Burney hesitated. Reuben Crabb was possibly a murderer,— at the best could but be a burden. The burden, however, had fallen in his way, and he lifted it.

"I tell ye now, Reuben Crabb," he said, "I ain't a-goin' ter holp no man ter break the law an' hender jestice; but ef ye will go an' stand yer trial, I'll take keer of ye agin them Grims ez long ez I kin fire a rifle. An' arter the jury hev done let ye off, ye air welcome ter live along o' me at my house till ye die. Ye air no-'count ter work, I know, but I ain't a-goin' ter grudge ye fur a livin' at my house."

And so it came to pass that the reward set upon the head of the harnt that walked Chilhowee was never claimed.

With his powerful ally, the forlorn little spectre went to stand his trial, and the jury acquitted him without leaving the box. Then he came back to the mountains to live with Simon Burney. The cruel gibes of his burly mockers that had beset his feeble life from his childhood up, the deprivation and loneliness and despair and fear that had filled those days when he walked Chilhowee, had not improved the harnt's temper. He was a helpless creature, not able to carry a gun or hold a plow, and the years that he spent smoking his cob-pipe in Simon Burney's door were idle years and unhappy. But Mrs. Giles said she thought he was "a mighty lucky little critter: fust, he hed Joel ter take keer of him an' feed him, when he tuk ter the woods ter pertend he war a harnt; an' they do say now that Clarsie Pratt, afore she war married, used ter kerry him vittles, too; an' then old Simon Burney tuk him up an' fed him ez plenty ez ef he war a good workin' hand, an' gin him clothes an' house-room, an' put up with his jawin' jes' like he never hearn a word of it. But law! some folks dunno when they air well off."

There was only a sluggish current of peasant blood in Simon Burney's veins, but a prince could not have dispensed hospitality with a more royal hand. Ungrudgingly he gave of his best; valiantly he defended his thankless guest at the risk of his life; with a moral gallantry he struggled with his sloth, and worked early and late, that there might be enough to divide. There was no possibility of a recompense for him, not even in the encomiums of discriminating friends, nor the satisfaction of tutored feelings and a practiced spiritual discernment; for he was an uncouth creature, and densely ignorant.

The grace of culture is, in its way, a fine thing, but the best that art can do—the polish of a gentleman—is hardly equal to the best that Nature can do in her higher moods.

Atlantic Monthly, May 1883; *In the Tennessee Mountains,* 1884

MARY E. WILKINS FREEMAN
1852-1930

Born October 31, 1852, in Randolph, Massachusetts, to Warren E. and Eleanor Lothrop Wilkins, Mary Ella Wilkins Freeman (she later changed her middle name to "Eleanor") knew New England village life as the daughter of a housewright in a period of decline in the building trades. When Freeman was fifteen, the Wilkinses moved to Brattleboro, Vermont, in an attempt to improve their financial situation. Here her father opened a dry goods business. The business failed, however, and so, to support the family, her mother became a live-in housekeeper, caring for Mary and her younger sister Nan in someone else's house. Freeman grew up with close ties to "best friends"—Mary Wales in Randolph and Evelyn Sawyer in Brattleboro—as well as to her sister, mother, and her mother's extended family of female relatives in Randolph. Yet early in life, before she became a writer, she suffered major losses: her friend Evelyn married and moved away; and her sister died in 1876, followed by her mother, in 1880, when Freeman was twenty-eight, and her father in 1883. In 1884, with her immediate family dead and at the beginning of her career, having published her first significant fiction in *Harper's Bazar* shortly before her father's death, she moved back to Randolph and lived with Mary Wales and her family. For almost twenty years her friendship with Mary Wales primarily sustained her emotional life.

In 1902, after a decade of acquaintance and three years of apparent wavering on the question of marriage—she alternately broke then renewed her engagement and postponed wedding dates—Mary Wilkins married Charles Manning Freeman, a Columbia University M.D. She was forty-nine years old. The Freemans moved to Metuchen, New Jersey, where Freeman continued to write, although her critics unanimously agree that the New Jersey novels she published late in her career—conventional books with melodramatic and unbelievable outcomes—are inferior to her regional short fiction, collected in *A Humble Romance* (1887) and *A New England Nun* (1891), and to the New England novels that earned her a reputation as a realist as well as a regionalist. Both *Pembroke* (1894) and *By the Light of the Soul* (1906) demonstrate Freeman's attempt to enlarge regionalism into the novel form; both also reflect her use of family history and autobiographical material. *By the Light of the Soul* particularly documents her ambivalence about her marriage. Although the Freemans' marriage appears to have worked well enough in its early years, by 1909 Charles had begun to enter sanitariums for drinking and by 1919 Freeman had committed him to the New Jersey State Hospital for the Insane to be treated for alcoholism. She secured a formal separation before Charles's death in 1923.

Freeman's circle of friends and acquaintances included Hamlin Garland,

William Dean Howells, Rudyard Kipling, Julia Ward Howe, and other prominent figures in the late-nineteenth-century literary world. She also exchanged
letters with Sarah Orne Jewett, expressed her praise of Jewett's "A White
Heron," and met Jewett on several occasions. She sat next to Mark Twain at
a banquet given to honor his seventieth birthday, and in April 1926 received
the Howells Medal for Fiction from the American Academy of Arts and
Letters. Later that year, she and Edith Wharton were among the first women
to be elected to membership in the National Institute of Arts and Letters. The
bronze doors at the entrance of the National Institute, installed in 1938, bear
the inscription "Dedicated to the Memory of Mary E. Wilkins Freeman and
the Women Writers of America." She died of a heart attack March 13, 1930,
in Metuchen.

○ ○ ○

By the time Mary Wilkins Freeman began to publish her short stories in
Harper's Bazar in 1883, the work of Stowe, Cooke, Jewett and others had
identified the topography and character of the New England village for American readers and had even ensured that the word "village" would conjure up
such topography. Thus Freeman in writing her fiction could indicate her region
with a few generic brush-strokes: her characters drop some of their vowels and
call herbs "yarbs," they cultivate the plants and bushes that grow well in New
England, they live near a church. Able to identify region and establish dialect
with relatively little effort, Freeman could choose to focus her attention on
narrative form. Freeman carefully frames her fiction and carefully fills the
space she frames. Within this fictional frame, and indeed because of it, her
stories generate extraordinary power of the kind witnessed in the revolt of
Candace Whitcomb in "A Village Singer." When she is dismissed from her
position in the choir, Candace Whitcomb feels rage and contempt for a congregation that retains an old minister and an old tenor but "retires" an old
soprano. As a result of her revolution of feeling and perception, Candace loses
that respect for men and male authority that has presumably kept her quiet
before; she finds voice to express her rage, delivering a devastating final
comment on the spiritual state of her community: " 'You flatted a little on—
soul.' " Yet although Candace has the last word, at the end of the story she is
nevertheless dead. In the very brilliance of her formal achievement, Freeman
may have identified the limitations of regionalism, limitations that only Sarah
Orne Jewett and Mary Austin were able to transcend in discovering how to
link sketches together to create a larger form. Candace's capitulation seems
forced, less the result of her character than of Freeman's inability to imagine
a larger form for the development of her rebellion.

The way Freeman tells a story resembles the story she tells. In fact, many
of Freeman's characters, like Freeman herself, choose an art form to express
their vision, and to negotiate identity and survival in a world in which what
they have to "eat"—both literally and symbolically—is as "tough" as the
doughnuts Harriet and Charlotte Shattuck are given in "A Mistaken Charity."
In "On the Walpole Road," Freeman suggests that storytelling is literally the
way home for two women faced with the possibility of bad weather. Although
she has no food in the house, Betsey Dole of "A Poetess" grows flowering
plants instead of vegetables, suggesting that art can offer nurturance to women
who live on the margins of their society. And in "Sister Liddy" Polly Moss
moves herself from margin to center by telling her listeners the story they most
want to hear—a story that confirms their origins and establishes their identity.

Polly's narrative transforms her listeners' present in a way that their own memories have failed to do. And by telling her story Polly transforms the relationship among these women from one of competitive bickering to one of communal collaboration; her fiction about sisters literally creates sisterhood.

Unlike Jewett, Freeman does not dramatize the shift in the center of perception; instead she writes from a position where such a shift has already occurred. Her carefully framed stories, filled with images of literal framing devices such as the black border that encloses Betsey Dole's poem or the frame that surrounds Hetty Fifield's worsted work in "A Church Mouse," create the territory from within which both characters and narrator can articulate the perspective of marginal women as central. Freeman's fierceness in framing, bordering, bounding her stories acknowledges her awareness of the pressure exerted on her vision from other external, and more dominant, points of view. It equally acknowledges what is required of her characters to establish and maintain a home and to survive.

Candace Whitcomb, Polly Moss, and Betsey Dole ultimately die from the exertions entailed by their marginality; Hetty Fifield, the fierce protagonist of "A Church Mouse," digs in on the margins and ultimately lives to triumph over her adversaries. From the deacon's opening assertion, " 'I never heard of a woman's bein' saxton,' " to the closing lines, in which Hetty wakes up on Christmas morning in a room of her own inside the meetinghouse, "A Church Mouse" defines Hetty Fifield's heroism and her defense of the right of women to a home of their own and to their own way of seeing the world. In the story's final scene, Hetty manages to gather the collective power of the women in the congregation, symbolized by the deacon's wife, who dissuades the men from forcing the entrance to the meetinghouse and thereby putting Hetty out of her home. While the young daughters of the congregation watch from the sidelines, Hetty assumes her own "pulpit" and speaks out on behalf of women's right to " 'keep a footin' on the earth.' "

On the Walpole Road

Walpole was a lively little rural emporium of trade; thither the villagers from the small country hamlets thereabouts went to make the bulk of their modest purchases.

One summer afternoon two women were driving slowly along a road therefrom, in a dusty old-fashioned chaise,[1] whose bottom was heaped up with brown-paper parcels.

One woman might have been seventy, but she looked younger, she was so hale and portly. She had a double, bristling chin, her gray eyes twinkled humorously over her spectacles, and she wore a wide-flaring black straw bonnet with purple bows on the inside of the rim. The afternoon was very warm, and she held in one black-mitted hand a palm-leaf fan, which she waved gently, now and then, over against her capacious bosom.

The other woman was younger—forty, perhaps; her face was plain-

1. A light, open, horse-drawn carriage.

featured and energetic. She wore a gray serge dress and drab cotton gloves, and held tightly on to the reins as she drove. Now and then she would slap them briskly upon the horse's back. He was a heavy, hard-worked farm animal, and was disposed to jog along at an easy pace this warm afternoon.

There had not been any rain for a long time, and everything was very dusty. This road was not much traveled, and grass was growing between the wheel-ruts; but the soil flew up like smoke from the horse's hoofs and the wheels. The blackberry vines climbing over the stone walls on either side, and the meadow-sweet and hardhack bushes were powdered thickly with dust, and had gray leaves instead of green. The big-leaved things, such as burdock, growing close to the ground, had their veins all outlined in dust.

The two women rode in a peaceful sort of way; the old lady fanned herself mildly, and the younger one slapped the horse mechanically. Neither spoke, till they emerged into a more open space on a hill-crest. There they had an uninterrupted view of the northwest sky; the trees had hidden it before.

"I declare, Almiry," said the old lady, "we air goin' to hev a thunder-shower."

"It won't get up till we get home," replied the other, "an' ten chances to one it'll go round by the north anyway, and not touch us at all. That's the way they do half the time here. If I'd 'a seen a cloud as black as that down where I used to live, I'd 'a known for sure there was goin' to be a heavy tempest, but here there's no knowin' anything about it. I wouldn't worry anyway, Mis' Green, if it should come up before we get home: the horse ain't afraid of lightnin'."

The old lady looked comical. "He ain't afraid of anything, is he, Almiry?"

"No," answered her companion, giving the horse a spiteful slap; "he don't know enough to get scared even, that's a fact. I don't believe anything short of Gabriel's trumpet[2] would start him up a bit."

"I don't think you ought to speak that way, Almiry," said the old lady; "it's kinder makin' light o' sacred things, seems to me. But as long as you've spoke of it, I don't believe that would start him up either. Though I'll tell you one thing, Almiry: I don't believe thar's goin' to be anything very frightful 'bout Gabriel's trumpet. I think it's goin' to come kinder like the robins an' the flowers do in the spring, kinder meltin' right into everything else, sweet an' nateral like."

"That ain't accordin' to Scripture," said Almira, stoutly.

"It's accordin' to my Scripture. I tell you what 'tis, Almiry, I've found out one thing a-livin' so long, an' that is, thar ain't so much difference in things on this airth as thar is in the folks that see 'em. It's me a-seein' the Scripturs, an' it's you a-seein' the Scripturs, Almiry, an' you see one

2. The summons to Judgment Day in the Book of Revelation is accompanied by the archangel's trumpet call; see Revelation 10.7.

thing an' I another, an' I dare say we both see crooked mostly, with maybe a little straight mixed up with it, an' we'll never reely know how much is straight till we see to read it by the light of the New Jerusalem."[3]

"You ought to ha' ben a minister, Mis' Green."

"Wa'al, so I would ha' ben ef I had been a man; I allers thought I would. But I s'pose the Lord thought there was more need of an extra hand just then to raise up children, an' bake an' brew an' wash dishes. You'd better drive along a leetle faster ef you kin, Almiry."

Almira jerked the reins viciously and clucked, but the horse jogged along undisturbed. "It ain't no use," said she. "You might as well try to start up a stone post."

"Wa'al, mebbe the shower won't come up," said the old lady, and she leaned back and began peacefully fanning herself.

"That cloud makes me think of Aunt Rebecca's funeral," she broke out, suddenly. "Did I ever tell you about it, Almiry?"

"No; I don't think you ever did, Mis' Green."

"Wa'al, mebbe you'll like to hear it, as we're joggin' along. It'll keep us from getting aggervated at the horse, poor, dumb thing!"

"Wa'al, you see, Almiry, Aunt Rebecca was my aunt on my mother's side—my mother's oldest sister she was—an' I'd allers thought a sight of her. This happened twenty year ago or more, before Israel died. She was allers such an own-folks sort of a woman, an' jest the best hand when any one was sick. I'll never forget how she nussed me through the typhus fever, the year after mother died. Thar I was took sick all of a sudden, an' four leetle children cryin', an' Israel couldn't get anybody but that shiftless Lyons woman, far and near, to come an' help. When Aunt Rebecca heerd of it she jest left everything an' come. She packed off that Lyons woman, bag an' baggage, an' tuk right hold, as nobody but her could ha' known how to. I allers knew I should ha' died ef it hadn't been for her.

"She lived ten miles off, on this very road, too, but we allers used to visit back an' forth. I couldn't get along without goin' to see Aunt Rebecca once in so often; I'd get jest as lonesome an' homesick as could be.

"So, feelin' that way, it ain't surprisin' that it gave me an awful shock when I heerd she was dead that mornin'. They sent the word by a man that they hailed, drivin' by. He was comin' down here to see about sellin' a horse, an' he said he'd jest as soon stop an' tell us as not. A real nice sort of a man he was—a store-keeper from Comstock. Wa'al, I see Israel standin' out in the road an' talkin' with the man, an' I wondered what it could be about. But when he came in an' told me that Aunt Rebecca was dead, I jest sat right down, kinder stunned like. I couldn't ha' felt much worse ef it had been my mother. An' it was so awful

---

3. The Book of Revelation predicts the end of the world followed by the creation of a new heaven, a new earth, and a heavenly Jerusalem.

sudden! Why, I'd seen her only the week before, an' she looked uncommon smart for her, I thought. Ef it had been Uncle Enos, her husband, I shouldn't ha' wondered. He'd had the heart-disease for years, an' we'd thought he might die any minute; but to think of her—

"I jest stared at Israel. I felt too bad to cry. I didn't, till I happened to look down at the apron I had on. It was like a dress she had; she had a piece left, an' she gave it to me for an apron. When I saw that, I bust right out sobbin'.

" 'O Lord,' says I, 'this apron she give me! Oh dear! dear! dear!'

" 'Sarah,' says Israel, 'it's the will of the Lord.'

" 'I know it,' says I, 'but she's dead, an' she gave me this apron, dear blessed woman,' an' I went right on cryin', though he tried to stop me. Every time I looked at that apron, it seemed as if I should die.

"Thar wa'n't any particulars, Israel said. All the man that told him knew was that a woman hailed him from one of the front windows as he was drivin' by, and asked him to stop an' tell us. I s'posed most likely the woman that hailed him was Mis' Simmons, a widder woman that used to work for Aunt Rebecca busy times.

"Wa'al, Israel kinder hurried me to get ready. The funeral was app'inted at two o'clock, an' we had a horse that wa'n't much swifter on the road than the one you're drivin' now.

"So I got into my best black gown the quickest I could. I had a good black shawl, and a black bunnit too; so I looked quite decent. I felt reel glad I had em'. They were things I had when mother died. I don't see hardly how I had happened to keep the bunnit, but it was lucky I did. I got ready in such a flutter that I got on my black gown over the caliker one I'd been wearin', an' never knew it till I came to go to bed that night, but I don't think it was much wonder.

"We'd been havin' a terrible dry spell, jest as we've been havin' now, an' everything was like powder. I thought my dress would be spoilt before we got thar. The horse was dreadful lazy, an' it was nothin' but g'langin'[4] an' slappin' an' whippin' all the way, an' it didn't amount to nothin' then.

"When we'd got half-way thar or so, thar come up an awful thunder-shower from the northwest, jest as it's doin' today. Wa'al, thar wa'n't nowhar to stop, an' we driv right along. The horse wa'n't afraid of lightnin', an' we got in under the shay top as far as we could, an' pulled the blanket up over us; but we got drippin' wet. An' thar was Israel in his meetin' coat, an' me in my best gown. Take it with the dust an' everything, they never looked anyhow again.

"Wa'al, Israel g'langed to the horse, an' put the whip over her, but she jest jogged right along. What with feelin' so about Aunt Rebecca, an' worryin' about Israel's coat an' my best gown, I thought I should never live to git thar.

"When we driv by the meetin'-house at Four Corners, where Aunt

4. The act of telling a horse to "go along" or "giddyup."

Rebecca lived, it was five minutes after two, an' two was the time sot for the funeral. I did feel reel worked up to think we was late, an' we chief mourners. When we got to the house thar seemed to be consider'-ble goin' on around it, folks goin' in an' out, an' standin' in the yard, an' Israel said he didn't believe we was late, after all. He hollered to a man standin' by the fence, an' asked him if they had had the funeral. The man said no; they was goin' to hev it at the meetin'-house at three o'clock. We was glad enough to hear that, an' Israel said he would drive round an' hitch the horse, an' I'd better go in an' get dried off a little, an' see the folks.

"It had slacked up then, an' was only drizzlin' a leetle, an' lightnin' a good ways off now an' then.

"Wa'al, I got out, an' went up to the house. Thar was quite a lot of men I knew standin' round the door an' in the entry, but they only bowed kinder stiff an' solemn, an' moved to let me pass. I noticed the entry floor was drippin' wet too. 'Been rainin' in,' thinks I. 'I wonder why they didn't shet the door.' I went right into the room on the left-hand side of the entry—that was the settin'-room—an' thar, a-set-tin' in a cheer by the winder, jest as straight an' smart as could be, in her new black bunnit an' gown, was—Aunt Rebecca.

"Wa'al, ef I was to tell you what I did, Almiry, I s'pose you'd think it was awful. But I s'pose the sudden change from feelin' so bad made me kinder highstericky. I jest sot right down in the first cheer I come to an' laughed; I laughed till the tears was runnin' down my cheeks, an' it was all I could do to breathe. There was quite a lot of Uncle Enos's folks settin' round the room—his brother's family an' some cousins—an' they looked at me as ef they thought I was crazy. But seein' them look only sot me off again. Some of the folks came in from the entry, an' stood starin' at me, but I jest laughed harder. Finally Aunt Rebecca comes up to me.

" 'For mercy's sake, Sarah,' says she, 'what air you doin' so for?'

" 'Oh, dear!' says I. 'I thought you was dead, an' thar you was a-settin'. Oh dear!'

"And then I begun to laugh again. I was awful 'shamed of myself, but I couldn't stop to save my life.

" 'For the land's sake, Aunt Rebecca,' says I, 'is thar a funeral or a weddin'? An' ef thar is a funeral, who's dead?'

" 'Come into the bedroom with me a minute, Sarah,' says she.

"Then we went into her bedroom, that opened out of the settin-room, an' sot down, an' she told me that it was Uncle Enos that was dead. It seems she was the one that hailed the man, an' he was a little hard of hearin', an' thar was a misunderstandin' between 'em some way.

"Uncle Enos had died very sudden, the day before, of heart-disease. He went into the settin'-room after breakfast, an' sot down by the winder, an' Aunt Rebecca found him thar dead in his cheer when she went in a few minutes afterwards.

"It was such awful hot weather they had to hurry about the funeral. But that wa'n't all. Then she went on to tell me the rest. They had had the awfulest time that ever was. The shower had come up about one o'clock, and the barn had been struck by lightnin'. It was a big new one that Uncle Enos had sot great store by. He had laid out consider'ble money on it, an' they'd jest got in twelve ton of hay. I s'pose that was how it happened to be struck. A barn is a good deal more likely to be when they've jest got hay in. Well, everybody sot to an' put the fire in the barn out. They handed buckets of water up to the men on the roof, an' put that out without much trouble by takin' it in time.

"But after they'd got that put out they found the house was on fire. The same thunderbolt that struck the barn had struck that too, an' it was blazin' away at one end of the roof pretty lively.

"Wa'al, they went to work at that then, an' they'd jest got that fairly put out a few minutes before we come. Nothin' was hurt much, only thar was a good deal of water round: we had hard work next day cleanin' of it up.

"Aunt Rebecca allers was a calm sort of woman, an' she didn't seem near as much flustered by it all as most folks would have been.

"I couldn't help wonderin', an' lookin' at her pretty sharp to see how she took Uncle Enos's death, too. You see, thar was something kinder curious about their gittin' married. I'd heerd about it all from mother. I don't s'pose she ever wanted him, nor cared about him the best she could do, any more than she would have about any good, respectable man that was her neighbor. Uncle Enos was a pretty good sort of a man, though he was allers dreadful sot in his ways, an' I believe it would have been wuss than death, any time, for him to have given up anything he had determined to hev. But I must say I never thought so much of him after mother told me what she did. You see, the way of it was, my grandmother Wilson, Aunt Rebecca's mother, was awful sot on her hevin' him, an' she was dreadful nervous an' feeble, an' Aunt Rebecca jest give in to her. The wust of it was, thar was someone else she wanted too, an' he wanted her. Abner Lyons his name was; he wa'n't any relation to the Lyons woman I had when I was sick. He was a real likely young feller, an' thar wa'n't a thing agin him that anyone else could see; but grandmother fairly hated him, an' mother said she did believe her mother would rather hev buried Rebecca than seen her married to him. Well, grandmother took on, an' acted so, that Aunt Rebecca give in an' said she'd marry Uncle Enos, an' the weddin'-day come.

"Mother said she looked handsome as a pictur', but thar was some-thin' kinder awful[5] about her when she stood up before the minister with Uncle Enos to be married.

"She was dressed in green silk, an' had some roses in her hair. I kin imagine jest how she must hev looked. She was a good-lookin' woman

---

5. Inspiring reverence, dread, or fear.

when I knew her, an' they said when she was young there wa'n't many to compare with her.

"Mother said Uncle Enos looked nice, but he had his mouth kinder hard sot, as ef now he'd got what he wanted, an' meant to hang on to it. He'd known all the time jest how matters was. Aunt Rebecca'd told him the whole story; she declared she wouldn't marry him, without she did.

"I s'pose, at the last minute, that Aunt Rebecca got kinder desp'rate, an' a realizin' sense of what she was doin' come over her, an' she thought she'd make one more effort to escape; for when the minister asked that question 'bout thar bein' any obstacles to their gettin' married, an' ef thar were, let' em speak up, or forever hold their peace, Aunt Rebecca did speak up. Mother said she looked straight at the parson, an' her eyes was shinin' an her cheeks white as lilies.

" 'Yes,' says she, 'thar is an obstacle, an' I will speak, an' then I will forever hold my peace. I don't love this man I'm standin' beside of, an' I love another man. Now ef Enos Fairweather wants me after what I've said, I've promised to marry him, an' you kin go on; but I won't tell or act a lie before God an' man.'

"Mother said it was awful. You could hev heerd a pin drop anywheres in the room. The minister jest stopped short an' looked at Uncle Enos, an' Uncle Enos nodded his head for him to go on.

"But then the minister begun to hev doubts as to whether or no he ought to marry 'em after what Aunt Rebecca had said, an' it seemed for a minute as ef thar wouldn't be any weddin' at all.

"But grandmother begun to cry, an' take on, an' Aunt Rebecca jest turned round an' looked at her. 'Go on,' says she to the minister.

"Mother said ef thar was ever anybody looked fit to be a martyr, Aunt Rebecca did then. But it never seemed to me t'was right. Marryin' to please your relations an' dyin' to please the Lord is two things.

"Wa'al, I never thought much of Uncle Enos after I heerd that story, though, as I said before, I guess he was a pretty good sort of a man. The principal thing that was bad about him, I guess, was, he was bound to hev Aunt Rebecca, an' he didn't let anything, even proper self-respect stand in his way.

"Aunt Rebecca allers did her duty by him, an' was a good wife an' good housekeeper. They never had any children. But I don't s'pose she was ever really happy or contented, an' I don't see how she could hev respected Uncle Enos, scursly, for my part, but you'd never hev known but what she did.

"So I looked at her pretty sharp, as we sot thar in her little bedroom that opened out of the settin'-room; thar was jest room for one cheer beside the bed, an' I sot on the bed. It seemed rather awful, with *him* a-layin' dead in the best room, but I couldn't help wonderin' ef she wouldn't marry Abner Lyons now. He'd never got married, but lived, all by himself, jest at the rise of the hill from where Aunt Rebecca lived. He'd never had a housekeeper, but jest shifted for himself, an' folks said his house was as neat as wax, an' he could cook an' wash dishes as handy as a woman. He used to hev his washin' out on the line by seven o'clock of a Monday mornin', anyhow; that I know, for I've seen it myself; an' the clothes looked white as snow. I shouldn't hev been ashamed of 'em myself.

"Aunt Rebecca looked very calm, an' I don't think she'd ben cryin'. But then that wa'n't nothin' to go by; 'twa'n't her way. I don't believe she'd a cried ef it had been Abner Lyons. Though I don't know, maybe, ef she'd married the man she'd wanted, she'd cried easier. For all Aunt Rebecca was so kind an' sympathizin' to other folks, she'd always seemed like a stone 'bout her own troubles. I don't s'pose, ef the barn an' house had both burned down, an' left her without a roof over her head, she'd 'a seemed any different. I kin see her now, jest as she looked, settin' thar, tellin' me the story that would hev flustrated[6] any other woman most to death. But her voice was jest as low an' even, an' never shook. Her hair was gray, but it was kinder crinkly, an' her forehead was as white an' smooth as a young girl's.

"Aunt Rebecca's troubles always stayed in her heart, I s'pose, an' never pricked through. Except for her gray hair, she never looked as ef she'd had one.

"She never took on any more when she went to the funeral, for they buried him at last, poor man. He had 'most as hard a time gittin' buried as he did gittin' married. I couldn't help peekin' round to see ef Abner Lyons was thar, an' he was, on the other side of the aisle from me. An' he was lookin' straight at Uncle Enos's coffin, that stood up in front under the pulpit, with the curiousest expression that I ever did see.

"He didn't look glad reely. I couldn't say he did, but all I could think of was a man who'd been runnin' an' runnin' to get to a place, an' at length had got in sight of it.

"Maybe 'twas dreadful for him to go to a man's funeral an' look that way, but natur' is natur', an' I always felt somehow that ef Uncle Enos chose to do as he did 'twa'n't anythin' more than he ought to hev expected when he was dead.

"But I did feel awful ashamed an' wicked, thinkin' of such things, with the poor man layin' dead before me. An' when I went up to look at him, layin' thar so helpless, I cried like a baby. Poor Uncle Enos! it ain't for us to be down on folks after everything's all over.

"Well, Aunt Rebecca married Abner Lyons 'bout two years after Uncle Enos died, an' they lived together jest five years an' seven months; then she was took sudden with cholera-morbus[7] from eatin' currants, an' died. He lived a year an' a half or so longer, an' then he died in a kind of consumption.

" 'Twa'n't long they had to be happy together, an' sometimes I used to think they wa'n't so happy after all; for thar's no mistake about it,

6. Flustered.
7. Stomach and intestinal inflammation marked by severe cramp, diarrhea, and vomiting.

Abner Lyons was awful fussy. I s'pose his livin' alone so long made him so; but I don't believe Aunt Rebecca ever made a loaf of bread, after she was married, without his havin' something to say about it; an' ef thar's anything that's aggervatin' to a woman, it's havin' a man fussin' around in her kitchen.

"But ef Aunt Rebecca didn't find anything just as she thought it was goin' to be, she never let on she was disapp'inted.

"I declare, Almiry, thar's the house in sight, an' the shower has gone round to the northeast, an' we ain't had a speck of rain to lay the dust.

"Well, my story's gone round to the northeast too. Ain't you tired out hearin' me talk, Almiry?"

"No indeed, Mis' Green," replied Almira, slapping the reins; "I liked to hear you, only it's kind of come to me, as I've been listening, that I *had* heard it before. The last time I took you to Walpole, I guess, you told it."

"Wa'al, I declare, I shouldn't wonder ef I did."

Then the horse turned cautiously around the corner, and stopped willingly before the house.

Harper's Bazar, 9 February 1884; *A Humble Romance*, 1887

A Mistaken Charity

There were in a green field a little, low, weather-stained cottage, with a foot-path leading to it from the highway several rods distant, and two old women—one with a tin pan and old knife searching for dandelion greens among the short young grass, and the other sitting on the door-step watching her, or, rather, having the appearance of watching her.

"Air there enough for a mess,[1] Harriét?" asked the old woman on the door-step. She accented oddly the last syllable of the Harriet, and there was a curious quality in her feeble, cracked old voice. Besides the question denoted by the arrangement of her words and the rising inflection, there was another, broader and subtler, the very essence of all questioning, in the tone of her voice itself; the cracked, quavering notes that she used reached out of themselves, and asked, and groped like fingers in the dark. One would have known by the voice that the old woman was blind.

The old woman on her knees in the grass searching for dandelions did not reply; she evidently had not heard the question. So the old woman on the doorstep, after waiting a few minutes with her head turned expectantly, asked again, varying her question slightly, and speaking louder:

"Air there enough for a mess, do ye s'pose, Harriét?"

1. An amount of food sufficient for a meal, course, or dish.

The old woman in the grass heard this time. She rose slowly and laboriously; the effort of straightening out the rheumatic old muscles was evidently a painful one; then she eyed the greens heaped up in the tin pan, and pressed them down with her hand.

"Wa'al, I don't know, Charlotte," she replied, hoarsely. "There's plenty on 'em here, but I 'ain't got near enough for a mess; they do bile down so when you get 'em in the pot; an' it's all I can do to bend my j'ints enough to dig 'em."

"I'd give consider'ble to help ye, Harriét," said the old woman on the door-step.

But the other did not hear her; she was down on her knees in the grass again, anxiously spying out the dandelions.

So the old woman on the door-step crossed her little shriveled hands over her calico knees, and sat quite still, with the soft spring wind blowing over her.

The old wooden door-step was sunk low down among the grasses, and the whole house to which it belonged had an air of settling down and mouldering into the grass as into its own grave.

When Harriet Shattuck grew deaf and rheumatic, and had to give up her work as tailoress, and Charlotte Shattuck lost her eyesight, and was unable to do any more sewing for her livelihood, it was a small and trifling charity for the rich man who held a mortgage on the little house in which they had been born and lived all their lives to give them the use of it, rent and interest free. He might as well have taken credit to himself for not charging a squirrel for his tenement in some old decaying tree in his woods.

So ancient was the little habitation, so wavering and mouldering, the hands that had fashioned it had lain still so long in their graves, that it almost seemed to have fallen below its distinctive rank as a house. Rain and snow had filtered through its roof, mosses had grown over it, worms had eaten it, and birds built their nests under its eaves; nature had almost completely overrun and obliterated the work of man, and taken her own to herself again, till the house seemed as much a natural ruin as an old tree-stump.

The Shattucks had always been poor people and common people; no especial grace and refinement or fine ambition had ever characterized any of them; they had always been poor and coarse and common. The father and his father before him had simply lived in the poor little house, grubbed for their living, and then unquestioningly died. The mother had been of no rarer stamp, and the two daughters were cast in the same mould.

After their parents' death Harriet and Charlotte had lived along in the old place from youth to old age, with the one hope of ability to keep a roof over their heads, covering on their backs, and victuals in their mouths—an all-sufficient one with them.

Neither of them had ever had a lover; they had always seemed to repel rather than attract the opposite sex. It was not merely because they were poor, ordinary, and homely; there were plenty of men in the place who would have matched them well in that respect; the fault lay deeper—in their characters. Harriet, even in her girlhood, had a blunt, defiant manner that almost amounted to surliness, and was well calculated to alarm timid adorers, and Charlotte had always had the reputation of not being any too strong in her mind.

Harriet had gone about from house to house doing tailor-work after the primitive country fashion, and Charlotte had done plain sewing and mending for the neighbors. They had been, in the main, except when pressed by some temporary anxiety about their work or the payment thereof, happy and contented, with that negative kind of happiness and contentment which comes not from gratified ambition, but a lack of ambition itself. All that they cared for they had had in tolerable abundance, for Harriet at least had been swift and capable about her work. The patched, mossy old roof had been kept over their heads, the coarse, hearty food that they loved had been set on their table, and their cheap clothes had been warm and strong.

After Charlotte's eyes failed her, and Harriet had the rheumatic fever, and the little hoard of earnings went to the doctors, times were harder with them, though still it could not be said that they actually suffered.

When they could not pay the interest on the mortgage they were allowed to keep the place interest free; there was as much fitness in a mortgage on the little house, anyway, as there would have been on a rotten old apple-tree; and the people about, who were mostly farmers, and good friendly folk, helped them out with their living. One would donate a barrel of apples from his abundant harvest to the two poor old women, one a barrel of potatoes, another a load of wood for the winter fuel, and many a farmer's wife had bustled up the narrow foot-path with a pound of butter, or a dozen fresh eggs, or a nice bit of pork. Besides all this, there was a tiny garden patch behind the house, with a straggling row of currant bushes in it, and one of gooseberries, where Harriet contrived every year to raise a few pumpkins, which were the pride of her life. On the right of the garden were two old apple-trees, a Baldwin and a Porter, both yet in a tolerably good fruit-bearing state.

The delight which the two poor old souls took in their own pumpkins, their apples and currants, was indescribable. It was not merely that they contributed largely towards their living; they were their own, their private share of the great wealth of nature, the little taste set apart for them alone out of her bounty, and worth more to them on that account, though they were not conscious of it, than all the richer fruits which they received from their neighbors' gardens.

This morning the two apple-trees were brave[2] with flowers, the currant bushes looked alive, and the pumpkin seeds were in the ground. Harriet cast complacent glances in their direction from time to time, as she painfully dug her dandelion greens. She was a short,

2. Making a fine display; splendid.

stoutly built old woman, with a large face coarsely wrinkled, with a suspicion of a stubble of beard on the square chin.

When her tin pan was filled to her satisfaction with the sprawling, spidery greens, and she was hobbling stiffly towards her sister on the door-step, she saw another woman standing before her with a basket in her hand.

"Good-morning, Harriet," she said, in a loud, strident voice, as she drew near. "I've been frying some doughnuts, and I brought you over some warm."

"I've been tellin' her it was real good in her," piped Charlotte from the door-step, with an anxious turn of her sightless face towards the sound of her sister's footstep.

Harriet said nothing but a hoarse "Good-mornin', Mis' Simonds." Then she took the basket in her hand, lifted the towel off the top, selected a doughnut, and deliberately tasted it.

"Tough," said she. "I s'posed so. If there is anything I 'spise on this airth it's a tough doughnut."

"Oh, Harriét!" said Charlotte, with a frightened look.

"They air tough," said Harriet, with hoarse defiance, "and if there is anything I 'spise on this airth it's a tough doughnut."

The woman whose benevolence and cookery were being thus ungratefully received only laughed. She was quite fleshy, and had a round, rosy, determined face.

"Well, Harriet," said she, "I am sorry they are tough, but perhaps you had better take them out on a plate, and give me my basket. You may be able to eat two or three of them if they are tough."

"They air tough—turrible tough," said Harriet, stubbornly; but she took the basket into the house and emptied it of its contents nevertheless.

"I suppose your roof leaked as bad as ever in that heavy rain day before yesterday?" said the visitor to Harriet, with an inquiring squint towards the mossy shingles, as she was about to leave with her empty basket.

"It was turrible," replied Harriet, with crusty acquiescence—"turrible. We had to set pails an' pans everywheres, an' move the bed out."

"Mr. Upton ought to fix it."

"There ain't any fix to it; the old ruff[3] ain't fit to nail new shingles on to; the hammerin' would bring the whole thing down on our heads," said Harriet, grimly.

"Well, I don't know as it can be fixed, it's so old. I suppose the wind comes in bad around the windows and doors too?"

"It's like livin' with a piece of paper, or mebbe a sieve, 'twixt you an' the wind an' the rain," quoth Harriet, with a jerk of her head.

"You ought to have a more comfortable home in your old age," said the visitor, thoughtfully.

"Oh, it's well enough," cried Harriet, in quick alarm, and with a

3. I.e., roof.

complete change of tone; the woman's remark had brought an old dread over her. "The old house'll last as long as Charlotte an' me do. The rain ain't so bad, nuther is the wind; there's room enough for us in the dry places, an' out of the way of the doors an' windows. It's enough sight better than goin' on the town."[4] Her square, defiant old face actually looked pale as she uttered the last words and stared apprehensively at the woman.

"Oh, I did not think of your doing that," she said, hastily and kindly. "We all know how you feel about that, Harriet, and not one of us neighbors will see you and Charlotte go to the poorhouse while we've got a crust of bread to share with you."

Harriet's face brightened. "Thank ye, Mis' Simonds," she said, with reluctant courtesy. "I'm much obleeged to you an' the neighbors. I think mebbe we'll be able to eat some of them doughnuts if they air tough," she added, mollifyingly, as her caller turned down the foot-path.

"My, Harriét," said Charlotte, lifting up a weakly, wondering, peaked old face, "what did you tell her them doughnuts was tough fur?"

"Charlotte, do you want everybody to look down on us, an' think we ain't no account at all, just like any beggars, 'cause they bring us in vittles?" said Harriet, with a grim glance at her sister's meek, unconscious face.

"No, Harriét," she whispered.

"Do you want *to go to the poor-house?*"

"No, Harriét." The poor little old woman on the door-step fairly cowered before her aggressive old sister.

"Then don't hender me agin when I tell folks their doughnuts is tough an' their pertaters is poor. If I don't kinder keep up an' show some sperrit, I sha'n't think nothing of myself, an' other folks won't nuther, and fust thing we know they'll kerry us to the poorhouse. You'd 'a been there before now if it hadn't been for me, Charlotte."

Charlotte looked meekly convinced, and her sister sat down on a chair in the doorway to scrape her dandelions.

"Did you git a good mess, Harriét?" asked Charlotte, in a humble tone.

"Toler'ble."

"They'll be proper relishin' with that piece of pork Mis' Mann brought in yesterday. O Lord, Harriet, it's a chink!"

Harriet sniffed.

Her sister caught with her sensitive ear the little contemptuous sound. "I guess," she said, querulously, and with more pertinacity than she had shown in the matter of the doughnuts, "that if you was in the dark, as I am, Harriet, you wouldn't make fun an' turn up your nose

---

4. Having to take charity from the townspeople; before the institution of social welfare, the way a rural community collectively supported its poor and indigent citizens.

at chinks. If you had seen the light streamin' in all of a sudden through some little hole that you hadn't known of before when you set down on the door-step this mornin', and the wind with the smell of the apple blows in it came in your face, an' when Mis' Simonds brought them hot doughnuts, an' when I thought of the pork an' greens jest now— O Lord, how it did shine in! An' it does now. If you was me, Harriét, you would know there was chinks."

Tears began starting from the sightless eyes, and streaming pitifully down the pale old cheeks.

Harriet looked at her sister, and her grim face softened. "Why, Charlotte, hev it that thar *is* chinks if you want to. Who cares?"

"Thar *is* chinks, Harriét."

"Wa'al, thar *is* chinks, then. If I don't hurry, I sha'n't get these greens in in time for dinner."

When the two old women sat down complacently to their meal of pork and dandelion greens in their little kitchen they did not dream how destiny slowly and surely was introducing some new colors into their web of life, even when it was almost completed, and that this was one of the last meals they would eat in their old home for many a day. In about a week from that day they were established in the "Old Ladies' Home" in a neighboring city. It came about in this wise: Mrs. Simonds, the woman who had brought the gift of hot doughnuts, was a smart, energetic person, bent on doing good, and she did a great deal. To be sure, she always did it in her own way. If she chose to give hot doughnuts, she gave hot doughnuts; it made not the slightest difference to her if the recipients of her charity would infinitely have preferred ginger cookies. Still, a great many would like hot doughnuts, and she did unquestionably a great deal of good.

She had a worthy coadjutor in the person of a rich and childless elderly widow in the place. They had fairly entered into a partnership in good works, with about an equal capital on both sides, the widow furnishing the money, and Mrs. Simonds, who had much the better head of the two, furnishing the active schemes of benevolence.

The afternoon after the doughnut episode she had gone to the widow with a new project, and the result was that entrance fees had been paid, and old Harriet and Charlotte made sure of a comfortable home for the rest of their lives. The widow was hand in glove with officers of missionary boards and trustees of charitable institutions. There had been an unusual mortality among the inmates of the "Home" this spring, there were several vacancies, and the matter of the admission of Harriet and Charlotte was very quickly and easily arranged. But the matter which would have seemed the least difficult—inducing the two old women to accept the bounty which Providence, the widow, and Mrs. Simonds were ready to bestow on them— proved the most so. The struggle to persuade them to abandon their tottering old home for a better was a terrible one. The widow had pleaded with mild surprise, and Mrs. Simonds with benevolent determination; the counsel and reverend eloquence of the minister had been called in; and when they yielded at last it was with a sad grace for the recipients of a worthy charity.

It had been hard to convince them that the "Home" was not an almshouse under another name, and their yielding at length to anything short of actual force was only due probably to the plea, which was advanced most eloquently to Harriet, that Charlotte would be so much more comfortable.

The morning they came away, Charlotte cried pitifully, and trembled all over her little shriveled body. Harriet did not cry. But when her sister had passed out the low, sagging door she turned the key in the lock, then took it out and thrust it slyly into her pocket, shaking her head to herself with an air of fierce determination.

Mrs. Simonds's husband, who was to take them to the depot, said to himself, with disloyal defiance of his wife's active charity, that it was a shame, as he helped the two distressed old souls into his light wagon, and put the poor little box, with their homely clothes in it, in behind.

Mrs. Simonds, the widow, the minister, and the gentleman from the "Home" who was to take charge of them, were all at the depot, their faces beaming with the delight of successful benevolence. But the two poor old women looked like two forlorn prisoners in their midst. It was an impressive illustration of the truth of the saying "that it is more blessed to give than to receive."

Well, Harriet and Charlotte Shattuck went to the "Old Ladies' Home" with reluctance and distress. They stayed two months, and then—they ran away.

The "Home" was comfortable, and in some respects even luxurious; but nothing suited those two unhappy, unreasonable old women.

The fare was of a finer, more delicately served variety than they had been accustomed to; those finely flavored nourishing soups for which the "Home" took great credit to itself failed to please palates used to common, coarser food.

"O Lord, Harriét, when I set down to the table here there ain't no chinks," Charlotte used to say. "If we could hev some cabbage, or some pork an' greens, how the light would stream in!"

Then they had to be more particular about their dress. They had always been tidy enough, but now it had to be something more; the widow, in the kindness of her heart, had made it possible, and the good folks in charge of the "Home," in the kindness of their hearts, tried to carry out the widow's designs.

But nothing could transform these two unpolished old women into two nice old ladies. They did not take kindly to white lace caps and delicate neckerchiefs. They liked their new black cashmere dresses well enough, but they felt as if they broke a commandment when they put them on every afternoon. They had always worn calico with long aprons at home, and they wanted to now; and they wanted to twist up their scanty gray locks into little knots at the back of their heads, and go without caps, just as they always had done.

Charlotte in a dainty white cap was pitiful, but Harriet was both pitiful and comical. They were totally at variance with their surroundings, and they felt it keenly, as people of their stamp always do. No amount of kindness and attention—and they had enough of both—sufficed to reconcile them to their new abode. Charlotte pleaded continually with her sister to go back to their old home.

"O Lord, Harriét, she would exclaim (by the way, Charlotte's "O Lord," which, as she used it, was innocent enough, had been heard with much disfavor in the "Home," and she, not knowing at all why, had been remonstrated with concerning it), "let us go home. I can't stay here no ways in this world. I don't like their vittles, an' I don't like to wear a cap; I want to go home and do different. The currants will be ripe, Harriét. O Lord, thar was almost a chink, thinking about 'em. I want some of 'em; an' the Porter apples will be gittin' ripe, an' we could have some apple-pie. This here ain't good; I want merlasses fur sweeting. Can't we get back no ways, Harriét? It ain't far, an' we could walk, an' they don't lock us in, nor nothin'. I don't want to die here; it ain't so straight up to heaven from here. O Lord, I've felt as if I was slantendicular[5] from heaven ever since I've been here, an' it's been so awful dark. I ain't had any chinks. I want to go home, Harriét."

"We'll go tomorrow mornin'," said Harriet, finally; "we'll pack up our things an' go; we'll put on our old dresses, an' we'll do up the new ones in bundles, an' we'll jest shy out the back way tomorrow mornin'; an' we'll go. I kin find the way, an' I reckon we kin git thar, if it is fourteen mile. Mebbe somebody will give us a lift."

And they went. With a grim humor Harriet hung the new white lace caps with which she and Charlotte had been so pestered, one on each post at the head of the bedstead, so they would meet the eyes of the first person who opened the door. Then they took their bundles, stole slyly out, and were soon on the high-road, hobbling along, holding each other's hands, as jubilant as two children, and chuckling to themselves over their escape, and the probable astonishment there would be in the "Home" over it.

"O Lord, Harriét, what do you s'pose they will say to them caps?" cried Charlotte, with a gleeful cackle.

"I guess they'll see as folks ain't goin' to be made to wear caps agin their will in a free kentry," returned Harriet, with an echoing cackle, as they sped feebly and bravely along.

The "Home" stood on the very outskirts of the city, luckily for them. They would have found it a difficult undertaking to traverse the crowded streets. As it was, a short walk brought them into the free country road—free comparatively, for even here at ten o'clock in the morning there was considerable traveling to and from the city on business or pleasure.

People whom they met on the road did not stare at them as curiously as might have been expected. Harriet held her bristling chin high in air,

5. Slanting, sloping, oblique; neither perpendicular nor horizontal.

and hobbled along with an appearance of being well aware of what she was about, that led folks to doubt their own first opinion that there was something unusual about the two old women.

Still their evident feebleness now and then occasioned from one and another more particular scrutiny. When they had been on the road a half-hour or so, a man in a covered wagon drove up behind them. After he had passed them, he poked his head around the front of the vehicle and looked back. Finally he stopped, and waited for them to come up to him.

"Like a ride, ma'am?" said he, looking at once bewildered and compassionate.

"Thankee," said Harriet, "we'd be much obleeged."

After the man had lifted the old women into the wagon, and established them on the back seat, he turned around, as he drove slowly along, and gazed at them curiously.

"Seems to me you look pretty feeble to be walking far," said he. "Where were you going?"

Harriet told him with an air of defiance.

"Why," he exclaimed, "it is fourteen miles out. You could never walk it in the world. Well, I am going within three miles of there, and I can go on a little farther as well as not. But I don't see— Have you been in the city?"

"I have been visitin' my married darter in the city," said Harriet, calmly.

Charlotte started, and swallowed convulsively.

Harriet had never told a deliberate falsehood before in her life, but this seemed to her one of the tremendous exigencies of life which justify a lie. She felt desperate. If she could not contrive to deceive him in some way, the man might turn directly around and carry Charlotte and her back to the "Home" and the white caps.

"I should not have thought your daughter would have let you start for such a walk as that," said the man. "Is this lady your sister? She is blind, isn't she? She does not look fit to walk a mile."

"Yes, she's my sister," replied Harriet, stubbornly: "an' she's blind; an' my darter didn't want us to walk. She felt reel bad about it. But she couldn't help it. She's poor, and her husband's dead, an' she's got four leetle children."

Harriet recounted the hardships of her imaginary daughter with a glibness that was astonishing. Charlotte swallowed again.

"Well," said the man, "I am glad I overtook you, for I don't think you would ever have reached home alive."

About six miles from the city an open buggy passed them swiftly. In it were seated the matron and one of the gentlemen in charge of the "Home." They never thought of looking into the covered wagon—and indeed one can travel in one of those vehicles, so popular in some parts of New England, with as much privacy as he could in his tomb. The two in the buggy were seriously alarmed, and anxious for the safety of the old women, who were chuckling maliciously in the wagon they soon left far behind. Harriet had watched them breathlessly until they disappeared on a curve of the road; then she whispered to Charlotte.

A little after noon the two old women crept slowly up the foot-path across the field to their old home.

"The clover is up to our knees," said Harriet; "an' the sorrel and the white-weed; an' there's lots of yaller butterflies."

"O Lord, Harriét, thar's a chink, an' I do believe I saw one of them yaller butterflies go past it," cried Charlotte, trembling all over, and nodding her gray head violently.

Harriet stood on the old sunken door-step and fitted the key, which she drew triumphantly from her pocket, in the lock, while Charlotte stood waiting and shaking behind her.

Then they went in. Everything was there just as they had left it. Charlotte sank down on a chair and began to cry. Harriet hurried across to the window that looked out on the garden.

"The currants air ripe," said she; *"an'* them pumpkins hev run all over everything."

"O Lord, Harriét," sobbed Charlotte, "thar is so many chinks that they air all runnin' together!"

A Humble Romance, 1887

Sister Liddy

There were no trees near the almshouse; it stood in its bare, sandy lot, and there were no leaves or branches to cast shadows on its walls. It seemed like the folks whom it sheltered, out in the full glare of day, without any little kindly shade between itself and the dull, unfeeling stare of curiosity. The almshouse stood upon rising ground, so one could see it for a long distance. It was a new building, Mansard-roofed[1] and well painted. The village took pride in it: no town far or near had such a house for the poor. It was so fine and costly that the village did not feel able to give its insane paupers separate support in a regular asylum; so they lived in the almshouse with the sane paupers, and there was a padded cell in case they waxed too violent.

Around the almshouse lay the town fields. In summer they were green with corn and potatoes, now they showed ugly plough ridges sloping over the uneven ground, and yellow corn stubble. Beyond the field at the west of the almshouse was a little wood of elms and oaks and wild apple-trees. The yellow leaves had all fallen from the elms and the apple-trees, but most of the brown ones stayed on the oaks.

Polly Moss stood at the west window in the women's sitting-room

---

1. A roof having two slopes on all four sides, with the lower slope almost vertical and the upper almost horizontal.

and gazed over at the trees. "It's cur'us how them oak leaves hang on arter the others have all fell off," she remarked.

A tall old woman sitting beside the stove looked around suddenly. She had singular bright eyes, and a sardonic smile around her mouth. "It's a way they allers have," she returned, scornfully. "Guess there ain't nothin' very cur'us about it. When the oak leaves fall off an' the others hang on, then you can be lookin' for the end of the world; that's goin' to be one of the signs."

"Allers a-harpin' on the end of the world," growled another old woman, in a deep bass voice. "I've got jest about sick on't. Seems as if I should go crazy myself, hearin' on't the whole time." She was sewing a seam in coarse cloth, and she sat on a stool on the other side of the stove. She was short and stout, and she sat with a heavy settle as if she were stuffed with lead.

The tall old woman took no further notice. She sat rigidly straight, and fixed her bright eyes upon the top of the door, and her sardonic smile deepened.

The stout old woman gave an ugly look at her; then she sewed with more impetus. Now and then she muttered something in her deep voice.

There were, besides herself, three old women in the room—Polly Moss, the tall one, and a pretty one in a white cap and black dress. There was also a young woman; she sat in a rocking-chair and leaned her head back. She was handsome, but she kept her mouth parted miserably, and there were ghastly white streaks around it and her nostrils. She never spoke. Her pretty black hair was rough, and her dress sagged at the neck. She had been living out at a large farm, and had overworked. She had no friends or relatives to take her in; so she had come to the almshouse to rest and try to recover. She had no refuge but the almshouse or the hospital, and she had a terrible horror of a hospital. Dreadful visions arose in her ignorant childish mind whenever she thought of one. She had a lover, but he had not been to see her since she came to the almshouse, six weeks before; she wept most of the time over that and her physical misery.

Polly Moss stood at the window until a little boy trudged into the room, bringing his small feet down with a clapping noise. He went up to Polly and twitched her dress. She looked around at him. "Well, now, Tommy, what do ye want?"

"Come out-doors an' play hide an' coot wis me, Polly."

Tommy was a stout little boy. He wore a calico tier[2] that sagged to his heels in the back, and showed in front his little calico trousers. His round face was pleasant and innocent and charming.

Polly put her arms around the boy and hugged him. "Tommy's a darlin'," she said; "can't he give poor Polly a kiss?"

Tommy put up his lips. "Come out-doors an' play hide an' coot wis me," he said again, breathing the words out with the kiss.

2. A pinafore or apron.

"Now, Tommy, jest look out of the winder. Don't he see that it's rainin', hey?"

The child shook his head stubbornly, although he was looking straight at the window, which revealed plainly enough that long sheets of rain were driving over the fields. "Come out-doors and play hide an' coot wis me, Polly."

"Now, Tommy, jest listen to Polly. Don't he know he can't go out-doors when it's rainin' this way? He'd get all wet, an' Polly too. But I'll tell you what Polly an' Tommy can do. We'll jest go out in the hall an' we'll roll the ball. Tommy go run quick an' get his ball."

Tommy raised a shout, and clapped out of the room; his sweet nature was easily diverted. Polly followed him. She had a twisting limp, and was so bent that she was not much taller than Tommy, her little pale triangular face seemed to look from the middle of her flat chest.

"The wust-lookin' objeck," growled the stout old woman when Polly was out of the room: "looks more like an old cat that's had to airn it's own livin' than a human bein'. It 'bout makes me sick to look at her." Her deep tones traveled far; Polly, out in the corridor waiting for Tommy, heard every word.

"She is a dretful-lookin' cretur," assented the pretty old woman. As she spoke she puckered her little red mouth daintily, and drew herself up with a genteel air.

The stout old woman surveyed her contemptuously. "Well, good looks don't amount to much, nohow," said she, "if folks ain't got common-sense to balance 'em. I'd enough sight ruther know a leetle somethin' than have a dolly-face myself."

"Seems to me she is about the dretfulest-lookin' cretur that I ever did see," repeated the pretty old woman, quite unmoved. Aspersions on her intellect never aroused her in the least.

The stout old woman looked baffled. "Jest turn your head a leetle that way, will you, Mis' Handy?" she said, presently.

The pretty old woman turned her head obediently. "What is it?" she inquired, with a conscious simper.

"Jest turn your head a leetle more. Yes, it's funny I ain't never noticed it afore. Your nose is a leetle grain crooked—ain't it, Mis' Handy?"

Mrs. Handy's face turned a deep pink—even her little ears and her delicate old neck were suffused; her blue eyes looked like an enraged bird's. "Crooked! H'm! I shouldn't think that folks that's got a nose like some folks had better say much about other folks' noses. There can't nobody tell me nothin' about my nose; I know all about it. Folks that wouldn't wipe their feet on some folks, nor look twice at 'em, has praised it. My nose ain't crooked an' never was, an' if anybody says so it's 'cause they're so spity,[3] 'cause they're so mortal homely themselves. Guess I know." She drew breath, and paused for

3. Spiteful.

a return shot, but she got none. The stout old woman sewed and chuckled to herself, the tall one still fixed her eyes upon the top of the door, and the young woman leaned back with her lips parted, and her black eyes rolled.

The pretty old woman began again in defence of her nose; she talked fiercely, and kept feeling of it. Finally she arose and went out of the room with a flirt.

Then the stout old woman laughed. "She's gone to look at her nose in the lookin'-glass, an' make sure it ain't crooked: if it ain't a good joke!" she exclaimed, delightedly.

But she got no response. The young woman never stirred, and the tall old one only lowered her gaze from the door to the stove, which she regarded disapprovingly. "I call it the devil's stove," she remarked, after a while.

The stout old woman gave a grunt and sewed her seam; she was done with talking to such an audience. The shouts of children out in the corridor could be heard. "Pesky young ones!" she muttered.

In the corridor Polly Moss played ball with the children. She never caught the ball, and she threw it with weak, aimless jerks; her back ached, but she was patient, and her face was full of simple childish smiles. There were two children besides Tommy—his sister and a little boy.

The corridor was long; doors in both sides led into the paupers' bedrooms. Suddenly one of the doors flew open, and a little figure shot out. She went down the corridor with a swift trot like a child. She had on nothing but a woollen petticoat and a calico waist;[4] she held her head down, and her narrow shoulders worked as she ran; her mop of soft white hair flew out. The children looked around at her; she was a horrible caricature of themselves.

The stout old woman came pressing out of the sitting-room. She went directly to the room that the running figure had left, and peered in; then she looked around significantly. "I knowed it," she said; "it's tore all to pieces agin. I'd jest been thinkin' to myself that Sally was dretful still, an' I'd bet she was pullin' her bed to pieces. There 'tis, an' made up jest as nice a few minutes ago! I'm goin' to see Mis' Arms."

Mrs. Arms was the matron. The old woman went off with an important air, and presently she returned with her. The matron was a large woman with a calm, benignant, and weary face.

Polly Moss continued to play ball, but several other old women had assembled, and they all talked volubly. They demonstrated that Sally had torn her bed to pieces, that it had been very nicely made, and that she should be punished.

The matron listened; she did not say much. Then she returned to the kitchen, where she was preparing dinner. Some of the paupers assisted her. An old man, with his baggy trousers hitched high, chopped some-

4. An undergarment, worn especially by children, to which petticoats and drawers are buttoned.

thing in a tray, an old woman peeled potatoes, and a young one washed pans at the sink. The young woman, as she washed, kept looking over her shoulder and rolling her dark eyes at the other people in the room. She was mindful of every motion behind her back.

Mrs. Arms herself worked and directed the others. When dinner was ready the old man clanged a bell in the corridor, and everybody flocked to the dining-room except the young woman at the kitchen sink; she still stood there washing dishes. The dinner was coarse and abundant. The paupers, with the exception of the sick young woman, ate with gusto. The children were all hearty, and although the world had lost all its savor for the hearts and minds of the old ones, it was still somewhat salt to their palates. Now that their thoughts had ceased reaching and grasping, they could still put out their tongues, for that primitive instinct of life with which they had been born still survived and gave them pleasure. In this world it is the child only that is immortal.

The old people and the children ate after the same manner. There was a loud smacking of lips and gurgling noises. The rain drove against the windows of the dining-room, with its bare floor, its board tables and benches, and rows of feeding paupers. The smooth yellow heads of the children seemed to catch all the light in the room. Once in a while they raised imperious clamors. The overseer sat at one end of the table and served the beef. He was stout, and had a handsome, heavy face.

The meal was nearly finished when there was a crash of breaking crockery, a door slammed, and there was a wild shriek out in the corridor. The overseer and one of the old men who was quite able-bodied sprang and rushed out of the room. The matron followed, and the children tagged at her heels. The others continued feeding as if nothing had happened. "That Agnes is wuss agin," remarked the stout old woman. "I've seed it a-comin' on fer a couple of days. They'd orter have put her in the cell yesterday; I told Mis' Arms so, but they're allers puttin' off, an' puttin' off."

"They air a-takin' on her up to the cell now," said the pretty old woman; and she brought around her knifeful of cabbage with a side-wise motion, and stretched her little red mouth to receive it.

Out in the corridor shriek followed shriek; there were loud voices and scuffling. The children were huddled in the doorway, peeping, but the old paupers continued to eat. The sick young woman laid down her knife and fork and wept.

Presently the shrieks and the scuffling grew faint in the distance; the children had followed on. Then, after a little, they all returned and the dinner was finished.

After dinner, when the women paupers had done their share of the clearing away, they were again assembled in their sitting-room. The windows were cloudy with fine mist; the rain continued to drive past them from over the yellow stubbly fields. There was a good fire in the stove, and the room was hot and close. The stout old woman sewed again on her coarse seam, the others were idle. There were now six old women present; one of them was the little creature whom they called Sally. She sat close to the stove, bent over and motionless. Her clothing hardly covered her. The sick young woman was absent; she was lying down on the lounge in the matron's room, and the children too were in there.

Polly Moss sat by the window. The old women began talking among themselves. The pretty old one had taken off her cap and had it in her lap, perking up the lace and straightening it. It was a flimsy rag, like a soiled cobweb. The stout old woman cast a contemptuous glance at it. She raised her nose and her upper lip scornfully. "I don't see how you can wear that nasty thing nohow, Mis' Handy," said she.

Mrs. Handy flushed pink again. She bridled and began to speak, then she looked at the little soft soiled mass in her lap, and paused. She had not the force of character to proclaim black white while she was looking at it. Had the old cap been in the bureau drawer, or even on her head, she might have defended it to the death, but here before her eyes it silenced her.

But after her momentary subsidence she aroused herself; her blue eyes gleamed dimly at the stout old woman. "It was a handsome cap when it was new, anyhow!" said she; "better'n some folks ever had, I'll warrant. Folks that ain't got no caps at all can't afford to be flingin' at them that has, if they ain't quite so nice as they was. You'd orter have seen the cap I had when my daughter was married! All white wrought lace, an' bows of pink ribbon, an' long streamers, an' some artificial roses on't. I don't s'pose you ever seen anythin' like it, Mis' Paine."

The stout woman was Mrs. Paine. "Mebbe I ain't," said she, sarcastically.

The tall old woman chimed in suddenly; her thin, nervous voice clanged after the others like a sharply struck bell. "I ain't never had any caps to speak of," she proclaimed; "never thought much of 'em, anyhow; heatin' things; an' I never heard that folks in heaven wore caps. But I have had some good clothes. I've got a piece of silk in my bureau drawer. That silk would stand alone. An' I had a good thibet;[5] there was rows an' rows of velvet ribbon on it. I always had good clothes; my husband, he wanted I should, an' he got 'em fer me. I airned some myself, too. I 'ain't got any now, an' I dunno as I care if I ain't, fer the signs are increasin'."

"Allers a-harpin' on that," muttered the stout old woman.

"I had a handsome blue silk when I was marri'd," vouchsafed Mrs. Handy.

"I've seen the piece of it," returned the tall one; "it ain't near so thick as mine is."

---

5. E.g., tibet; originally used to refer to wool obtained from Tibet and to garments made from this wool or in imitation of it; later and here, reference is to a fine cloth used for women's dresses.

The old woman who had not been present in the morning now spoke. She had been listening with a superior air. She was the only one in the company who had possessed considerable property, and had fallen from a widely differing estate. She was tall and dark and gaunt; she towered up next the pretty old woman like a scraggy old pine beside a faded lily. She was a single woman, and she had lost all her property through an injudicious male relative. "Well," she proclaimed, "everybody knows I've had things if I ain't got 'em now. There I had a whole house, with Brussels carpets[6] on all the rooms except the kitchen, an' stuffed furniture, an' beddin' packed away in chists, an' bureau drawers full of things. An' I ruther think I've had silk dresses an' bunnits an' caps."

"I remember you had a real handsome blue bunnit once, but it warn't so becomin' as some you'd had, you was so dark-complected," remarked the pretty old woman, in a soft, spiteful voice. "I had a white one, drawn silk, an' white feathers on't, when I was married, and they all said it was real becomin'. I was allers real white myself. I had a white muslin dress with a flounce on it, once, too, an' a black silk spencer cape."

"I had a fitch tippet[7] an' muff that cost twenty-five dollars," remarked the stout old woman, emphatically, "an' a cashmire shawl."

"I had two cashmire shawls, an' my tippet cost fifty dollars," retorted the dark old woman, with dignity.

"My fust baby had an elegant blue cashmire cloak, all worked with silk as deep as that," said Mrs. Handy. She now had the old cap on her head, and looked more assertive.

"Mine had a little wagon with a velvet cushion to ride in; an' I had a tea-set, real chiny, with a green sprig on't," said the stout old woman.

"I had a Brittany teapot," returned Mrs. Handy.

"I had gilt vases as tall as that on my parlor mantelshelf," said the dark old woman.

"I had a chiny figger, a girl with a basket of flowers on her arm, once," rejoined the tall one; "it used to set side of the clock. An' when I was fust married I used to live in a white house, with a flower-garden to one side. I can smell them pinks an' roses now, an' I s'pose I allers shall, jest as far as I go."

"I had a pump in my kitchen sink, an' things real handy," said the stout old one; "an' I used to look as well as anybody, an' my husband too, when we went to meetin'. I remember one winter I had a new brown alpaca with velvet buttons, an' he had a new great-coat with a velvet collar."

Suddenly the little cowering Sally raised herself and gave testimony to her own little crumb of past comfort. Her wits were few and scattering, and had been all her days, but the conversation of the other

---

6. Thick, richly patterned carpets made by machine.

7. A "tippet" is a cape or short cloak, often with hanging ends; "fitch" is the fur of the fitchew or polecat, a small, dark brown, weasel-like mammal.

women seemed to set some vibrating into momentary concord. She laughed, and her bleared blue eyes twinkled. "I had a pink caliker gownd once," she quavered out. "Mis' Thompson, she gin it me when I lived there."

"Do hear the poor cretur," said the pretty old woman, with an indulgent air.

Now everybody had spoken but Polly Moss. She sat by the misty window, and her little pale triangular face looked from her sunken chest at the others. This conversation was a usual one. Many and many an afternoon the almshouse old women sat together and bore witness to their past glories. Now they had nothing, but at one time or another they had had something over which to plume themselves and feel that precious pride of possession. Their present was to them a state of simple existence, they regarded their future with a vague resignation; they were none of them thinkers, and there was no case of rapturous piety among them. In their pasts alone they took real comfort, and they kept, as it were, feeling of them to see if they were not still warm with life.

The old women delighted in these inventories and comparing of notes. Polly Moss alone had never spoken. She alone had never had anything in which to take pride. She had been always deformed and poor and friendless. She had worked for scanty pay as long as she was able, and had then drifted and struck on the almshouse, where she had grown old. She had not even a right to the charity of this particular village: this was merely the place where her working powers had failed her; but no one could trace her back to her birthplace, or the town which was responsible for her support. Polly Moss herself did not know—she went humbly where she was told. All her life the world had seemed to her simply standing-ground; she had gotten little more out of it.

Every day, when the others talked, she listened admiringly, and searched her memory for some little past treasure of her own, but she could not remember any. The dim image of a certain delaine dress, with bright flowers scattered over it, which she had once owned, away back in her girlhood, sometimes floated before her eyes when they were talking, and she had a half-mind to mention that, but her heart would fail her. She feared that it was not worthy to be compared with the others' fine departed gowns; it paled before even Sally's pink calico. Polly's poor clothes, covering her pitiful crookedness, had never given her any firm stimulus to gratulation. So she was always silent, and the other old women had come to talk at her. Their conversation acquired a gusto from this listener who could not join in. When a new item of past property was given, there was always a side-glance in Polly's direction.

None of the old women expected to ever hear a word from Polly, but this afternoon, when they had all, down to Sally, testified, she spoke up:

"You'd orter have seen my sister Liddy," said she; her voice was very small, it sounded like the piping of a feeble bird in a bush.

There was a dead silence. The other old women looked at each other. "Didn't know you ever had a sister Liddy," the stout old woman blurted out, finally, with an amazed air.

"My sister Liddy was jest as handsome as a pictur'," Polly returned.

The pretty old woman flushed jealously. "Was she fair-complected?" she inquired.

"She was jest as fair as a lily—a good deal fairer than you ever was, Mis' Handy, an' she had long yaller curls a-hangin' clean down to her waist, an' her cheeks were jest as pink, an' she had the biggest blue eyes I ever see, an' the beautifulest leetle red mouth."

"Lor'!" ejaculated the stout old woman, and the pretty old woman sniffed.

But Polly went on; she was not to be daunted; she had been silent all this time; and now her category poured forth, not piecemeal, but in a flood, upon her astonished hearers.

"Liddy, she could sing the best of anybody anywheres around," she continued; "nobody ever heerd sech singin'. It was so dretful loud an' sweet that you could hear it 'way down the road when the winders was shut. She used to sing in the meetin'-house, she did, an' all the folks used to sit up an' look at her when she begun. She used to wear a black silk dress to meetin', an' a white cashmire shawl, an' a bunnit with a pink wreath around the face, an' she had white kid gloves. Folks used to go to that meetin'-house jest to hear Liddy sing an' see her. They thought 'nough sight more of that than they did of the preachin'.

"Liddy had a feather fan, an' she used to sit an' fan her when she wa'n't singin', an' she allers had scent on her handkercher. An' when meetin' was done in the evenin' all the young fellars used to be crowdin' 'round, an' pushin' and bowin' an' scrapin', a-tryin' to get a chance to see her home. But Liddy she wouldn't look at none of them; she married a real rich fellar from Bostown. He was jest as straight as an arrer, an' he had black eyes an' hair, an' he wore a beautiful coat an' a satin vest, an' he spoke jest as perlite.

"When Liddy was married she had a whole chistful of clothes, real fine cotton cloth, all tucks an' laid-work, an' she had a pair of silk stockin's, an' some white shoes. An' her weddin' dress was white satin, with a great long trail to it, an' she had a lace veil, an' she wore great long ear-drops that shone like everythin'. *An'* she come out bride in a blue silk dress, an' a black lace mantilly, an' a white bunnit trimmed with lutestring ribbon."

"Where did your sister Liddy live arter she was married?" inquired the pretty old woman, with a subdued air.

"She lived in Bostown, an' she had a great big house with a parlor an' settin'-room, an' a room to eat in besides the kitchen. An' she had real velvet carpets on all the floors down to the kitchen, an' great pictur's in gilt frames a-hangin' on all the walls. An' her furnitur' was all stuffed, an' kivered with red velvet, an' she had a pianner, an' great big marble images a-settin' on her mantel-shelf. An' she had a coach with lamps on the sides, an' blue satin cushings, to ride in, an' four horses to draw it, an' a man to drive. An' she allers had a hired girl in the kitchen. I never knowed Liddy to be without a hired girl.

"Liddy's husband, he thought everythin' of her; he never used to come home from his work without he brought her somethin', an' she used to run out to meet him. She was allers dretful lovin', an' had a good disposition. Liddy, she had the beautifulest baby you ever see, an' she had a cradle lined with blue silk to rock him in, an' he had a white silk cloak, an' a leetle lace cap—"

"I shouldn't think your beautiful sister Liddy an' her husband would let you come to the poor-house," interrupted the dark old woman.

"Liddy's dead, or she wouldn't."

"Are her husband an' the baby dead, too?"

"They're all dead," responded Polly Moss. She looked out of the window again, her face was a burning red, and there were tears in her eyes.

There was silence among the other old women. They were at once overawed and incredulous. Polly left the room before long, then they began to discuss the matter. "I dun know whether to believe it or not," said the dark old woman.

"Well, I dun know, neither; I never knowed her to tell anythin' that wa'n't so," responded the stout old one, doubtfully.

The old women could not make up their minds whether to believe or disbelieve. The pretty one was the most incredulous of any. She said openly that she did not believe it possible that such a "homely cretur" as Polly Moss could have had such a handsome sister.

But, credulous or not, their interest and curiosity were lively. Every day Polly Moss was questioned and cross-examined concerning her sister Liddy. She rose to the occasion; she did not often contradict herself, and the glories of her sister were increased daily. Old Polly Moss, her little withered face gleaming with reckless enthusiasm, sang the praises of her sister Liddy as wildly and faithfully as any minnesinger[8] his angel mistress, and the old women listened with ever-increasing bewilderment and awe.

It was two weeks before Polly Moss died with pneumonia that she first mentioned her sister Liddy, and there was not one afternoon until the day when she was taken ill that she did not relate the story, with new and startling additions, to the old women.

Polly was not ill long, she settled meekly down under the disease: her little distorted frame had no resistance in it. She died at three o'clock in the morning. The afternoon before, she seemed better; she was quite rational, and she told the matron that she wanted to see her comrades, the old women. "I've got somethin' to tell 'em, Mis' Arms," Polly whispered, and her eyes were piteous.

8. A German troubadour.

So the other old women came into the room. They stood around Polly's little iron bed and looked at her. "I—want to—tell you—somethin'," she began. But there was a soft rush, and the sick young woman entered. She pressed straight to the matron; she disregarded the others. Her wan face seemed a very lamp of life—to throw a light over and above all present darkness, even of the grave. She moved nimbly; she was so full of joy that her sickly body seemed permeated by it, and almost a spiritual one. She did not appear in the least feeble. She caught the matron's arm. "Charley has come, Mis' Arms!" she cried out. "Charley has come! He's got a house ready. He's goin' to marry me, an' take me home, an' take care of me till I get well. I'm goin' right away!"

The old women all turned away from Polly and stared at the radiant girl. The matron sent her away, with a promise to see her in a few minutes. "Polly's dyin'," she whispered, and the girl stole out with a hushed air, but the light in her face was not dimmed. What was death to her, when she had just stepped on a height of life where one can see beyond it?

"Tell them what you wanted to, now, Polly," said the matron.

"I—want to tell you—somethin'," Polly repeated. "I s'pose I've been dretful wicked, but I ain't never had nothin' in my whole life. I—s'pose the Lord orter have been enough, but it's dretful hard sometimes to keep holt of him, an' not look anywheres else, when you see other folks a-clawin' an' gettin' other things, an' actin' as if they was wuth havin'. I ain't never had nothin' as fur as them other things go; I don't want nothin' else now. I've—got past 'em. I see I don't want nothin' but the Lord. But I used to feel dretful bad an' wicked when I heerd you all talkin' 'bout things you'd had, an' I hadn't never had nothin', so—"Polly Moss stopped talking, and coughed. The matron supported her. The old women nudged each other; their awed, sympathetic, yet sharply inquiring eyes never left her face. The children were peeping in at the open door; old Sally trotted past—she had just torn her bed to pieces. As soon as she got breath enough, Polly Moss finished what she had to say. "I—s'pose I—was dretful wicked," she whispered; "but—I never had any sister Liddy."

Harper's Bazar, 2 March 1889; *A New England Nun,* 1891

A Village Singer

The trees were in full leaf, a heavy south wind was blowing, and there was a loud murmur among the new leaves. The people noticed it, for it was the first time that year that the trees had so murmured in the wind. The spring had come with a rush during the last few days.

The murmur of the trees sounded loud in the village church, where the people sat waiting for the service to begin. The windows were open; it was a very warm Sunday for May.

The church was already filled with this soft sylvan music—the tender harmony of the leaves and the south wind, and the sweet, desultory whistles of birds—when the choir arose and began to sing.

In the center of the row of women singers stood Alma Way. All the people stared at her, and turned their ears critically. She was the new leading soprano. Candace Whitcomb, the old one, who had sung in the choir for forty years, had lately been given her dismissal. The audience considered that her voice had grown too cracked and uncertain on the upper notes. There had been much complaint, and after long deliberation the church-officers had made known their decision as mildly as possible to the old singer. She had sung for the last time the Sunday before, and Alma Way had been engaged to take her place. With the exception of the organist, the leading soprano was the only paid musician in the large choir. The salary was very modest, still the village people considered it large for a young woman. Alma was from the adjoining village of East Derby; she had quite a local reputation as a singer.

Now she fixed her large solemn blue eyes; her long, delicate face, which had been pretty, turned paler; the blue flowers on her bonnet trembled; her little thin gloved hands, clutching the singing-book, shook perceptibly; but she sang out bravely. That most formidable mountain-height of the world, self-distrust and timidity, arose before her, but her nerves were braced for its ascent. In the midst of the hymn she had a solo; her voice rang out piercingly sweet; the people nodded admiringly at each other; but suddenly there was a stir; all the faces turned toward the windows on the south side of the church. Above the din of the wind and the birds, above Alma Way's sweetly straining tones, arose another female voice, singing another hymn to another tune.

"It's her," the women whispered to each other; they were half aghast, half smiling.

Candace Whitcomb's cottage stood close to the south side of the church. She was playing on her parlor organ, and singing, to drown out the voice of her rival.

Alma caught her breath; she almost stopped; the hymn-book waved like a fan; then she went on. But the long husky drone of the parlor organ and the shrill clamor of the other voice seemed louder than anything else.

When the hymn was finished, Alma sat down. She felt faint; the woman next her slipped a peppermint into her hand. "It ain't worth minding," she whispered, vigorously. Alma tried to smile; down in the audience a young man was watching her with a kind of fierce pity.

In the last hymn Alma had another solo. Again the parlor organ droned above the carefully delicate accompaniment of the church organ, and again Candace Whitcomb's voice clamored forth in another tune.

After the benediction, the other singers pressed around Alma. She did not say much in return for their expressions of indignation and sympathy. She wiped her eyes furtively once or twice, and tried to smile. William Emmons, the choir leader, elderly, stout, and smooth-faced, stood over her, and raised his voice. He was the old musical dignitary of the village, the leader of the choral club and the singing-schools. "A most outrageous proceeding," he said. People had coupled his name with Candace Whitcomb's. The old bachelor tenor and old maiden soprano had been wont to walk together to her home next door after the Saturday night rehearsals, and they had sung duets to the parlor organ. People had watched sharply her old face, on which the blushes of youth sat pitifully, when William Emmons entered the singing-seats. They wondered if he would ever ask her to marry him.

And now he said further to Alma Way that Candace Whitcomb's voice had failed utterly of late, that she sang shockingly, and ought to have had sense enough to know it.

When Alma went down into the audience-room, in the midst of the chattering singers, who seemed to have descended, like birds, from song flights to chirps, the minister approached her. He had been waiting to speak to her. He was a steady-faced, fleshy old man, who had preached from that one pulpit over forty years. He told Alma, in his slow way, how much he regretted the annoyance to which she had been subjected, and intimated that he would endeavor to prevent a recurrence of it. "Miss Whitcomb—must be—reasoned with," said he; he had a slight hesitation of speech, not an impediment. It was as if his thoughts did not slide readily into his words, although both were present. He walked down the aisle with Alma, and bade her good-morning when he saw Wilson Ford waiting for her in the door-way. Everybody knew that Wilson Ford and Alma were lovers;[1] they had been for the last ten years.

Alma colored softly, and made a little imperceptible motion with her head; her silk dress and the lace on her mantle fluttered, but she did not speak. Neither did Wilson, although they had not met before that day. They did not look at each other's faces—they seemed to see each other without that—and they walked along side by side.

They reached the gate before Candace Whitcomb's little house. Wilson looked past the front yard, full of pink and white spikes on flowering bushes, at the lace-curtained windows; a thin white profile, stiffly inclined, apparently over a book, was visible at one of them. Wilson gave his head a shake. He was a stout man, with features so strong that they overcame his flesh. "I'm going up home with you, Alma," said he; "and then—I'm just coming back, to give Aunt Candace one blowing up."

"Oh, don't, Wilson."

"Yes, I shall. If you want to stand this kind of a thing you may; I sha'n't."

---

1. Sweethearts.

"There's no need of your talking to her. Mr. Pollard's going to."

"Did he say he was?"

"Yes. I think he's going in before the afternoon meeting, from what he said."

"Well, there's one thing about it, if she does that thing again this afternoon, I'll go in there and break that old organ up into kindling-wood." Wilson set his mouth hard, and shook his head again.

Alma gave little side glances up at him, her tone was deprecatory, but her face was full of soft smiles. "I suppose she does feel dreadfully about it," said she. "I can't help feeling kind of guilty, taking her place."

"I don't see how you're to blame. It's outrageous, her acting so."

"The choir gave her a photograph album last week, didn't they?"

"Yes. They went there last Thursday night, and gave her an album and a surprise-party. She ought to behave herself."

"Well, she's sung there so long, I suppose it must be dreadful hard for her to give it up."

Other people going home from church were very near Wilson and Alma. She spoke softly that they might not hear; he did not lower his voice in the least. Presently Alma stopped before a gate.

"What are you stopping here for?" asked Wilson.

"Minnie Lansing wanted me to come and stay with her this noon."

"You're going home with me."

"I'm afraid I'll put your mother out."

"Put mother out! I told her you were coming, this morning. She's got all ready for you. Come along; don't stand here."

He did not tell Alma of the pugnacious spirit with which his mother had received the announcement of her coming, and how she had stayed at home to prepare the dinner, and make a parade of her hard work and her injury.

Wilson's mother was the reason why he did not marry Alma. He would not take his wife home to live with her, and was unable to support separate establishments. Alma was willing enough to be married and put up with Wilson's mother, but she did not complain of his decision. Her delicate blond features grew sharper, and her blue eyes more hollow. She had had a certain fine prettiness, but now she was losing it, and beginning to look old, and there was a prim, angular, old maiden carriage about her narrow shoulders.

Wilson never noticed it, and never thought of Alma as not possessed of eternal youth, or capable of losing or regretting it.

"Come along, Alma," said he; and she followed meekly after him down the street.

Soon after they passed Candace Whitcomb's house, the minister went up the front walk and rang the bell. The pale profile at the window had never stirred as he opened the gate and came up the walk. However, the door was promptly opened, in response to his ring. "Good-morning, Miss Whitcomb," said the minister.

"*Good*-morning." Candace gave a sweeping toss of her head as she spoke. There was a fierce upward curl to her thin nostrils and her lips, as if she scented an adversary. Her black eyes had two tiny cold sparks of fury in them, like an enraged bird's. She did not ask the minister to enter, but he stepped lumberingly into the entry, and she retreated rather than led the way into her little parlor. He settled into the great rocking-chair and wiped his face. Candace sat down again in her old place by the window. She was a tall woman, but very slender and full of pliable motions, like a blade of grass.

"It's a—very pleasant day," said the minister.

Candace made no reply. She sat still, with her head drooping. The wind stirred the looped lace-curtains; a tall rose-tree outside the window waved; soft shadows floated through the room. Candace's parlor organ stood in front of an open window that faced the church; on the corner was a pitcher with a bunch of white lilacs. The whole room was scented with them. Presently the minister looked over at them and sniffed pleasantly.

"You have—some beautiful—lilacs there."

Candace did not speak. Every line of her slender figure looked flexible, but it was a flexibility more resistant than rigor.

The minister looked at her. He filled up the great rocking-chair; his arms in his shiny black coat-sleeves rested squarely and comfortably upon the hair-cloth arms of the chair.

"Well, Miss Whitcomb, I suppose I—may as well come to—the point. There was—a little—matter I wished to speak to you about. I don't suppose you were—at least I can't suppose you were—aware of it, but—this morning, during the singing by the choir, you played and— sung a little too—loud. That is, with—the windows open. It—disturbed us—a little. I hope you won't feel hurt—my dear Miss Candace, but I knew you would rather I would speak of it, for I knew—you would be more disturbed than anybody else at the idea of such a thing."

Candace did not raise her eyes; she looked as if his words might sway her through the window. "I ain't disturbed at it," said she. "I did it on purpose; I meant to."

The minister looked at her.

"You needn't look at me. I know jest what I'm about. I sung the way I did on purpose, an' I'm goin' to do it again, an' I'd like to see you stop me. I guess I've got a right to set down to my own organ, an' sing a psalm tune on a Sabbath day, 'f I want to; an' there ain't no amount of talkin' an' palaverin' a-goin' to stop me. See there!" Candace swung aside her skirts a little. "Look at that!"

The minister looked. Candace's feet were resting on a large red-plush photograph album.

"Makes a nice footstool, don't it?" said she.

The minister looked at the album, then at her; there was a slowly gathering alarm in his face; he began to think she was losing her reason.

Candace had her eyes full upon him now, and her head up. She laughed, and her laugh was almost a snarl. "Yes; I thought it would make a beautiful footstool," said she. "I've been wantin' one for some time." Her tone was full of vicious irony.

"Why, miss—" began the minister; but she interrupted him:

"I know what you're a-goin' to say, Mr. Pollard, an' now I'm goin' to have my say; I'm a-goin' to speak. I want to know what you think of folks that pretend to be Christians treatin' anybody the way they've treated me? Here I've sung in those singin'-seats forty year. I 'ain't never missed a Sunday, except when I've been sick, an' I've gone an' sung a good many times when I'd better been in bed, an' now I'm turned out without a word of warnin'. My voice is jest as good as ever 'twas; there can't anybody say it ain't. It wa'n't ever quite so high-pitched as that Way girl's, mebbe; but she flats the whole durin' time. My voice is as good an' high today as it was twenty year ago; an' if it wa'n't, I'd like to know where the Christianity comes in. I'd like to know if it wouldn't be more to the credit of folks in a church to keep an old singer an' an old minister, if they didn't sing an' hold forth quite so smart as they used to, ruther than turn 'em off an' hurt their feelin's. I guess it would be full as much to the glory of God. S'pose the singin' an' the preachin' wa'n't quite so good, what difference would it make? Salvation don't hang on anybody's hittin' a high note, that I ever heard of. Folks are gettin' as high-steppin' an' fussy in a meetin'-house as they are in a tavern, nowadays. S'pose they should turn you off, Mr. Pollard, come an' give you a photograph album, an' tell you to clear out, how'd you like it? I ain't findin' any fault with your preachin'; it was always good enough to suit me; but it don't stand to reason folks'll be as took up with your sermons as when you was a young man. You can't expect it. S'pose they should turn you out in your old age, an' call in some young bob squirt,[2] how'd you feel? There's William Emmons, too; he's three years older'n I am, if he does lead the choir an' run all the singin' in town. If my voice has gi'en out, it stan's to reason his has. It ain't, though. William Emmons sings jest as well as he ever did. Why don't they turn him out the way they have me, an' give him a photograph album? I dun know but it would be a good idea to send everybody, as soon as they get a little old an' gone by, an' young folks begin to push, onto some desert island, an' give 'em each a photograph album. Then they can sit down an' look at pictures the rest of their days. Mebbe government'll take it up.

"There they come here last week Thursday, all the choir, jest about eight o'clock in the evenin', an' pretended they'd come to give me a nice little surprise. Surprise! h'm! Brought cake an' oranges, an' was jest as nice as they could be, an' I was real tickled. I never had a surprise-party before in my life. Jenny Carr she played, an' they wanted me to sing alone, an' I never suspected a thing. I've been mad

2. An insignificant but arrogant person.

ever since to think what a fool I was, an' how they must have laughed in their sleeves.

"When they'd gone I found this photograph album on the table, all done up as nice as you please, an' directed to Miss Candace Whitcomb from her many friends, an' I opened it, an' there was the letter inside givin' me notice to quit.

"If they'd gone about it any decent way, told me right out honest that they'd got tired of me, an' wanted Alma Way to sing instead of me, I wouldn't minded so much; I should have been hurt 'nough, for I'd felt as if some that had pretended to be my friends wa'n't; but it wouldn't have been as bad as this. They said in the letter that they'd always set great value on my services, an' it wa'n't from any lack of appreciation that they turned me off, but they thought the duty was gettin' a little too arduous for me. H'm! I hadn't complained. If they'd turned me right out fair an' square, showed me the door, an' said, 'Here, you get out,' but to go an' spill molasses, as it were, all over the threshold, tryin' to make me think it's all nice an' sweet—

"I'd sent that photograph album back quick's I could pack it, but I didn't know who started it, so I've used it for a footstool. It's all it's good for, 'cordin' to my way of thinkin'. An' I ain't been particular to get the dust off my shoes before I used it neither."

Mr. Pollard, the minister, sat staring. He did not look at Candace; his eyes were fastened upon a point straight ahead. He had a look of helpless solidity, like a block of granite. This country minister, with his steady, even temperament, treading with heavy precision his one track for over forty years, having nothing new in his life except the new sameness of the seasons, and desiring nothing new, was incapable of understanding a woman like this, who had lived as quietly as he, and all the time held within herself the elements of revolution. He could not account for such violence, such extremes, except in a loss of reason. He had a conviction that Candace was getting beyond herself. He himself was not a typical New-Englander; the national elements of character were not pronounced in him. He was aghast and bewildered at this outbreak, which was tropical, and more than tropical, for a New England nature has a floodgate, and the power which it releases is an accumulation. Candace Whitcomb had been a quiet woman, so delicately resolute that the quality had been scarcely noticed in her, and her ambition had been unsuspected. Now the resolution and the ambition appeared raging over her whole self.

She began to talk again. "I've made up my mind that I'm goin' to sing Sundays the way I did this mornin', an' I don't care what folks say," said she. "I've made up my mind that I'm goin' to take matters into my own hands. I'm goin' to let folks see that I ain't trod down quite flat, that there's a little rise left in me. I ain't goin' to give up beat yet a while; an' I'd like to see anybody stop me. If I ain't got a right to play a psalm tune on my organ an' sing, I'd like to know. If you don't like it, you can move the meetin'-house."

Candace had had an inborn reverence for clergymen. She had always treated Mr. Pollard with the utmost deference. Indeed, her manner toward all men had been marked by a certain delicate stiffness and dignity. Now she was talking to the old minister with the homely freedom with which she might have addressed a female gossip[3] over the back fence. He could not say much in return. He did not feel competent to make headway against any such tide of passion; all he could do was to let it beat against him. He made a few expostulations, which increased Candace's vehemence; he expressed his regret over the whole affair, and suggested that they should kneel and ask the guidance of the Lord in the matter, that she might be led to see it all in a different light.

Candace refused flatly. "I don't see any use prayin' about it," said she. "I don't think the Lord's got much to do with it, anyhow."

It was almost time for the afternoon service when the minister left. He had missed his comfortable noontide rest, through this encounter with his revolutionary parishioner. After the minister had gone, Candace sat by the window and waited. The bell rang, and she watched the people file past. When her nephew Wilson Ford with Alma appeared, she grunted to herself. "She's thin as a rail," said she; "guess there won't be much left of her by the time Wilson gets her. Little soft-spoken nippin' thing, she wouldn't make him no kind of a wife, anyway. Guess it's jest as well."

When the bell had stopped tolling, and all the people entered the church, Candace went over to her organ and seated herself. She arranged a singing-book before her, and sat still, waiting. Her thin, colorless neck and temples were full of beating pulses; her black eyes were bright and eager; she leaned stiffly over toward the music-rack, to hear better. When the church organ sounded out she straightened herself; her long skinny fingers pressed her own organ-keys with nervous energy. She worked the pedals with all her strength; all her slender body was in motion. When the first notes of Alma's solo began, Candace sang. She had really possessed a fine voice, and it was wonderful how little she had lost it. Straining her throat with jealous fury, her notes were still for the main part true. Her voice filled the whole room; she sang with wonderful fire and expression. That, at least, mild little Alma Way could never emulate. She was full of steadfastness and unquestioning constancy, but there were in her no smouldering fires of ambition and resolution. Music was not to her what it had been to her older rival. To this obscure woman, kept relentlessly by circumstances in a narrow track, singing in the village choir had been as much as Italy was to Napoleon[4]—and now on her island of exile she was still showing fight.

After the church service was done, Candace left the organ and went

3. A close friend or neighbor.
4. Napoleon Bonaparte's appointment as com- mander-in-chief of the army of Italy in 1796 marked the beginning of his rise to power.

over to her old chair by the window. Her knees felt weak, and shook under her. She sat down, and leaned back her head. There were red spots on her cheeks. Pretty soon she heard a quick slam of her gate, and an impetuous tread on the gravel-walk. She looked up, and there was her nephew Wilson Ford hurrying up to the door. She cringed a little, then she settled herself more firmly in her chair.

Wilson came into the room with a rush. He left the door open, and the wind slammed it to after him.

"Aunt Candace, where are you?" he called out, in a loud voice.

She made no reply. He looked around fiercely, and his eyes seemed to pounce upon her.

"Look here, Aunt Candace," said he, "are you crazy?" Candace said nothing. "Aunt Candace!" She did not seem to see him. "If you don't answer me," said Wilson, "I'll just go over there and pitch that old organ out of the window!"

"Wilson Ford!" said Candace, in a voice that was almost a scream.

"Well, what say! What have you got to say for yourself, acting the way you have? I tell you what 'tis, Aunt Candace, I won't stand it."

"I'd like to see you help yourself."

"I will help myself. I'll pitch that old organ out of the window, and then I'll board up the window on that side of your house. Then we'll see."

"It ain't your house, and it won't never be."

"Who said it was my house? You're my aunt, and I've got a little lookout for the credit of the family. Aunt Candace, what are you doing this way for?"

"It don't make no odds what I'm doin' so for. I ain't bound to give my reasons to a young fellar like you, if you do act so mighty toppin'. But I'll tell you one thing, Wilson Ford, after the way you've spoke today, you sha'n't never have one cent of my money, an' you can't never marry that Way girl if you don't have it. You can't never take her home to live with your mother, an' this house would have been mighty nice an' convenient for you some day. Now you won't get it. I'm goin' to make another will. I'd made one, if you did but know it. Now you won't get a cent of my money, you nor your mother neither. An' I ain't goin' to live a dreadful while longer, neither. Now I wish you'd go home; I want to lay down. I'm 'bout sick."

Wilson could not get another word from his aunt. His indignation had not in the least cooled. Her threat of disinheriting him did not cow him at all; he had too much rough independence, and indeed his aunt Candace's house had always been too much of an air-castle[5] for him to contemplate seriously. Wilson, with his burly frame and his headlong common-sense, could have little to do with air-castles, had he been hard enough to build them over graves. Still, he had not admitted that he never could marry Alma. All his hopes were based upon a rise in his

---

5. Castle in the air, a dream.

own fortunes, not by some sudden convulsion, but by his own long and steady labor. Some time, he thought, he should have saved enough for the two homes.

He went out of his aunt's house still storming. She arose after the door had shut behind him, and got out into the kitchen. She thought that she would start a fire and make a cup of tea. She had not eaten anything all day. She put some kindling-wood into the stove and touched a match to it; then she went back to the sitting-room, and settled down again into the chair by the window. The fire in the kitchen-stove roared, and the light wood was soon burned out. She thought no more about it. She had not put on the teakettle. Her head ached, and once in a while she shivered. She sat at the window while the afternoon waned and the dusk came on. At seven o'clock the meeting bell rang again, and the people flocked by. This time she did not stir. She had shut her parlor organ. She did not need to out-sing her rival this evening; there was only congregational singing at the Sunday-night prayer-meeting.

She sat still until it was nearly time for meeting to be done; her head ached harder and harder, and she shivered more. Finally she arose. "Guess I'll go to bed," she muttered. She went about the house, bent over and shaking, to lock the doors. She stood a minute in the back door, looking over the fields to the woods. There was a red light over there. "The woods are on fire," said Candace. She watched with a dull interest the flames roll up, withering and destroying the tender green spring foliage. The air was full of smoke, although the fire was half a mile away.

Candace locked the door and went in. The trees with their delicate garlands of new leaves, with the new nests of song birds, might fall, she was in the roar of an intenser fire; the growths of all her springs and the delicate wontedness of her whole life were going down in it. Candace went to bed in her little room off the parlor, but she could not sleep. She lay awake all night. In the morning she crawled to the door and hailed a little boy who was passing. She bade him go for the doctor as quickly as he could, then to Mrs. Ford's, and ask her to come over. She held on to the door while she was talking. The boy stood staring wonderingly at her. The spring wind fanned her face. She had drawn on a dress skirt and put her shawl over her shoulders, and her gray hair was blowing over her red cheeks.

She shut the door and went back to her bed. She never arose from it again. The doctor and Mrs. Ford came and looked after her, and she lived a week. Nobody but herself thought until the very last that she would die; the doctor called her illness merely a light run of fever; she had her senses fully.

But Candace gave up at the first. "It's my last sickness," she said to Mrs. Ford that morning when she first entered; and Mrs. Ford had laughed at the notion; but the sick woman held to it. She did not seem to suffer much physical pain; she only grew weaker and weaker, but she was distressed mentally. She did not talk much, but her eyes followed everybody with an agonized expression.

On Wednesday William Emmons came to inquire for her. Candace heard him out in the parlor. She tried to raise herself on one elbow that she might listen better to his voice.

"William Emmons come in to ask how you was," Mrs. Ford said, after he was gone.

"I—heard him," replied Candace. Presently she spoke again. "Nancy," said she, "where's that photograph album?"

"On the table," replied her sister, hesitatingly.

"Mebbe—you'd better—brush it up a little."

"Well."

Sunday morning Candace wished that the minister should be asked to come in at the noon intermission. She had refused to see him before. He came and prayed with her, and she asked his forgiveness for the way she had spoken the Sunday before. "I—hadn't ought to—spoke so," said she. "I was—dreadful wrought up."

"Perhaps it was your sickness coming on," said the minister, soothingly.

Candace shook her head. "No—it wa'n't. I hope the Lord will—forgive me."

After the minister had gone, Candace still appeared unhappy. Her pitiful eyes followed her sister everywhere with the mechanical persistency of a portrait.

"What is it you want, Candace?" Mrs. Ford said at last. She had nursed her sister faithfully, but once in a while her impatience showed itself.

"Nancy!"

"What say?"

"I wish—you'd go out when—meetin's done, an'—head off Alma an' Wilson, an'—ask 'em to come in. I feel as if—I'd like to—hear her sing."

Mrs. Ford stared. "Well," said she.

The meeting was now in session. The windows were all open, for it was another warm Sunday. Candace lay listening to the music when it began, and a look of peace came over her face. Her sister had smoothed her hair back, and put on a clean cap. The white curtain in the bedroom window waved in the wind like a white sail. Candace almost felt as if she were better, but the thought of death seemed easy.

Mrs. Ford at the parlor window watched for the meeting to be out. When the people appeared, she ran down the walk and waited for Alma and Wilson. When they came she told them what Candace wanted, and they all went in together.

"Here's Alma an' Wilson, Candace," said Mrs. Ford, leading them to the bedroom door.

Candace smiled. "Come in," she said, feebly. And Alma and Wilson entered and stood beside the bed. Candace continued to look at them, the smile straining her lips.

"Wilson!"

"What is it, Aunt Candace?"

"I ain't altered that—will. You an' Alma can—come here an'— live—when I'm—gone. Your mother won't mind livin' alone. Alma can have—all—my things."

"Don't, Aunt Candace." Tears were running over Wilson's cheeks, and Alma's delicate face was all of a quiver.

"I thought—maybe—Alma 'd be willin' to—sing for me," said Candace.

"What do you want me to sing?" Alma asked, in a trembling voice.

" 'Jesus, lover of my soul.' "

Alma, standing there beside Wilson, began to sing. At first she could hardly control her voice, then she sang sweetly and clearly.

Candace lay and listened. Her face had a holy and radiant expression. When Alma stopped singing it did not disappear, but she looked up and spoke, and it was like a secondary glimpse of the old shape of a forest tree through the smoke and flame of the transfiguring fire the instant before it falls. "You flatted a little on—soul," said Candace.

Harper's Bazar, 6 July 1889; *A New England Nun*, 1891

A Church Mouse

"I never heard of a woman's bein' saxton."[1]

"I dun' know what difference that makes; I don't see why they shouldn't have women saxtons as well as men saxtons, for my part, nor nobody else neither. They'd keep dusted 'nough sight cleaner. I've seen the dust layin' on my pew thick enough to write my name in a good many times, an' ain't said nothin' about it. An' I ain't goin' to say nothin' now again Joe Sowen, now he's dead an' gone. He did jest as well as most men do. Men git in a good many places where they don't belong, an' where they set as awkward as a cow on a hen-roost, jest because they push in ahead of women. I ain't blamin' 'em; I s'pose if I could push in I should, jest the same way. But there ain't no reason that I can see, nor nobody else neither, why a woman shouldn't be saxton."

Hetty Fifield stood in the rowen hay-field before Caleb Gale. He was a deacon, the chairman of the selectmen, and the rich and influential man of the village. One looking at him would not have guessed it. There was nothing imposing about his lumbering figure in his calico shirt and baggy trousers. However, his large face, red and moist with

---

1. I.e., sexton; a person responsible for maintenance in a church and sometimes for bell-ringing or supervising burials.

perspiration, scanned the distant horizon with a stiff and reserved air; he did not look at Hetty.

"How'd you go to work to ring the bell?" said he. "It would have to be tolled, too, if anybody died."

"I'd jest as lief ring that little meetin'-house bell as to stan' out here an' jingle a cow-bell," said Hetty; "an' as for tollin', I'd jest as soon toll the bell for Methusaleh,[2] if he was livin' here! I'd laugh if I ain't got strength 'nough for that."

"It takes a kind of a knack."

"If I ain't got as much knack as old Joe Sowen ever had, I'll give up the ship."

"You couldn't tend the fires."

"Couldn't tend the fires—when I've cut an' carried in all the wood I've burned for forty year! Couldn't keep the fires a-goin' in them two little wood-stoves!"

"It's consider'ble work to sweep the meetin'-house."

"I guess I've done 'bout as much work as to sweep that little meeting'-house, I ruther guess I have."

"There's one thing you ain't thought of."

"What's that?"

"Where'd you live? All old Sowen got for bein' saxton was twenty dollar a year, an' we couldn't pay a woman so much as that. You wouldn't have enough to pay for your livin' anywheres."

"Where am I goin' to live whether I'm saxton or not?"

Caleb Gale was silent.

There was a wind blowing, the rowen hay drifted round Hetty like a brown-green sea touched with ripples of blue and gold by the asters and golden-rod. She stood in the midst of it like a May-weed that had gathered a slender toughness through the long summer; her brown cotton gown clung about her like a wilting leaf, outlining her harsh little form. She was as sallow as a squaw, and she had pretty black eyes; they were bright, although she was old. She kept them fixed upon Caleb. Suddenly she raised herself upon her toes; the wind caught her dress and made it blow out; her eyes flashed. "I'll tell you where I'm goin' to live," said she. *"I'm going' to live in the meetin'-house."*

Caleb looked at her. *"Goin' to live in the meetin'-house!"*

"Yes, I be."

"Live in the meetin'-house!"

"I'd like to know why not."

"Why—you couldn't—live in the meetin'-house. You're crazy."

Caleb flung out the rake which he was holding, and drew it in full of rowen. Hetty moved around in front of him, he raked imperturbably; she moved again right in the path of the rake, then he stopped. "There ain't no sense in such talk."

"All I want is jest the east corner of the back gall'ry, where the

2. One of the Old Testament patriarchs; he lived for 969 years; see Genesis 5.27.

chimbly goes up. I'll set up my cookin'-stove there, an' my bed, an' I'll curtain it off with my sunflower quilt, to keep off the wind."

"A cookin'-stove an' a bed in the meetin'-house!"

"Mis' Grout she give me that cookin'-stove, an' that bed I've allers slept on, before she died. She give 'em to me before Mary Anne Thomas, an' I moved 'em out. They air settin' out in the yard now, an' if it rains that stove an' that bed will be spoilt. It looks some like rain now. I guess you'd better give me the meetin'-house key right off."

"You don't think you can move that cookin'-stove an' that bed into the meetin'-house—I ain't goin' to stop to hear such talk."

"My worsted-work, all my mottoes I've done, an' my wool flowers, air out there in the yard."

Caleb raked. Hetty kept standing herself about until he was forced to stop, or gather her in with the rowen hay. He looked straight at her, and scowled; the perspiration trickled down his cheeks. "If I go up to the house can Mis' Gale git me the key to the meetin'-house?" said Hetty.

"No, she can't."

"Be you goin' up before long?"

"No, I ain't." Suddenly Caleb's voice changed: it had been full of stubborn vexation, now it was blandly argumentative. "Don't you see it ain't no use talkin' such nonsense, Hetty? You'd better go right along, an' make up your mind it ain't to be thought of."

"Where be I goin' tonight, then?"

"Tonight?"

"Yes; where be I a-goin'?"

"Ain't you got any place to go to?"

"Where do you s'pose I've got any place? Them folks air movin' into Mis' Grout's house, an' they as good as told me to clear out. I ain't got no folks to take me in. I dun' know where I'm goin'; mebbe I can go to your house?"

Caleb gave a start. "We've got company to home," said he, hastily. "I'm 'fraid Mis' Gale wouldn't think it was convenient."

Hetty laughed. "Most everybody in the town has got company," said she.

Caleb dug his rake into the ground as if it were a hoe, then he leaned on it, and stared at the horizon. There was a fringe of yellow birches on the edge of the hay-field; beyond them was a low range of misty blue hills. "You ain't got no place to go to, then?"

"I dun' know of any. There ain't no poor-house here, an' I ain't got no folks."

Caleb stood like a statue. Some crows flew cawing over the field. Hetty waited. "I s'pose that key is where Mis' Gale can find it?" she said, finally.

Caleb turned and threw out his rake with a jerk. "She knows where 'tis; it's hangin' up behind the settin'-room door. I s'pose you can stay there tonight, as long as you ain't got no other place. We shall have to see what can be done."

Hetty scuttled off across the field. "You mustn't take no stove nor bed into the meetin'-house," Caleb called after her; "we can't have that, nohow."

Hetty went on as if she did not hear.

The golden-rod at the sides of the road was turning brown; the asters were in their prime, blue and white ones; here and there were rows of thistles with white tops. The dust was thick; Hetty, when she emerged from Caleb's house, trotted along in a cloud of it. She did not look to the right or left, she kept her small eager face fixed straight ahead, and moved forward like some little animal with the purpose to which it was born strong within it.

Presently she came to a large cottage-house on the right of the road; there she stopped. The front yard was full of furniture, tables and chairs standing among the dahlias and clumps of marigolds. Hetty leaned over the fence at one corner of the yard, and inspected a little knot of household goods set aside from the others. There were a small cooking-stove, a hair trunk, a yellow bedstead stacked up against the fence, and a pile of bedding. Some children in the yard stood in a group and eyed Hetty. A woman appeared in the door—she was small, there was a black smutch on her face, which was haggard with fatigue, and she scowled in the sun as she looked over at Hetty. "Well, got a place to stay in?" said she, in an unexpectedly deep voice.

"Yes, I guess so," replied Hetty.

"I dun' know how in the world I can have you. All the beds will be full—I expect his mother some tonight, an' I'm dreadful stirred up anyhow."

"Everybody's havin' company; I never see anything like it." Hetty's voice was inscrutable. The other woman looked sharply at her.

"You've got a place, ain't you?" she asked, doubtfully.

"Yes, I have."

At the left of this house, quite back from the road, was a little unpainted cottage, hardly more than a hut. There was smoke coming out of the chimney, and a tall youth lounged in the door. Hetty, with the woman and children staring after her, struck out across the field in the little foot-path towards the cottage. "I wonder if she's goin' to stay there?" the woman muttered, meditating.

The youth did not see Hetty until she was quite near him, then he aroused suddenly as if from sleep, and tried to slink off around the cottage. But Hetty called after him. "Sammy," she cried, "Sammy, come back here, I want you!"

"What d'ye want?"

"Come back here!"

The youth lounged back sulkily, and a tall woman came to the door. She bent out of it anxiously to hear Hetty.

"I want you to come an' help me move my stove an' things," said Hetty.

"Where to?"

"Into the meetin'-house."

"The meetin'-house?"

"Yes, the meetin'-house."

The woman in the door had sodden hands; behind her arose the steam of a wash-tub. She and the youth stared at Hetty, but surprise was too strong an emotion for them to grasp firmly.

"I want Sammy to come right over an' help me," said Hetty.

"He ain't strong enough to move a stove," said the woman.

"Ain't strong enough!"

"He's apt to git lame."

"Most folks are. Guess I've got lame. Come right along, Sammy!"

"He ain't able to lift much."

"I s'pose he's able to be lifted, ain't he?"

"I dun' know what you mean."

"The stove don't weigh nothin'," said Hetty; "I could carry it myself if I could git hold of it. Come, Sammy!"

Hetty turned down the path, and the youth moved a little way after her, as if perforce. Then he stopped, and cast an appealing glance back at his mother. Her face was distressed. "Oh, Sammy, I'm afraid you'll git sick," said she.

"No, he ain't goin' to git sick," said Hetty. "Come, Sammy." And Sammy followed her down the path.

It was four o'clock then. At dusk Hetty had her gay sunflower quilt curtaining off the chimney-corner of the church gallery; her stove and little bedstead were set up, and she had entered upon a life which endured successfully for three months. All that time a storm brewed; then it broke; but Hetty sailed in her own course for the three months.

It was on a Saturday that she took up her habitation in the meeting-house. The next morning, when the boy who had been supplying the dead sexton's place came and shook the door, Hetty was prompt on the other side. "Deacon Gale said for you to let me in so I could ring the bell," called the boy.

"Go away," responded Hetty. "I'm goin' to ring the bell; I'm sax-ton."

Hetty rang the bell with vigor, but she made a wild, irregular jangle at first; at the last it was better. The village people said to each other that a new hand was ringing. Only a few knew that Hetty was in the meeting-house. When the congregation had assembled, and saw that gaudy tent pitched in the house of the Lord,[3] and the resolute little pilgrim at the door of it, there was a commotion. The farmers and their wives were stirred out of their Sabbath decorum. After the service was over, Hetty, sitting in a pew corner of the gallery, her little face dark

---

3. See Genesis 26.25.

and watchful against the flaming background of her quilt, saw the
people below gathering in groups, whispering, and looking at her.

Presently the minister, Caleb Gale, and the other deacon came up
the gallery stairs. Hetty sat stiffly erect. Caleb Gale went up to the
sunflower quilt, slipped it aside, and looked in. He turned to Hetty with
a frown. Today his dignity was supported by important witnesses. "Did
you bring that stove an' bedstead here?"

Hetty nodded.

"What made you do such a thing?"

"What was I goin' to do if I didn't? How's a woman as old as me
goin' to sleep in a pew, an' go without a cup of tea?"

The men looked at each other. They withdrew to another corner of
the gallery and conferred in low tones; then they went downstairs and
out of the church. Hetty smiled when she heard the door shut. When
one is hard pressed, one, however simple, gets wisdom as to vantage-
points. Hetty comprehended hers perfectly. She was the propounder of
a problem; as long as it was unguessed, she was sure of her foothold
as propounder. This little village in which she had lived all her life had
removed the shelter from her head; she being penniless, it was be-
holden to provide her another; she asked it what. When the old woman
with whom she had lived died, the town promptly seized the estate for
taxes—none had been paid for years. Hetty had not laid up a cent;
indeed, for the most of the time she had received no wages. There had
been no money in the house; all she had gotten for her labor for a
sickly, impecunious old woman was a frugal board. When the old
woman died, Hetty gathered in the few household articles for which
she had stipulated, and made no complaint. She walked out of the
house when the new tenants came in; all she asked was, "What are
you going to do with me?" This little settlement of narrow-minded,
prosperous farmers, however hard a task charity might be to them,
could not turn an old woman out into the fields and highways to seek
for food as they would a Jersey cow. They had their Puritan consciences, and her note of distress would sound louder in their ears than
the Jersey's bell echoing down the valley in the stillest night. But the
question as to Hetty Fifield's disposal was a hard one to answer. There
was no almshouse in the village, and no private family was willing to
take her in. Hetty was strong and capable; although she was old, she
could well have paid for her food and shelter by her labor; but this
could not secure her an entrance even among this hard-working and
thrifty people, who would ordinarily grasp quickly enough at service
without wage in dollars and cents. Hetty had somehow gotten for
herself an unfortunate name in the village. She was held in the light of
a long-thorned brier among the beanpoles, or a fierce little animal with
claws and teeth bared. People were afraid to take her into their families; she had the reputation of always taking her own way, and never
heeding the voice of authority. "I'd take her in an' have her give me
a lift with the work," said one sickly farmer's wife; "but, near's I can

find out, I couldn't never be sure that I'd get molasses in the beans, nor saleratus[4] in my sour-milk cakes, if she took a notion not to put it in. I don't dare to risk it."

Stories were about concerning Hetty's authority over the old woman with whom she had lived. "Old Mis' Grout never dared to say her soul was her own," people said. Then Hetty's sharp, sarcastic sayings were repeated; the justice of them made them sting. People did not want a tongue like that in their homes.

Hetty as a church sexton was directly opposed to all their ideas of church decorum and propriety in general; her pitching her tent in the Lord's house was almost sacrilege; but what could they do? Hetty jangled the Sabbath bells for the three months; once she tolled the bell for an old man, and it seemed by the sound of the bell as if his long, calm years had swung by in a weak delirium; but people bore it. She swept and dusted the little meeting-house, and she garnished the walls with her treasures of worsted-work. The neatness and the garniture went far to quiet the dissatisfaction of the people. They had a crude taste. Hetty's skill in fancy-work was quite celebrated. Her wool flowers were much talked of, and young girls tried to copy them. So these wreaths and clusters of red and blue and yellow wool roses and lilies hung as acceptably between the meeting-house windows as pictures of saints in a cathedral.

Hetty hung a worsted motto over the pulpit; on it she set her chiefest treasure of art, a white wax cross with an ivy vine trailing over it, all covered with silver frost-work. Hetty always surveyed this cross with a species of awe; she felt the irresponsibility and amazement of a genius at his own work.

When she set it on the pulpit, no queen casting her rich robes and her jewels upon a shrine could have surpassed her in generous enthusiasm. "I guess when they see that they won't say no more," she said.

But the people, although they shared Hetty's admiration for the cross, were doubtful. They, looking at it, had a double vision of a little wax Virgin upon an altar. They wondered if it savored of popery.[5] But the cross remained, and the minister was mindful not to jostle it in his gestures.

It was three months from the time Hetty took up her abode in the church, and a week before Christmas, when the problem was solved. Hetty herself precipitated the solution. She prepared a boiled dish in the meeting-house, upon a Saturday, and the next day the odors of turnip and cabbage were strong in the senses of the worshippers. They sniffed and looked at one another. This superseding the legitimate savor of the sanctuary, the fragrance of peppermint lozenges and wintergreen, the breath of Sunday clothes, by the homely week-day

4. Baking soda.
5. Since Protestant churches do not worship the Virgin Mary, the congregation here disparagingly associates Hetty's figure with the doctrines, practices, and rituals of the Roman Catholic Church.

odors of kitchen vegetables, was too much for the sensibilities of the
people. They looked indignantly around at Hetty, sitting before her
sunflower hanging, comfortable from her good dinner of the day
before, radiant with the consciousness of a great plateful of cold vegetables in her tent for her Sabbath dinner.

Poor Hetty had not many comfortable dinners. The selectmen doled
out a small weekly sum to her, which she took with dignity as being her
hire; then she had a mild forage in the neighbors' cellars and kitchens,
of poor apples and stale bread and pie, paying for it in teaching her art
of worsted-work to the daughters. Her Saturday's dinner had been a
banquet to her: she had actually bought a piece of pork to boil with the
vegetables; somebody had given her a nice little cabbage and some
turnips, without a thought of the limitations of her housekeeping.
Hetty herself had not a thought. She made the fires as usual that
Sunday morning; the meeting-house was very clean, there was not a
speck of dust anywhere, the wax cross on the pulpit glistened in a
sunbeam slanting through the house. Hetty, sitting in the gallery,
thought innocently how nice it looked.

After the meeting, Caleb Gale approached the other deacon. "Somethin's got to be done," said he. And the other deacon nodded. He had
not smelt the cabbage until his wife nudged him and mentioned it;
neither had Caleb Gale.

In the afternoon of the next Thursday, Caleb and the other two
selectmen waited upon Hetty in her tabernacle.[6] They stumped up the
gallery stairs, and Hetty emerged from behind the quilt and stood
looking at them scared and defiant. The three men nodded stiffly;
there was a pause; Caleb Gale motioned meaningly to one of the
others, who shook his head; finally he himself had to speak. "I'm 'fraid
you find it pretty cold here, don't you, Hetty?" said he.

"No, thank ye; it's very comfortable," replied Hetty, polite and
wary.

"It ain't very convenient for you to do your cookin' here, I guess."

"It's jest as convenient as I want. I don't find no fault."

"I guess it's rayther lonesome here nights, ain't it?"

"I'd 'nough sight ruther be alone than have comp'ny, any day."

"It ain't fit for an old woman like you to be livin' alone here this
way."

"Well, I dun' know of anything that's any fitter; mebbe you do."

Caleb looked appealingly at his companions; they stood stiff
and irresponsive. Hetty's eyes were sharp and watchful upon them
all.

"Well, Hetty," said Caleb, "we've found a nice, comfortable place
for you, an' I guess you'd better pack up your things, an' I'll carry you
right over there." Caleb stepped back a little closer to the other men.
Hetty, small and trembling and helpless before them, looked vicious.

6. A temporary place of worship, often a tent.

She was like a little animal driven from its cover, for whom there is nothing left but desperate warfare and death.

"Where to?" asked Hetty. Her voice shrilled up into a squeak.

Caleb hesitated. He looked again at the other selectmen. There was a solemn, far-away expression upon their faces. "Well," said he, "Mis' Radway wants to git somebody, an'—"

"You ain't goin' to take me to that woman's!"

"You'd be real comfortable—"

"I ain't goin'."

"Now, why not, I'd like to know?"

"I don't like Susan Radway, hain't never liked her, an' I ain't goin' to live with her."

"Mis' Radway's a good Christian woman. You hadn't ought to speak that way about her."

"You know what Susan Radway is, jest as well's I do; an' everybody else does too. I ain't goin' a step, an' you might jest as well make up your mind to it."

Then Hetty seated herself in the corner of the pew nearest her tent, and folded her hands in her lap. She looked over at the pulpit as if she were listening to preaching. She panted, and her eyes glittered, but she had an immovable air.

"Now, Hetty, you've got sense enough to know you can't stay here," said Caleb. "You'd better put on your bonnet, an' come right along before dark. You'll have a nice ride."

Hetty made no response.

The three men stood looking at her. "Come, Hetty," said Caleb, feebly; and another selectman spoke. "Yes, you'd better come," he said, in a mild voice.

Hetty continued to stare at the pulpit.

The three men withdrew a little and conferred. They did not know how to act. This was a new emergency in their simple, even lives. They were not constables; these three steady, sober old men did not want to drag an old woman by main force out of the meeting-house, and thrust her into Caleb Gale's buggy as if it were a police wagon.

Finally Caleb brightened. "I'll go over an' git mother," said he. He started with a brisk air, and went down the gallery stairs; the others followed. They took up their stand in the meeting-house yard, and Caleb got into his buggy and gathered up the reins. The wind blew cold over the hill. "Hadn't you better go inside and wait out of the wind?" said Caleb.

"I guess we'll wait out here," replied one; and the other nodded.

"Well, I sha'n't be gone long," said Caleb. "Mother'll know how to manage her." He drove carefully down the hill; his buggy wings rattled in the wind. The other men pulled up their coat collars, and met the blast stubbornly.

"Pretty ticklish piece of business to tackle," said one, in a low grunt.

"That's so," assented the other. Then they were silent, and waited for Caleb. Once in a while they stamped their feet and slapped their mittened hands. They did not hear Hetty slip the bolt and turn the key of the meeting-house door, nor see her peeping at them from a gallery window.

Caleb returned in twenty minutes; he had not far to go. His wife, stout and handsome and full of vigor, sat beside him in the buggy. Her face was red with the cold wind; her thick cashmere shawl was pinned tightly over her broad bosom. "Has she come down yet?" she called out, in an imperious way.

The two selectmen shook their heads. Caleb kept the horse quiet while his wife got heavily and briskly out of the buggy. She went up the meeting-house steps, and reached out confidently to open the door. Then she drew back and looked around. "Why," said she, "the door's locked; she's locked the door. I call this pretty work!"

She turned again quite fiercely, and began beating on the door. "Hetty!" she called; "Hetty, Hetty Fifield! Let me in! What have you locked this door for?"

She stopped and turned to her husband.

"Don't you s'pose the barn key would unlock it?" she asked.

"I don't b'lieve 'twould."

"Well, you'd better go home and fetch it."

Caleb again drove down the hill, and the other men searched their pockets for keys. One had the key of his corn-house, and produced it hopefully; but it would not unlock the meeting-house door.

A crowd seldom gathered in the little village for anything short of a fire; but today in a short time quite a number of people stood on the meeting-house hill, and more kept coming. When Caleb Gale returned with the barn key his daughter, a tall, pretty young girl, sat beside him, her little face alert and smiling in her red hood. The other selectmen's wives toiled eagerly up the hill, with a young daughter of one of them speeding on ahead. Then the two young girls stood close to each other and watched the proceedings. Key after key was tried; men brought all the large keys they could find, running importantly up the hill, but none would unlock the meeting-house door. After Caleb had tried the last available key, stooping and screwing it anxiously, he turned around. "There ain't no use in it, any way," said he; "most likely the door's bolted."

"You don't mean there's a bolt on that door?" cried his wife.

"Yes, there is."

"Then you might jest as well have tore 'round for hen's feathers as keys. Of course she's bolted it if she's got any wit, an' I guess she's got most as much as some of you men that have been bringin' keys. Try the windows."

But the windows were fast. Hetty had made her sacred castle impregnable except to violence. Either the door would have to be forced or a window broken to gain an entrance.

The people conferred with one another. Some were for retreating, and leaving Hetty in peaceful possession until time drove her to capitulate. "She'll open it tomorrow," they said. Others were for extreme measures, and their impetuosity gave them the lead. The project of forcing the door was urged; one man started for a crow-bar.

"They are a parcel of fools to do such a thing," said Caleb Gale's wife to another woman. "Spoil that good door! They'd better leave the poor thing alone till tomorrow. I dun' know what's goin' to be done with her when they git in. I ain't goin' to have father draggin' her over to Mis' Radway's by the hair of her head."

"That's jest what I say," returned the other woman.

Mrs. Gale went up to Caleb and nudged him. "Don't you let them break that door down, father," said she.

"Well, well, we'll see," Caleb replied. He moved away a little; his wife's voice had been drowned out lately by a masculine clamor, and he took advantage of it.

All the people talked at once; the wind was keen, and all their garments fluttered; the two young girls had their arms around each other under their shawls; the man with the crow-bar came stalking up the hill.

"Don't you let them break down that door, father," said Mrs. Gale.

"Well, well," grunted Caleb.

Regardless of remonstrances, the man set the crow-bar against the door; suddenly there was a cry, "There she is!" Everybody looked up. There was Hetty looking out of a gallery window.

Everybody was still. Hetty began to speak. Her dark old face, peering out of the window, looked ghastly; the wind blew her poor gray locks over it. She extended her little wrinkled hands. "Jest let me say one word," said she; "jest one word." Her voice shook. All her coolness was gone. The magnitude of her last act of defiance had caused it to react upon herself like an overloaded gun.

"Say all you want to, Hetty, an' don't be afraid," Mrs. Gale called out.

"I jest want to say a word," repeated Hetty. "Can't I stay here, nohow? It don't seem as if I could go to Mis' Radway's. I ain't nothin' again' her. I s'pose she's a good woman, but she's used to havin' her own way, and I've been livin' all my life with them that was, an' I've had to fight to keep a footin' on the earth, an' now I'm gittin' too old for't. If I can jest stay here in the meetin'-house, I won't ask for nothin' any better. I sha'n't need much to keep me, I wa'n't never a hefty eater; an' I'll keep the meetin'-house jest as clean as I know how. An' I'll make some more of them wool flowers. I'll make a wreath to go the whole length of the gallery, if I can git wool 'nough. Won't you let me stay? I ain't complainin', but I've always had a dretful hard time; seems as if now I might take a little comfort the last of it, if I could stay here. I can't go to Mis' Radway's nohow." Hetty covered her face with her hands; her words ended in a weak wail.

Mrs. Gale's voice rang out clear and strong and irrepressible. "Of

course you can stay in the meetin'-house," said she; "I should laugh if
you couldn't. Don't you worry another mite about it. You sha'n't go one
step to Mis' Radway's; you couldn't live a day with her. You can stay
jest where you are; you've kept the meetin'-house enough sight
cleaner than I've ever seen it. Don't you worry another mite, Hetty."

Mrs. Gale stood majestically, and looked defiantly around; tears
were in her eyes. Another woman edged up to her. "Why couldn't she
have that little room side of the pulpit, where the minister hangs his
hat?" she whispered. "He could hang it somewhere else."

"Course she could," responded Mrs. Gale, with alacrity, "jest as
well as not. The minister can have a hook in the entry for his hat. She
can have her stove an' her bed in there, an' be jest as comfortable as
can be. I should laugh if she couldn't. Don't you worry, Hetty."

The crowd gradually dispersed, sending out stragglers down the hill
until it was all gone. Mrs. Gale waited until the last, sitting in the
buggy in state. When her husband gathered up the reins, she called
back to Hetty: "Don't you worry one mite more about it, Hetty. I'm
comin' up to see you in the mornin'!"

It was almost dusk when Caleb drove down the hill; he was the last
of the besiegers, and the feeble garrison was left triumphant.

The next day but one was Christmas, the next night Christmas Eve.
On Christmas Eve Hetty had reached what to her was the flood-tide
of peace and prosperity. Established in that small, lofty room, with her
bed and her stove, with gifts of a rocking-chair and table, and a goodly
store of food, with no one to molest or disturb her, she had nothing to
wish for on earth. All her small desires were satisfied. No happy girl
could have a merrier Christmas than this old woman with her little
measure full of gifts. That Christmas Eve Hetty lay down under her
sunflower quilt, and all her old hardships looked dim in the distance,
like far-away hills, while her new joys came out like stars.

She was a light sleeper; the next morning she was up early. She
opened the meeting-house door and stood looking out. The smoke from
the village chimneys had not yet begun to rise blue and rosy in the clear
frosty air. There was no snow, but over all the hill there was a silver
rime of frost; the bare branches of the trees glistened. Hetty stood
looking. "Why, it's Christmas mornin'," she said, suddenly. Christmas
had never been a gala-day to this old woman. Christmas had not been
kept at all in this New England village when she was young. She was
led to think of it now only in connection with the dinner Mrs. Gale had
promised to bring her today.

Mrs. Gale had told her she should have some of her Christmas
dinner, some turkey and plum-pudding. She called it to mind now with
a thrill of delight. Her face grew momentarily more radiant. There was
a certain beauty in it. A finer morning light than that which lit up the
wintry earth seemed to shine over the furrows of her old face. "I'm
goin' to have turkey an' plum-puddin' today," said she; "it's Christmas." Suddenly she started, and went into the meeting-house, straight

up the gallery stairs. There in a clear space hung the bell-rope. Hetty grasped it. Never before had a Christmas bell been rung in this village; Hetty had probably never heard of Christmas bells. She was prompted by pure artless enthusiasm and grateful happiness. Her old arms pulled on the rope with a will, the bell sounded peal on peal. Down in the village, curtains rolled up, letting in the morning light, happy faces looked out of the windows. Hetty had awakened the whole village to Christmas Day.

Harper's Bazar, 28 December 1889; *A New England Nun*, 1891

A New England Nun

It was late in the afternoon, and the light was waning. There was a difference in the look of the tree shadows out in the yard. Somewhere in the distance cows were lowing and a little bell was tinkling; now and then a farm-wagon tilted by, and the dust flew; some blue-shirted laborers with shovels over their shoulders plodded past; little swarms of flies were dancing up and down before the peoples' faces in the soft air. There seemed to be a gentle stir arising over everything for the mere sake of subsidence—a very premonition of rest and hush and night.

This soft diurnal commotion was over Louisa Ellis also. She had been peacefully sewing at her sitting-room window all the afternoon. Now she quilted her needle carefully into her work, which she folded precisely, and laid in a basket with her thimble and thread and scissors. Louisa Ellis could not remember that ever in her life she had mislaid one of these little feminine appurtenances, which had become, from long use and constant association, a very part of her personality.

Louisa tied a green apron round her waist, and got out a flat straw hat with a green ribbon. Then she went into the garden with a little blue crockery bowl, to pick some currants for her tea. After the currants were picked she sat on the back door-step and stemmed them, collecting the stems carefully in her apron, and afterwards throwing them into the hen-coop. She looked sharply at the grass beside the step to see if any had fallen there.

Louisa was slow and still in her movements; it took her a long time to prepare her tea; but when ready it was set forth with as much grace as if she had been a veritable guest to her own self. The little square table stood exactly in the center of the kitchen, and was covered with a starched linen cloth whose border pattern of flowers glistened. Louisa had a damask napkin on her tea-tray, where were arranged a cut-glass tumbler full of teaspoons, a silver cream-pitcher, a china sugar-bowl, and one pink china cup and saucer. Louisa used china every day—something which none of her neighbors did. They whispered about it among themselves. Their daily tables were laid with common crockery, their sets of best china stayed in the parlor closet, and Louisa Ellis was no richer nor better bred than they. Still she would use the china. She had for her supper a glass dish full of sugared currants, a plate of little cakes, and one of light white biscuits. Also a leaf or two of lettuce, which she cut up daintily. Louisa was very fond of lettuce, which she raised to perfection in her little garden. She ate quite heartily, though in a delicate, pecking way; it seemed almost surprising that any considerable bulk of the food should vanish.

After tea she filled a plate with nicely baked thin corn-cakes, and carried them out into the back-yard.

"Cæsar!" she called. "Cæsar! Cæsar!"

There was a little rush, and the clank of a chain, and a large yellow-and-white dog appeared at the door of his tiny hut, which was half hidden among the tall grasses and flowers. Louisa patted him and gave him the corn-cakes. Then she returned to the house and washed the tea-things, polishing the china carefully. The twilight had deepened; the chorus of the frogs floated in at the open window wonderfully loud and shrill, and once in a while a long sharp drone from a tree-toad pierced it. Louisa took off her green gingham apron, disclosing a shorter one of pink and white print. She lighted her lamp, and sat down again with her sewing.

In about half an hour Joe Dagget came. She heard his heavy step on the walk, and rose and took off her pink-and-white apron. Under that was still another—white linen with a little cambric edging on the bottom; that was Louisa's company apron. She never wore it without her calico sewing apron over it unless she had a guest. She had barely folded the pink and white one with methodical haste and laid it in a table-drawer when the door opened and Joe Dagget entered.

He seemed to fill up the whole room. A little yellow canary that had been asleep in his green cage at the south window woke up and fluttered wildly, beating his little yellow wings against the wires. He always did so when Joe Dagget came into the room.

"Good-evening," said Louisa. She extended her hand with a kind of solemn cordiality.

"Good-evening, Louisa," returned the man, in a loud voice.

She placed a chair for him, and they sat facing each other, with the table between them. He sat bolt-upright, toeing out his heavy feet squarely, glancing with a good-humored uneasiness around the room. She sat gently erect, folding her slender hands in her white-linen lap.

"Been a pleasant day," remarked Dagget.

"Real pleasant," Louisa assented, softly. "Have you been haying?" she asked, after a little while.

"Yes, I've been haying all day, down in the ten-acre lot. Pretty hot work."

"It must be."

"Yes, it's pretty hot work in the sun."

"Is your mother well today?"

"Yes, mother's pretty well."

"I suppose Lily Dyer's with her now?"

Dagget colored. "Yes, she's with her," he answered, slowly.

He was not very young, but there was a boyish look about his large face. Louisa was not quite as old as he, her face was fairer and smoother, but she gave people the impression of being older.

"I suppose she's a good deal of help to your mother," she said, further.

"I guess she is; I don't know how mother'd get along without her," said Dagget, with a sort of embarrassed warmth.

"She looks like a real capable girl. She's pretty-looking too," remarked Louisa.

"Yes, she is pretty fair looking."

Presently Dagget began fingering the books on the table. There was a square red autograph album, and a Young Lady's Gift-Book[1] which had belonged to Louisa's mother. He took them up one after the other and opened them; then laid them down again, the album on the Gift-Book.

Louisa kept eying them with mild uneasiness. Finally she rose and changed the position of the books, putting the album underneath. That was the way they had been arranged in the first place.

Dagget gave an awkward little laugh. "Now what difference did it make which book was on top?" said he.

Louisa looked at him with a deprecating smile. "I always keep them that way," murmured she.

"You do beat everything," said Dagget, trying to laugh again. His large face was flushed.

He remained about an hour longer, then rose to take leave. Going out, he stumbled over a rug, and trying to recover himself, hit Louisa's work-basket on the table, and knocked it on the floor.

He looked at Louisa, then at the rolling spools; he ducked himself awkwardly toward them, but she stopped him. "Never mind," said she; "I'll pick them up after you're gone."

She spoke with a mild stiffness. Either she was a little disturbed, or his nervousness affected her, and made her seem constrained in her effort to reassure him.

When Joe Dagget was outside he drew in the sweet evening air with a sigh, and felt much as an innocent and perfectly well-intentioned bear might after his exit from a china shop.

Louisa, on her part, felt much as the kind-hearted, long-suffering owner of the china shop might have done after the exit of the bear.

She tied on the pink, then the green apron, picked up all the scattered treasures and replaced them in her work-basket, and straightened the rug. Then she set the lamp on the floor, and began sharply

---

1. A common title for illustrated volumes of poems, stories, and moral essays, often given as gifts. Auto- graph album: a special book set aside for signatures and brief messages from friends and visitors.

examining the carpet. She even rubbed her fingers over it, and looked at them.

"He's tracked in a good deal of dust," she murmured. "I thought he must have."

Louisa got a dust-pan and brush, and swept Joe Dagget's track carefully.

If he could have known it, it would have increased his perplexity and uneasiness, although it would not have disturbed his loyalty in the least. He came twice a week to see Louisa Ellis, and every time, sitting there in her delicately sweet room, he felt as if surrounded by a hedge of lace. He was afraid to stir lest he should put a clumsy foot or hand through the fairy web, and he had always the consciousness that Louisa was watching fearfully lest he should.

Still the lace and Louisa commanded perforce his perfect respect and patience and loyalty. They were to be married in a month, after a singular courtship which had lasted for a matter of fifteen years. For fourteen out of the fifteen years the two had not once seen each other, and they had seldom exchanged letters. Joe had been all those years in Australia, where he had gone to make his fortune, and where he had stayed until he made it. He would have stayed fifty years if it had taken so long, and come home feeble and tottering, or never come home at all, to marry Louisa.

But the fortune had been made in the fourteen years, and he had come home now to marry the woman who had been patiently and unquestioningly waiting for him all that time.

Shortly after they were engaged he had announced to Louisa his determination to strike out into new fields, and secure a competency before they should be married. She had listened and assented with the sweet serenity which never failed her, not even when her lover set forth on that long and uncertain journey. Joe, buoyed up as he was by his sturdy determination, broke down a little at the last, but Louisa kissed him with a mild blush, and said good-by.

"It won't be for long," poor Joe had said, huskily; but it was for fourteen years.

In that length of time much had happened. Louisa's mother and brother had died, and she was all alone in the world. But greatest happening of all—a subtle happening which both were too simple to understand—Louisa's feet had turned into a path, smooth maybe under a calm, serene sky, but so straight and unswerving that it could only meet a check at her grave, and so narrow that there was no room for anyone at her side.

Louisa's first emotion when Joe Dagget came home (he had not apprised her of his coming) was consternation, although she would not admit it to herself, and he never dreamed of it. Fifteen years ago she had been in love with him—at least she considered herself to be. Just at that time, gently acquiescing with and falling into the natural drift of girlhood, she had seen marriage ahead as a reasonable feature and a probable desirability of life. She had listened with calm docility to her mother's views upon the subject. Her mother was remarkable for her cool sense and sweet, even temperament. She talked wisely to her daughter when Joe Dagget presented himself, and Louisa accepted him with no hesitation. He was the first lover she had ever had.

She had been faithful to him all these years. She had never dreamed of the possibility of marrying anyone else. Her life, especially for the last seven years, had been full of a pleasant peace, she had never felt discontented nor impatient over her lover's absence; still she had always looked forward to his return and their marriage as the inevitable conclusion of things. However, she had fallen into a way of placing it so far in the future that it was almost equal to placing it over the boundaries of another life.

When Joe came she had been expecting him, and expecting to be married for fourteen years, but she was as much surprised and taken aback as if she had never thought of it.

Joe's consternation came later. He eyed Louisa with an instant confirmation of his old admiration. She had changed but little. She still kept her pretty manner and soft grace, and was, he considered, every whit as attractive as ever. As for himself, his stent[2] was done; he had turned his face away from fortune-seeking, and the old winds of romance whistled as loud and sweet as ever through his ears. All the song which he had been wont to hear in them was Louisa; he had for a long time a loyal belief that he heard it still, but finally it seemed to him that although the winds sang always that one song, it had another name. But for Louisa the wind had never more than murmured; now it had gone down, and everything was still. She listened for a little while with half-wistful attention; then she turned quietly away and went to work on her wedding clothes.

Joe had made some extensive and quite magnificent alterations in his house. It was the old homestead; the newly married couple would live there, for Joe could not desert his mother, who refused to leave her old home. So Louisa must leave hers. Every morning, rising and going about among her neat maidenly possessions, she felt as one looking her last upon the faces of dear friends. It was true that in a measure she could take them with her, but, robbed of their old environments, they would appear in such new guises that they would almost cease to be themselves. Then there were some peculiar features of her happy solitary life which she would probably be obliged to relinquish altogether. Sterner tasks than these graceful but half needless ones would probably devolve upon her. There would be a large house to care for; there would be company to entertain; there would be Joe's rigorous and feeble old mother to wait upon; and it would be contrary to all thrifty village traditions for her to keep more than one servant. Louisa had a little still, and she used to occupy herself pleasantly in summer

2. Stint.

weather with distilling the sweet and aromatic essences[3] from roses
and peppermint and spearmint. By-and-by her still must be laid away.
Her store of essences was already considerable, and there would be no
time for her to distil for the mere pleasure of it. Then Joe's mother
would think it foolishness; she had already hinted her opinion in the
matter. Louisa dearly loved to sew a linen seam, not always for use, but
for the simple, mild pleasure which she took in it. She would have been
loath to confess how more than once she had ripped a seam for the
mere delight of sewing it together again. Sitting at her window during
long sweet afternoons, drawing her needle gently through the dainty
fabric, she was peace itself. But there was small chance of such foolish
comfort in the future. Joe's mother, domineering, shrewd old matron
that she was even in her old age, and very likely even Joe himself, with
his honest masculine rudeness, would laugh and frown down all these
pretty but senseless old maiden ways.

Louisa had almost the enthusiasm of an artist over the mere order
and cleanliness of her solitary home. She had throbs of genuine triumph at the sight of the window-panes which she had polished until
they shone like jewels. She gloated gently over her orderly bureau-
drawers, with their exquisitely folded contents redolent with lavender
and sweet clover and very purity. Could she be sure of the endurance
of even this? She had visions, so startling that she half repudiated them
as indelicate, of coarse masculine belongings strewn about in endless
litter; of dust and disorder arising necessarily from a coarse masculine
presence in the midst of all this delicate harmony.

Among her forebodings of disturbance, not the least was with regard
to Cæsar. Cæsar was a veritable hermit of a dog. For the greater part
of his life he had dwelt in his secluded hut, shut out from the society
of his kind and all innocent canine joys. Never had Cæsar since his
early youth watched at a woodchuck's hole; never had he known the
delights of a stray bone at a neighbor's kitchen door. And it was all on
account of a sin committed when hardly out of his puppyhood. No one
knew the possible depth of remorse of which this mild-visaged, altogether innocent-looking old dog might be capable; but whether or not
he had encountered remorse, he had encountered a full measure of
righteous retribution. Old Cæsar seldom lifted up his voice in a growl
or a bark; he was fat and sleepy; there were yellow rings which looked
like spectacles around his dim old eyes; but there was a neighbor who
bore on his hand the imprint of several of Cæsar's sharp white youthful
teeth, and for that he had lived at the end of a chain, all alone in a little
hut, for fourteen years. The neighbor, who was choleric and smarting
with the pain of his wound, had demanded either Cæsar's death or
complete ostracism. So Louisa's brother, to whom the dog had belonged, had built him his little kennel and tied him up. It was now

3. Louisa is not distilling alcohol but rather the concentrated liquids, or essences, from the aromatic leaves
of herbs.

fourteen years since, in a flood of youthful spirits, he had inflicted that memorable bite, and with the exception of short excursions, always at the end of the chain, under the strict guardianship of his master or Louisa, the old dog had remained a close prisoner. It is doubtful if, with his limited ambition, he took much pride in the fact, but it is certain that he was possessed of considerable cheap fame. He was regarded by all the children in the village and by many adults as a very monster of ferocity. St. George's dragon[4] could hardly have surpassed in evil repute Louisa Ellis's old yellow dog. Mothers charged their children with solemn emphasis not to go too near to him, and the children listened and believed greedily, with a fascinated appetite for terror, and ran by Louisa's house stealthily, with many sidelong and backward glances at the terrible dog. If perchance he sounded a hoarse bark, there was a panic. Wayfarers chancing into Louisa's yard eyed him with respect, and inquired if the chain was stout. Cæsar at large might have seemed a very ordinary dog, and excited no comment whatever; chained, his reputation overshadowed him, so that he lost his own proper outlines and looked darkly vague and enormous. Joe Dagget, however, with his good-humored sense and shrewdness, saw him as he was. He strode valiantly up to him and patted him on the head, in spite of Louisa's soft clamor of warning, and even attempted to set him loose. Louisa grew so alarmed that he desisted, but kept announcing his opinion in the matter quite forcibly at intervals. "There ain't a better-natured dog in town," he would say, "and it's downright cruel to keep him tied up there. Some day I'm going to take him out."

Louisa had very little hope that he would not, one of these days, when their interests and possessions should be more completely fused in one. She pictured to herself Cæsar on the rampage through the quiet and unguarded village. She saw innocent children bleeding in his path. She was herself very fond of the old dog, because he had belonged to her dead brother, and he was always very gentle with her; still she had great faith in his ferocity. She always warned people not to go too near him. She fed him on ascetic fare of corn-mush and cakes, and never fired his dangerous temper with heating and sanguinary diet of flesh and bones. Louisa looked at the old dog munching his simple fare, and thought of her approaching marriage and trembled. Still no anticipation of disorder and confusion in lieu of sweet peace and harmony, no forebodings of Cæsar on the rampage, no wild fluttering of her little yellow canary, were sufficient to turn her a hair's-breadth. Joe Dagget had been fond of her and working for her all these years. It was not for her, whatever came to pass, to prove untrue and break his heart. She put the exquisite little stitches into her wedding-garments, and the time went on until it was only a week before her wedding-day. It was a Tuesday evening, and the wedding was to be a week from Wednesday.

---

4. The monster of English lore, slain by St. George; the dragon terrorized the countryside and demanded the daily sacrifice of a young woman.

There was a full moon that night. About nine o'clock Louisa strolled down the road a little way. There were harvest-fields on either hand, bordered by low stone walls. Luxuriant clumps of bushes grew beside the wall, and trees—wild cherry and old apple-trees—at intervals. Presently Louisa sat down on the wall and looked about her with mildly sorrowful reflectiveness. Tall shrubs of blueberry and meadow-sweet, all woven together and tangled with blackberry vines and horsebriers, shut her in on either side. She had a little clear space between them. Opposite her, on the other side of the road, was a spreading tree; the moon shone between its boughs, and the leaves twinkled like silver. The road was bespread with a beautiful shifting dapple of silver and shadow; the air was full of a mysterious sweetness. "I wonder if it's wild grapes?" murmured Louisa. She sat there some time. She was just thinking of rising, when she heard footsteps and low voices, and remained quiet. It was a lonely place, and she felt a little timid. She thought she would keep still in the shadow and let the persons, whoever they might be, pass her.

But just before they reached her the voices ceased, and the foot-steps. She understood that their owners had also found seats upon the stone wall. She was wondering if she could not steal away unobserved, when the voice broke the stillness. It was Joe Dagget's. She sat still and listened.

The voice was announced by a loud sigh, which was as familiar as itself. "Well," said Dagget, "you've made up your mind, then, I sup-pose?"

"Yes," returned another voice; "I'm going day after tomorrow."

"That's Lily Dyer," thought Louisa to herself. The voice embodied itself in her mind. She saw a girl tall and full-figured, with a firm, fair face, looking fairer and firmer in the moonlight, her strong yellow hair braided in a close knot. A girl full of a calm rustic strength and bloom, with a masterful way which might have beseemed a princess. Lily Dyer was a favorite with the village folk; she had just the qualities to arouse the admiration. She was good and handsome and smart. Louisa had often heard her praises sounded.

"Well," said Joe Dagget, "I ain't got a word to say."

"I don't know what you could say," returned Lily Dyer.

"Not a word to say," repeated Joe, drawing out the words heavily. Then there was a silence. "I ain't sorry," he began at last, "that that happened yesterday—that we kind of let on how we felt to each other. I guess it's just as well we knew. Of course I can't do anything any different. I'm going right on an' get married next week. I ain't going back on a woman that's waited for me fourteen years, an' break her heart."

"If you should jilt her tomorrow, I wouldn't have you," spoke up the girl, with sudden vehemence.

"Well, I ain't going to give you the chance," said he; "but I don't believe you would, either."

"You'd see I wouldn't. Honor's honor, an' right's right. An' I'd never think anything of any man that went against 'em for me or any other girl; you'd find that out, Joe Dagget."

"Well, you'll find out fast enough that I ain't going against 'em for you or any other girl," returned he. Their voices sounded almost as if they were angry with each other. Louisa was listening eagerly.

"I'm sorry you feel as if you must go away," said Joe, "but I don't know but it's best."

"Of course it's best. I hope you and I have got common-sense."

"Well, I suppose you're right." Suddenly Joe's voice got an undertone of tenderness. "Say, Lily," said he, "I'll get along well enough myself, but I can't bear to think—You don't suppose you're going to fret much over it?"

"I guess you'll find out I sha'n't fret much over a married man."

"Well, I hope you won't—I hope you won't, Lily. God knows I do. And—I hope—one of these days—you'll—come across somebody else—"

"I don't see any reason why I shouldn't." Suddenly her tone changed. She spoke in a sweet, clear voice, so loud that she could have been heard across the street. "No, Joe Dagget," said she, "I'll never marry any other man as long as I live. I've got good sense, an' I ain't going to break my heart nor make a fool of myself; but I'm never going to be married, you can be sure of that. I ain't that sort of a girl to feel this way twice."

Louisa heard an exclamation and a soft commotion behind the bushes; then Lily spoke again—the voice sounded as if she had risen. "This must be put a stop to," said she. "We've stayed here long enough. I'm going home."

Louisa sat there in a daze, listening to their retreating steps. After a while she got up and slunk softly home herself. The next day she did her housework methodically; that was as much a matter of course as breathing; but she did not sew on her wedding-clothes. She sat at her window and meditated. In the evening Joe came. Louisa Ellis had never known that she had any diplomacy in her, but when she came to look for it that night she found it, although meek of its kind, among her little feminine weapons. Even now she could hardly believe that she had heard aright, and that she would not do Joe a terrible injury should she break her troth-plight.[5] She wanted to sound him without betraying too soon her own inclinations in the matter. She did it successfully, and they finally came to an understanding; but it was a difficult thing, for he was as afraid of betraying himself as she.

She never mentioned Lily Dyer. She simply said that while she had no cause of complaint against him, she had lived so long in one way that she shrank from making a change.

"Well, I never shrank, Louisa," said Dagget. "I'm going to be honest enough to say that I think maybe it's better this way; but if you'd

5. A promise to marry that accompanies engagement or betrothal.

wanted to keep on, I'd have stuck to you till my dying day. I hope you know that."

"Yes, I do," said she.

That night she and Joe parted more tenderly than they had done for a long time. Standing in the door, holding each other's hands, a last great wave of regretful memory swept over them.

"Well, this ain't the way we've thought it was all going to end, is it, Louisa?" said Joe.

She shook her head. There was a little quiver on her placid face.

"You let me know if there's ever anything I can do for you," said he. "I ain't ever going to forget you, Louisa." Then he kissed her, and went down the path.

Louisa, all alone by herself that night, wept a little, she hardly knew why; but the next morning, on waking, she felt like a queen who, after fearing lest her domain be wrested away from her, sees it firmly insured in her possession.

Now the tall weeds and grasses might cluster around Cæsar's little hermit hut, the snow might fall on its roof year in and year out, but he never would go on a rampage through the unguarded village. Now the little canary might turn itself into a peaceful yellow ball night after night, and have no need to wake and flutter with wild terror against its bars. Louisa could sew linen seams, and distil roses, and dust and polish and fold away in lavender, as long as she listed. That afternoon she sat with her needle-work at the window, and felt fairly steeped in peace. Lily Dyer, tall and erect and blooming, went past; but she felt no qualm. If Louisa Ellis had sold her birthright she did not know it, the taste of the pottage was so delicious, and had been her sole satisfaction for so long.[6] Serenity and placid narrowness had become to her as the birthright itself. She gazed ahead through a long reach of future days strung together like pearls in a rosary, every one like the others, and all smooth and flawless and innocent, and her heart went up in thankfulness. Outside was the fervid summer afternoon; the air was filled with the sounds of the busy harvest of men and birds and bees; there were halloos, metallic clatterings, sweet calls, and long hummings. Louisa sat, prayerfully numbering her days, like an uncloistered nun.

A New England Nun, 1891

A Poetess

The garden-patch at the right of the house was all a gay spangle with sweet-peas and red-flowering beans, and flanked with feathery asparagus. A woman in blue was moving about there. Another woman, in a

---

6. Esau, the elder twin brother of Jacob, who sells his birthright to Jacob for a plate of stew. See Genesis 25.31 ff.

black bonnet, stood at the front door of the house. She knocked and waited. She could not see from where she stood the blue-clad woman in the garden. The house was very close to the road, from which a tall evergreen hedge separated it, and the view to the side was in a measure cut off.

The front door was open; the woman had to reach to knock on it, as it swung into the entry. She was a small woman and quite young, with a bright alertness about her which had almost the effect of prettiness. It was to her what greenness and crispness are to a plant. She poked her little face forward, and her sharp pretty eyes took in the entry and a room at the left, of which the door stood open. The entry was small and square and unfurnished, except for a well-rubbed old card-table against the back wall. The room was full of green light from the tall hedge, and bristling with grasses and flowers and asparagus stalks.

"Betsey, you there?" called the woman. When she spoke, a yellow canary, whose cage hung beside the front door, began to chirp and twitter.

"Betsey, you there?" the woman called again. The bird's chirps came in a quick volley; then he began to trill and sing.

"She ain't there," said the woman. She turned and went out of the yard through the gap in the hedge; then she looked around. She caught sight of the blue figure in the garden. "There she is," said she.

She went around the house to the garden. She wore a gay cashmere-patterned calico dress with her mourning bonnet, and she held it carefully away from the dewy grass and vines.

The other woman did not notice her until she was close to her and said, "Good-mornin', Betsey." Then she started and turned around.

"Why, Mis' Caxton! That you?" said she.

"Yes. I've been standin' at your door for the last half-hour. I was jest goin' away when I caught sight of you out here."

In spite of her brisk speech her manner was subdued. She drew down the corners of her mouth sadly.

"I declare I'm dreadful sorry you had to stan' there so long!" said the other woman.

She set a pan partly filled with beans on the ground, wiped her hands, which were damp and green from the wet vines, on her apron, then extended her right one with a solemn and sympathetic air.

"It don't make much odds, Betsey," replied Mrs. Caxton. "I ain't got much to take up my time nowadays." She sighed heavily as she shook hands, and the other echoed her.

"We'll go right in now. I'm dreadful sorry you stood there so long," said Betsey.

"You'd better finish pickin' your beans."

"No; I wa'n't goin' to pick any more. I was jest goin' in."

"I declare, Betsey Dole, I shouldn't think you'd got enough for a cat!" said Mrs. Caxton, eying the pan.

"I've got pretty near all there is. I guess I've got more flowerin' beans than eatin' ones, anyway."

"I should think you had," said Mrs. Caxton, surveying the row of bean-poles topped with swarms of delicate red flowers. "I should think they were pretty near all flowerin' ones. Had any peas?"

"I didn't have more'n three or four messes.[1] I guess I planted sweet-peas mostly. I don't know hardly how I happened to."

"Had any summer squash?"

"Two or three. There's some more set, if they ever get ripe. I planted some gourds. I think they look real pretty on the kitchen shelf in the winter."

"I should think you'd got a sage bed big enough for the whole town."

"Well, I have got a pretty good-sized one. I always liked them blue sage-blows.[2] You'd better hold up your dress real careful goin' through here, Mis' Caxton, or you'll get it wet."

The two women picked their way through the dewy grass, around a corner of the hedge, and Betsey ushered her visitor into the house.

"Set right down in the rockin-chair," said she. "I'll jest carry these beans out into the kitchen."

"I should think you'd better get another pan and string 'em, or you won't get 'em done for dinner."

"Well, mebbe I will, if you'll excuse it, Mis' Caxton. The beans had ought to boil quite a while; they're pretty old."

Betsey went into the kitchen and returned with a pan and an old knife. She seated herself opposite Mrs. Caxton, and began to string and cut the beans.

"If I was in your place I shouldn't feel as if I'd got enough to boil a kettle for," said Mrs. Caxton, eying the beans. "I should 'most have thought when you didn't have any more room for a garden than you've got that you'd planted more real beans and peas instead of so many flowerin' ones. I'd rather have a good mess of green peas boiled with a piece of salt pork than all the sweet-peas you could give me. I like flowers well enough, but I never set up for a butterfly, an' I want something else to live on." She looked at Betsey with pensive superiority.

Betsey was near-sighted; she had to bend low over the beans in order to string them. She was fifty years old, but she wore her streaky light hair in curls like a young girl. The curls hung over her faded cheeks and almost concealed them. Once in a while she flung them back with a childish gesture which sat strangely upon her.

"I dare say you're in the right of it," she said, meekly.

"I know I am. You folks that write poetry wouldn't have a single thing to eat growin' if they were left alone. And that brings to mind what I come for. I've been thinkin' about it ever since—our—little Willie—left us." Mrs. Caxton's manner was suddenly full of shame-faced dramatic fervor, her eyes reddened with tears.

Betsey looked up inquiringly, throwing back her curls. Her face took

---

1. Amounts of food sufficient for a meal.
2. Blooms of the sage plant, an herb used in cooking.

on unconsciously lines of grief so like the other woman's that she looked like her for the minute.

"I thought maybe," Mrs. Caxton went on, tremulously, "you'd be willin' to—write a few lines."

"Of course I will, Mis' Caxton. I'll be glad to, if I can do 'em to suit you," Betsey said, tearfully.

"I thought jest a few—lines. You could mention how—handsome he was, and good, and I never had to punish him but once in his life, and how pleased he was with his little new suit, and what a sufferer he was, and—how we hope he is at rest—in a better land."

"I'll try, Mis' Caxton, I'll try," sobbed Betsey. The two women wept together for a few minutes.

"It seems as if—I couldn't have it so sometimes," Mrs. Caxton said, brokenly. "I keep thinkin' he's in the other—room. Every time I go back home when I've been away it's like—losin' him again. Oh, it don't seem as if I could go home and not find him there—it don't, it don't! Oh, you don't know anything about it, Betsey. You never had any children!"

"I don't s'pose I do, Mis' Caxton; I don't s'pose I do."

Presently Mrs. Caxton wiped her eyes. "I've been thinkin'," said she, keeping her mouth steady with an effort, "that it would be real pretty to have—some lines printed on some sheets of white paper with a neat black border. I'd like to send some to my folks, and one to the Perkinses in Brigham, and there's a good many others I thought would value 'em."

"I'll do jest the best I can, Mis' Caxton, an' be glad to. It's little enough anybody can do at such times."

Mrs. Caxton broke out weeping again. "Oh, it's true, it's true, Betsey!" she sobbed. "Nobody can do anything, and nothin' amounts to anything—poetry or anything else—when he's *gone*. Nothin' can bring him back. Oh, what shall I do, what shall I do?"

Mrs. Caxton dried her tears again, and arose to take leave. "Well, I must be goin', or Wilson won't have any dinner," she said, with an effort at self-control.

"Well, I'll do jest the best I can with the poetry," said Betsey. "I'll write it this afternoon." She had set down her pan of beans and was standing beside Mrs. Caxton. She reached up and straightened her black bonnet, which had slipped backward.

"I've got to get a pin," said Mrs. Caxton, tearfully. "I can't keep it anywheres. It drags right off my head, the veil is so heavy."

Betsey went to the door with her visitor. "It's dreadful dusty, ain't it?" she remarked, in that sad, contemptuous tone with which one speaks of discomforts in the presence of affliction.

"Terrible," replied Mrs. Caxton. "I wouldn't wear my black dress in it nohow; a black bonnet is bad enough. This dress is 'most too good. It's enough to spoil everything. Well, I'm much obliged to you, Betsey, for bein' willin' to do that."

"I'll do jest the best I can, Mis' Caxton."

After Betsey had watched her visitor out of the yard she returned to the sitting-room and took up the pan of beans. She looked doubtfully at the handful of beans all nicely strung and cut up. "I declare I don't know what to do," said she. "Seems as if I should kind of relish these, but it's goin' to take some time to cook 'em, tendin' the fire an' everything, an' I'd ought to go to work on that poetry. Then, there's another thing, if I have 'em today, I can't tomorrow. Mebbe I shall take more comfort thinkin' about 'em. I guess I'll leave 'em over till tomorrow."

Betsey carried the pan of beans out into the kitchen and set them away in the pantry. She stood scrutinizing the shelves like a veritable Mother Hubbard. There was a plate containing three or four potatoes and a slice of cold boiled pork, and a spoonful of red jelly in a tumbler; that was all the food in sight. Betsey stooped and lifted the lid from an earthen jar on the floor. She took out two slices of bread. "There!" said she. "I'll have this bread and that jelly this noon, an' tonight I'll have a kind of dinner-supper with them potatoes warmed up with the pork. An' then I can sit right down an' go to work on that poetry."

It was scarcely eleven o'clock, and not time for dinner. Betsey returned to the sitting-room, got an old black portfolio and pen and ink out of the chimney cupboard, and seated herself to work. She meditated, and wrote one line, then another. Now and then she read aloud what she had written with a solemn intonation. She sat there thinking and writing, and the time went on. The twelve-o'clock bell rang, but she never noticed it; she had quite forgotten the bread and jelly. The long curls drooped over her cheeks; her thin yellow hand, cramped around the pen, moved slowly and fitfully over the paper. The light in the room was dim and green, like the light in an arbor, from the tall hedge before the windows. Great plumy bunches of asparagus waved over the tops of the looking-glass; a framed sampler,[3] a steel engraving of a female head taken from some old magazine, and sheaves of dried grasses hung on or were fastened to the walls; vases and tumblers of flowers stood on the shelf and table. The air was heavy and sweet.

Betsey in this room, bending over her portfolio, looked like the very genius of gentle, old-fashioned, sentimental poetry. It seemed as if one, given the premises of herself and the room, could easily deduce what she would write, and read without seeing those lines where in flowers rhymed sweetly with vernal bowers, home with beyond the tomb, and heaven with even.

The summer afternoon wore on. It grew warmer and closer; the air was full of the rasping babble of insects, with the cicadas shrilling over them; now and then a team passed, and a dust cloud floated over the top of the hedge; the canary at the door chirped and trilled, and Betsey wrote poor little Willie Caxton's obituary poetry.

Tears stood in her pale blue eyes; occasionally they rolled down her

3. Needlework illustrating a variety of decorative stitches and knots.

cheeks, and she wiped them away. She kept her handkerchief in her lap with her portfolio. When she looked away from the paper she seemed to see two childish forms in the room—one purely human, a boy clad in his little girl petticoats, with a fair chubby face; the other in a little straight white night-gown, with long, shining wings, and the same face. Betsey had not enough imagination to change the face. Little Willie Caxton's angel was still himself to her, although decked in the paraphernalia of the resurrection.

"I s'pose I can't feel about it nor write about it anything the way I could if I'd had any children of my own an' lost 'em. I s'pose it *would* have come home to me different," Betsey murmured once, sniffing. A soft color flamed up under her curls at the thought. For a second the room seemed all aslant with white wings, and smiling with the faces of children that had never been. Betsey straightened herself as if she were trying to be dignified to her inner consciousness. "That's one trouble I've been clear of, anyhow," said she; "an' I guess I can enter into her feelin's considerable."

She glanced at a great pink shell on the shelf, and remembered how she had often given it to the dead child to play with when he had been in with his mother, and how he had put it to his ear to hear the sea.

"Dear little fellow!" she sobbed, and sat awhile with her handker-chief at her face.

Betsey wrote her poem upon backs of old letters and odd scraps of paper. She found it difficult to procure enough paper for fair copies[4] of her poems when composed; she was forced to be very economical with the first draft. Her portfolio was piled with a loose litter of written papers when she at length arose and stretched her stiff limbs. It was near sunset; men with dinner-pails were tramping past the gate, going home from their work.

Betsey laid the portfolio on the table. "There! I've wrote sixteen verses," said she, "an' I guess I've got everything in. I guess she'll think that's enough. I can copy it off nice tomorrow. I can't see tonight to do it, anyhow."

There were red spots on Betsey's cheeks; her knees were unsteady when she walked. She went into the kitchen and made a fire, and set on the tea-kettle. "I guess I won't warm up them potatoes tonight," said she; "I'll have the bread an' jelly, an' save 'em for breakfast. Somehow I don't seem to feel so much like 'em as I did, an' fried potatoes is apt to lay heavy at night."

When the kettle boiled, Betsey drank her cup of tea and soaked her slice of bread in it; then she put away her cup and saucer and plate, and went out to water her garden. The weather was so dry and hot it had to be watered every night. Betsey had to carry the water from a neighbor's well; her own was dry. Back and forth she went in the deepening twilight, her slender body strained to one side with the

4. Neat, exact final copies.

heavy water-pail, until the garden-mould looked dark and wet. Then she took in the canary-bird, locked up her house, and soon her light went out. Often on these summer nights Betsey went to bed without lighting a lamp at all. There was no moon, but it was a beautiful starlight night. She lay awake nearly all night, thinking of her poem. She altered several lines in her mind.

She arose early, made herself a cup of tea, and warmed over the potatoes, then sat down to copy the poem. She wrote it out on both sides of note-paper, in a neat, cramped hand. It was the middle of the afternoon before it was finished. She had been obliged to stop work and cook the beans for dinner, although she begrudged the time. When the poem was fairly copied, she rolled it neatly and tied it with a bit of black ribbon; then she made herself ready to carry it to Mrs. Caxton's.

It was a hot afternoon. Betsey went down the street in her thinnest dress—an old delaine,[5] with delicate bunches of faded flowers on a faded green ground. There was a narrow green belt ribbon around her long waist. She wore a green barège bonnet, stiffened with rattans,[6] scooping over her face, with her curls pushed forward over her thin cheeks in two bunches, and she carried a small green parasol with a jointed handle. Her costume was obsolete, even in the little country village where she lived. She had worn it every summer for the last twenty years. She made no more change in her attire than the old perennials in her garden. She had no money with which to buy new clothes, and the old satisfied her. She had come to regard them as being as unalterably a part of herself as her body.

Betsey went on, setting her slim, cloth-gaitered feet daintily in the hot sand of the road. She carried her roll of poetry in a black-mitted hand. She walked rather slowly. She was not very strong; there was a limp feeling in her knees; her face, under the green shade of her bonnet, was pale and moist with the heat.

She was glad to reach Mrs. Caxton's and sit down in her parlor, damp and cool and dark as twilight, for the blinds and curtains had been drawn all day. Not a breath of the fervid outdoor air had penetrated it.

"Come right in this way; it's cooler than the sittin'-room," Mrs. Caxton said; and Betsey sank into the hair-cloth rocker and waved a palm-leaf fan.

Mrs. Caxton sat close to the window in the dim light, and read the poem. She took out her handkerchief and wiped her eyes as she read. "It's beautiful, beautiful," she said, tearfully, when she had finished. "It's jest as comfortin' as it can be, and you worked that in about his new suit so nice. I feel real obliged to you, Betsey, and you shall have one of the printed ones when they're done. I'm goin' to see to it right off."

5. A light fabric of wool or cotton and wool.   sheer fabric of silk, cotton, or wool, first woven in
6. Stems of palms used as fabric stays. Barège: a   Barèges, France.

Betsey flushed and smiled. It was to her as if her poem had been approved and accepted by one of the great magazines. She had the pride and self-wonderment of recognized genius. She went home buoyantly, under the wilting sun, after her call was done. When she reached home there was no one to whom she could tell her triumph, but the hot spicy breath of the evergreen hedge and the fervent sweetness of the sweet-peas seemed to greet her like the voices of friends.

She could scarcely wait for the printed poem. Mrs. Caxton brought it, and she inspected it, neatly printed in its black border. She was quite overcome with innocent pride.

"Well, I don't know but it does read pretty well," said she.

"It's beautiful," said Mrs. Caxton, fervently. "Mr. White said he never read anything any more touchin', when I carried it to him to print. I think folks are goin' to think a good deal of havin' it. I've had two dozen printed."

It was to Betsey like a large edition of a book. She had written obituary poems before, but never one had been printed in this sumptuous fashion. "I declare I think it would look pretty framed!" said she.

"Well, I don't know but it would," said Mrs. Caxton. "Anybody might have a neat little black frame, and it would look real appropriate."

"I wonder how much it would cost?" said Betsey.

After Mrs. Caxton had gone, she sat long, staring admiringly at the poem, and speculating as to the cost of a frame. "There ain't no use; I can't have it nohow, not if it don't cost more'n a quarter of a dollar," said she.

Then she put the poem away and got her supper. Nobody knew how frugal Betsey Dole's suppers and breakfasts and dinners were. Nearly all her food in the summer came from the scanty vegetables which flourished between the flowers in her garden. She ate scarcely more than her canary-bird, and sang as assiduously. Her income was almost infinitesimal: the interest at a low per cent. of a tiny sum in the village savings-bank, the remnant of her father's little hoard after his funeral expenses had been paid. Betsey had lived upon it for twenty years, and considered herself well-to-do. She had never received a cent for her poems; she had not thought of such a thing as possible. The appearance of this last in such shape was worth more to her than its words represented in as many dollars.

Betsey kept the poem pinned on the wall under the looking-glass; if any one came in, she tried with delicate hints to call attention to it. It was two weeks after she received it that the downfall of her innocent pride came.

One afternoon Mrs. Caxton called. It was raining hard. Betsey could scarcely believe it was she when she went to the door and found her standing there.

"Why, Mis' Caxton!" said she. "Ain't you wet to your skin?"

"Yes, I guess I be, pretty near. I s'pose I hadn't ought to come 'way down here in such a soak; but I went into Sarah Rogers's a minute after dinner, and something she said made me so mad, I made up my mind I'd come down here and tell you about it if I got drowned." Mrs. Caxton was out of breath; rain-drops trickled from her hair over her face; she stood in the door and shut her umbrella with a vicious shake to scatter the water from it. "I don't know what you're goin' to do with this," said she; "it's drippin'."

"I'll take it out an' put it in the kitchen sink."

"Well, I'll take off my shawl here too, and you can hang it out in the kitchen. I spread this shawl out. I thought it would keep the rain off me some. I know one thing, I'm goin' to have a waterproof[7] if I live."

When the two women were seated in the sitting-room, Mrs. Caxton was quiet for a moment. There was a hesitating look on her face, fresh with the moist wind, with strands of wet hair clinging to the temples.

"I don't know as I had ought to tell you," she said, doubtfully.

"Why hadn't you ought to?"

"Well, I don't care; I'm goin' to, anyhow. I think you'd ought to know, an' it ain't so bad for you as it is for me. It don't begin to be. I put considerable money into 'em. I think Mr. White was pretty high, myself."

Betsey looked scared. "What is it?" she asked, in a weak voice.

"*Sarah Rogers says that the minister told her Ida that that poetry you wrote was jest as poor as it could be, an' it was in dreadful bad taste to have it printed an' sent round that way.* What do you think of that?"

Betsey did not reply. She sat looking at Mrs. Caxton as a victim whom the first blow had not killed might look at her executioner. Her face was like a pale wedge of ice between her curls.

Mrs. Caxton went on. "Yes, she said that right to my face, word for word. An' there was something else. She said the minister said that you had never wrote anything that could be called poetry, an' it was a dreadful waste of time. I don't s'pose he thought 'twas comin' back to you. You know he goes with Ida Rogers, an' I s'pose he said it to her kind of confidential when she showed him the poetry. There! I gave Sarah Rogers one of them nice printed ones, an' she acted glad enough to have it. Bad taste! H'm! If anybody wants to say anything against that beautiful poetry, printed with that nice black border, they can. I don't care if it's the minister, or who it is. I don't care if he does write poetry himself, an' has had some printed in a magazine. Maybe his ain't quite so fine as he thinks 'tis. Maybe them magazine folks jest took his for lack of something better. I'd like to have you send that poetry there. Bad taste! I jest got right up. 'Sarah Rogers,' says I, 'I hope you won't never do anything yourself in any worse taste.' I trembled so I could hardly speak, and I made up my mind I'd come right straight over here."

Mrs. Caxton went on and on. Betsey sat listening, and saying noth-

---

7. A garment rendered impervious to water by treatment with india rubber; thus, a raincoat or poncho.

ing. She looked ghastly. Just before Mrs. Caxton went home she noticed it. "Why, Betsey Dole," she cried, "you look as white as a sheet. You ain't takin' it to heart as much as all that comes to, I hope. Goodness, I wish I hadn't told you!"

"I'd a good deal ruther you told me," replied Betsey, with a certain dignity. She looked at Mrs. Caxton. Her back was as stiff as if she were bound to a stake.

"Well, I thought you would," said Mrs. Caxton, uneasily; "and you're dreadful silly if you take it to heart, Betsey, that's all I've got to say. Goodness, I guess I don't, and it's full as hard on me as 'tis on you!"

Mrs. Caxton arose to go. Betsey brought her shawl and umbrella from the kitchen, and helped her off. Mrs. Caxton turned on the doorstep and looked back at Betsey's white face. "Now don't go to thinkin' about it any more," said she. "I ain't goin' to. It ain't worth mindin'. Everybody knows what Sarah Rogers is. Good-by."

"Good-by, Mis' Caxton," said Betsey. She went back into the sitting-room. It was a cold rain, and the room was gloomy and chilly. She stood looking out of the window, watching the rain pelt on the hedge. The bird-cage hung at the other window. The bird watched her with his head on one side; then he begun to chirp.

Suddenly Betsey faced about and began talking. It was not as if she were talking to herself; it seemed as if she recognized some other presence in the room. "I'd like to know if it's fair," said she. "I'd like to know if you think it's fair. Had I ought to have been born with the wantin' to write poetry if I couldn't write it—had I? Had I ought to have been let to write all my life, an' not know before there wa'n't any use in it? Would it be fair if that canary-bird there, that ain't never done anything but sing, should turn out not to be singin'? Would it, I'd like to know? S'pose them sweet-peas shouldn't be smellin' the right way? I ain't been dealt with as fair as they have, I'd like to know if I have."

The bird trilled and trilled. It was as if the golden down on his throat bubbled. Betsey went across the room to a cupboard beside the chimney. On the shelves were neatly stacked newspapers and little white rolls of writing-paper. Betsey began clearing the shelves. She took out the newspapers first, got the scissors, and cut a poem neatly out of the corner of each. Then she took up the clipped poems and the white rolls in her apron, and carried them into the kitchen. She cleaned out the stove carefully, removing every trace of ashes; then she put in the papers, and set them on fire. She stood watching them as their edges curled and blackened, then leaped into flame. Her face twisted as if the fire were curling over it also. Other women might have burned their lovers' letters in agony of heart. Betsey had never had any lover, but she was burning all the love-letters that had passed between her and life. When the flames died out she got a blue china sugar-bowl from the pantry and dipped the ashes into it with one of her thin silver teaspoons; then she put on the cover and set it away in the sitting-room cupboard.

The bird, who had been silent while she was out, began chirping again. Betsey went back to the pantry and got a lump of sugar, which she stuck between the cage wires. She looked at the clock on the kitchen shelf as she went by. It was after six. "I guess I don't want any supper tonight," she muttered.

She sat down by the window again. The bird pecked at his sugar. Betsey shivered and coughed. She had coughed more or less for years. People said she had the old-fashioned consumption.[8] She sat at the window until it was quite dark; then she went to bed in her little bedroom out of the sitting-room. She shivered so she could not hold herself upright crossing the room. She coughed a great deal in the night.

Betsey was always an early riser. She was up at five the next morning. The sun shone, but it was very cold for the season. The leaves showed white in a north wind, and the flowers looked brighter than usual, though they were bent with the rain of the day before. Betsey went out in the garden to straighten her sweet-peas.

Coming back, a neighbor passing in the street eyed her curiously. "Why, Betsey, you sick?" said she.

"No; I'm kinder chilly, that's all," replied Betsey.

But the woman went home and reported that Betsey Dole looked dreadfully, and she didn't believe she'd ever see another summer.

It was now late August. Before October it was quite generally recognized that Betsey Dole's life was nearly over. She had no relatives, and hired nurses were rare in this little village. Mrs. Caxton came voluntarily and took care of her, only going home to prepare her husband's meals. Betsey's bed was moved into the sitting room, and the neighbors came every day to see her, and brought little delicacies. Betsey had talked very little all her life; she talked less now, and there was a reticence about her which somewhat intimidated the other women. They would look pityingly and solemnly at her, and whisper in the entry when they went out.

Betsey never complained; but she kept asking if the minister had got home. He had been called away by his mother's illness, and returned only a week before Betsey died.

He came over at once to see her. Mrs. Caxton ushered him in one afternoon.

"Here's Mr. Lang come to see you, Betsey," said she, in the tone she would have used toward a little child. She placed the rocking-chair for the minister, and was about to seat herself, when Betsey spoke:

"Would you mind goin' out in the kitchen jest a few minutes, Mis' Caxton?" said she.

Mrs. Caxton arose, and went out with an embarrassed trot. Then

---

8. Tuberculosis.

there was silence. The minister was a young man—a country boy who had worked his way through a country college. He was gaunt and awkward, but sturdy in his loose clothes. He had a homely, impetuous face, with a good forehead.

He looked at Betsey's gentle, wasted face, sunken in the pillow, framed by its clusters of curls; finally he began to speak in the stilted fashion, yet with a certain force by reason of his unpolished honesty, about her spiritual welfare. Betsey listened quietly; now and then she assented. She had been a church member for years. It seemed now to the young man that this elderly maiden, drawing near the end of her simple, innocent life, had indeed her lamp, which no strong winds of temptation had ever met, well trimmed and burning.[9]

When he paused, Betsey spoke. "Will you go to the cupboard side of the chimney and bring me the blue sugar-bowl on the top shelf?" said she, feebly.

The young man stared at her a minute; then he went to the cupboard, and brought the sugar-bowl to her. He held it, and Betsey took off the lid with her weak hand. "Do you see what's in there?" said she.

"It looks like ashes."

"It's—the ashes of all—the poetry I—ever wrote."

"Why, what made you burn it, Miss Dole?"

"I found out it wa'n't worth nothin'."

The minister looked at her in a bewildered way. He began to question if she were not wandering in her mind. He did not once suspect his own connection with the matter.

Betsey fastened her eager, sunken eyes upon his face. "What I want to know is—if you'll 'tend to—havin' this—buried with me."

The minister recoiled. He thought to himself that she certainly was wandering.

"No, I ain't out of my head," said Betsey. "I know what I'm sayin'. Maybe it's queer soundin', but it's a notion I've took. If you'll—'tend to it, I shall be—much obliged. I don't know anybody else I can ask."

"Well, I'll attend to it, if you wish me to, Miss Dole," said the minister, in a serious, perplexed manner. She replaced the lid on the sugar-bowl, and left it in his hands.

"Well, I shall be much obliged if you will tend to it; an' now there's something else," said she.

"What is it, Miss Dole?"

She hesitated a moment. "You write poetry, don't you?"

The minister colored. "Why, yes; a little sometimes."

"It's good poetry, ain't it? They printed some in a magazine."

The minister laughed confusedly. "Well, Miss Dole, I don't know how good poetry it may be, but they did print some in a magazine."

9. Matthew 25.1–13 tells the parable of the wise and foolish maidens; in it, Jesus compares the soul ready to enter the kingdom of heaven to the wick of a lamp well-trimmed and ready to be lighted at a moment's notice.

Betsey lay looking at him. "I never wrote none that was—good," she whispered, presently; "but I've been thinkin'—if you would jest write a few—lines about me—afterward—I've been thinkin' that—mebbe my—dyin' was goin' to make me—a good subject for—poetry, if I never wrote none. If you would jest write a few lines."

The minister stood holding the sugar-bowl; he was quite pale with bewilderment and sympathy. "I'll—do the best I can, Miss Dole," he stammered.

"I'll be much obliged," said Betsey, as if the sense of grateful obligation was immortal like herself. She smiled, and the sweetness of the smile was as evident through the drawn lines of her mouth as the old red in the leaves of a withered rose. The sun was setting; a red beam flashed softly over the top of the hedge and lay along the opposite wall; then the bird in his cage began to chirp. He chirped faster and faster until he trilled into a triumphant song.

A New England Nun, 1891

GRACE ELIZABETH KING
1852–1932

Grace Elizabeth King was born November 29, 1852, and lived her entire life in New Orleans, with the exception of several years during the Civil War when the Kings took refuge in a remote plantation in south-central Louisiana. Although both parents were Protestant and of Anglo-Saxon background, they moved comfortably in the circle of upper-class New Orleans Creole society, whose members were descendants of the original French settlers of Louisiana and predominantly Roman Catholic. Her father, William Woodson King, practiced law and served in the Louisiana state legislature. As a member of the Confederate government, King's father was forced to flee New Orleans when Union troops occupied the city in 1862; King's mother, Sarah Ann Miller, demonstrated her character by escaping the occupied city with her family of seven children and five servants and joining her husband at L'Embarras Plantation. When the Kings returned to New Orleans in 1866, they were no longer wealthy, and they lived among Gascons, or working-class French-speaking Creoles. King and her three sisters, however, attended a private Creole school, and after graduation she studied writing at a second private school and received tutoring in French. Both of her parents as well as her maternal grandmother contributed to King's love of storytelling. In her autobiography, King describes her mother in particular as "a charming raconteuse" who entertained her children with endless stories of her girlhood as the only Protestant day boarder in a Creole school (1).

Though she wanted to be a writer from the age of ten, King did not begin her career until 1884, when Julia Ward Howe arrived in New Orleans to direct the Women's Division of the Centennial Exposition. King joined Howe's literary club, and a paper she prepared for the club appeared as her first publication in the New Orleans *Times-Democrat* of May 31, 1885. During the same spring she met Richard Watson Gilder, George Washington Cable's editor at *Century* magazine. After a controversial discussion with Gilder, during which she maintained that Cable had betrayed New Orleans by championing the rights of the freed Negroes and questioning the superiority of Creole culture, Gilder challenged her to write something better. Although *Century* magazine later rejected the story that King immediately went home to write ("Monsieur Motte"), Gilder's challenge led to King's first significant publication, in the *New Princeton Review*, January 1886. This and a series of related stories formed her first collection, *Monsieur Motte* (1888); *Tales of a Time and Place* (1892) would include stories that appeared in *Harper's* during the same period.

From the very beginning of her career Grace King entered the ranks of prominent southern writers. Charles Dudley Warner, literary critic of *Harper's*, became her friend and supporter and introduced her to Samuel and

Olivia Clemens, who would also become close friends. In her autobiography King recalls an incident from a visit to Hartford in 1887. One morning while dressing, she noticed a figure near the pond. She was shocked to learn that she had seen Harriet Beecher Stowe, whose name she associated only with *Uncle Tom's Cabin*—a book she had not been allowed to mention in her household as a child. During a trip to Europe in 1891, King met Madame Marie Thérèse Blanc (Th. Bentzon), a close friend of Sarah Orne Jewett and Annie Fields, and the connection stimulated her interest in writing about French culture.

After the publication of *Balcony Stories* in 1892, King turned almost exclusively to the writing of history and became more a scholar than a writer. A final series of stories appeared in 1916 (*The Pleasant Ways of St. Medard*). For the rest of her life she wrote nonfiction books about the Creole families of New Orleans, a historical romance, and *Memories of a Southern Woman of Letters* (published posthumously in 1932). She died November 29, 1932, apparently of complications following a stroke.

°   °   °

"There is much of life passed on the balcony in a country where the summer unrolls in six moon-lengths," Grace King writes in the opening sketch of *Balcony Stories* (1893). "The Balcony" establishes King's fiction against a background of hot New Orleans nights, oral culture, and women's voices—the secure "noise" that soothes night fears in sleeping children. Unlike their frequently laconic New England counterparts, who turn to writing for self-expression, the women who sit on Grace King's balcony—"men are not balcony sitters"—are talkative—openly expressive and inquisitive. King's characters belong to an oral tradition. They are interested in other women's "destinies" told "as only women know how to relate them"; the stories begin once women have "embarked" on their own lives; and, although the women's stories may seem strikingly similar, to the teller each appears unique as she "inflects" her story, "trying to make the point visible to her apparent also to her hearers."

Unlike another regionalist whose work she admired, Mary Noialles Murfree, who learned about the mountaineers as a summer observer, King acquired her knowledge of Creole life first-hand. Yet King does not write about Creoles because she views them as marginal; rather, by stressing the ties between Creole culture and its origins in France, and by insisting that Creole culture gives New Orleans its regional inflection or identity, she removes from her fiction the American perspective that would make her Creole characters marginal. She presents her characters as speaking French (rather than the broken English of another New Orleans writer, George Washington Cable, or the mountain dialect of Murfree), and she does this, as her biographer notes, "by imitating in English the tone, the lilt, the expression of French and by occasionally using a French phrase or a literally translated phrase" (Bush 94).

Both " 'One of Us' " and "Pupasse" contain elements of self-portraiture for Grace King. Despite the comedy, Pupasse's cries of "quelle injustice" earn King's own sympathies. Perhaps Pupasse is less unable to learn than she is unwilling to grow up, with its prospect of having to leave home and mother. In " 'One of Us,' " King's narrator views the opera singer, an unmarried, professional woman and artist like King herself, from the point of view of a child under her potential care. The singer's charm for the narrator is her capacity for maternal love. This story suggests that for King one of the strengths of the regionalist perspective was the opportunity it offered to write out of her own "mother-knowledge"—as she uses the term in "The Balcony" and as she herself experienced it as the rapt listener to her mother's own stories. The regionalist sketch thus served the same purpose for Grace King that it did for Celia Thaxter and other New England writers: it enabled King to create a soothing "mother-voice" that made the child in her feel central, despite the unpleasantness of the adult's marginality.

Much of Grace King's fiction depicts the humiliation of Reconstruction and the loss of status she and her family endured; her treatment of working-class Creoles and former slaves reflects her position as a member of the fallen aristocracy. In "La Grande Demoiselle," for example, the former plantation owner, Champigny—an avowed misogynist and a member of what King describes as the *nouveaux pauvres*—marries "la grande demoiselle" simply to rescue her from teaching in a public school for former slaves as if she were " 'some Northern lady on a mission.' " King's themes are conservative, and she herself disliked life on the margins, defining it, through the experience of the protagonist in "The Old Lady's Restoration," as a "descent into poverty." Yet—a paradox of sorts—the success King achieves as a regionalist derives from her efforts to write empathically about the disenfranchised.

The Balcony

There is much of life passed on the balcony in a country where the summer unrolls in six moon-lengths, and where the nights have to come with a double endowment of vastness and splendor to compensate for the tedious, sun-parched days.

And in that country the women love to sit and talk together of summer nights, on balconies, in their vague, loose, white garments,—men are not balcony sitters,—with their sleeping children within easy hearing, the stars breaking the cool darkness, or the moon making a show of light—oh, such a discreet show of light!—through the vines. And the children inside, waking to go from one sleep into another, hear the low, soft mother-voices on the balcony, talking about this person and that, old times, old friends, old experiences; and it seems to them, hovering a moment in wakefulness, that there is no end of the world or time, or of the mother-knowledge; but, illimitable as it is, the mother-voices and the mother-love and protection fill it all,—with their mother's hand in theirs, children are not afraid even of God,—and they drift into slumber again, their little dreams taking all kinds of pretty reflections from the great unknown horizon outside, as their fragile soap-bubbles take on reflections from the sun and clouds.

Experiences, reminiscences, episodes, picked up as only women know how to pick them up from other women's lives,—or other women's destinies, as they prefer to call them,—and told as only women know how to relate them; what God has done or is doing with some other woman whom they have known—that is what interests women once embarked on their own lives,—the embarkation takes place at marriage, or after the marriageable time,—or, rather, that is what interests the women who sit of summer nights on balconies. For in those long-moon countries life is open and accessible, and romances seem to be furnished real and gratis, in order to save, in a languor-breeding climate, the ennui of reading and writing books. Each woman has a different way of picking up and relating her stories, as each one selects different pieces, and has a personal way of playing them on the piano.

Each story *is* different, or appears so to her; each has some unique and peculiar pathos in it. And so she dramatizes and inflects it, trying to make the point visible to her apparent also to her hearers. Some-times the pathos and interest to the hearers lie only in this—that the relater has observed it, and gathered it, and finds it worth telling. For do we not gather what we have not, and is not our own lacking our one motive? It may be so, for it often appears so.

And if a child inside be wakeful and precocious, it is not dreams alone that take on reflections from the balcony outside: through the half-open shutters the still, quiet eyes look across the dim forms on the balcony to the star-spangled or the moon-brightened heavens beyond; while memory makes stores for the future, and germs are sown, out of which the slow, clambering vine of thought issues, one day, to decorate or hide, as it may be, the structures or ruins of life.

Century, December 1892; *Balcony Stories,* 1893

A Drama of Three

It was a regular dramatic performance every first of the month in the little cottage of the old General and Madame B——.

It began with the waking up of the General by his wife, standing at the bedside with a cup of black coffee.

"Hé! Ah! Oh, Honorine! Yes; the first of the month, and affairs—affairs to be transacted."

On those mornings when affairs were to be transacted there was not much leisure for the household; and it was Honorine who constituted the household. Not the old dressing-gown and slippers, the old, old trousers, and the antediluvian neck-foulard of other days! Far from it. It was a case of warm water (with even a fling of cologne in it), of the trimming of beard and mustache by Honorine, and the black broad-cloth suit, and the brown satin stock, and that *je ne sais quoi de dégagé*[1] which no one could possess or assume like the old General. Whether he possessed or assumed it is an uncertainty which hung over the fine manners of all the gentlemen of his day, who were kept through their youth in Paris to cultivate *bon ton*[2] and an education.

It was also something of a gala-day for Madame la Générale too, as it must be a gala-day for all old wives to see their husbands

---

1. Indefinable graceful something.   2. Good form.

pranked[3] in the manners and graces that had conquered their maiden-hood, and exhaling once more that ambrosial fragrance which once so well incensed their compelling presence.

Ah, to the end a woman loves to celebrate her conquest! It is the last touch of misfortune with her to lose in the old, the ugly, and the commonplace her youthful lord and master. If one could look under the gray hairs and wrinkles with which time thatches old women, one would be surprised to see the flutterings, the quiverings, the thrills, the emotions, the coals of the heart-fires which death alone extinguishes, when he commands the tenant to vacate.

Honorine's hands chilled with the ice of sixteen as she approached scissors to the white mustache and beard. When her finger-tips brushed those lips, still well formed and roseate, she felt it, strange to say, on her lips. When she asperged[4] the warm water with cologne,—it was her secret delight and greatest effort of economy to buy this cologne,—she always had one little moment of what she called faint-ness—that faintness which had veiled her eyes, and chained her hands, and stilled her throbbing bosom, when as a bride she came from the church with him. It was then she noticed the faint fragrance of the cologne bath. Her lips would open as they did then, and she would stand for a moment and think thoughts to which, it must be confessed, she looked forward from month to month. What a man he had been! In truth he belonged to a period that would accept nothing less from Nature than physical beauty; and Nature is ever subservient to the period. If it is today all small men, and tomorrow gnomes and dwarfs, we may know that the period is demanding them from Nature.

When the General had completed—let it be called no less than the ceremony of—his toilet, he took his chocolate and his *pain de Paris*.[5] Honorine could not imagine him breakfasting on anything but *pain de Paris*. Then he sat himself in his large armchair before his escritoire, and began transacting his affairs with the usual—

"But where is that idiot, that dolt, that sluggard, that snail, with my mail?"

Honorine, busy in the breakfast-room:

"In a moment, husband. In a moment."

"But he should be here now. It is the first of the month, it is nine o'clock, I am ready; he should be here."

"It is not yet nine o'clock, husband."

"Not yet nine! Not yet nine! Am I not up? Am I not dressed? Have I not breakfasted before nine?"

"That is so, husband. That is so."

Honorine's voice, prompt in cheerful acquiescence, came from the next room, where she was washing his cup, saucer, and spoon.

"It is getting worse and worse every day. I tell you, Honorine,

---

3. Dressed ostentatiously.   5. French bread.
4. Sprinkled.

Pompey must be discharged. He is worthless. He is trifling. Discharge him! Discharge him! Do not have him about! Chase him out of the yard! Chase him as soon as he makes his appearance! Do you hear, Honorine?"

"You must have a little patience, husband."

It was perhaps the only reproach one could make to Madame Honorine, that she never learned by experience.

"Patience! Patience! Patience is the invention of dullards and sluggards. In a well-regulated world there should be no need of such a thing as patience. Patience should be punished as a crime, or at least as a breach of the peace. Wherever patience is found police investigation should be made as for smallpox. Patience! Patience! I never heard the word—I assure you, I never heard the word in Paris. What do you think would be said there to the messenger who craved patience of you? Oh, they know too well in Paris—a rataplan[6] from the walking-stick on his back, that would be the answer; and a, 'My good fellow, we are not hiring professors of patience, but legs.' "

"But, husband, you must remember we do not hire Pompey. He only does it to oblige us, out of his kindness."

"Oblige us! Oblige me! Kindness! A Negro oblige me! Kind to me! That is it; that is it. That is the way to talk under the new régime. It is favor, and oblige, and education, and monsieur, and madame, now. What child's play to call this a country—a government! I would not be surprised"—jumping to his next position on this ever-recurring first of the month theme—"I would not be surprised if Pompey has failed to find the letter in the box. How do I know that the mail has not been tampered with? From day to day I expect to hear it. What is to prevent? Who is to interpose? The honesty of the officials? Honesty of the officials—that is good! What a farce—honesty of officials! That is evidently what has happened. The thought has not occurred to me in vain. Pompey has gone. He has not found the letter, and—well; that is the end."

But the General had still another theory to account for the delay in the appearance of his mail which he always posed abruptly after the exhaustion of the arraignment of the post-office.

"And why not Journel?" Journel was their landlord, a fellow of means, but no extraction, and a favorite aversion of the old gentleman's. "Journel himself? You think he is above it, hé? You think Journel would not do such a thing? Ha! your simplicity, Honorine—your simplicity is incredible. It is miraculous. I tell you, I have known the Journels, from father to son, for—yes, for seventy-five years. Was not his grandfather the overseer on my father's plantation? I was not five years old when I began to know the Journels. And this fellow, I know him better than he knows himself. I know him as well as God knows him. I have made up my mind. I have made it up carefully that the first

6. Ratatat.

time that letter fails on the first of the month I shall have Journel arrested as a thief. I shall land him in the penitentiary. What! You think I shall submit to have my mail tampered with by a Journel? Their contents appropriated? What! You think there was no coincidence in Journel's offering me his post-office box just the month—just the month, before those letters began to arrive? You think he did not have some inkling of them? Mark my words, Honorine, he did—by some of his subterranean methods. And all these five years he has been arranging his plans—that is all. He was arranging theft, which no doubt has been consummated today. Oh, I have regretted it—I assure you I have regretted it, that I did not promptly reject his proposition, that, in fact, I ever had anything to do with the fellow."

It was almost invariably, so regularly do events run in this world,—it was almost invariably that the Negro messenger made his appearance at this point. For five years the General had perhaps not been interrupted as many times, either above or below the last sentence. The mail, or rather the letter, was opened, and the usual amount—three ten-dollar bills—was carefully extracted and counted. And as if he scented the bills, even as the General said he did, within ten minutes after their delivery, Journel made his appearance to collect the rent.

It could only have been in Paris, among that old retired nobility, who counted their names back, as they expressed it, "au de çà du déluge," that could have been acquired the proper manner of treating a "roturier"[7] landlord: to measure him with the eyes from head to foot; to hand the rent—the ten-dollar bill—with the tips of the fingers; to scorn a look at the humbly tendered receipt; to say: "The cistern needs repairing, the roof leaks; I must warn you that unless such notifications meet with more prompt attention than in the past, you must look for another tenant," etc., in the monotonous tone of supremacy, and in the French, not of Journel's dictionary, nor of the dictionary of any such as he, but in the French of Racine and Corneille; in the French of the above suggested circle, which inclosed the General's memory, if it had not inclosed—as he never tired of recounting—his star-like personality.

A sheet of paper always infolded the bank-notes. It always bore, in fine but sexless tracery, "From one who owes you much."

There, that was it, that sentence, which, like a locomotive, bore the General and his wife far on these firsts of the month to two opposite points of the horizon, in fact, one from the other—"From one who owes you much."

The old gentleman would toss the paper aside with the bill receipt. In the man to whom the bright New Orleans itself almost owed its brightness, it was a paltry act to search and pick for a debtor. Friends had betrayed and deserted him; relatives had forgotten him; merchants had failed with his money; bank presidents had stooped to deceive him; for he was an old man, and had about run the gamut of

7. Plebian, common. Au de çà du déluge: on this side of the flood, or, in other words, pretty far back.

human disappointments—a gamut that had begun with a C major of trust, hope, happiness, and money.

His political party had thrown him aside. Neither for ambassador, plenipotentiary, senator, congressman, not even for a clerkship, could he be nominated by it. Certes! "From one who owed him much." He had fitted the cap to a new head, the first of every month, for five years, and still the list was not exhausted. Indeed, it would have been hard for the General to look anywhere and not see someone whose obligations to him far exceeded this thirty dollars a month. Could he avoid being happy with such eyes?

But poor Madame Honorine! She who always gathered up the receipts, and the "From one who owes you much"; who could at an instant's warning produce the particular ones for any month of the past half-decade. She kept them filed, not only in her armoire, but the scrawled papers—skewered, as it were, somewhere else—where women from time immemorial have skewered such unsigned papers. She was not original in her thoughts—no more, for the matter of that, than the General was. Tapped at any time on the first of the month, when she would pause in her drudgery to reimpale her heart by a sight of the written characters on the scrap of paper, her thoughts would have been found flowing thus, "One can give everything, and yet be sure of nothing."

When Madame Honorine said "everything," she did not, as women in such cases often do, exaggerate. When she married the General, she in reality gave the youth of sixteen, the beauty (ah, do not trust the denial of those wrinkles, the thin hair, the faded eyes!) of an angel, the dot[8] of an heiress. Alas! It was too little at the time. Had she in her own person united all the youth, all the beauty, all the wealth, sprinkled parsimoniously so far and wide over all the women in this land, would she at that time have done aught else with this than immolate it on the burning pyre of the General's affection? "And yet be sure of nothing."

It is not necessary, perhaps, to explain that last clause. It is very little consolation for wives that their husbands have forgotten, when someone else remembers. Someone else! Ah! there could be so many someone elses in the General's life, for in truth he had been irresistible to excess. But this was one particular someone else who had been faithful for five years. Which one?

When Madame Honorine solves that enigma she has made up her mind how to act.

As for Journel, it amused him more and more. He would go away from the little cottage rubbing his hands with pleasure (he never saw Madame Honorine, by the way, only the General). He would have given far more than thirty dollars a month for this drama; for he was not only rich, but a great *farceur*.[9]

Century, December 1892; *Balcony Stories*, 1893

---

8. Dowry.   9. Practical joker.

La Grande Demoiselle[1]

That was what she was called by everybody as soon as she was seen or described. Her name, besides baptismal titles,[2] was Idalie Sainte Foy Mortemart des Islets. When she came into society, in the brilliant little world of New Orleans, it was the event of the season, and after she came in, whatever she did became also events. Whether she went, or did not go; what she said, or did not say; what she wore, and did not wear—all these became important matters of discussion, quoted as much or more than what the president said, or the governor thought. And in those days, the days of '59, New Orleans was not, as it is now, a one-heiress place,[3] but it may be said that one could find heiresses then as one finds type-writing girls now.

Mademoiselle Idalie received her birth, and what education she had, on her parents' plantation, the famed old Reine Sainte Foy place, and it is no secret that, like the ancient kings of France, her birth exceeded her education.

It was a plantation, the Reine Sainte Foy, the richness and luxury of which are really well described in those perfervid pictures of tropical life, at one time the passion of philanthropic imaginations, excited and exciting over the horrors of slavery. Although these pictures were then often accused of being purposely exaggerated, they seem now to fall short of, instead of surpassing, the truth. Stately walls, acres of roses, miles of oranges, unmeasured fields of cane, colossal sugar-house— they were all there, and all the rest of it, with the slaves, slaves, slaves everywhere, whole villages of Negro cabins. And there were also, most noticeable to the natural, as well as to the visionary, eye—there were the ease, idleness, extravagance, self-indulgence, pomp, pride, arrogance, in short the whole enumeration, the moral *sine qua non*,[4] as some people considered it, of the wealthy slaveholder of aristocratic descent and tastes.

What Mademoiselle Idalie cared to learn she studied, what she did not she ignored; and she followed the same simple rule untrammeled in her eating, drinking, dressing, and comportment generally; and whatever discipline may have been exercised on the place, either in fact or fiction, most assuredly none of it, even so much as in a threat, ever attainted her sacred person. When she was just turned sixteen, Mademoiselle Idalie made up her mind to go into society. Whether she was beautiful or not, it is hard to say. It is almost impossible to appreciate properly the beauty of the rich, the very rich. The unfettered development, the limitless choice of accessories, the confidence, the self-esteem, the sureness of expression, the simplicity of purpose, the ease of execution—all these produce a certain effect of beauty behind which one really cannot get to measure length of nose, or brilliancy of

1. The great gentlewoman, the great lady.
2. Names given upon the occasion of baptism.
3. An allusion to the relative poverty of the New
Orleans aristocracy in the post–Civil War period.
4. The essential condition.

eye. This much can be said: there was nothing in her that positively contradicted any assumption of beauty on her part, or credit of it on the part of others. She was very tall and very thin with small head, long neck, black eyes, and abundant straight black hair,—for which her hair-dresser deserved more praise than she,—good teeth, of course, and a mouth that, even in prayer, talked nothing but commands; that is about all she had *en fait d'ornements*,[5] as the modistes say. It may be added that she walked as if the Reine Sainte Foy plantation extended over the whole earth, and the soil of it were too vile for her tread. Of course she did not buy her toilets[6] in New Orleans. Everything was ordered from Paris, and came as regularly through the custom-house as the modes and robes to the milliners. She was furnished by a certain house there, just as one of a royal family would be at the present day. As this had lasted from her layette up to her sixteenth year, it may be imagined what took place when she determined to make her début. Then it was literally, not metaphorically, *carte blanche*, at least so it got to the ears of society. She took a sheet of note-paper, wrote the date at the top, added, "I make my début in November," signed her name at the extreme end of the sheet, addressed it to her dressmaker in Paris, and sent it.

It was said that in her dresses the very handsomest silks were used for linings, and that real lace was used where others put imitation,— around the bottoms of the skirts, for instance,—and silk ribbons of the best quality served the purposes of ordinary tapes; and sometimes the buttons were of real gold and silver, sometimes set with precious stones. Not that she ordered these particulars, but the dressmakers, when given *carte blanche* by those who do not condescend to details, so soon exhaust the outside limits of garments that perforce they take to plastering them inside with gold, so to speak, and, when the bill goes in, they depend upon the furnishings to carry out a certain amount of the contract in justifying the price. And it was said that these costly dresses, after being worn once or twice, were cast aside, thrown upon the floor, given to the Negroes—anything to get them out of sight. Not an inch of the real lace, not one of the jeweled buttons, not a scrap of ribbon, was ripped off to save. And it was said that if she wanted to romp with her dogs in all her finery, she did it; she was known to have ridden horseback, one moonlight night, all around the plantation in a white silk dinner-dress flounced with Alençon.[7] And at night, when she came from the balls, tired, tired to death as only balls can render one, she would throw herself down upon her bed in her tulle skirts,—on top, or not, of the exquisite flowers, she did not care,—and make her maid undress her in that position; often having her bodices cut off her, because she was too tired to turn over and have them unlaced.

That she was admired, raved about, loved even, goes without saying.

5. In the way of adornment, embellishment.
6. Dress or attire.

7. Fine lace from Alençon, in northwest France.

After the first month she held the refusal of half the beaux of New Orleans. Men did absurd, undignified, preposterous things for her; and she? Love? Marry? The idea never occurred to her. She treated the most exquisite of her pretenders no better than she treated her Paris gowns, for the matter of that. She could not even bring herself to listen to a proposal patiently; whistling to her dogs, in the middle of the most ardent protestations, or jumping up and walking away with a shrug of the shoulders, and a "Bah!"

Well! Everyone knows what happened after '59.[8] There is no need to repeat. The history of one is the history of all. But there was this difference—for there is every shade of difference in misfortune, as there is every shade of resemblance in happiness. Mortemart des Islets went off to fight. That was natural; his family had been doing that, he thought, or said, ever since Charlemagne.[9] Just as naturally he was killed in the first engagement. They, his family, were always among the first killed; so much so that it began to be considered assassination to fight a duel with any of them. All that was in the ordinary course of events. One difference in their misfortunes lay in that after the city was captured, their plantation, so near, convenient, and rich in all kinds of provisions, was selected to receive a contingent of troops—a colored company. If it had been a colored company raised in Louisiana it might have been different; and these Negroes mixed with the Negroes in the neighborhood,—and Negroes are no better than whites, for the proportion of good and bad among them,—and the officers were always off duty when they should have been on, and on when they should have been off.

One night the dwelling caught fire. There was an immediate rush to save the ladies. Oh, there was no hesitation about that! They were seized in their beds, and carried out in the very arms of their enemies; carried away off to the sugar-house, and deposited there. No danger of their doing anything but keep very quiet and still in their *chemises de nuit*,[1] and their one sheet apiece, which was about all that was saved from the conflagration—that is, for them. But it must be remembered that this is all hearsay. When one has not been present, one knows nothing of one's own knowledge; one can only repeat. It has been repeated, however, that although the house was burned to the ground, and everything in it destroyed, wherever, for a year afterward, a man of that company or of that neighborhood was found, there could have been found also, without search-warrant, property that had belonged to the Des Islets. That is the story; and it is believed or not, exactly according to prejudice.

How the ladies ever got out of the sugar-house, history does not relate; nor what they did. It was not a time for sociability, either

---

8. A reference to John Brown's raid on Harpers Ferry in October 1859, an attempt to create a slave rebellion; this event increased support in the South for secession, leading ultimately to the Civil War by 1861.

9. Charles the Great (742–814), king of the Franks and later emperor of the Romans.

1. Nightshirts.

personal or epistolary. At one offensive word your letter, and you, very likely, examined; and Ship Island[2] for a hotel, with soldiers for hostesses! Madame Des Islets died very soon after the accident—of rage, they say; and that was about all the public knew.

Indeed, at that time the society of New Orleans had other things to think about than the fate of the Des Islets. As for *la grande demoiselle*, she had prepared for her own oblivion in the hearts of her female friends. And the gentlemen,—her *preux chevaliers*,[3] —they were burning with other passions than those which had driven them to her knees, encountering a little more serious response than "bahs" and shrugs. And, after all, a woman seems the quickest thing forgotten when once the important affairs of life come to men for consideration.

It might have been ten years according to some calculations, or ten eternities,—the heart and the almanac never agree about time,—but one morning old Champigny (they used to call him Champignon) was walking along his levee front,[4] calculating how soon the water would come over, and drown him out, as the Louisianians say. It was before a seven-o'clock breakfast, cold, wet, rainy, and discouraging. The road was knee-deep in mud, and so broken up with hauling, that it was like walking upon waves to get over it. A shower poured down. Old Champigny was hurrying in when he saw a figure approaching. He had to stop to look at it, for it was worth while. The head was hidden by a green barege veil, which the showers had plentifully besprinkled with dew; a tall, thin figure. Figure! No; not even could it be called a figure: straight up and down, like a finger or a post; high-shouldered, and a step—a step like a plowman's. No umbrella; no—nothing more, in fact. It does not sound so peculiar as when first related—something must be forgotten. The feet—oh, yes, the feet—they were like waffle-irons, or frying-pans, or anything of that shape.

Old Champigny did not care for women—he never had; they simply did not exist for him in the order of Nature. He had been married once, it is true, about a half century before; but that was not reckoned against the existence of his prejudice, because he was *célibataire*[5] to his finger-tips, as any one could see a mile away. But that woman *intrigué'd* him.

He had no servant to inquire from. He performed all of his own domestic work in the wretched little cabin that replaced his old home. For Champigny also belonged to the great majority of the *nouveaux pauvres*.[6] He went out into the rice-field, where were one or two hands that worked on shares with him, and he asked them. They knew immediately; there is nothing connected with the parish that a field-hand does not know at once. She was the teacher of the colored public school some three or four miles away. "Ah," thought Champigny,

2. An island in the Gulf of Mexico off the coast of Mississippi.
3. Proven chevaliers, or devoted admirers.
4. A waterfront at a raised embankment or landing-place on a river. Champignon: mushroom.
5. Bachelor.
6. Newly poor.

"some Northern lady on a mission." He watched to see her return in the evening, which she did, of course; in a blinding rain. Imagine the green barege veil then; for it remained always down over her face.

Old Champigny could not get over it that he had never seen her before. But he must have seen her, and, with his abstraction and old age, not have noticed her, for he found out from the Negroes that she had been teaching four or five years there. And he found out also—how, is not important—that she was Idalie Sainte Foy Mortemart des Islets. *La grande demoiselle!* He had never known her in the old days, owing to his uncomplimentary attitude toward women, but he knew of her, of course, and of her family. It should have been said that his plantation was about fifty miles higher up the river, and on the opposite bank to Reine Sainte Foy. It seemed terrible. The old gentleman had had reverses of his own, which would bear the telling, but nothing was more shocking to him than this—that Idalie Sainte Foy Mortemart des Islets should be teaching a public colored school for—it makes one blush to name it—seven dollars and a half a month. For seven dollars and a half a month to teach a set of—well! He found out where she lived, a little cabin—not so much worse than his own, for that matter—in the corner of a field; no companion, no servant, nothing but food and shelter. Her clothes have been described.

Only the good God himself knows what passed in Champigny's mind on the subject. We know only the results. He went and married *la grande demoiselle.* How? Only the good God knows that too. Every first of the month, when he goes to the city to buy provisions, he takes her with him—in fact, he takes her everywhere with him.

Passengers on the railroad know them well, and they always have a chance to see her face. When she passes her old plantation *la grande demoiselle* always lifts her veil for one instant—the inevitable green barege veil. What a face! Thin, long, sallow, petrified! And the neck! If she would only tie something around the neck! And her plain, coarse cottonade gown! The Negro women about her were better dressed than she.

Poor old Champignon! It was not an act of charity to himself, no doubt cross and disagreeable, besides being ugly. And as for love, gratitude!

Century, January 1893; *Balcony Stories,* 1893

"One of Us"

At the first glance one might have been inclined to doubt; but at the second anybody would have recognized her—that is, with a little mental rehabilitation: the bright little rouge spots in the hollow of her cheek, the eyebrows well accentuated with paint, the thin lips rose-tinted, and the dull, straight hair frizzed and curled and twisted and turned by that consummate rascal and artist, the official beautifier and rectifier of stage humanity, Robert, the opera *coiffeur*. Who in the world knows better than he the gulf between the real and the ideal, the limitations between the natural and the romantic?

Yes, one could see her, in that time-honored thin silk dress of hers stiffened into brocade by buckram underneath; the high, low-necked waist, hiding any evidences of breast, if there were such evidences to hide, and bringing the long neck into such faulty prominence; and the sleeves, crisp puffs of tulle divided by bands of red velvet, through which the poor lean arm runs like a wire, stringing them together like beads. Yes, it was she, the whilom *dugazon*[1] of the opera troupe. Not that she ever was a *dugazon*, but that was what her voice once aspired to be: a *dugazon manquée*[2] would better describe her.

What a ghost! But they always appeared like mere evaporations of real women. For what woman of flesh and blood can seriously maintain through life the rôle of sham attendant on sham sensations, and play public celebrant of other women's loves and lovers, singing, or rather saying, nothing more enlivening than: "Oh, madame!" and "Ah, madame!" and *"Quelle ivresse!"* or *"Quelle horreur!"*[3] or, in recitative, detailing whatever dreary platitudes and inanities the librettist and Heaven connive to put upon the tongues of confidantes and attendants?

Looking at her—how it came over one! The music, the lights, the scene; the fat soprano confiding to her the fact of the "amour extrême" she bears for the tenor, to which she, the *dugazon*, does not even try to listen; her eyes wandering listlessly over the audience. The calorous secret out, and in her possession, how she stumbles over her train to the back of the stage, there to pose in abject patience and awkwardness, while the gallant baritone, touching his sword, and flinging his cape over his shoulder, defies the world and the tenor, who is just recovering from his "ut de poitrine"[4] behind the scenes.

She was talking to me all the time, apologizing for the intrusion, explaining her mission, which involved a short story of her life, as women's intrusions and missions usually do. But my thoughts, also as usual, distracted me from listening, as so often they have distracted me from following what was perhaps more profitable.

The composer, of course, wastes no music upon her; flinging to her only an occasional recitative in two notes, but always ending in a reef of a scale, trill, or roulade, for her to wreck her voice on before the audience. The *chef d'orchestre*, if he is charitable, starts her off with a contribution from his own lusty lungs, and then she—oh, her voice is always thinner and more osseous than her arms, and her smile no more graceful than her train!

---

1. The singer who takes the young coquettish roles in light opera; from French singer Rosalie Dugazon (1755–1821). Whilom: former.
2. Unsuccessful, failed.

3. "What wildness!"; "what horror!"
4. A vocal exercise of hitting the note C deep in the chest.

As well think of the simulated trees, waterfalls, and châteaux leaving the stage, as the *dugazon!* One always imagines them singing on into dimness, dustiness, unsteadiness, and uselessness, until, like any other piece of stage property, they are at last put aside and simply left there at the end of some season—there seems to be a superstition against selling or burning useless and dilapidated stage property. As it came to me, the idea was not an impossibility. The last representation of the season is over. She, tired beyond judgment—haply, beyond feeling— by her tireless rôle, sinks upon her chair to rest in her dressing-room; sinks, further, to sleep. She has no maid. The troupe, hurrying away to France on the special train waiting not half a dozen blocks away, forget her—the insignificant are so easily forgotten! The porter, more tired, perhaps, than any one of the beautiful ideal world about him, and savoring already in advance the good onion-flavored *grillade* awaiting him at home, locks up everything fast and tight; the tighter and faster for the good fortnight's vacation he has promised himself.

No doubt if the old opera-house were ever cleaned out, just such a heap of stiff, wire-strung bones would be found, in some such hole as the *dugazon's* dressing-room, desiccating away in its last costume— perhaps in that very costume of *Inez;*[5] and if one were venturesome enough to pass Allhallowe'en there, the spirit of those bones might be seen availing itself of the privilege of unasperged corpses to roam. Not singing, not talking—it is an anachronism to say that ghosts talk: their medium of communication must be pure thought; and one should be able to see their thoughts working, just as one sees the working of the digestive organs in the clear viscera of transparent animalculæ.[6] The hard thing of it is that ghosts are chained to the same scenes that chained their bodies, and when they sleep-walk, so to speak, it must be through phases of former existence. What a nightmare for them to go over once again the lived and done, the suffered and finished! What a comfort to wake up and find one's self dead, well dead!

I could have continued and put the whole opera troupe in "costume de ghost," but I think it was the woman's eyes that drew me back to her face and her story. She had a sensible face, now that I observed her naturally, as it were; and her hands,—how I have agonized over those hands on the stage!—all knuckles and exaggerated veins, clutching her dress as she sang, or, petrified, outstretched to *Leonore's* "Pourquoi ces larmes?"[7]—her hands were the hands of an honest, hard-working woman who buckrams[8] her own skirts, and at need could scrub her own floor. Her face (my description following my wandering glance)— her face was careworn, almost to desuetude; not dissipation-worn, as, alas! the faces of the more gifted ladies of opera troupes too often are. There was no fattening in it of pastry, truffles, and bonbons; upon it

---

5. The name of Leonora's confidante in Donizetti's opera *La Favorita* (1840).
6. Microscopic organisms, such as amoebas.
7. The aria "Why these tears?" sung by Leonore,

heroine of *La Favorita.*
8. Adds glue as sizing to coarse fabric so that it becomes stiff.

none of the tracery left by nightly champagne tides and ripples; and consequently her figure, under her plain dress, had not that for display which the world has conventioned to call charms. Where a window-cord would hardly have sufficed to girdle *Leonore,* a necklace would have served her. She had not beauty enough to fear the flattering dangers of masculine snares and temptations,—or there may have been other reasons,—but as a wife—there was something about her that guaranteed it—she would have blossomed love and children as a fig-tree does figs.

In truth, she was just talking about children. The first part of her story had passed: her birthplace, education, situation; and now she was saying:

"I have always had the temptation, but I have always resisted it. Now,"—with a blush at her excuse,—"it may be your spring weather, your birds, your flowers, your sky—and your children in the streets. The longing came over me yesterday: I thought of it on the stage, I thought of it afterward—it was better than sleeping; and this morning"—her eyes moistened, she breathed excitedly—"I was determined. I gave up, I made inquiry, I was sent to you. Would it be possible? Would there be any place" ("any rôle," she said first) "in any of your asylums, in any of your charitable institutions, for me? I would ask nothing but my clothes and food, and very little of that; the recompense would be the children—the little girl children," with a smile— can you imagine the smile of a woman dreaming of children that might be? "Think! Never to have held a child in my arms more than a moment, never to have felt a child's arms about my neck! Never to have known a child! Born on a stage, my mother born on a stage!" Ah, there were tragic possibilities in that voice and movement! "Pardon, madam. You see how I repeat. And you must be very wearied hearing about me. But I could be their nurse and their servant. I would bathe and dress them, play with them, teach them their prayers; and when they are sick they would see no difference. They would not know but what their mother was there!"

Oh, she had her program all prepared; one could see that.

"And I would sing to them—no! no!" with a quick gesture, "nothing from the stage; little songs and lullabys I have picked up traveling around, and," hesitating, "little things I have composed myself—little things that I thought children would like to hear some day." What did she not unconsciously throw into those last words? "I dream of it," she pursued, talking with as little regard to me as on the stage she sang to the prima donna.[9] "Their little arms, their little faces, their little lips! And in an asylum there would be so many of them! When they cried and were in trouble I would take them in my lap, and I would say to them, with all sorts of tenderness—" She had arranged that in her program, too—all the minutiæ of what she would say to them in their

---

9. The leading female soloist in an opera company.

distress. But women are that way. When once they begin to love, their hearts are magnifying-lenses for them to feel through. "And my heart hungers to commence right here, now, at once! It seems to me I cannot wait. Ah, madam, no more stage, no more opera!" speaking quickly, feverishly. "As I said, it may be your beautiful spring, your flowers, your birds, and your numbers of children. I have always loved that place most where there are most children; and you have more children here than I ever saw anywhere. Children are so beautiful! It is strange, is it not, when you consider my life and my rearing?"

Her life, her rearing, how interesting they must have been! What a pity I had not listened more attentively!

"They say you have much to do with asylums here."

Evidently, when rôles do not exist in life for certain characters, God has to create them. And thus He had to create a rôle in an asylum for my friend, for so she became from the instant she spoke of children as she did. It was the poorest and neediest of asylums; and the poor little orphaned wretches—but it is better not to speak of them. How can God ever expect to rear children without their mothers!

But the rôle I craved to create for my friend was far different—some good, honest bourgeois interior, where lips are coarse and cheeks are ruddy, and where life is composed of real scenes, set to the real music of life, the homely successes and failures, and loves and hates, and embraces and tears, that fill out the orchestra of the heart; where romance and poetry abound *au naturel;*[1] and where—yes, where children grow as thick as Nature permits: the domestic interior of the opera porter, for instance, or the clockmaker over the way. But what a loss the orphan-asylum would have suffered, and the dreary lacking there would have been in the lives of the children! For there must have been moments in the lives of the children in that asylum when they felt, awake, as they felt in their sleep when they dreamed their mothers were about them.

Century, August 1893; *Balcony Stories*, 1893

The Old Lady's Restoration

The news came out in the papers that the old lady had been restored to her fortune. She had been deprived of it so long ago that the real manner of her dispossession had become lost, or at least hidden under the many versions that had been invented to replace lapses of memory, or to remedy the unpicturesqueness of the original truth. The face of truth, like the face of many a good woman, is liable to the accident of ugliness, and the desire to embellish one as well as the other need not

1. In their natural setting.

necessarily proceed from anything more harmful than an over-weighted love of the beautiful.

If the old lady had not been restored to her fortune, her *personalia*[1] would have remained in the oblivion which, as one might say, had accumulated upon everything belonging to her. But after that newspaper paragraph, there was such a flowering of memory around her name as would have done credit to a whole cemetery on All Saints.[2] It took three generations to do justice to the old lady, for so long and so slow had been her descent into poverty that a grandmother was needed to remember her setting out upon the road to it.

She set out as most people do, well provided with money, diamonds, pretty clothing, handsome residence, equipage,[3] opera-box, beaus (for she was a widow), and so many, many friends that she could never indulge in a small party—she always had to give a grand ball to accommodate them. She made quite an occasion of her first reverse,—some litigation decided against her,—and said it came from the court's having only one ear, and that preëmpted by the other party.

She always said whatever she thought, regardless of the consequences, because she averred truth was so much more interesting than falsehood. Nothing annoyed her more in society than to have to listen to the compositions women make as a substitute for the original truth. It was as if, when she went to the theater to hear Shakspeare and Molière, the actors should try to impose upon the audience by reciting lines of their own. Truth was the wit of life and the wit of books. She traveled her road from affluence so leisurely that nothing escaped her eyes or her feelings, and she signaled unhesitatingly every stage in it.

"My dear, do you know there is really such a thing as existence without a carriage and horses?"—"I assure you it is perfectly new to me to find that an opera-box is not a necessity. It is a luxury. In theory one can really never tell the distinction between luxuries and necessities."—"How absurd! At one time I thought hair was given us only to furnish a profession to hair-dressers; just as we wear artificial flowers to support the flower-makers."—"Upon my word, it is not uninteresting. There is always some *haute nouveauté*[4] in economy. The ways of depriving oneself are infinite. There is wine, now."—"Not own your residence! As soon not own your tomb as your residence! My mama used to scream that in my ears. According to her, it was not *comme il faut*[5] to board or live in a rented house. How little she knew!"

When her friends, learning her increasing difficulties, which they did from the best authority (herself), complimented her, as they were forced to do, upon her still handsome appearance, pretty laces, feathers, jewelry, silks, "Fat," she would answer—"fat. I am living off my

1. Personhood.
2. All Saints Day, November 1, commemorates all the saints of the Roman Catholic church, both known and unknown.
3. A carriage that is elegantly equipped with horses and footmen.
4. Lofty novelty or charm.
5. Proper or suitable.

fat, as bears do in winter. In truth, I remind myself of an animal in more ways than one."

And so everyone had something to contribute to the conversation about her—bits which, they said, affection and admiration had kept alive in their memory.

Each city has its own roads to certain ends, its ways of Calvary,[6] so to speak. In New Orleans the victim seems ever to walk down Royal Street and up Chartres, or *vice versa*. One would infer so, at least, from the display in the shops and windows of those thoroughfares. Old furniture, cut glass, pictures, books, jewelry, lace, china—the fleece (sometimes the flesh still sticking to it) left on the brambles by the driven herd. If there should some day be a trump of resurrection for defunct fortunes, those shops would be emptied in the same twinkling of the eye allowed to tombs for their rendition of property.

The old lady must have made that promenade many, many times, to judge by the samples of her "fat or fleece" displayed in the windows. She took to hobbling, as if from tired or sore feet.

"It is nothing," in answer to an inquiry. "Made-to-order feet learning to walk in ready-made shoes: that is all. One's feet, after all, are the most unintelligent part of one's body." Tea was her abomination, coffee her adoration; but she explained: "Tea, you know, is so detestable that the very worst is hardly worse than the very best; while coffee is so perfect that the smallest shade of impurity is not to be tolerated. The truly economical, I observe, always drink tea." "At one time I thought if all the luxuries of the world were exposed to me, and but one choice allowed, I should select gloves. Believe me, there is no superfluity in the world so easily dispensed with."

As may be supposed, her path led her farther and farther away from her old friends. Even her intimates became scarce; so much so, that these observations, which, of course, could be made only to intimates, became fewer and fewer, unfortunately, for her circumstances were becoming such that the remarks became increasingly valuable. The last thing related of her was apropos of friends.

"My friends! My dear, I cannot tell you just so, on the spur of the moment, but with a little reflection and calculation I could tell you, to a picayune,[7] the rent of every friend in the market. You can lease, rent, or hire them, like horses, carriages, opera-boxes, servants, by year, month, day, or hour; and the tariff is just as fixed.

"Christians! Christians are the most discreet people in the world. If you should ask me what Christianity has most promoted in the world, I should answer without hesitation, discretion. Of course, when I say the world I mean society, and when I say Christianity I mean our interpretation of it. If only duns[8] could be pastors, and pastors duns!

---

6. The hill outside Jerusalem where Jesus was crucified.
7. A small copper coin once used in parts of the South; worth about five cents or less.
8. Bill collectors.

But of course you do not know what duns are; they are the guardian angels of the creditor, the pursuing fiends of the debtor."

After that, the old lady made her disappearance under the waves of that sea into the depths of which it is very improbable that a single friend ever attempted to pursue her. And there she remained until the news came that she was restored to fortune.

A week passed, two weeks; no sight or sound of her. It was during this period that her old friends were so occupied resuscitating their old friendships for her—when all her antique sayings and doings became current ball-room and dinner-table gossip—that she arose from her obscurity like Cinderella from her ashes, to be decked with every gift that fairy minds could suggest. Those who had known her intimately made no effort to conceal their importance. Those who did not know her personally put forward claims of inherited friendship, and those who did not know her traditionally or otherwise—the *nouveaux riches* and *parvenus*,[9] who alone feel the moneyed value of such social connections—began making their resolutions to capture her as soon as she came in sight of society.

The old residence was to be rebought, and refurnished from France; the *avant scène*[1] at the opera had been engaged; the old cook was to be hired back from the club at a fabulous price; the old balls and the old dinners were to gladden the city—so said they who seemed to know. Nothing was to be spared, nothing stinted—at her age, with no child or relative, and life running short for pleasure. Diamonds, laces, velvets, champagne, Château Yquem[2]—"Grand Dieu Seigneur!" the old Creole servants exclaimed, raising their hands at the enumeration of it.

Where the news came from nobody knew, but everything was certified and accepted as facts, although, as between women, the grain of salt should have been used. Impatience waxed, until nearly every day someone would ring the bell of the old residence, to ask when the mistress was going to move in. And such affectionate messages! And people would not, simply could not, be satisfied with the incomprehensible answers. And then it leaked out. The old lady was simply waiting for everything to arrive—furniture, toilets,[3] carriage, etc.—to make a grand *entrée* into her old sphere; to come riding on a throne, as it were. And still the time passed, and she did not come. Finally two of the clever-heads penetrated the enigma: *mauvaise honte*, shyness—so long out of the world, so old; perhaps not sure of her welcome. So they determined to seek her out.

"We will go to her, like children to a grandmother, etc. The others have no delicacy of sentiment, etc. And she will thus learn who really remember, really love her, etc."

Provided with congratulatory bouquets, they set forth. It is very hard

---

9. Upstarts. *Nouveaux riches:* newly rich.
1. The proscenium of a stage.

2. A fine dessert wine, or sauterne.
3. Clothing, attire.

to find a dweller on the very sea-bottom of poverty. Perhaps that is why the effort is so seldom made. One has to ask at grocers' shops, groggeries,[4] market-stalls, Chinese restaurants; interview corner cobblers, ragpickers, gutter children. But nothing is impossible to the determined. The two ladies overcame all obstacles, and needled their way along, where under other circumstances they would not have glanced, would have thought it improper to glance.

They were directed through an old, old house, out on an old, old gallery, to a room at the very extreme end.

"Poor thing! Evidently she has not heard the good news yet. We will be the first to communicate it," they whispered, standing before the dilapidated, withered-looking door.

Before knocking, they listened, as it is the very wisdom of discretion to do. There was life inside, a little kind of voice, like someone trying to hum a song with a very cracked old throat.

The ladies opened the door. "Ah, my friend!"

"Ah, my friend!"

"Restored!"

"Restored!"

"At last!"

"At last!"

"Just the same!"

"Exactly the same!"

It was which one would get to her first with bouquet and kiss, competition almost crowding friendship.

"The good news!"

"The good news!"

"We could not stay!"

"We had to come!"

"It has arrived at last!"

"At last it has arrived!"

The old lady was very much older, but still the same.

"You will again have a chance!"

"Restored to your friends!"

"The world!"

"Your luxuries!"

"Your comforts!"

"Comforts! Luxuries!" At last the old lady had an opportunity to slip in a word. "And friends! You say right."

There was a pause—a pause which held not a small measure of embarrassment. But the two visitors, although they were women of the world, and so dreaded an embarrassment more than they did sin, had prepared themselves even to stand this.

The old lady standing there—she was very much thinner, very much bent, but still the same—appeared to be looking not at them, but at their enumeration.

---

4. Taverns.

"Comfort!" She opened a pot bubbling on the fire. "Bouillon! A good five-cent bouillon. Luxury!" She picked up something from a chair, a handful of new cotton chemises. "Luxury!" She turned back her bedspread: new cotton sheets. "Did you ever lie in your bed at night and dream of sheets? Comfort! Luxury! I should say so! And friends! My dear, look!" Opening her door, pointing to an opposite gallery, to the yard, her own gallery; to the washing, ironing, sewing women, the cobbling, chair-making, carpentering men; to the screaming, laughing, crying, quarreling, swarming children. "Friends! All friends—friends for fifteen years. Ah, yes, indeed! We are all glad—elated in fact. As you say, I am restored."

The visitors simply reported that they had found the old lady, and that she was imbecile; mind completely gone under stress of poverty and old age. Their opinion was that she should be interdicted.[5]

Century, September 1893; *Balcony Stories,* 1893

Pupasse

Every day, every day, it was the same overture in Madame Joubert's room in the Institut St. Denis; the strident:

"Mesdemoiselles; à vos places! Notre Père qui est dans le ciel—Quit a fait ce bruit?"[1]

"It's Pupasse, madame! It's Pupasse!" The answer invariably was unanimous.

"But, Madame Joubert,—I assure you, Madame Joubert,—I could not help it! They know I could not help it!"

By this time the fresh new fool's cap made from yesterday's "Bee" would have been pinned on her head.

"Quelle injustice! Quelle injustice!"

This last apostrophe in a high, whining nasal voice, always procured Pupasse's elevation on the tall three-legged stool in the corner.

It was a theory of the little girls in the primary class that Madame Joubert would be much more lenient to their own little inevitabilities of bad conduct and lessons if Pupasse did not invariably comb her the wrong way every morning after prayers, by dropping something, or sniffling, or sneezing. Therefore, while they distractedly got together books, slates, and copy-books, their infantile eyes found time to dart deadly reproaches toward the corner of penitence, and their little lips, still shaped from their first nourishment, pouted anything but sympathy for the occupant of it.

Indeed, it would have been a most startling unreality to have ever entered Madame Joubert's room and not seen Pupasse in that corner, on that stool, her tall figure shooting up like a post, until her tall, pointed *bonnet d' âne*[2] came within an inch or two of the ceiling. It was

5. Banned from Communion and Christian burial.
1. "Girls; to your places! Our Father who art in   heaven—who made that noise?"
2. Fool's cap.

her hoop-skirt that best testified to her height. It was the period of those funnel-shaped hoop-skirts that spread out with such nice mathematical proportions, from the waist down, that it seemed they must have emanated from the brains of astronomers, like the orbits, and diameters, and other things belonging to the heavenly bodies. Pupasse could not have come within three feet of the wall with her hoop-skirt distended. To have forced matters was not to be thought of an instant. So even in her greatest grief and indignation, she had to pause before the three-legged black stool, and gather up steel after steel of her circumference in her hands behind, until her calico skirt careened and flattened; and so she could manage to accommodate herself to the limited space of her punishment, the circles drooping far over her feet as she stood there, looking like the costumed stick of a baby's rattle.

Her thinness continued into her face, which, unfortunately, had nothing in the way of toilet to assist it. Two little black eyes fixed in the sides of a mere fence of a nose, and a mouth with the shape and expression of all mouths made to go over sharp-pointed teeth planted very far apart; the smallest amount possible of fine, dry, black hair—a perfect rat-tail when it was plaited in one, as almost all wore their hair. But sometimes Pupasse took it into her head to plait it in two braids, as none but the thick-haired ventured to wear it. As the little girls said, it was a petition to Heaven for "eau Quinquina."[3] When Marcelite, the hair-dresser, came at her regular periods to visit the hair of the boarders, she would make an effort with Pupasse, plaiting her hundred hairs in a ten-strand braid. The effect was a half yard of black worsted galloon;[4] nothing more, or better. Had Pupasse possessed as many heads as the hydra,[5] she could have "coiffe'd" them all with fools' caps during one morning's recitations. She entirely monopolized the "Daily Bee." Madame Joubert was forced to borrow from "madame" the stale weekly "Courrier des Etats-Unis" for the rest of the room. From grammar, through sacred history, arithmetic, geography, mythology, down to dictation, Pupasse could pile up an accumulation of penitences that would have tasked the limits of the current day had not recreation been wisely set as a term which disbarred, by proscription, previous offenses. But even after recreation, with that day's lessons safely out, punished and expiated, Pupasse's doom seemed scarcely lightened; there was still a whole criminal code of conduct to infract. The only difference was that instead of books, slates, or copy-books, leathern medals, bearing various legends and mottos, were hung around her neck—a travestied decoration worse than the books for humiliation.

The "abécédaires,"[6] their torment for the day over, thankful for any distraction from the next day's lessons, and eager for any relief from the intolerable ennui of goodness, were thankful enough now for Pu-

3. Quinine water, a tonic used to treat malaria.
4. A narrow braid of wool or thread used as trimming.

5. In Greek mythology, a many-headed monster.
6. A French term for spelling books (ABC); hence, the youngest students in the school.

passe. They naturally watched her in preference to Madame Joubert, holding their books and slates quite cunningly to hide their faces. Pupasse had not only the genius, but that which sometimes fails genius, the means for grimacing: little eyes, long nose, foolish mouth, and pointed tongue. And she was so amusing, when Madame Joubert's head was turned, that the little girls, being young and innocent, would forget themselves and all burst out laughing. It sounded like a flight of singing birds through the hot, close, stupid little room; but not so to Madame Joubert.

"Young ladies! But what does this mean?"

And, terror-stricken, the innocents would call out with one voice, "It's Pupasse, madame! It's Pupasse who made us laugh!" There was nothing but fools' caps to be gained by prevaricating, and there was frequently nothing less gained by confession. And oh, the wails and the sobs as the innocents would be stood up, one by one, in their places! Even the pigtails at the backs of their little heads were convulsed with grief. Oh, how they hated Pupasse then! When their *bonnes*[7] came for them at three o'clock,—washing their tear-stained faces at the cistern before daring to take them through the streets,—how passionately they would cry out, the tears breaking afresh into the wet handker-chiefs:

"It's that Pupasse! It's that *vilaine* Pupasse!"

To Pupasse herself would be meted out that "peine forte et dure,"[8] that acme of humiliation and disgrace, so intensely horrible that many a little girl in that room solemnly averred and believed she would kill herself before submitting to it. Pupasse's voluminous calico skirt would be gathered up by the hem and tied up over her head! Oh, the horrible monstrosity on the stool in the corner then! There were no eyes in that room that had any desire to look upon it. And the cries and the "Quelle injustice!" that fell on the ears then from the hidden feelings had all the weirdness of the unseen, but heard. And all the other girls in the room, in fear and trembling, would begin to move their lips in a perfect whirlwind of study, or write violently on their slates, or begin at that very instant to rule off their copy-books for the next day's verb.

Pupasse—her name was Marie Pupasse, but no one thought of calling her anything but Pupasse, with emphasis on the first syllable and sibilance on the last—had no parents, only a grandmother, to describe whom, all that is necessary to say is that she was as short as Pupasse was tall, and that her face resembled nothing so much as a little yellow apple shriveling from decay. The old lady came but once a week, to fetch Pupasse fresh clothes, and a great brown paper bag of nice things to eat. There was no boarder in the school who received handsomer bags of cake and fruit than Pupasse. And although, not two

7. Servant-maids, nursery-maids.
8. From the French term *"condamné à la peine forte et dure,"* i.e., condemned to be pressed to death, in which a prisoner may choose between making a confession or being pressed under large weights; hence, any protracted and harsh punishment.

hours before, a girl might have been foremost in the shrill cry, "It is Pupasse who made the noise! It is Pupasse who made me laugh!" there was nothing in that paper bag reserved even from such a one. When the girl herself with native delicacy would, under the circumstances, judge it discreet to refuse, Pupasse would plead, "Oh, but take it to give me pleasure!" And if still the refusal continued, Pupasse would take her bag and go into the summer-house in the corner of the garden, and cry until the unforgiving one would relent. But the first offering of the bag was invariably to the stern dispenser of fools' caps and the unnamed humiliation of the reversed skirt: Madame Joubert.

Pupasse was in the fifth class. The sixth—the abécédaires—was the lowest in the school. Green was the color of the fifth; white—innocence—of the abécédaires. Exhibition[9] after exhibition, the same green sash and green ribbons appeared on Pupasse's white muslin, the white muslin getting longer and longer every year, trying to keep up with her phenomenal growth; and always, from all over the room, buzzed the audience's suppressed merriment at Pupasse's appearance in the ranks of the little ones of nine and ten. It was that very merriment that brought about the greatest change in the Institut St. Denis. The sitting order of the classes was reversed. The first class—the graduates—went up to the top step of the *estrade;*[1] and the little ones put on the lowest, behind the pianos. The graduates grumbled that it was not *comme il faut*[2] to have young ladies of their position stepping like camels up and down those great steps; and the little girls said it was a shame to hide them behind the pianos after their mamas had taken so much pains to make them look pretty. But madame said—going also to natural history for her comparison—that one must be a rhinoceros to continue the former routine.

Religion cannot be kept waiting forever on the intelligence. It was always in the fourth class that the first communion was made; that is, when the girls stayed one year in each class. But Pupasse had spent three years in the sixth class, and had already been four in the fifth, and Madame Joubert felt that longer delay would be disrespectful to the good Lord. It was true that Pupasse could not yet distinguish the ten commandments from the seven capital sins, and still would answer that Jeanne d'Arc was the foundress of the "Little Sisters of the Poor." But, as Madame Joubert always said in the little address she made to the catechism class[3] every year before handing it over to Father Dolomier, God judged from the heart, and not from the mind.

Father Dolomier—from his face he would have been an able contestant of *bonnets d' âne* with Pupasse, if subjected to Madame Joubert's discipline—evidently had the same method of judging as God, although the catechism class said they could dance a waltz on the end of his long nose without his perceiving it.

---

9. A school program to show students' progress.
1. Platform.
2. Proper, suitable.

3. Students learning the basics of Catholic doctrine in preparation for an examination.

There is always a little air of mystery about the first communion: not that there is any in reality, but the little ones assume it to render themselves important. The going to early mass, the holding their dog-eared catechisms as if they were relics, the instruction from the priest, even if he were only old Father Dolomier—it all put such a little air of devotion into their faces that it imposed (as it did every year) upon their companions, which was a vastly gratifying effect. No matter how young and innocent she may be, a woman's devotion always seems to have two aims—God and her own sex.

The week of retreat came. Oh, the week of retreat! That was the *bonne bouche*[4] of it all, for themselves and for the others. It was the same every year. By the time the week of retreat arrived, interest and mystery had been frothed to the point of indiscretion; so that the little girls would stand on tiptoe to peep through the shutters at the postu-lants[5] inside, and even the larger girls, to whom first communion was a thing of an infantile past, would condescend to listen to their reports with ill-feigned indifference.

As the day of the first communion neared, the day of the general confession naturally neared, too, leading it. And then the little girls, peeping through the shutters, and holding their breath to see better, saw what they beheld every year; but it was always new and awe-some—mysterious scribbling in corners with lead-pencils on scraps of paper; consultations; rewritings; copyings; the list of their sins, of all the sins of their lives.

"*Ma chère!*"—pigtails and sunbonnets hiving outside would shud-der. "Oh, *Mon Dieu!* To have to confess all—but *all* your sins! As for me, it would kill me, sure!"

And the frightful recoils of their consciences would make all in-stantly blanch and cross themselves.

"And look at Pupasse's sins! Oh, but they are long! *Ma chère*, but look! But look, I ask you, at them!"

The longest record was of course the most complimentary and hon-orable to the possessor, as each girl naturally worked not only for absolution but for fame.

Between catechisms and instructions Madame Joubert would have "La Vie des Saints"[6] read aloud, to stimulate their piety and to engage their thoughts; for the thoughts of first communicants are worse than flies for buzzing around the forbidden. The lecture must have been a great quickener of conscience; for they would dare punishment and cheat Madame Joubert, under her own eyes, in order surreptitiously to add a new sin to their list. Of course the one hour's recreation could not afford time enough for observation now, and the little girls were driven to all sorts of excuses to get out of the classroom for one moment's peep through the shutters; at which whole swarms of them would some-times be caught and sent into punishment.

---

4. The climax, the moment worth waiting for. Re-treat: A period of seclusion and contemplation.

5. Those petitioning to take first communion.

6. The Life of the Saints.

Only two days more. Madame Joubert put them through the rehearsal, a most important part of the preparation, almost as important as catechism—how to enter the church, how to hold the candle, how to advance, how to kneel, retire—everything, in fact.

Only one day more, the quietest, most devotional day of all. Pupasse lost her sins!

Of course every year the same accident happened to someone. But it was a new accident to Pupasse. And such a long list!

The commotion inside that retreat! Pupasse's nasal whine, carrying her lament without any mystery to the outside garden. Such searching of pockets, rummaging of corners, microscopic examination of the floor! Such crimination and recrimination, protestation, asseveration, assurances, backed by divine and saintly invocations! Pupasse accused companion after companion of filching her sins, which each after each would violently deny, producing each her own list from her own pocket,—proof to conviction of innocence, and, we may say, of guilt also.

Pupasse declared they had filched it to copy, because her list was the longest and most complete. She could not go to confession without her sins; she could not go to communion without confession. The tears rolled down her long thin nose unchecked, for she never could remember to use her handkerchief until reminded by Madame Joubert.

She had committed it to memory, as all the others had done theirs; but how was she to know without the list if she had not forgotten something? And to forget one thing in a general confession they knew was a mortal sin.

"I shall tell Madame Joubert! I shall tell Madame Joubert!"

"*Ma chère!*" whispered the little ones outside. "Oh, but look at them! *Elles font les quatre cents coups!*" which is equivalent to "cutting up like the mischief."

And with reason. As if such an influx of the world upon them at this moment were not sufficient of itself to damn them. But to tell Madame Joubert! With all their dresses made and ready, wreaths, veils, candles, prayer-books, picture-cards, mother-of-pearl prayer-beads, and festival breakfasts with admiring family and friends prepared. Tell Madame Joubert! She would simply cancel it all. In a body they chorused:

"But, Pupasse!"

"*Chère* Pupasse!"

"*Voyons*, Pupasse!"

"I assure you, Pupasse!"

"On the cross, Pupasse!"

"Ah, Pupasse!"

"We implore you, Pupasse!"

The only response—tears, and "I shall tell Madame Joubert."

Consultations, caucuses, individual appeals, general outbursts. Pupasse stood in the corner. Curiously, she always sought refuge in the very sanctum of punishment, her face hidden in her bended arms, her hoops standing out behind, vouchsafing nothing but tears, and the promise to tell Madame Joubert. And three o'clock approaching! And Madame Joubert imminent! But Pupasse really could not go to confession without her sins. They all recognized that; they were reasonable, as they assured her.

A crisis quickens the wits. They heard the cathedral clock strike the quarter to three. They whispered, suggested, argued—bunched in the farthest corner from Pupasse.

"Console yourself, Pupasse! We will help you, Pupasse! Say no more about it! We will help you!"

A delegate was sent to say that. She was only four feet and a half high, and had to stand on tiptoe to pluck the six-foot Pupasse's dress to gain her attention.

And they did help her generously. A new sheet of fool's-cap was procured, and torn in two, lengthwise, and pinned in a long strip. One by one, each little girl took it, and, retiring as far as possible, would put her hand into her pocket, and, extracting her list, would copy it in full on the new paper. Then she would fold it down, and give it to the next one, until all had written.

"Here, Pupasse; here are all our sins. We give them to you; you can have them."

Pupasse was radiant; she was more than delighted, and the more she read the better pleased she was. Such a handsome long list, and so many sins she had never thought of—never dreamed of! She set herself with zeal to commit them to memory. But a hand on the door— Madame Joubert! You never could have told that those little girls had not been sitting during the whole time, with their hands clasped and eyes cast up to the ceiling, or moving their lips as the prayer-beads glided through their fingers. Their versatility was really marvelous.

Poor Pupasse! God solved the dilemma of her education, and madame's increasing sensitiveness about her appearance in the fifth class, by the death of the old grandmother. She went home to the funeral, and never returned—or at least she returned, but only for madame. There was a little scene in the parlor: Pupasse, all dressed in black, with her bag of primary books in her hand, ready and eager to get back to her classes and fools' caps; madame, hesitating between her interests and her fear of ridicule; Madame Joubert, between her loyalty to school and her conscience. Pupasse the only one free and untrammeled, simple and direct.

That little school parlor had been the stage for so many scenes! Madame Joubert detested acting—the comedy, as she called it. There was nothing she punished with more pleasure up in her room. And yet—

"Pupasse, *ma fille*,[7] give me your grammar."

The old battered, primitive book was gotten out of the bag, the string

7. My girl, my daughter.

still tied between the leaves for convenience in hanging around the neck.

"Your last punishment: the rule for irregular verbs. Commence!"

"I know it, Madame Joubert; I know it perfectly, I assure you."

"Commence!"

"Irregular verbs—but I assure you I know it—I know it by heart—"

"Commence, *ma fille!*"

"Irregular verbs—irregular verbs—I know it, Madame Joubert—one moment—" and she shook her right hand, as girls do to get inspiration, they say. "Irregular verbs—give me one word, Madame Joubert; only one word!"

"That—"

"Irregular verbs, that—irregular verbs, that—"

"See here, Pupasse; you do not know that lesson any more than a cat does"—Madame Joubert's favorite comparison.

"Yes, I do, Madame Joubert! Yes, I do!"

"Silence!"

"But, Madame Joubert—"

"Will you be silent!"

"Yes, Madame Joubert; only—"

"Pupasse, one more word—and—" Madame Joubert was forgetting her comedy—"Listen, Pupasse, and obey! You go home and learn that lesson. When you know it, you can reënter your class. That is the punishment I have thought of to correct your 'want of attention.' "

That was the way Madame Joubert put it—"want of attention."

Pupasse looked at her—at madame, a silent but potent spectator. To be sent from home because she did not know the rule of the irregular verbs! To be sent from home, family, friends!—for that was the way Pupasse put it. She had been in that school—it may only be whispered—fifteen years. Madame Joubert knew it; so did madame, although they accounted for only four or five years in each class. That school was her home; Madame Joubert—God help her!—her mother; madame, her divinity; fools' caps and turned-up skirts, her life. The old grandmother—she it was who had done everything for her (a *ci-devant*[8] rag-picker, they say); she it was who was nothing to her.

Madame must have felt something of it besides the loss of the handsome salary for years from the little old withered woman. But conventionality is inexorable; and the St. Denis's great recommendation was its conventionality. Madame Joubert must have felt something of it,—she must have felt something of it,—for why should she volunteer? Certainly madame could not have imposed *that* upon *her*. *It must* have been an inspiration of the moment, or a movement, a *tressaillement,*[9] of the heart.

"Listen, Pupasse, my child. Go home, study your lesson well. I shall come every evening myself and hear it; and as soon as you know it, I shall fetch you back myself. You know I always keep my word."

---

8. Former, ex-.   9. Thrill or flutter.

Keep her word! That she did. Could the inanimate past testify, what a fluttering of fools' caps in that parlor—"Daily Bees," and "Weekly Couriers," by the year-full!

What could Pupasse say or do? It settled the question, as Madame Joubert assured madame, when the tall, thin black figure with the bag of books disappeared through the gate.

Madame Joubert was never known to break her word; that is all one knows about her part of the bargain.

One day, not three years ago, ringing a bell to inquire for a servant, a familiar murmuring fell upon the ear, and an old abécédaire's eyes could not resist the temptation to look through the shutters. There sat Pupasse; there was her old grammar; there were both fingers stopping her ears—as all studious girls do, or used to do; and there sounded the old words composing the rule for irregular verbs.

And you all remember how long it is since we wore funnel-shaped hoop-skirts!

Century, October 1893; *Balcony Stories*, 1893

KATE CHOPIN
1851-1904

Although she would write primarily of Louisiana Creoles, Kate O'Flaherty Chopin on her mother's side could trace her origins to the earliest Creole settlers of St. Louis. Born February 8, 1850, Chopin grew up in St. Louis in a household dominated by her mother Eliza, her grandmother, and her great-grandmother, all Creole widows of elite ancestry. Her great-grandmother, Mme. Charleville, who lived with the O'Flahertys and took over the care and education of Kate after her father's death in 1855, gave her a love of storytelling, particularly about women and their passions, and encouraged her independence and curiosity. Kate began her formal education in 1855 at the St. Louis Academy of the Sacred Heart, which she attended until her graduation in 1868. In 1870, she met and married Oscar Chopin, a Louisiana Creole who had moved to St. Louis to work for a bank, and after a three-month honeymoon in Europe the Chopins moved to New Orleans, where Oscar began business as a cotton factor, the agent who provided the planters' supplies and brokered their cotton.

During the 1870s, Kate Chopin lived the life of the society matron, giving birth to six children by the end of the decade. As a pastime, she explored New Orleans, going about on foot (Chopin was an avid walker) and keeping a notebook of her observations. She often traveled with her children back to St. Louis or to Grand Isle, a resort fifty miles south of New Orleans on the Gulf of Mexico, which would become the fictional location of her novel *The Awakening*. In 1879, in order to recover from business losses, Oscar Chopin moved his family to Natchitoches County in northwestern Louisiana where he owned and managed some small plantations. In 1882 Oscar died, leaving Kate to carry on the work of managing, which she successfully did. However, in response to her mother's repeated urgings, she returned with her children to her mother's home in St. Louis in 1884. In 1885 her mother died unexpectedly.

During the period of mourning for husband and mother in St. Louis, Chopin developed a close friendship with her obstetrician, Dr. Kolbenheyer, who had admired her letters from Louisiana and encouraged her to write fiction. She did begin to write, poetry at first, and published a poem in the Chicago magazine *America* in January 1889; during this same period she began to work on short stories reflecting her life in Natchitoches County. For literary models she turned to Guy de Maupassant and to her compatriot regionalists Sarah Orne Jewett and Mary Wilkins Freeman. She wrote in a diary that Freeman was a "great genius," and that "I know of no one better than Miss Jewett to study for technique and nicety of construction" (Seyersted 52). Chopin's first published story, "Wiser Than a God," appeared in December 1889, in the *Philadelphia Musical Journal*, and when a publisher rejected her first novel, *At Fault*, she published it in St. Louis at her own expense, in April 1890.

408

After failing to find a publisher for a second novel, which she later destroyed, Chopin turned her attention to short fiction in the early 1890s. Her first significant regional publication, included in this collection, was "At the 'Cadian Ball," first published in *Two Tales* on October 22, 1892. By 1894 she had enough material for a collection, publishing *Bayou Folk* with Houghton Mifflin. In the same year Richard Watson Gilder published two regional stories in *Century*, an event that marked her first appearance in a nationally known eastern magazine. Perhaps as a reply to Gilder, who had rejected the title story, Chopin called her second collection *A Night in Acadie*, which she published in 1897 with a relatively unknown publisher; and in 1899 she published *The Awakening*. *The Awakening* was not a critical success; it elicited a series of negative, even hostile, reviews. With the exception of a few last stories, such as "A Little Country Girl" (included here), Chopin essentially stopped writing following publication of *The Awakening*. Kate Chopin died August 22, 1904, two days following a brain hemorrhage, at the age of fifty-three.

o o o

Kate Chopin's regionalist fiction assumes hierarchies of race, class, and gender. Her characters accord superiority to the Creoles, descendants of the original French settlers of Louisiana, and lower-class status to the Cajuns, descendants of the French Acadians exiled from Nova Scotia in the late eighteenth century. And they relegate black characters to the lowest social position. Black male characters appear, but are insignificant in Chopin's fiction. Her black women characters may occupy significant positions in her stories (as in "Odalie Misses Mass" and "Ozème's Holiday," included here), but while Chopin, in *The Awakening*, may be aware that Creole society silences the black woman, she does not use her own fiction to explore possibilities for reversing that silence.

A story like "Madame Celestin's Divorce," however, realizes the conception of regionalism as fiction that moves the regional voice, here understood as that of the Creole woman, into the center and challenges the hegemony of the "New England" view characteristic of local-color writing. Lawyer Paxton, desiring Madame Celestin's divorce for professional as well as personal reasons, and unable to imagine a perspective or culture other than his own, misreads Madame Celestin, who, despite his efforts to speak for her, manages to determine her own life. Similarly, in "A Gentleman of Bayou Têche" (reminiscent of Murfree's "The Star in the Valley" and Jewett's "The Circus at Denby" in the conscious distinctions it draws between local colorist and regionalist perspectives), the Yankee Sublet identifies Evariste as a "tempting" subject to an artist looking for "bits of 'local color.'" It is the black woman in the story, Aunt Dicey, who alerts Martinette to the patronizing quality of Sublet's request to paint Evariste as if he had just emerged from the swamp. So enlightened, Martinette dares to confront the "smile of intelligence" that passes among the white men when she returns the money and states that her father does not want his portrait painted. While Evariste does finally agree to a portrait of himself as if he has just emerged from the swamp, Martinette in her confrontation with the painter asserts the authority of the regional voice and the importance of retaining control over one's story.

In Chopin's fiction, Creole men have both the leisure time and the sense of personal identity to indulge their sensuality, and they have the class privilege that attracts both Creole and Cajun women. Cajun men, unable to compete sexually with Creole men, become nurturing and maternal—quite unlike the male characters in the fiction by New England women regionalists. In

"Ozème's Holiday" Ozème begins his holiday desiring attention from the "mother" he stops to visit; but he willingly misses his holiday when he perceives the mother's greater need. This story, like "Odalie Misses Mass," locates Chopin's work in relation to the New England regionalist vision. In both stories, the younger person gives the gift of a home visit to an older person whose welfare others have disregarded. The significant difference between these stories and those of Freeman or Jewett, however, is that the redeeming characters are not women, but, in "Ozème's Holiday," a Cajun man, and, in "Odalie Misses Mass," a Creole child.

Able to portray the regional male as maternal, and to allow him to occupy the cultural and literary space held by women in the fiction she admired of Freeman and Jewett, Chopin is free to investigate what other emotional territory women may occupy. That there are few literal or even surrogate mothers in Chopin's fiction suggests that she saw in mothering an end to, not the beginning of, female development. In particular, a daughter's development of autonomous sexuality seems to depend on her mother's disappearance, death, or displacement. Chopin's white female protagonists attempt to escape their position in the hierarchy of gender by affirming their own sensuality as a primary path to personal development. While many of her Creole and Cajun women characters choose to return to their position in the traditional hierarchy, many others begin to explore female sexuality in a way that equates sexuality with autonomy, individuation, and freedom.

In the little-known story "Lilacs," Chopin prefigures an awareness of the reception her own later works will receive. Adrienne's attempt to experience her sensuality fully, including its origins in the apparently austere world of the convent, fares no better with the world than Chopin's attempt to describe this experience in fiction; both are censured, and Adrienne is exiled. Yet the story testifies to the primacy and power of women's sensuality. In *The Awakening*, Chopin further associates regional identity with the adult woman's discovery of sensuality, an association that contrasts markedly with the regional themes of her New England counterparts and predecessors. In chapter 21, Edna Pontellier pays a visit to Mlle. Reisz, whose neighbors describe her as the "most disagreeable and unpopular woman who ever lived in Bienville Street." Mlle. Reisz's lack of popularity apparently derives from the fact that she is a woman who defies convention, lives singly and likes it, and is also an artist. In these features she resembles many of the characters in Jewett's and Freeman's fiction. Though Edna is drawn to Mlle. Reisz and to the "region of the gasoline stove" that is her garret apartment, she leaves her mentor having experienced a reawakening of the sensuality that Mlle. Reisz has, like her New England counterparts, apparently renounced for herself. In "The Storm" Chopin shows Calixta experiencing the sexual fulfillment denied her in "At the 'Cadian Ball" and denied Edna Pontellier in *The Awakening*. In "A New England Nun" Freeman identified women's birthright as the right to remain single, free from the experience and consequences of their sexuality; in "The Storm" Chopin identifies passionate sexual experience as woman's birthright. It is particularly unfortunate that "The Storm" was not published during Chopin's lifetime, since with this story she realized most fully the connection between regionalism and the expression of women's sexuality.

Among the fiction included in this collection, only the selections from *Bayou Folk* and *A Night in Acadie* received the kind of public attention that might have allowed Chopin's work to influence other women writers, and hence the development of regionalism. For Chopin, regionalist fiction opened up possibilities that were not publishable—the "region" of women's sexuality. In daring to extend regionalism in this direction, Chopin also discovered the limits of what was culturally acceptable for women writers of her era.

At the 'Cadian Ball

Bobinôt, that big, brown, good-natured Bobinôt, had no intention of going to the ball, even though he knew Calixta would be there. For what came of those balls but heartache, and a sickening disinclination for work the whole week through, till Saturday night came again and his tortures began afresh? Why could he not love Ozéina, who would marry him tomorrow; or Fronie, or any one of a dozen others, rather than that little Spanish vixen? Calixta's slender foot had never touched Cuban soil; but her mother's had, and the Spanish was in her blood all the same. For that reason the prairie people forgave her much that they would not have overlooked in their own daughters or sisters.

Her eyes,—Bobinôt thought of her eyes, and weakened,—the bluest, the drowsiest, most tantalizing that ever looked into a man's; he thought of her flaxen hair that kinked worse than a mulatto's[1] close to her head; that broad, smiling mouth and tiptilted nose, that full figure; that voice like a rich contralto song, with cadences in it that must have been taught by Satan, for there was no one else to teach her tricks on that 'Cadian prairie. Bobinôt thought of them all as he plowed his rows of cane.

There had even been a breath of scandal whispered about her a year ago, when she went to Assumption,—but why talk of it? No one did now. "C'est Espagnol, ça,"[2] most of them said with lenient shoulder-shrugs. "Bon chien tient de race,"[3] the old men mumbled over their pipes, stirred by recollections. Nothing was made of it, except that Fronie threw it up to Calixta when the two quarreled and fought on the church steps after mass one Sunday, about a lover. Calixta swore roundly in fine 'Cadian French and with true Spanish spirit, and slapped Fronie's face. Fronie had slapped her back; "Tiens, cocotte, va!' "Espèce de lionèse; prends ça, et ça!"[4] till the curé himself was obliged to hasten and make peace between them. Bobinôt thought of it all, and would not go to the ball.

But in the afternoon, over at Friedheimer's store, where he was buying a trace-chain, he heard someone say that Alcée Laballière would be there. Then wild horses could not have kept him away. He knew how it would be—or rather he did not know how it would be—if the handsome young planter came over to the ball as he sometimes did.

---

1. A person of mixed black and white parentage.
2. That's a Spaniard for you, that is.
3. A version of "bon chien chasse de race," i.e., like father, like son; here perhaps referring to Calixta's

mother.
4. Listen, you flirt, go away. Espèce de lionèse, prends ça et ça: you lioness, take that and that.

If Alcée happened to be in a serious mood, he might only go to the card-room and play a round or two; or he might stand out on the galleries talking crops and politics with the old people. But there was no telling. A drink or two could put the devil in his head,—that was what Bobinôt said to himself, as he wiped the sweat from his brow with his red bandanna; a gleam from Calixta's eyes, a flash of her ankle, a twirl of her skirts could do the same. Yes, Bobinôt would go to the ball.

∘ ∘ ∘

That was the year Alcée Laballière put nine hundred acres in rice. It was putting a good deal of money into the ground, but the returns promised to be glorious. Old Madame Laballière, sailing about the spacious galleries in her white *volante*,[5] figured it all out in her head. Clarisse, her goddaughter, helped her a little, and together they built more air-castles than enough. Alcée worked like a mule that time; and if he did not kill himself, it was because his constitution was an iron one. It was an every-day affair for him to come in from the field well-nigh exhausted, and wet to the waist. He did not mind if there were visitors; he left them to his mother and Clarisse. There were often guests: young men and women who came up from the city, which was but a few hours away, to visit his beautiful kinswoman. She was worth going a good deal farther than that to see. Dainty as a lily; hardy as a sunflower; slim, tall, graceful, like one of the reeds that grew in the marsh. Cold and kind and cruel by turn, and everything that was aggravating to Alcée.

He would have liked to sweep the place of those visitors, often. Of the men, above all, with their ways and their manners; their swaying of fans like women, and dandling about hammocks. He could have pitched them over the levee[6] into the river, if it hadn't meant murder. That was Alcée. But he must have been crazy the day he came in from the rice-field, and, toil-stained as he was, clasped Clarisse by the arms and panted a volley of hot, blistering love-words into her face. No man had ever spoken love to her like that.

"Monsieur!" she exclaimed, looking him full in the eyes, without a quiver. Alcée's hands dropped and his glance wavered before the chill of her calm, clear eyes.

"Par exemple!" she muttered disdainfully, as she turned from him, deftly adjusting the careful toilet[7] that he had so brutally disarranged.

That happened a day or two before the cyclone came that cut into the rice like fine steel. It was an awful thing, coming so swiftly, without a moment's warning in which to light a holy candle or set a piece of blessed palm burning. Old madame wept openly and said her beads, just as her son Didier, the New Orleans one, would have done. If such a thing had happened to Alphonse, the Laballière planting cotton up in Natchitoches, he would have raved and stormed like a second cy-

---

5. Loose robe or dress.
6. A raised embankment at the river's edge.

7. Dress or attire. Par exemple: Upon my word!

clone, and made his surroundings unbearable for a day or two. But Alcée took the misfortune differently. He looked ill and gray after it, and said nothing. His speechlessness was frightful. Clarisse's heart melted with tenderness; but when she offered her soft, purring words of condolence, he accepted them with mute indifference. Then she and her nénaine[8] wept afresh in each other's arms.

A night or two later, when Clarisse went to her window to kneel there in the moonlight and say her prayers before retiring, she saw that Bruce, Alcée's Negro servant, had led his master's saddle-horse noiselessly along the edge of the sward that bordered the gravel-path, and stood holding him near by. Presently, she heard Alcée quit his room, which was beneath her own, and traverse the lower portico. As he emerged from the shadow and crossed the strip of moonlight, she perceived that he carried a pair of well-filled saddle-bags which he at once flung across the animal's back. He then lost no time in mounting, and after a brief exchange of words with Bruce, went cantering away, taking no precaution to avoid the noisy gravel as the Negro had done.

Clarisse had never suspected that it might be Alcée's custom to sally forth from the plantation secretly, and at such an hour; for it was nearly midnight. And had it not been for the telltale saddle-bags, she would only have crept to bed, to wonder, to fret and dream unpleasant dreams. But her impatience and anxiety would not be held in check. Hastily unbolting the shutters of her door that opened upon the gallery, she stepped outside and called softly to the old Negro.

"Gre't Peter! Miss Clarisse. I wasn' sho it was a ghos' o' w'at, stan'in' up dah, plumb in de night, dataway."

He mounted halfway up the long, broad flight of stairs. She was standing at the top.

"Bruce, w'ere has Monsieur Alcée gone?" she asked.

"W'y, he gone 'bout he business, I reckin," replied Bruce, striving to be non-committal at the outset.

"W'ere has Monsieur Alcée gone?" she reiterated, stamping her bare foot. "I won't stan' any nonsense or any lies; mine,[9] Bruce."

"I don' ric'lic ez I eva tole you lie *yit*, Miss Clarisse. Mista Alcée, he all broke up, sho."

"W'ere—has—he gone? Ah, Sainte Vierge! faut de la patience! butor, *va!*"[1]

"W'en I was in he room, a-breshin' off he clo'es today," the darkey began, settling himself against the stair-rail, "he look dat speechless an' down, I say, 'You 'pear to me like some pussun w'at gwine have a spell o' sickness, Mista Alcée.' He say, 'You reckin?' 'I dat he git up, go look hisse'f stiddy in de glass. Den he go to de chimbly an' jerk up de quinine bottle an' po' a gre't hoss-dose on to he han'. An' he swalla

---

8. Perhaps, nanny; here, a reference to Alcée's mother.
9. Mind.

1. Blessed Virgin! I need patience! Stupid fellow, get along!

dat mess in a wink, an' wash hit down wid a big dram o' w'iskey w'at he keep in he room, aginst he come all soppin' wet outen de fiel'.

"He 'lows, 'No, I ain' gwine be sick, Bruce.' Den he square off. He say, 'I kin mak out to stan' up an' gi' an' take wid any man I knows, lessen hit's John L. Sulvun.[2] But w'en God A'mighty an' a 'oman jines fo'ces agin me, dat's one too many fur me.' I tell 'im, 'Jis so,' whils' I'se makin' out to bresh a spot off w'at ain' dah, on he coat colla. I tell 'im, 'You wants li'le res', suh.' He say, 'No, I wants li'le fling; dat w'at I wants; an' I gwine git it. Pitch me a fis'ful o' clo'es in dem 'ar saddle-bags.' Dat w'at he say. Don't you bodda, missy. He jis' gone a-caperin' yonda to de Cajun ball. Uh—uh—de skeeters is fair' a-swarmin' like bees roun' yo' foots!'"

The mosquitoes were indeed attacking Clarisse's white feet savagely. She had unconsciously been alternately rubbing one foot over the other during the darkey's recital.

"The 'Cadian ball," she repeated contemptuously. "Humph! *Par exemple!* Nice conduc' for a Laballière. An' he needs a saddle-bag, fill' with clothes, to go to the 'Cadian ball."

"Oh, Miss Clarisse; you go on to bed, chile; git yo' soun' sleep. He 'low he come back in couple weeks o' so. I kiarn be repeatin' lot o' truck w'at young mans say, out heah face o' young gal."

Clarisse said no more, but turned and abruptly reëntered the house.

"You done talk too much wid yo' mouf a'ready, you ole fool nigga, you," muttered Bruce to himself as he walked away.

Alcée reached the ball very late, of course—too late for the chicken gumbo which had been served at midnight.

The big, low-ceiled room—they called it a hall—was packed with men and women dancing to the music of three fiddles. There were broad galleries all around it. There was a room at one side where sober-faced men were playing cards. Another, in which babies were sleeping, was called *le parc aux petits.*[3] Anyone who is white may go to a 'Cadian ball, but he must pay for his lemonade, his coffee and chicken gumbo. And he must behave himself like a 'Cadian. Grosbœuf was giving this ball. He had been giving them since he was a young man, and he was a middle-aged one, now. In that time he could recall but one disturbance, and that was caused by American railroaders, who were not in touch with their surroundings and had no business there. "Ces maudits gens du raiderode,"[4] Grosbœuf called them.

Alcée Laballière's presence at the ball caused a flutter even among the men, who could not but admire his "nerve" after such misfortune befalling him. To be sure, they knew the Laballières were rich—that there were resources East, and more again in the city. But they felt it took a *brave homme*[5] to stand a blow like that philosophically. One old

2. John L. Sullivan (1858–1918), American heavy-weight boxing champion.
3. The children's playpen.
4. These cursed railroad people.
5. Honest, worthy fellow.

gentleman, who was in the habit of reading a Paris newspaper and knew things, chuckled gleefully to everybody that Alcée's conduct was altogether *chic, mais chic*. That he had more *panache* than Boulanger. Well, perhaps he had.

But what he did not show outwardly was that he was in a mood for ugly things tonight. Poor Bobinôt alone felt it vaguely. He discerned a gleam of it in Alcée's handsome eyes, as the young planter stood in the doorway, looking with rather feverish glance upon the assembly, while he laughed and talked with a 'Cadian farmer who was beside him.

Bobinôt himself was dull-looking and clumsy. Most of the men were. But the young women were very beautiful. The eyes that glanced into Alcée's as they passed him were big, dark, soft as those of the young heifers standing out in the cool prairie grass.

But the belle was Calixta. Her white dress was not nearly so handsome or well made as Fronie's (she and Fronie had quite forgotten the battle on the church steps, and were friends again), nor were her slippers so stylish as those of Ozéina; and she fanned herself with a handkerchief, since she had broken her red fan at the last ball, and her aunts and uncles were not willing to give her another. But all the men agreed she was at her best tonight. Such animation! and abandon! such flashes of wit!

"Hé, Bobinôt! *Mais* w'at's the matta? W'at you standin' *planté là* like ole Ma'ame Tina's cow in the bog, you?"

That was good. That was an excellent thrust at Bobinôt, who had forgotten the figure[6] of the dance with his mind bent on other things, and it started a clamor of laughter at his expense. He joined good-naturedly. It was better to receive even such notice as that from Calixta than none at all. But Madame Suzonne, sitting in a corner, whispered to her neighbor that if Ozéina were to conduct herself in a like manner, she should immediately be taken out to the mule-cart and driven home. The women did not always approve of Calixta.

Now and then were short lulls in the dance, when couples flocked out upon the galleries for a brief respite and fresh air. The moon had gone down pale in the west, and in the east was yet no promise of day. After such an interval, when the dancers again assembled to resume the interrupted quadrille, Calixta was not among them.

She was sitting upon a bench out in the shadow, with Alcée beside her. They were acting like fools. He had attempted to take a little gold ring from her finger; just for the fun of it, for there was nothing he could have done with the ring but replace it again. But she clinched her hand tight. He pretended that it was a very difficult matter to open it. Then he kept the hand in his. They seemed to forget about it. He played with her earring, a thin crescent of gold hanging from her small brown ear. He caught a wisp of the kinky hair that had escaped its fastening, and rubbed the ends of it against his shaven cheek.

6. The group of steps that form a particular dance.

"You know, last year in Assumption, Calixta?" They belonged to the younger generation, so preferred to speak English.

"Don't come say Assumption to me, M'sieur Alcée. I done yeard Assumption till I'm plumb sick."

"Yes, I know. The idiots! Because you were in Assumption, and I happened to go to Assumption, they must have it that we went together. But it was nice—*hein,* Calixta?—in Assumption?"

They saw Bobinôt emerge from the hall and stand a moment outside the lighted doorway, peering uneasily and searchingly into the darkness. He did not see them, and went slowly back.

"There is Bobinôt looking for you. You are going to set poor Bobinôt crazy. You'll marry him some day; *hein,* Calixta?"

"I don't say no, me," she replied, striving to withdraw her hand, which he held more firmly for the attempt.

"But come, Calixta; you know you said you would go back to Assumption, just to spite them."

"No, I neva said that, me. You mus' dreamt that."

"Oh, I thought you did. You know I'm going down to the city."

"W'en?"

"Tonight."

"Betta make has'e, then; it's mos' day."

"Well, tomorrow'll do."

"W'at you goin' do, yonda?"

"I don't know. Drown myself in the lake, maybe; unless you go down there to visit your uncle."

Calixta's senses were reeling; and they well-nigh left her when she felt Alcée's lips brush her ear like the touch of a rose.

"Mista Alcée! Is dat Mista Alcée?" the thick voice of a Negro was asking; he stood on the ground, holding to the banister-rails near which the couple sat.

"W'at do you want now?" cried Alcée impatiently. "Can't I have a moment of peace?"

"I ben huntin' you high an' low, suh," answered the man. "Dey— dey someone in de road, onda de mulbare-tree, want see you a minute."

"I wouldn't go out to the road to see the Angel Gabriel. And if you come back here with any more talk, I'll have to break your neck." The Negro turned mumbling away.

Alcée and Calixta laughed softly about it. Her boisterousness was all gone. They talked low, and laughed softly, as lovers do.

"Alcée! Alcée Laballière!"

It was not the Negro's voice this time; but one that went through Alcée's body like an electric shock, bringing him to his feet.

Clarisse was standing there in her riding-habit, where the Negro had stood. For an instant confusion reigned in Alcée's thoughts, as with one who awakes suddenly from a dream. But he felt that something of serious import had brought his cousin to the ball in the dead of night.

"W'at does this mean, Clarisse?" he asked.

"It means something has happen' at home. You mus' come."

"Happened to maman?" he questioned, in alarm.

"No; nénaine is well, and asleep. It is something else. Not to frighten you. But you mus' come. Come with me, Alcée."

There was no need for the imploring note. He would have followed the voice anywhere.

She had now recognized the girl sitting back on the bench.

"Ah, c'est vous, Calixta? Comment ça va, mon enfant?"[7]

"Tcha va b'en;[8] et vous, mam'zélle?"

Alcée swung himself over the low rail and started to follow Clarisse, without a word, without a glance back at the girl. He had forgotten he was leaving her there. But Clarisse whispered something to him, and he turned back to say "Good-night, Calixta," and offer his hand to press through the railing. She pretended not to see it.

°   °   °

"How come that? You settin' yere by yo'se'f, Calixta?" It was Bobinôt who had found her there alone. The dancers had not yet come out. She looked ghastly in the faint, gray light struggling out of the east.

"Yes, that's me. Go yonda in the *parc aux petits* an' ask Aunt Olisse fu' my hat. She knows w'ere 't is. I want to go home, me."

"How you came?"

"I come afoot, with the Cateaus. But I'm goin' now. I ent goin' wait fu' 'em. I'm plumb wo' out, me."

"Kin I go with you, Calixta?"

"I don' care."

They went together across the open prairie and along the edge of the fields, stumbling in the uncertain light. He told her to lift her dress that was getting wet and bedraggled; for she was pulling at the weeds and grasses with her hands.

"I don't care; it's got to go in the tub, anyway. You been sayin' all along you want to marry me, Bobinôt. Well, if you want, yet, I don' care, me."

The glow of a sudden and overwhelming happiness shone out in the brown, rugged face of the young Acadian. He could not speak, for very joy. It choked him.

"Oh well, if you don't want," snapped Calixta, flippantly, pretending to be piqued at his silence.

"*Bon Dieu!* You know that makes me crazy, w'at you sayin'. You mean that, Calixta? You ent goin' turn roun' agin?"

"I neva tole you that much *yet*, Bobinôt. I mean that. *Tiens*," and she held out her hand in the business-like manner of a man who clinches a bargain with a hand-clasp. Bobinôt grew bold with happiness and asked Calixta to kiss him. She turned her face, that was almost ugly after the night's dissipation, and looked steadily into his.

---

7. It's you; how's it going, my child?   8. Everything's going okay.

"I don' want to kiss you, Bobinôt," she said, turning away again, "not today. Some other time. *Bonté divine!*[9] ent you satisfy, *yet!*"

"Oh, I'm satisfy, Calixta," he said.

* * *

Riding through a patch of wood, Clarisse's saddle became ungirted, and she and Alcée dismounted to readjust it.

For the twentieth time he asked her what had happened at home.

"But, Clarisse, w'at is it? Is it a misfortune?"

"Ah Dieu sait! It's only something that happen' to me."

"To you!"

"I saw you go away las' night, Alcée, with those saddle-bags," she said, haltingly, striving to arrange something about the saddle, "an' I made Bruce tell me. He said you had gone to the ball, an' wouldn' be home for weeks an' weeks. I thought, Alcée—maybe you were going to—to Assumption. I got wild. An' then I knew if you didn't come back, *now*, tonight, I couldn't stan' it,—again."

She had her face hidden in her arm that she was resting against the saddle when she said that.

He began to wonder if this meant love. But she had to tell him so, before he believed it. And when she told him, he thought the face of the Universe was changed—just like Bobinôt. Was it last week the cyclone had well-nigh ruined him? The cyclone seemed a huge joke, now. It was he, then, who, an hour ago was kissing little Calixta's ear and whispering nonsense into it. Calixta was like a myth, now. The one, only, great reality in the world was Clarisse standing before him, telling him that she loved him.

In the distance they heard the rapid discharge of pistol-shots; but it did not disturb them. They knew it was only the Negro musicians who had gone into the yard to fire their pistols into the air, as the custom is, and to announce *"le bal est fini."*[1]

Two Tales, October 1892; *Bayou Folk*, 1894

Madame Célestin's Divorce

Madame Célestin always wore a neat and snugly fitting calico wrapper when she went out in the morning to sweep her small gallery.[1] Lawyer Paxton thought she looked very pretty in the gray one that was made with a graceful Watteau fold at the back: and with which she invariably wore a bow of pink ribbon at the throat. She was always sweeping her gallery when lawyer Paxton passed by in the morning on his way to his office in St. Denis Street.

Sometimes he stopped and leaned over the fence to say good-morning at his ease; to criticise or admire her rosebushes; or, when he had

9. Good gracious.   1. Verandah.
1. The ball is over.

time enough, to hear what she had to say. Madame Célestin usually
had a good deal to say. She would gather up the train of her calico
wrapper in one hand, and balancing the broom gracefully in the other,
would go tripping down to where the lawyer leaned, as comfortably as
he could, over her picket fence.

Of course she had talked to him of her troubles. Everyone knew
Madame Célestin's troubles.

"Really, madame," he told her once, in his deliberate, calculating,
lawyer-tone, "it's more than human nature—woman's nature—should
be called upon to endure. Here you are, working your fingers off"—she
glanced down at two rosy finger-tips that showed through the rents in
her baggy doeskin gloves—"taking in sewing; giving music lessons;
doing God knows what in the way of manual labor to support yourself
and those two little ones"—Madame Célestin's pretty face beamed
with satisfaction at this enumeration of her trials.

"You right, Judge. Not a picayune,[2] not one, not one, have I lay my
eyes on in the pas' fo' months that I can say Célestin give it to me or
sen' it to me."

"The scoundrel!" muttered lawyer Paxton in his beard.

"An' *pourtant*,"[3] she resumed, "they say he's making money down
roun' Alexandria w'en he wants to work."

"I dare say you haven't seen him for months?" suggested the lawyer.

"It's good six month' since I see a sight of Célestin," she admitted.

"That's it, that's what I say; he has practically deserted you; fails to
support you. It wouldn't surprise me a bit to learn that he has ill treated
you."

"Well, you know, Judge," with an evasive cough, "a man that
drinks—w'at can you expec'? An' if you would know the promises he
has made me! Ah, if I had as many dolla' as I had promise from
Célestin, I wouldn' have to work, *je vous garantis*."[4]

"And in my opinion, Madame, you would be a foolish woman to
endure it longer, when the divorce court is there to offer you redress."

"You spoke about that befo', Judge; I'm goin' think about that
divo'ce. I believe you right."

Madame Célestin thought about the divorce and talked about it, too;
and lawyer Paxton grew deeply interested in the theme.

"You know, about that divo'ce, Judge," Madame Célestin was waiting for him that morning, "I been talking to my family an' my frien's,
an' it's me that tells you, they all plumb agains' that divo'ce."

"Certainly, to be sure; that's to be expected, Madame, in this community of Creoles. I warned you that you would meet with opposition,
and would have to face it and brave it."

"Oh, don't fear, I'm going to face it! Maman says it's a disgrace like

---

2. A small copper coin formerly used in parts of the
southern United States; worth about five cents or
less.

3. However.

4. I guarantee you.

it's neva been in the family. But it's good for Maman to talk, her. W'at trouble she ever had? She says I mus' go by all means consult with Père[5] Duchéron—it's my confessor, you undastan'—Well, I'll go, Judge, to please Maman. But all the confessor' in the worl' ent goin' make me put up with that conduc' of Célestin any longa."

A day or two later, she was there waiting for him again. "You know, Judge, about that divo'ce."

"Yes, yes," responded the lawyer, well pleased to trace a new determination in her brown eyes and in the curves of her pretty mouth. "I suppose you saw Père Duchéron and had to brave it out with him, too."

"Oh, fo' that, a perfec' sermon, I assho you. A talk of giving scandal an' bad example that I thought would neva en'! He says, fo' him, he wash' his hands; I mus' go see the bishop."

"You won't let the bishop dissuade you, I trust," stammered the lawyer more anxiously than he could well understand.

"You don't know me yet, Judge," laughed Madame Célestin with a turn of the head and a flirt of the broom which indicated that the interview was at an end.

"Well, Madame Célestin! And the bishop!" Lawyer Paxton was standing there holding to a couple of the shaky pickets. She had not seen him. "Oh, it's you, Judge?" and she hastened towards him with an *empressement*[6] that could not but have been flattering.

"Yes, I saw Monseigneur," she began. The lawyer had already gathered from her expressive countenance that she had not wavered in her determination. "Ah, he's a eloquent man. It's not a mo' eloquent man in Natchitoches parish. I was fo'ced to cry, the way he talked to me about my troubles; how he undastan's them, an' feels for me. It would move even you, Judge, to hear how he talk' about that step I want to take; its danga, its temptation. How it is the duty of a Catholic to stan' everything till the las' extreme. An' that life of retirement an' self-denial I would have to lead,—he told me all that."

"But he hasn't turned you from your resolve, I see," laughed the lawyer complacently.

"For that, no," she returned emphatically. "The bishop don't know w'at it is to be married to a man like Célestin, an' have to endu' that conduc' like I have to endu' it. The Pope himse'f can't make me stan' that any longer, if you say I got the right in the law to sen' Célestin sailing."

A noticeable change had come over lawyer Paxton. He discarded his work-day coat and began to wear his Sunday one to the office. He grew solicitous as to the shine of his boots, his collar, and the set of his tie. He brushed and trimmed his whiskers with a care that had not before been apparent. Then he fell into a stupid habit of dreaming as he walked the streets of the old town. It would be very good to take unto himself a wife, he dreamed. And he could dream of no other than

5. Father.   6. Eagerness.

pretty Madame Célestin filling that sweet and sacred office as she filled his thoughts, now. Old Natchitoches would not hold them comfortably, perhaps; but the world was surely wide enough to live in, outside of Natchitoches town.

His heart beat in a strangely irregular manner as he neared Madame Célestin's house one morning, and discovered her behind the rose-bushes, as usual plying her broom. She had finished the gallery and steps and was sweeping the little brick walk along the edge of the violet border.

"Good-morning, Madame Célestin."

"Ah, it's you, Judge? Good-morning." He waited. She seemed to be doing the same. Then she ventured, with some hesitancy, "You know, Judge, about that divo'ce. I been thinking,—I reckon you betta neva mine about that divo'ce." She was making deep rings in the palm of her gloved hand with the end of the broomhandle, and looking at them critically. Her face seemed to the lawyer to be unusually rosy; but maybe it was only the reflection of the pink bow at the throat. "Yes, I reckon you needn' mine. You see, Judge, Célestin came home las' night. An' he's promise me on his word an' honor he's going to turn ova a new leaf."

No magazine publication; *Bayou Folk*, 1894

A Gentleman of Bayou Têche

It was no wonder Mr. Sublet, who was staying at the Hallet plantation, wanted to make a picture of Evariste. The 'Cadian was rather a pictur-esque subject in his way, and a tempting one to an artist looking for bits of "local color" along the Têche.

Mr. Sublet had seen the man on the back gallery just as he came out of the swamp, trying to sell a wild turkey to the housekeeper. He spoke to him at once, and in the course of conversation engaged him to return to the house the following morning and have his picture drawn. He handed Evariste a couple of silver dollars to show that his intentions were fair, and that he expected the 'Cadian to keep faith with him.

"He tell' me he want' put my picture in one fine '*Mag*'zine,' " said Evariste to his daughter, Martinette, when the two were talking the matter over in the afternoon. "W'at fo' you reckon he want' do dat?" They sat within the low, homely cabin of two rooms, that was not quite so comfortable as Mr. Hallet's Negro quarters.

Martinette pursed her red lips that had little sensitive curves to them, and her black eyes took on a reflective expression.

"Mebbe he yeard 'bout that big fish w'at you ketch las' winta in Carancro lake. You know it was all wrote about in the 'Suga Bowl.' " Her father set aside the suggestion with a deprecatory wave of the hand.

"Well, anyway, you got to fix yo'se'f up," declared Martinette, dismissing further speculation; "put on yo' otha pant'loon an' yo' good coat; an' you betta ax Mr. Léonce to cut yo' hair, an' you' w'sker' a li'le bit."

"It's w'at I say," chimed in Evariste. "I tell dat gent'man I'm goin' make myse'f fine. He say', 'No, no,' like he ent please'. He want' me like I come out de swamp. So much betta if my pant'loon' an' coat is tore, he say, an' color' like de mud." They could not understand these eccentric wishes on the part of the strange gentleman, and made no effort to do so.

An hour later Martinette, who was quite puffed up over the affair, trotted across to Aunt Dicey's cabin to communicate the news to her. The negress was ironing; her irons stood in a long row before the fire of logs that burned on the hearth. Martinette seated herself in the chimney corner and held her feet up to the blaze; it was damp and a little chilly out of doors. The girl's shoes were considerably worn and her garments were a little too thin and scant for the winter season. Her father had given her the two dollars he had received from the artist, and Martinette was on her way to the store to invest them as judiciously as she knew how.

"You know, Aunt Dicey," she began a little complacently after listening awhile to Aunt Dicey's unqualified abuse of her own son, Wilkins, who was dining-room boy at Mr. Hallet's, "you know that stranger gentleman up to Mr. Hallet's? he want' to make my popa's picture; an' he say' he goin' put it in one fine *Mag'*zine yonda."

Aunt Dicey spat upon her iron to test its heat. Then she began to snicker. She kept on laughing inwardly, making her whole fat body shake, and saying nothing.

"W'at you laughin' 'bout, Aunt Dice?" inquired Martinette mistrustfully.

"I is n' laughin', chile!"

"Yas, you' laughin'."

"Oh, don't pay no 'tention to me. I jis studyin' how simple you an' yo' pa is. You is bof de simplest somebody I eva come 'crost."

"You got to say plumb out w'at you mean, Aunt Dice," insisted the girl doggedly, suspicious and alert now.

"Well, dat w'y I say you is simple," proclaimed the woman, slamming down her iron on an inverted, battered pie pan, "jis like you says, dey gwine put yo' pa's picture yonda in de picture paper. An' you know w'at readin' dey gwine sot down on'neaf dat picture?" Martinette was intensely attentive. "Dey gwine sot down on'neaf: 'Dis heah is one dem low-down 'Cajuns o' Bayeh Têche!' "

The blood flowed from Martinette's face, leaving it deathly pale; in another instant it came beating back in a quick flood, and her eyes smarted with pain as if the tears that filled them had been fiery hot.

"I knows dem kine o' folks," continued Aunt Dicey, resuming her interrupted ironing. "Dat stranger he got a li'le boy w'at ain't none too big to spank. Dat li'le imp he come a hoppin' in heah yistiddy wid a

kine o' box on'neaf his arm. He say' 'Good mo'nin', madam. Will you
be so kine an' stan' jis like you is dah at you' i'onin', an' lef me take yo'
picture?' I 'lowed I gwine make a picture outen him wid dis heah
flati'on, ef he don' cl'ar hisse'f quick. An' he say he baig my pardon fo'
his intrudement. All dat kine o' talk to a ole nigga 'oman! Dat plainly
sho' he don' know his place."

"W'at you want 'im to say, Aunt Dice?" asked Martinette, with an
effort to conceal her distress.

"I wants 'im to come in heah an' say: 'Howdy, Aunt Dicey! will you
be so kine and go put on yo' noo calker dress an' yo' bonnit w'at you
w'ars to meetin', an' stan' 'side f'om dat i'onin'-boa'd w'ilse I gwine
take yo photygraph.' Dat de way fo' a boy to talk w'at had good
raisin'."

Martinette had arisen, and began to take slow leave of the woman.
She turned at the cabin door to observe tentatively: "I reckon it's
Wilkins tells you how the folks they talk, yonda up to Mr. Hallet's."

She did not go to the store as she had intended, but walked with a
dragging step back to her home. The silver dollars clicked in her pocket
as she walked. She felt like flinging them across the field; they seemed
to her somehow the price of shame.

The sun had sunk, and twilight was settling like a silver beam upon
the bayou and enveloping the fields in a gray mist. Evariste, slim and
slouchy, was waiting for his daughter in the cabin door. He had lighted
a fire of sticks and branches, and placed the kettle before it to boil. He
met the girl with his slow, serious, questioning eyes, astonished to see
her empty-handed.

"How come you didn' bring nuttin' f'om de sto', Martinette?"

She entered and flung her gingham sunbonnet upon a chair. "No, I
didn't go yonda;" and with sudden exasperation: "You got to go take
back that money; you mus'n' git no picture took."

"But, Martinette," her father mildly interposed, "I promise' 'im; an'
he's goin' give me some mo' money w'en he finish."

"If he give you a ba'el o' money, you mus'n' git no picture took. You
know w'at he want to put un'neath that picture, fo' ev'body to read?"
She could not tell him the whole hideous truth as she had heard it
distorted from Aunt Dicey's lips; she would not hurt him that much.
"He's goin' to write: 'This is one 'Cajun' o' the Bayou Têche.'" Evariste winced.

"How you know?" he asked.

"I yeard so. I know it 's true."

The water in the kettle was boiling. He went and poured a small
quantity upon the coffee which he had set there to drip. Then he said
to her: "I reckon you jus' as well go care dat two dolla' back, tomo'
mo'nin'; me, I'll go yonda ketch a mess o' fish in Carancro lake."

ø   ø   ø

Mr. Hallet and a few masculine companions were assembled at a
rather late breakfast the following morning. The dining-room was a
big, bare one, enlivened by a cheerful fire of logs that blazed in the

wide chimney on massive andirons. There were guns, fishing tackle, and other implements of sport lying about. A couple of fine dogs strayed unceremoniously in and out behind Wilkins, the Negro boy who waited upon the table. The chair beside Mr. Sublet, usually occupied by his little son, was vacant, as the child had gone for an early morning outing and had not yet returned.

When breakfast was about half over, Mr. Hallet noticed Martinette standing outside upon the gallery.[1] The dining-room door had stood open more than half the time.

"Isn't that Martinette out there, Wilkins?" inquired the jovial-faced young planter.

"Dat 's who, suh," returned Wilkins. "She ben standin' dah sense mos' sun-up; look like she studyin' to take root to de gall'ry."

"What in the name of goodness does she want? Ask her what she wants. Tell her to come in to the fire."

Martinette walked into the room with much hesitancy. Her small, brown face could hardly be seen in the depths of the gingham sunbonnet. Her blue cottonade skirt scarcely reached the thin ankles that it should have covered.

"Bonjou'," she murmured, with a little comprehensive nod that took in the entire company. Her eyes searched the table for the "stranger gentleman," and she knew him at once, because his hair was parted in the middle and he wore a pointed beard. She went and laid the two silver dollars beside his plate and motioned to retire without a word of explanation.

"Hold on, Martinette!" called out the planter, "what 's all this pantomime business? Speak out, little one."

"My poppa don't want any picture took," she offered, a little timorously. On her way to the door she had looked back to say this. In that fleeting glance she detected a smile of intelligence pass from one to the other of the group. She turned quickly, facing them all, and spoke out, excitement making her voice bold and shrill: "My popa ent one lowdown 'Cajun. He ent goin' to stan' to have that kine o' writin' put down un'neath his picture!"

She almost ran from the room, half blinded by the emotion that had helped her to make so daring a speech.

Descending the gallery steps she ran full against her father who was ascending, bearing in his arms the little boy, Archie Sublet. The child was most grotesquely attired in garments far too large for his diminutive person—the rough jeans clothing of some Negro boy. Evariste himself had evidently been taking a bath without the preliminary ceremony of removing his clothes, that were now half dried upon his person by the wind and sun.

"Yere you' li'le boy," he announced, stumbling into the room. "You ought not lef dat li'le chile go by hisse'f *comme ça* in de pirogue."[2] Mr.

1. Verandah.
2. A canoe made from a hollowed tree trunk. Comme ça: like that.

Sublet darted from his chair; the others following suit almost as hastily. In an instant, quivering with apprehension, he had his little son in his arms. The child was quite unharmed, only somewhat pale and nervous, as the consequence of a recent very serious ducking.

Evariste related in his uncertain, broken English how he had been fishing for an hour or more in Carancro lake, when he noticed the boy paddling over the deep, black water in a shell-like pirogue. Nearing a clump of cypress-trees that rose from the lake, the pirogue became entangled in the heavy moss that hung from the tree limbs and trailed upon the water. The next thing he knew, the boat had overturned, he heard the child scream, and saw him disappear beneath the still, black surface of the lake.

"W'en I done swim to de sho' wid 'im," continued Evariste, "I hurry yonda to Jake Baptiste's cabin, an' we rub 'im an' warm 'im up, an' dress 'im up dry like you see. He all right now, M'sieur; but you mus'n lef 'im go no mo' by hisse'f in one pirogue."

Martinette had followed into the room behind her father. She was feeling and tapping his wet garments solicitously, and begging him in French to come home. Mr. Hallet at once ordered hot coffee and a warm breakfast for the two; and they sat down at the corner of the table, making no manner of objection in their perfect simplicity. It was with visible reluctance and ill-disguised contempt that Wilkins served them.

When Mr. Sublet had arranged his son comfortably, with tender care, upon the sofa, and had satisfied himself that the child was quite uninjured, he attempted to find words with which to thank Evariste for this service which no treasure of words or gold could pay for. These warm and heart-felt expressions seemed to Evariste to exaggerate the importance of his action, and they intimidated him. He attempted shyly to hide his face as well as he could in the depths of his bowl of coffee.

"You will let me make your picture now, I hope, Evariste," begged Mr. Sublet, laying his hand upon the 'Cadian's shoulder. "I want to place it among things I hold most dear, and shall call it 'A hero of Bayou Têche.' " This assurance seemed to distress Evariste greatly.

"No, no," he protested, "it's nuttin' hero' to take a li'le boy out de water. I jus' as easy do dat like I stoop down an' pick up a li'le chile w'at fall down in de road. I ent goin' to 'low dat, me. I don't git no picture took, *va!*"

Mr. Hallet, who now discerned his friend's eagerness in the matter, came to his aid.

"I tell you, Evariste, let Mr. Sublet draw your picture, and you yourself may call it whatever you want. I'm sure he'll let you."

"Most willingly," agreed the artist.

Evariste glanced up at him with shy and child-like pleasure. "It's a bargain?" he asked.

"A bargain," affirmed Mr. Sublet.

"Popa," whispered Martinette, "you betta come home an' put on yo' otha pant'loon' an' yo' good coat."

"And now, what shall we call the much talked-of picture?" cheerily inquired the planter, standing with his back to the blaze.

Evariste in a business-like manner began carefully to trace on the tablecloth imaginary characters with an imaginary pen; he could not have written the real characters with a real pen—he did not know how.

"You will put on'neat' de picture," he said, deliberately, " 'Dis is one picture of Mista Evariste Anatole Bonamour, a gent'man of de Bayou Têche.' "

No magazine publication; *Bayou Folk,* 1894

Odalie Misses Mass

Odalie sprang down from the mulecart, shook out her white skirts, and firmly grasping her parasol, which was blue to correspond with her sash, entered Aunt Pinky's gate and proceeded towards the old woman's cabin. She was a thick-waisted young thing who walked with a firm tread and carried her head with a determined poise. Her straight brown hair had been rolled up overnight in papillotes,[1] and the artificial curls stood out in clusters, stiff and uncompromising beneath the rim of her white chip hat. Her mother, sister, and brother remained seated in the cart before the gate.

It was the fifteenth of August, the great feast of the Assumption, so generally observed in the Catholic parishes of Louisiana. The Chotard family were on their way to mass, and Odalie had insisted upon stopping to "show herself" to her old friend and protegée, Aunt Pinky.

The helpless, shriveled old Negress sat in the depths of a large, rudely fashioned chair. A loosely hanging unbleached cotton gown enveloped her mite of a figure. What was visible of her hair beneath the bandana turban looked like white sheep's wool. She wore round, silver-rimmed spectacles, which gave her an air of wisdom and respectability, and she held in her hand the branch of a hickory sapling, with which she kept mosquitoes and flies at bay, and even chickens and pigs that sometimes penetrated the heart of her domain.

Odalie walked straight up to the old woman and kissed her on the cheek.

"Well, Aunt Pinky, yere I am," she announced with evident self-complacency, turning herself slowly and stiffly around like a mechanical dummy. In one hand she held her prayer-book, fan, and handkerchief, in the other the blue parasol, still open; and on her plump hands were blue cotton mitts. Aunt Pinky beamed and chuckled; Odalie hardly expected her to be able to do more.

"Now you saw me," the child continued. "I reckon you satisfied. I mus' go; I ain't got a minute to was'e." But at the threshold she turned to inquire, bluntly:

"W'ere's Pug?"

1. Curl papers.

"Pug," replied Aunt Pinky, in her tremulous old-woman's voice. "She's gone to chu'ch; done gone; she done gone," nodding her head in seeming approval of Pug's action.

"To church!" echoed Odalie with a look of consternation settling in her round eyes.

"She gone to chu'ch," reiterated Aunt Pinky. "Say she kain't miss chu'ch on de fifteent'; de debble gwine pester her twell jedgment, she miss chu'ch on de fifteent'."

Odalie's plump cheeks fairly quivered with indignation and she stamped her foot. She looked up and down the long, dusty road that skirted the river. Nothing was to be seen save the blue cart with its dejected looking mule and patient occupants. She walked to the end of the gallery and called out to a Negro boy whose black bullet-head showed up in bold relief against the white of the cotton patch:

"Hé, Baptiste! w'ere's yo' ma? Ask yo' ma if she can't come set with Aunt Pinky."

"Mammy, she gone to chu'ch," screamed Baptiste in answer.

"Bonté![2] w'at's taken you all darkies with yo' 'church' today? You come along yere Baptiste an' set with Aunt Pinky. That Pug! I'm goin' to make yo' ma wear her out fo' that trick of hers—leavin' Aunt Pinky like that."

But at the first intimation of what was wanted of him, Baptiste dipped below the cotton like a fish beneath water, leaving no sight nor sound of himself to answer Odalie's repeated calls. Her mother and sister were beginning to show signs of impatience.

"But, I can't go," she cried out to them. "It's nobody to stay with Aunt Pinky. I can't leave Aunt Pinky like that, to fall out of her chair, maybe, like she already fell out once."

"You goin' to miss mass on the fifteenth, you, Odalie! W'at you thinkin' about?" came in shrill rebuke from her sister. But her mother offering no objection, the boy lost not a moment in starting the mule forward at a brisk trot. She watched them disappear in a cloud of dust; and turning with a dejected, almost tearful countenance, re-entered the room.

Aunt Pinky seemed to accept her reappearance as a matter of course; and even evinced no surprise at seeing her remove her hat and mitts, which she laid carefully, almost religiously, on the bed, together with her book, fan, and handkerchief.

Then Odalie went and seated herself some distance from the old woman in her own small, low rocking-chair. She rocked herself furiously, making a great clatter with the rockers over the wide, uneven boards of the cabin floor; and she looked out through the open door.

"Puggy, she done gone to chu'ch; done gone. Say de debble gwine pester her twell jedgment—"

"You done tole me that, Aunt Pinky; neva mine; don't le's talk about it."

2. Gracious!

Aunt Pinky, thus rebuked, settled back into silence and Odalie continued to rock and stare out of the door.

Once she arose, and taking the hickory branch from Aunt Pinky's nerveless hand, made a bold and sudden charge upon a little pig that seemed bent upon keeping her company. She pursued him with flying heels and loud cries as far as the road. She came back flushed and breathless and her curls hanging rather limp around her face; she began again to rock herself and gaze silently out of the door.

"You gwine make yo' fus' c'mmunion?"

This seemingly sober inquiry on the part of Aunt Pinky at once shattered Odalie's ill-humor and dispelled every shadow of it. She leaned back and laughed with wild abandonment.

"Mais w'at you thinkin' about, Aunt Pinky? How you don't remember I made my firs' communion las' year, with this same dress w'at maman let out the tuck," holding up the altered skirt for Aunt Pinky's inspection. "An' with this same petticoat w'at maman added this ruffle an' crochet' edge; excep' I had a w'ite sash."

These evidences proved beyond question convincing and seemed to satisfy Aunt Pinky. Odalie rocked as furiously as ever, but she sang now, and the swaying chair had worked its way nearer to the old woman.

"You gwine git mar'ied?"

"I declare, Aunt Pinky," said Odalie, when she had ceased laughing and was wiping her eyes, "I declare, sometime' I think you gittin' plumb foolish. How you expec' me to git married w'en I'm on'y thirteen?"

Evidently Aunt Pinky did not know why or how she expected anything so preposterous; Odalie's holiday attire that filled her with contemplative rapture had doubtless incited her to these vagaries.

The child now drew her chair quite close to the old woman's knee after she had gone out to the rear of the cabin to get herself some water and had brought a drink to Aunt Pinky in the gourd dipper.

There was a strong, hot breeze blowing from the river, and it swept fitfully and in gusts through the cabin, bringing with it the weedy smell of cacti that grew thick on the bank, and occasionally a shower of reddish dust from the road. Odalie for a while was greatly occupied in keeping in place her filmy skirt, which every gust of wind swelled balloon-like about her knees. Aunt Pinky's little black, scrawny hand had found its way among the droopy curls, and strayed often caressingly to the child's plump neck and shoulders.

"You riclics, honey, dat day yo' granpappy say it wur pinchin' times an' he reckin he bleege to sell Yallah Tom an' Susan an' Pinky? Don' know how come he think 'bout Pinky, 'less caze he sees me playin' an' trapsin' roun' wid you alls, day in an' out. I riclics yit how you tu'n w'ite like milk an' fling yo' arms roun' li'le black Pinky; an' you cries out you don' wan' no saddle-mar'; you don' wan' no silk dresses and fing' rings an' sich; an' don' wan' no idication; des wants Pinky. An' you cries an'

screams an' kicks, an' 'low you gwine kill fus' pusson w'at dar come an'
buy Pinky an' kiars her off. You riclics dat, honey?"

Odalie had grown accustomed to these flights of fancy on the part of
her old friend; she liked to humor her as she chose to sometimes humor
very small children; so she was quite used to impersonating one dearly
beloved but impetuous, "Paulette," who seemed to have held her
place in old Pinky's heart and imagination through all the years of her
suffering life.

"I rec'lec' like it was yesterday, Aunt Pinky. How I scream an' kick
an' maman gave me some med'cine; an' how you scream an' kick an'
Susan took you down to the quarters an' give you 'twenty'."[3]

"Das so, honey; des like you says," chuckled Aunt Pinky. "But you
don' riclic dat time you cotch Pinky cryin' down in de holler behine de
gin; an' you say you gwine give me 'twenty' ef I don't tell you w'at I
cryin' 'bout?"

"I rec'lec' like it happen'd today, Aunt Pinky. You been cryin' because you want to marry Hiram, ole Mr. Benitou's servant."

"Das true like you says, Miss Paulette; an' you goes home an' cries
and kiars on an' won' eat, an' breaks dishes, an' pesters yo' gran'pap
'tell he bleedge to buy Hi'um f'om de Benitous."

"Don't talk, Aunt Pink! I can see all that jus' as plain!" responded
Odalie sympathetically, yet in truth she took but a languid interest in
these reminiscences which she had listened to so often before.

She leaned her flushed cheek against Aunt Pinky's knee.

The air was rippling now, and hot and caressing. There was the hum
of bumble bees outside; and busy mud-daubers[4] kept flying in and out
through the door. Some chickens had penetrated to the very threshold
in their aimless roamings, and the little pig was approaching more
cautiously. Sleep was fast overtaking the child, but she could still hear
through her drowsiness the familiar tones of Aunt Pinky's voice.

"But Hi'um, he done gone; he nuva come back; an' Yallah Tom nuva
come back; an' ole Marster an' de chillun—all gone—nuva come back.
Nobody nuva come back to Pinky 'cep you, my honey. You ain' gwine
'way f'om Pinky no mo', is you, Miss Paulette?"

"Don' fret, Aunt Pinky—I'm goin'—to stay with—you."

"No pussun nuva come back 'cep' you."

Odalie was fast asleep. Aunt Pinky was asleep with her head leaning
back on her chair and her fingers thrust into the mass of tangled brown
hair that swept across her lap. The chickens and little pig walked
fearlessly in and out. The sunlight crept close up to the cabin door and
stole away again.

Odalie awoke with a start. Her mother was standing over her arous-
ing her from sleep. She sprang up and rubbed her eyes. "Oh, I been
asleep!" she exclaimed. The cart was standing in the road waiting.
"An' Aunt Pinky, she's asleep, too."

---

3. I.e., twenty lashes with the whip.　　　　4. Wasps.

"Yes, chérie, Aunt Pinky is asleep," replied her mother, leading Odalie away. But she spoke low and trod softly as gentle-souled women do, in the presence of the dead.

Shreveport Times, July 1895; *A Night in Acadie*, 1897

Ozème's Holiday

Ozème often wondered why there was not a special dispensation of providence to do away with the necessity for work. There seemed to him so much created for man's enjoyment in this world, and so little time and opportunity to profit by it. To sit and do nothing but breathe was a pleasure to Ozème; but to sit in the company of a few choice companions, including a sprinkling of ladies, was even a greater delight; and the joy which a day's hunting or fishing or picnicking afforded him is hardly to be described. Yet he was by no means indolent. He worked faithfully on the plantation the whole year long, in a sort of methodical way; but when the time came around for his annual week's holiday, there was no holding him back. It was often decidedly inconvenient for the planter that Ozème usually chose to take his holiday during some very busy season of the year.

He started out one morning in the beginning of October. He had borrowed Mr. Laballière's buckboard and Padue's old gray mare, and a harness from the negro Séverin. He wore a light blue suit which had been sent all the way from St. Louis, and which had cost him ten dollars; he had paid almost as much again for his boots; and his hat was a broad-rimmed gray felt which he had no cause to be ashamed of. When Ozème went "broading,"[1] he dressed—well, regardless of cost. His eyes were blue and mild; his hair was light, and he wore it rather long; he was clean shaven, and really did not look his thirty-five years.

Ozème had laid his plans weeks beforehand. He was going visiting along Cane River; the mere contemplation filled him with pleasure. He counted upon reaching Fédeaus' about noon, and he would stop and dine there. Perhaps they would ask him to stay all night. He really did not hold to staying all night, and was not decided to accept if they did ask him. There were only the two old people, and he rather fancied the notion of pushing on to Beltrans', where he would stay a night, or even two, if urged. He was quite sure that there would be something agreeable going on at Beltrans', with all those young people—perhaps a fish-fry, or possibly a ball!

Of course he would have to give a day to Tante Sophie and another to Cousine Victoire; but none to the St. Annes unless entreated—after St. Anne reproaching him last year with being a fainéant[2] for broading at such a season! At Cloutierville, where he would linger as long as

1. Going abroad, going on holiday. 2. Loiterer, loafer.

possible, he meant to turn and retrace his course, zigzagging back and forth across Cane River so as to take in the Duplans, the Velcours, and others that he could not at the moment recall. A week seemed to Ozème a very, very little while in which to crowd so much pleasure.

There were steam-gins[3] at work; he could hear them whistling far and near. On both sides of the river the fields were white with cotton, and everybody in the world seemed busy but Ozème. This reflection did not distress or disturb him in the least; he pursued his way at peace with himself and his surroundings.

At Lamérie's cross-roads store, where he stopped to buy a cigar, he learned that there was no use heading for Fédeaus', as the two old people had gone to town for a lengthy visit, and the house was locked up. It was at Fédeaus' that Ozème had intended to dine.

He sat in the buckboard, given up to a moment or two of reflection. The result was that he turned away from the river, and entered the road that led between two fields back to the woods and into the heart of the country. He had determined upon taking a short cut to the Beltrans' plantation, and on the way he meant to keep an eye open for old Aunt Tildy's cabin, which he knew lay in some remote part of this cut-off. He remembered that Aunt Tildy could cook an excellent meal if she had the material at hand. He would induce her to fry him a chicken, drip a cup of coffee, and turn him out a pone of corn-bread,[4] which he thought would be sumptuous enough fare for the occasion.

Aunt Tildy dwelt in the not unusual log cabin, of one room, with its chimney of mud and stone, and its shallow gallery formed by the jutting of the roof. In close proximity to the cabin was a small cotton-field, which from a long distance looked like a field of snow. The cotton was bursting and overflowing foam-like from bolls on the drying stalk. On the lower branches it was hanging ragged and tattered, and much of it had already fallen to the ground. There were a few chinaberry-trees in the yard before the hut, and under one of them an ancient and rusty-looking mule was eating corn from a wood trough. Some common little Creole chickens were scratching about the mule's feet and snatching at the grains of corn that occasionally fell from the trough.

Aunt Tildy was hobbling across the yard when Ozème drew up before the gate. One hand was confined in a sling; in the other she carried a tin pan, which she let fall noisily to the ground when she recognized him. She was broad, black, and misshapen, with her body bent forward almost at an acute angle. She wore a blue cottonade of large plaids, and a bandana awkwardly twisted around her head.

"Good God A'mighty, man! Whar you come from?" was her startled exclamation at beholding him.

"F'om home, Aunt Tildy; w'ere else do you expec'?" replied Ozème, dismounting composedly.

He had not seen the old woman for several years—since she was

---

3. Steam-powered cotton gins.   4. A cornmeal patty made without milk or eggs.

cooking in town for the family with which he boarded at the time. She had washed and ironed for him, atrociously, it is true, but her intentions were beyond reproach if her washing was not. She had also been clumsily attentive to him during a spell of illness. He had paid her with an occasional bandana, a calico dress, or a checked apron, and they had always considered the account between themselves square, with no sentimental feeling of gratitude remaining on either side.

"I like to know," remarked Ozème, as he took the gray mare from the shafts, and led her up to the trough where the mule was—"I like to know w'at you mean by makin' a crop like that an' then lettin' it go to was'e? Who you reckon's goin' to pick that cotton? You think maybe the angels goin' to come down an' pick it fo' you, an' gin it an' press it, an' then give you ten cents a poun' fo' it, hein?"

"Ef de Lord don' pick it, I don' know who gwine pick it, Mista Ozème. I tell you, me an' Sandy we wuk dat crap[5] day in an' day out; it's him done de mos' of it."

"Sandy? That little—"

"He ain' dat li'le Sandy no mo' w'at you rec'lec's; he 'mos' a man, an' he wuk like a man now. He wuk mo' 'an fittin' fo' his strenk, an' now he layin' in dah sick—God A'mighty knows how sick. An' me wid a risin' twell[6] I bleeged to walk de flo' o' nights, an' don' know ef I ain' gwine to lose de han' atter all."

"W'y, in the name o' conscience, you don' hire somebody to pick?"

"Whar I got money to hire? An' you knows well as me ev'y chick an' chile is pickin' roun' on de plantations an' gittin' good pay."

The whole outlook appeared to Ozème very depressing, and even menacing, to his personal comfort and peace of mind. He foresaw no prospect of dinner unless he should cook it himself. And there was that Sandy—he remembered well the little scamp of eight, always at his grandmother's heels when she was cooking or washing. Of course he would have to go in and look at the boy, and no doubt dive into his traveling-bag for quinine, without which he never traveled.

Sandy was indeed very ill, consumed with fever. He lay on a cot covered up with a faded patchwork quilt. His eyes were half closed, and he was muttering and rambling on about hoeing and bedding and cleaning and thinning out the cotton; he was hauling it to the gin, wrangling about weight and bagging and ties and the price offered per pound. That bale or two of cotton had not only sent Sandy to bed, but had pursued him there, holding him through his fevered dreams, and threatening to end him. Ozème would never have known the black boy, he was so tall, so thin, and seemingly so wasted, lying there in bed.

"See yere, Aunt Tildy," said Ozème, after he had, as was usual with him when in doubt, abandoned himself to a little reflection; "between us—you an' me—we got to manage to kill an' cook one o' those chick-

---

5. I.e., crop.   6. I.e., until.

ens I see scratchin' out yonda, fo' I'm jus' about starved. I reckon you ain't got any quinine in the house? No; I didn't suppose an instant you had. Well, I'm goin' to give Sandy a good dose o' quinine tonight, an' I'm goin' stay an' see how that'll work on 'im. But sun-up, min' you, I mus' get out o' yere."

Ozème had spent more comfortable nights than the one passed in Aunt Tildy's bed, which she considerately abandoned to him.

In the morning Sandy's fever was somewhat abated, but had not taken a decided enough turn to justify Ozème in quitting him before noon, unless he was willing "to feel like a dog," as he told himself. He appeared before Aunt Tildy stripped to the undershirt, and wearing his second-best pair of trousers.

"That's a nice pickle o' fish you got me in, ol' woman. I guarantee, nex' time I go abroad, 'tain't me that'll take any cut-off. W'ere's that cotton-basket an' cotton-sack o' yo's?"

"I knowed it!" chanted Aunt Tildy—"I knowed de Lord war gwine sen' somebody to holp me out. He war n' gwine let de crap was'e atter he give Sandy an' me de strenk to make hit. De Lord gwine shove you 'long de row, Mista Ozème. De Lord gwine give you plenty mo' fingers an' han's to pick dat cotton nimble an' clean."

"Neva you min' w'at the Lord's goin' to do; go get me that cotton-sack. An' you put that poultice like I tol' you on yo' han', an' set down there an' watch Sandy. It looks like you are 'bout as helpless as a' ol' cow tangled up in a potato-vine."

Ozème had not picked cotton for many years, and he took to it a little awkwardly at first; but by the time he had reached the end of the first row the old dexterity of youth had come back to his hands, which flew rapidly back and forth with the motion of a weaver's shuttle; and his ten fingers became really nimble in clutching the cotton from its dry shell. By noon he had gathered about fifty pounds. Sandy was not then quite so well as he had promised to be, and Ozème concluded to stay that day and one more night. If the boy were no better in the morning, he would go off in search of a doctor for him, and he himself would continue on down to Tante Sophie's; the Beltrans' was out of the question now.

Sandy hardly needed a doctor in the morning. Ozème's doctoring was beginning to tell favorably; but he would have considered it criminal indifference and negligence to go away and leave the boy to Aunt Tildy's awkward ministrations just at the critical moment when there was a turn for the better; so he stayed that day out, and picked his hundred and fifty pounds.

On the third day it looked like rain, and a heavy rain just then would mean a heavy loss to Aunt Tildy and Sandy, and Ozème again went to the field, this time urging Aunt Tildy with him to do what she might with her one good hand.

"Aunt Tildy," called out Ozème to the bent old woman moving

ahead of him between the white rows of cotton, "if the Lord gets me safe out o' this ditch, 't ain't tomorro' I'll fall in anotha with my eyes open, I bet you."

"Keep along, Mista Ozème; don' grumble, don' stumble; de Lord's a-watchin' you. Look at yo' Aunt Tildy; she doin' mo' wid her one han' 'an you doin' wid yo' two, man. Keep right along, honey. Watch dat cotton how it fallin' in yo' Aunt Tildy's bag."

"I am watchin' you, ol' woman; you don' fool me. You got to work that han' o' yo's spryer than you doin', or I'll take the rawhide.[7] You done fo'got w'at the rawhide tas'e like, I reckon"—a reminder which amused Aunt Tildy so powerfully that her big Negro-laugh resounded over the whole cotton-patch, and even caused Sandy, who heard it, to turn in his bed.

The weather was still threatening on the succeeding day, and a sort of dogged determination or characteristic desire to see his undertakings carried to a satisfactory completion urged Ozème to continue his efforts to drag Aunt Tildy out of the mire into which circumstances seemed to have thrust her.

One night the rain did come, and began to beat softly on the roof of the old cabin. Sandy opened his eyes, which were no longer brilliant with the fever flame. "Granny," he whispered, "de rain! Des listen, granny; de rain a-comin', an' I ain' pick dat cotton yit! W'at time it is? Gi' me my pants—I got to go—"

"You lay whar you is, chile alive. Dat cotton put aside clean and dry. Me an' de Lord an' Mista Ozème done pick dat cotton."

Ozème drove away in the morning looking quite as spick and span as the day he left home in his blue suit and his light felt drawn a little over his eyes.

"You want to take care o' that boy," he instructed Aunt Tildy at parting, "an' get 'im on his feet. An', let me tell you, the nex' time I start out to broad, if you see me passin' in this yere cut-off, put on yo' specs an' look at me good, because it won't be me; it'll be my ghos', ol' woman."

Indeed, Ozème, for some reason or other, felt quite shamefaced as he drove back to the plantation. When he emerged from the lane which he had entered the week before, and turned into the river road, Lamérie, standing in the store door, shouted out:

"Hé, Ozème! you had good times yonda? I bet you danced holes in the sole of them new boots."

"Don't talk, Lamérie!" was Ozème's rather ambiguous reply, as he flourished the remainder of a whip over the old gray mare's sway-back, urging her to a gentle trot.

When he reached home, Bodé, one of Padue's boys, who was assisting him to unhitch, remarked:

"How come you didn' go yonda down de coas' like you said, Mista

7. I'll get the whip.

Ozème? Nobody didn' see you in Cloutierville, an' Mailitte say you neva cross' de twenty-fo'-mile ferry, an' nobody didn' see you no place."

Ozème returned, after his customary moment of reflection:

"You see, it's 'mos' always the same thing on Cane riva, my boy; a man gets tired o' that à la fin.[8] This time I went back in the woods, 'way yonda in the Fédeau cut-off; kin' o' campin' an' roughin' like, you might say. I tell you, it was sport, Bodé."

Century, August 1896; *A Night in Acadie,* 1897

Lilacs

Mme. Adrienne Farival never announced her coming; but the good nuns knew very well when to look for her. When the scent of the lilac blossoms began to permeate the air, Sister Agathe would turn many times during the day to the window; upon her face the happy, beatific expression with which pure and simple souls watch for the coming of those they love.

But it was not Sister Agathe; it was Sister Marceline who first espied her crossing the beautiful lawn that sloped up to the convent. Her arms were filled with great bunches of lilacs which she had gathered along her path. She was clad all in brown; like one of the birds that come with the spring, the nuns used to say. Her figure was rounded and graceful, and she walked with a happy, buoyant step. The cabriolet[1] which had conveyed her to the convent moved slowly up the gravel drive that led to the imposing entrance. Beside the driver was her modest little black trunk, with her name and address printed in white letters upon it: "Mme. A. Farival, Paris." It was the crunching of the gravel which had attracted Sister Marceline's attention. And then the commotion began.

White-capped heads appeared suddenly at the windows; she waved her parasol and her bunch of lilacs at them. Sister Marceline and Sister Marie Anne appeared, fluttered and expectant at the doorway. But Sister Agathe, more daring and impulsive than all, descended the steps and flew across the grass to meet her. What embraces, in which the lilacs were crushed between them! What ardent kisses! What pink flushes of happiness mounting the cheeks of the two women!

Once within the convent Adrienne's soft brown eyes moistened with tenderness as they dwelt caressingly upon the familiar objects about her, and noted the most trifling details. The white, bare boards of the floor had lost nothing of their luster. The stiff, wooden chairs, standing in rows against the walls of hall and parlor, seemed to have taken on an extra polish since she had seen them, last lilac time. And there was

---

8. In the end.   1. A two-wheeled, one-horse carriage.

a new picture of the Sacré-Coeur[2] hanging over the hall table. What had they done with Ste. Catherine de Sienne, who had occupied that position of honor for so many years? In the chapel—it was no use trying to deceive her—she saw at a glance that St. Joseph's mantle had been embellished with a new coat of blue, and the aureole about his head freshly gilded. And the Blessed Virgin there neglected! Still wearing her garb of last spring, which looked almost dingy by contrast. It was not just—such partiality! The Holy Mother had reason to be jealous and to complain.

But Adrienne did not delay to pay her respects to the Mother Superior, whose dignity would not permit her to so much as step outside the door of her private apartments to welcome this old pupil. Indeed, she was dignity in person; large, uncompromising, unbending. She kissed Adrienne without warmth, and discussed conventional themes learnedly and prosaically during the quarter of an hour which the young woman remained in her company.

It was then that Adrienne's latest gift was brought in for inspection. For Adrienne always brought a handsome present for the chapel in her little black trunk. Last year it was a necklace of gems for the Blessed Virgin, which the Good Mother was only permitted to wear on extra occasions, such as great feast days of obligation. The year before it had been a precious crucifix—an ivory figure of Christ suspended from an ebony cross, whose extremities were tipped with wrought silver. This time it was a linen embroidered altar cloth of such rare and delicate workmanship that the Mother Superior, who knew the value of such things, chided Adrienne for the extravagance.

"But, dear Mother, you know it is the greatest pleasure I have in life—to be with you all once a year, and to bring some such trifling token of my regard."

The Mother Superior dismissed her with the rejoinder: "Make yourself at home, my child. Sister Thérèse will see to your wants. You will occupy Sister Marceline's bed in the end room, over the chapel. You will share the room with Sister Agathe."

There was always one of the nuns detailed to keep Adrienne company during her fortnight's stay at the convent. This had become almost a fixed regulation. It was only during the hours of recreation that she found herself with them all together. Those were hours of much harmless merry-making under the trees or in the nuns' refectory.

This time it was Sister Agathe who waited for her outside of the Mother Superior's door. She was taller and slenderer than Adrienne, and perhaps ten years older. Her fair blonde face flushed and paled with every passing emotion that visited her soul. The two women linked arms and went together out into the open air.

There was so much which Sister Agathe felt that Adrienne must see. To begin with, the enlarged poultry yard, with its dozens upon dozens

2. Sacred Heart of Jesus.

of new inmates. It took now all the time of one of the lay sisters to attend to them. There had been no change made in the vegetable garden, but—yes there had; Adrienne's quick eye at once detected it. Last year old Philippe had planted his cabbages in a large square to the right. This year they were set out in an oblong bed to the left. How it made Sister Agathe laugh to think Adrienne should have noticed such a trifle! And old Philippe, who was nailing a broken trellis not far off, was called forward to be told about it.

He never failed to tell Adrienne how well she looked, and how she was growing younger each year. And it was his delight to recall certain of her youthful and mischievous escapades. Never would he forget that day she disappeared; and the whole convent in a hubbub about it! And how at last it was he who discovered her perched among the tallest branches of the highest tree on the grounds, where she had climbed to see if she could get a glimpse of Paris! And her punishment afterwards!—half of the Gospel of Palm Sunday to learn by heart!

"We may laugh over it, my good Philippe, but we must remember that Madame is older and wiser now."

"I know well, Sister Agathe, that one ceases to commit follies after the first days of youth." And Adrienne seemed greatly impressed by the wisdom of Sister Agathe and old Philippe, the convent gardener.

A little later when they sat upon a rustic bench which overlooked the smiling landscape about them, Adrienne was saying to Sister Agathe, who held her hand and stroked it fondly:

"Do you remember my first visit, four years ago, Sister Agathe? and what a surprise it was to you all!"

"As if I could forget it, dear child!"

"And I! Always shall I remember that morning as I walked along the boulevard with a heaviness of heart—oh, a heaviness which I hate to recall. Suddenly there was wafted to me the sweet odor of lilac blossoms. A young girl had passed me by, carrying a great bunch of them. Did you ever know, Sister Agathe, that there is nothing which so keenly revives a memory as a perfume—an odor?"

"I believe you are right, Adrienne. For now that you speak of it, I can feel how the odor of fresh bread—when Sister Jeanne bakes—always makes me think of the great kitchen of ma tante[3] de Sierge, and crippled Julie, who sat always knitting at the sunny window. And I never smell the sweet scented honeysuckle without living again through the blessed day of my first communion."

"Well, that is how it was with me, Sister Agathe, when the scent of the lilacs at once changed the whole current of my thoughts and my despondency. The boulevard, its noises, its passing throng, vanished from before my senses as completely as if they had been spirited away. I was standing here with my feet sunk in the green sward as they are now. I could see the sunlight glancing from that old white stone wall,

3. My aunt.

could hear the notes of birds, just as we hear them now, and the humming of insects in the air. And through all I could see and could smell the lilac blossoms, nodding invitingly to me from their thick-leaved branches. It seems to me they are richer than ever this year, Sister Agathe. And do you know, I became like an *enragée;*[4] nothing could have kept me back. I do not remember now where I was going; but I turned and retraced my steps homeward in a perfect fever of agitation: 'Sophie! my little trunk—quick—the black one! A mere handful of clothes! I am going away. Don't ask me any questions. I shall be back in a fortnight.' And every year since then it is the same. At the very first whiff of a lilac blossom, I am gone! There is no holding me back."

"And how I wait for you, and watch those lilac bushes, Adrienne! If you should once fail to come, it would be like the spring coming without the sunshine or the song of birds.

"But do you know, dear child, I have sometimes feared that in moments of despondency such as you have just described, I fear that you do not turn as you might to our Blessed Mother in heaven, who is ever ready to comfort and solace an afflicted heart with the precious balm of her sympathy and love."

"Perhaps I do not, dear Sister Agathe. But you cannot picture the annoyances which I am constantly submitted to. That Sophie alone, with her detestable ways! I assure you she of herself is enough to drive me to St. Lazare."[5]

"Indeed, I do understand that the trials of one living in the world must be very great, Adrienne; particularly for you, my poor child, who have to bear them alone, since Almighty God was pleased to call to himself your dear husband. But on the other hand, to live one's life along the lines which our dear Lord traces for each one of us, must bring with it resignation and even a certain comfort. You have your household duties, Adrienne, and your music, to which, you say, you continue to devote yourself. And then, there are always good works—the poor—who are always with us—to be relieved; the afflicted to be comforted."

"But, Sister Agathe! Will you listen! Is it not La Rose that I hear moving down there at the edge of the pasture? I fancy she is reproach-ing me with being an ingrate, not to have pressed a kiss yet on that white forehead of hers. Come, let us go."

The two women arose and walked again, hand in hand this time, over the tufted grass down the gentle decline where it sloped toward the broad, flat meadow, and the limpid stream that flowed cool and fresh from the woods. Sister Agathe walked with her composed, nun-like tread; Adrienne with a balancing motion, a bounding step, as though the earth responded to her light footfall with some subtle impulse all its own.

---

4. Madwoman.   5. A sanitarium in Paris.

They lingered long upon the foot-bridge that spanned the narrow stream which divided the convent grounds from the meadow beyond. It was to Adrienne indescribably sweet to rest there in soft, low converse with this gentle-faced nun, watching the approach of evening. The gurgle of the running water beneath them; the lowing of cattle approaching in the distance, were the only sounds that broke upon the stillness, until the clear tones of the angelus bell pealed out from the convent tower. At the sound both women instinctively sank to their knees, signing themselves with the sign of the cross. And Sister Agathe repeated the customary invocation, Adrienne responding in musical tones:

"The Angel of the Lord declared unto Mary,
And she conceived by the Holy Ghost—"
and so forth, to the end of the brief prayer, after which they arose and retraced their steps toward the convent.

It was with subtle and naïve pleasure that Adrienne prepared herself that night for bed. The room which she shared with Sister Agathe was immaculately white. The walls were a dead white, relieved only by one florid print depicting Jacob's dream at the foot of the ladder, upon which angels mounted and descended.[6] The bare floors, a soft yellow-white, with two little patches of gray carpet beside each spotless bed. At the head of the white-draped beds were two *bénitiers*[7] containing holy water absorbed in sponges.

Sister Agathe disrobed noiselessly behind her curtains and glided into bed without having revealed, in the faint candlelight, as much as a shadow of herself. Adrienne pattered about the room, shook and folded her garments with great care, placing them on the back of a chair as she had been taught to do when a child at the convent. It secretly pleased Sister Agathe to feel that her dear Adrienne clung to the habits acquired in her youth.

But Adrienne could not sleep. She did not greatly desire to do so. These hours seemed too precious to be cast into the oblivion of slumber.

"Are you not asleep, Adrienne?"

"No, Sister Agathe. You know it is always so the first night. The excitement of my arrival—I don't know what—keeps me awake."

"Say your 'Hail, Mary,' dear child, over and over."

"I have done so, Sister Agathe; it does not help."

"Then lie quite still on your side and think of nothing but your own respiration. I have heard that such inducement to sleep seldom fails."

"I will try. Good night, Sister Agathe."

"Good night, dear child. May the Holy Virgin guard you."

An hour later Adrienne was still lying with wide, wakeful eyes, listening to the regular breathing of Sister Agathe. The trailing of the passing wind through the treetops, the ceaseless babble of the rivulet were some of the sounds that came to her faintly through the night.

---

6. See Genesis 28:12–17.   7. Basins for holy-water.

The days of the fortnight which followed were in character much like the first peaceful, uneventful day of her arrival, with the exception only that she devoutly heard mass every morning at an early hour in the convent chapel, and on Sundays sang in the choir in her agreeable, cultivated voice, which was heard with delight and the warmest appreciation.

When the day of her departure came, Sister Agathe was not satisfied to say good-by at the portal as the others did. She walked down the drive beside the creeping old cabriolet, chattering her pleasant last words. And then she stood—it was as far as she might go—at the edge of the road, waving good-by in response to the fluttering of Adrienne's handkerchief. Four hours later Sister Agathe, who was instructing a class of little girls for their first communion, looked up at the classroom clock and murmured: "Adrienne is at home now."

Yes, Adrienne was at home. Paris had engulfed her.

At the very hour when Sister Agathe looked up at the clock, Adrienne, clad in a charming negligé, was reclining indolently in the depths of a luxurious armchair. The bright room was in its accustomed state of picturesque disorder. Musical scores were scattered upon the open piano. Thrown carelessly over the backs of chairs were puzzling and astonishing-looking garments.

In a large gilded cage near the window perched a clumsy green parrot. He blinked stupidly at a young girl in street dress who was exerting herself to make him talk.

In the center of the room stood Sophie, that thorn in her mistress's side. With hands plunged in the deep pockets of her apron, her white starched cap quivering with each emphatic motion of her grizzled head, she was holding forth, to the evident ennui of the two young women. She was saying:

"Heaven knows I have stood enough in the six years I have been with Mademoiselle; but never such indignities as I have had to endure in the past two weeks at the hands of that man who calls himself a manager! The very first day—and I, good enough to notify him at once of Mademoiselle's flight—he arrives like a lion; I tell you, like a lion. He insists upon knowing Mademoiselle's whereabouts. How can I tell him any more than the statue out there in the square? He calls me a liar! Me, me—a liar! He declares he is ruined. The public will not stand La Petite Gilberta in the role which Mademoiselle has made so famous—La Petite Gilberta, who dances like a jointed wooden figure and sings like a *traînée* of a *café chantant*.[8] If I were to tell La Gilberta that, as I easily might, I guarantee it would not be well for the few straggling hairs which he has left on that miserable head of his!

"What could he do? He was obliged to inform the public that Mademoiselle was ill; and then began my real torment! Answering this one and that one with their cards, their flowers, their dainties in covered

8. Streetwalker who frequents a café where concerts take place.

dishes! which, I must admit, saved Florine and me much cooking. And all the while having to tell them that the physician had advised for Mademoiselle a rest of two weeks at some watering-place, the name of which I had forgotten!"

Adrienne had been contemplating old Sophie with quizzical, half-closed eyes, and pelting her with hot-house roses which lay in her lap, and which she nipped off short from their graceful stems for that purpose. Each rose struck Sophie full in the face; but they did not disconcert her or once stem the torrent of her talk.

"Oh, Adrienne!" entreated the young girl at the parrot's cage. "Make her hush; please do something. How can you ever expect Zozo to talk? A dozen times he has been on the point of saying something! I tell you, she stupefies him with her chatter."

"My good Sophie," remarked Adrienne, not changing her attitude, "you see the roses are all used up. But I assure you, anything at hand goes," carelessly picking up a book from the table beside her. "What is this? Mons. Zola![9] Now I warn you, Sophie, the weightiness, the heaviness of Mons. Zola are such that they cannot fail to prostrate you; thankful you may be if they leave you with energy to regain your feet."

"Mademoiselle's pleasantries are all very well; but if I am to be shown the door for it—if I am to be crippled for it—I shall say that I think Mademoiselle is a woman without conscience and without heart. To torture a man as she does! A man? No, an angel!

"Each day he has come with sad visage and drooping mien. 'No news, Sophie?'

"'None, Monsieur Henri.' 'Have you no idea where she has gone?' 'Not any more than the statue in the square, Monsieur.' 'Is it perhaps possible that she may not return at all?' with his face blanching like that curtain.

"I assure him you will be back at the end of the fortnight. I entreat him to have patience. He drags himself, *désolé*,[1] about the room, picking up Mademoiselle's fan, her gloves, her music, and turning them over and over in his hands. Mademoiselle's slipper, which she took off to throw at me in the impatience of her departure, and which I purposely left lying where it fell on the chiffonier—he kissed it—I saw him do it—and thrust it into his pocket, thinking himself unobserved.

"The same song each day. I beg him to eat a little good soup which I have prepared. 'I cannot eat, my dear Sophie.' The other night he came and stood long gazing out of the window at the stars. When he turned he was wiping his eyes; they were red. He said he had been riding in the dust, which had inflamed them. But I knew better; he had been crying.

"*Ma foi!* in his place I would snap my finger at such cruelty. I would go out and amuse myself. What is the use of being young!"

9. Emile Zola (1840–1902), French novelist.   1. Disconsolate.

Adrienne arose with a laugh. She went and seizing old Sophie by the shoulders shook her till the white cap wobbled on her head.

"What is the use of all this litany, my good Sophie? Year after year the same! Have you forgotten that I have come a long, dusty journey by rail, and that I am perishing of hunger and thirst? Bring us a bottle of Château Yquem and a biscuit and my box of cigarettes." Sophie had freed herself, and was retreating toward the door. "And, Sophie! If Monsieur Henri is still waiting, tell him to come up."

° ° °

It was precisely a year later. The spring had come again, and Paris was intoxicated.

Old Sophie sat in her kitchen discoursing to a neighbor who had come in to borrow some trifling kitchen utensil from the old *bonne*.[2]

"You know, Rosalie, I begin to believe it is an attack of lunacy which seizes her once a year. I wouldn't say it to everyone, but with you I know it will go no further. She ought to be treated for it; a physician should be consulted; it is not well to neglect such things and let them run on.

"It came this morning like a thunder clap. As I am sitting here, there had been no thought or mention of a journey. The baker had come into the kitchen—you know what a gallant he is—with always a girl in his eye. He laid the bread down upon the table and beside it a bunch of lilacs. I didn't know they had bloomed yet. 'For Mam'selle Florine, with my regards,' he said with his foolish simper.

"Now, you know I was not going to call Florine from her work in order to present her the baker's flowers. All the same, it would not do to let them wither. I went with them in my hand into the dining room to get a majolica pitcher which I had put away in the closet there, on an upper shelf, because the handle was broken. Mademoiselle, who rises early, had just come from her bath, and was crossing the hall that opens into the dining room. Just as she was, in her white *peignoir*, she thrust her head into the dining room, snuffling the air and exclaiming, 'What do I smell?'

"She espied the flowers in my hand and pounced upon them like a cat upon a mouse. She held them up to her, burying her face in them for the longest time, only uttering a long 'Ah!'

"Sophie, I am going away. Get out the little black trunk; a few of the plainest garments I have; my brown dress that I have not yet worn."

" 'But, Mademoiselle,' I protested, 'you forget that you have ordered a breakfast of a hundred francs for tomorrow.'

" 'Shut up!' she cried, stamping her foot.

" 'You forget how the manager will rave,' I persisted, 'and vilify me. And you will go like that without a word of adieu to Monsieur Paul, who is an angel if ever one trod the earth.'

"I tell you, Rosalie, her eyes flamed.

---

2. Maid.

" 'Do as I tell you this instant,' she exclaimed, 'or I will strangle you—with your Monsieur Paul and your manager and your hundred francs!' "

"Yes," affirmed Rosalie, "it is insanity. I had a cousin seized in the same way one morning, when she smelled calf's liver frying with onions. Before night it took two men to hold her."

"I could well see it was insanity, my dear Rosalie, and I uttered not another word as I feared for my life. I simply obeyed her every command in silence. And now—whiff, she is gone! God knows where. But between us, Rosalie—I wouldn't say it to Florine—but I believe it is for no good. I, in Monsieur Paul's place, should have her watched. I would put a detective upon her track.

"Now I am going to close up; barricade the entire establishment. Monsieur Paul, the manager, visitors, all—all may ring and knock and shout themselves hoarse. I am tired of it all. To be vilified and called a liar—at my age, Rosalie!"

°   °   °

Adrienne left her trunk at the small railway station, as the old cabriolet was not at the moment available; and she gladly walked the mile or two of pleasant roadway which led to the convent. How infinitely calm, peaceful, penetrating was the charm of the verdant, undulating country spreading out on all sides of her! She walked along the clear smooth road, twirling her parasol; humming a gay tune; nipping here and there a bud or a waxlike leaf from the hedges along the way; and all the while drinking deep draughts of complacency and content.

She stopped, as she had always done, to pluck lilacs in her path.

As she approached the convent she fancied that a whitecapped face had glanced fleetingly from a window; but she must have been mistaken. Evidently she had not been seen, and this time would take them by surprise. She smiled to think how Sister Agathe would utter a little joyous cry of amazement, and in fancy she already felt the warmth and tenderness of the nun's embrace. And how Sister Marceline and the others would laugh, and make game of her puffed sleeves! For puffed sleeves had come into fashion since last year; and the vagaries of fashion always afforded infinite merriment to the nuns. No, they surely had not seen her.

She ascended lightly the stone steps and rang the bell. She could hear the sharp metallic sound reverberate through the halls. Before its last note had died away the door was opened very slightly, very cautiously by a lay sister who stood there with downcast eyes and flaming cheeks. Through the narrow opening she thrust forward toward Adrienne a package and a letter, saying, in confused tones: "By order of our Mother Superior." After which she closed the door hastily and turned the heavy key in the great lock.

Adrienne remained stunned. She could not gather her faculties to grasp the meaning of this singular reception. The lilacs fell from her arms to the stone portico on which she was standing. She turned the note and the parcel stupidly over in her hands, instinctively dreading what their contents might disclose.

The outlines of the crucifix were plainly to be felt through the wrapper of the bundle, and she guessed, without having courage to assure herself, that the jeweled necklace and the altar cloth accompanied it.

Leaning against the heavy oaken door for support, Adrienne opened the letter. She did not seem to read the few bitter reproachful lines word by word—the lines that banished her forever from this haven of peace, where her soul was wont to come and refresh itself. They imprinted themselves as a whole upon her brain, in all their seeming cruelty—she did not dare to say injustice.

There was no anger in her heart; that would doubtless possess her later, when her nimble intelligence would begin to seek out the origin of this treacherous turn. Now, there was only room for tears. She leaned her forehead against the heavy oaken panel of the door and wept with the abandonment of a little child.

She descended the steps with a nerveless and dragging tread. Once as she was walking away, she turned to look back at the imposing façade of the convent, hoping to see a familiar face, or a hand, even, giving a faint token that she was still cherished by some one faithful heart. But she saw only the polished windows looking down at her like so many cold and glittering and reproachful eyes.

In the little white room above the chapel, a woman knelt beside the bed on which Adrienne had slept. Her face was pressed deep in the pillow in her efforts to smother the sobs that convulsed her frame. It was Sister Agathe.

After a short while, a lay sister came out of the door with a broom, and swept away the lilac blossoms which Adrienne had let fall upon the portico.

New Orleans Times Democrat, December 1896;
The Complete Works of Kate Chopin, 1969

From The Awakening

Chapter 21

Some people contended that the reason Mademoiselle Reisz always chose apartments up under the roof was to discourage the approach of beggars, peddlars, and callers. There were plenty of windows in her little front room. They were for the most part dingy, but as they were nearly always open it did not make so much difference. They often admitted into the room a good deal of smoke and soot; but at the same time all the light and air that there was came through them. From her windows could be seen the crescent of the river, the masts of ships, and the big chimneys of the Mississippi steamers. A magnificent piano crowded the apartment. In the next room she slept, and in the third and last she harbored a gasoline stove on which she cooked her meals when disinclined to descend to the neighboring restaurant. It was there also that she ate, keeping her belongings in a rare old buffet, dingy and battered from a hundred years of use.

When Edna knocked at Mademoiselle Reisz's front room door and entered, she discovered that person standing beside the window, engaged in mending or patching an old prunella gaiter.[1] The little musician laughed all over when she saw Edna. Her laugh consisted of a contortion of the face and all the muscles of the body. She seemed strikingly homely, standing there in the afternoon light. She still wore the shabby lace and the artificial bunch of violets on the side of her head.

"So you remembered me at last," said Mademoiselle. "I had said to myself, 'Ah, bah! she will never come.'"

"Did you want me to come?" asked Edna with a smile.

"I had not thought much about it," answered Mademoiselle. The two had seated themselves on a little bumpy sofa which stood against the wall. "I am glad, however, that you came. I have the water boiling back there, and was just about to make some coffee. You will drink a cup with me. And how is *la belle dame?*[2] Always handsome! always healthy! always contented!" She took Edna's hand between her strong wiry fingers, holding it loosely without warmth, and executing a sort of double theme upon the back and palm.

"Yes," she went on; "I sometimes thought: 'She will never come. She promised as those women in society always do, without meaning it. She will not come.' For I really don't believe you like me, Mrs. Pontellier."

"I don't know whether I like you or not," replied Edna, gazing down at the little woman with a quizzical look.

The candor of Mrs. Pontellier's admission greatly pleased Mademoiselle Reisz. She expressed her gratification by repairing forthwith to the region of the gasoline stove and rewarding her guest with the promised cup of coffee. The coffee and the biscuit accompanying it proved very acceptable to Edna, who had declined refreshment at Madame Lebrun's and was now beginning to feel hungry. Mademoiselle set the tray which she brought in upon a small table near at hand, and seated herself once again on the lumpy sofa.

"I have had a letter from your friend," she remarked, as she poured a little cream into Edna's cup and handed it to her.

"My friend?"

"Yes, your friend Robert. He wrote to me from the City of Mexico."

---

1. Shoe upper or covering for the ankle made of heavy fabric. 2. The beautiful lady.

"Wrote to *you?*" repeated Edna in amazement, stirring her coffee absently.

"Yes, to me. Why not? Don't stir all the warmth out of your coffee; drink it. Though the letter might as well have been sent to you; it was nothing but Mrs. Pontellier from beginning to end."

"Let me see it," requested the young woman, entreatingly.

"No; a letter concerns no one but the person who writes it and the one to whom it is written."

"Haven't you just said it concerned me from beginning to end?"

"It was written about you, not to you. 'Have you seen Mrs. Pontellier? How is she looking?' he asks. 'As Mrs. Pontellier says,' or 'as Mrs. Pontellier once said.' 'If Mrs. Pontellier should call upon you, play for her that Impromptu of Chopin's,[3] my favorite. I heard it here a day or two ago, but not as you play it. I should like to know how it affects her,' and so on, as if he supposed we were constantly in each other's society."

"Let me see the letter."

"Oh, no."

"Have you answered it?"

"No."

"Let me see the letter."

"No, and again, no."

"Then play the Impromptu for me."

"It is growing late; what time do you have to be home?"

"Time doesn't concern me. Your question seems a little rude. Play the Impromptu."

"But you have told me nothing of yourself. What are you doing?"

"Painting!" laughed Edna. "I am becoming an artist. Think of it!"

"Ah! an artist! You have pretensions, Madame."

"Why pretensions? Do you think I could not become an artist?"

"I do not know you well enough to say. I do not know your talent or your temperament. To be an artist includes much; one must possess many gifts—absolute gifts—which have not been acquired by one's own effort. And, moreover, to succeed, the artist must possess the courageous soul."

"What do you mean by the courageous soul?"

"Courageous, *ma foi!* The brave soul. The soul that dares and defies."

"Show me the letter and play for me the Impromptu. You see that I have persistence. Does that quality count for anything in art?"

"It counts with a foolish old woman whom you have captivated," replied Mademoiselle, with her wriggling laugh.

The letter was right there at hand in the drawer of the little table upon which Edna had just placed her coffee cup. Mademoiselle opened the drawer and drew forth the letter, the topmost one. She placed it in

3. Frédéric Chopin (1810–1849), Polish-French composer and pianist.

Edna's hands, and without further comment arose and went to the piano.

Mademoiselle played a soft interlude. It was an improvisation. She sat low at the instrument, and the lines of her body settled into ungraceful curves and angles that gave it an appearance of deformity. Gradually and imperceptibly the interlude melted into the soft opening minor chords of the Chopin Impromptu.

Edna did not know when the Impromptu began or ended. She sat in the sofa corner reading Robert's letter by the fading light. Mademoiselle had glided from the Chopin into the quivering love-notes of Isolde's song, and back again to the Impromptu with its soulful and poignant longing.

The shadows deepened in the little room. The music grew strange and fantastic—turbulent, insistent, plaintive and soft with entreaty. The shadows grew deeper. The music filled the room. It floated out upon the night, over the housetops, the crescent of the river, losing itself in the silence of the upper air.

Edna was sobbing, just as she had wept one midnight at Grand Isle when strange, new voices awoke in her. She arose in some agitation to take her departure. "May I come again, Mademoiselle?" she asked at the threshold.

"Come whenever you feel like it. Be careful; the stairs and landings are dark; don't stumble."

Mademoiselle reëntered and lit a candle. Robert's letter was on the floor. She stopped and picked it up. It was crumpled and damp with tears. Mademoiselle smoothed the letter out, restored it to the envelope, and replaced it in the table drawer.

1899

The Storm

A Sequel to "The 'Cadian Ball"

I

The leaves were so still that even Bibi thought it was going to rain. Bobinôt, who was accustomed to converse on terms of perfect equality with his little son, called the child's attention to certain somber clouds that were rolling with sinister intention from the west, accompanied by a sullen, threatening roar. They were at Friedheimer's store and decided to remain there till the storm had passed. They sat within the door on two empty kegs. Bibi was four years old and looked very wise.

"Mama'll be 'fraid, yes," he suggested with blinking eyes.

"She'll shut the house. Maybe she got Sylvie helpin' her this evenin'," Bobinôt responded reassuringly.

"No; she ent got Sylvie. Sylvie was helpin' her yistiday," piped Bibi.

Bobinôt arose and going across to the counter purchased a can of shrimps, of which Calixta was very fond. Then he returned to his perch on the keg and sat stolidly holding the can of shrimps while the storm burst. It shook the wooden store and seemed to be ripping great furrows in the distant field. Bibi laid his little hand on his father's knee and was not afraid.

II

Calixta, at home, felt no uneasiness for their safety. She sat at a side window sewing furiously on a sewing machine. She was greatly occupied and did not notice the approaching storm. But she felt very warm and often stopped to mop her face on which the perspiration gathered in beads. She unfastened her white sacque[1] at the throat. It began to grow dark, and suddenly realizing the situation she got up hurriedly and went about closing windows and doors.

Out on the small front gallery[2] she had hung Bobinôt's Sunday clothes to air and she hastened out to gather them before the rain fell. As she stepped outside, Alcée Laballière rode in at the gate. She had not seen him very often since her marriage, and never alone. She stood there with Bobinôt's coat in her hands, and the big rain drops began to fall. Alcée rode his horse under the shelter of a side projection where the chickens had huddled and there were plows and a harrow piled up in the corner.

"May I come and wait on your gallery till the storm is over, Calixta?" he asked.

"Come 'long in, M'sieur Alcée."

His voice and her own startled her as if from a trance, and she seized Bobinôt's vest. Alcée, mounting to the porch, grabbed the trousers and snatched Bibi's braided jacket that was about to be carried away by a sudden gust of wind. He expressed an intention to remain outside, but it was soon apparent that he might as well have been out in the open: the water beat in upon the boards in driving sheets, and he went inside, closing the door after him. It was even necessary to put something beneath the door to keep the water out.

"My! what a rain! It's good two years sence it rain' like that," exclaimed Calixta as she rolled up a piece of bagging and Alcée helped her to thrust it beneath the crack.

She was a little fuller of figure than five years before when she married; but she had lost nothing of her vivacity. Her blue eyes still retained their melting quality; and her yellow hair, disheveled by the wind and rain, kinked more stubbornly than ever about her ears and temples.

---

1. A short, loose-fitting coat.   2. Verandah.

The rain beat upon the low, shingled roof with a force and clatter that threatened to break an entrance and deluge them there. They were in the dining room—the sitting room—the general utility room. Adjoining was her bedroom, with Bibi's couch along side her own. The door stood open, and the room with its white, monumental bed, its closed shutters, looked dim and mysterious.

Alcée flung himself into a rocker and Calixta nervously began to gather up from the floor the lengths of a cotton sheet which she had been sewing.

"If this keeps up, *Dieu sait* if the levees[3] goin' to stan' it!" she exclaimed.

"What have you got to do with the levees?"

"I got enough to do! An' there's Bobinôt with Bibi out in that storm—if he only didn't left Friedheimer's!"

"Let us hope, Calixta, that Bobinôt's got sense enough to come in out of a cyclone."

She went and stood at the window with a greatly disturbed look on her face. She wiped the frame that was clouded with moisture. It was stiflingly hot. Alcée got up and joined her at the window, looking over her shoulder. The rain was coming down in sheets obscuring the view of far-off cabins and enveloping the distant wood in a gray mist. The playing of the lightning was incessant. A bolt struck a tall chinaberry tree at the edge of the field. It filled all visible space with a blinding glare and the crash seemed to invade the very boards they stood upon.

Calixta put her hands to her eyes, and with a cry, staggered backward. Alcée's arm encircled her, and for an instant he drew her close and spasmodically to him.

"*Bonté!*"[4] she cried, releasing herself from his encircling arm and retreating from the window, "the house'll go next! If I only knew we're Bibi was!" She would not compose herself; she would not be seated. Alcée clasped her shoulders and looked into her face. The contact of her warm, palpitating body when he had unthinkingly drawn her into his arms, had aroused all the old-time infatuation and desire for her flesh.

"Calixta," he said, "don't be frightened. Nothing can happen. The house is too low to be struck, with so many tall trees standing about. There! aren't you going to be quiet? say, aren't you?" He pushed her hair back from her face that was warm and steaming. Her lips were as red and moist as pomegranate seed. Her white neck and a glimpse of her full, firm bosom disturbed him powerfully. As she glanced up at him the fear in her liquid blue eyes had given place to a drowsy gleam that unconsciously betrayed a sensuous desire. He looked down into her eyes and there was nothing for him to do but to gather her lips in a kiss. It reminded him of Assumption.

"Do you remember—in Assumption, Calixta?" he asked in a low

---

3. Embankments raised to prevent a river from overflowing. Dieu sait: God knows.   4. Gracious.

voice broken by passion. Oh! she remembered; for in Assumption he had kissed her and kissed and kissed her; until his senses would well nigh fail, and to save her he would resort to a desperate flight. If she was not an immaculate dove in those days, she was still inviolate; a passionate creature whose very defenselessness had made her defense, against which his honor forbade him to prevail. Now—well, now—her lips seemed in a manner free to be tasted, as well as her round, white throat and her whiter breasts.

They did not heed the crashing torrents, and the roar of the elements made her laugh as she lay in his arms. She was a revelation in that dim, mysterious chamber; as white as the couch she lay upon. Her firm, elastic flesh that was knowing for the first time its birthright, was like a creamy lily that the sun invites to contribute its breath and perfume to the undying life of the world.

The generous abundance of her passion, without guile or trickery, was like a white flame which penetrated and found response in depths of his own sensuous nature that had never yet been reached.

When he touched her breasts they gave themselves up in quivering ecstasy, inviting his lips. Her mouth was a fountain of delight. And when he possessed her, they seemed to swoon together at the very borderland of life's mystery.

He stayed cushioned upon her, breathless, dazed, enervated, with his heart beating like a hammer upon her. With one hand she clasped his head, her lips lightly touching his forehead. The other hand stroked with a soothing rhythm his muscular shoulders.

The growl of the thunder was distant and passing away. The rain beat softly upon the shingles, inviting them to drowsiness and sleep. But they dared not yield.

The rain was over; and the sun was turning the glistening green world into a palace of gems. Calixta, on the gallery, watched Alcée ride away. He turned and smiled at her with a beaming face; and she lifted her pretty chin in the air and laughed aloud.

III

Bobinôt and Bibi, trudging home, stopped without at the cistern to make themselves presentable.

"My! Bibi, w'at will yo' mama say! You ought to be ashame'. You oughtn' put on those good pants. Look at 'em! An' that mud on yo' collar! How you got that mud on yo' collar, Bibi? I never saw such a boy!" Bibi was the picture of pathetic resignation. Bobinôt was the embodiment of serious solicitude as he strove to remove from his own person and his son's the signs of their tramp over heavy roads and through wet fields. He scraped the mud off Bibi's bare legs and feet with a stick and carefully removed all traces from his heavy brogans. Then, prepared for the worst—the meeting with an over-scrupulous housewife, they entered cautiously at the back door.

Calixta was preparing supper. She had set the table and was dripping coffee at the hearth. She sprang up as they came in.

"Oh, Bobinôt! You back! My! but I was uneasy. W'ere you been during the rain? An' Bibi? he ain't wet? he ain't hurt?" She had clasped Bibi and was kissing him effusively. Bobinôt's explanations and apologies which he had been composing all along the way, died on his lips as Calixta felt him to see if he were dry, and seemed to express nothing but satisfaction at their safe return.

"I brought you some shrimps, Calixta," offered Bobinôt, hauling the can from his ample side pocket and laying it on the table.

"Shrimps! Oh, Bobinôt! you too good fo' anything!" and she gave him a smacking kiss on the cheek that resounded. *"J'vous réponds,*[5] we'll have a feas' to night! umph-umph!"

Bobinôt and Bibi began to relax and enjoy themselves, and when the three seated themselves at table they laughed much and so loud that anyone might have heard them as far away as Laballière's.

IV

Alcée Laballière wrote to his wife, Clarisse, that night. It was a loving letter, full of tender solicitude. He told her not to hurry back, but if she and the babies liked it at Biloxi, to stay a month longer. He was getting on nicely; and though he missed them, he was willing to bear the separation a while longer—realizing that their health and pleasure were the first things to be considered.

V

As for Clarisse, she was charmed upon receiving her husband's letter. She and the babies were doing well. The society was agreeable; many of her old friends and acquaintances were at the bay. And the first free breath since her marriage seemed to restore the pleasant liberty of her maiden days. Devoted as she was to her husband, their intimate conjugal life was something which she was more than willing to forego for a while.

So the storm passed and every one was happy.

No magazine publication; *The Complete Works of Kate Chopin,*
1969

A Little Country Girl

Ninette was scouring the tin milk-pail with sand and lye-soap, and bringing it to a high polish. She used for that purpose the native

5. I tell you.

scrub-brush, the fibrous root of the palmetto, which she called *latanier*. The long table on which the tins were ranged stood out in the yard under a mulberry tree. It was there that the pots and kettles were washed, the chickens, the meats, and vegetables cut up and prepared for cooking.

Occasionally a drop of water fell with a faint splash on the shining surface of the tin; whereupon Ninette would wipe it away and carrying the corner of her checked apron up to her eyes, she would wipe them and proceed with her task. For the drops were falling from Ninette's eyes; trickling down her cheeks and sometimes dropping from the end of her nose.

It was all because two disagreeable old people, who had long out-lived their youth, no longer believed in the circus as a means of cheering the human heart; nor could they see the use of it.

Ninette had not even mentioned the subject to them. Why should she? She might as well have said: "Grandfather and Grandmother, with your permission and a small advance of fifty cents, I should like, after my work is done, to make a visit to one of the distant planets this afternoon."

It was very warm and Ninette's face was red with heat and ill-humor. Her hair was black and straight and kept falling over her face. It was an untidy length; her grandmother having decided to let it grow, about six months before. She was barefooted and her calico skirt reached a little above her thick, brown ankles.

Even the Negroes were all going to the circus. Suzan's daughter, who was known as Black-Gal, had lingered beside the table a moment on her way through the yard.

"You ain't gwine to de suckus?" she inquired with condescension.

"No," and bread-pan went bang on the table.

"We all's goin'. Pap an' Mammy an' all us is goin'," with a complacent air and a restful pose against the table.

"Where you all goin' to get the money, I like to know."

"Oh, Mr. Ben advance' Mammy a dollar on de crap;[1] an' Joe, he got six bits lef' f'om las' pickin'; an' pap sole a ole no'count plow to Dennis. We all's goin'.

"Joe say he seed 'em pass yonder back Mr. Ben's lane. Dey a elephant mos' as big as dat corn-crib, walkin' long des like he some-body. An' a whole pa'cel wild critters shet up in a cage. An' all kind o' dogs an' hosses; an' de ladies rarin' an' pitchin' in red skirts all fill' up wid gole an' diamonds.

"We all's goin'. Did you ax yo' gran'ma? How come you don't ax yo' gran'pap?"

"That's my business; 'tain't none o' yo's, Black-Gal. You better be gettin' yonder home, tendin' to yo' work, I think."

"I ain't got no work, 'cep' iron out my pink flounce' dress fo' de

---

1. I.e., crop.

suckus." But she took herself off with an air of lofty contempt, swinging her tattered skirts. It was after that that Ninette's tears began to drop and spatter.

Resentment rose and rose within her like a leaven, causing her to ferment with wickedness and to make all manner of diabolical wishes in regard to the circus. The worst of these was that she wished it would rain.

"I hope to goodness it'll po' down rain; po' down rain; po' down rain!" She uttered the wish with the air of a young Medusa[2] pronouncing a blighting curse.

"I like to see 'em all drippin' wet. Black-Gal with her pink flounces, all drippin' wet." She spoke these wishes in the very presence of her grandfather and grandmother, for they understood not a word of English; and she used that language to express her individual opinion on many occasions.

"What do you say, Ninette?" asked her grandmother. Ninette had brought in the last of the tin pails and was ranging them on a shelf in the kitchen.

"I said I hoped it would rain," she answered, wiping her face and fanning herself with a pie pan as though the oppressive heat had suggested the desire for a change of weather.

"You are a wicked girl," said her grandmother, turning on her, "when you know your grandfather has acres and acres of cotton ready to fall, that the rain would ruin. He's angry enough, too, with every man, woman, and child leaving the fields today to take themselves off to the village. There ought to be a law to compel them to pick their cotton; those trifling creatures! Ah! it was different in the good old days."

Ninette possessed a sensitive soul, and she believed in miracles. For instance, if she were to go to the circus that afternoon she would consider it a miracle. Hope follows on the heels of Faith. And the white-winged goddess—which is Hope—did not leave her, but prompted her to many little surreptitious acts of preparation in the event of the miracle coming to pass.

She peeped into the clothes-press to see that her gingham dress was where she had folded and left it the Sunday before, after Mass. She inspected her shoes and got out a clean pair of stockings which she hid beneath the pillow. In the tin basin behind the house, she scrubbed her face and neck till they were red as a boiled crawfish. And her hair, which was too short to plait, she plastered and tied back with a green ribbon; it stood out in a little bristling, stiff tail.

The noon hour had hardly passed, than an unusual agitation began to be visible throughout the surrounding country. The fields were deserted. People, black and white, began passing along the road in

2. From Greek mythology; beheaded by Perseus; the severed head of Medusa turned all who looked upon it into stone.

squads and detachments. Ponies were galloping on both sides of the river, carrying two and as many as three, on their backs. Blue and green carts with rampant mules; top-buggies and no-top buggies; family carriages that groaned with age and decrepitude; heavy wagons filled with piccaninnies[3] made a passing procession that nothing short of a circus in town could have accounted for.

Grandfather Bézeau was too angry to look at it. He retired to the hall, where he sat gloomily reading a two-weeks-old paper. He looked about ninety years old; he was in reality, not more than seventy.

Grandmother Bézeau stayed out on the gallery,[4] apparently to cast ridicule and contempt upon the heedless and extravagant multitude; in reality, to satisfy a womanly curiosity and a natural interest in the affairs of her neighbors.

As for Ninette, she found it difficult to keep her attention fixed upon her task of shelling peas and her inward supplications that something might happen.

Something *did* happen. Jules Perrault, with a family load in his big farm-wagon, stopped before their gate. He handed the reins to one of the children and he, himself, got down and came up to the gallery where Ninette and her grandmother were sitting.

"What's this! what's this!" he cried out in French, "Ninette not going to the circus? not even ready to go?"

"*Par exemple*[5]!" exclaimed the old lady, looking daggers over her spectacles. She was binding the leg of a wounded chicken that squawked and fluttered with terror.

" '*Par exemple*' or no '*par exemple*' she's going and she's going with me; and her grandfather will give her the money. Run in, little one; get ready; make haste, we shall be late." She looked appealingly at her grandmother who said nothing, being ashamed to say what she felt in the face of her neighbor, Perrault, of whom she stood a little in awe. Ninette, taking silence for consent, darted into the house to get ready.

And when she came out, wonder of wonders! There was her grandfather taking his purse from his pocket. He was drawing it out slowly and painfully, with a hideous grimace, as though it were some vital organ that he was extracting. What arguments could Mons. Perrault have used! They were surely convincing. Ninette had heard them in wordy discussion as she nervously laced her shoes; dabbed her face with flour; hooked the gingham dress; and balanced upon her head a straw "flat" whose roses looked as though they had stayed out overnight in a frost.

But no triumphant queen on her throne could have presented a more beaming and joyful countenance than did Ninette when she ascended and seated herself in the big wagon in the midst of the Perrault family. She at once took the baby from Mme. Perrault and held it and felt supremely happy.

---

3. Refers to Negro children; derives from Portuguese *pequenino*, meaning "little one."
4. Verandah.
5. Upon my word!

The more the wagon jolted and bounced, the more did it convey to her a sense of reality; and less did it seem like a dream. They passed Black-Gal and her family in the road, trudging ankle-deep in dust. Fortunately the girl was barefooted; though the pink flounces were all there, and she carried a green parasol. Her mother was *semi-décol-letée*[6] and her father wore a heavy winter coat; while Joe had secured piecemeal a species of cakewalk[7] costume for the occasion. It was with a feeling of lofty disdain that Ninette passed and left the Black-Gal family in a cloud of dust.

Even after they reached the circus grounds, which were just outside the the village, Ninette continued to carry the baby. She would willingly have carried three babies, had such a thing been possible. The infant took a wild and noisy interest in the merry-go-round with its hurdy-gurdy accompaniment. Oh! that she had had more money! that she might have mounted one of those flying horses and gone spinning round in a whirl of ecstasy!

There were side-shows, too. She would have liked to see the lady who weighed six hundred pounds and the gentleman who tipped the scales at fifty. She would have wanted to peep in at the curious monster, captured after a desperate struggle in the wilds of Africa. Its picture, in red and green on the flapping canvas, was surely not like anything she had ever seen or even heard of.

The lemonade was tempting: the pop-corn, the peanuts, the oranges were delights that she might only gaze upon and sigh for. Mons. Perrault took them straight to the big tent, bought the tickets and entered.

Ninette's pulses were thumping with excitement. She sniffed the air, heavy with the smell of saw-dust and animals, and it lingered in her nostrils like some delicious odor. Sure enough! There was the elephant which Black-Gal had described. A chain was about his ponderous leg and he kept reaching out his trunk for tempting morsels. The wild creatures were all there in cages, and the people walked solemnly around, looking at them; awed by the unfamiliarity of the scene.

Ninette never forgot that she had the baby in her arms. She talked to it, and it listened and looked with round, staring eyes. Later on she felt as if she were a person of distinction assisting at some royal pageant when the be-spangled Knights and Ladies in plumes and flowing robes went prancing round on their beautiful horses.

The people all sat on the circus benches and Ninette's feet hung down, because an irritable old lady objected to having them thrust into the small of her back. Mme. Perrault offered to take the baby, but Ninette clung to it. It was something to which she might communicate her excitement. She squeezed it spasmodically when her emotions became uncontrollable.

"Oh! *bébé!* I believe I'm goin' to split my sides! Oh, la! la! if

---

6. Partially bared neck and shoulders.
7. A promenade or walk in which those performing the most complex and unusual steps won cakes as prizes.

gran'ma could see that, I know she'd laugh herse'f sick." It was none
other than the clown who was producing this agreeable impression
upon Ninette. She had only to look at his chalky face to go into contortions of mirth.

No one had noticed a gathering obscurity, and the ominous growl of
thunder made every one start with disappointment or apprehension. A
flash and a second clap, that was like a crash, followed. It came just as
the ring-master was cracking his whip with a "hip-la! hip-la!" at the
bareback rider, and the clown was standing on his head. There was a
sinister roar; a terrific stroke of the wind; the center pole swayed and
snapped; the great canvas swelled and beat the air with bellowing
resistance.

Pandemonium reigned. In the confusion Ninette found herself down
beneath piled up benches. Still clutching the baby, she proceeded to
crawl out of an opening in the canvas. She stayed huddled up against
the fallen tent, thinking her end had come, while the baby shrieked
lustily.

The rain poured in sheets. The cries and howls of the frightened
animals were like unearthly sounds. Men called and shouted; children
screamed; women went into hysterics and the Negroes were having
fits.

Ninette got on her knees and prayed God to keep her and the baby
and everyone from injury and to take them safely home. It was thus
that Mons. Perrault discovered her and the baby, half covered by the
fallen tent.

* * *

She did not seem to recover from the shock. Days afterward, Ninette
was going about in a most unhappy frame of mind, with a wretched
look upon her face. She was often discovered in tears.

When her condition began to grow monotonous and depressing, her
grandmother insisted upon knowing the cause of it. Then it was that
she confessed her wickedness and claimed the guilt of having caused
the terrible catastrophe at the circus.

It was her fault that a horse had been killed; it was her fault if an
old gentleman had had a collar-bone broken and a lady an arm dis-
located. She was the cause of several persons having been thrown into
fits and hysterics. All her fault! She it was who had called the rain
down upon their heads and thus had she been punished!

It was a very delicate matter for grandmother Bézeau to pronounce
upon—far too delicate. So the next day she went and explained it all
to the priest and got him to come over and talk to Ninette.

The girl was at the table under the mulberry tree peeling potatoes
when the priest arrived. He was a jolly little man who did not like to
take things too seriously. So he advanced over the short, tufted grass,
bowing low to the ground and making deep salutations with his hat.

"I am overwhelmed," he said, "at finding myself in the presence of
the wonderful Magician! who has but to call upon the rain and down

it comes. She whistles for the wind and—there it is! Pray, what weather will you give us this afternoon, fair Sorceress?"

Then he became serious and frowning, straightened himself and rapped his stick upon the table.

"What foolishness is this I hear? look at me; look at me!" for she was covering her face, "and who are you, I should like to know, that you dare think you can control the elements!"

Well, they made a great deal of fuss of Ninette and she felt ashamed.

But Mons. Perrault came over; he understood best of all. He took grandmother and grandfather aside and told them the girl was morbid from staying so much with old people, and never associating with those of her own age. He was very impressive and convincing. He frightened them, for he hinted vaguely at terrible consequences to the child's intellect.

He must have touched their hearts, for they both consented to let her go to a birthday party over at his house the following day. Grandfather Bézeau even declared that *if it was necessary* he would contribute towards providing her with a suitable toilet[8] for the occasion.

No magazine publication; *The Complete Works of Kate Chopin*, 1969

8. Clothing, attire.

ALICE DUNBAR-NELSON
1875–1935

Alice Ruth Moore Dunbar-Nelson was born in New Orleans on July 19, 1875, to Patricia Wright Moore, a former slave from Opelousas, Louisiana, and Joseph Moore, a seaman whom Gloria Hull identifies as "probably of white Creole extraction" (*Diary* 297). Her mother appears to have been of Indian as well as Negro heritage, and although Dunbar-Nelson was light-skinned and passed for white when it suited her, she also identified herself as Creole and, later in life, gave public lectures on Negro history which included observations on the Creole people. Alice grew up in a single-mother household; whether or not her father remained in contact with the family seems uncertain. Patricia Moore raised Alice and her older sister Mary Leila strictly, supporting them by her work as a seamstress, and, for much of Dunbar-Nelson's adulthood and married life, continued to make her home with her daughters. The young Alice Moore attended public schools in New Orleans, graduated from a two-year teacher's program at Straight College in 1892, and for the next four years taught in New Orleans. In 1896, like so many African-Americans of her generation, Dunbar-Nelson left New Orleans and the South for what were perceived to be the wider opportunities of the North. She moved first to Medford, Massachusetts; then in 1897 to Brooklyn, New York, and finally in 1902 to Wilmington, Delaware. She made her living primarily as a teacher, eventually becoming head of the English department of Wilmington's Howard High School. At various points in her career she also studied at several northern colleges, including Cornell, Columbia, Pennsylvania School of Industrial Art, and the University of Pennsylvania, apparently always supporting her desire for education by her own teaching.

Before the age of twenty, Alice Ruth Moore had begun to publish poetry in the Boston *Monthly Review*, and in 1895 her first book, *Violets and Other Tales*, appeared. After seeing one of her poems in the *Monthly Review*, the poet Paul Laurence Dunbar initiated a two-year correspondence with her in April 1895, which led to their meeting and engagement two years later, then eventually to marriage on March 8, 1898. In 1899 Dunbar-Nelson published *The Goodness of St. Rocque and Other Stories*, her second and final collection of short stories, which was designed as a companion volume to Dunbar's *Poems of Cabin and Field*. Following a brief residence in New York, the Dunbars moved to Washington, D.C., where Paul's career as a poet eclipsed Alice's reputation as a fiction writer. After a volatile marriage marked by separations, infidelities, and her husband's alcoholism, Alice left Paul in 1902 and moved with her mother, sister, and sister's family to Wilmington, Delaware. Though she would never see her husband again, following Dunbar's death in 1906 Alice accepted the public role of his widow, even after she married Robert J. Nelson, a journalist, in 1916.

Although Dunbar-Nelson continued to write poetry, short fiction, and several unpublished novels, after the dissolution of her "literary" marriage she increasingly turned to journalism as a means of self-expression and social and political activism. Throughout her life Dunbar-Nelson devoted herself to improving the social position of black women and men. She helped to found the White Rose Home for Girls in Harlem in 1898; she campaigned for women's suffrage in 1915; she was a political organizer among black women in 1920 as a representative to the State Republican Committee of Delaware; she headed the Anti-Lynching Crusade in Delaware in 1922; and she participated actively in the National Federation of Colored Women's Clubs (see Hull, *Works,* 1. 57–60).

Dunbar-Nelson also kept a personal diary during 1921 and between the years 1926 and 1931, which Gloria Hull has described as her most significant literary work. In this diary she addresses issues that shed light on the complexities of life for a twentieth-century light-skinned black woman. Despite her apparent conformity to the norms of the traditional feminine role, and despite her visible attachments to her husbands, Dunbar-Nelson, like many of the nineteenth-century writers in this volume, derived a great deal of her emotional support from women—from the women in her household, from the larger system of black female support located in the club movement, and within her lesbian relationships, which Gloria Hull documents in the diary. Alice Dunbar-Nelson died September 18, 1935, in Philadelphia of a heart ailment; she was cremated and her husband scattered her ashes into the Delaware River.

o   o   o

In a letter to Alice Moore dated February 16, 1896, Paul Dunbar captures the outsider's view of New Orleans as "a kind of romance land," ripe with opportunity for the local artist: "Its very atmosphere must teem with stories and its streets and by-ways be redolent of dramatic incident that lingers as a sort of perfume from a fragrant past. No wonder you have Grace King and Geo. W. Cable, no wonder you will have Alice R. M." (Metcalf 80). In *Violets and Other Tales*, which included short stories, sketches, poems, brief essays, and reviews, Dunbar-Nelson does indeed turn for the material of her fiction to New Orleans Creole culture, a culture with which she identified, which formed her own social milieu at the time, and which writers like Grace King and George Washington Cable had, as Dunbar indicates, made familiar to readers throughout the nation. However, that Dunbar-Nelson did not share Paul Dunbar's sentimental view of her as a writer absorbing the "perfume from a fragrant past," that she wished to avoid the local-color impulse that distances narrator from character, seems evident in all her work but is particularly clear in a story like "M'sieu Fortier's Violin." Here one of her characters implicitly criticizes local color when he objects to his friend's desire to own M'sieu Fortier's violin: " 'You are like the rest of these nineteenth-century vandals, you can see nothing picturesque that you do not wish to deface for a souvenir . . .' "

Writing about her native region gave the young Dunbar-Nelson a readily identifiable inspiration for literary expression and an opportunity to experiment with developing a literary voice. Yet the issue of race is noticeably absent from the fiction collected in *Violets* and in *The Goodness of St. Rocque*. Arguing that Dunbar-Nelson inherited notions of art that led her to separate her lived experience from what she viewed as literature, Gloria Hull suggests giving more critical attention to the work Dunbar-Nelson produced in the nontraditional genre of the diary and in the weekly newspaper columns she wrote between 1926 and 1930 in order to understand her perceptions of racial experience. Still, according to Hull, Dunbar-Nelson "considered the short story her most representative genre" (*Color* 25).

Dunbar-Nelson herself provides a possible clue to her relation to the regional sketch in her first letter to Paul Dunbar, May 7, 1895, in which she remarks that she hasn't "much liking for those writers that wedge the Negro problem and social equality and long dissertations on the Negro in general into their stories. . . . Somehow when I start a story I always think of my folk characters as simple human beings, not as types of a race or an idea, and I seem to be on more friendly terms with them" (Metcalf 38). Perhaps Dunbar-Nelson viewed fiction as a kind of free space in which she did not have to deal with explicitly racial concerns or identify herself clearly as either black or white. Yet while fiction in general may have presented itself to Dunbar-Nelson as a place to experiment with passing for white, a strategy that light-skinned African-Americans used early in the twentieth century as a way of increasing their social and professional opportunities, in some of her regional fiction she nevertheless explored the complexities of the experience of passing and of the racial ambiguity that made such experience possible. In "The Stones of the Village," Victor Grabert is light-skinned, easily "passes" in white society, and successfully repudiates his Negro grandmother and the rural Louisiana village of his childhood torments when he becomes a lawyer and a judge. Yet his terror of exposure and his contempt for his own cowardice and self-betrayal combine to kill him and he dies believing that the village boys had come to hurl stones at the "white nigger."

Since, for Dunbar-Nelson, Creole ethnicity clearly included persons whom others would consider black, in writing fiction about Creole culture she also found a way, however indirectly, to explore the experience of persons of color, including women. Indeed, she may have correctly surmised that turn-of-the-century audiences would not be receptive to explicitly racial fiction, for when she approached the *Atlantic Monthly* about expanding "The Stones of the Village" into a novel, the editor, Bliss Perry, informed her that the American public had a " 'dislike' for treatment of 'the color-line' " (*Color* 57). In "Sister Josepha" and "The Praline Woman," Dunbar-Nelson invites identification between Creole and Negro. In "Sister Josepha," Dunbar-Nelson hints at racial identity for her protagonist. Outside the convent there is no meaningful existence for a woman of unknown parentage possessed of "a glorious tropical beauty." Hull describes this story as an exploration of the " 'heavy door' of illegitimacy, racism, sexism, female vulnerability, and forced convent life" (*Color* 52). In "The Praline Woman," she comes close to identifying Tante Marie as black; is she the "praline woman" simply because she sells pralines, or because of the color of her skin? And Tante Marie has adopted a child whom she describes as brown. More strikingly, perhaps, in stories like "The Goodness of St. Rocque" and "Mr. Baptiste," Dunbar-Nelson explores human conflict in terms of light and dark, and, like Mr. Baptiste himself, sides with the dark. Although St. Rocque may be a good saint, he alone cannot win Theophilé for Manuela. Unlike Claralie, Manuela has access to the Wizened One, and the power of the "black arts" allows the dark Manuela to triumph over her blonde and pink rival. Mr. Baptiste, though desperate to see the cotton unloaded so that the fruit boats which provide his food can land, forgets the precariousness of his own position. Caught up in the sight of the Negro stevedores "with muscles standing out like cables through their blue cotton shirts, and sweat rolling from glossy black skins," he cries, "Bravo." The Irish, on strike because they refuse to work with Negroes, turn on him with stones and he dies "with a great ugly gash in his wrinkled brown temple."

Dunbar-Nelson's empathic stance towards her characters, especially in her portraits of Creole life, defines her place in the tradition of regionalist writers. Writing with a regional perspective created an opening for Dunbar-Nelson, just as it did for other writers in the tradition, to create a base for her literary authority. And it is precisely such a base that enabled her to write about women characters, about Creole ethnicity, and, in a few stories, about explicitly black characters.

The Goodness of Saint Rocque

Manuela was tall and slender and graceful, and once you knew her the lithe form could never be mistaken. She walked with the easy spring that comes from a perfectly arched foot. Today she swept swiftly down Marais Street, casting a quick glance here and there from under her heavy veil as if she feared she was being followed. If you had peered under the veil, you would have seen that Manuela's dark eyes were swollen and discolored about the lids, as though they had known a sleepless, tearful night.

There had been a picnic the day before, and as merry a crowd of giddy, chattering Creole[1] girls and boys as ever you could see boarded the ramshackle dummy-train[2] that puffed its way wheezily out wide Elysian Fields Street, around the lily-covered bayous, to Milneburg-on-the-Lake. Now, a picnic at Milneburg is a thing to be remembered forever. One charters a rickety-looking, weather-beaten dancing-pavilion, built over the water, and after storing the children—for your true Creole never leaves the small folks at home—and the baskets and mothers downstairs, the young folks go upstairs and dance to the tune of the best band you ever heard. For what can equal the music of a violin, a guitar, a cornet, and a bass viol to trip the quadrille[3] to at a picnic?

Then one can fish in the lake and go bathing under the prim bath-houses, so severely separated sexually, and go rowing on the lake in a trim boat, followed by the shrill warnings of anxious mamans. And in the evening one comes home, hat crowned with cool gray Spanish moss, hands burdened with fantastic latanier[4] baskets woven by the brown bayou boys, hand in hand with your dearest one, tired but happy.

At this particular picnic, however, there had been bitterness of spirit. Theophilé was Manuela's own especial property, and Theophilé

1. The French-speaking descendants of the early French and Spanish settlers in Louisiana.
2. Train pulled by a locomotive with condensing engines and consequently no noise of escaping steam.
3. To dance a French square dance performed by four couples.
4. Palm branch.

had proven false. He had not danced a single waltz or quadrille with
Manuela, but had deserted her for Claralie, blonde and petite. It was
Claralie whom Theophilé had rowed out on the lake; it was Claralie
whom Theophilé had gallantly led to dinner; it was Claralie's hat that
he wreathed with Spanish moss, and Claralie whom he escorted home
after the jolly singing ride in town on the little dummy-train.

Not that Manuela lacked partners or admirers. Dear no! she was too
graceful and beautiful for that. There had been more than enough for
her. But Manuela loved Theophilé, you see, and no one could take his
place. Still, she had tossed her head and let her silvery laughter ring out
in the dance, as though she were the happiest of mortals, and had
tripped home with Henri, leaning on his arm, and looking up into his
eyes as though she adored him.

This morning she showed the traces of a sleepless night and an
aching heart as she walked down Marais Street. Across wide St.
Rocque Avenue she hastened. "Two blocks to the river and one
below—" she repeated to herself breathlessly. Then she stood on the
corner gazing about her, until with a final summoning of a desperate
courage she dived through a small wicket gate into a garden of weed-
choked flowers.

There was a hoarse, rusty little bell on the gate that gave querulous
tongue as she pushed it open. The house that sat back in the yard was
little and old and weather-beaten. Its one-story frame had once been
painted, but that was a memory remote and traditional. A straggling
morning-glory strove to conceal its time-ravaged face. The little walk
of broken bits of brick was reddened carefully, and the one little step
was scrupulously yellow-washed, which denoted that the occupants
were cleanly as well as religious.

Manuela's timid knock was answered by a harsh "Entrez."

It was a small somber room within, with a bare yellow-washed floor
and ragged curtains at the little window. In a corner was a diminutive
altar draped with threadbare lace. The red glow of the taper lighted
a cheap print of St. Joseph and a brazen crucifix. The human element
in the room was furnished by a little, wizened yellow woman, who,
black-robed, turbaned, and stern, sat before an uncertain table
whereon were greasy cards.

Manuela paused, her eyes blinking at the semi-obscurity within. The
Wizened One called in croaking tones:

"An' fo' w'y you come here? Assiez-là,[5] ma'amzelle."

Timidly Manuela sat at the table facing the owner of the voice.

"I want," she began faintly; but the Mistress of the Cards understood: she had had much experience. The cards were shuffled in her
long grimy talons and stacked before Manuela.

"Now you cut dem in t'ree part, so—un, deux, trois, bien[6]! You mek'
you' weesh wid all you' heart, bien! Yaas, I see, I see!"

---

5. Sit over there.   6. One, two, three, good!

Breathlessly did Manuela learn that her lover was true, but "dat light gal, yaas, she mek' nouvena[7] in St. Rocque fo' hees love."

"I give you one lil' charm, yaas," said the Wizened One when the séance was over, and Manuela, all white and nervous, leaned back in the rickety chair. "I give you one lil' charm fo' to ween him back, yaas. You wear h'it 'roun' you' wais', an' he come back. Den you mek prayer at St. Rocque an' burn can'le. Den you come back an' tell me, yaas. Cinquante sous,[8] ma'amzelle. Merci. Good luck go wid you."

Readjusting her veil, Manuela passed out the little wicket gate, treading on air. Again the sun shone, and the breath of the swamps came as healthful sea-breeze unto her nostrils. She fairly flew in the direction of St. Rocque.

There were quite a number of persons entering the white gates of the cemetery, for this was Friday, when all those who wish good luck pray to the saint, and wash their steps promptly at twelve o'clock with a wondrous mixture to guard the house. Manuela bought a candle from the keeper of the little lodge at the entrance, and pausing one instant by the great sun-dial to see if the heavens and the hour were propitious, glided into the tiny chapel, dim and stifling with heavy air from myriad wish-candles blazing on the wide table before the altar-rail. She said her prayer and lighting her candle placed it with the others.

Mon Dieu! how brightly the sun seemed to shine now, she thought, pausing at the door on her way out. Her small finger-tips, still bedewed with holy water, rested caressingly on a gamin's[9] head. The ivy which enfolds the quaint chapel never seemed so green; the shrines which serve as the Way of the Cross[1] never seemed so artistic; the baby graves, even, seemed cheerful.

Theophilé called Sunday. Manuela's heart leaped. He had been spending his Sundays with Claralie. His stay was short and he was plainly bored. But Manuela knelt to thank the good St. Rocque that night, and fondled the charm about her slim waist. There came a box of bonbons during the week, with a decorative card all roses and fringe, from Theophilé; but being a Creole, and therefore superstitiously careful, and having been reared by a wise and experienced maman to mistrust the gifts of a recreant lover, Manuela quietly thrust bonbons, box, and card into the kitchen fire, and the Friday following placed the second candle of her nouvena in St. Rocque.

Those of Manuela's friends who had watched with indignation Theophilé gallantly leading Claralie home from High Mass on Sundays, gasped with astonishment when the next Sunday, with his usual bow, the young man offered Manuela his arm as the worshippers filed out in step to the organ's march. Claralie tossed her head as she crossed

---

7. I.e., novena; in the Roman Catholic Church, a recitation of prayers and devotions performed for nine consecutive days.
8. Fifty French copper coins worth five centimes each.

9. A street urchin, a waif.
1. A series of images, ranged around the interior of a church or shrine, representing the "Stations of the Cross," i.e., successive incidents in the event of Christ's crucifixion.

herself with holy water, and the pink in her cheeks was brighter than usual.

Manuela smiled a bright good-morning when she met Claralie in St. Rocque the next Friday. The little blonde blushed furiously, and Manuela rushed post-haste to the Wizened One to confer upon this new issue.

"H'it ees good," said the dame, shaking her turbaned head. "She ees 'fraid, she will work, mais you' charm, h'it weel beat her."

And Manuela departed with radiant eyes.

Theophilé was not at Mass Sunday morning, and murderous glances flashed from Claralie to Manuela before the tinkling of the Host-Bell.[2] Nor did Theophilé call at either house. Two hearts beat furiously at the sound of every passing footstep, and two minds wondered if the other were enjoying the beloved one's smiles. Two pair of eyes, however, blue and black, smiled on others, and their owners laughed and seemed none the less happy. For your Creole girls are proud, and would die rather than let the world see their sorrows.

Monday evening Theophilé, the missing, showed his rather sheepish countenance in Manuela's parlour, and explained that he, with some chosen spirits, had gone for a trip—"over the Lake."

"I did not ask you where you were yesterday," replied the girl, saucily.

Theophilé shrugged his shoulders and changed the conversation.

The next week there was a birthday fète[3] in honor of Louise, Theophilé's young sister. Everyone was bidden, and no one thought of refusing, for Louise was young, and this would be her first party. So, though the night was hot, the dancing went on as merrily as light young feet could make it go. Claralie fluffed her dainty white skirts, and cast mischievous sparkles in the direction of Theophilé, who with the maman and Louise was bravely trying not to look self-conscious. Manuela, tall and calm and proud-looking, in a cool, pale yellow gown, was apparently enjoying herself without paying the slightest attention to her young host.

"Have I the pleasure of this dance?" he asked her finally, in a lull of the music.

She bowed assent, and as if moved by a common impulse they strolled out of the dancing-room into the cool, quaint garden, where jessamines gave out an overpowering perfume, and a caged mocking-bird complained melodiously to the full moon in the sky.

It must have been an engrossing tête-a-tête,[4] for the call to supper had sounded twice before they heard and hurried into the house. The march had formed with Louise radiantly leading on the arm of papa. Claralie tripped by with Leon. Of course, nothing remained for Theo-

---

2. A bell announcing communion; the Host is a consecrated wafer regarded as the body of Christ.

3. Party.

4. Private conversation between two persons.

philé and Manuela to do but to bring up the rear, for which they received much good-natured chaffing.

But when the party reached the dining-room, Theophilé proudly led his partner to the head of the table, at the right hand of maman, and smiled benignly about at the delighted assemblage. Now you know, when a Creole young man places a girl at his mother's right hand at his own table, there is but one conclusion to be deduced therefrom.

If you had asked Manuela, after the wedding was over, how it happened, she would have said nothing, but looked wise.

If you had asked Claralie, she would have laughed and said she always preferred Leon.

If you had asked Theophilé, he would have wondered that you thought he had ever meant more than to tease Manuela.

If you had asked the Wizened One, she would have offered you a charm.

But St. Rocque knows, for he is a good saint, and if you believe in him and are true and good, and make your nouvenas with a clean heart, he will grant your wish.

No magazine publication; *The Goodness of St. Rocque,* 1899

M'sieu Fortier's Violin

Slowly, one by one, the lights in the French Opera[1] go out, until there is but a single glimmer of pale yellow flickering in the great dark space, a few moments ago all a-glitter with jewels and the radiance of womanhood and a-clash with music. Darkness now, and silence, and a great haunted hush over all, save for the distant cheery voice of a stage hand humming a bar of the opera.

The glimmer of gas makes a halo about the bowed white head of a little old man putting his violin carefully away in its case with aged, trembling, nervous fingers. Old M'sieu Fortier was the last one out every night.

Outside the air was murky, foggy. Gas and electricity were but faint splotches of light on the thick curtain of fog and mist. Around the opera was a mighty bustle of carriages and drivers and footmen, with a car gaining headway in the street now and then, a howling of names and numbers, the laughter and small talk of cloaked society stepping slowly to its carriages, and the more bourgeoisie[2] vocalisation of the foot passengers who streamed along and hummed little bits of music. The fog's denseness was confusing, too, and at one moment it seemed that the little narrow street would become inextricably choked and remain so until some mighty engine would blow the crowd into atoms. It had

1. The French Opera House in New Orleans, 1859–   2. Middle class.
1913.

been a crowded night. From around Toulouse Street, where led the entrance to the troisièmes, from the grand stairway, from the entrance to the quatrièmes,[3] the human stream poured into the street, nearly all with a song on their lips.

M'sieu Fortier stood at the corner, blinking at the beautiful ladies in their carriages. He exchanged a hearty salutation with the saloon-keeper at the corner, then, tenderly carrying his violin case, he trudged down Bourbon Street, a little old, bent, withered figure, with shoulders shrugged up to keep warm, as though the faded brown overcoat were not thick enough.

Down on Bayou Road, not so far from Claiborne Street, was a house, little and old and queer, but quite large enough to hold M'sieu Fortier, a wrinkled dame, and a white cat. He was home but little, for on nearly every day there were rehearsals; then on Tuesday, Thursday, and Saturday nights, and twice Sundays there were performances, so Ma'am Jeanne and the white cat kept house almost always alone. Then, when M'sieu Fortier was at home, why, it was practice, practice all the day, and smoke, snore, sleep at night. Altogether it was not very exhilarating.

M'sieu Fortier had played first violin in the orchestra ever since—well, no one remembered his not playing there. Sometimes there would come breaks in the seasons, and for a year the great building would be dark and silent. Then M'sieu Fortier would do jobs of playing here and there, one night for this ball, another night for that soirée dansante,[4] and in the day, work at his trade,—that of a cigar-maker. But now for seven years there had been no break in the season, and the little old violinist was happy. There is nothing sweeter than a regular job and good music to play, music into which one can put some soul, some expression, and which one must study to understand. Dance music, of the frivolous, frothy kind deemed essential to soirées, is trivial, easy, uninteresting.

So M'sieu Fortier, Ma'am Jeanne, and the white cat lived a peaceful, uneventful existence out on Bayou Road. When the opera season was over in February, M'sieu went back to cigar-making, and the white cat purred none the less contentedly.

It had been a benefit tonight for the leading tenor, and he had chosen "Roland à Ronceveaux,"[5] a favorite this season, for his farewell. And, mon Dieu, mused the little M'sieu, but how his voice had rung out bell-like, piercing above the chorus of the first act! Encore after encore was given, and the bravos of the troisièmes were enough to stir the most sluggish of pulses.

"Superbes Pyrenées
Qui dressez dans le ciel,

3. Balconies in the opera house; the *troisièmes* are seats on the third balcony; *quatrièmes*, the fourth balcony.

4. An evening dance.

5. An opera by the French composer Auguste Mermet (1810–1889) popular in New Orleans after 1869.

Vos cimes couronnées
D'un hiver éternelle,
Pour nous livrer passage
Ouvrez vos larges flancs,
Faîtes taire l'orage,
Voici, venir les Francs!"[6]

M'sieu quickened his pace down Bourbon Street as he sang the chorus to himself in a thin old voice, and then, before he could see in the thick fog, he had run into two young men.

"I—I—beg your pardon,—messieurs," he stammered.

"Most certainly," was the careless response; then the speaker, taking a second glance at the object of the rencontre,[7] cried joyfully:

"Oh, M'sieu Fortier, is it you? Why, you are so happy, singing your love sonnet to your lady's eyebrow, that you didn't see a thing but the moon, did you? And who is the fair one who should clog your senses so?"

There was a deprecating shrug from the little man.

"Ma foi, but monsieur must know fo' sho', dat I am too old for love songs!"

"I know nothing save that I want that violin of yours. When is it to be mine, M'sieu Fortier?"

"Nevare, nevare!" exclaimed M'sieu, gripping on as tightly to the case as if he feared it might be wrenched from him. "Me a lovere, and to sell mon violon! Ah, so ver' foolish!"

"Martel," said the first speaker to his companion as they moved on up town, "I wish you knew that little Frenchman. He's a unique specimen. He has the most exquisite violin I've seen in years; beautiful and mellow as a genuine Cremona,[8] and he can make the music leap, sing, laugh, sob, skip, wail, anything you like from under his bow when he wishes. It's something wonderful. We are good friends. Picked him up in my French-town[9] rambles. I've been trying to buy that instrument since—"

"To throw it aside a week later?" lazily inquired Martel. "You are like the rest of these nineteenth-century vandals, you can see nothing picturesque that you do not wish to deface for a souvenir; you cannot even let simple happiness alone, but must needs destroy it in a vain attempt to make it your own or parade it as an advertisement."

As for M'sieu Fortier, he went right on with his song and turned into Bayou Road, his shoulders still shrugged high as though he were cold, and into the quaint little house, where Ma'am Jeanne and the white

6. Stately Pyrenées Mountains
That rise up into the heavens,
Your peaks crowned
With an eternal winter
For us yield a passage,
Open your large flanks,
Silence the storm,

Behold, here come the French!
7. Meeting, encounter.
8. A violin made in Cremona, Italy, during the 16th through the 18th centuries by the Amati family and their pupils, Guarneri and Stradivari.
9. The French Quarter of New Orleans.

cat, who always waited up for him at nights, were both nodding over the fire.

It was not long after this that the opera closed, and M'sieu went back to his old out-of-season job. But somehow he did not do as well this spring and summer as always. There is a certain amount of cunning and finesse required to roll a cigar just so, that M'sieu seemed to be losing, whether from age or deterioration it was hard to tell. Nevertheless, there was just about half as much money coming in as formerly, and the quaint little pucker between M'sieu's eyebrows which served for a frown came oftener and stayed longer than ever before.

"Minesse," he said one day to the white cat,—he told all his troubles to her; it was of no use to talk to Ma'am Jeanne, she was too deaf to understand,—"Minesse, we are gettin' po'. You' père git h'old, an' hees han's dey go no mo' rapidement, an' dere be no mo' soirées dese day. Minesse, eef la saison[1] don' hurry up, we shall eat ver' lil' meat."

And Minesse curled her tail and purred.

Before the summer had fairly begun, strange rumors began to float about in musical circles. M. Maugé would no longer manage the opera, but it would be turned into the hands of Americans, a syndicate. Bah! These English-speaking people could do nothing unless there was a trust, a syndicate, a company immense and dishonest. It was going to be a guarantee business, with a strictly financial basis. But worse than all this, the new manager, who was now in France, would not only procure the artists, but a new orchestra, a new leader. M'sieu Fortier grew apprehensive at this, for he knew what the loss of his place would mean to him.

September and October came, and the papers were filled with accounts of the new artists from France and of the new orchestra leader too. He was described as a most talented, progressive, energetic young man. M'sieu Fortier's heart sank at the word "progressive." He was anything but that. The New Orleans Creole blood flowed too sluggishly in his old veins.

November came; the opera reopened. M'sieu Fortier was not re-engaged.

"Minesse," he said with a catch in his voice that strongly resembled a sob, "Minesse, we mus' go hongry sometime. Ah, mon pauvre violon! Ah, mon Dieu, dey put us h'out, an' dey will not have us. Nev' min', we will sing anyhow." And drawing his bow across the strings, he sang in his thin, quavering voice, "Salut demeure, chaste et pure."[2]

It is strange what a peculiar power of fascination former haunts have for the human mind. The criminal, after he has fled from justice, steals back and skulks about the scene of his crime; the employee thrown from work hangs about the place of his former industry; the schoolboy, truant or expelled, peeps in at the school-gate and taunts the good boys within. M'sieu Fortier was no exception. Night after night of the

---

1. Here, the opera season.   2. "Salvation remains, virtuous and pure."

performances he climbed the stairs of the opera and sat, an attentive listener to the orchestra, with one ear inclined to the stage, and a quizzical expression on his wrinkled face. Then he would go home, and pat Minesse, and fondle the violin.

"Ah, Minesse, dose new player! Not one bit can dey play. Such tones, Minesse, such tones! All the time portemento,[3] oh, so ver' bad! Ah, mon chère violon, we can play." And he would play and sing a romance, and smile tenderly to himself.

At first it used to be into the deuxièmes[4] that M'sieu Fortier went, into the front seats. But soon they were too expensive, and after all, one could hear just as well in the fourth row as in the first. After a while even the rear row of the deuxièmes was too costly, and the little musician wended his way with the plebeians around on Toulouse Street, and climbed the long, tedious flight of stairs into the troisièmes. It makes no difference to be one row higher. It was more to the liking, after all. One felt more at home up here among the people. If one was thirsty, one could drink a glass of wine or beer being passed about by the libretto boys,[5] and the music sounded just as well.

But it happened one night that M'sieu could not even afford to climb the Toulouse Street stairs. To be sure, there was yet another gallery, the quatrièmes, where the peanut boys went for a dime, but M'sieu could not get down to that yet. So he stayed outside until all the beautiful women in their warm wraps, a bright-hued chattering throng, came down the grand staircase to their carriages.

It was on one of these nights that Courcey and Martel found him shivering at the corner.

"Hello, M'sieu Fortier," cried Courcey, "are you ready to let me have that violin yet?"

"For shame!" interrupted Martel.

"Fifty dollars, you know," continued Courcey, taking no heed of his friend's interpolation.

M'sieu Fortier made a courtly bow. "Eef Monsieur will call at my 'ouse on de morrow, he may have mon violon," he said huskily; then turned abruptly on his heel, and went down Bourbon Street, his shoulders drawn high as though he were cold.

When Courcey and Martel entered the gate of the little house on Bayou Road the next day, there floated out to their ears a wordless song thrilling from the violin, a song that told more than speech or tears or gestures could have done of the utter sorrow and desolation of the little old man. They walked softly up the short red brick walk and tapped at the door. Within, M'sieu Fortier was caressing the violin, with silent tears streaming down his wrinkled gray face.

There was not much said on either side. Courcey came away with

---

3. Portamento, a continuous glide from one tone to another with the bow of a stringed instrument; evidently to M'sieu Fortier less technically exacting than accenting each note individually.

4. The second story of seats in the opera house.
5. The boys selling copies of the libretto, or text, of the opera.

the instrument, leaving the money behind, while Martel grumbled at the essentially sordid, mercenary spirit of the world. M'sieu Fortier turned back into the room, after bowing his visitors out with old-time French courtliness, and turning to the sleepy white cat, said with a dry sob:

"Minesse, dere's only me an' you now."

About six days later, Courcey's morning dreams were disturbed by the announcement of a visitor. Hastily doing a toilet,[6] he descended the stairs to find M'sieu Fortier nervously pacing the hall floor.

"I come fo' bring back you' money, yaas. I cannot sleep, I cannot eat, I only cry, and t'ink, and weesh fo' mon violon; and Minesse, an' de ol' woman too, dey mope an' look bad too, all for mon violon. I try fo' to use dat money, but eet burn an' sting lak blood money. I feel lak' I done sol' my child. I cannot go at l'opéra no mo', I t'ink of mon violon. I starve befo' I live widout. My heart, he is broke, I die for mon violon."

Courcey left the room and returned with the instrument.

"M'sieu Fortier," he said, bowing low, as he handed the case to the little man, "take your violin; it was a whim with me, a passion with you. And as for the money, why, keep that too; it was worth a hundred dollars to have possessed such an instrument even for six days."

No magazine publication; *The Goodness of St. Rocque*, 1899

Mr. Baptiste

He might have had another name; we never knew. Someone had christened him Mr. Baptiste long ago in the dim past, and it sufficed. No one had ever been known who had the temerity to ask him for another cognomen, for though he was a mild-mannered little man, he had an uncomfortable way of shutting up oyster-wise and looking disagreeable when approached concerning his personal history.

He was small: most Creole men are small when they are old. It is strange, but a fact. It must be that age withers them sooner and more effectually than those of un-Latinised extraction. Mr. Baptiste was, furthermore, very much wrinkled and lame. Like the Son of Man,[1] he had nowhere to lay his head, save when some kindly family made room for him in a garret or a barn. He subsisted by doing odd jobs, whitewashing, cleaning yards, doing errands, and the like.

The little old man was a frequenter of the levee.[2] Never a day passed that his quaint little figure was not seen moving up and down about the ships. Chiefly did he haunt the Texas and Pacific warehouses and the landing-place of the Morgan-line steamships. This seemed like madness, for these spots are almost the busiest on the levee, and the rough

6. Grooming and dressing oneself.
1. Jesus Christ.
2. A raised embankment at the river's edge that served as a Landing-place for ships and the center of river commerce.

seamen and 'longshoremen[3] have least time to be bothered with small weak folks. Still there was method in the madness of Mr. Baptiste. The Morgan steamships, as everyone knows, ply between New Orleans and Central and South American ports, doing the major part of the fruit trade; and many were the baskets of forgotten fruit that Mr. Baptiste took away with him unmolested. Sometimes, you know, bananas and mangoes and oranges and citrons will half spoil, particularly if it has been a bad voyage over the stormy Gulf, and the officers of the ships will give away stacks of fruit, too good to go into the river, too bad to sell to the fruit-dealers.

You could see Mr. Baptiste trudging up the street with his quaint one-sided walk, bearing his dilapidated basket on one shoulder, a nondescript head-cover pulled over his eyes, whistling cheerily. Then he would slip in at the back door of one of his clients with a brisk,—

"Ah, bonjour, madame. Now here ees jus' a lil' bit fruit, some bananas. Perhaps madame would cook some for Mr. Baptiste?"

And madame, who understood and knew his ways, would fry him some of the bananas, and set it before him, a tempting dish, with a bit of madame's bread and meat and coffee thrown in for lagniappe;[4] and Mr. Baptiste would depart, filled and contented, leaving the load of fruit behind as madame's pay. Thus did he eat, and his clients were many, and never too tired or too cross to cook his meals and get their pay in baskets of fruit.

One day he slipped in at Madame Garcia's kitchen door with such a woe-begone air, and slid a small sack of nearly ripe plantains on the table with such a misery-laden sigh, that madame, who was fat and excitable, threw up both hands and cried out:

"Mon Dieu, Mistare Baptiste, fo' w'y you look lak dat? What ees de mattare?"

For answer, Mr. Baptiste shook his head gloomily and sighed again. Madame Garcia moved heavily about the kitchen, putting the plantains in a cool spot and punctuating her footsteps with sundry "Mon Dieux" and "Misères."[5]

"Dose cotton!" ejaculated Mr. Baptiste, at last.

"Ah, mon Dieu!" groaned Madame Garcia, rolling her eyes heavenwards.

"Hit will drive de fruit away!" he continued.

"Misère!" said Madame Garcia.

"Hit will."

"Oui, oui," said Madame Garcia. She had carefully inspected the plantains, and seeing that they were good and wholesome, was inclined to agree with anything Mr. Baptiste said.

He grew excited. "Yaas, dose cotton-yardmans,[6] dose 'longsho'-

---

3. Dock workers who load and unload ships.
4. A small gift presented to a customer with a purchase.

5. Exclamations of "My God" and "Misery."
6. Longshoremen or stevedores particularly hired to load cotton.

mans, dey go out on one strik'. Dey t'row down dey tool an' say dey work no mo' wid niggers. Les veseaux,[7] dey lay in de river, no work, no cargo, yaas. Den de fruit ship, dey can' mak' lan', de mans, dey t'reaten an' say t'ings. Dey mak' big fight, yaas. Dere no mo' work on de levee, lak dat. Ever'body jus' walk roun' an' say cuss word, yaas!"

"Oh, mon Dieu, mon Dieu!" groaned Madame Garcia, rocking her guinea-blue-clad self to and fro.

Mr. Baptiste picked up his nondescript head-cover and walked out through the brick-reddened alley, talking excitedly to himself. Madame Garcia called after him to know if he did not want his luncheon, but he shook his head and passed on.

Down on the levee it was even as Mr. Baptiste had said. The 'long-shoremen, the cotton-yardmen, and the stevedores[8] had gone out on a strike. The levee lay hot and unsheltered under the glare of a noonday sun. The turgid Mississippi scarce seemed to flow, but gave forth a brazen gleam from its yellow bosom. Great vessels lay against the wharf, silent and unpopulated. Excited groups of men clustered here and there among bales of uncompressed cotton, lying about in disorderly profusion. Cargoes of molasses and sugar gave out a sticky sweet smell, and now and then the fierce rays of the sun would kindle tiny blazes in the cotton and splinter-mixed dust underfoot.

Mr. Baptiste wandered in and out among the groups of men, exchanging a friendly salutation here and there. He looked the picture of woe-begone misery.

"Hello, Mr. Baptiste," cried a big, brawny Irishman, "sure an' you look, as if you was about to be hanged."

"Ah, mon Dieu," said Mr. Baptiste, "dose fruit ship be ruined fo' dees strik'."

"Damn the fruit!" cheerily replied the Irishman, artistically disposing of a mouthful of tobacco juice. "It ain't the fruit we care about, it's the cotton."

"Hear! hear!" cried a dozen lusty comrades.

Mr. Baptiste shook his head and moved sorrowfully away.

"Hey, by howly[9] St. Patrick, here's that little fruit-eater!" called the center of another group of strikers perched on cotton-bales.

"Hello! Where—" began a second; but the leader suddenly held up his hand for silence, and the men listened eagerly.

It might not have been a sound, for the levee lay quiet and the mules on the cotton-drays[1] dozed languidly, their ears pitched at varying acute angles. But the practiced ears of the men heard a familiar sound stealing up over the heated stillness.

"Oh—ho—ho—humph—humph —humph—ho—ho—ho—oh—o—o—humph!"

---

7. Vessels, ships.
8. Persons employed in the loading or unloading of ships.
9. I.e., holy.
1. Low, heavy carts without sides used to haul cotton.

Then the faint rattle of chains, and the steady thump of a machine pounding.

If ever you go on the levee you'll know that sound, the rhythmic song of the stevedores heaving cotton-bales, and the steady thump, thump, of the machine compressing them within the hold of the ship.

Finnegan, the leader, who had held up his hand for silence, uttered an oath.

"Scabs!² Men, come on!"

There was no need for a further invitation. The men rose in sullen wrath and went down the levee, the crowd gathering in numbers as it passed along. Mr. Baptiste followed in its wake, now and then sighing a mournful protest which was lost in the roar of the men.

"Scabs!" Finnegan had said; and the word was passed along, until it seemed that the half of the second District knew and had risen to investigate.

"Oh—ho—ho—humph—humph—humph—oh—ho—ho—oh—o—o—humph!"

The rhythmic chorus sounded nearer, and the cause manifested itself when the curve of the levee above the French Market was passed. There rose a White Star steamer, insolently settling itself to the water as each consignment of cotton bales was compressed into her hold.

"Niggers!" roared Finnegan wrathily.

"Niggers! niggers! Kill 'em, scabs!" chorused the crowd.

With muscles standing out like cables through their blue cotton shirts, and sweat rolling from glossy black skins, the Negro stevedores were at work steadily laboring at the cotton, with the rhythmic song swinging its cadence in the hot air. The roar of the crowd caused the men to look up with momentary apprehension, but at the overseer's reassuring word they bent back to work.

Finnegan was a Titan.³ With livid face and bursting veins he ran into the street facing the French Market, and uprooted a huge block of paving stone. Staggering under its weight, he rushed back to the ship, and with one mighty effort hurled it into the hold.

The delicate poles of the costly machine tottered in the air, then fell forward with a crash as the whole iron framework in the hold collapsed.

"Damn ye," shouted Finnegan, "now yez can pack yer cotton!"

The crowd's cheers at this changed to howls, as the Negroes, infuriated at their loss, for those costly machines belong to the laborers and not to the ship-owners, turned upon the mob and began to throw brickbats, pieces of iron, chunks of wood, anything that came to hand.

---

2. Strikebreakers.
3. In Greek mythology, the Titans were the sons and daughters of Uranus and Ge, who rose up against Uranus and deposed him; by association the term has come to mean having colossal size or strength.

It was pandemonium turned loose over a turgid stream, with a malarial sun to heat the passions to fever point.

Mr. Baptiste had taken refuge behind a bread-stall on the outside of the market. He had taken off his cap, and was weakly cheering the Negroes on.

"Bravo!" cheered Mr. Baptiste.

"Will yez look at that damned fruit-eatin' Frinchman!" howled McMahon. "Cheerin' the niggers, are you?" and he let fly a brickbat in the direction of the bread-stall.

"Oh, mon Dieu, mon Dieu!" wailed the bread-woman.

Mr. Baptiste lay very still, with a great ugly gash in his wrinkled brown temple. Fishmen and vegetable marchands[4] gathered around him in a quick, sympathetic mass. The individual, the concrete bit of helpless humanity, had more interest for them than the vast, vague fighting mob beyond.

The noon-hour pealed from the brazen throats of many bells, and the numerous hoarse whistles of the steam-boats called the unheeded luncheon-time to the levee workers. The war waged furiously, and groans of the wounded mingled with curses and roars from the combatants.

"Killed instantly," said the surgeon, carefully lifting Mr. Baptiste into the ambulance.

Tramp, tramp, tramp, sounded the militia steadily marching down Decatur Street.

"Whist! do yez hear!" shouted Finnegan; and the conflict had ceased ere the yellow river could reflect the sun from the polished bayonets.

You remember, of course, how long the strike lasted, and how many battles were fought and lives lost before the final adjustment of affairs. It was a fearsome war, and many forgot afterwards whose was the first life lost in the struggle,—poor little Mr. Baptiste's, whose body lay at the Morgue unclaimed for days before it was finally dropped unnamed into Potter's Field.[5]

No magazine publication; *The Goodness of St. Rocque*, 1899

Sister Josepha

Sister Josepha told her beads[1] mechanically, her fingers numb with the accustomed exercise. The little organ creaked a dismal "O Salutaris,"[2] and she still knelt on the floor, her white-bonneted head nodding suspiciously. The Mother Superior gave a sharp glance at the tired

4. Merchants.
5. Burying ground for the poor and unknown; mentioned in Matthew 27.7.
1. Said one prayer for each bead on her rosary.

2. O Salutaris Hostia (Oh Saving Victim) is a Roman Catholic hymn associated with the service of benediction.

figure; then, as a sudden lurch forward brought the little sister back to consciousness, Mother's eyes relaxed into a genuine smile.

The bell tolled the end of vespers,[3] and the somber-robed nuns filed out of the chapel to go about their evening duties. Little Sister Josepha's work was to attend to the household lamps, but there must have been as much oil spilled upon the table tonight as was put in the vessels. The small brown hands trembled so that most of the wicks were trimmed with points at one corner which caused them to smoke that night.

"Oh, cher Seigneur,"[4] she sighed, giving an impatient polish to a refractory chimney,[5] "it is wicked and sinful, I know, but I am so tired. I can't be happy and sing any more. It doesn't seem right for le bon Dieu[6] to have me all cooped up here with nothing to see but stray visitors, and always the same old work, teaching those mean little girls to sew, and washing and filling the same old lamps. Pah!" And she polished the chimney with a sudden vigorous jerk which threatened destruction.

They were rebellious prayers that the red mouth murmured that night, and a restless figure that tossed on the hard dormitory bed. Sister Dominica called from her couch to know if Sister Josepha were ill.

"No," was the somewhat short response; then a muttered, "Why can't they let me alone for a minute? That pale-eyed Sister Dominica never sleeps; that's why she is so ugly."

About fifteen years before this night someone had brought to the orphan asylum connected with this convent, du Sacré Coeur,[7] a round, dimpled bit of three-year-old humanity, who regarded the world from a pair of gravely twinkling black eyes, and only took a chubby thumb out of a rosy mouth long enough to answer in monosyllabic French. It was a child without an identity; there was but one name that anyone seemed to know, and that, too, was vague,—Camille.

She grew up with the rest of the waifs; scraps of French and American civilization thrown together to develop a seemingly inconsistent miniature world. Mademoiselle Camille was a queen among them, a pretty little tyrant who ruled the children and dominated the more timid sisters in charge.

One day an awakening came. When she was fifteen, and almost fully ripenèd into a glorious tropical beauty of the type that matures early, some visitors to the convent were fascinated by her and asked the Mother Superior to give the girl into their keeping.

Camille fled like a frightened fawn into the yard, and was only unearthed with some difficulty from behind a group of palms. Sulky and pouting, she was led into the parlor, picking at her blue pinafore like a spoiled infant.

3. Evening prayers or worship services.
4. Dear Lord.
5. A glass cover of an oil lamp.
6. The good God.
7. Of the Sacred Heart.

"The lady and gentleman wish you to go home with them, Camille," said the Mother Superior, in the language of the convent. Her voice was kind and gentle apparently; but the child, accustomed to its various inflections, detected a steely ring behind its softness, like the proverbial iron hand in the velvet glove.

"You must understand, madame," continued Mother, in stilted English, "that we never force children from us. We are ever glad to place them in comfortable—how you say that?—quarters—maisons—homes—bien! But we will not make them go if they do not wish."

Camille stole a glance at her would-be guardians, and decided instantly, impulsively, finally. The woman suited her; but the man! It was doubtless intuition of the quick, vivacious sort which belonged to her blood that served her. Untutored in worldly knowledge, she could not divine the meaning of the pronounced leers and admiration of her physical charms which gleamed in the man's face, but she knew it made her feel creepy, and stoutly refused to go.

Next day Camille was summoned from a task to the Mother Superior's parlor. The other girls gazed with envy upon her as she dashed down the courtyard with impetuous movement. Camille, they decided crossly, received too much notice. It was Camille this, Camille that; she was pretty, it was to be expected. Even Father Ray lingered longer in his blessing when his hands pressed her silky black hair.

As she entered the párlor, a strange chill swept over the girl. The room was not an unaccustomed one, for she had swept it many times, but today the stiff black chairs, the dismal crucifixes, the gleaming whiteness of the walls, even the cheap lithograph of the Madonna which Camille had always regarded as a perfect specimen of art, seemed cold and mean.

"Camille, ma chère," said Mother, "I am extremely displeased with you. Why did you not wish to go with Monsieur and Madame Lafayé yesterday?"

The girl uncrossed her hands from her bosom, and spread them out in a deprecating gesture.

"Mais, ma mère, I was afraid."

Mother's face grew stern. "No foolishness now," she exclaimed.

"It is not foolishness, ma mère; I could not help it, but that man looked at me so funny, I felt all cold chills down my back. Oh, dear Mother, I love the convent and the sisters so, I just want to stay and be a sister too, may I?"

And thus it was that Camille took the white veil at sixteen years. Now that the period of novitiate[8] was over, it was just beginning to dawn upon her that she had made a mistake.

"Maybe it would have been better had I gone with the funny-looking lady and gentleman," she mused bitterly one night. "Oh, Sei-

---

8. The probationary period of a novice, one who has entered a religious order, before finally taking religious vows.

gneur, I'm so tired and impatient; it's so dull here, and, dear God, I'm so young."

There was no help for it. One must arise in the morning, and help in the refectory[9] with the stupid Sister Francesca, and go about one's duties with a prayerful mien, and not even let a sigh escape when one's head ached with the eternal telling of beads.

A great fête[1] day was coming, and an atmosphere of preparation and mild excitement pervaded the brown walls of the convent like a delicate aroma. The old Cathedral around the corner had stood a hundred years, and all the city was rising to do honour to its age and time-softened beauty. There would be a service, oh, but such a one! with two Cardinals, and Archbishops and Bishops, and all the accompanying glitter of soldiers and orchestras. The little sisters of the Convent du Sacré Coeur clasped their hands in anticipation of the holy joy. Sister Josepha curled her lip, she was so tired of churchly pleasures.

The day came, a gold and blue spring day, when the air hung heavy with the scent of roses and magnolias, and the sunbeams fairly laughed as they kissed the houses. The old Cathedral stood gray and solemn, and the flowers in Jackson Square smiled cheery birthday greetings across the way. The crowd around the door surged and pressed and pushed in its eagerness to get within. Ribbons stretched across the banquette[2] were of no avail to repress it, and important ushers with cardinal colors could do little more.

The Sacred Heart sisters filed slowly in at the side door, creating a momentary flutter as they paced reverently to their seats, guarding the blue-bonneted orphans. Sister Josepha, determined to see as much of the world as she could, kept her big black eyes opened wide, as the church rapidly filled with the fashionably dressed, perfumed, rustling, and self-conscious throng.

Her heart beat quickly. The rebellious thoughts that will arise in the most philosophical of us surged in her small heavily gowned bosom. For her were the gray things, the neutral tinted skies, the ugly garb, the coarse meats; for them the rainbow, the ethereal airiness of earthly joys, the bonbons and glacés[3] of the world. Sister Josepha did not know that the rainbow is elusive, and its colors but the illumination of tears; she had never been told that earthly ethereality is necessarily ephemeral, nor that bonbons and glacés, whether of the palate or of the soul, nauseate and pall upon the taste. Dear God, forgive her, for she bent with contrite tears over her worn rosary, and glanced no more at the worldly glitter of femininity.

The sunbeams streamed through the high windows in purple and crimson lights upon a veritable fugue of color. Within the seats, crush upon crush of spring millinery; within the aisles erect lines of gold-braided, gold-buttoned military. Upon the altar, broad sweeps of

9. A room where meals are served.
1. Festival.
2. Railing.
3. Ice cream; bonbons: sweets.

golden robes, great dashes of crimson skirts, miters and gleaming crosses, the soft neutral hue of rich lace vestments;[4] the tender heads of childhood in picturesque attire; the proud, golden magnificence of the domed altar with its weighting mass of lilies and wide-eyed roses, and the long candles that sparkled their yellow star points above the reverent throng within the altar rails.

The soft baritone of the Cardinal intoned a single phrase in the suspended silence. The censer[5] took up the note in its delicate clink clink, as it swung to and fro in the hands of a fair-haired child. Then the organ, pausing an instant in a deep, mellow, long-drawn note, burst suddenly into a magnificent strain, and the choir sang forth, "Kyrie Eleïson, Christe Eleïson."[6] One voice, flute-like, piercing, sweet, rang high over the rest. Sister Josepha heard and trembled, as she buried her face in her hands, and let her tears fall, like other beads, through her rosary.

It was when the final word of the service had been intoned, the last peal of the exit march had died away, that she looked up meekly, to encounter a pair of youthful brown eyes gazing pityingly upon her. That was all she remembered for a moment, that the eyes were youthful and handsome and tender. Later, she saw that they were placed in a rather beautiful boyish face, surmounted by waves of brown hair, curling and soft, and that the head was set on a pair of shoulders decked in military uniform. Then the brown eyes marched away with the rest of the rear guard, and the white-bonneted sisters filed out the side door, through the narrow court, back into the brown convent.

That night Sister Josepha tossed more than usual on her hard bed, and clasped her fingers often in prayer to quell the wickedness in her heart. Turn where she would, pray as she might, there was ever a pair of tender, pitying brown eyes, haunting her persistently. The squeaky organ at vespers intoned the clank of military accoutrements to her ears, the white bonnets of the sisters about her faded into mists of curling brown hair. Briefly, Sister Josepha was in love.

The days went on pretty much as before, save for the one little heart that beat rebelliously now and then, though it tried so hard to be submissive. There was the morning work in the refectory, the stupid little girls to teach sewing, and the insatiable lamps that were so greedy for oil. And always the tender, boyish brown eyes, that looked so sorrowfully at the fragile, beautiful little sister, haunting, following, pleading.

Perchance, had Sister Josepha been in the world, the eyes would have been an incident. But in this home of self-repression and retrospection, it was a life-story. The eyes had gone their way, doubtless forgetting the little sister they pitied; but the little sister?

---

4. Ritual robes worn by the clergy. Miters: tall pointed hats with peaks in front and back, worn by bishops.

5. A container in which incense is burned.
6. "Lord have mercy, Christ have mercy"; part of the Ordinary of the Mass.

The days glided into weeks, the weeks into months. Thoughts of escape had come to Sister Josepha, to flee into the world, to merge in the great city where recognition was impossible, and, working her way like the rest of humanity, perchance encounter the eyes again.

It was all planned and ready. She would wait until some morning when the little band of black-robed sisters wended their way to mass at the Cathedral. When it was time to file out the side-door into the courtway, she would linger at prayers, then slip out another door, and unseen glide up Chartres Street to Canal, and once there, mingle in the throng that filled the wide thoroughfare. Beyond this first plan she could think no further. Penniless, garbed, and shaven[7] though she would be, other difficulties never presented themselves to her. She would rely on the mercies of the world to help her escape from this torturing life of inertia. It seemed easy now that the first step of decision had been taken.

The Saturday night before the final day had come, and she lay feverishly nervous in her narrow little bed, wondering with wide-eyed fear at the morrow. Pale-eyed Sister Dominica and Sister Francesca were whispering together in the dark silence, and Sister Josepha's ears pricked up as she heard her name.

"She is not well, poor child," said Francesca. "I fear the life is too confining."

"It is best for her," was the reply. "You know, sister, how hard it would be for her in the world, with no name but Camille, no friends, and her beauty; and then—"

Sister Josepha heard no more, for her heart beating tumultously in her bosom drowned the rest. Like the rush of the bitter salt tide over a drowning man clinging to a spar came the complete submerging of her hopes of another life. No name but Camille, that was true; no nationality, for she could never tell from whom or whence she came; no friends, and a beauty that not even an ungainly bonnet and shaven head could hide. In a flash she realised the deception of the life she would lead, and the cruel self-torture of wonder at her own identity. Already, as if in anticipation of the world's questionings, she was asking herself, "Who am I? What am I?"

The next morning the sisters du Sacré Cœur filed into the Cathedral at High Mass, and bent devout knees at the general confession. "Confiteor Deo omnipotenti,"[8] murmured the priest; and tremblingly one little sister followed the words, "Je confesse à Dieu, tout puissant—que j'ai beaucoup péché par pensées—c'est ma faute—c'est ma faute—c'est ma très grande faute."[9]

The organ pealed forth as mass ended, the throng slowly filed out, and the sisters paced through the courtway back into the brown con-

---

7. Refers to the practice of shaving the heads of novices.
8. "Confess to God the omnipotent."

9. "I confess to God, all powerful—that I have sinned much in my thoughts—it is my failing—it is my failing—it is my great failing."

vent walls. One paused at the entrance, and gazed with swift longing eyes in the direction of narrow, squalid Chartres Street, then, with a gulping sob, followed the rest, and vanished behind the heavy door.

No magazine publication; *The Goodness of St. Rocque*, 1899

The Praline Woman

The praline woman sits by the side of the Archbishop's quaint little old chapel on Royal Street, and slowly waves her latanier[1] fan over the pink and brown wares.

"Pralines, pralines. Ah, ma'amzelle, you buy? S'il vous plaît, ma'amzelle, ces pralines, dey be fine, ver' fresh.

"Mais non, maman, you are not sure?

"Sho', chile, ma bébé, ma petite, she put dese up hissef. He's hans' so small, ma'amzelle, lak you's, mais brune.[2] She put dese up dis morn'. You tak' none? No husban' fo' you den!

"Ah, ma petite, you tak'? Cinq sous,[3] bébé, may le bon Dieu keep you good!

"Mais oui, madame, I know you étrangér.[4] You don' look lak dese New Orleans peop'. You lak' dose Yankee dat come down 'fo' de war."

Ding-dong, ding-dong, ding-dong, chimes the Cathedral bell across Jackson Square, and the praline woman crosses herself.

"Hail, Mary, full of grace—

"Pralines, madame? You buy lak' dat? Dix sous, madame, an' one lil' piece fo' lagniappe[5] fo' madame's lil' bébé. Ah, c'est bon!

"Pralines, pralines, so fresh, so fine! M'sieu would lak' some fo' he's lil' gal' at home? Mais non, what's dat you say? She's daid! Ah, m'sieu, 'tis my lil' gal what died long year ago. Misère, misère!

"Here come dat lazy Indien squaw. What she good fo', anyhow? She jes' sit lak dat in de French Market an' sell her filé,[6] an' sleep, sleep, sleep, lak' so in he's blanket. Hey, dere, you, Tonita, how goes you' beezness?

"Pralines, pralines! Holy Father, you give me dat blessin' sho'? Tak' one, I know you lak dat w'ite one. It tas' good, I know, bien.

"Pralines, madame? I lak' you' face. What fo' you wear black? You' lil' boy daid? You tak' one, jes' see how it tas'. I had one lil' boy once, he jes' grow 'twell he's big lak' dis, den one day he tak' sick an' die. Oh, madame, it mos' brek my po' heart. I burn candle in St. Rocque, I say my beads,[7] I sprinkle holy water roun' he's bed; he jes' lay so, he's eyes

---

1. Palm branch.
2. Dark-complexioned. Hisself: even though she uses the masculine pronoun, she is referring to a female child.
3. Five French copper coins.
4. Stranger.

5. A small gift presented to a customer with a purchase. Dix sous: ten sous.
6. Powdered sassafras leaves, used to thicken soup.
7. Say a prayer for each bead on a rosary. St. Rocque: here, the chapel or church named for St. Roch, the patron saint of invalids.

turn up, he say 'Maman, maman,' den he die! Madame, you tak' one. Non, non, no l'argent,[8] you tak' one fo' my lil' boy's sake.

"Pralines, pralines, m'sieu? Who mak' dese? My lil' gal, Didele, of co'se. Non, non, I don't mak' no mo'. Po' Tante Marie get too ol'. Didele? She's one lil' gal I 'dopt. I see her one day in de strit. He walk so; hit col' she shiver, an' I say, 'Where you gone, lil' gal?' and he can' tell. He jes' crip close to me, an' cry so! Den I tak' her home wid me, and she say he's name Didele. You see dey wa'nt nobody dere. My lil' gal, she's daid of de yellow fever; my lil' boy, he's daid, po' Tante Marie all alone. Didele, she grow fine, she keep house an' mek' pralines. Den, when night come, she sit wid he's guitar an' sing,

> " 'Tu l'aime ces trois jours,
> Tu l'aime ces trois jours,
> Ma cœur à toi,
> Ma cœur à toi,
> Tu l'aime ces trois jours!'[9]

"Ah, he's fine gal, is Didele!

"Pralines, pralines! Dat lil' cloud, h'it look lak' rain, I hope no.

"Here come dat lazy I'ishman down de strit. I don't lak' I'ishman, me, non, dey so funny. One day one I'ishman, he say to me, 'Auntie, what fo' you talk so?' and I jes' say back, 'What fo' you say "Faith an' be jabers"?'[1] Non, I don' lak I'ishman, me!

"Here come de rain! Now I got fo' to go. Didele, she be wait fo' me. Down h'it come! H'it fall in de Meesseesip, an' fill up—up—so, clean to de levee, den we have big crivasse,[2] an' po' Tante Marie float away. Bonjour, madame, you come again? Pralines! Pralines!"

No magazine publication; *The Goodness of St. Rocque*, 1899

The Stones of the Village

Victor Grabért strode down the one, wide, tree-shaded street of the village, his heart throbbing with a bitterness and anger that seemed too great to bear. So often had he gone home in the same spirit, however, that it had grown nearly second nature to him—this dull, sullen resentment, flaming out now and then into almost murderous vindictiveness. Behind him there floated derisive laughs and shouts, the taunts of little brutes, boys of his own age.

He reached the tumbledown cottage at the farther end of the street and flung himself on the battered step. Grandmére Grabért sat rocking herself to and fro, crooning a bit of song brought over from the West

8. Money.
9. You love him these three days; my heart is yours.
1. An expletive commonly associated in the 19th

century with the Irish.
2. Crevasse, or crack in a levee. Levee: an embankment raised to prevent a river from overflowing.

Indies years ago; but when the boy sat silent, his head bowed in his hands, she paused in the midst of a line and regarded him with keen, piercing eyes.

"Eh, Victor?" she asked. That was all, but he understood. He raised his head and waved a hand angrily down the street towards the lighted square that marked the village center.

"Dose boy," he gulped.

Grandmére Grabért laid a sympathetic hand on his black curls, but withdrew it the next instant.

"Bien," she said angrily, "Fo' what you go by dem, eh? W'y not keep to yo'self? Dey don' want you, dey don' care fo' you. H'ain' you got no sense?"

"Oh, but Grandmére," he wailed piteously, "I wan' fo' to play."

The old woman stood up in the doorway, her tall, spare form towering menacingly over him.

"You wan' fo' to play, eh? Fo' w'y? You don' need no play. Dose boy," she swept a magnificent gesture down the street, "Dey fools!"

"Eef I could play wid—" began Victor, but his grandmother caught him by the wrist, and held him as in a vise.

"Hush," she cried, "You mus' be goin' crazy," and still holding him by the wrist, she pulled him indoors.

It was a two room house, bare and poor and miserable but never had it seemed so meager before to Victor as it did this night. The supper was frugal almost to the starvation point. They ate in silence, and afterwards Victor threw himself on his cot in the corner of the kitchen and closed his eyes. Grandmére Grabért thought him asleep, and closed the door noiselessly as she went into her own room. But he was awake, and his mind was like a shifting kaleidoscope of miserable incidents and heartaches. He had lived fourteen years, and he could remember most of them as years of misery. He had never known a mother's love, for his mother had died, so he was told, when he was but a few months old. No one ever spoke to him of a father, and Grandmére Grabért had been all to him. She was kind, after a stern, unloving fashion, and she provided for him as best she could. He had picked up some sort of an education at the parish school. It was a good one after its way, but his life there had been such a succession of miseries, that he rebelled one day and refused to go any more.

His earliest memories were clustered about this poor little cottage. He could see himself toddling about its broken steps, playing alone with a few broken pieces of china which his fancy magnified into glorious toys. He remembered his first whipping too. Tired one day of the loneliness which even the broken china could not mitigate, he had toddled out the side gate after a merry group of little black and yellow boys of his own age. When Grandmére Grabért, missing him from his accustomed garden corner, came to look for him, she found him sitting contentedly in the center of the group in the dusty street, all of them gravely scooping up handsful of the gravelly dirt and trickling it down their chubby bare legs. Grandmére snatched at him fiercely, and he whimpered, for he was learning for the first time what fear was.

"What you mean?" she hissed at him, "What you mean playin' in de strit wid dose niggers?" And she struck at him wildly with her open hand.

He looked up into her brown face surmounted by a wealth of curly black hair faintly streaked with gray, but he was too frightened to question.

It had been loneliness ever since. For the parents of the little black and yellow boys, resenting the insult Grandmére had offered their offspring, sternly bade them have nothing more to do with Victor. Then when he toddled after some other little boys, whose faces were white like his own, they ran him away with derisive hoots of "Nigger! Nigger!" And again, he could not understand.

Hardest of all, though, was when Grandmére sternly bade him cease speaking the soft, Creole patois[1] that they chattered together, and forced him to learn English. The result was a confused jumble which was no language at all; that when he spoke it in the streets or in the school, all the boys, white and black and yellow, hooted at him and called him "White nigger! White nigger!"

He writhed on his cot that night and lived over all the anguish of his years until hot tears scalded their way down a burning face, and he fell into a troubled sleep wherein he sobbed over some dreamland miseries.

The next morning, Grandmére eyed his heavy swollen eyes sharply, and a momentary thrill of compassion passed over her and found expression in a new tenderness of manner toward him as she served his breakfast. She, too, had thought over the matter in the night, and it bore fruit in an unexpected way.

Some few weeks after, Victor found himself timidly ringing the door-bell of a house on Hospital Street in New Orleans. His heart throbbed in painful unison to the jangle of the bell. How was he to know that old Madame Guichard, Grandmére's one friend in the city, to whom she had confided him, would be kind? He had walked from the river landing to the house, timidly inquiring the way of busy pedestrians. He was hungry and frightened. Never in all his life had he seen so many people before, and in all the busy streets there was not one eye which would light up with recognition when it met his own. Moreover, it had been a weary journey down the Red River, thence into the Mississippi, and finally here. Perhaps it had not been devoid of interest, after its fashion, but Victor did not know. He was too heartsick at leaving home.

However, Mme. Guichard was kind. She welcomed him with a volubility and overflow of tenderness that acted like balm to the boy's sore spirit. Thence they were firm friends, even confidants.

---

1. A regional dialect.

Victor must find work to do. Grandmére Grabért's idea in sending him to New Orleans was that he might "mek one man of himse'f" as she phrased it. And Victor, grown suddenly old in the sense that he had a responsibility to bear, set about his search valiantly.

It chanced one day that he saw a sign in an old bookstore on Royal Street that stated in both French and English the need of a boy. Almost before he knew it, he had entered the shop and was gasping out some choked words to the little old man who sat behind the counter.

The old man looked keenly over his glasses at the boy and rubbed his bald head reflectively. In order to do this, he had to take off an old black silk cap which he looked at with apparent regret.

"Eh, what you say?" he asked sharply, when Victor had finished.

"I—I—want a place to work," stammered the boy again.

"Eh, you do? Well, can you read?"

"Yes sir," replied Victor.

The old man got down from his stool, came from behind the counter, and putting his finger under the boy's chin, stared hard into his eyes. They met his own unflinchingly, though there was the suspicion of pathos and timidity in their brown depths.

"Do you know where you live, eh?"

"On Hospital Street," said Victor. It did not occur to him to give the number, and the old man did not ask.

"Très bien," grunted the book-seller, and his interest relaxed. He gave a few curt directions about the manner of work Victor was to do, and settled himself again upon his stool, poring into his dingy book with renewed ardor.

Thus began Victor's commercial life. It was an easy one. At seven, he opened the shutters of the little shop and swept and dusted. At eight, the book-seller came downstairs, and passed out to get his coffee at the restaurant across the street. At eight in the evening, the shop was closed again. That was all.

Occasionally, there came a customer, but not often, for there were only odd books and rare ones in the shop, and those who came were usually old, yellow, querulous book-worms, who nosed about for hours, and went away leaving many bank notes behind them. Sometimes there was an errand to do, and sometimes there came a customer when the proprietor was out. It was an easy matter to wait on them. He had but to point to the shelves and say, "Monsieur will be in directly," and all was settled, for those who came here to buy had plenty of leisure and did not mind waiting.

So a year went by, then two and three, and the stream of Victor's life flowed smoothly on its uneventful way. He had grown tall and thin, and often Mme. Guichard would look at him and chuckle to herself, "Ha, he is lak one bean-pole, yaas, mais—" and there would be a world of unfinished reflection in that last word.

Victor had grown pale from much reading. Like a shadow of the old book-seller he sat day after day poring into some dusty yellow-paged book, and his mind was a queer jumble of ideas. History and philoso-

phy and old-fashioned social economy were tangled with French romance and classic mythology and astrology and mysticism. He had
made few friends, for his experience in the village had made him chary
of strangers. Every week, he wrote to Grandmére Grabért and sent her
part of his earnings. In his way he was happy, and if he was lonely, he
had ceased to care about it, for his world was peopled with images of
his own fancying.

Then all at once, the world he had built about him tumbled down,
and he was left, staring helplessly at its ruins. The little book-seller
died one day, and his shop and its books were sold by an unscrupulous
nephew who cared not for bindings nor precious yellowed pages, but
only for the grossly material things that money can buy. Victor ground
his teeth as the auctioneer's strident voice sounded through the shop
where all once had been hushed quiet, and wept as he saw some of his
favorite books carried away by men and women whom he was sure
could not appreciate their value.

He dried his tears, however, the next day when a grave-faced lawyer
came to the little house on Hospital Street, and informed him that he
had been left a sum of money by the book-seller.

Victor sat staring at him helplessly. Money meant little to him. He
never needed it, never used it. After he had sent Grandmére her sum
each week, Mme. Guichard kept the rest and doled it out to him as he
needed it for carfare and clothes.

"The interest of the money," continued the lawyer, clearing his
throat, "is sufficient to keep you very handsomely without touching the
principal. It was my client's wish that you should enter Tulane College,
and there fit yourself for your profession. He had great confidence in
your ability."

"Tulane College!" cried Victor. "Why—why—why—" then he
stopped suddenly, and the hot blood mounted to his face. He glanced
furtively about the room. Mme. Guichard was not near; the lawyer
had seen no one but him. Then why tell him? His heart leaped wildly
at the thought. Well, Grandmére would have willed it so.

The lawyer was waiting politely for him to finish his sentence.

"Why—why—I should have to study in order to enter there," finished Victor lamely.

"Exactly so," said Mr. Buckley, "and as I have, in a way, been
appointed your guardian, I will see to that."

Victor found himself murmuring confused thanks and good-byes to
Mr. Buckley. After he had gone, the boy sat down and gazed blankly
at the wall. Then he wrote a long letter to Grandmére.

A week later, he changed boarding places at Mr. Buckley's advice,
and entered a preparatory school for Tulane. And still, Mme. Guichard
and Mr. Buckley had not met.

* * *

It was a handsomely furnished office on Carondelet Street in which
Lawyer Grabért sat some years later. His day's work done, he was
leaning back in his chair and smiling pleasantly out of the window.

Within, was warmth and light and cheer; without, the wind howled and gusty rains beat against the window pane. Lawyer Grabért smiled again as he looked about at the comfort, and found himself half pitying those without who were forced to buffet the storm afoot. He rose finally, and, donning his overcoat, called a cab and was driven to his rooms in the most fashionable part of the city. There he found his old-time college friend, awaiting him with some impatience.

"Thought you never were coming, old man," was his greeting.

Grabért smiled pleasantly, "Well, I was a bit tired, you know," he answered, "and I have been sitting idle for an hour or more, just relaxing, as it were."

Vannier laid his hand affectionately on the other's shoulder. "That was a mighty effort you made today," he said earnestly, "I, for one, am proud of you."

"Thank you," replied Grabért simply, and the two sat silent for a minute.

"Going to the Charles' dance tonight?" asked Vannier finally.

"I don't believe I am. I am tired and lazy."

"It will do you good. Come on."

"No, I want to read and ruminate."

"Ruminate over your good fortune of today?"

"If you will have it so, yes."

But it was not simply over his good fortune of that day over which Grabért pondered. It was over the good fortune of the past fifteen years. From school to college, and from college to law school he had gone, and thence into practice, and he was now accredited a successful young lawyer. His small fortune, which Mr. Buckley, with generous kindness, had invested wisely, had almost doubled, and his school career, while not of the brilliant, meteoric kind, had been pleasant and profitable. He had made friends, at first, with the boys he met and they, in turn, had taken him into their homes. Now and then, the Buckleys asked him to dinner, and he was seen occasionally in their box at the opera. He was rapidly becoming a social favorite, and girls vied with each other to dance with him. No one had asked any questions, and he had volunteered no information concerning himself. Vannier, who had known him in preparatory school days, had said that he was a young country fellow with some money, no connections, and a ward of Mr. Buckley's, and somehow, contrary to the usual social custom of the South, this meager account had passed muster. But Vannier's family had been a social arbiter for many years, and Grabért's personality was pleasing, without being aggressive, so he had passed through the portals of the social world and was in the inner circle.

One year, when he and Vannier were in Switzerland, pretending to climb impossible mountains and in reality smoking many cigars a day on hotel porches, a letter came to Grabért from the priest of his old-time town, telling him that Grandmére Grabért had been laid away in the parish church-yard. There was no more to tell. The little old hut had been sold to pay funeral expenses.

"Poor Grandmére," sighed Victor, "She did care for me after her fashion. I'll go take a look at her grave when I go back."

But he did not go, for when he returned to Louisiana, he was too busy, then he decided that it would be useless, sentimental folly. Moreover, he had no love for the old village. Its very name suggested things that made him turn and look about him nervously. He had long since eliminated Mme. Guichard from his list of acquaintances.

And yet, as he sat there in his cozy study that night, and smiled as he went over in his mind triumph after triumph which he had made since the old bookstore days in Royal Street, he was conscious of a subtle undercurrent of annoyance; a sort of mental reservation that placed itself on every pleasant memory.

"I wonder what's the matter with me?" he asked himself as he rose and paced the floor impatiently. Then he tried to recall his other triumph, the one of the day. The case of Tate vs. Tate, a famous will contest, had been dragging through the courts for seven years and his speech had decided it that day. He could hear the applause of the courtroom as he sat down, but it rang hollow in his ears, for he remembered another scene. The day before he had been in another court, and found himself interested in the prisoner before the bar. The offense was a slight one, a mere technicality. Grabért was conscious of a something pleasant in the man's face; a scrupulous neatness in his dress, an unostentatious conforming to the prevailing style. The Recorder, however, was short and brusque.

"Wilson—Wilson—" he growled, "Oh, yes, I know you, always kicking up some sort of a row about theater seats and cars. Hum-um. What do you mean by coming before me with a flower in your buttonhole?"

The prisoner looked down indifferently at the bud on his coat, and made no reply.

"Hey?" growled the Recorder. "You niggers are putting yourselves up too much for me."

At the forbidden word, the blood rushed to Grabért's face, and he started from his seat angrily. The next instant, he had recovered himself and buried his face in a paper. After Wilson had paid his fine, Grabért looked at him furtively as he passed out. His face was perfectly impassive, but his eyes flashed defiantly. The lawyer was tingling with rage and indignation, although the affront had not been given him.

"If Recorder Grant had any reason to think that I was in any way like Wilson, I would stand no better show," he mused bitterly.

However, as he thought it over tonight, he decided that he was a sentimental fool. "What have I to do with them?" he asked himself, "I must be careful."

The next week, he discharged the man who cared for his office. He was a Negro, and Grabért had no fault to find with him generally, but he found himself with a growing sympathy toward the man, and since the episode in the courtroom, he was morbidly nervous lest a something in his manner would betray him. Thereafter, a round-eyed Irish boy cared for his rooms.

The Vanniers were wont to smile indulgently at his every move. Elise Vannier, particularly, was more than interested in his work. He had a way of dropping in of evenings and talking over his cases and speeches with her in a cosy corner of the library. She had a gracious sympathetic manner that was soothing and a cheery fund of repartee[2] to whet her conversation. Victor found himself drifting into sentimental bits of talk now and then. He found himself carrying around in his pocketbook a faded rose which she had once worn, and when he laughed at it one day and started to throw it in the wastebasket, he suddenly kissed it instead, and replaced it in the pocketbook. That Elise was not indifferent to him he could easily see. She had not learned yet how to veil her eyes and mask her face under a cool assumption of superiority. She would give him her hand when they met with a girlish impulsiveness, and her color came and went under his gaze. Sometimes, when he held her hand a bit longer than necessary, he could feel it flutter in his own, and she would sigh a quick little gasp that made his heart leap and choked his utterance.

They were tucked away in their usual cosy corner one evening, and the conversation had drifted to the problem of where they would spend the summer.

"Papa wants to go to the country house," pouted Elise, "and mama and I don't want to go. It isn't fair, of course, because when we go so far away, Papa can be with us only for a few weeks when he can get away from his office, while if we go to the country place, he can run up every few days. But it is so dull there, don't you think so?"

Victor recalled some pleasant vacation days at the plantation home and laughed, "Not if you are there."

"Yes, but you see, I can't take myself for a companion. Now if you'll promise to come up sometimes, it will be better."

"If I may, I shall be delighted to come."

Elise laughed intimately, "If you may—" she replied, "as if such a word had to enter into our plans. Oh, but Victor, haven't you some sort of plantation somewhere? It seems to me that I heard Steven years ago speak of your home in the country, and I wondered sometimes that you never spoke of it, or ever mentioned having visited it."

The girl's artless words were bringing cold sweat to Victor's brow, his tongue felt heavy and useless, but he managed to answer quietly, "I have no home in the country."

"Well, didn't you ever own one, or your family?"

"It was old quite a good many years ago," he replied, and a vision of the little old hut with its tumbledown steps and weed-grown garden came into his mind.

"Where was it?" pursued Elise innocently.

2. Witty and spirited conversation.

"Oh, away up in St. Landry parish, too far away from civilization to mention." He tried to laugh, but it was a hollow forced attempt that rang false. But Elise was too absorbed in her own thoughts of the summer to notice.

"And you haven't a relative living?" she continued.

"Not one."

"How strange. Why it seems to me if I did not have a half a hundred cousins and uncles and aunts that I should feel somehow out of touch with the world."

He did not reply, and she chattered away on another topic.

When he was alone in his room that night, he paced the floor again, chewing wildly at a cigar that he had forgotten to light.

"What did she mean? What did she mean?" he asked himself over and over. Could she have heard or suspected anything that she was trying to find out about? Could any action, any unguarded expression of his have set the family thinking? But he soon dismissed the thought as unworthy of him. Elise was too frank and transparent a girl to stoop to subterfuge. If she wished to know anything, she was wont to ask out at once, and if she had once thought anyone was sailing under false colors, she would say so frankly, and dismiss them from her presence.

Well, he must be prepared to answer questions if he were going to marry her. The family would want to know all about him, and Elise, herself, would be curious for more than her brother, Steve Vannier's, meager account. But was he going to marry Elise? That was the question.

He sat down and buried his head in his hands. Would it be right for him to take a wife, especially such a woman as Elise, and from such a family as the Vanniers? Would it be fair? Would it be just? If they knew and were willing, it would be different. But they did not know, and they would not consent if they did. In fancy, he saw the dainty girl whom he loved shrinking from him as he told her of Grandmère Grabért and the village boys. This last thought made him set his teeth hard, and the hot blood rushed to his face.

Well, why not, after all, why not? What was the difference between him and the hosts of other suitors who hovered about Elise? They had money; so had he. They had education, polite training, culture, social position; so had he. But they had family traditions, and he had none. Most of them could point to a long line of family portraits with justifiable pride; while if he had had a picture of Grandmére Grabért, he would have destroyed it fearfully, lest it fall into the hands of some too curious person. This was the subtle barrier that separated them. He recalled with a sting how often he had had to sit silent and constrained when the conversation turned to ancestors and family traditions. He might be one with his companions and friends in everything but this. He must ever be on the outside, hovering at the gates, as it were. Into the inner life of his social world, he might never enter. The charming impoliteness of an intercourse begun by their fathers and grandfathers was not for him. There must always be a certain formality with him, even though they were his most intimate friends. He had not fifty cousins, therefore, as Elise phrased it, he was "out of touch with the world."

"If ever I have a son or a daughter," he found himself saying unconsciously, "I would try to save him from this."

Then he laughed bitterly as he realized the irony of the thought. Well, anyway, Elise loved him. There was a sweet consolation in that. He had but to look into her frank eyes and read her soul. Perhaps she wondered why he had not spoken. Should he speak? There he was back at the old question again.

"According to the standard of the world," he mused reflectively, "my blood is tainted in two ways. Who knows it? No one but myself, and I shall not tell. Otherwise, I am quite as good as the rest, and Elise loves me."

But even this thought failed of its sweetness in a moment. Elise loved him because she did not know. He found a sickening anger and disgust rising in himself at a people whose prejudices made him live a life of deception. He would cater to their traditions no longer; he would be honest. Then he found himself shrinking from the alternative with a dread that made him wonder. It was the old problem of his life in the village; and the boys, both white and black and yellow, stood as before, with stones in their hands to hurl at him.

He went to bed worn out with the struggle, but still with no definite idea what to do. Sleep was impossible. He rolled and tossed miserably, and cursed the fate that had thrown him in such a position. He had never thought very seriously over the subject before. He had rather drifted with the tide and accepted what came to him as a sort of recompense the world owed him for his unhappy childhood. He had known fear, yes, and qualms now and then, and a hot resentment occasionally when the outsideness of his situation was inborne to him; but that was all. Elise had awakened a disagreeable conscientiousness within him, which he decided was as unpleasant as it was unnecessary.

He could not sleep, so he arose, and dressing, walked out and stood on the banquette.[3] The low hum of the city came to him like the droning of some sleepy insect, and ever and anon, the quick flash and fire of the gas houses[4] like a huge winking fiery eye lit up the south of the city. It was inexpressingly soothing to Victor; the great unknowing city, teeming with life and with lives whose sadness mocked his own teacup tempest. He smiled and shook himself as a dog shakes off the water from his coat.

"I think a walk will help me out," he said absently, and presently he was striding down St. Charles Avenue, around Lee Circle and down to Canal Street, where the lights and glare absorbed him for a while. He walked out the wide boulevard towards Claiborne Street, hardly think-

---

3. Sidewalk.   4. Factories producing natural gas.

ing, hardly realizing that he was walking. When he was thoroughly
worn out, he retraced his steps and dropped wearily into a restaurant
near Bourbon Street.

"Hullo!" said a familiar voice from a table as he entered. Victor
turned and recognized Frank Ward, a little oculist, whose office was in
the same building as his own.

"Another night owl besides myself," laughed Ward, making room
for him at his table. "Can't you sleep too, old fellow?"

"Not very well," said Victor, taking the proffered seat, "I believe I'm
getting nerves. Think I need toning up."

"Well, you'd have been toned up if you had been in here a few
minutes ago. Why—why—" and Ward went off into peals of laughter
at the memory of the scene.

"What was it?" asked Victor.

"Why—a fellow came in here, nice sort of fellow, apparently, and
wanted to have supper. Well, would you believe it, when they
wouldn't serve him, he wanted to fight everything in sight. It was
positively exciting for a time."

"Why wouldn't the waiter serve him?" Victor tried to make his tone
indifferent, but he felt the quaver in his voice.

"Why? Why, he was a darkey, you know."

"Well, what of it?" demanded Grabért fiercely, "Wasn't he quiet,
well-dressed, polite? Didn't he have money?"

"My dear fellow," began Ward mockingly, "Upon my word, I believe you are losing your mind. You do need toning up or something.
Would you—could you—?"

"Oh, pshaw," broke in Grabért, "I—I—believe I am losing my
mind. Really, Ward, I need something to make me sleep. My head
aches."

Ward was at once all sympathy and advice, and chiding to the waiter
for his slowness in filling their order. Victor toyed with his food, and
made an excuse to leave the restaurant as soon as he could decently.

"Good heavens," he said when he was alone, "What will I do next?"
His outburst of indignation at Ward's narrative had come from his lips
almost before he knew it, and he was frightened, frightened at his own
unguardedness. He did not know what had come over him.

"I must be careful, I must be careful," he muttered to himself. "I
must go to the other extreme, if necessary." He was pacing his rooms
again, and suddenly he faced the mirror.

"You wouldn't fare any better than the rest, if they knew," he told
the reflection, "You poor wretch, what are you?"

When he thought of Elise, he smiled. He loved her, but he hated the
traditions which she represented. He was conscious of a blind fury
which bade him wreak vengeance on those traditions, and of a cowardly fear which cried out to him to retain his position in the world's
and Elise's eyes at any cost.

❄   ❄   ❄

Mrs. Grabért was delighted to have visiting her her old school friend from Virginia, and the two spent hours laughing over their girlish escapades, and comparing notes about their little ones. Each was confident that her darling had said the cutest things, and their polite deference to each other's opinions on the matter was a sham through which each saw without resentment.

"But Elise," remonstrated Mrs. Allen, "I think it so strange you don't have a mammy for Baby Vannier. He would be so much better cared for than by that harum-scarum young white girl you have."

"I think so too, Adelaide," sighed Mrs. Grabért, "It seems strange for me not to have a darkey maid about, but Victor can't bear them. I cried and cried for my old mammy, but he was stern. He doesn't like darkies, you know, and he says old mammies just frighten children, and ruin their childhood. I don't see how he could say that, do you?" She looked wistfully to Mrs. Allen for sympathy.

"I don't know," mused that lady, "We were all looked after by our mammies, and I think they are the best kind of nurses."

"And Victor won't have any kind of darkey servant either here or at the office. He says they're shiftless and worthless and generally no-account. Of course, he knows, he's had lots of experience with them in his business."

Mrs. Allen folded her hands behind her head and stared hard at the ceiling. "Oh, well, men don't know everything," she said, "and Victor may come around to our way of thinking after all."

It was late that evening when the lawyer came in for dinner. His eyes had acquired a habit of veiling themselves under their lashes as if they were constantly concealing something which they feared might be wrenched from them by a stare. He was nervous and restless, with a habit of glancing about him furtively, and a twitching compressing of his lips when he had finished a sentence, which somehow reminded you of a kindhearted judge, who is forced to give a death sentence.

Elise met him at the door as was her wont, and she knew from the first glance into his eyes that something had disturbed him more than usual that day, but she forbore asking questions, for she knew he would tell her when the time had come.

They were in their room that night when the rest of the household lay in slumber. He sat for a long while gazing at the open fire, then he passed his hand over his forehead wearily.

"I have had a rather unpleasant experience today," he began.

"Yes."

"Pavageau, again."

His wife was brushing her hair before the mirror. At the name she turned hastily with the brush in her uplifted hand.

"I can't understand, Victor, why you must have dealings with that man. He is constantly irritating you. I simply wouldn't associate with him."

"I don't," and he laughed at her feminine argument. "It isn't a

question of association, chérie, it's a purely business and unsocial relation, if relation it may be called, that throws us together."

She threw down the brush petulantly, and came to his side, "Victor,"
she began hesitatingly, her arms about his neck, her face close to his,
"Won't you—won't you give up politics for me? It was ever so much
nicer when you were just a lawyer and wanted only to be the best
lawyer in the state, without all this worry about corruption and votes
and such things. You've changed, oh, Victor, you've changed so. Baby
and I won't know you after a while."

He put her gently on his knee. "You mustn't blame the poor politics,
darling. Don't you think, perhaps, it's the inevitable hardening and
embittering that must come to us all as we grow older?"

"No, I don't," she replied emphatically, "Why do you go into this
struggle, anyhow? You have nothing to gain but an empty honor. It
won't bring you more money, or make you more loved or respected.
Why must you be mixed up with such—such—awful people?"

"I don't know," he said wearily.

And in truth, he did not know. He had gone on after his marriage
with Elise making one success after another. It seemed that a beneficent Providence had singled him out as the one man in the state upon
whom to heap the most lavish attentions. He was popular after the
fashion of those who are high in the esteem of the world; and this very
fact made him tremble the more, for he feared that should some
disclosure come, he could not stand the shock of public opinion that
must overwhelm him.

"What disclosure?" he would say impatiently when such a thought
would come to him, "Where could it come from, and then, what is
there to disclose?"

Thus he would deceive himself for as much as a month at a
time.

He was surprised to find awaiting him in his office one day the man
Wilson, whom he remembered in the courtroom before Recorder
Grant. He was surprised and annoyed. Why had the man come to his
office? Had he seen the telltale flush on his face that day?

But it was soon evident that Wilson did not even remember having
seen him before.

"I came to see if I could retain you in a case of mine," he began, after
the usual formalities of greeting were over.

"I am afraid, my good man," said Grabért brusquely, "that you have
mistaken the office."

Wilson's face flushed at the appellation, but he went on bravely, "I
have not mistaken the office. I know you are the best civil lawyer in the
city, and I want your services."

"An impossible thing."

"Why? Are you too busy? My case is a simple thing, a mere point in
law, but I want the best authority and the best opinion brought to bear
on it."

"I could not give you any help—and—I fear, we do not understand each other—I do not wish to." He turned to his desk abruptly.

"What could he have meant by coming to me?" he questioned himself fearfully, as Wilson left the office. "Do I look like a man likely to take up his impossible contentions?"

He did not look like it, nor was he. When it came to a question involving the Negro, Victor Grabért was noted for his stern, unrelenting attitude; it was simply impossible to convince him that there was anything but sheerest incapacity in that race. For him, no good could come out of this Nazareth.[5] He was liked and respected by men of his political belief, because, even when he was a candidate for a judgeship, neither money nor the possible chance of a deluge of votes from the First and Fourth Wards could cause him to swerve one hair's breadth from his opinion of the black inhabitants of those wards.

Pavageau, however, was his *bête noir*.[6] Pavageau was a lawyer, a coolheaded, calculating man with steely eyes set in a grim brown face. They had first met in the courtroom in a case which involved the question whether a man may set aside the will of his father, who, disregarding the legal offspring of another race than himself, chooses to leave his property to educational institutions which would not have granted admission to that son. Pavageau represented the son. He lost, of course. The judge, the jury, the people and Grabért were against him; but he fought his fight with a grim determination which commanded Victor's admiration and respect.

"Fools," he said between his teeth to himself, when they were crowding about him with congratulations, "Fools, can't they see who is the abler man of the two?"

He wanted to go up to Pavageau and give him his hand; to tell him that he was proud of him and that he had really won the case, but public opinion was against him; but he dared not. Another one of his colleagues might; but he was afraid. Pavageau and the world might misunderstand, or would it be understanding?

Thereafter they met often. Either by some freak of nature, or because there was a shrewd sense of the possibilities in his position, Pavageau was of the same political side of the fence as Grabért. Secretly, he admired the man; he respected him; he liked him, and because of this he was always ready with sneer and invective for him. He fought him bitterly when there was no occasion for fighting, and Pavageau became his enemy, and his name a very synonym of horror to Elise, who learned to trace her husband's fits of moodiness and depression to the one source.

Meanwhile, Vannier Grabért was growing up, a handsome lad, with his father's and mother's physical beauty, and a strength and force of character that belonged to neither. In him, Grabért saw the reparation

5. A reference to Jesus, who grew up in the town of Nazareth. See John 1.46.

6. Literally, black beast; someone or something that one especially dislikes or avoids.

of all his childhood's wrongs and sufferings. The boy realized all his own longings. He had family traditions, and a social position which was his from birth and an inalienable right to hold up his head without an unknown fear gripping at his heart. Grabért felt that he could forgive all; the village boys of long ago, and the imaginary village boys of today when he looked at his son. He had bought and paid for Vannier's freedom and happiness. The coins may have been each a drop of his heart's blood, but he had reckoned the cost before he had given it.

It was a source of great pride for him to take the boy to court with him, and one Saturday morning, when he was starting out, Vannier asked if he might go.

"There is nothing that would interest you today, mon fils," he said tenderly, "but you may go."

In fact, there was nothing interesting that day; merely a troublesome old woman, who instead of taking her fair-skinned grandchild out of the school where it had been found it did not belong, had preferred to bring the matter to court. She was represented by Pavageau. Of course, there was not the ghost of a show for her. Pavageau had told her that. The law was very explicit about the matter. The only question lay in proving the child's affinity to the Negro race, which was not such a difficult matter to do, so the case was quickly settled, since the child's grandmother accompanied him. The judge, however, was irritated. It was a hot day and he was provoked that such a trivial matter should have taken up his time. He lost his temper as he looked at his watch.

"I don't see why these people want to force their children into the white schools," he declared, "There should be a rigid inspection to prevent it, and all the suspected children put out and made to go where they belong."

Pavageau, too, was irritated that day. He looked up from some papers which he was folding, and his gaze met Grabért's with a keen, cold, penetrating flash.

"Perhaps Your Honor would like to set the example by taking your son from the schools."

There was an instant silence in the courtroom, a hush intense and eager. Every eye turned upon the judge who sat still, a figure carven in stone with livid face and fear-stricken eyes. After the first flash of his eyes, Pavageau had gone on coolly sorting the papers.

The courtroom waited, waited, for the judge to rise and thunder forth a fine against the daring Negro lawyer for contempt. A minute passed, which seemed like an hour. Why did not Grabért speak? Pavageau's implied accusation was too absurd for denial; but he should be punished. Was His Honor ill, or did he merely hold the man in too much contempt to notice him or his remark?

Finally Grabért spoke; he moistened his lips, for they were dry and parched, and his voice was weak and sounded far away in his own ears. "My son—does—not—attend the public schools."

Someone in the rear of the room laughed, and the atmosphere

lightened at once. Plainly Pavageau was an idiot, and His Honor too far above him; too much of a gentleman to notice him. Grabért continued calmly; "The gentleman," there was an unmistakable sneer in this word, habit if nothing else, and not even fear could restrain him, "The gentleman doubtless intended a little pleasantry, but I shall have to fine him for contempt of court."

"As you will," replied Pavageau, and he flashed another look at Grabért. It was a look of insolent triumph and derision. His Honor's eyes dropped beneath it.

"What did that man mean, father, by saying you should take me out of school?" asked Vannier on his way home.

"He was provoked, my son, because he had lost his case, and when a man is provoked he is likely to say silly things. By the way, Vannier, I hope you won't say anything to your mother about the incident. It would only annoy her."

For the public, the incident was forgotten as soon as it had closed, but for Grabért, it was indelibly stamped on his memory; a scene that shrieked in his mind and stood out before him at every footstep he took. Again and again as he tossed on a sleepless bed did he see the cold flash of Pavageau's eyes, and hear his quiet accusation. How did he know? Where had he gotten his information? For he spoke, not as one who makes a random shot in anger; but as one who knows, who has known a long while, and who is betrayed by irritation into playing his trump card[7] too early in the game.

He passed a wretched week, wherein it seemed that his every footstep was dogged, his every gesture watched and recorded. He fancied that Elise, even, was suspecting him. When he took his judicial seat each morning, it seemed that every eye in the courtroom was fastened upon him in derision; everyone who spoke, it seemed, were but biding their time to shout the old village street refrain which had haunted him all his life, "Nigger!—Nigger!—White nigger!"

Finally, he could stand it no longer, and with leaden feet and furtive glances to the right and left for fear he might be seen, he went up a flight of dusty stairs in an Exchange Alley building, which led to Pavageau's office.

The latter was frankly surprised to see him. He made a polite attempt to conceal it, however. It was the first time in his legal life that Grabért had ever sought out a Negro; the first time that he had ever voluntarily opened conversation with one.

He mopped his forehead nervously as he took the chair Pavageau offered him; he stared about the room for an instant; then with a sudden, almost brutal directness, he turned on the lawyer.

"See here, what did you mean by that remark you made in court the other day?"

7. In card games, a card declared to out rank all others; thus, a key resource to be used at the opportune moment.

"I meant just what I said," was the cool reply.

Grabért paused, "Why did you say it?" he asked slowly.

"Because I was a fool. I should have kept my mouth shut until another time, should I not?"

"Pavageau," said Grabért softly, "let's not fence. Where did you get your information?"

Pavageau paused for an instant. He put his fingertips together and closed his eyes as one who meditates. Then he said with provoking calmness.

"You seem anxious—well, I don't mind letting you know. It doesn't really matter."

"Yes, yes," broke in Grabért impatiently.

"Did you ever hear of a Mme. Guichard of Hospital Street?"

The sweat broke out on the judge's brow as he replied weakly, "Yes."

"Well, I am her nephew."

"And she?"

"Is dead. She told me about you once—with pride, let me say. No one else knows."

Grabért sat dazed. He had forgotten about Mme. Guichard. She had never entered into his calculations at all. Pavageau turned to his desk with a sigh as if he wished the interview were ended. Grabért rose.

"If—if—this were known—to—to—my—my wife," he said thickly, "it would hurt her very much."

His head was swimming. He had had to appeal to this man, and to appeal in his wife's name. His wife, whose name he scarcely spoke to men whom he considered his social equals.

Pavageau looked up quickly. "It happens that I often have cases in your court," he spoke deliberately, "I am willing, if I lose fairly, to give up; but I do not like to have a decision made against me because my opponent is of a different complexion from mine, or because the decision against me would please a certain class of people. I only ask what I have never had from you—fair play."

"I understand," said Grabért.

He admired Pavageau more than ever as he went out of his office, yet this admiration was tempered by the knowledge that this man was the only person in the whole world who possessed positive knowledge of his secret. He groveled in a self-abasement at his position; and yet he could not but feel a certain relief that the vague formless fear which had hitherto dogged his life and haunted it had taken on a definite shape. He knew where it was now; he could lay his hands on it, and fight it.

But with what weapons? There were none offered him save a substantial backing down from his position on certain questions; the position that had been his for so long that he was almost known by it. For in the quiet deliberate sentence of Pavageau's, he read that he must cease all the oppression, all the little injustices which he had offered

Pavageau's clientele. He must act now as his convictions and secret sympathies and affiliations had bidden him act; not as prudence and fear and cowardice had made him act.

Then what would be the result? he asked himself. Would not the suspicions of the people be aroused by this sudden change in his manner? Would not they begin to question and to wonder? Would not someone remember Pavageau's remark that morning, and, putting two and two together, start some rumor flying? His heart sickened again at the thought.

There was a banquet that night. It was in his honor, and he was to speak, and the thought was distasteful to him beyond measure. He knew how it all would be. He would be hailed with shouts and acclamations, as the finest flower of civilization. He would be listened to deferentially, and younger men would go away holding him in their hearts as a truly worthy model. When all the while—

He threw back his head and laughed. Oh, what a glorious revenge he had on those little white village boys! How he had made a race atone for Wilson's insult in the courtroom; for the man in the restaurant at whom Ward had laughed so uproariously; for all the affronts seen and unseen given these people of his own whom he had denied. He had taken a diploma from their most exclusive college; he had broken down the barriers of their social world; he had taken the highest possible position among them; and, aping their own ways, had shown them that he, too, could despise this inferior race they despised. Nay, he had taken for his wife the best woman among them all, and she had borne him a son. Ha, ha! What a joke on them all!

And he had not forgotten the black and yellow boys either. They had stoned him too, and he had lived to spurn them; to look down upon them, and to crush them at every possible turn from his seat on the bench. Truly, his life had not been wasted.

He had lived forty-nine years now, and the zenith of his power was not yet reached. There was much more to do, much more, and he was going to do it. He owed it to Elise and the boy. For their sake he must go on and on and keep his tongue still, and truckle to Pavageau and suffer alone. Some day, perhaps, he would have a grandson, who would point with pride to "My grandfather, the famous Judge Grabért!" Ah, that in itself, was a reward. To have founded a dynasty; to bequeath to others that which he had never possessed himself, and the lack of which had made his life a misery.

It was a banquet with a political significance; one that meant a virtual triumph for Judge Grabért in the next contest for the District Judge. He smiled around at the eager faces which were turned up to his as he arose to speak. The tumult of applause which had greeted his rising had died away, and an expectant hush fell on the room.

"What a sensation I could make now," he thought. He had but to open his mouth and cry out, "Fools! Fools! I whom you are honoring, I am one of the despised ones. Yes, I'm a nigger—do you hear, a nigger!" What a temptation it was to end the whole miserable farce. If he were alone in the world, if it were not for Elise and the boy; he would, just to see their horror and wonder. How they would shrink from him! But what could they do? They could take away his office; but his wealth, and his former successes, and his learning, they could not touch. Well, he must speak, and he must remember Elise and the boy.

Every eye was fastened on him in eager expectancy. Judge Grabért's speech was expected to outline the policy of their faction in the coming campaign. He turned to the chairman at the head of the table.

"Mr. Chairman," he began, and paused again. How peculiar it was that in the place of the chairman there sat Grandmére Grabért as she had been wont to sit on the steps of the tumbledown cottage in the village. She was looking at him sternly and bidding him give an account of his life since she had kissed him good-bye ere he had sailed down the river to New Orleans. He was surprised, and not a little annoyed. He had expected to address the chairman; not Grandmére Grabért. He cleared his throat and frowned.

"Mr. Chairman," he said again. Well, what was the use of addressing her that way? She would not understand him. He would call her Grandmére, of course. Were they not alone again on the cottage steps at twilight with the cries of the little brutish boys ringing derisively from the distant village square?

"Grandmére," he said softly, "you don't understand—" and then he was sitting down in his seat pointing one finger angrily at her because the other words would not come. They stuck in his throat, and he choked and beat the air with his hands. When the men crowded around him with water and hastily improvised fans, he fought them away wildly and desperately with furious curses that came from his blackened lips. For were they not all boys with stones to pelt him because he wanted to play with them? He would run away to Grandmére who would soothe him and comfort him. So he arose, and stumbling, shrieking and beating them back from him, ran the length of the hall, and fell across the threshold of the door.

The secret died with him, for Pavageau's lips were ever sealed.

Manuscript unpublished in Dunbar-Nelson's lifetime;
The Works of Alice Dunbar-Nelson, 1988

SUI SIN FAR
(EDITH MAUD EATON)
1867–1914

The facts concerning Sui Sin Far's origins, date of birth, and early childhood remain uncertain, but she characterized herself as Eurasian. As a young man, her father, Edward Eaton, of a well-to-do English family, traveled to the Far East on business, where he met and married a Chinese woman who had apparently been unofficially "adopted" by English missionaries and raised in England. In her autobiographical sketch titled "Leaves from the Mental Portfolio of an Eurasian," Sui Sin Far described her mother as having been "stolen" (128) from her native land at an early age. While the details of her mother's history are unknown, many young girls did leave China during the nineteenth century; families resorted to "mortgaging, infanticide, and the abandonment or selling of children," particularly female children, in order to ease the burdens of extreme poverty (Hirata 228).

The young Edith Eaton, the oldest daughter in a family of fourteen children, emigrated with her family from England first to Hudson, New York, at about the age of six, then to eastern Canada. In her autobiographical sketch, Eaton recalls discovering her difference as a biracial child very early in life. She writes about a memory from the age of four, of overhearing one nursemaid tell another that Edith's mother was Chinese. When she tries to tell her mother what she has overheard, she recalls, "My mother does not understand, and when the nurse declares to her, 'Little Miss Sui is a story-teller,' my mother slaps me" ("Leaves" 125). Yet the nursemaid's description of "little Miss Sui" would be prophetic, for after contributing to her family's income by selling lace and her father's paintings door-to-door, then supporting herself as a stenographer, Edith Eaton became a journalist and a storyteller, taking as her subject the situation of the Chinese in America and the plight of biracial identity. Both in Canada and later in Seattle where she settled as an adult, she encountered prejudice against the Chinese which she believed contributed to her lifelong ill health. Perhaps it was her own belief that as an Eurasian she belonged neither to her father's nationality nor to her mother's that led her to remain unmarried. She died in Montreal on April 7, 1914.

        o   o   o

Sui Sin Far's decision to depict Chinese-American life in her fiction contrasts markedly with the work of her sister Winnifred, twelve years her junior, who adopted an apparently false Japanese ancestry, capitalizing on the attitudes turn-of-the-century Americans held towards Japan as an exotic world that, unlike China, had not lost its romantic allure through the reality of immigration. Unlike Sui Sin Far, who collected her short sketches into only one book, *Mrs. Spring Fragrance* (1912), Winnifred, under the pseudonym Onoto Watanna, wrote fifteen books, most of them romantic novels set in Japan. Sui Sin Far credits the editor of the *Land of Sunshine*, the California magazine that published her first Chinese stories, with providing a supportive context for her writing. Such support enabled her to resist both renouncing her Chinese identity as her sister had done and the equally pernicious alternative of trading on the stereotypes of her nationality. Sue Sin Far clearly understood the compromise this option imposed in saying, "If I wish to succeed in literature in America I should dress in Chinese costume, carry a fan in my hand, wear a pair of scarlet beaded slippers, live in New York, and come of high birth. Instead of making myself familiar with the Chinese-Americans around me, I should discourse on my spirit acquaintance with Chinese ancestors . . . ." ("Leaves" 132). The editor who helped her find her own voice was Charles Lummis, who was host to numerous turn-of-the-century writers at his Southern California ranch, including Mary Austin as well as Sui Sin Far.

Sui Sin Far shared with other regionalist writers the desire to find a form to express the experience of those living within her region. Although Mrs. Spring Fragrance finds the natural setting of Seattle beautiful, and although the Sing Song Woman lovingly recalls the landscape of her native China, Sui Sin Far's region is "the street below—a populous thoroughfare of Chinatown," the "unbeautiful" urban environment within which Chinese immigrants and second-generation Chinese-Americans seek to resolve the tensions of divided cultural identities and loyalties. Opposed to the exploitation of her region by local-color journalists, Sui Sin Far creates in " 'Its Wavering Image' " a devastating portrait of the American reporter who would "sell his soul for a story." When Mr. Spring Fragrance's neighbor identifies himself as an "honorary reporter" and asks to be the only white man present in order to write a piece titled "a high-class Chinese stag party," Mr. Spring Fragrance, absorbed with other matters, does not appear offended, though he does inquire whether the reporter's interests extend to "my brother in the Detention Pen." However, when Mark Carson publishes a "special-feature article" on life in Chinatown, the biracial Pan despises him for the betrayal which has "cruelly unveiled and ruthlessly spread before the ridiculing and uncomprehending foreigner" things "sacred and secret." " 'Its Wavering Image' " recalls other works, such as Chopin's "The Gentleman of Bayou Têche" and Jewett's "A White Heron," in which regionalist writers distinguish between the insider's portrait of regional life and the potential betrayal of the outsider whose perspective is that of the "local color" journalist.

In attempting to present the insider's view of the Chinese-American experience, Sui Sin Far offers literature, in contrast to journalism, as a way of interpreting one culture to another. Most of her fiction, like " 'Its Wavering Image,' " seeks to correct the profoundly inaccurate reading of the Chinese-American character contained in Mark Carson's "lesson" to Pan and to offer as her own lesson a more informed alternative reading. In Mrs. Spring Fragrance, Sui Sin Far creates a character who has defined for herself the role of cultural interpreter and mediator, not simply between the Chinese and the Americans but also between Americans of different classes. Despite her pretensions to being a "woman suffragist," Mrs. Carman rejects the "inferior woman," not because she is Chinese, but because she is uneducated, poor, and without identifiable family background. Although her attitudes towards Mrs.

Carman and Ethel Evebrook, the suffragist lecturer, may be ambivalent, Sui Sin Far, in contrast to other writers included in this anthology, includes women's political concerns as an explicit subject of fiction.

While her desire to help two star-crossed lovers motivates Mrs. Spring Fragrance to intervene on behalf of her neighbors, this conventional concern for romance can be seen as masking the radical challenge posed by her own perspective. Mrs. Spring Fragrance is not so much interested in interpreting the mysterious Chinese to the Americans; instead, gaining literary authority from the example of American women rather than from "the divine right of learning" embodied in the Chinese writers her husband shares with their neighbor, she intends to write a book "about Americans for her Chinese women friends. The American people were so interesting and mysterious." If Sui Sin Far in her fiction shifts the center of perception from the American reporter to the Chinese-American writer, Mrs. Spring Fragrance takes the process one step further by establishing the Chinese-American woman reader as the point of reference and by defining the Americans as exotic outsiders who need to be explained to her reader. Both Sui Sin Far and Mrs. Spring Fragrance show us that literature, in the hands of the Chinese-American woman, has the potential to translate between cultures and to promote empathy between people deemed "inferior" and those who consider themselves "superior."

Like Alice Dunbar-Nelson, Sui Sin Far explores the issue of racial ambiguity in her fiction, particularly as it is experienced by those of mixed racial background confronted by those who seek to order the world in absolute categories. Thus Mark Carson intends his lesson to redefine Pan as white; paradoxically, his lesson succeeds in "teaching" her that she is Chinese. Indeed, only Mrs. Spring Fragrance successfully negotiates cultural differences to create an identity that combines an admiration of things American—poetry (including the "noble American," the British poet Alfred, Lord Tennyson), American fudge, and American attitudes toward love and women's social roles—with things Chinese, as expressed by the traditions and rituals of a sophisticated Chinese woman. By her ability to convert both her Chinese and American friends, and even her husband, to her own way of thinking, Mrs. Spring Fragrance represents the power and appeal of the Chinese-American personality and stands no doubt as a version of Sui Sin Far herself. Yet " 'Its Wavering Image' " suggests the immense difficulties of withstanding the pressure to be either definitively Chinese or definitively American. In this context "The Sing Song Woman" may represent the ultimate fantasy of resolving the tension by reversing the process that originally brought the Chinese to America. Against this fantasy, however, we must set the image of Pan, who remains in America and for whom the negotiation of identity will be a daily struggle.

The Sing Song Woman

I

Ah Oi, the Chinese actress, threw herself down on the floor of her room and, propping her chin on her hands, gazed up at the narrow strip of blue sky which could be seen through her window. She seemed to have lost her usually merry spirits. For the first time since she had left her home her thoughts were seriously with the past, and she longed with a great longing for the Chinese Sea, the boats, and the wet, blowing sands. She had been a fisherman's daughter, and many a spring had she watched the gathering of the fishing fleet to which her father's boat belonged. Well could she remember clapping her hands as the vessels steered out to sea for the season's work, her father's amongst them, looking as bright as paint could make it, and flying a neat little flag at its stern; and well could she also remember how her mother had taught her to pray to "Our Lady of Pootoo,"[1] the goddess of sailors. One does not need to be a Christian to be religious, and Ah Oi's parents had carefully instructed their daughter according to their light, and it was not their fault if their daughter was a despised actress in an American Chinatown.

The sound of footsteps outside her door seemed to chase away Ah Oi's melancholy mood, and when a girl crossed her threshold, she was gazing amusedly into the street below—a populous thoroughfare of Chinatown.

The newcomer presented a strange appearance. She was crying so hard that red paint, white powder, and carmine lip salve were all besmeared over a naturally pretty face.

Ah Oi began to laugh.

"Why, Mag-gee," said she, "how odd you look with little red rivers running over your face! What is the matter?"

"What is the matter?" echoed Mag-gee, who was a half-white girl. "The matter is that I wish that I were dead! I am to be married tonight to a Chinaman whom I have never seen, and whom I can't bear. It isn't natural that I should. I always took to other men, and never could put up with a Chinaman. I was born in America, and I'm not Chinese in looks nor in any other way. See! My eyes are blue, and there is gold in my hair; and I love potatoes and beef, and every time I eat rice it makes me sick, and so does chopped up food. He came down about a week ago and made arrangements with father, and now everything is fixed and I'm going away forever to live in China. I shall be a Chinese woman next year—I commenced to be one today, when father made me put the paint and powder on my face, and dress in Chinese clothes. Oh! I never want anyone to feel as I do. To think of having to marry a Chinaman! How I hate the Chinese! And the worst of it is, loving somebody else all the while."

The girl burst into passionate sobs. The actress, who was evidently accustomed to hearing her compatriots reviled by the white and half-white denizens of Chinatown, laughed—a light, rippling laugh. Her eyes glinted mischievously.

"Since you do not like the Chinese men," said she, "why do you give

1. P'Ut'O, an island sacred to Buddhists, where visions of the goddess were reported in 847 A.D.; it became a resort for pilgrims and a site for numerous monasteries and temples.

yourself to one? And if you care so much for somebody else, why do you not fly to that somebody?"

Bold words for a Chinese woman to utter! But Ah Oi was not as other Chinese women, who all their lives have been sheltered by a husband or father's care.

The half-white girl stared at her companion.

"What do you mean?" she asked.

"This," said Ah Oi. The fair head and dark head drew near together; and two women passing the door heard whispers and suppressed laughter.

"Ah Oi is up to some trick," said one.

II

"The Sing Song Woman! The Sing Song Woman!" It was a wild cry of anger and surprise.

The ceremony of unveiling the bride had just been performed, and Hwuy Yen, the father of Mag-gee, and his friends, were in a state of great excitement, for the unveiled, brilliantly clothed little figure standing in the middle of the room was not the bride who was to have been; but Ah Oi, the actress, the Sing Song Woman.

Every voice but one was raised. The bridegroom, a tall, handsome man, did not understand what had happened, and could find no words to express his surprise at the uproar. But he was so newly wedded that it was not until Hwuy Yen advanced to the bride and shook his hand threateningly in her face, that he felt himself a husband, and interfered by placing himself before the girl.

"What is all this?" he inquired. "What has my wife done to merit such abuse?"

"Your wife!" scornfully ejaculated Hwuy Yen. "She is no wife of yours. You were to have married my daughter, Mag-gee. This is not my daughter; this is an impostor, an actress, a Sing Song Woman. Where is my daughter?"

Ah Oi laughed her peculiar, rippling, amused laugh. She was in no wise abashed, and, indeed, appeared to be enjoying the situation. Her bright, defiant eyes met her questioner's boldly as she answered:

"Mag-gee has gone to eat beef and potatoes with a white man. Oh, we had such a merry time making this play!"

"See how worthless a thing she is," said Hwuy Yen to the young bridegroom.

The latter regarded Ah Oi compassionately. He was a man, and perhaps a little tenderness crept into his heart for the girl towards whom so much bitterness was evinced. She was beautiful. He drew near to her.

"Can you not justify yourself?" he asked sadly.

For a moment Ah Oi gazed into his eyes—the only eyes that had looked with true kindness into hers for many a moon.

"You justify me," she replied with an upward, pleading glance.

Then Ke Leang, the bridegroom, spoke. He said: "The daughter of Hwuy Yen cared not to become my bride and has sought her happiness with another. Ah Oi, having a kind heart, helped her to that happiness, and tried to recompense me my loss by giving me herself. She has been unwise and indiscreet; but the good that is in her is more than the evil, and now that she is my wife, none shall say a word against her."

Ah Oi pulled at his sleeve.

"You give me credit for what I do not deserve," said she. "I had no kind feelings. I thought only of mischief, and I am not your wife. It is but a play like the play I shall act tomorrow."

"Hush!" bade Ke Leang. "You shall act no more. I will marry you again and take you to China."

Then something in Ah Oi's breast, which for a long time had been hard as stone, became soft and tender, and her eyes ran over with tears.

"Oh, sir," said she, "it takes a heart to make a heart, and you have put one today in the bosom of a Sing Song Woman."

Land of Sunshine, October 1898; *Mrs. Spring Fragrance*, 1912

Mrs. Spring Fragrance

I

When Mrs. Spring Fragrance first arrived in Seattle, she was unacquainted with even one word of the American language. Five years later her husband, speaking of her, said: "There are no more American words for her learning." And everyone who knew Mrs. Spring Fragrance agreed with Mr. Spring Fragrance.

Mr. Spring Fragrance, whose business name was Sing Yook, was a young curio merchant. Though conservatively Chinese in many respects, he was at the same time what is called by the Westerners, "Americanized." Mrs. Spring Fragrance was even more "Americanized."

Next door to the Spring Fragrances lived the Chin Yuens. Mrs. Chin Yuen was much older than Mrs. Spring Fragrance; but she had a daughter of eighteen with whom Mrs. Spring Fragrance was on terms of great friendship. The daughter was a pretty girl whose Chinese name was Mai Gwi Far (a rose) and whose American name was Laura. Nearly everybody called her Laura, even her parents and Chinese friends. Laura had a sweetheart, a youth named Kai Tzu. Kai Tzu, who was American-born, and as ruddy and stalwart as any young Westerner, was noted amongst baseball players as one of the finest pitchers on the Coast. He could also sing, "Drink to me only with thine eyes," to Laura's piano accompaniment.

Now the only person who knew that Kai Tzu loved Laura and that Laura loved Kai Tzu, was Mrs. Spring Fragrance. The reason for this was that, although the Chin Yuen parents lived in a house furnished in American style, and wore American clothes, yet they religiously observed many Chinese customs, and their ideals of life were the ideals of their Chinese forefathers. Therefore, they had betrothed their daughter, Laura, at the age of fifteen, to the eldest son of the Chinese Government school-teacher in San Francisco. The time for the consummation of the betrothal was approaching.

Laura was with Mrs. Spring Fragrance and Mrs. Spring Fragrance was trying to cheer her.

"I had such a pretty walk today," said she. "I crossed the banks above the beach and came back by the long road. In the green grass the daffodils were blowing, in the cottage gardens the currant bushes were flowering, and in the air was the perfume of the wallflower. I wished, Laura, that you were with me."

Laura burst into tears. "That is the walk," she sobbed, "Kai Tzu and I so love; but never, ah, never, can we take it together again."

"Now, Little Sister," comforted Mrs. Spring Fragrance "you really must not grieve like that. Is there not a beautiful American poem written by a noble American named Tennyson, which says:

> " 'Tis better to have loved and lost,
> Than never to have loved at all"?[1]

Mrs. Spring Fragrance was unaware that Mr. Spring Fragrance, having returned from the city, tired with the day's business, had thrown himself down on the bamboo settee on the veranda, and that although his eyes were engaged in scanning the pages of the *Chinese World,* his ears could not help receiving the words which were borne to him through the open window.

> " 'Tis better to have loved and lost,
> Than never to have loved at all,"

repeated Mr. Spring Fragrance. Not wishing to hear more of the secret talk of women, he arose and sauntered around the veranda to the other side of the house. Two pigeons circled around his head. He felt in his pocket for a li-chi[2] which he usually carried for their pecking. His fingers touched a little box. It contained a jadestone pendant, which Mrs. Spring Fragrance had particularly admired the last time she was down town. It was the fifth anniversary of Mr. and Mrs. Spring Fragrance's wedding day.

Mr. Spring Fragrance pressed the little box down into the depths of his pocket.

1. Alfred, Lord Tennyson, *In Memoriam.*
2. The fruit of the Chinese Pi-chi tree; also called "litchi nut."

A young man came out of the back door of the house at Mr. Spring Fragrance's left. The Chin Yuen house was at his right.

"Good evening," said the young man. "Good evening," returned Mr. Spring Fragrance. He stepped down from his porch and went and leaned over the railing which separated this yard from the yard in which stood the young man.

"Will you please tell me," said Mr. Spring Fragrance, "the meaning of two lines of an American verse which I have heard?"

"Certainly," returned the young man with a genial smile. He was a star student at the University of Washington, and had not the slightest doubt that he could explain the meaning of all things in the universe.

"Well," said Mr. Spring Fragrance, "it is this:

> " 'Tis better to have loved and lost,
> Than never to have loved at all."

"Ah!" responded the young man with an air of profound wisdom. "That, Mr. Spring Fragrance, means that it is a good thing to love anyway—even if we can't get what we love, or, as the poet tells us, lose what we love. Of course, one needs experience to feel the truth of this teaching."

The young man smiled pensively and reminiscently. More than a dozen young maidens "loved and lost" were passing before his mind's eye.

"The truth of the teaching!" echoed Mr. Spring Fragrance, a little testily. "There is no truth in it whatever. It is disobedient to reason. Is it not better to have what you do not love than to love what you do not have?"

"That depends," answered the young man, "upon temperament."

"I thank you. Good evening," said Mr. Spring Fragrance. He turned away to muse upon the unwisdom of the American way of looking at things.

Meanwhile, inside the house, Laura was refusing to be comforted.

"Ah, no! no!" cried she. "If I had not gone to school with Kai Tzu, nor talked nor walked with him, nor played the accompaniments to his songs, then I might consider with complacency, or at least without horror, my approaching marriage with the son of Man You. But as it is—oh, as it is—!"

The girl rocked herself to and fro in heart-felt grief.

Mrs. Spring Fragrance knelt down beside her, and clasping her arms around her neck, cried in sympathy:

"Little Sister, oh, Little Sister! Dry your tears—do not despair. A moon has yet to pass before the marriage can take place. Who knows what the stars may have to say to one another during its passing? A little bird has whispered to me—"

For a long time Mrs. Spring Fragrance talked. For a long time Laura listened. When the girl arose to go, there was a bright light in her eyes.

II

Mrs. Spring Fragrance, in San Francisco on a visit to her cousin, the wife of the herb doctor of Clay Street, was having a good time. She was invited everywhere that the wife of an honorable Chinese merchant could go. There was much to see and hear, including more than a dozen babies who had been born in the families of her friends since she last visited the city of the Golden Gate. Mrs. Spring Fragrance loved babies. She had had two herself, but both had been transplanted into the spirit land before the completion of even one moon. There were also many dinners and theatre-parties given in her honor. It was at one of the theatre-parties that Mrs. Spring Fragrance met Ah Oi, a young girl who had the reputation of being the prettiest Chinese girl in San Francisco, and the naughtiest. In spite of gossip, however, Mrs. Spring Fragrance took a great fancy to Ah Oi and invited her to a tête-à-tête[3] picnic on the following day. This invitation Ah Oi joyfully accepted. She was a sort of bird girl and never felt so happy as when out in the park or woods.

On the day after the picnic Mrs. Spring Fragrance wrote to Laura Chin Yuen thus:

My Precious Laura,—May the bamboo ever wave. Next week I accompany Ah Oi to the beauteous town of San José. There will we be met by the son of the Illustrious Teacher, and in a little Mission, presided over by a benevolent American priest, the little Ah Oi and the son of the Illustrious Teacher will be joined together in love and harmony— two pieces of music made to complete one another.

The Son of the Illustrious Teacher, having been through an American Hall of Learning, is well able to provide for his orphan bride and fears not the displeasure of his parents, now that he is assured that your grief at his loss will not be inconsolable. He wishes me to waft to you and to Kai Tzu—and the little Ah Oi joins with him—ten thousand rainbow wishes for your happiness.

My respects to your honorable parents, and to yourself, the heart of your loving friend,

Jade Spring Fragrance

To Mr. Spring Fragrance, Mrs. Spring Fragrance also indited a letter:

Great and Honored Man,—Greeting from your plum blossom,[4] who is desirous of hiding herself from the sun of your presence for a week of seven days more. My honorable cousin is preparing for the Fifth Moon

---

3. Private meeting between two persons.
4. The plum blossom is the Chinese flower of virtue. It has been adopted by the Japanese, just in the same way as they have adopted the Chinese national flower, the chrysanthemum [Sui Sin Far's note].

Festival,[5] and wishes me to compound for the occasion some American "fudge," for which delectable sweet, made by my clumsy hands, you have sometimes shown a slight prejudice. I am enjoying a most agreeable visit, and American friends, as also our own, strive benevolently for the accomplishment of my pleasure. Mrs. Samuel Smith, an American lady, known to my cousin, asked for my accompaniment to a magniloquent lecture the other evening. The subject was "America, the Protector of China!" It was most exhilarating, and the effect of so much expression of benevolence leads me to beg of you to forget to remember that the barber charges you one dollar for a shave while he humbly submits to the American man a bill of fifteen cents. And murmur no more because your honored elder brother, on a visit to this country, is detained under the roof-tree of this great Government instead of under your own humble roof. Console him with the reflection that he is protected under the wing of the Eagle, the Emblem of Liberty. What is the loss of ten hundred years or ten thousand times ten dollars compared with the happiness of knowing oneself so securely sheltered? All of this I have learned from Mrs. Samuel Smith, who is as brilliant and great of mind as one of your own superior sex.

For me it is sufficient to know that the Golden Gate Park is most enchanting, and the seals on the rock at the Cliff House extremely entertaining and amiable. There is much feasting and merry-making under the lanterns in honor of your Stupid Thorn.

I have purchased for your smoking a pipe with an amber mouth. It is said to be very sweet to the lips and to emit a cloud of smoke fit for the gods to inhale.

Awaiting, by the wonderful wire of the telegram message, your gracious permission to remain for the celebration of the Fifth Moon Festival and the making of American "fudge," I continue for ten thousand times ten thousand years,

Your ever loving and obedient woman,

Jade

P.S. Forget not to care for the cat, the birds, and the flowers. Do not eat too quickly nor fan too vigorously now that the weather is warming.

Mrs. Spring Fragrance smiled as she folded this last epistle. Even if he were old-fashioned, there was never a husband so good and kind as hers. Only on one occasion since their marriage had he slighted her wishes. That was when, on the last anniversary of their wedding, she had signified a desire for a certain jadestone pendant, and he had failed to satisfy that desire.

But Mrs. Spring Fragrance, being of a happy nature, and disposed

---

5. The great summer festival in Chinese culture, which occurs on the fifth day of the fifth moon and celebrates the fertilizing rain; sometimes called the Dragon Boat festival.

to look upon the bright side of things, did not allow her mind to dwell upon the jadestone pendant. Instead, she gazed complacently down upon her bejeweled fingers and folded in with her letter to Mr. Spring Fragrance a bright little sheaf of condensed love.

III

Mr. Spring Fragrance sat on his doorstep. He had been reading two letters, one from Mrs. Spring Fragrance, and the other from an elderly bachelor cousin in San Francisco. The one from the elderly bachelor cousin was a business letter, but contained the following postscript:

Tsen Hing, the son of the Government school-master, seems to be much in the company of your young wife. He is a good-looking youth, and pardon me, my dear cousin; but if women are allowed to stray at will from under their husbands' mulberry roofs, what is to prevent them from becoming butterflies?

"Sing Foon is old and cynical," said Mr. Spring Fragrance to himself. "Why should I pay any attention to him? This is America, where a man may speak to a woman, and a woman listen, without any thought of evil."

He destroyed his cousin's letter and re-read his wife's. Then he became very thoughtful. Was the making of American fudge sufficient reason for a wife to wish to remain a week longer in a city where her husband was not?

The young man who lived in the next house came out to water the lawn.

"Good evening," said he. "Any news from Mrs. Spring Fragrance?"

"She is having a very good time," returned Mr. Spring Fragrance.

"Glad to hear it. I think you told me she was to return the end of this week."

"I have changed my mind about her," said Mr. Spring Fragrance. "I am bidding her remain a week longer, as I wish to give a smoking party during her absence. I hope I may have the pleasure of your company."

"I shall be delighted," returned the young fellow. "But, Mr. Spring Fragrance, don't invite any other white fellows. If you do not I shall be able to get in a scoop. You know, I'm a sort of honorary reporter for the *Gleaner*."

"Very well," absently answered Mr. Spring Fragrance.

"Of course, your friend the Consul will be present. I shall call it 'A high-class Chinese stag party!'"

In spite of his melancholy mood, Mr. Spring Fragrance smiled.

"Everything is 'high-class' in America," he observed.

"Sure!" cheerfully assented the young man. "Haven't you ever heard that all Americans are princes and princesses, and just as soon as a foreigner puts his foot upon our shores, he also becomes of the nobility—I mean, the royal family."

"What about my brother in the Detention Pen?"[6] dryly inquired Mr. Spring Fragrance.

"Now, you've got me," said the young man, rubbing his head. "Well, that is a shame—'a beastly shame,' as the Englishman says. But understand, old fellow, we that are real Americans are up against that—even more than you. It is against our principles."

"I offer the real Americans my consolations that they should be compelled to do that which is against their principles."

"Oh, well, it will all come right some day. We're not a bad sort, you know. Think of the indemnity money returned to the Dragon by Uncle Sam."[7]

Mr. Spring Fragrance puffed his pipe in silence for some moments. More than politics was troubling his mind.

At last he spoke. "Love," said he, slowly and distinctly, "comes before the wedding in this country, does it not?"

"Yes, certainly."

Young Carman knew Mr. Spring Fragrance well enough to receive with calmness his most astounding queries.

"Presuming," continued Mr. Spring Fragrance—"presuming that some friend of your father's, living—presuming—in England—has a daughter that he arranges with your father to be your wife. Presuming that you have never seen that daughter, but that you marry her, knowing her not. Presuming that she marries you, knowing you not.—After she marries you and knows you, will that woman love you?"

"Emphatically, no," answered the young man.

"That is the way it would be in America—that the woman who marries the man like that—would not love him?"

"Yes, that is the way it would be in America. Love, in this country, must be free, or it is not love at all."

"In China, it is different!" mused Mr. Spring Fragrance.

"Oh, yes, I have no doubt that in China it is different."

"But the love is in the heart all the same," went on Mr. Spring Fragrance.

"Yes, all the same. Everybody falls in love some time or another. Some"—pensively—"many times."

Mr. Spring Fragrance arose.

"I must go down town," said he.

As he walked down the street he recalled the remark of a business acquaintance who had met his wife and had had some conversation with her: "She is just like an American woman."

He had felt somewhat flattered when this remark had been made. He looked upon it as a compliment to his wife's cleverness; but it

---

6. During the late 19th and early 20th centuries, when Chinese persons, primarily men, attempted to secure papers to work in California, they were taken to Angel Island in San Francisco Bay for questioning by officials of the Immigration Service; many remained imprisoned on Angel Island for months.

7. As indemnity for foreign lives and property destroyed in the Boxer Uprising (1898–1901), the Qing government agreed to pay foreign governments the sum of $333 million in gold. The U.S. returned half its portion as scholarship money to educate Chinese in American colleges.

rankled in his mind as he entered the telegraph office. If his wife was becoming as an American woman, would it not be possible for her to love as an American woman—a man to whom she was not married? There also floated in his memory the verse which his wife had quoted to the daughter of Chin Yuen. When the telegraph clerk handed him a blank, he wrote this message:

"Remain as you wish, but remember that ' 'Tis better to have loved and lost, than never to have loved at all.' "

◦ ◦ ◦

When Mrs. Spring Fragrance received this message, her laughter tinkled like falling water. How droll! How delightful! Here was her husband quoting American poetry in a telegram. Perhaps he had been reading her American poetry books since she had left him! She hoped so. They would lead him to understand her sympathy for her dear Laura and Kai Tzu. She need no longer keep from him their secret. How joyful! It had been such a hardship to refrain from confiding in him before. But discreetness had been most necessary, seeing that Mr. Spring Fragrance entertained as old-fashioned notions concerning marriage as did the Chin Yuen parents. Strange that that should be so, since he had fallen in love with her picture before *ever* he had seen her, just as she had fallen in love with his! And when the marriage veil was lifted and each beheld the other for the first time in the flesh, there had been no disillusion—no lessening of the respect and affection, which those who had brought about the marriage had inspired in each young heart.

Mrs. Spring Fragrance began to wish she could fall asleep and wake to find the week flown, and she in her own little home pouring tea for Mr. Spring Fragrance.

IV

Mr. Spring Fragrance was walking to business with Mr. Chin Yuen. As they walked they talked.

"Yes," said Mr. Chin Yuen, "the old order is passing away, and the new order is taking its place, even with us who are Chinese. I have finally consented to give my daughter in marriage to young Kai Tzu."

Mr. Spring Fragrance expressed surprise. He had understood that the marriage between his neighbor's daughter and the San Francisco school-teacher's son was all arranged.

"So 'twas," answered Mr. Chin Yuen; "but it seems the young renegade, without consultation or advice, has placed his affections upon some untrustworthy female, and is so under her influence that he refuses to fulfil his parents' promise to me for him."

"So!" said Mr. Spring Fragrance. The shadow on his brow deepened.

"But," said Mr. Chin Yuen, with affable resignation, "it is all ordained by Heaven. Our daughter, as the wife of Kai Tzu, for whom she has long had a loving feeling, will not now be compelled to dwell with a mother-in-law and where her own mother is not. For that, we are thankful, as she is our only one and the conditions of life in this Western country are not as in China. Moreover, Kai Tzu, though not so much of a scholar as the teacher's son, has a keen eye for business and that, in America, is certainly much more desirable than scholarship. What do you think?"

"Eh! What!" exclaimed Mr. Spring Fragrance. The latter part of his companion's remarks had been lost upon him.

That day the shadow which had been following Mr. Spring Fragrance ever since he had heard his wife quote, " 'Tis better to have loved," etc., became so heavy and deep that he quite lost himself within it.

At home in the evening he fed the cat, the bird, and the flowers. Then, seating himself in a carved black chair—a present from his wife on his last birthday—he took out his pipe and smoked. The cat jumped into his lap. He stroked it softly and tenderly. It had been much fondled by Mrs. Spring Fragrance, and Mr. Spring Fragrance was under the impression that it missed her. "Poor thing!" said he. "I suppose you want her back!" When he arose to go to bed he placed the animal carefully on the floor, and thus apostrophized it:

"O Wise and Silent One, your mistress returns to you, but her heart she leaves behind her, with the Tommies[8] in San Francisco."

The Wise and Silent One made no reply. He was not a jealous cat.

Mr. Spring Fragrance slept not that night; the next morning he ate not. Three days and three nights without sleep and food went by.

There was a springlike freshness in the air on the day that Mrs. Spring Fragrance came home. The skies overhead were as blue as Puget Sound stretching its gleaming length toward the mighty Pacific, and all the beautiful green world seemed to be throbbing with springing life.

Mrs. Spring Fragrance was never so radiant.

"Oh," she cried light-heartedly, "is it not lovely to see the sun shining so clear, and everything so bright to welcome me?"

Mr. Spring Fragrance made no response. It was the morning after the fourth sleepless night.

Mrs. Spring Fragrance noticed his silence, also his grave face.

"Everything—everyone is glad to see me but you," she declared, half seriously, half jestingly.

Mr. Spring Fragrance set down her valise. They had just entered the house.

"If my wife is glad to see me," he quietly replied, "I also am glad to see her!"

Summoning their servant boy, he bade him look after Mrs. Spring Fragrance's comfort.

---

8. Slang for British soldiers; here, slang for Americans of English extraction.

"I must be at the store in half an hour," said he, looking at his watch. "There is some very important business requiring attention."

"What is the business?" inquired Mrs. Spring Fragrance, her lip quivering with disappointment.

"I cannot just explain to you," answered her husband.

Mrs. Spring Fragrance looked up into his face with honest and earnest eyes. There was something in his manner, in the tone of her husband's voice, which touched her.

"Yen," said she, "you do not look well. You are not well. What is it?"

Something arose in Mr. Spring Fragrance's throat which prevented him from replying.

"O darling one! O sweetest one!" cried a girl's joyous voice. Laura Chin Yuen ran into the room and threw her arms around Mrs. Spring Fragrance's neck.

"I spied you from the window," said Laura, "and I couldn't rest until I told you. We are to be married next week, Kai Tzu and I. And all through you, all through you—the sweetest jade jewel in the world!"

Mr. Spring Fragrance passed out of the room.

"So the son of the Government teacher and little Happy Love are already married," Laura went on, relieving Mrs. Spring Fragrance of her cloak, her hat, and her folding fan.

Mr. Spring Fragrance paused upon the doorstep.

"Sit down, Little Sister, and I will tell you all about it," said Mrs. Spring Fragrance, forgetting her husband for a moment.

When Laura Chin Yuen had danced away, Mr. Spring Fragrance came in and hung up his hat.

"You got back very soon," said Mrs. Spring Fragrance, covertly wiping away the tears which had begun to fall as soon as she thought herself alone.

"I did not go," answered Mr. Spring Fragrance. "I have been listening to you and Laura."

"But if the business is very important, do not you think you should attend to it?" anxiously queried Mrs. Spring Fragrance.

"It is not important to me now," returned Mr. Spring Fragrance. "I would prefer to hear again about Ah Oi and Man You and Laura and Kai Tzu."

"How lovely of you to say that!" exclaimed Mrs. Spring Fragrance, who was easily made happy. And she began to chat away to her husband in the friendliest and wifeliest fashion possible. When she had finished she asked him if he were not glad to hear that those who loved as did the young lovers whose secrets she had been keeping, were to be united; and he replied that indeed he was; that he would like every man to be as happy with a wife as he himself had ever been and ever would be.

"You did not always talk like that," said Mrs. Spring Fragrance slyly. "You must have been reading my American poetry books!"

"American poetry!" ejaculated Mr. Spring Fragrance almost fiercely, "American poetry is detestable, *abhorrable!*"

"Why! why!" exclaimed Mrs. Spring Fragrance, more and more surprised.

But the only explanation which Mr. Spring Fragrance vouchsafed was a jadestone pendant.

Hampton, January 1910; *Mrs. Spring Fragrance*, 1912

The Inferior Woman

I

Mrs. Spring Fragrance walked through the leafy alleys of the park, admiring the flowers and listening to the birds singing. It was a beautiful afternoon with the warmth from the sun cooled by a refreshing breeze. As she walked along she meditated upon a book which she had some notion of writing. Many American women wrote books. Why should not a Chinese? She would write a book about Americans for her Chinese women friends. The American people were so interesting and mysterious. Something of pride and pleasure crept into Mrs. Spring Fragrance's heart as she pictured Fei and Sie and Mai Gwi Far listening to Lae-Choo reading her illuminating paragraphs.

As she turned down a by-path she saw Will Carman, her American neighbor's son, coming towards her, and by his side a young girl who seemed to belong to the sweet air and brightness of all the things around her. They were talking very earnestly and the eyes of the young man were on the girl's face.

"Ah!" murmured Mrs. Spring Fragrance, after one swift glance. "It is love."

She retreated behind a syringa bush, which completely screened her from view.

Up the winding path went the young couple.

"It is love," repeated Mrs. Spring Fragrance, "and it is the 'Inferior Woman.' "

She had heard about the Inferior Woman from the mother of Will Carman.

After tea that evening Mrs. Spring Fragrance stood musing at her front window. The sun hovered over the Olympic mountains like a great, golden red-bird with dark purple wings, its long tail of light trailing underneath in the waters of Puget Sound.

"How very beautiful!" exclaimed Mrs. Spring Fragrance; then she sighed.

"Why do you sigh?" asked Mr. Spring Fragrance.

"My heart is sad," answered his wife.

"Is the cat sick?" inquired Mr. Spring Fragrance.

Mrs. Spring Fragrance shook her head. "It is not our Wise One who troubles me today," she replied. "It is our neighbors. The sorrow of the

Carman household is that the mother desires for her son the Superior
Woman, and his heart enshrines but the Inferior. I have seen them
together today, and I know."

"What do you know?"

"That the Inferior Woman is the mate for young Carman."

Mr. Spring Fragrance elevated his brows. Only the day before, his
wife's arguments had all been in favor of the Superior Woman. He
uttered some words expressive of surprise, to which Mrs. Spring Fragrance retorted:

"Yesterday, O Great Man, I was a caterpillar!"

Just then young Carman came strolling up the path. Mr. Spring
Fragrance opened the door to him. "Come in, neighbor," said he. "I
have received some new books from Shanghai."

"Good," replied young Carman, who was interested in Chinese
literature. While he and Mr. Spring Fragrance discussed the "Odes of
Chow" and the "Sorrows of Han,"[1] Mrs. Spring Fragrance, sitting in
a low easy-chair of rose-colored silk, covertly studied her visitor's
countenance. Why was his expression so much more grave than gay?
It had not been so a year ago—before he had known the Inferior
Woman. Mrs. Spring Fragrance noted other changes, also, both in
speech and manner. "He is no longer a boy," mused she. "He is a man,
and it is the work of the Inferior Woman."

"And when, Mr. Carman," she inquired, "will you bring home a
daughter to your mother?"

"And when, Mrs. Spring Fragrance, do you think I should?" returned the young man.

Mrs. Spring Fragrance spread wide her fan and gazed thoughtfully
over its silver edge.

"The summer moons will soon be over," said she. "You should not
wait until the grass is yellow."

> "The woodmen's blows responsive ring,
> As on the trees they fall,
> And when the birds their sweet notes sing,
> They to each other call.
> From the dark valley comes a bird,
> And seeks the lofty tree,
> Ying goes its voice, and thus it cries:
> 'Companion, come to me.'
> The bird, although a creature small,
> Upon its mate depends,
> And shall we men, who rank o'er all,
> Not seek to have our friends?"[2]

quoted Mr. Spring Fragrance.

Mrs. Spring Fragrance tapped his shoulder approvingly with her fan.

1. Classical Chinese works. "Odes of Chow," presumably a reference to classical Chinese poetry of
the Chow Dynasty (1122–255 B.C.); writers Lao Tzu,
Confucius, and Mencius all belong to this period;
"Sorrows of Han": presumably a reference to classical Chinese poetry of the Han Dynasty (202 B.C.–220
A.D.).
2. From The Book of Songs, ancient Chinese poetry.

"I perceive," said young Carman, "that you are both allied against my peace."

"It is for your mother," replied Mrs. Spring Fragrance soothingly. "She will be happy when she knows that your affections are fixed by marriage."

There was a slight gleam of amusement in the young man's eyes as he answered: "But if my mother has no wish for a daughter—at least, no wish for the daughter I would want to give her?"

"When I first came to America," returned Mrs. Spring Fragrance, "my husband desired me to wear the American dress. I protested and declared that never would I so appear. But one day he brought home a gown fit for a fairy, and ever since then I have worn and adored the American dress."

"Mrs. Spring Fragrance," declared young Carman, "your argument is incontrovertible."

II

A young man with a determined set to his shoulders stood outside the door of a little cottage perched upon a bluff overlooking the Sound. The chill sea air was sweet with the scent of roses, and he drew in a deep breath of inspiration before he knocked.

"Are you not surprised to see me?" he inquired of the young person who opened the door.

"Not at all," replied the young person demurely.

He gave her a quick almost fierce look. At their last parting he had declared that he would not come again unless she requested him, and that she assuredly had not done.

"I wish I could make you feel," said he.

She laughed—a pretty infectious laugh which exorcised all his gloom. He looked down upon her as they stood together under the cluster of electric lights in her cozy little sitting-room. Such a slender, girlish figure! Such a soft cheek, red mouth, and firm little chin! Often in his dreams of her he had taken her into his arms and coaxed her into a good humor. But, alas! dreams are not realities, and the calm friendliness of this young person made any demonstration of tenderness well-nigh impossible. But for the shy regard of her eyes, you might have thought that he was no more to her than a friendly acquaintance.

"I hear," said she, taking up some needlework, "that your Welland case comes on tomorrow."

"Yes," answered the young lawyer, "and I have all my witnesses ready."

"So, I hear, has Mr. Greaves," she retorted. "You are going to have a hard fight."

"What of that, when in the end I'll win."

He looked over at her with a bright gleam in his eyes.

"I wouldn't be too sure," she warned demurely. "You may lose on a technicality."

He drew his chair a little nearer to her side and turned over the pages of a book lying on her work-table. On the fly-leaf[3] was inscribed in a man's writing: "To the dear little woman whose friendship is worth a fortune."

Another book beside it bore the inscription: "With the love of all the firm, including the boys," and a volume of poems above it was dedicated to the young person "with the high regards and stanch affection" of some other masculine person.

Will Carman pushed aside these evidences of his sweetheart's popularity with his own kind and leaned across the table.

"Alice," said he, "once upon a time you admitted that you loved me."

A blush suffused the young person's countenance.

"Did I?" she queried.

"You did, indeed."

"Well?"

"Well! If you love me and I love you—"

"Oh, please!" protested the girl, covering her ears with her hands.

"I *will* please," asserted the young man. "I have come here tonight, Alice, to ask you to marry me—and at once."

"Deary me!" exclaimed the young person; but she let her needlework fall into her lap as her lover, approaching nearer, laid his arm around her shoulders and, bending his face close to hers, pleaded his most important case.

If for a moment the small mouth quivered, the firm little chin lost its firmness, and the proud little head yielded to the pressure of a lover's arm, it was only for a moment so brief and fleeting that Will Carman had hardly become aware of it before it had passed.

"No," said the young person sorrowfully but decidedly. She had arisen and was standing on the other side of the table facing him. "I cannot marry you while your mother regards me as beneath you."

"When she knows you she will acknowledge you are above me. But I am not asking you to come to my mother, I am asking you to come to me, dear. If you will put your hand in mine and trust to me through all the coming years, no man or woman born can come between us."

But the young person shook her head.

"No," she repeated. "I will not be your wife unless your mother welcomes me with pride and with pleasure."

The night air was still sweet with the perfume of roses as Will Carman passed out of the little cottage door; but he drew in no deep breath of inspiration. His impetuous Irish heart was too heavy with disappointment. It might have been a little lighter, however, had he known that the eyes of the young person who gazed after him were misty with a love and yearning beyond expression.

---

3. A blank leaf at the beginning or end of a book.

III

"Will Carman has failed to snare his bird," said Mr. Spring Fragrance to Mrs. Spring Fragrance. Their neighbor's son had just passed their veranda without turning to bestow upon them his usual cheerful greeting.

"It is too bad," sighed Mrs. Spring Fragrance sympathetically. She clasped her hands together and exclaimed:

"Ah, these Americans! These mysterious, inscrutable, incomprehensible Americans! Had I the divine right of learning I would put them into an immortal book!"

"The divine right of learning," echoed Mr. Spring Fragrance, "Humph!"

Mrs. Spring Fragrance looked up into her husband's face in wonderment.

"Is not the authority of the scholar, the student, almost divine?" she queried.

"So 'tis said," responded he. "So it seems."

The evening before, Mr. Spring Fragrance, together with several Seattle and San Francisco merchants, had given a dinner to a number of young students who had just arrived from China. The morning papers had devoted several columns to laudation of the students, prophecies as to their future, and the great influence which they would exercise over the destiny of their nation; but no comment whatever was made on the givers of the feast, and Mr. Spring Fragrance was therefore feeling somewhat unappreciated. Were not he and his brother merchants worthy of a little attention? If the students had come to learn things in America, they, the merchants, had accomplished things. There were those amongst them who had been instrumental in bringing several of the students to America. One of the boys was Mr. Spring Fragrance's own young brother, for whose maintenance and education he had himself sent the wherewithal every year for many years. Mr. Spring Fragrance, though well read in the Chinese classics, was not himself a scholar. As a boy he had come to the shores of America, worked his way up, and by dint of painstaking study after working hours acquired the Western language and Western business ideas. He had made money, saved money, and sent money home. The years had flown, his business had grown. Through his efforts trade between his native town and the port city in which he lived had greatly increased. A school in Canton[4] was being builded in part with funds furnished by him, and a railway syndicate, for the purpose of constructing a line of railway from the big city of Canton to his own native town, was under process of formation, with the name of Spring Fragrance at its head.

---

4. The capital of Kwangtung Province in southeastern China and the first Chinese port to which foreign trade was attracted; during the late 19th century, the city from which generations of Chinese men emigrated to work in the U.S.

No wonder then that Mr. Spring Fragrance muttered "Humph!" when Mrs. Spring Fragrance dilated upon the "divine right of learning," and that he should feel irritated and humiliated, when, after explaining to her his grievances, she should quote in the words of Confutze:[5] "Be not concerned that men do not know you; be only concerned that you do not know them." And he had expected wifely sympathy.

He was about to leave the room in a somewhat chilled state of mind when she surprised him again by pattering across to him and following up a low curtsy with these words:

"I bow to you as the grass bends to the wind. Allow me to detain you for just one moment."

Mr. Spring Fragrance eyed her for a moment with suspicion.

"As I have told you, O Great Man," continued Mrs. Spring Fragrance, "I desire to write an immortal book, and now that I have learned from you that it is not necessary to acquire the 'divine right of learning' in order to accomplish things, I will begin the work without delay. My first subject will be 'The Inferior Woman of America.' Please advise me how I shall best inform myself concerning her."

Mr. Spring Fragrance, perceiving that his wife was now serious, and being easily mollified, sat himself down and rubbed his head. After thinking for a few moments he replied:

"It is the way in America, when a person is to be illustrated, for the illustrator to interview the person's friends. Perhaps, my dear, you had better confer with the Superior Woman."

"Surely," cried Mrs. Spring Fragrance, "no sage was ever so wise as my Great Man."

"But I lack the 'divine right of learning,' " dryly deplored Mr. Spring Fragrance.

"I am happy to hear it," answered Mrs. Spring Fragrance. "If you were a scholar you would have no time to read American poetry and American newspapers."

Mr. Spring Fragrance laughed heartily.

"You are no Chinese woman," he teased. "You are an American."

"Please bring me my parasol and my folding fan," said Mrs. Spring Fragrance. "I am going out for a walk."

And Mr. Spring Fragrance obeyed her.

IV

"This is from Mary Carman, who is in Portland," said the mother of the Superior Woman, looking up from the reading of a letter, as her daughter came in from the garden.

"Indeed," carelessly responded Miss Evebrook.

"Yes, it's chiefly about Will."

5. Confucius (551–479 B.C.), Chinese philosopher.

"Oh, is it? Well, read it then, dear. I'm interested in Will Carman, because of Alice Winthrop."

"I had hoped, Ethel, at one time that you would have been interested in him for his own sake. However, this is what she writes:

"I came here chiefly to rid myself of a melancholy mood which has taken possession of me lately, and also because I cannot bear to see my boy so changed towards me, owing to his infatuation for Alice Winthrop. It is incomprehensible to me how a son of mine can find any pleasure whatever in the society of such a girl. I have traced her history, and find that she is not only uneducated in the ordinary sense, but her environment, from childhood up, has been the sordid and demoralizing one of extreme poverty and ignorance. This girl, Alice, entered a law office at the age of fourteen, supposedly to do the work of an office boy. Now, after seven years in business, through the friendship and influence of men far above her socially, she holds the position of private secretary to the most influential man in Washington—a position which by rights belongs only to a well-educated young woman of good family. Many such applied. I myself sought to have Jane Walker appointed. Is it not disheartening to our woman's cause to be compelled to realize that girls such as this one can win men over to be their friends and lovers, when there are so many splendid young women who have been carefully trained to be companions and comrades of educated men?"

"Pardon me, mother," interrupted Miss Evebrook, "but I have heard enough. Mrs. Carman is your friend and a well-meaning woman sometimes; but a woman suffragist,[6] in the true sense, she certainly is not. Mark my words: If any young man had accomplished for himself what Alice Winthrop has accomplished, Mrs. Carman could not have said enough in his praise. It is women such as Alice Winthrop who, in spite of every drawback, have raised themselves to the level of those who have had every advantage, who are the pride and glory of America. There are thousands of them, all over this land: women who have been of service to others all their years and who have graduated from the university of life with honor. Women such as I, who are called the Superior Women of America, are after all nothing but school-girls in comparison.

Mrs. Evebrook eyed her daughter mutinously. "I don't see why you should feel like that," said she. "Alice is a dear bright child, and it is prejudice engendered by Mary Carman's disappointment about you and Will which is the real cause of poor Mary's bitterness towards her; but to my mind, Alice does not compare with my daughter. She would be frightened to death if she had to make a speech."

"You foolish mother!" rallied Miss Evebrook. "To stand upon a platform at woman suffrage meetings and exploit myself is certainly a

6. An advocate of the extension of voting rights to women.

great recompense to you and father for all the sacrifices you have made in my behalf. But since it pleases you, I do it with pleasure even on the nights when my beau should 'come a courting.' "

"There is many a one who would like to come, Ethel. You're the handsomest girl in this Western town—and you know it."

"Stop that, mother. You know very well I have set my mind upon having ten years' freedom; ten years in which to love, live, suffer, see the world, and learn about men (not schoolboys) before I choose one."

"Alice Winthrop is the same age as you are, and looks like a child beside you."

"Physically, maybe; but her heart and mind are better developed. She has been out in the world all her life, I only a few months."

"Your lecture last week on 'The Opposite Sex' was splendid."

"Of course. I have studied one hundred books on the subject and attended fifty lectures. All that was necessary was to repeat in an original manner what was not by any means original."

Miss Evebrook went over to a desk and took a paper therefrom.

"This," said she, "is what Alice has written me in reply to my note suggesting that she attend next week the suffrage meeting, and give some of the experiences of her business career. The object I had in view when I requested the relation of her experiences was to use them as illustrations of the suppression and oppression of women by men. Strange to say, Alice and I have never conversed on this particular subject. If we had I would not have made this request of her, nor written her as I did. Listen:

"I should dearly love to please you, but I am afraid that my experiences, if related, would not help the cause. It may be, as you say, that men prevent women from rising to their level; but if there are such men, I have not met them. Ever since, when a little girl, I walked into a law office and asked for work, and the senior member kindly looked me over through his spectacles and inquired if I thought I could learn to index books, and the junior member glanced under my hat and said: "This is a pretty little girl and we must be pretty to her," I have loved and respected the men amongst whom I have worked and wherever I have worked. I may have been exceptionally fortunate, but I know this: the men for whom I have worked and amongst whom I have spent my life, whether they have been business or professional men, students or great lawyers and politicians, all alike have upheld me, inspired me, advised me, taught me, given me a broad outlook upon life for a woman; interested me in themselves and in their work. As to corrupting my mind and my morals, as you say so many men do, when they have young and innocent girls to deal with: As a woman I look back over my years spent amongst business and professional men, and see myself, as I was at first, an impressionable, ignorant little girl, born a Bohemian,[7] easy to lead and easy to win, but borne aloft and morally

7. One who spurns convention for artistic or literary pursuits.

supported by the goodness of my brother men, the men amongst whom I worked. That is why, dear Ethel, you will have to forgive me, because I cannot carry out your design, and help your work, as otherwise I would like to do."

"That, mother," declared Miss Evebrook, "answers all Mrs. Carman's insinuations, and should make her ashamed of herself. Can any one know the sentiments which little Alice entertains toward men, and wonder at her winning out as she has?"

Mrs. Evebrook was about to make reply, when her glance happening to stray out of the window, she noticed a pink parasol.

"Mrs. Spring Fragrance!" she ejaculated, while her daughter went to the door and invited in the owner of the pink parasol, who was seated in a veranda rocker calmly writing in a note-book.

"I'm so sorry that we did not hear your ring, Mrs. Spring Fragrance," said she.

"There is no necessity for you to sorrow," replied the little Chinese woman. "I did not expect you to hear a ring which rang not. I failed to pull the bell."

"You forgot, I suppose," suggested Ethel Evebrook.

"Is it wise to tell secrets?" ingenuously inquired Mrs. Spring Fragrance.

"Yes, to your friends. Oh, Mrs. Spring Fragrance, you are *so* refreshing."

"I have pleasure, then, in confiding to you. I have an ambition to accomplish an immortal book about the Americans, and the conversation I heard through the window was so interesting to me that I thought I would take some of it down for my book before I intruded myself. With your kind permission I will translate for your correction."

"I shall be delighted—honored," said Miss Evebrook, her cheeks glowing and her laugh rippling, "if you will promise me that you will also translate for our friend, Mrs. Carman."

"Ah, yes, poor Mrs. Carman! My heart is so sad for her," murmured the little Chinese woman.

V

When the mother of Will Carman returned from Portland, the first person upon whom she called was Mrs. Spring Fragrance. Having lived in China while her late husband was in the customs service there, Mrs. Carman's prejudices did not extend to the Chinese, and ever since the Spring Fragrances had become the occupants of the villa beside the Carmans, there had been social good feeling between the American and Chinese families. Indeed, Mrs. Carman was wont to declare that amongst all her acquaintances there was not one more congenial and interesting than little Mrs. Spring Fragrance. So after she had sipped a cup of delicious tea, tasted some piquant candied limes, and told Mrs. Spring Fragrance all about her visit to the Oregon city and the Chinese people she had met there, she reverted to a personal trouble confided to Mrs. Spring Fragrance some months before and dwelt upon it for more than half an hour. Then she checked herself and gazed at Mrs. Spring Fragrance in surprise. Hitherto she had found the little Chinese woman sympathetic and consoling. Chinese ideas of filial duty chimed in with her own. But today Mrs. Spring Fragrance seemed strangely uninterested and unresponsive.

"Perhaps," gently suggested the American woman, who was nothing if not sensitive, "you have some trouble yourself. If so, my dear, tell me all about it."

"Oh, no!" answered Mrs. Spring Fragrance brightly. "I have no troubles to tell; but all the while I am thinking about the book I am writing."

"A book!"

"Yes, a book about Americans, an immortal book."

"My dear Mrs. Spring Fragrance!" exclaimed her visitor in amazement.

"The American woman writes books about the Chinese. Why not a Chinese woman write books about the Americans?"

"I see what you mean. Why, yes, of course. What an original idea!"

"Yes, I think that is what it is. My book I shall take from the words of others."

"What do you mean, my dear?"

"I listen to what is said, I apprehend, I write it down. Let me illustrate by the 'Inferior Woman' subject. The Inferior Woman is most interesting to me because you have told me that your son is in much love with her. My husband advised me to learn about the Inferior Woman from the Superior Woman. I go to see the Superior Woman. I sit on the veranda of the Superior Woman's house. I listen to her converse with her mother about the Inferior Woman. With the speed of flames I write down all I hear. When I enter the house the Superior Woman advises me that what I write is correct. May I read to you?"

"I shall be pleased to hear what you have written; but I do not think you were wise in your choice of subject," returned Mrs. Carman somewhat primly.

"I am sorry I am not wise. Perhaps I had better not read?" said Mrs. Spring Fragrance with humility.

"Yes, yes, do, please."

There was eagerness in Mrs. Carman's voice. What could Ethel Evebrook have to say about that girl!

When Mrs. Spring Fragrance had finished reading, she looked up into the face of her American friend—a face in which there was nothing now but tenderness.

"Mrs. Mary Carman," said she, "you are so good as to admire my husband because he is what the Americans call 'a man who has made himself.' Why then do you not admire the Inferior Woman who is a woman who has made herself?"

"I think I do," said Mrs. Carman slowly.

VI

It was an evening that invited to reverie. The far stretches of the sea were gray with mist, and the city itself, lying around the sweep of the Bay, seemed dusky and distant. From her cottage window Alice Winthrop looked silently at the open world around her. It seemed a long time since she had heard Will Carman's whistle. She wondered if he were still angry with her. She was sorry that he had left her in anger, and yet not sorry. If she had not made him believe that she was proud and selfish, the parting would have been much harder; and perhaps had he known the truth and realized that it was for his sake, and not for her own, that she was sending him away from her, he might have refused to leave her at all. His was such an imperious nature. And then they would have married—right away. Alice caught her breath a little, and then she sighed. But they would not have been happy. No, that could not have been possible if his mother did not like her. When a gulf of prejudice lies between the wife and mother of a man, that man's life is not what it should be. And even supposing she and Will could have lost themselves in each other, and been able to imagine themselves perfectly satisfied with life together, would it have been right? The question of right and wrong was a very real one to Alice Winthrop. She put herself in the place of the mother of her lover—a lonely elderly woman, a widow with an only son, upon whom she had expended all her love and care ever since, in her early youth, she had been bereaved of his father. What anguish of heart would be hers if that son deserted her for one whom she, his mother, deemed unworthy! Prejudices are prejudices. They are like diseases.

The poor, pale, elderly woman, who cherished bitter and resentful feelings towards the girl whom her son loved, was more an object of pity than condemnation to the girl herself.

She lifted her eyes to the undulating line of hills beyond the water. From behind them came a silver light. "Yes," said she aloud to herself—and, though she knew it not, there was an infinite pathos in such philosophy from one so young—"if life cannot be bright and beautiful for me, at least it can be peaceful and contented."

The light behind the hills died away; darkness crept over the sea. Alice withdrew from the window and went and knelt before the open fire in her sitting-room. Her cottage companion, the young woman who rented the place with her, had not yet returned from town.

Alice did not turn on the light. She was seeing pictures in the fire, and in every picture was the same face and form—the face and form of a fine, handsome young man with love and hope in his eyes. No, not always love and hope. In the last picture of all there was an expression which she wished she could forget. And yet she would remember— ever—always—and with it, these words: "Is it nothing to you—nothing—to tell a man that you love him, and then to bid him go?"

Yes, but when she had told him she loved him she had not dreamed that her love for him and his for her would estrange him from one who, before ever she had come to this world, had pillowed his head on her breast.

Suddenly this girl, so practical, so humorous, so clever in every-day life, covered her face with her hands and sobbed like a child. Two roads of life had lain before her and she had chosen the hardest.

The warning bell of an automobile passing the cross-roads checked her tears. That reminded her that Nellie Blake would soon be home. She turned on the light and went to the bedroom and bathed her eyes. Nellie must have forgotten her key. There she was knocking.

° ° °

The chill sea air was sweet with the scent of roses as Mary Carman stood upon the threshold of the little cottage, and beheld in the illumination from within the young girl whom she had called "the Inferior Woman."

"I have come, Miss Winthrop," said she, "to beg of you to return home with me. Will, reckless boy, met with a slight accident while out shooting, so could not come for you himself. He has told me that he loves you, and if you love him, I want to arrange for the prettiest wedding of the season. Come, dear!"

"I am so glad," said Mrs. Spring Fragrance, "that Will Carman's bird is in his nest and his felicity is assured."

"What about the Superior Woman?" asked Mr. Spring Fragrance.

"Ah, the Superior Woman! Radiantly beautiful, and gifted with the divine right of learning! I love well the Inferior Woman; but, O Great Man, when we have a daughter, may Heaven ordain that she walk in the groove of the Superior Woman."

Hampton, May 1910; *Mrs. Spring Fragrance,* 1912

"Its Wavering Image"

I

Pan was a half-white, half-Chinese girl. Her mother was dead, and Pan lived with her father who kept an Oriental Bazaar on Dupont Street. All her life had Pan lived in Chinatown,[1] and if she were different in any sense from those around her, she gave little thought to it. It was only after the coming of Mark Carson that the mystery of her nature began to trouble her.

They met at the time of the boycott of the Sam Yups by the See Yups. After the heat and dust and unsavoriness of the highways and byways of Chinatown, the young reporter who had been sent to find a story had stepped across the threshold of a cool, deep room, fragrant with the odor of dried lilies and sandalwood, and found Pan.

---

1. The Chinese district within U.S. cities.

She did not speak to him, nor he to her. His business was with the spectacled merchant, who, with a pointed brush, was making up accounts in brown paper books and rolling balls in an abacus box.[2] As to Pan, she always turned from whites. With her father's people she was natural and at home; but in the presence of her mother's she felt strange and constrained, shrinking from their curious scrutiny as she would from the sharp edge of a sword.

When Mark Carson returned to the office, he asked some questions concerning the girl who had puzzled him. What was she? Chinese or white? The city editor answered him, adding: "She is an unusually bright girl, and could tell more stories about the Chinese than any other person in this city—if she would."

Mark Carson had a determined chin, clever eyes, and a tone to his voice which easily won for him the confidence of the unwary. In the reporter's room he was spoken of as "a man who would sell his soul for a story."

After Pan's first shyness had worn off, he found her bewilderingly frank and free with him; but he had all the instincts of a gentleman save one, and made no ordinary mistake about her. He was Pan's first white friend. She was born a Bohemian,[3] exempt from the conventional restrictions imposed upon either the white or Chinese woman; and the Oriental who was her father mingled with his affection for his child so great a respect for and trust in the daughter of the dead white woman, that everything she did or said was right to him. And Pan herself! A white woman might pass over an insult; a Chinese woman fail to see one. But Pan! He would be a brave man indeed who offered one to childish little Pan.

All this Mark Carson's clear eyes perceived, and with delicate tact and subtlety he taught the young girl that, all unconscious until his coming, she had lived her life alone. So well did she learn this lesson that it seemed at times as if her white self must entirely dominate and trample under foot her Chinese.

Meanwhile, in full trust and confidence, she led him about Chinatown, initiating him into the simple mystery and history of many things, for which she, being of her father's race, had a tender regard and pride. For her sake he was received as a brother by the yellow-robed priest in the joss house,[4] the Astrologer of Prospect Place, and other conservative Chinese. The Water Lily Club opened its doors to him when she knocked, and the Sublimely Pure Brothers' organization admitted him as one of its honorary members, thereby enabling him not only to see but to take part in a ceremony in which no American had ever before participated. With her by his side, he was welcomed wherever he went. Even the little Chinese women in the midst of their

2. A manual counting device consisting of a frame holding parallel rods strung with movable counters.
3. One who spurns convention for artistic or literary pursuits.
4. A Chinese temple or shrine containing idols.

babies received him with gentle smiles, and the children solemnly munched his candies and repeated nursery rhymes for his edification.

He enjoyed it all, and so did Pan. They were both young and light-hearted. And when the afternoon was spent, there was always that high room open to the stars, with its China bowls full of flowers and its big colored lanterns, shedding a mellow light.

Sometimes there was music. A Chinese band played three evenings a week in the gilded restaurant beneath them, and the louder the gongs sounded and the fiddlers fiddled, the more delighted was Pan. Just below the restaurant was her father's bazaar. Occasionally Mun You would stroll upstairs and inquire of the young couple if there was anything needed to complete their felicity, and Pan would answer: "Thou only." Pan was very proud of her Chinese father. "I would rather have a Chinese for a father than a white man," she often told Mark Carson. The last time she had said that he had asked whom she would prefer for a husband, a white man or a Chinese. And Pan, for the first time since he had known her, had no answer for him.

II

It was a cool, quiet evening, after a hot day. A new moon was in the sky.

"How beautiful above! How unbeautiful below!" exclaimed Mark Carson involuntarily.

He and Pan had been gazing down from their open retreat into the lantern-lighted, motley-thronged street beneath them.

"Perhaps it isn't very beautiful," replied Pan, "but it is here I live. It is my home." Her voice quivered a little.

He leaned towards her suddenly and grasped her hands.

"Pan," he cried, "you do not belong here. You are white—white."

"No! no!" protested Pan.

"You are," he asserted. "You have no right to be here."

"I was born here," she answered, "and the Chinese people look upon me as their own."

"But they do not understand you," he went on. "Your real self is alien to them. What interest have they in the books you read—the thoughts you think?"

"They have an interest in me," answered faithful Pan. "Oh, do not speak in that way any more."

"But I must," the young man persisted. "Pan, don't you see that you have got to decide what you will be—Chinese or white? You cannot be both."

"Hush! Hush!" bade Pan. "I do not love you when you talk to me like that."

A little Chinese boy brought tea and saffron cakes. He was a picturesque little fellow with a quaint manner of speech. Mark Carson jested merrily with him, while Pan holding a tea-bowl between her two small hands laughed and sipped.

When they were alone again, the silver stream and the crescent moon became the objects of their study. It was a very beautiful evening.

After a while Mark Carson, his hand on Pan's shoulder, sang:

> "And forever, and forever,
> As long as the river flows,
> As long as the heart has passions,
> As long as life has woes,
> The moon and its broken reflection,
> And its shadows shall appear,
> As the symbol of love in heaven,
> And its wavering image here."

Listening to that irresistible voice singing her heart away, the girl broke down and wept. She was so young and so happy.

"Look up at me," bade Mark Carson. "Oh, Pan! Pan! Those tears prove that you are white."

Pan lifted her wet face.

"Kiss me, Pan," said he. It was the first time.

Next morning Mark Carson began work on the special-feature article which he had been promising his paper for some weeks.

III

"Cursed be his ancestors," bayed Man You.

He cast a paper at his daughter's feet and left the room.

Startled by her father's unwonted passion, Pan picked up the paper, and in the clear passionless light of the afternoon read that which forever after was blotted upon her memory.

"Betrayed! Betrayed! Betrayed to be a betrayer!"

It burnt red hot; agony unrelieved by words, unassuaged by tears.

So till evening fell. Then she stumbled up the dark stairs which led to the high room open to the stars and tried to think it out. Someone had hurt her. Who was it? She raised her eyes. There shone: "Its Wavering Image." It helped her to lucidity. He had done it. Was it unconsciously dealt—that cruel blow? Ah, well did he know that the sword which pierced her through others, would carry with it to her own heart, the pain of all those others. None knew better than he that she, whom he had called "a white girl, a white woman," would rather that her own naked body and soul had been exposed, than that things, sacred and secret to those who loved her, should be cruelly unveiled and ruthlessly spread before the ridiculing and uncomprehending foreigner. And knowing all this so well, so well, he had carelessly sung her heart away and with her kiss upon his lips, had smilingly turned and stabbed her. She, who was of the race that remembers.

IV

Mark Carson, back in the city after an absence of two months, thought of Pan. He would see her that very evening. Dear little Pan, pretty Pan, clever Pan, amusing Pan; Pan, who was always so frankly glad to have him come to her; so eager to hear all that he was doing; so appreciative, so inspiring, so loving. She would have forgotten that article by now. Why should a white woman care about such things? Her true self was above it all. Had he not taught her *that* during the weeks in which they had seen so much of one another? True, his last lesson had been a little harsh, and as yet he knew not how she had taken it; but even if its roughness had hurt and irritated, there was a healing balm, a wizard's oil which none knew so well as he how to apply.

But for all these soothing reflections, there was an undercurrent of feeling which caused his steps to falter on his way to Pan. He turned into Portsmouth Square and took a seat on one of the benches facing the fountain erected in memory of Robert Louis Stevenson.[5] Why had Pan failed to answer the note he had written telling her of the assignment which would keep him out of town for a couple of months and giving her his address? Would Robert Louis Stevenson have known why? Yes—and so did Mark Carson. But though Robert Louis Stevenson would have boldly answered himself the question, Mark Carson thrust it aside, arose, and pressed up the hill.

"I knew they would not blame you, Pan!"

"Yes."

"And there was no word of you, dear. I was careful about that, not only for your sake, but for mine."

Silence.

"It is mere superstition anyway. These things have got to be exposed and done away with."

Still silence.

Mark Carson felt strangely chilled. Pan was not herself tonight. She did not even look herself. He had been accustomed to seeing her in American dress. Tonight she wore the Chinese costume. But for her clear-cut features she might have been a Chinese girl. He shivered.

"Pan," he asked, "why do you wear that dress?"

Within her sleeves Pan's small hands struggled together; but her face and voice were calm.

"Because I am a Chinese woman," she answered.

"You are not," cried Mark Carson, fiercely. "You cannot say that now, Pan. You are a white woman—white. Did your kiss not promise me that?"

"A white woman!" echoed Pan her voice rising high and clear to the

---

5. Scottish novelist, essayist, and poet (1850–1894), author of *Treasure Island* and *A Child's Garden of Verses*.

stars above them. "I would not be a white woman for all the world. You are a white man. And *what* is a promise to a white man!"

＊　＊　＊

When she was lying low, the element of Fire[6] having raged so fiercely within her that it had almost shriveled up the childish frame, there came to the house of Man You a little toddler who could scarcely speak. Climbing upon Pan's couch, she pressed her head upon the sick girl's bosom. The feel of that little head brought tears.

"Lo!" said the mother of the toddler. "Thou wilt bear a child thyself some day, and all the bitterness of this will pass away."

And Pan, being a Chinese woman, was comforted.

Mrs. Spring Fragrance, 1912

---

6. In ancient Chinese religion, fire is the revered life force or fluid associated with truth and justice.

ZITKALA-SÄ
(GERTRUDE SIMMONS BONNIN)
1876–1938

Born at the Yankton Sioux Agency in South Dakota on February 22, 1876, Gertrude Simmons spent the first eight years of her life on the reservation. Her mother, Ellen Tate'Iyohiwin (Reaches for the Wind), was a full-blooded Sioux whose first husband, a white man named Felker, deserted her before his daughter was born. Thus, Gertrude was given the name of her mother's second husband, John Haysting Simmons, another white man. Later she would give herself her own tribal name, Zitkala-Sä, which means Red Bird. At the age of eight, and against her mother's wishes, Zitkala-Sä left Yankton with the Quaker missionaries who had come to the reservation to recruit children for Indian schools back East. "Impressions of an Indian Childhood" records the early period of Zitkala-Sä's life and her early separation from her mother and from the reservation.

For the next three years she attended White's Indiana Manual Labor Institute in Wabash, Indiana, where she experienced humiliation and insensitive treatment as the school educated her and her classmates for assimilation into American society. At the end of three years, she returned to Yankton and to her mother's house, where she began to discover that she no longer felt at home in either white or Indian worlds. "Miserable in this state of cultural dislocation" (Young 199), she returned to White's and received a diploma three years later, then enrolled for two years at Earlham College in Richmond, Indiana. While a student at Earlham, she won two prizes in oratory. "The School Days of an Indian Girl" recounts her experiences at White's Institute, and later at Earlham College, where she won second-place in an oratory contest and was mocked by a banner depicting her college as represented by a "squaw."

In 1897 she left Earlham to teach for two years at the Carlisle (Pa.) Indian School, followed by a period at the New England Conservatory of Music in Boston, where she studied the violin. In 1900 she attended the Paris Exposition as a violin soloist with the Carlisle Indian Band, then returned to begin a brief literary career. In the same year she published three autobiographical essays in the *Atlantic Monthly* ("Impressions" and "School Days," included here, and "An Indian Teacher Among Indians"), followed by a fourth *Atlantic* essay in December 1902 ("Why I Am a Pagan"). During the same period, *Harper's* magazine published two short stories, "The Soft-Hearted Sioux" and "The Trial Path" (included here). She later collected these and other work in a 1921 volume, *American Indian Stories*. A collection of Sioux myths and tribal legends written for children appeared as *Old Indian Legends* in 1901.

In a letter dated February 20, 1901, to Carlos Montezuma, a Yavapai physician to whom she was briefly engaged, Zitkala-Sä expressed uncertainty about her future as a writer.

> As for my plans,—I do not mean to give up my literary work—but while the old people last I want to get from them their treasured ideas of life. This I can do by living among them. Thus I mean to divide my time between teaching and getting story material (Fisher, "Zitkala-Sä," 229).

In fact, she did give up a literary career and began instead the lifelong work of teaching and advocacy on behalf of Indians. Her decision coincided with her marriage to Raymond T. Bonnin, a Sioux employed by the Bureau of Indian Affairs, on May 10, 1902. The couple moved to the Uintah and Ouray Reservation in Utah, where Bonnin gave birth to her only child, Raymond O. Bonnin, and worked to organize community activities for Indian women. During this period she also collaborated on an opera, *Sun Dance*, which was performed at Brigham Young University and later in New York.

In 1916 Zitkala-Sä was elected secretary of the Society of the American Indian and she and her husband moved to Washington, D.C. Her work for the society, which included editing the *American Indian Magazine* during 1918–19, gave her a forum from which to lecture across the country on behalf of "Indian citizenship, employment of Indians in the Bureau of Indian Affairs, equitable settlement of tribal land claims, and stabilization of laws relating to Indians" (Fisher, "Zitkala-Sä," 235). After the society dissolved, she began to work with the General Federation of Women's Clubs, forming an Indian Welfare committee that allowed her to continue and to enhance her reform efforts. And in 1926 she founded her own organization, the National Council of American Indians, which she served as president until she died January 26, 1938, of heart failure and kidney disease. She is buried in Arlington National Cemetery.

◦   ◦   ◦

In "The Transportation of Tradition," Fisher terms Zitkala-Sä a "transitional writer," an Indian caught between the tradition of oral storytelling and the written forms she would be able to choose for her own work because she could write in the English language. And, unlike other Native American women who told their life stories, Zitkala-Sä is also, "perhaps, the first Indian woman to write her own story without the aid of an editor, an interpreter, or an ethnographer" (34). Thus, instead of a voice mediated by the interests of a white ethnographic interviewer, Zitkala-Sä presents her own voice directly, risking alienating both white and Indian readers in the process. For, as both "Impressions" and "School Days" reveal, Zitkala-Sä is critical both of reservation life and the assimilation policies of the Indian boarding schools and the Bureau of Indian Affairs. Her choice to leave the reservation created a rift with her mother that she was never able to mend; and yet she failed to assimilate into the white world. At the end of "An Indian Teacher Among Indians," she describes the extent of her alienation:

In the process of my education I had lost all consciousness of the nature world about me . . . For the white man's papers I had given up my faith in the Great Spirit. For these same papers I had forgotten the healing in trees and brooks. On account of my mother's simple view of life, and my lack of any, I gave her up, also. I made no friends among the race of people I loathed. Like a slender tree, I had been uprooted from my mother, nature, and God (*Atlantic Monthly*, March 1900, p. 386).

Zitkala-Sä shares with the other writers in this volume a concern with the way place—her early years on the reservation—and her relationship with her mother formed her identity and became the subject matter for her writing, and she expresses the desire to tell Indian legends and stories in an Indian voice, demonstrating once again the impulse shared by regionalist writers to shift the center of perception to the native speaker. In "The Trial Path," the relationship between the grandmother-storyteller and her granddaughter-listener may remind some readers of the relationship between narrator and listener in Jewett's fiction. Yet, in this story, the grandmother who tries to tell a story filled with "sacred knowledge" only manages to put her granddaughter to sleep.

As important as Zitkala-Sä believed the storyteller could be, she valued political activity even more, and perhaps believed that only such activity could wake her people up. The regionalist elements of her autobiographical sketches and "The Trial Path" suggest that, had she chosen a literary career, she might have continued to develop as a regionalist writer. Her choice to spend her life as a reformer may indicate that the price she paid for attaining the language that could have made such a career possible was the loss of place. Fisher suggests that she inhabited a "middle ground" between two worlds ("Transportation," 41), but unlike the reservation of her early childhood, such "middle ground" is not either an actual or a literary region. In her preface to *Old Indian Legends*, Zitkala-Sä wrote that in attempting to translate oral tales into written form, she "tried to transplant the native spirit" of the tales (quoted in Fisher, "Transportation," 49). Yet for this "transitional writer," working in written English may have created an intolerable opposition to the oral storytelling tradition she hoped to "transplant." Unable to fully affirm the old Indian traditions in her writing, she compromised by ceasing to write, but continued, in her career as a public speaker and reformist, to tell oral stories of advocacy and political change.

Impressions of an Indian Childhood

I. My Mother

A wigwam of weather-stained canvas stood at the base of some irregu-
larly ascending hills. A footpath wound its way gently down the sloping
land till it reached the broad river bottom; creeping through the long
swamp grasses that bent over it on either side, it came out on the edge
of the Missouri.

Here, morning, noon, and evening, my mother came to draw water
from the muddy stream for our household use. Always, when my
mother started for the river, I stopped my play to run along with her.
She was only of medium height. Often she was sad and silent, at which
times her full arched lips were compressed into hard and bitter lines,
and shadows fell under her black eyes. Then I clung to her hand and
begged to know what made the tears fall.

"Hush; my little daughter must never talk about my tears"; and
smiling through them, she patted my head and said, "Now let me see
how fast you can run today." Whereupon I tore away at my highest
possible speed, with my long black hair blowing in the breeze.

I was a wild little girl of seven. Loosely clad in a slip of brown
buckskin, and light-footed with a pair of soft moccasins on my feet, I
was as free as the wind that blew my hair, and no less spirited than a
bounding deer. These were my mother's pride,—my wild freedom and
overflowing spirits. She taught me no fear save that of intruding myself
upon others.

Having gone many paces ahead I stopped, panting for breath, and
laughing with glee as my mother watched my every movement. I was
not wholly conscious of myself, but was more keenly alive to the fire
within. It was as if I were the activity, and my hands and feet were only
experiments for my spirit to work upon.

Returning from the river, I tugged beside my mother, with my hand
upon the bucket I believed I was carrying. One time, on such a return,
I remember a bit of conversation we had. My grown-up cousin, Warca-
Ziwin (Sunflower), who was then seventeen, always went to the river
alone for water for her mother. Their wigwam was not far from ours;
and I saw her daily going to and from the river. I admired my cousin
greatly. So I said: "Mother, when I am tall as my cousin Warca-Ziwin,
you shall not have to come for water. I will do it for you."

With a strange tremor in her voice which I could not understand, she
answered, "If the paleface does not take away from us the river we
drink."

"Mother, who is this bad paleface?" I asked.

"My little daughter, he is a sham,—a sickly sham! The bronzed
Dakota is the only real man."

I looked up into my mother's face while she spoke; and seeing her bite her lips, I knew she was unhappy. This aroused revenge in my small soul. Stamping my foot on the earth, I cried aloud, "I hate the paleface that makes my mother cry!"

Setting the pail of water on the ground, my mother stopped, and stretching her left hand out on the level with my eyes, she placed her other arm about me; she pointed to the hill where my uncle and my only sister lay buried.

"There is what the paleface has done! Since then your father too has been buried in a hill nearer the rising sun. We were once very happy. But the paleface has stolen our lands and driven us hither. Having defrauded us of our land, the paleface forced us away.

"Well, it happened on the day we moved camp that your sister and uncle were both very sick. Many others were ailing, but there seemed to be no help. We traveled many days and nights; not in the grand happy way that we moved camp when I was a little girl, but we were driven, my child, driven like a herd of buffalo. With every step, your sister, who was not as large as you are now, shrieked with the painful jar until she was hoarse with crying. She grew more and more feverish. Her little hands and cheeks were burning hot. Her little lips were parched and dry, but she would not drink the water I gave her. Then I discovered that her throat was swollen and red. My poor child, how I cried with her because the Great Spirit had forgotten us!

"At last, when we reached this western country, on the first weary night your sister died. And soon your uncle died also, leaving a widow and an orphan daughter, your cousin Warca-Ziwin. Both your sister and uncle might have been happy with us today, had it not been for the heartless paleface."

My mother was silent the rest of the way to our wigwam. Though I saw no tears in her eyes, I knew that was because I was with her. She seldom wept before me.

II. The Legends

During the summer days, my mother built her fire in the shadow of our wigwam.

In the early morning our simple breakfast was spread upon the grass west of our tepee. At the farthest point of the shade my mother sat beside her fire, toasting a savory piece of dried meat. Near her, I sat upon my feet, eating my dried meat with unleavened bread, and drinking strong black coffee.

The morning meal was our quiet hour, when we two were entirely alone. At noon, several who chanced to be passing by stopped to rest, and to share our luncheon with us, for they were sure of our hospitality.

My uncle, whose death my mother ever lamented, was one of our nation's bravest warriors. His name was on the lips of old men when talking of the proud feats of valor; and it was mentioned by younger men, too, in connection with deeds of gallantry. Old women praised him for his kindness toward them; young women held him up as an ideal to their sweethearts. Everyone loved him, and my mother worshiped his memory. Thus it happened that even strangers were sure of welcome in our lodge, if they but asked a favor in my uncle's name.

Though I heard many strange experiences related by these wayfarers, I loved best the evening meal, for that was the time old legends were told. I was always glad when the sun hung low in the west, for then my mother sent me to invite the neighboring old men and women to eat supper with us. Running all the way to the wigwams, I halted shyly at the entrances. Sometimes I stood long moments without saying a word. It was not any fear that made me so dumb when out upon such a happy errand; nor was it that I wished to withhold the invitation, for it was all I could do to observe this very proper silence. But it was a sensing of the atmosphere, to assure myself that I should not hinder other plans. My mother used to say to me, as I was almost bounding away for the old people: "Wait a moment before you invite anyone. If other plans are being discussed, do not interfere, but go elsewhere."

The old folks knew the meaning of my pauses; and often they coaxed my confidence by asking, "What do you seek, little granddaughter?"

"My mother says you are to come to our tepee this evening," I instantly exploded, and breathed the freer afterwards.

"Yes, yes, gladly, gladly I shall come!" each replied. Rising at once and carrying their blankets across one shoulder, they flocked leisurely from their various wigwams toward our dwelling.

My mission done, I ran back, skipping and jumping with delight. All out of breath, I told my mother almost the exact words of the answers to my invitation. Frequently she asked, "What were they doing when you entered their tepee?" This taught me to remember all I saw at a single glance. Often I told my mother my impressions without being questioned.

While in the neighboring wigwams sometimes an old Indian woman asked me, "What is your mother doing?" Unless my mother had cautioned me not to tell, I generally answered her questions without reserve.

At the arrival of our guests I sat close to my mother, and did not leave her side without first asking her consent. I ate my supper in quiet, listening patiently to the talk of the old people, wishing all the time that they would begin the stories I loved best. At last, when I could not wait any longer, I whispered in my mother's ear, "Ask them to tell an Iktomi[1] story, mother."

Soothing my impatience, my mother said aloud, "My little daughter is anxious to hear your legends." By this time all were through eating, and the evening was fast deepening into twilight.

As each in turn began to tell a legend, I pillowed my head in my mother's lap; and lying flat upon my back, I watched the stars as they

1. The Sioux word for spider, a fabulous creature in Indian folklore.

peeped down upon me, one by one. The increasing interest of the tale
aroused me, and I sat up eagerly listening for every word. The old
women made funny remarks, and laughed so heartily that I could not
help joining them.

The distant howling of a pack of wolves or the hooting of an owl in
the river bottom frightened me, and I nestled into my mother's lap. She
added some dry sticks to the fire, and the bright flames heaped up into
the faces of the old folks as they sat around in a great circle.

On such an evening, I remember the glare of the fire shone on a
tattooed star upon the brow of the old warrior who was telling a story.
I watched him curiously as he made his unconscious gestures. The blue
star upon his bronzed forehead was a puzzle to me. Looking about, I
saw two parallel lines on the chin of one of the old women. The rest
had none. I examined my mother's face, but found no sign there.

After the warrior's story was finished, I asked the old woman the
meaning of the blue lines on her chin, looking all the while out of the
corners of my eyes at the warrior with the star on his forehead. I was
a little afraid that he would rebuke me for my boldness.

Here the old woman began: "Why, my grandchild, they are signs,—
secret signs I dare not tell you. I shall, however, tell you a wonderful
story about a woman who had a cross tattooed upon each of her
cheeks."

It was a long story of a woman whose magic power lay hidden
behind the marks upon her face. I fell asleep before the story was
completed.

Ever after that night I felt suspicious of tattooed people. Whenever
I saw one I glanced furtively at the mark and round about it, wondering what terrible magic power was covered there.

It was rarely that such a fearful story as this one was told by the
camp fire. Its impression was so acute that the picture still remains
vividly clear and pronounced.

III. The Beadwork

Soon after breakfast, mother sometimes began her beadwork. On a
bright clear day, she pulled out the wooden pegs that pinned the skirt
of our wigwam to the ground, and rolled the canvas part way up on its
frame of slender poles. Then the cool morning breezes swept freely
through our dwelling, now and then wafting the perfume of sweet
grasses from newly burnt prairie.

Untying the long tasseled strings that bound a small brown buckskin
bag, my mother spread upon a mat beside her bunches of colored
beads, just as an artist arranges the paints upon his palette. On a
lapboard she smoothed out a double sheet of soft white buckskin; and
drawing from a beaded case that hung on the left of her wide belt a
long, narrow blade, she trimmed the buckskin into shape. Often she
worked upon small moccasins for her small daughter. Then I became

intensely interested in her designing. With a proud, beaming face, I watched her work. In imagination, I saw myself walking in a new pair of snugly fitting moccasins. I felt the envious eyes of my playmates upon the pretty red beads decorating my feet.

Close beside my mother I sat on a rug, with a scrap of buckskin in one hand and an awl in the other. This was the beginning of my practical observation lessons in the art of beadwork. From a skein of finely twisted threads of silvery sinews my mother pulled out a single one. With an awl she pierced the buckskin, and skillfully threaded it with the white sinew. Picking up the tiny beads one by one, she strung them with the point of her thread, always twisting it carefully after every stitch.

It took many trials before I learned how to knot my sinew thread on the point of my finger, as I saw her do. Then the next difficulty was in keeping my thread stiffly twisted, so that I could easily string my beads upon it. My mother required of me original designs for my lessons in beading. At first I frequently ensnared many a sunny hour into working a long design. Soon I learned from self-inflicted punishment to refrain from drawing complex patterns, for I had to finish whatever I began.

After some experience I usually drew easy and simple crosses and squares. These were some of the set forms. My original designs were not always symmetrical nor sufficiently characteristic, two faults with which my mother had little patience. The quietness of her oversight made me feel strongly responsible and dependent upon my own judgment. She treated me as a dignified little individual as long as I was on my good behavior; and how humiliated I was when some boldness of mine drew forth a rebuke from her!

In the choice of colors she left me to my own taste. I was pleased with an outline of yellow upon a background of dark blue, or a combination of red and myrtle-green. There was another of red with a bluish gray that was more conventionally used. When I became a little familiar with designing and the various pleasing combinations of color, a harder lesson was given me. It was the sewing on, instead of beads, some tinted porcupine quills, moistened and flattened between the nails of the thumb and forefinger. My mother cut off the prickly ends and burned them at once in the center fire. These sharp points were poisonous, and worked into the flesh wherever they lodged. For this reason, my mother said, I should not do much alone in quills until I was as tall as my cousin Warca-Ziwin.

Always after these confining lessons I was wild with surplus spirits, and found joyous relief in running loose in the open again. Many a summer afternoon, a party of four or five of my playmates roamed over the hills with me. We each carried a light sharpened rod about four feet long, with which we pried up certain sweet roots. When we had eaten all the choice roots we chanced upon, we shouldered our rods and strayed off into patches of a stalky plant under whose yellow blossoms we found little crystal drops of gum. Drop by drop we gath-

ered this nature's rockcandy, until each of us could boast of a lump the
size of a small bird's egg. Soon satiated with its woody flavor, we tossed
away our gum, to return again to the sweet roots.

I remember well how we used to exchange our necklaces, beaded
belts, and sometimes even our moccasins. We pretended to offer them
as gifts to one another. We delighted in impersonating our own mothers. We talked of things we had heard them say in their conversations.
We imitated their various manners, even to the inflection of their
voices. In the lap of the prairie we seated ourselves upon our feet; and
leaning our painted cheeks in the palms of our hands, we rested our
elbows on our knees, and bent forward as old women were most
accustomed to do.

While one was telling of some heroic deed recently done by a near
relative, the rest of us listened attentively, and exclaimed in under-
tones, "Han! han!" (yes! yes!) whenever the speaker paused for
breath, or sometimes for our sympathy. As the discourse became more
thrilling, according to our ideas, we raised our voices in these interjec-
tions. In these impersonations our parents were led to say only those
things that were in common favor.

No matter how exciting a tale we might be rehearsing, the mere
shifting of a cloud shadow in the landscape near by was sufficient to
change our impulses; and soon we were all chasing the great shadows
that played among the hills. We shouted and whooped in the chase;
laughing and calling to one another, we were like little sportive
nymphs on that Dakota sea of rolling green.

On one occasion, I forgot the cloud shadow in a strange notion to
catch up with my own shadow. Standing straight and still, I began to
glide after it, putting out one foot cautiously. When, with the greatest
care, I set my foot in advance of myself, my shadow crept onward too.
Then again I tried it; this time with the other foot. Still again my
shadow escaped me. I began to run; and away flew my shadow, always
just a step beyond me. Faster and faster I ran, setting my teeth and
clenching my fists, determined to overtake my own fleet shadow. But
ever swifter it glided before me, while I was growing breathless and
hot. Slackening my speed, I was greatly vexed that my shadow should
check its pace also. Daring it to the utmost, as I thought, I sat down
upon a rock imbedded in the hillside.

So! My shadow had the impudence to sit down beside me!

Now my comrades caught up with me, and began to ask why I was
running away so fast.

"Oh, I was chasing my shadow! Didn't you ever do that?" I inquired,
surprised that they should not understand.

They planted their moccasined feet firmly upon my shadow to stay
it, and I arose. Again my shadow slipped away, and moved as often as
I did. Then we gave up trying to catch my shadow.

Before this peculiar experience I have no distinct memory of having
recognized any vital bond between myself and my own shadow. I
never gave it an afterthought.

Returning our borrowed belts and trinkets, we rambled homeward. That evening, as on other evenings. I went to sleep over my legends.

IV. The Coffee-Making

One summer afternoon, my mother left me alone in our wigwam, while she went across the way to my aunt's dwelling.

I did not much like to stay alone in our tepee, for I feared a tall, broad-shouldered crazy man, some forty years old, who walked loose among the hills. Wiyaka-Napbina (Wearer of a Feather Necklace) was harmless, and whenever he came into a wigwam he was driven there by extreme hunger. He went nude except for the half of a red blanket he girdled around his waist. In one tawny arm he used to carry a heavy bunch of wild sunflowers that he gathered in his aimless ramblings. His black hair was matted by the winds, and scorched into a dry red by the constant summer sun. As he took great strides, placing one brown bare foot directly in front of the other, he swung his long lean arm to and fro.

Frequently he paused in his walk and gazed far backward, shading his eyes with his hand. He was under the belief that an evil spirit was haunting his steps. This was what my mother told me once, when I sneered at such a silly big man. I was brave when my mother was near by, and Wiyaka-Napbina walking farther and farther away.

"Pity the man, my child. I knew him when he was a brave and handsome youth. He was overtaken by a malicious spirit among the hills, one day, when he went hither and thither after his ponies. Since then he cannot stay away from the hills," she said.

I felt so sorry for the man in his misfortune that I prayed to the Great Spirit to restore him. But though I pitied him at a distance, I was still afraid of him when he appeared near our wigwam.

Thus, when my mother left me by myself that afternoon, I sat in a fearful mood within our tepee. I recalled all I had ever heard about Wiyaka-Napbina; and I tried to assure myself that though he might pass nearby, he would not come to our wigwam because there was no little girl around our grounds.

Just then, from without a hand lifted the canvas covering of the entrance; the shadow of a man fell within the wigwam, and a large roughly moccasined foot was planted inside.

For a moment I did not dare to breathe or stir, for I thought that could be no other than Wiyaka-Napbina. The next instant I sighed aloud in relief. It was an old grandfather who had often told me Iktomi legends.

"Where is your mother, my little grandchild?" were his first words.

"My mother is soon coming back from my aunt's tepee," I replied.

"Then I shall wait awhile for her return," he said, crossing his feet and seating himself upon a mat.

At once I began to play the part of a generous hostess. I turned to my mother's coffeepot.

Lifting the lid, I found nothing but coffee grounds in the bottom. I set the pot on a heap of cold ashes in the center, and filled it half full of warm Missouri River water. During this performance I felt conscious of being watched. Then breaking off a small piece of our unleavened bread, I placed it in a bowl. Turning soon to the coffeepot, which would never have boiled on a dead fire had I waited forever, I poured out a cup of worse than muddy warm water. Carrying the bowl in one hand and cup in the other, I handed the light luncheon to the old warrior. I offered them to him with the air of bestowing generous hospitality.

"How! how!"[2] he said, and placed the dishes on the ground in front of his crossed feet. He nibbled at the bread and sipped from the cup. I sat back against a pole watching him. I was proud to have succeeded so well in serving refreshments to a guest all by myself. Before the old warrior had finished eating, my mother entered. Immediately she wondered where I had found coffee, for she knew I had never made any, and that she had left the coffeepot empty. Answering the question in my mother's eyes, the warrior remarked, "My granddaughter made coffee on a heap of dead ashes, and served me the moment I came."

They both laughed, and mother said, "Wait a little longer, and I shall build a fire." She meant to make some real coffee. But neither she nor the warrior, whom the law of our custom had compelled to partake of my insipid hospitality, said anything to embarrass me. They treated my best judgment, poor as it was, with the utmost respect. It was not till long years afterward that I learned how ridiculous a thing I had done.

V. The Dead Man's Plum Bush

One autumn afternoon, many people came streaming toward the dwelling of our near neighbor. With painted faces, and wearing broad white bosoms of elk's teeth, they hurried down the narrow footpath to Haraka Wambdi's wigwam. Young mothers held their children by the hand, and half pulled them along in their haste. They overtook and passed by the bent old grandmothers who were trudging along with crooked canes toward the center of excitement. Most of the young braves galloped hither on their ponies. Toothless warriors, like the old women, came more slowly, though mounted on lively ponies. They sat proudly erect on their horses. They wore their eagle plumes, and waved their various trophies of former wars.

In front of the wigwam a great fire was built, and several large black kettles of venison were suspended over it. The crowd were seated about it on the grass in a great circle. Behind them some of the braves stood leaning against the necks of their ponies, their tall figures draped in loose robes which were well drawn over their eyes.

Young girls, with their faces glowing like bright red autumn leaves,

2. Or *hao*, Indian greeting.

their glossy braids falling over each ear, sat coquettishly beside their chaperons. It was a custom for young Indian women to invite some older relative to escort them to the public feasts. Though it was not an iron law, it was generally observed.

Haraka Wambdi was a strong young brave, who had just returned from his first battle, a warrior. His near relatives, to celebrate his new rank, were spreading a feast to which the whole of the Indian village was invited.

Holding my pretty striped blanket in readiness to throw over my shoulders, I grew more and more restless as I watched the gay throng assembling. My mother was busily broiling a wild duck that my aunt had that morning brought over.

"Mother, mother, why do you stop to cook a small meal when we are invited to a feast?" I asked, with a snarl in my voice.

"My child, learn to wait. On our way to the celebration we are going to stop at Chanyu's wigwam. His aged mother-in-law is lying very ill, and I think she would like a taste of this small game."

Having once seen the suffering on the thin, pinched features of this dying woman, I felt a momentary shame that I had not remembered her before.

On our way, I ran ahead of my mother, and was reaching out my hand to pick some purple plums that grew on a small bush, when I was checked by a low "Sh!" from my mother.

"Why, mother, I want to taste the plums!" I exclaimed, as I dropped my hand to my side in disappointment.

"Never pluck a single plum from this bush, my child, for its roots are wrapped around an Indian's skeleton. A brave is buried here. While he lived, he was so fond of playing the game of striped plum seeds that, at his death, his set of plum seeds were buried in his hands. From them sprang up this little bush."

Eyeing the forbidden fruit, I trod lightly on the sacred ground, and dared to speak only in whispers, until we had gone many paces from it. After that time, I halted in my ramblings whenever I came in sight of the plum bush. I grew sober with awe, and was alert to hear a long-drawn-out whistle rise from the roots of it. Though I had never heard with my own ears this strange whistle of departed spirits, yet I had listened so frequently to hear the old folks describe it that I knew I should recognize it at once.

The lasting impression of that day, as I recall it now, is what my mother told me about the dead man's plum bush.

VI. The Ground Squirrel

In the busy autumn days, my cousin Warca-Ziwin's mother came to our wigwam to help my mother preserve foods for our winter use. I was very fond of my aunt, because she was not so quiet as my mother. Though she was older, she was more jovial and less reserved. She was slender and remarkably erect. While my mother's hair was heavy and black, my aunt had unusually thin locks.

Ever since I knew her, she wore a string of large blue beads around her neck,—beads that were precious because my uncle had given them to her when she was a younger woman. She had a peculiar swing in her gait, caused by a long stride rarely natural to so slight a figure. It was during my aunt's visit with us that my mother forgot her accustomed quietness, often laughing heartily at some of my aunt's witty remarks.

I loved my aunt threefold: for her hearty laughter, for the cheerfulness she caused my mother, and most of all for the times she dried my tears and held me in her lap, when my mother had reproved me.

Early in the cool mornings, just as the yellow rim of the sun rose above the hills, we were up and eating our breakfast. We awoke so early that we saw the sacred hour when a misty smoke hung over a pit surrounded by an impassable sinking mire. This strange smoke appeared every morning, both winter and summer; but most visibly in midwinter it rose immediately above the marshy spot. By the time the full face of the sun appeared above the eastern horizon, the smoke vanished. Even very old men, who had known this country the longest, said that the smoke from this pit had never failed a single day to rise heavenward.

As I frolicked about our dwelling, I used to stop suddenly, and with a fearful awe watch the smoking of the unknown fires. While the vapor was visible, I was afraid to go very far from our wigwam unless I went with my mother.

From a field in the fertile river bottom my mother and aunt gathered an abundant supply of corn. Near our tepee, they spread a large canvas upon the grass, and dried their sweet corn in it. I was left to watch the corn, that nothing should disturb it. I played around it with dolls made of ears of corn. I braided their soft fine silk for hair, and gave them blankets as various as the scraps I found in my mother's workbag.

There was a little stranger with a black-and-yellow-striped coat that used to come to the drying corn. It was a little ground squirrel; who was so fearless of me that he came to one corner of the canvas and carried away as much of the sweet corn as he could hold. I wanted very much to catch him, and rub his pretty fur back, but my mother said he would be so frightened if I caught him that he would bite my fingers. So I was as content as he to keep the corn between us. Every morning he came for more corn. Some evenings I have seen him creeping about our grounds; and when I gave a sudden whoop of recognition, he ran quickly out of sight.

When mother had dried all the corn she wished, then she sliced great pumpkins into thin rings; and these she doubled and linked together into long chains. She hung them on a pole that stretched between two forked posts. The wind and sun soon thoroughly dried the chains of pumpkin. Then she packed them away in a case of thick and stiff buckskin.

In the sun and wind she also dried many wild fruits,—cherries, berries, and plums. But chiefest among my early recollections of autumn is that one of the corn drying and the ground squirrel.

I have few memories of winter days, at this period of my life, though many of the summer. There is one only which I can recall.

Some missionaries gave me a little bag of marbles. They were all sizes and colors. Among them were some of colored glass. Walking with my mother to the river, on a late winter day, we found great chunks of ice piled all along the bank. The ice on the river was floating in huge pieces. As I stood beside one large block, I noticed for the first time the colors of the rainbow in the crystal ice. Immediately I thought of my glass marbles at home. With my bare fingers I tried to pick out some of the colors, for they seemed so near the surface. But my fingers began to sting with the intense cold, and I had to bite them hard to keep from crying.

From that day on, for many a moon, I believed that glass marbles had river ice inside of them.

VII. The Big Red Apples

The first turning away from the easy, natural flow of my life occurred in an early spring. It was in my eighth year; in the month of March, I afterward learned. At this age I knew but one language, and that was my mother's native tongue.

From some of my playmates I heard that two paleface missionaries were in our village. They were from that class of white men who wore big hats and carried large hearts, they said. Running direct to my mother, I began to question her why these two strangers were among us. She told me, after I had teased much, that they had come to take away Indian boys and girls to the East. My mother did not seem to want me to talk about them. But in a day or two, I gleaned many wonderful stories from my playfellows concerning the strangers.

"Mother, my friend Judéwin is going home with the missionaries. She is going to a more beautiful country than ours; the palefaces told her so!" I said wistfully, wishing in my heart that I too might go.

Mother sat in a chair, and I was hanging on her knee. Within the last two seasons my big brother Dawée had returned from a three years' education in the East, and his coming back influenced my mother to take a farther step from her native way of living. First it was a change from the buffalo skin to the white man's canvas that covered our wigwam. Now she had given up her wigwam of slender poles, to live, a foreigner, in a home of clumsy logs.

"Yes, my child, several others besides Judéwin are going away with the palefaces. Your brother said the missionaries had inquired about his little sister," she said, watching my face very closely.

My heart thumped so hard against my breast, I wondered if she could hear it.

"Did he tell them to take me, mother?" I asked, fearing lest Dawée had forbidden the palefaces to see me, and that my hope of going to the Wonderland would be entirely blighted.

With a sad, slow smile, she answered: "There! I knew you were wishing to go, because Judéwin has filled your ears with the white men's lies. Don't believe a word they say! Their words are sweet, but, my child, their deeds are bitter. You will cry for me, but they will not even soothe you. Stay with me, my little one! Your brother Dawée says that going East, away from your mother, is too hard an experience for his baby sister."

Thus my mother discouraged my curiosity about the lands beyond our eastern horizon; for it was not yet an ambition for Letters that was stirring me. But on the following day the missionaries did come to our very house. I spied them coming up the footpath leading to our cottage. A third man was with them, but he was not my brother Dawée. It was another, a young interpreter, a paleface who had a smattering of the Indian language. I was ready to run out to meet them, but I did not dare to displease my mother. With great glee, I jumped up and down on our ground floor. I begged my mother to open the door, that they would be sure to come to us. Alas! They came, they saw, and they conquered!

Judéwin had told me of the great tree where grew red, red apples; and how we could reach out our hands and pick all the red apples we could eat. I had never seen apple trees. I had never tasted more than a dozen red apples in my life; and when I heard of the orchards of the East, I was eager to roam among them. The missionaries smiled into my eyes, and patted my head. I wondered how mother could say such hard words against them.

"Mother, ask them if little girls may have all the red apples they want, when they go East," I whispered aloud, in my excitement.

The interpreter heard me, and answered: "Yes, little girl, the nice red apples are for those who pick them; and you will have a ride on the iron horse if you go with these good people."

I had never seen a train, and he knew it.

"Mother, I'm going East! I like big red apples, and I want to ride on the iron horse! Mother, say yes!" I pleaded.

My mother said nothing. The missionaries waited in silence; and my eyes began to blur with tears, though I struggled to choke them back. The corners of my mouth twitched, and my mother saw me.

"I am not ready to give you any word," she said to them. "Tomorrow I shall send you my answer by my son."

With this they left us. Alone with my mother, I yielded to my tears, and cried aloud, shaking my head so as not to hear what she was saying to me. This was the first time I had ever been so unwilling to give up my own desire that I refused to hearken to my mother's voice.

There was a solemn silence in our home that night. Before I went to bed I begged the Great Spirit to make my mother willing I should go with the missionaries.

The next morning came, and my mother called me to her side. "My daughter, do you still persist in wishing to leave your mother?" she asked.

"Oh, mother, it is not that I wish to leave you, but I want to see the wonderful Eastern land," I answered.

My dear old aunt came to our house that morning, and I heard her say, "Let her try it."

I hoped that, as usual, my aunt was pleading on my side. My brother Dawée came for mother's decision. I dropped my play, and crept close to my aunt.

"Yes, Dawée, my daughter, though she does not understand what it all means, is anxious to go. She will need an education when she is grown, for then there will be fewer real Dakotas, and many more palefaces. This tearing her away, so young, from her mother is necessary, if I would have her an educated woman. The palefaces, who owe us a large debt for stolen lands, have begun to pay a tardy justice in offering some education to our children. But I know my daughter must suffer keenly in this experiment. For her sake, I dread to tell you my reply to the missionaries. Go, tell them that they may take my little daughter, and that the Great Spirit shall not fail to reward them according to their hearts."

Wrapped in my heavy blanket, I walked with my mother to the carriage that was soon to take us to the iron horse. I was happy. I met my playmates, who were also wearing their best thick blankets. We showed one another our new beaded moccasins, and the width of the belts that girdled our new dresses. Soon we were being drawn rapidly away by the white man's horses. When I saw the lonely figure of my mother vanish in the distance, a sense of regret settled heavily upon me. I felt suddenly weak, as if I might fall limp to the ground. I was in the hands of strangers whom my mother did not fully trust. I no longer felt free to be myself, or to voice my own feelings. The tears trickled down my cheeks, and I buried my face in the folds of my blanket. Now the first step, parting me from my mother, was taken, and all my belated tears availed nothing.

Having driven thirty miles to the ferryboat, we crossed the Missouri in the evening. Then riding again a few miles eastward, we stopped before a massive brick building. I looked at it in amazement, and with a vague misgiving, for in our village I had never seen so large a house. Trembling with fear and distrust of the palefaces, my teeth chattering from the chilly ride, I crept noiselessly in my soft moccasins along the narrow hall, keeping very close to the bare wall. I was as frightened and bewildered as the captured young of a wild creature.

Atlantic Monthly, January 1900

The School Days of an Indian Girl

I. The Land of Red Apples

There were eight in our party of bronzed children who were going East
with the missionaries. Among us were three young braves, two tall
girls, and we three little ones, Judéwin, Thowin, and I.

We had been very impatient to start on our journey to the Red Apple
Country, which, we were told, lay a little beyond the great circular
horizon of the Western prairie. Under a sky of rosy apples we dreamt
of roaming as freely and happily as we had chased the cloud shadows
on the Dakota plains. We had anticipated much pleasure from a ride
on the iron horse, but the throngs of staring palefaces disturbed and
troubled us.

On the train, fair women, with tottering babies on each arm, stopped
their haste and scrutinized the children of absent mothers. Large men,
with heavy bundles in their hands, halted near by, and riveted their
glassy blue eyes upon us.

I sank deep into the corner of my seat, for I resented being watched.
Directly in front of me, children who were no larger than I hung
themselves upon the backs of their seats, with their bold white faces
toward me. Sometimes they took their forefingers out of their mouths
and pointed at my moccasined feet. Their mothers, instead of reprov-
ing such rude curiosity, looked closely at me, and attracted their children's further notice to my blanket. This embarrassed me, and kept me
constantly on the verge of tears.

I sat perfectly still, with my eyes downcast, daring only now and
then to shoot long glances around me. Chancing to turn to the window
at my side, I was quite breathless upon seeing one familiar object. It
was the telegraph pole which strode by at short paces. Very near my
mother's dwelling, along the edge of a road thickly bordered with wild
sunflowers, some poles like these had been planted by white men.
Often I had stopped, on my way down the road, to hold my ear against
the pole, and, hearing its low moaning, I used to wonder what the
paleface had done to hurt it. Now I sat watching for each pole that
glided by to be the last one.

In this way I had forgotten my uncomfortable surroundings, when I
heard one of my comrades call out my name. I saw the missionary
standing very near, tossing candies and gums into our midst. This
amused us all, and we tried to see who could catch the most of the
sweetmeats. The missionary's generous distribution of candies was
impressed upon my memory by a disastrous result which followed. I
had caught more than my share of candies and gums, and soon after
our arrival at the school I had a chance to disgrace myself, which, I am
ashamed to say, I did.

Though we rode several days inside of the iron horse, I do not recall a single thing about our luncheons.

It was night when we reached the school grounds. The lights from the windows of the large buildings fell upon some of the icicled trees that stood beneath them. We were led toward an open door, where the brightness of the lights within flooded out over the heads of the excited palefaces who blocked the way. My body trembled more from fear than from the snow I trod upon.

Entering the house, I stood close against the wall. The strong glaring light in the large whitewashed room dazzled my eyes. The noisy hurrying of hard shoes upon a bare wooden floor increased the whirring in my ears. My only safety seemed to be in keeping next to the wall. As I was wondering in which direction to escape from all this confusion, two warm hands grasped me firmly, and in the same moment I was tossed high in midair. A rosy-cheeked paleface woman caught me in her arms. I was both frightened and insulted by such trifling. I stared into her eyes, wishing her to let me stand on my own feet, but she jumped me up and down with increasing enthusiasm. My mother had never made a plaything of her wee daughter. Remembering this I began to cry aloud.

They misunderstood the cause of my tears, and placed me at a white table loaded with food. There our party were united again. As I did not hush my crying, one of the older ones whispered to me, "Wait until you are alone in the night."

It was very little I could swallow besides my sobs, that evening.

"Oh, I want my mother and my brother Dawée! I want to go to my aunt!" I pleaded; but the ears of the palefaces could not hear me.

From the table we were taken along an upward incline of wooden boxes, which I learned afterward to call a stairway. At the top was a quiet hall, dimly lighted. Many narrow beds were in one straight line down the entire length of the wall. In them lay sleeping brown faces, which peeped just out of the coverings. I was tucked into bed with one of the tall girls, because she talked to me in my mother tongue and seemed to soothe me.

I had arrived in the wonderful land of rosy skies, but I was not happy, as I had thought I should be. My long travel and the bewildering sights had exhausted me. I fell asleep, heaving deep, tired sobs. My tears were left to dry themselves in streaks, because neither my aunt nor my mother was near to wipe them away.

II. The Cutting of My Long Hair

The first day in the land of apples was a bitter-cold one; for the snow still covered the ground, and the trees were bare. A large bell rang for breakfast, its loud metallic voice crashing through the belfry overhead and into our sensitive ears. The annoying clatter of shoes on bare floors gave us no peace. The constant clash of harsh noises, with an undercurrent of many voices murmuring an unknown tongue, made a bedlam within which I was securely tied. And though my spirit tore itself in struggling for its lost freedom, all was useless.

A paleface woman, with white hair, came up after us. We were placed in a line of girls who were marching into the dining room. These were Indian girls, in stiff shoes and closely clinging dresses. The small girls wore sleeved aprons and shingled[1] hair. As I walked noiselessly in my soft moccasins, I felt like sinking to the floor, for my blanket had been stripped from my shoulders. I looked hard at the Indian girls, who seemed not to care that they were even more immodestly dressed than I, in their tightly fitting clothes. While we marched in, the boys entered at an opposite door. I watched for the three young braves who came in our party. I spied them in the rear ranks, looking as uncomfortable as I felt.

A small bell was tapped, and each of the pupils drew a chair from under the table. Supposing this act meant they were to be seated, I pulled out mine and at once slipped into it from one side. But when I turned my head, I saw that I was the only one seated, and all the rest at our table remained standing. Just as I began to rise, looking shyly around to see how chairs were to be used, a second bell was sounded. All were seated at last, and I had to crawl back into my chair again. I heard a man's voice at one end of the hall, and I looked around to see him. But all the others hung their heads over their plates. As I glanced at the long chain of tables, I caught the eyes of a paleface woman upon me. Immediately I dropped my eyes, wondering why I was so keenly watched by the strange woman. The man ceased his mutterings, and then a third bell was tapped. Every one picked up his knife and fork and began eating. I began crying instead, for by this time I was afraid to venture anything more.

But this eating by formula was not the hardest trial in that first day. Late in the morning, my friend Judéwin gave me a terrible warning. Judéwin knew a few words of English; and she had overheard the paleface woman talk about cutting our long, heavy hair. Our mothers had taught us that only unskilled warriors who were captured had their hair shingled by the enemy. Among our people, short hair was worn by mourners, and shingled hair by cowards!

We discussed our fate some moments, and when Judéwin said, "We have to submit, because they are strong," I rebelled.

"No, I will not submit! I will struggle first!" I answered.

I watched my chance, and when no one noticed I disappeared. I crept up the stairs as quietly as I could in my squeaking shoes,—my moccasins had been exchanged for shoes. Along the hall I passed, without knowing whither I was going. Turning aside to an open door, I found a large room with three white beds in it. The windows were

---

1. Bobbed, cut short.

covered with dark green curtains, which made the room very dim. Thankful that no one was there, I directed my steps toward the corner farthest from the door. On my hands and knees I crawled under the bed, and cuddled myself in the dark corner.

From my hiding place I peered out, shuddering with fear whenever I heard footsteps near by. Though in the hall loud voices were calling my name, and I knew that even Judéwin was searching for me, I did not open my mouth to answer. Then the steps were quickened and the voices became excited. The sounds came nearer and nearer. Women and girls entered the room. I held my breath, and watched them open closet doors and peep behind large trunks. Someone threw up the curtains, and the room was filled with sudden light. What caused them to stoop and look under the bed I do not know. I remember being dragged out, though I resisted by kicking and scratching wildly. In spite of myself, I was carried downstairs and tied fast in a chair.

I cried aloud, shaking my head all the while until I felt the cold blades of the scissors against my neck, and heard them gnaw off one of my thick braids. Then I lost my spirit. Since the day I was taken from my mother I had suffered extreme indignities. People had stared at me. I had been tossed about in the air like a wooden puppet. And now my long hair was shingled like a coward's! In my anguish I moaned for my mother, but no one came to comfort me. Not a soul reasoned quietly with me, as my own mother used to do; for now I was only one of many little animals driven by a herder.

III. The Snow Episode

A short time after our arrival we three Dakotas were playing in the snowdrifts. We were all still deaf to the English language, excepting Judéwin, who always heard such puzzling things. One morning we learned through her ears that we were forbidden to fall lengthwise in the snow, as we had been doing, to see our own impressions. However, before many hours we had forgotten the order, and were having great sport in the snow, when a shrill voice called us. Looking up, we saw an imperative hand beckoning us into the house. We shook the snow off ourselves, and started toward the woman as slowly as we dared.

Judéwin said: "Now the paleface is angry with us. She is going to punish us for falling into the snow. If she looks straight into your eyes and talks loudly, you must wait until she stops. Then, after a tiny pause, say, 'No.' " The rest of the way we practiced upon the little word "no."

As it happened, Thowin was summoned to judgment first. The door shut behind her with a click.

Judéwin and I stood silently listening at the keyhole. The paleface woman talked in very severe tones. Her words fell from her lips like crackling embers, and her inflection ran up like the small end of a switch! I understood her voice better than the things she was saying. I was certain we had made her very impatient with us. Judéwin heard enough of the words to realize all too late that she had taught us the wrong reply.

"Oh, poor Thowin!" she gasped, as she put both hands over her ears.

Just then I heard Thowin's tremulous answer, "No."

With an angry exclamation, the woman gave her a hard spanking. Then she stopped to say something. Judéwin said it was this: "Are you going to obey my word the next time?"

Thowin answered again with the only word at her command, "No."

This time the woman meant her blows to smart, for the poor frightened girl shrieked at the top of her voice. In the midst of the whipping the blows ceased abruptly, and the woman asked another question: "Are you going to fall in the snow again?"

Thowin gave her bad password another trial. We heard her say feebly, "No! No!"

With this the woman hid away her half-worn slipper, and led the child out, stroking her black shorn head. Perhaps it occurred to her that brute force is not the solution for such a problem. She did nothing to Judéwin nor to me. She only returned to us our unhappy comrade, and left us alone in the room.

During the first two or three seasons misunderstandings as ridiculous as this one of the snow episode frequently took place, bringing unjustifiable frights and punishments into our little lives.

Within a year I was able to express myself somewhat in broken English. As soon as I comprehended a part of what was said and done, a mischievous spirit of revenge possessed me. One day I was called in from my play for some misconduct. I had disregarded a rule which seemed to me very needlessly binding. I was sent into the kitchen to mash the turnips for dinner. It was noon, and steaming dishes were hastily carried into the dining room. I hated turnips, and their odor which came from the brown jar was offensive to me. With fire in my heart, I took the wooden tool that the paleface woman held out to me. I stood upon a step, and, grasping the handle with both hands, I bent in hot rage over the turnips. I worked my vengeance upon them. All were so busily occupied that no one noticed me. I saw that the turnips were in a pulp, and that further beating could not improve them; but the order was, "Mash these turnips," and mash them I would! I renewed my energy; and as I sent the masher into the bottom of the jar, I felt a satisfying sensation that the weight of my body had gone into it.

Just here a paleface woman came up to my table. As she looked into the jar, she shoved my hands roughly aside. I stood fearless and angry. She placed her red hands upon the rim of the jar. Then she gave one lift and a stride away from the table. But lo! the pulpy contents fell through the crumbled bottom to the floor! She spared me no scolding phrases that I had earned. I did not heed them. I felt triumphant in my revenge, though deep within me I was a wee bit sorry to have broken the jar.

As I sat eating my dinner, and saw that no turnips were served, I whooped in my heart for having once asserted the rebellion within me.

IV. The Devil

Among the legends the old warriors used to tell me were many stories of evil spirits. But I was taught to fear them no more than those who stalked about in material guise. I never knew there was an insolent chieftain among the bad spirits, who dared to array his forces against the Great Spirit, until I heard this white man's legend from a paleface woman.

Out of a large book she showed me a picture of the white man's devil. I looked in horror upon the strong claws that grew out of his fur-covered fingers. His feet were like his hands. Trailing at his heels was a scaly tail tipped with a serpent's open jaws. His face was a patchwork: he had bearded cheeks, like some I had seen palefaces wear; his nose was an eagle's bill, and his sharp-pointed ears were pricked up like those of a sly fox. Above them a pair of cow's horns curved upward. I trembled with awe, and my heart throbbed in my throat, as I looked at the king of evil spirits. Then I heard the paleface woman say that this terrible creature roamed loose in the world, and that little girls who disobeyed school regulations were to be tortured by him.

That night I dreamt about this evil divinity. Once again I seemed to be in my mother's cottage. An Indian woman had come to visit my mother. On opposite sides of the kitchen stove, which stood in the center of the small house, my mother and her guest were seated in straight-backed chairs. I played with a train of empty spools hitched together on a string. It was night, and the wick burned feebly. Suddenly I heard someone turn our door-knob from without.

My mother and the woman hushed their talk, and both looked toward the door. It opened gradually. I waited behind the stove. The hinges squeaked as the door was slowly, very slowly pushed inward.

Then in rushed the devil! He was tall! He looked exactly like the picture I had seen of him in the white man's papers. He did not speak to my mother, because he did not know the Indian language, but his glittering yellow eyes were fastened upon me. He took long strides around the stove, passing behind the woman's chair. I threw down my spools, and ran to my mother. He did not fear her, but followed closely after me. Then I ran round and round the stove, crying aloud for help. But my mother and the woman seemed not to know my danger. They sat still, looking quietly upon the devil's chase after me. At last I grew dizzy. My head revolved as on a hidden pivot. My knees became numb, and doubled under my weight like a pair of knife blades without a spring. Beside my mother's chair I fell in a heap. Just as the devil stooped over me with outstretched claws my mother awoke from her quiet indifference, and lifted me on her lap. Whereupon the devil vanished, and I was awake.

On the following morning I took my revenge upon the devil. Stealing into the room where a wall of shelves was filled with books, I drew forth The Stories of the Bible. With a broken slate pencil I carried in my apron pocket, I began by scratching out his wicked eyes. A few moments later, when I was ready to leave the room, there was a ragged hole in the page where the picture of the devil had once been.

V. Iron Routine

A loud-clamoring bell awakened us at half past six in the cold winter mornings. From happy dreams of Western rolling lands and unlassoed freedom we tumbled out upon chilly bare floors back again into a paleface day. We had short time to jump into our shoes and clothes, and wet our eyes with icy water, before a small hand bell was vigorously run for roll call.

There were too many drowsy children and too numerous orders for the day to waste a moment in any apology to nature for giving her children such a shock in the early morning. We rushed downstairs, bounding over two high steps at a time, to land in the assembly room.

A paleface woman, with a yellowcovered roll book open on her arm and a gnawed pencil in her hand, appeared at the door. Her small, tired face was coldly lighted with a pair of large gray eyes.

She stood still in a halo of authority, while over the rim of her spectacles her eyes pried nervously about the room. Having glanced at her long list of names and called out the first one, she tossed up her chin and peered through the crystals of her spectacles to make sure of the answer "Here."

Relentlessly her pencil black-marked our daily records if we were not present to respond to our names, and no chum of ours had done it successfully for us. No matter if a dull headache or the painful cough of slow consumption[2] had delayed the absentee, there was only time enough to mark the tardiness. It was next to impossible to leave the iron routine after the civilizing machine had once begun its day's buzzing; and as it was inbred in me to suffer in silence rather than to appeal to the ears of one whose open eyes could not see my pain, I have many times trudged in the day's harness heavy-footed, like a dumb sick brute.

Once I lost a dear classmate. I remember well how she used to mope along at my side, until one morning she could not raise her head from her pillow. At her deathbed I stood weeping, as the paleface woman sat near her moistening the dry lips. Among the folds of the bedclothes

---

2. Old term for tuberculosis.

I saw the open pages of the white man's Bible. The dying Indian girl talked disconnectedly of Jesus the Christ and the paleface who was cooling her swollen hands and feet.

I grew bitter, and censured the woman for cruel neglect of our physical ills. I despised the pencils that moved automatically, and the one teaspoon which dealt out, from a large bottle, healing to a row of variously ailing Indian children. I blamed the hard-working, well-meaning, ignorant woman who was inculcating in our hearts her superstitious ideas. Though I was sullen in all my little troubles, as soon as I felt better I was ready again to smile upon the cruel woman. Within a week I was again actively testing the chains which tightly bound my individuality like a mummy for burial.

The melancholy of those black days has left so long a shadow that it darkens the path of years that have since gone by. These sad memories rise above those of smoothly grinding school days. Perhaps my Indian nature is the moaning wind which stirs them now for their present record. But, however tempestuous this is within me, it comes out as the low voice of a curiously colored seashell, which is only for those ears that are bent with compassion to hear it.

VI. Four Strange Summers

After my first three years of school, I roamed again in the Western country through four strange summers.

During this time I seemed to hang in the heart of chaos, beyond the touch or voice of human aid. My brother, being almost ten years my senior, did not quite understand my feelings. My mother had never gone inside of a schoolhouse, and so she was not capable of comforting her daughter who could read and write. Even nature seemed to have no place for me. I was neither a wee girl nor a tall one; neither a wild Indian nor a tame one. This deplorable situation was the effect of my brief course in the East, and the unsatisfactory "teenth" in a girl's years.

It was under these trying conditions that, one bright afternoon, as I sat restless and unhappy in my mother's cabin, I caught the sound of the spirited step of my brother's pony on the road which passed by our dwelling. Soon I heard the wheels of a light buckboard[3] and Dawée's familiar "Ho!" to his pony. He alighted upon the bare ground in front of our house. Tying his pony to one of the projecting corner logs of the low-roofed cottage, he stepped upon the wooden doorstep.

I met him there with a hurried greeting, and, as I passed by, he looked a quiet "What?" into my eyes.

When he began talking with my mother, I slipped the rope from the pony's bridle. Seizing the reins and bracing my feet against the dashboard, I wheeled around in an instant. The pony was ever ready to try

---

3. A four-wheeled open carriage.

his speed. Looking backward, I saw Dawée waving his hand to me. I turned with the curve in the road and disappeared. I followed the winding road which crawled upward between the bases of little hillocks. Deep water-worn ditches ran parallel on either side. A strong wind blew against my cheeks and fluttered my sleeves. The pony reached the top of the highest hill, and began an even race on the level lands. There was nothing moving within that great circular horizon of the Dakota prairies save the tall grasses, over which the wind blew and rolled off in long, shadowy waves.

Within this vast wigwam of blue and green I rode reckless and insignificant. It satisfied my small consciousness to see the white foam fly from the pony's mouth.

Suddenly, out of the earth a coyote came forth at a swinging trot that was taking the cunning thief toward the hills and the village beyond. Upon the moment's impulse, I gave him a long chase and a wholesome fright. As I turned away to go back to the village, the wolf sank down upon his haunches for rest, for it was a hot summer day; and as I drove slowly homeward, I saw his sharp nose pointed at me, until I vanished below the margin of the hilltops.

In a little while I came in sight of my mother's house. Dawée stood in the yard, laughing at an old warrior who was pointing his forefinger, and again waving his whole hand, toward the hills. With his blanket drawn over one shoulder, he talked and motioned excitedly. Dawée turned the old man by the shoulder and pointed me out to him.

"Oh han!" (Oh yes) the warrior muttered, and went his way. He had climbed the top of his favorite barren hill to survey the surrounding prairies, when he spied my chase after the coyote. His keen eyes recognized the pony and driver. At once uneasy for my safety, he had come running to my mother's cabin to give her warning. I did not appreciate his kindly interest, for there was an unrest gnawing at my heart.

As soon as he went away, I asked Dawée about something else.

"No, my baby sister, I cannot take you with me to the party tonight," he replied. Though I was not far from fifteen, and I felt that before long I should enjoy all the privileges of my tall cousin, Dawée persisted in calling me his baby sister.

That moonlight night, I cried in my mother's presence when I heard the jolly young people pass by our cottage. They were no more young braves in blankets and eagle plumes, nor Indian maids with prettily painted cheeks. They had gone three years to school in the East, and had become civilized. The young men wore the white man's coat and trousers, with bright neckties. The girls wore tight muslin dresses; with ribbons at neck and waist. At these gatherings they talked English. I could speak English almost as well as my brother, but I was not properly dressed to be taken along. I had no hat, no ribbons, and no close-fitting gown. Since my return from school I had thrown away my shoes, and wore again the soft moccasins.

While Dawée was busily preparing to go I controlled my tears. But when I heard him bounding away on his pony, I buried my face in my arms and cried hot tears.

My mother was troubled by my unhappiness. Coming to my side, she offered me the only printed matter we had in our home. It was an Indian Bible, given her some years ago by a missionary. She tried to console me. "Here, my child, are the white man's papers. Read a little from them," she said most piously.

I took it from her hand, for her sake; but my enraged spirit felt more like burning the book, which afforded me no help, and was a perfect delusion to my mother. I did not read it, but laid it unopened on the floor, where I sat on my feet. The dim yellow light of the braided muslin burning in a small vessel[4] of oil flickered and sizzled in the awful silent storm which followed my rejection of the Bible.

Now my wrath against the fates consumed my tears before they reached my eyes. I sat stony, with a bowed head. My mother threw a shawl over her head and shoulders, and stepped out into the night.

After an uncertain solitude, I was suddenly aroused by a loud cry piercing the night. It was my mother's voice wailing among the barren hills which held the bones of buried warriors. She called aloud for her brothers' spirits to support her in her helpless misery. My fingers grew icy cold, as I realized that my unrestrained tears had betrayed my suffering to her, and she was grieving for me.

Before she returned, though I knew she was on her way, for she had ceased her weeping, I extinguished the light, and leaned my head on the window sill.

Many schemes of running away from my surroundings hovered about in my mind. A few more moons of such a turmoil drove me away to the Eastern school. I rode on the white man's iron steed, thinking it would bring me back to my mother in a few winters, when I should be grown tall, and there would be congenial friends awaiting me.

VII. Incurring my Mother's Displeasure

In the second journey to the East I had not come without some precautions. I had a secret interview with one of our best medicine men, and when I left his wigwam I carried securely in my sleeve a tiny bunch of magic roots. This possession assured me of friends wherever I should go. So absolutely did I believe in its charms that I wore it through all the school routine for more than a year. Then, before I lost my faith in the dead roots, I lost the little buckskin bag containing all my good luck.

At the close of this second term of three years I was the proud owner of my first diploma. The following autumn I ventured upon a college career against my mother's will.

I had written for her approval, but in her reply I found no encour-

---

4. An oil lamp with a wick made of braided cotton.

agement. She called my notice to her neighbors' children, who had completed their education in three years. They had returned to their homes, and were then talking English with the frontier settlers. Her few words hinted that I had better give up my slow attempt to learn the white man's ways, and be content to roam over the prairies and find my living upon wild roots. I silenced her by deliberate disobedience.

Thus, homeless and heavy-hearted, I began anew my life among strangers.

As I hid myself in my little room in the college dormitory, away from the scornful and yet curious eyes of the students, I pined for sympathy. Often I wept in secret, wishing I had gone West, to be nourished by my mother's love, instead of remaining among a cold race whose hearts were frozen hard with prejudice.

During the fall and winter seasons I scarcely had a real friend, though by that time several of my classmates were courteous to me at a safe distance.

My mother had not yet forgiven my rudeness to her, and I had no moment for letter-writing. By daylight and lamplight, I spun with reeds and thistles, until my hands were tired from their weaving, the magic design which promised me the white man's respect.

At length, in the spring term, I entered an oratorical contest among the various classes. As the day of competition approached, it did not seem possible that the event was so near at hand, but it came. In the chapel the classes assembled together, with their invited guests. The high platform was carpeted, and gayly festooned with college colors. A bright while light illumined the room, and outlined clearly the great polished beams that arched the domed ceiling. The assembled crowds filled the air with pulsating murmurs. When the hour for speaking arrived all were hushed. But on the wall the old clock which pointed out the trying moment ticked calmly on.

One after another I saw and heard the orators. Still, I could not realize that they longed for the favorable decision of the judges as much as I did. Each contestant received a loud burst of applause, and some were cheered heartily. Too soon my turn came, and I paused a moment behind the curtains for a deep breath. After my concluding words, I heard the same applause that the others had called out.

Upon my retreating steps, I was astounded to receive from my fellow students a large bouquet of roses tied with flowing ribbons. With the lovely flowers I fled from the stage. This friendly token was a rebuke to me for the hard feelings I had borne them.

Later, the decision of the judges awarded me the first place. Then there was a mad uproar in the hall, where my classmates sang and shouted my name at the top of their lungs; and the disappointed students howled and brayed in fearfully dissonant tin trumpets. In this excitement, happy students rushed forward to offer their congratulations. And I could not conceal a smile when they wished to escort me in a procession to the students' parlor, where all were going to calm themselves. Thanking them for the kind spirit which prompted them to make such a proposition, I walked alone with the night to my own little room.

A few weeks afterward, I appeared as the college representative in another contest. This time the competition was among orators from different colleges in our state. It was held at the state capital, in one of the largest opera houses.

Here again was a strong prejudice against my people. In the evening, as the great audience filled the house, the student bodies began warring among themselves. Fortunately, I was spared witnessing any of the noisy wrangling before the contest began. The slurs against the Indian that stained the lips of our opponents were already burning like a dry fever within my breast.

But after the orations were delivered a deeper burn awaited me. There, before that vast ocean of eyes, some college rowdies threw out a large white flag, with a drawing of a most forlorn Indian girl on it. Under this they had printed in bold black letters words that ridiculed the college which was represented by a "squaw." Such worse than barbarian rudeness embittered me. While we waited for the verdict of the judges, I gleamed fiercely upon the throngs of palefaces. My teeth were hard set, as I saw the white flag still floating insolently in the air.

Then anxiously we watched the man carry toward the stage the envelope containing the final decision.

There were two prizes given, that night, and one of them was mine!

The evil spirit laughed within me when the white flag dropped out of sight, and the hands which furled it hung limp in defeat.

Leaving the crowd as quickly as possible, I was soon in my room. The rest of the night I sat in an armchair and gazed into the crackling fire. I laughed no more in triumph when thus alone. The little taste of victory did not satisfy a hunger in my heart. In my mind I saw my mother far away on the Western plains, and she was holding a charge against me.

Atlantic Monthly, February 1900

The Trial Path

It was an autumn night on the plain. The smoke-lapels of the cone-shaped tepee flapped gently in the breeze. From the low night sky, with its myriad fire points, a large bright star peeped in at the smoke-hole of the wigwam between its fluttering lapels, down upon two Dakotas[1] talking in the dark. The mellow stream from the star above, a maid of twenty summers, on a bed of sweet-grass, drank in with her

---

1. A large group of tribes of North American Plains Indians, commonly called Sioux, now living on reser-vations in North and South Dakota, Minnesota, and Montana.

wakeful eyes. On the opposite side of the tepee, beyond the center fireplace, the grandmother spread her rug. Though once she had lain down, the telling of a story has aroused her to a sitting posture.

Her eyes are tight closed. With a thin palm she strokes her wind-shorn hair.

"Yes, my grandchild, the legend says the large bright stars are wise old warriors, and the small dim ones are handsome young braves," she reiterates, in a high, tremulous voice.

"Then this one peeping in at the smoke-hole yonder is my dear old grandfather," muses the young woman, in long-drawn-out words.

Her soft rich voice floats through the darkness within the tepee, over the cold ashes heaped on the center fire, and passes into the ear of the toothless old woman, who sits dumb in silent reverie. Thence it flies on swifter wing over many winter snows, till at last it cleaves the warm light atmosphere of her grandfather's youth. From there her grandmother made answer:

"Listen! I am young again. It is the day of your grandfather's death. The elder one, I mean, for there were two of them. They were like twins, though they were not brothers. They were friends, inseparable! All things, good and bad, they shared together, save one, which made them mad. In that heated frenzy the younger man slew his most intimate friend. He killed his elder brother, for long had their affection made them kin."

The voice of the old woman broke. Swaying her stopped shoulders to and fro as she sat upon her feet, she muttered vain exclamations beneath her breath. Her eyes, closed tight against the night, beheld behind them the light of bygone days. They saw again a rolling black cloud spread itself over the land. Her ear heard the deep rumbling of a tempest in the West. She bent low a cowering head, while angry thunder-birds shrieked across the sky. "Heyä! heyä!" (No! no!) groaned the toothless grandmother at the fury she had awakened. But the glorious peace afterward, when yellow sunshine made the people glad, now lured her memory onward through the storm.

"How fast, how loud my heart beats as I listen to the messenger's horrible tale!" she ejaculates. "From the fresh grave of the murdered man he hurried to our wigwam. Deliberately crossing his bare shins, he sat down unbidden beside my father, smoking a long-stemmed pipe. He had scarce caught his breath when, panting, he began:

" 'He was an only son, and a much-adored brother.'

"With wild, suspecting eyes he glanced at me as if I were in league with the man-killer, my lover. My father, exhaling sweet-scented smoke, assented—'How.' Then interrupting the 'Eya' on the lips of the round-eyed tale-bearer, he asked, 'My friend, will you smoke?' He took the pipe by its red-stone bowl, and pointed the long slender stem toward the man. 'Yes, yes, my friend,' replied he, and reached out a long brown arm.

"For many heart-throbs he puffed out the blue smoke, which hung

like a cloud between us. But even through the smoke-mist I saw his
sharp black eyes glittering toward me. I longed to ask what doom
awaited the young murderer, but dared not open my lips, lest I burst
forth into screams instead. My father plied the question. Returning the
pipe, the man replied: 'Oh, the chieftain and his chosen men have had
counsel together. They have agreed it is not safe to allow a man-killer
loose in our midst. He who kills one of our tribe is an enemy, and must
suffer the fate of a foe.'

"My temples throbbed like a pair of hearts!

"While I listened, a crier passed by my father's tepee. Mounted, and
swaying with his pony's steps, he proclaimed in a loud voice these
words (hark! I hear them now!): 'Ho-po! Give ear, all you people. A
terrible deed is done. Two friends—ay, brothers in heart—have quarrelled together. Now one lies buried on the hill, while the other sits, a
dreaded man-killer, within his dwelling. Says our chieftain: "He who
kills one of our tribe commits the offence of an enemy. As such he must
be tried. Let the father of the dead man choose the mode of torture or
taking of life. He has suffered livid pain, and he alone can judge how
great the punishment must be to avenge his wrong." It is done.

" 'Come, every one, to witness the judgment of a father upon him
who was once his son's best friend. A wild pony is now lassoed. The
man-killer must mount and ride the ranting beast. Stand you all in two
parallel lines from the center tepee of the bereaved family to the
wigwam opposite in the great outer ring. Between you, in the wide
space, is the given trailway. From the outer circle the rider must mount
and guide his pony toward the center tepee. If, having gone the entire
distance, the man-killer gains the center tepee still sitting on the pony's
back, his life is spared and pardon given. But should he fall, then he
himself has chosen death.'

"The crier's words now cease. A lull holds the village breathless.
Then hurrying feet tear along, swish, swish, through the tall grass.
Sobbing women hasten toward the trailway. The muffled groan of the
round camp-ground is unbearable. With my face hid in the folds of my
blanket, I run with the crowd toward the open place in the outer circle
of our village. In a moment the two long files of solemn-faced people
mark the path of the public trial. Ah! I see strong men trying to lead
the lassoed pony, pitching and rearing, with white foam flying from his
mouth. I choke with pain as I recognize my handsome lover desolately
alone, striding with set face toward the lassoed pony. 'Do not fall!
Choose life and me!' I cry in my breast, but over my lips I hold my thick
blanket.

"In an instant he has leaped astride the frightened beast, and the
men have let go their hold. Like an arrow sprung from a strong bow,
the pony, with extended nostrils, plunges halfway to the center tepee.
With all his might the rider draws the strong reins in. The pony halts
with wooden legs. The rider is thrown forward by force, but does not
fall. Now the maddened creature pitches, with flying heels. The line of

men and women sways outward. Now it is back in place, safe from the
kicking, snorting thing.

"The pony is fierce, with its large black eyes bulging out of their
sockets. With humped back and nose to the ground, it leaps into the air.
I shut my eyes. I cannot see him fall.

"A loud shout goes up from the hoarse throats of men and women.
I look. So! The wild horse is conquered. My lover dismounts at the
doorway of the center wigwam. The pony, wet with sweat and shaking
with exhaustion, stands like a guilty dog at his master's side. Here at
the entranceway of the tepee sit the bereaved father, mother, and
sister. The old warrior father rises. Stepping forward two long strides,
he grasps the hand of the murderer of his only son. Holding it so the
people can see, he cries, with compassionate voice, 'My son!' A murmur of surprise sweeps like a puff of sudden wind along the lines.

"The mother, with swollen eyes, with her hair cut square with her
shoulders, now rises. Hurrying to the young man, she takes his right
hand. 'My son!' she greets him. But on the second word her voice
shook, and she turned away in sobs.

"The young people rivet their eyes upon the young woman. She does
not stir. With bowed head, she sits motionless. The old warrior speaks
to her. 'Shake hands with the young brave, my little daughter. He was
your brother's friend for many years. Now he must be both friend and
brother to you.'

"Hereupon the girl rises. Slowly reaching out her slender hand, she
cries, with twitching lips, 'My brother!' The trial ends."

"Grandmother!" exploded the girl on the bed of sweet-grass. "Is this
true?"

"Tosh!" answered the grandmother, with a warmth in her voice. "It
is all true. During the fifteen winters of our wedded life many ponies
passed from our hands, but this little winner, Ohiyesa, was a constant
member of our family. At length, on that sad day your grandfather
died, Ohiyesa was killed at the grave."

Though the various groups of stars which move across the sky,
marking the passing of time, told how the night was in its zenith, the
old Dakota woman ventured an explanation of the burial ceremony.

"My grandchild, I have scarce ever breathed the sacred knowledge
in my heart. To-night I must tell you one of them. Surely you are old
enough to understand.

"Our wise medicine-man said I did well to hasten Ohiyesa after his
master. Perchance on the journey along the ghostpath your grandfather will weary, and in his heart wish for his pony. The creature,
already bound on the spirit-trail, will be drawn by that subtle wish.
Together master and beast will enter the next camp-ground."

The woman ceased her talking. But only the deep breathing of the
girl broke the quiet, for now the night wind had lulled itself to sleep.

"Hinnu! hinnu! Asleep! I have been talking in the dark, unheard. I did wish the girl would plant in her heart this sacred tale," muttered she, in a querulous voice.

Nestling into her bed of sweet-scented grass, she dozed away into another dream. Still the guardian star in the night sky beamed compassionately down upon the little tepee on the plain.

Harper's Monthly, October 1901; *American Indian Stories*, 1921

MARY AUSTIN
1868–1934

By the time Mary Austin was four, she had discovered an inner self whom she named "I-Mary," who comforted her and later inspired her to write. As a child she needed such comfort; from an early age she felt unwanted and unmothered for reasons she could never understand. She associated the birth of I-Mary with her mother's rejection, describing this second self as solitary and strong: "I-Mary suffered no need of being taken up and comforted; to be I-Mary was more solid and satisfying than to be Mary-by-herself" (*Earth Horizon* 47). Then, at the age of five, she had a vision: "God happened to Mary under the walnut tree" (*EH* 51). Walking through the orchard near her family's farm, she became aware of a Presence and a Voice, which she would look for again and again in the California desert and in the mountains and cañons of the Southwest.

Mary Austin was born September 9, 1868, to Susanna Savilla Graham and George Hunter of Carlinville, Illinois. She began school at five and a half, before she was legally entitled to attend, because "her mother did not know . . . what to do with her" (*EH* 58). Once enrolled, she was promoted to the third grade on the basis of her reading achievement. The resulting two years' difference between Austin and her school peers contributed to the loneliness she experienced and to her tendencies toward willfulness and nonconformity. She earned acceptance from her classmates, however, by telling stories. When Austin was ten, her father died, followed two months later by the death of her beloved sister Jennie. At her father's death, she overheard her mother tell a relative, "Why couldn't it have been Mary?" (Fink 20). Following these deaths, Susanna Hunter moved her family into town, separating Austin from the natural world she associated with the source of her own nurturance. So that she could work, her mother required Austin to take over domestic responsibilities; and she elevated Austin's older brother Jim to "head" of the family, enforcing a hierarchy based on male privilege that further alienated her daughter. Austin writes in her autobiography that her own simple requests became "a constantly annoying snag in the perfect family gesture of subservience to the Head," and that she continued to feel her own oddity as an anomaly, "not in the least realizing that there was growing up in the mind of thousands of young American women at that moment, the notion that [home], at least, *shouldn't* be the place of the apotheosis of its male members" (*EH* 129).

Although she suffered a nervous breakdown in the process, Austin graduated from Blackburn College at the age of nineteen, with a major in science, and shortly after moved to California with her mother and younger brother to join Jim, who had gone West to homestead public lands. She spent her first six months in the California desert in a state of malnutrition and near-collapse, for Jim's land had no irrigation and she arrived in a year of drought. Even so, she writes in her autobiography about being taken with the land, as a naturalist is; about finding unexpected nourishment in the wild grapes growing in parched surroundings, and about the moment, in the spring of 1889, when she went walking through a hollow and experienced again "the warm pervasive sweetness of ultimate reality" that she had known under the walnut tree in Illinois (198). In her relationship with nature, she was able to locate I-Mary, her source of inspiration, and to mother herself.

Unable to convince her mother and brother that she had a right to share the proceeds from the sale of the family home in Carlinville, and after twice failing to pass an examination in order to keep her teaching position, Austin resigned herself to marriage as her only means of economic support. After an apparently uninspired courtship, she and Stanford Wallace Austin, a novice vineyardist, were married May 18, 1891. Marriage temporarily gave Austin time to write, and through Ina Coolbrith, the western poet and former editor whom she met during a two-months' residence in San Francisco, she published her first story, "The Mother of Felipe," in the *Overland Monthly* in November 1892. When she presented the story to her mother, Susanna's only comment was, "I think you could have made more of it" (*EH* 240).

During the decade that elapsed between this story and her first significant publication in 1903, *The Land of Little Rain*, Austin endured several major disappointments. Her husband moved them east of the Sierra Nevadas to the borders of Death Valley, first to Lone Pine and later to Independence, where she wrote *The Land of Little Rain*. Wallace proved a financial as well as an emotional failure, and although they did not finally separate until 1906, Austin began to face the reality of her marriage during her years in the desert. Adding to her distress, the year after their arrival in Lone Pine, Austin gave birth to a mentally retarded daughter. Forced to physically restrain Ruth for hours each day in order to make time to write, she eventually decided to place her in an institution when she was twelve and to never see her daughter again. Finally, Susanna Hunter died during the summer of 1896, when Austin was twenty-seven.

At the encouragement of Charles Lummis, her editor at the Los Angeles magazine the *Land of Sunshine*, which had begun to publish her work, Austin left the desert in 1906, in order to affiliate with other writers and artists. She built a house in Carmel, on the central California coast, where she wrote *Lost Borders* (1909) and associated with a bohemian group that included the writers George Sterling and Jack London. She made trips to Italy and England, where she walked in suffragist parades. For twelve years she lived in New York, where she entered into literary and artistic circles as a friend of Mabel Dodge, known for her literary and artistic salons, as well as into a disappointing love affair with the journalist Lincoln Steffens. In 1924 she moved to Santa Fe, where she built Casa Querida, the "beloved house," and renewed her connection to the landscape of the Southwest. During the final years of her life she worked to preserve and encourage the arts of the Pueblo Indians of New Mexico. She also wrote *Earth Horizon*, opened her house to Willa Cather so that Cather would have a conducive environment for completing her novel, *Death Comes for the Archbishop*, and fought a series of debilitating illnesses, including breast cancer and gall bladder and heart attacks. She died in her sleep August 13, 1934. Her ashes are encased in cement amid boulders near the summit of Mt. Picacho, on the edge of the Sangre de Cristo Mountains, within view of Casa Querida.

°   °   °

The themes and short sketch forms Austin chose for much of her writing locate her in the tradition of literary regionalism. She most closely resembles Celia Thaxter and Sarah Orne Jewett in her attention to natural detail; and her narrator in *The Land of Little Rain*, as well as her Walking Woman, both possess the mystical and visionary qualities of Jewett's Mrs. Todd. In *The Land of Little Rain*, Austin writes that "the manner of the country makes the usage of life there, and the land will not be lived in except in its own fashion." The connection between character and landscape, so central to regionalist fiction, yet muted in less extreme environments, comes into focus clearly in the desert, where inevitably the land informs the life. Still, like the Ohio frontier of Alice Cary's *Clovernook* sketches fifty years earlier, the desert could become the topic of regional fiction for Austin only after explorers and pioneers became its settlers and inhabitants. In "Regionalism and American Fiction," one of the few explicitly theoretical pieces produced by writers in this tradition, Austin proposes that the influence of regional environment creates a "pattern of response common to a group of people who have lived together" long enough (97). She distinguishes between local color and regionalism, suggesting that local color might use region as a scenic backdrop, but that "the first of the indispensable conditions" of regionalism "is that the region must enter constructively into the story, as another character, as the instigator of plot" (105). The second condition is that the story must reflect "in some fashion the essential qualities of the land" (107). Her own regional writing, at its best in *The Land of Little Rain* and *Lost Borders*, conveys the intensity of connection between natural landscape and human life.

As the title essay demonstrates, *The Land of Little Rain* is a book about patterns. In "The Basket Maker," Seyavi's life is patterned after the land she has lived in, and she captures this same pattern in her baskets. Austin identifies Seyavi as her own creative and visionary guide, and, taking Seyavi as her model and mirror and creating a book to capture the patterns of her own regional experience, Austin learns to make "baskets" of her own. Like her regionalist predecessors, Austin explored the meaning of women's lives—both Indian and white women—in her writing; she locates in their lives the source of creative power. This feminist value that informs *The Land of Little Rain* and *Lost Borders*, as well as several of her novels, especially *A Woman of Genius* (1912), links Austin to a tradition that allows women to speak for themselves through their own creativity.

In *The Land of Little Rain*, people resemble desert creatures; in *Lost Borders* Austin understands human behavior in light of the desert's mysteries. Truth in the country of lost borders extends the limits of conventional knowledge; as she writes in "The Land," appropriately introducing the tales that follow, "I have seen things happen that I do not believe myself." In "The Return of Mr. Wills" Austin executes a shift of perspective that reverses traditional patterns when Mr. Wills betrays Mrs. Wills, not by leaving but by returning home. However, Mrs. Wills finds hope in "the inscrutable grim spaces" that might once again lure him away. The Walking Woman of Austin's last tale in *Lost Borders*, an imaginative projection of Austin herself, also finds in the desert the possibility of creating her own radical truth. Driven to the open to become "sobered and healed at last by the large soundness of nature," she has managed to "walk off" society-made values and, "knowing the best when the best came to her, was able to take it." Though the narrator has heard her called lame, she finds no trace of a limp in the track the Walking Woman's feet make as she disappears.

"If the desert were a woman, I know well what like she would be," Austin writes in "The Land," and she proceeds to describe the tawny, sphinx-like, deep-breasted and full-lipped woman who comes very close to resembling Austin herself, as photographs and *Earth Horizon* reveal. Both Mrs. Wills and the Walking Woman suggest the possibility that women can learn to nurture themselves beyond the cultural inheritance of deprivation, betrayal, and abandonment; but the desert, and the reflection of her own strengths that Mary Austin saw in the desert, remain the most powerful image of vision and desire in either *The Land of Little Rain* or *Lost Borders*. Like many of her regionalist predecessors and the characters they create, Austin allowed herself to be mothered, nourished, and given her creative power by the land. For her, telling stories about the land becomes the single water-trail to an oasis of emotional, artistic, and mystical fulfillment.

The Land of Little Rain

East away from the Sierras, south from Panamint and Amargosa, east and south many an uncounted mile, is the Country of Lost Borders.[1]

Ute, Paiute, Mojave, and Shoshone inhabit its frontiers, and as far into the heart of it as a man dare go. Not the law, but the land sets the limit. Desert is the name it wears upon the maps, but the Indian's is the better word. Desert is a loose term to indicate land that supports no man; whether the land can be bitted and broken to that purpose is not proven. Void of life it never is, however dry the air and villainous the soil.

This is the nature of that country. There are hills, rounded, blunt, burned, squeezed up out of chaos, chrome and vermilion painted, aspiring to the snowline. Between the hills lie high level-looking plains full of intolerable sun glare, or narrow valleys drowned in a blue haze. The hill surface is streaked with ash drift and black, unweathered lava flows. After rains water accumulates in the hollows of small closed valleys, and, evaporating, leaves hard dry levels of pure desertness that get the local name of dry lakes. Where the mountains are steep and the rains heavy, the pool is never quite dry, but dark and bitter, rimmed about with the efflorescence of alkaline deposits. A thin crust of it lies along the marsh over the vegetating area, which has neither beauty nor freshness. In the broad wastes open to the wind the sand drifts in hummocks about the stubby shrubs, and between them the soil shows saline traces. The sculpture of the hills here is more wind than water work, though the quick storms do sometimes scar them past many a

1. Austin's landmarks here are the mountain ranges that form the northern (Panamint, Amargosa) and western (Sierra Nevadas) boundaries of the north-ern Mojave Desert in California. Her "country" here is about 100 miles north of Barstow, California, and just west of Death Valley.

year's redeeming. In all the Western desert edges there are essays in miniature at the famed, terrible Grand Cañon, to which, if you keep on long enough in this country, you will come at last.

Since this is a hill country one expects to find springs, but not to depend upon them; for when found they are often brackish and unwholesome, or maddening, slow dribbles in a thirsty soil. Here you find the hot sink of Death Valley, or high rolling districts where the air has always a tang of frost. Here are the long heavy winds and breathless calms on the tilted mesas[2] where dust devils dance, whirling up into a wide, pale sky. Here you have no rain when all the earth cries for it, or quick downpours called cloud-bursts for violence. A land of lost rivers, with little in it to love; yet a land that once visited must be come back to inevitably. If it were not so there would be little told of it.

This is the country of three seasons. From June on to November it lies hot, still, and unbearable, sick with violent unrelieving storms; then on until April, chill, quiescent, drinking its scant rain and scanter snows; from April to the hot season again, blossoming, radiant, and seductive. These months are only approximate; later or earlier the rain-laden wind may drift up the water gate of the Colorado from the Gulf, and the land sets its seasons by the rain.

The desert floras shame us with their cheerful adaptations to the seasonal limitations. Their whole duty is to flower and fruit, and they do it hardly, or with tropical luxuriance, as the rain admits. It is recorded in the report of the Death Valley expedition that after a year of abundant rains, on the Colorado desert was found a specimen of Amaranthus ten feet high. A year later the same species in the same place matured in the drought at four inches. One hopes the land may breed like qualities in her human offspring, not tritely to "try," but to do. Seldom does the desert herb attain the full stature of the type. Extreme aridity and extreme altitude have the same dwarfing effect, so that we find in the high Sierras and in Death Valley related species in miniature that reach a comely growth in mean temperatures. Very fertile are the desert plants in expedients to prevent evaporation, turning their foliage edgewise toward the sun, growing silky hairs, exuding viscid gum. The wind, which has a long sweep, harries and helps them. It rolls up dunes about the stocky stems, encompassing and protective, and above the dunes, which may be, as with the mesquite, three times as high as a man, the blossoming twigs flourish and bear fruit.

There are many areas in the desert where drinkable water lies within a few feet of the surface, indicated by the mesquite and the bunch grass (Sporobolus airoides). It is this nearness of unimagined help that makes the tragedy of desert deaths. It is related that the final breakdown of that hapless party that gave Death Valley its forbidding name occurred in a locality where shallow wells would have saved them. But how were they to know that? Properly equipped it is

---

2. Literally, tables; flat-topped elevations of land.

possible to go safely across that ghastly sink, yet every year it takes its toll of death, and yet men find there sun-dried mummies, of whom no trace or recollection is preserved. To underestimate one's thirst, to pass a given landmark to the right or left, to find a dry spring where one looked for running water—there is no help for any of these things.

Along springs and sunken watercourses one is surprised to find such water-loving plants as grow widely in moist ground, but the true desert breeds its own kind, each in its particular habitat. The angle of the slope, the frontage of a hill, the structure of the soil determines the plant. South-looking hills are nearly bare, and the lower tree-line higher here by a thousand feet. Cañons running east and west will have one wall naked and one clothed. Around dry lakes and marshes the herbage preserves a set and orderly arrangement. Most species have well-defined areas of growth, the best index the voiceless land can give the traveler of his whereabouts.

If you have any doubt about it, know that the desert begins with the creosote. This immortal shrub spreads down into Death Valley and up to the lower timber-line, odorous and medicinal as you might guess from the name, wandlike, with shining fretted foliage. Its vivid green is grateful to the eye in a wilderness of gray and greenish white shrubs. In the spring it exudes a resinous gum which the Indians of those parts know how to use with pulverized rock for cementing arrow points to shafts. Trust Indians not to miss any virtues of the plant world!

Nothing the desert produces expresses it better than the unhappy growth of the tree yuccas. Tormented, thin forests of it stalk drearily in the high mesas, particularly in that triangular slip that fans out eastward from the meeting of the Sierras and coastwise hills where the first swings across the southern end of the San Joaquin Valley. The yucca bristles with bayonet-pointed leaves, dull green, growing shaggy with age, tipped with panicles of fetid, greenish bloom. After death, which is slow, the ghostly hollow network of its woody skeleton, with hardly power to rot, makes the moonlight fearful. Before the yucca has come to flower, while yet its bloom is a creamy cone-shaped bud of the size of a small cabbage, full of sugary sap, the Indians twist it deftly out of its fence of daggers and roast it for their own delectation. So it is that in those parts where man inhabits one sees young plants of *Yucca arborensis* infrequently. Other yuccas, cacti, low herbs, a thousand sorts, one finds journeying east from the coastwise hills. There is neither poverty of soil nor species to account for the sparseness of desert growth, but simply that each plant requires more room. So much earth must be preëmpted to extract so much moisture. The real struggle for existence, the real brain of the plant, is underground; above there is room for a rounded perfect growth. In Death Valley, reputed the very core of desolation, are nearly two hundred identified species.

Above the lower tree-line, which is also the snow-line, mapped out abruptly by the sun, one finds spreading growth of piñon, juniper, branched nearly to the ground, lilac and sage, and scattering white pines.

There is no special preponderance of self-fertilized or wind-fertilized plants, but everywhere the demand for and evidence of insect life. Now where there are seeds and insects there will be birds and small mammals and where these are, will come the slinking, sharp-toothed kind that prey on them. Go as far as you dare in the heart of a lonely land, you cannot go so far that life and death are not before you. Painted lizards slip in and out of rock crevices, and pant on the white hot sands. Birds, hummingbirds even, nest in the cactus scrub; woodpeckers befriend the demoniac yuccas; out of the stark, treeless waste rings the music of the night-singing mockingbird. If it be summer and the sun well down, there will be a burrowing owl to call. Strange, furry, tricksy things dart across the open places, or sit motionless in the conning towers of the creosote. The poet may have "named all the birds without a gun,"[3] but not the fairy-footed, ground-inhabiting, furtive, small folk of the rainless regions. They are too many and too swift; how many you would not believe without seeing the footprint tracings in the sand. They are nearly all night workers, finding the days too hot and white. In mid-desert where there are no cattle, there are no birds of carrion, but if you go far in that direction the chances are that you will find yourself shadowed by their tilted wings. Nothing so large as a man can move unspied upon in that country, and they know well how the land deals with strangers. There are hints to be had here of the way in which a land forces new habits on its dwellers. The quick increase of suns at the end of spring sometimes overtakes birds in their nesting and effects a reversal of the ordinary manner of incubation. It becomes necessary to keep eggs cool rather than warm. One hot, stifling spring in the Little Antelope I had occasion to pass and repass frequently the nest of a pair of meadowlarks, located unhappily in the shelter of a very slender weed. I never caught them sitting[4] except near night, but at midday they stood, or drooped above it, half fainting with pitifully parted bills, between their treasure and the sun. Sometimes both of them together with wings spread and half lifted continued a spot of shade in a temperature that constrained me at last in a fellow feeling to spare them a bit of canvas for permanent shelter. There was a fence in that country shutting in a cattle range, and along its fifteen miles of posts one could be sure of finding a bird or two in every strip of shadow; sometime the sparrow and the hawk, with wings trailed and beaks parted, drooping in the white truce of noon.

If one is inclined to wonder at first how so many dwellers came to be in the loneliest land that ever came out of God's hands, what they do there and why stay, one does not wonder so much after having lived there. None other than this long brown land lays such a hold on the

---

3. First line of Ralph Waldo Emerson's 1842 poem,   4. E.g., on their eggs.
"Forbearance."

affections. The rainbow hills, the tender bluish mists, the luminous radiance of the spring, have the lotus charm. They trick the sense of time, so that once inhabiting there you always mean to go away without quite realizing that you have not done it. Men who have lived there, miners and cattle-men, will tell you this, not so fluently, but emphatically, cursing the land and going back to it. For one thing there is the divinest, cleanest air to be breathed anywhere in God's world. Some day the world will understand that, and the little oases on the windy tops of hills will harbor for healing its ailing, house-weary broods. There is promise there of great wealth in ores and earths, which is no wealth by reason of being so far removed from water and workable conditions, but men are bewitched by it and tempted to try the impossible.

You should hear Salty Williams tell how he used to drive eighteen and twenty-mule teams from the borax[5] marsh to Mojave, ninety miles, with the trail wagon full of water barrels. Hot days the mules would go so mad for drink that the clank of the water bucket set them into an uproar of hideous, maimed noises, and a tangle of harness chains, while Salty would sit on the high seat with the sun glare heavy in his eyes, dealing out curses of pacification in a level, uninterested voice until the clamor fell off from sheer exhaustion. There was a line of shallow graves along that road; they used to count on dropping a man or two of every new gang of coolies brought out in the hot season. But when he lost his swamper,[6] smitten without warning at the noon halt, Salty quit his job; he said it was "too durn hot." The swamper he buried by the way with stones upon him to keep the coyotes from digging him up, and seven years later I read the penciled lines on the pine headboard, still bright and unweathered.

But before that, driving up on the Mojave stage, I met Salty again crossing Indian Wells, his face from the high seat, tanned and ruddy as a harvest moon, looming through the golden dust above his eighteen mules. The land had called him.

The palpable sense of mystery in the desert air breeds fables, chiefly of lost treasure. Somewhere within its stark borders, if one believes report, is a hill strewn with nuggets; one seamed with virgin silver; an old clayey water-bed where Indians scooped up earth to make cooking pots and shaped them reeking with grains of pure gold. Old miners drifting about the desert edges, weathered into the semblance of the tawny hills, will tell you tales like these convincingly. After a little sojourn in that land you will believe them on their own account. It is a question whether it is not better to be bitten by the little horned snake of the desert that goes sidewise and strikes without coiling, than by the tradition of a lost mine.

---

5. Borax is a salt with many uses, obtained from deposits in Death Valley, California; early in the 20th century, mule teams were used to haul the mineral from the mines to railroad cars.
6. A mule driver's assistant. Coolies: laborers hired to build the railroads.

And yet—and yet—is it not perhaps to satisfy expectation that one falls into the tragic key in writing of desertness? The more you wish of it the more you get, and in the mean time lose much of pleasantness. In that country which begins at the foot of the east slope of the Sierras and spreads out by less and less lofty hill ranges toward the Great Basin, it is possible to live with great zest, to have red blood and delicate joys, to pass and repass about one's daily performance an area that would make an Atlantic sea-board State, and that with no peril, and, according to our way of thought, no particular difficulty. At any rate, it was not people who went into the desert merely to write it up who invented the fabled Hassaympa,[7] of whose waters, if any drink, they can no more see fact as naked fact, but all radiant with the color of romance. I, who must have drunk of it in my twice seven years' wanderings, am assured that it is worth while.

For all the toll the desert takes of a man it gives compensations, deep breaths, deep sleep, and the communion of the stars. It comes upon one with new force in the pauses of the night that the Chaldeans[8] were a desert-bred people. It is hard to escape the sense of mastery as the stars move in the wide clear heavens to risings and settings unobscured. They look large and near and palpitant; as if they moved on some stately service not needful to declare. Wheeling to their stations in the sky, they make the poor world-fret of no account. Of no account you who lie out there watching, nor the lean coyote that stands off in the scrub from you and howls and howls.

Atlantic Monthly, January 1903; *The Land of Little Rain*, 1903

The Basket Maker

"A man," says Seyavi of the campoodie,[1] "must have a woman, but a woman who has a child will do very well."

That was perhaps why, when she lost her mate in the dying struggle of his race,[2] she never took another, but set her wit to fend for herself and her young son. No doubt she was often put to it in the beginning to find food for them both. The Paiutes[3] had made their last stand at the border of the Bitter Lake; battle-driven they died in its waters, and the land filled with cattle-men and adventurers for gold: this while Seyavi and the boy lay up in the caverns of the Black Rock and ate tule roots and fresh-water clams that they dug out of the slough bottoms

---

7. According to Austin, this is a river whose name means "small rocks" in one dialect and "sacred bear" in another.

8. An ancient Semitic people who ruled in Babylonia.

1. "A group of Indian huts, from the Spanish *campo*, a field or prairie. In some localities written 'campody' " (Austin, *The Basket Woman*).

2. The Bannock War of 1878, during which many Paiutes died trying to protect their land from seizure by the U.S. Government.

3. "The name of a large tribe of Indians inhabiting middle California and Nevada. The name is derived from the Indian word *pah*, water, and is used to distinguish this tribe from the related tribe of Utes, who lived in the desert away from running water" (Austin, *The Basket Woman*).

with their toes. In the interim, while the tribes swallowed their defeat, and before the rumor of war died out, they must have come very near to the bare core of things. That was the time Seyavi learned the sufficiency of mother wit, and how much more easily one can do without a man than might at first be supposed.

To understand the fashion of any life, one must know the land it is lived in and the procession of the year. This valley is a narrow one, a mere trough between hills, a draught for storms, hardly a crow's flight from the sharp Sierras of the Snows to the curled, red and ochre, uncomforted, bare ribs of Waban.[4] Midway of the groove runs a burrowing, dull river, nearly a hundred miles from where it cuts the lava flats of the north to its widening in a thick, tideless pool of a lake. Hereabouts the ranges have no foothills, but rise up steeply from the bench lands above the river. Down from the Sierras, for the east ranges have almost no rain, pour glancing white floods toward the lowest land, and all beside them lie the campoodies, brown wattled brush heaps, looking east.

In the river are mussels, and reeds that have edible white roots, and in the soddy meadows tubers of joint grass; all these at their best in the spring. On the slope the summer growth affords seeds; up the steep the one-leafed pines, an oily nut. That was really all they could depend upon, and that only at the mercy of the little gods of frost and rain. For the rest it was cunning against cunning, caution against skill, against quacking hordes of wild-fowl in the tulares,[5] against pronghorn and bighorn and deer. You can guess, however, that all this warring of rifles and bowstrings, this influx of overlording whites, had made game wilder and hunters fearful of being hunted. You can surmise also, for it was a crude time and the land was raw, that the women became in turn the game of the conquerors.

There used to be in the Little Antelope a she dog, stray or outcast, that had a litter in some forsaken lair, and ranged and foraged for them, slinking savage and afraid, remembering and mistrusting humankind, wistful, lean, and sufficient for her young. I have thought Seyavi might have had days like that, and have had perfect leave to think, since she will not talk of it. Paiutes have the art of reducing life to its lowest ebb and yet saving it alive on grasshoppers, lizards, and strange herbs; and that time must have left no shift untried. It lasted long enough for Seyavi to have evolved the philosophy of life which I have set down at the beginning. She had gone beyond learning to do for her son, and learned to believe it worth while.

In our kind of society, when a woman ceases to alter the fashion of her hair, you guess that she has passed the crisis of her experience. If she goes on crimping and uncrimping with the changing mode, it is safe to suppose she has never come up against anything too big for her. The

---

4. A mountain near Oppapago and Mt. Whitney. Sierras of the Snows: the Sierra Nevadas.

5. "A marshy place overgrown with the bulrushes known as *tule*" (Austin, *The Basket Woman*).

Indian woman gets nearly the same personal note in the pattern of her baskets. Not that she does not make all kinds, carriers, water-bottles, and cradles,—these are kitchen ware,—but her works of art are all of the same piece. Seyavi made flaring, flat-bottomed bowls, cooking pots really, when cooking was done by dropping hot stones into water-tight food baskets, and for decoration a design in colored bark of the procession of plumed crests of the valley quail. In this pattern she had made cooking pots in the golden spring of her wedding year, when the quail went up two and two to their resting places about the foot of Oppapago.[6] In this fashion she made them when, after pillage, it was possible to reinstate the housewifely crafts. Quail ran then in the Black Rock by hundreds,—so you will still find them in fortunate years,—and in the famine time the women cut their long hair to make snares when the flocks came morning and evening to the springs.

Seyavi made baskets for love and sold them for money, in a generation that preferred iron pots for utility. Every Indian woman is an artist,—sees, feels, creates, but does not philosophize about her processes. Seyavi's bowls are wonders of technical precision, inside and out, the palm finds no fault with them, but the subtlest appeal is in the sense that warns us of humanness in the way the design spreads into the flare of the bowl. There used to be an Indian woman at Olancha who made bottle-neck trinket baskets in the rattlesnake pattern, and could accommodate the design to the swelling bowl and flat shoulder of the basket without sensible disproportion, and so cleverly that you might own one a year without thinking how it was done; but Seyavi's baskets had a touch beyond cleverness. The weaver and the warp lived next to the earth and were saturated with the same elements. Twice a year, in the time of white butterflies and again when young quail ran neck and neck in the chaparral, Seyavi cut willows for basketry by the creek where it wound toward the river against the sun and sucking winds. It never quite reached the river except in far-between times of summer flood, but it always tried, and the willows encouraged it as much as they could. You nearly always found them a little farther down than the trickle of eager water. The Paiute fashion of counting time appeals to me more than any other calendar. They have no stamp of heathen gods nor great ones, nor any succession of moons as have red men of the East and North, but count forward and back by the progress of the season; the time of *taboose*,[7] before the trout begin to leap, the end of the piñon harvest, about the beginning of deep snows. So they get nearer the sense of the season, which runs early or late according as the rains are forward or delayed. But whenever Seyavi cut willows for baskets was always a golden time, and the soul of the weather went into the wood. If you had ever owned one of Seyavi's golden russet

6. "A Mt. peak near Mt. Whitney. The name signifies 'the Weeper,' in reference to the streams that run down from it continually like tears" (Austin, *The Basket Woman*); also called Lone Pine Peak.

7. "Small tubercles of the joint grass; they appear on the joints of the roots early in spring, and are an important item of food to the Indians" (Austin, *The Basket Woman*).

cooking bowls with the pattern of plumed quail, you would understand
all this without saying anything.

Before Seyavi made baskets for the satisfaction of desire,—for that
is a house-bred theory of art that makes anything more of it,—she
danced and dressed her hair. In those days, when the spring was at
flood and the blood pricked to the mating fever, the maids chose their
flowers, wreathed themselves, and danced in the twilights, young desire crying out to young desire. They sang what the heart prompted,
what the flower expressed, what boded in the mating weather.

"And what flower did you wear, Seyavi?"

"I, ah,—the white flower of twining (clematis), on my body and my
hair, and so I sang:—

> "I am the white flower of twining,
> Little white flower by the river,
> Oh, flower that twines close by the river,
> Oh, trembling flower!
> So trembles the maiden heart."

So sang Seyavi of the campoodie before she made baskets, and in her
later days laid her arms upon her knees and laughed in them at the
recollection. But it was not often she would say so much, never understanding the keen hunger I had for bits of lore and the "fool talk" of
her people. She had fed her young son with meadowlarks' tongues, to
make him quick of speech; but in late years was loath to admit it,
though she had come through the period of unfaith in the lore of the
clan with a fine appreciation of its beauty and significance.

"What good will your dead get, Seyavi, of the baskets you burn?"
said I, coveting them for my own collection.

Thus Seyavi, "As much good as yours of the flowers you strew."

Oppapago looks on Waban, and Waban on Coso[8] and the Bitter
Lake, and the campoodie looks on these three; and more, it sees the
beginning of winds along the foot of Coso, the gathering of clouds
behind the high ridges, the spring flush, the soft spread of wild almond
bloom on the mesa. These first, you understand, are the Paiute's walls,
the other his furnishings. Not the wattled[9] hut is his home, but the
land, the winds, the hill front, the stream. These he cannot duplicate
at any furbisher's shop as you who live within doors, who, if your purse
allows, may have the same home at Sitka and Samarcand.[1] So you see
how it is that the homesickness of an Indian is often unto death, since
he gets no relief from it; neither wind nor weed nor sky-line, nor any
aspect of the hills of a strange land sufficiently like his own. So it was
when the government reached out for the Paiutes, they gathered into
the Northern Reservation only such poor tribes as could devise no
other end of their affairs. Here, all along the river, and south to Sho-

---

8. Coso Mountain Range, south of Oppapago.
9. Constructed with poles intertwined with twigs,
reeds, or branches.

1. Sitka, Alaska (on the west coast of Baranof Island); Samarcand, Russia (Uzbek province).

shone Land,[2] live the clans who owned the earth, fallen into the deplorable condition of hangers-on. Yet you hear them laughing at the hour when they draw in to the campoodie after labor, when there is a smell of meat and the steam of the cooking pots goes up against the sun. Then the children lie with their toes in the ashes to hear tales; then they are merry, and have the joys of repletion and the nearness of their kind. They have their hills, and though jostled are sufficiently free to get some fortitude for what will come. For now you shall hear of the end of the basket maker.

In her best days Seyavi was most like Deborah,[3] deep bosomed, broad in the hips, quick in counsel, slow of speech, esteemed of her people. This was that Seyavi who reared a man by her own hand, her own wit, and none other. When the townspeople began to take note of her—and it was some years after the war[4] before there began to be any towns—she was then in the quick maturity of primitive women; but when I knew her she seemed already old. Indian women do not often live to great age, though they look incredibly steeped in years. They have the wit to win sustenance from the raw material of life without intervention, but they have not the sleek look of the women whom the social organization conspires to nourish. Seyavi had somehow squeezed out of her daily round a spiritual ichor that kept the skill in her knotted fingers long after the accustomed time, but that also failed. By all counts she would have been about sixty years old when it came her turn to sit in the dust on the sunny side of the wickiup,[5] with little strength left for anything but looking. And in time she paid the toll of the smoky huts and became blind. This is a thing so long expected by the Paiutes that when it comes they find it neither bitter nor sweet, but tolerable because common. There were three other blind women in the campoodie, withered fruit on a bough, but they had memory and speech. By noon of the sun there were never any left in the campoodie but these or some mother of weanlings, and they sat to keep the ashes warm upon the hearth. If it were cold, they burrowed in the blankets of the hut; if it were warm, they followed the shadow of the wickiup around. Stir much out of their places they hardly dared, since one might not help another; but they called, in high, old cracked voices, gossip and reminder across the ash heaps.

Then, if they have your speech or you theirs, and have an hour to spare, there are things to be learned of life not set down in any books, folk tales, famine tales, love and long-suffering and desire, but no whimpering. Now and then one or another of the blind keepers of the camp will come across to where you sit gossiping, tapping her way among the kitchen middens, guided by your voice that carries far in the

2. The land inhabited by the Shoshones, an Indian tribe split in two by the Paiutes, and living north and south of them in the Mojave Desert; Austin refers to the southern division in her work.
3. An Old Testament prophetess; see Judges 4, 5.

4. Bannock War of 1878.
5. "An Indian hut of brush, or reeds. It is often pieced out with blankets and tin cans" (Austin, *The Basket Woman*).

clearness and stillness of mesa afternoons. But suppose you find Seyavi retired into the privacy of her blanket, you will get nothing for that day. There is no other privacy possible in a campoodie. All the processes of life are carried on out of doors or behind the thin, twig-woven walls of the wickiup, and laughter is the only corrective for behavior. Very early the Indian learns to possess his countenance in impassivity, to cover his head with his blanket. Something to wrap around him is as necessary to the Paiute as to you your closet to pray in.

So in her blanket Seyavi, sometime basket maker, sits by the unlit hearths of her tribe and digests her life, nourishing her spirit against the time of the spirit's need, for she knows in fact quite as much of these matters as you who have a larger hope, though she has none but the certainty that having borne herself courageously to this end she will not be reborn a coyote.

Atlantic Monthly, February 1903; *The Land of Little Rain*, 1903

The Walking Woman

The first time of my hearing of her was at Temblor. We had come all one day between blunt, whitish bluffs rising from mirage water, with a thick, pale wake of dust billowing from the wheels, all the dead wall of the foothills sliding and shimmering with heat, to learn that the Walking Woman had passed us somewhere in the dizzying dimness, going down to the Tulares on her own feet. We heard of her again in the Carrisal,[1] and again at Adobe Station, where she had passed a week before the shearing, and at last I had a glimpse of her at the Eighteen-Mile House as I went hurriedly northward on the Mojave stage; and afterward sheepherders at whose camps she slept, and cowboys at rodeos, told me as much of her way of life as they could understand. Like enough they told her as much of mine. That was very little. She was the Walking Woman, and no one knew her name, but because she was a sort of whom men speak respectfully, they called her to her face Mrs. Walker, and she answered to it if she was so inclined. She came and went about our western world on no discoverable errand, and whether she had some place of refuge where she lay by in the interim, or whether between her seldom, unaccountable appearances in our quarter she went on steadily walking, we never learned. She came and went, oftenest in a kind of muse of travel which the untrammeled space begets, or at rare intervals flooding wondrously with talk, never of herself, but of things she had known and seen. She must have seen some rare happenings, too—by report. She was at Maverick the time of the Big Snow, and at Tres Piños when they brought home the body of Morena; and if anybody could have told

---

1. Temblor, Tulares, Carrisal: One of various small towns in the Mojave Desert in the southwestern U.S.

whether De Borba killed Mariana for spite or defense, it would have
been she, only she could not be found when most wanted. She was at
Tunawai at the time of the cloud-burst, and if she had cared for it could
have known most desirable things of the ways of trail-making, burrow-
habiting small things.

All of which should have made her worth meeting, though it was not,
in fact, for such things I was wishful to meet her; and as it turned out,
it was not of these things we talked when at last we came together. For
one thing, she was a woman, not old, who had gone about alone in a
country where the number of women is as one in fifteen. She had eaten
and slept at the herder's camps, and laid by for days at one-man
stations whose masters had no other touch of human kind than the
passing of chance prospectors, or the halting of the tri-weekly stage.
She had been set on her way by teamsters who lifted her out of white,
hot desertness and put her down at the crossing of unnamed ways, days
distant from anywhere. And through all this she passed unarmed and
unoffended. I had the best testimony to this, the witness of the men
themselves. I think they talked of it because they were so much surprised at it. It was not, on the whole, what they expected of themselves.

Well I understand that nature which wastes its borders with too
eager burning, beyond which rim of desolation it flares forever quick
and white, and have had some inkling of the isolating calm of a desire
too high to stoop to satisfaction. But you could not think of these things
pertaining to the Walking Woman; and if there were ever any truth in
the exemption from offense residing in a frame of behavior called
ladylike, it should have been inoperative here. What this really means
is that you get no affront so long as your behavior in the estimate of the
particular audience invites none. In the estimate of the immediate
audience—conduct which affords protection in Mayfair[2] gets you no
consideration in Maverick. And by no canon could it be considered
ladylike to go about on your own feet, with a blanket and a black bag
and almost no money in your purse, in and about the haunts of rude
and solitary men.

There were other things that pointed the wish for a personal encounter with the Walking Woman. One of them was the contradiction of
reports of her—as to whether she was comely, for example. Report said
yes, and again, plain to the point of deformity. She had a twist to her
face, some said; a hitch to one shoulder; they averred she limped as
she walked. But by the distance she covered she should have been
straight and young. As to sanity, equal incertitude. On the mere evidence of her way of life she was cracked; not quite broken, but unser-
viceable. Yet in her talk there was both wisdom and information, and
the word she brought about trails and water-holes was as reliable as an
Indian's.

2. A fashionable district of London.

By her own account she had begun by walking off an illness. There had been an invalid to be taken care of for years, leaving her at last broken in body, and with no recourse but her own feet to carry her out of that predicament. It seemed there had been, besides the death of her invalid, some other worrying affairs, upon which, and the nature of her illness, she was never quite clear, so that it might very well have been an unsoundness of mind which drove her to the open, sobered and healed at last by the large soundness of nature. It must have been about that time that she lost her name. I am convinced that she never told it because she did not know it herself. She was the Walking Woman, and the country people called her Mrs. Walker. At the time I knew her, though she wore short hair and a man's boots, and had a fine down over all her face from exposure to the weather, she was perfectly sweet and sane.

I had met her occasionally at ranch-houses and road-stations, and had got as much acquaintance as the place allowed; but for the things I wished to know there wanted a time of leisure and isolation. And when the occasion came we talked altogether of other things.

It was at Warm Spring in the Little Antelope I came upon her in the heart of a clear forenoon. The spring lies off a mile from the main trail, and has the only trees about it known in that country. First you come upon a pool of waste full of weeds of a poisonous dark green, every reed ringed about the water-level with a muddy white incrustation. Then the three oaks appear staggering on the slope, and the spring sobs and blubbers below them in ashy-colored mud. All the hills of that country have the down plunge toward the desert and back abruptly toward the Sierra. The grass is thick and brittle and bleached straw-color toward the end of the season. As I rode up the swale of the spring I saw the Walking Woman sitting where the grass was deepest, with her black bag and blanket, which she carried on a stick, beside her. It was one of those days when the genius[3] of talk flows as smoothly as the rivers of mirage through the blue hot desert morning.

You are not to suppose that in my report of a Borderer I give you the words only, but the full meaning of the speech. Very often the words are merely the punctuation of thought; rather, the crests of the long waves of intercommunicative silences. Yet the speech of the Walking Woman was fuller than most.

The best of our talk that day began in some dropped word of hers from which I inferred that she had had a child. I was surprised at that, and then wondered why I should have been surprised, for it is the most natural of all experiences to have children. I said something of that purport, and also that it was one of the perquisites of living I should be least willing to do without. And that led to the Walking Woman saying that there were three things which if you had known you could cut out all the rest, and they were good any way you got them, but best if, as

3. In this sense, guiding spirit.

in her case, they were related to and grew each one out of the others. It was while she talked that I decided that she really did have a twist to her face, a sort of natural warp or skew into which it fell when it was worn merely as a countenance, but which disappeared the moment it became the vehicle of thought or feeling.

The first of the experiences the Walking Woman had found most worth while had come to her in a sand-storm on the south slope of Tehachapi in a dateless spring. I judged it should have been about the time she began to find herself, after the period of worry and loss in which her wandering began. She had come, in a day pricked full of intimations of a storm, to the camp of Filon Geraud, whose companion shepherd had gone a three days' *pasear*[4] to Mojave for supplies. Geraud was of great hardihood, red-blooded, of a full laughing eye, and an indubitable spark for women. It was the season of the year when there is a soft bloom on the days, but the nights are cowering cold and the lambs tender, not yet flockwise. At such times a sand-storm works incalculable disaster. The lift of the wind is so great that the whole surface of the ground appears to travel upon it slantwise, thinning out miles high in air. In the intolerable smother the lambs are lost from the ewes; neither dogs nor man make headway against it.

The morning flared through a horizon of yellow smudge, and by mid-forenoon the flock broke.

"There were but the two of us to deal with the trouble," said the Walking Woman. "Until that time I had not known how strong I was, nor how good it is to run when running is worth while. The flock traveled down the wind, the sand bit our faces; we called, and after a time heard the words broken and beaten small by the wind. But after a little we had not to call. All the time of our running in the yellow dusk of day and the black dark of night, I knew where Filon was. A flock-length away, I knew him. Feel? What should I feel? I knew. I ran with the flock and turned it this way and that as Filon would have.

"Such was the force of the wind that when we came together we held by one another and talked a little between pantings. We snatched and ate what we could as we ran. All that day and night until the next afternoon the camp kit was not out of the cayaques.[5] But we held the flock. We herded them under a butte when the wind fell off a little, and the lambs sucked; when the storm rose they broke, but we kept upon their track and brought them together again. At night the wind quieted, and we slept by turns; at least Filon slept. I lay on the ground when my turn was and beat with the storm. I was no more tired than the earth was. The sand filled in the creases of the blanket, and where I turned, dripped back upon the ground. But we saved the sheep. Some ewes there were that would not give down their milk because of the worry of the storm, and the lambs died. But we kept the flock together. And I was not tired."

4. Spanish for stroll or walk.
5. *Cayuse* is the name given to an Indian pony used for carrying supplies; perhaps means saddlebags.
Camp kit: the supplies or pack.

The Walking Woman stretched out her arms and clasped herself, rocking in them as if she would have hugged the recollection to her breast.

"For you see," said she, "I worked with a man, without excusing, without any burden on me of looking or seeming. Not fiddling or fumbling as women work, and hoping it will all turn out for the best. It was not for Filon to ask, Can you, or Will you. He said, Do, and I did. And my work was good. We held the flock. And that," said the Walking Woman, the twist coming in her face again, "is one of the things that make you able to do without the others."

"Yes," I said; and then, "What others?"

"Oh," she said, as if it pricked her, "the looking and the seeming."

And I had not thought until that time that one who had the courage to be the Walking Woman would have cared! We sat and looked at the pattern of the thick crushed grass on the slope, wavering in the fierce noon like the waterings in the coat of a tranquil beast; the ache of a world-old bitterness sobbed and whispered in the spring. At last—

"It is by the looking and the seeming," said I, "that the opportunity finds you out."

"Filon found out," said the Walking Woman. She smiled; and went on from that to tell me how, when the wind went down about four o'clock and left the afternoon clear and tender, the flock began to feed, and they had out the kit from the cayaques, and cooked a meal. When it was over, and Filon had his pipe between his teeth, he came over from his side of the fire, of his own notion, and stretched himself on the ground beside her. Of his own notion. There was that in the way she said it that made it seem as if nothing of the sort had happened before to the Walking Woman, and for a moment I thought she was about to tell me one of the things I wished to know; but she went on to say what Filon had said to her of her work with the flock. Obvious, kindly things, such as any man in sheer decency would have said, so that there must have something more gone with the words to make them so treasured of the Walking Woman.

"We were very comfortable," said she, "and not so tired as we expected to be. Filon leaned up on his elbow. I had not noticed until then how broad he was in the shoulders, and how strong in the arms. And we had saved the flock together. We felt that. There was something that said together, in the slope of his shoulders toward me. It was around his mouth and on the cheek high up under the shine of his eyes. And under the shine the look—the look that said, 'We are of one sort and one mind'—his eyes that were the color of the flat water in the toulares[6] —do you know the look?"

"I know it."

"The wind was stopped and all the earth smelled of dust, and Filon understood very well that what I had done with him I could not have done so well with another. And the look—the look in the eyes—"

---

6. "A marshy place overgrown with the bulrushes known as *tule*" (Austin, *The Basket Maker*).

"Ah-ah—!"

I have always said, I will say again, I do not know why at this point the Walking Woman touched me. If it were merely a response to my unconscious throb of sympathy, or the unpremeditated way of her heart to declare that this, after all, was the best of all indispensable experiences; or if in some flash of forward vision, encompassing the unimpassioned years, the stir, the movement of tenderness were for *me*—but no; as often as I have thought of it, I have thought of a different reason, but no conclusive one, why the Walking Woman should have put out her hand and laid it on my arm.

"To work together, to love together," said the Walking Woman, withdrawing her hand again; "there you have two of the things; the other you know."

"The mouth at the breast," said I.

"The lips and the hands," said the Walking Woman. "The little, pushing hands and the small cry." There ensued a pause of fullest understanding, while the land before us swam in the noon, and a dove in the oaks behind the spring began to call. A little red fox came out of the hills and lapped delicately at the pool.

"I stayed with Filon until the fall," said she. "All that summer in the Sierras, until it was time to turn south on the trail. It was a good time, and longer than he could be expected to have loved one like me. And besides, I was no longer able to keep the trail. My baby was born in October."

Whatever more there was to say to this, the Walking Woman's hand said it, straying with remembering gesture to her breast. There are so many ways of loving and working, but only one way of the first-born. She added, after an interval, that she did not know if she would have given up her walking to keep at home and tend him, or whether the thought of her son's small feet running beside her in the trails would have driven her to the open again. The baby had not stayed long enough for that. "And whenever the wind blows in the night," said the Walking Woman, "I wake and wonder if he is well covered."

She took up her black bag and her blanket; there was the ranch-house of Dos Palos to be made before night, and she went as outliers do, without a hope expressed of another meeting and no word of good-bye. She was the Walking Woman. That was it. She had walked off all sense of society-made values, and, knowing the best when the best came to her, was able to take it. Work—as I believed; love—as the Walking Woman had proved it; a child—as you subscribe to it. But look you: it was the naked thing the Walking Woman grasped, not dressed and tricked out, for instance, by prejudices in favor of certain occupations; and love, man love, taken as it came, not picked over and rejected if it carried no obligation of permanency; and a child; *any* way you get it, a child is good to have, say nature and the Walking Woman; to have it and not to wait upon a proper concurrence of so many decorations that the event may not come at all.

At least one of us is wrong. To work and to love and to bear children. *That* sounds easy enough. But the way we live establishes so many things of much more importance.

Far down the dim, hot valley I could see the Walking Woman with her blanket and black bag over her shoulder. She had a queer, sidelong gait, as if in fact she had a twist all through her.

Recollecting suddenly that people called her lame, I ran down to the open place below the spring where she had passed. There in the bare, hot sand the track of her two feet bore evenly and white.

Atlantic Monthly, August 1907; *Lost Borders,* 1909

The Return of Mr. Wills

Mrs. Wills had lived seventeen years with Mr. Wills, and when he left her for three, those three were so much the best of her married life that she wished he had never come back. And the only real trouble with Mr. Wills was that he should never have moved West. Back East I suppose they breed such men because they need them, but they ought really to keep them there.

I am quite certain that when Mr. Wills was courting Mrs. Wills he parted his hair in the middle, and the breast-pocket of his best suit had a bright silk lining which Mr. Wills pulled up to simulate a silk handkerchief. Mrs. Wills had a certain draggled prettiness, and a way of tossing her head which came back to her after Mr. Wills left, which made you think she might have been the prettiest girl of her town. They were happy enough at first, when Mr. Wills was a grocery clerk, assistant Sunday-school superintendent, and they owned a cabinet organ and four little Willses. It might have been that Mr. Wills thought he could go right on being the same sort of a man in the West—he was clerk at the Bed Rock Emporium, and had brought the organ and the children; or it might have been at bottom he thought himself a very different sort of man, and meant to be it if he got a chance.

There is a sort of man bred up in close communities, like a cask, to whom the church, public opinion, the social note, are a sort of hoop to hold him in serviceable shape.[1] Without these there are a good many ways of going to pieces. Mr. Wills' way was Lost Mines.

Being clerk at the Emporium, where miners and prospectors bought their supplies, he heard a lot of talk about mines, and was too new to it to understand that the man who has the most time to stop and talk about it has the least to do with mining. And of all he heard, the most fascinating to Mr. Wills, who was troubled with an imagination, was of the lost mines: incredibly rich ledges, touched and not found again. To go out into the unmapped hills on the mere chance of coming across

---

1. Here the implication is that without the support of social institutions like the church, Mr. Wills will fall apart, like the staves of a barrel if the hoops were removed.

something was, on the face of it, a risky business; but to look for a mine once located, sampled and proved, definitely situated in a particular mountain range or a certain cañon, had a smack of plausibility. Besides that, an ordinary prospect might or might not prove workable, but the lost mines were always amazingly rich. Of all the ways in the West for a man to go to pieces this is the most insidious. Out there beyond the towns the long Wilderness lies brooding, imperturbable; she puts out to adventurous minds glittering fragments of fortune or romance, like the lures men use to catch antelopes—clip! then she has them. If Mr. Wills had gambled or drank, his wife could have gone to the minister about it, his friends could have done something. There was a church in Maverick of twenty-seven members, and the Willses had brought letters to it,[2] but except for the effect it had on Mrs. Wills, it would not be worth mentioning. Though he might never have found it out in the East, Mr. Wills belonged to the church, not because of what it meant to himself, but for what it meant to other people. Back East it had meant social standing, repute, moral impeccability. To other people in Maverick it meant a weakness which was excused in you so long as you did not talk about it. Mr. Wills did not, because there was so much else to talk about in connection with lost mines.

He began by grub-staking[3] Pedro Ruiz to look for the Lost Ledge of Fisherman's Peak, and that was not so bad, for it had not been lost more than thirty years, the peak was not a hundred miles from Maverick, and, besides, I have a piece of the ore myself. Then he was bitten by the myth of the Gunsight, of which there was never anything more tangible than a dime's worth of virgin silver, picked up by a Jay-hawker,[4] hammered into a sight for a gun; and you had to take the gun on faith at that, for it and the man who owned it had quite disappeared; and afterward it was the Duke o' Wild Rose, which was never a mine at all, merely an arrow-mark on a map left by a penniless lodger found dead in a San Francisco hotel. Grub-staking is expensive, even to a clerk at the Bed Rock Emporium getting discounts on the grub, and grub-staked prospectors are about as dependable as the dreams they chase, often pure fakes, lying up at seldom-visited water-holes while the stake lasts, returning with wilder tales and clews more alluring. It was a late conviction that led Mr. Wills, when he put the last remnant of his means into the search for the White Cement mines, to resign his clerkship and go in charge of the expedition himself. There is no doubt whatever that there is a deposit of cement on Bald Mountain, with lumps of gold sticking out of it like plums in a pudding. It lies at the bottom of a small gulch near the middle fork of Owens River, and is overlaid by pumice. There is a camp kit buried somewhere near, and two skeletons. There is also an Indian in that vicinity who is thought

2. Individuals joining a new church would customarily bring letters of introduction from their home church.
3. Outfitting a prospector in return for a share of

future profits.
4. Originally one who fought in the guerrilla war (1854–60) waged in Kansas over slavery; later extended to mean any lawless marauder or robber.

to be able to point out the exact location—if he would. It is quite the sort of thing to appeal to the imagination of Mr. Wills, and he spent two years proving that he could not find it. After that he drifted out toward the Lee district to look for Lost Cabin mine, because a man who had immediate need of twenty dollars, had, for that amount, offered Wills some exact and unpublished information as to its location. By that time Wills' movements had ceased to interest anybody in Maverick. He could be got to believe anything about any sort of a prospect, providing it was lost.

The only visible mark left by all this was on Mrs. Wills. Everybody in a mining-town, except the minister and professional gamblers who wear frock-coats, dresses pretty much alike, and Wills very soon got to wear in his face the guileless, trustful fixity of the confirmed prospector. It seemed as if the desert had overshot him and struck at Mrs. Wills, and Richard Wills, Esther Wills, Benjy Wills, and the youngest Wills, who was called Mugsey. Desertness attacked the door-yard and the house; even the cabinet organ had a weathered look. During the time of the White Cement obsession the Wills family appeared to be in need of a grub-stake themselves. Mrs. Wills' eyes were like the eyes of trail-weary cattle; her hands grew to have that pitiful way of catching the front of her dress of the woman not so much a slattern as hopeless. It was when her husband went out after Lost Cabin she fell into the habit of sitting down to a cheap novel with the dishes unwashed, a sort of drugging of despair common among women of the camps. All this time Mr. Wills was drifting about from camp to camp of the desert borders, working when it could not be avoided, but mostly on long, fruitless trudges among the unmindful ranges. I do not know if the man was honest with himself; if he knew by this time that the clew of a lost mine was the baldest of excuses merely to be out and away from everything that savored of definiteness and responsibility. The fact was, the desert had got him. All the hoops were off the cask. The mind of Mr. Wills faded out at the edges like the desert horizon that melts in mists and mirages, and finally he went on an expedition from which he did not come back.

He had been gone nearly a year when Mrs. Wills gave up expecting him. She had grown so used to the bedraggled crawl of life that she might never have taken any notice of the disappearance of Mr. Wills had not the Emporium refused to make any more charges in his name. There had been a great many dry water-holes on the desert that year, and more than the usual complement of sun-dried corpses. In a general way this accounted for Mr. Wills, though nothing transpired of sufficient definiteness to justify Mrs. Wills in putting on a widow's dress, and, anyway, she could not have afforded it.

Mrs. Wills and the children went to work, and work was about the only thing in Maverick of which there was more than enough. It was a matter of a very few months when Mrs. Wills made the remarkable discovery that after the family bills were paid at the end of the month, there was a little over. A very little. Mrs. Wills had lived so long with the tradition that a husband is a natural provider that it took some months longer to realize that she not only did not need Mr. Wills, but got on better without him. This was about the time she was able to have the sitting-room repapered and put up lace curtains. And the next spring the children planted roses in the front yard. All up and down the wash of Salt Creek there were lean coyote mothers, and wild folk of every sort could have taught her that nature never makes the mistake of neglecting to make the child-bearer competent to provide. But Mrs. Wills had not been studying life in the lairs. She had most of her notions of it from the church and her parents, and all under the new sense of independence and power she had an ache of forlornness and neglect. As a matter of fact she filled out, grew stronger, had a spring in her walk. She was not pining for Mr. Wills; the desert had him—for whatever conceivable use, it was more than Mrs. Wills could put him to—let the desert keep what it had got.

It was in the third summer that she regained a certain air that made me think she must have been pretty when Mr. Wills married her. And no woman in a mining-town can so much as hint at prettiness without its being found out. Mrs. Wills had a good many prejudices left over from the time when Mr. Wills had been superintendent of the Sunday-school, and would not hear of divorce. Yet, as the slovenliness of despair fell away from her, as she held up her head and began to have company to tea, it is certain somebody would have broached it to her before the summer was over; but by that time Mr. Wills came back.

It happened that Benjy Wills, who was fourteen and driving the Bed Rock delivery wagon, had a runaway accident in which he had behaved very handsomely and gotten a fractured skull. News of it went by way of the local paper to Tonopah, and from there drifted south to the Funeral Mountains and the particular prospect that Mr. Wills was working on a grub-stake. He had come to that. Perhaps as much because he had found there was nothing in it, as from paternal anxiety, he came home the evening of the day the doctor had declared the boy out of danger.

It was my turn to sit up that night, I remember, and Mrs. Meyer, who had the turn before, was telling me about the medicines. There was a neighbor woman who had come in by the back door with a bowl of custard, and the doctor standing in the sitting-room with Mrs. Wills, when Mr. Wills came in through the black block of the doorway with his hand before his face to ward off the light—and perhaps some shamefacedness—who knows?

I saw Mrs. Wills quiver, and her hand went up to her bosom as if someone had struck her. I have seen horses start and check like that as they came over the Pass and the hot blast of the desert took them fairly. It was the stroke of desolation. I remember turning quickly at the

doctor's curt signal to shut the door between the sitting-room and
Benjy.

"Don't let the boy see you tonight, Wills," said the doctor, with no
hint of a greeting; "he's not to be excited." With that he got himself
off as quickly as possible, and the neighbor woman and I went out and
sat on the back steps a long time, and tried to talk about everything but
Mr. Wills. When I went in, at last, he was sitting in the Morris chair,
which had come with soap-wrappers, explaining to Mrs. Meyer about
the rich prospect he had left to come to his darling boy. But he did not
get so much as a glimpse of his darling boy while I was in charge.

Mr. Wills settled on his family like a blight. For a man who has
prospected lost mines to that extent is positively not good for anything
else. It was not only as if the desert had sucked the life out of him and
cast him back, but as if it would have Mrs. Wills in his room. As the
weeks went on you could see a sort of dinginess creeping up from her
dress to her hair and her face, and it spread to the house and the
doorway. Mr. Wills had enjoyed the improved condition of his home,
though he missed the point of it; his wife's cooking tasted good to him
after miner's fare, and he was proud of his boys. He didn't want any
more of the desert. Not he. "There's no place like home," said Mr.
Wills, or something to that effect.

But he had brought the desert with him on his back. If it had been
at any other time than when her mind was torn with anxiety for Benjy,
Mrs. Wills might have made a fight against it. But the only practical
way to separate the family from the blight was to divorce Mr. Wills,
and the church to which Mrs. Wills belonged admitted divorce only in
the event of there being another woman.

Mrs. Wills rose to the pitch of threatening, I believe, about the time
Mr. Wills insisted on his right to control the earnings of his sons. But
the minister called; the church put out its hand upon her poor, staggered soul that sunk aback. The minister himself was newly from the
East, and did not understand that the desert is to be dealt with as a
woman and a wanton; he was thinking of it as a place on the map.
Therefore, he was not of the slightest use to Mrs. Wills, which did not
prevent him from commanding her behavior. And the power of the
wilderness lay like a wasting sickness on the home.

About that time Mrs. Wills took to novel-reading again; the eldest
son drifted off up Tonopah way; and Benjy began to keep back a part
of the wages he brought home. And Mr. Wills is beginning to collect
misinformation about the exact locality where Peg-leg Smith is supposed to have found the sun-burnt nuggets. He does not mention the
matter often, being, as he says, done with mines; but whenever the
Peg-leg comes up in talk I can see Mrs. Wills chirk up[5] a little, her gaze
wandering to the inscrutable grim spaces, not with the hate you might

5. Cheer up.

suppose, but with something like hope in her eye, as if she had guessed what I am certain of—that in time its insatiable spirit will reach out and take Mr. Wills again.

And this time, if I know Mrs. Wills, he will not come back.

Century, April 1908; *Lost Borders*, 1909

The Land

When the Paiute nations broke westward through the Sierra wall they cut off a remnant of the Shoshones, and forced them south as far as Death Valley and the borders of the Mojaves, they penned the Washoes in and around Tahoe, and, passing between these two, established themselves along the snow-fed Sierra creeks.[1] And this it was proper they should do, for the root of their name-word is Pah, meaning water, to distinguish them from their brothers the Utes of the Great Basin.

In time they passed quite through the saw-cut cañons by Kern and Kings rivers and possessed all the east slope of the San Joaquin, but chiefly they settled by small clans and family groups where the pines leave off and the sage begins and the desert abuts on the great Sierra fault. On the northeast they touched the extreme flanks of the Utes, and with them and the southerly tribes swept a wide arc about that region of mysterious desertness of which you shall presently hear more particularly.

The boundaries between the tribes and between the clans within the tribe were plainly established by natural landmarks—peaks, hill-crests, creeks, and chains of water-holes—beginning at the foot of the Sierra and continuing eastward past the limit of endurable existence. Out there, a week's journey from everywhere, the land was not worth parceling off, and the boundaries which should logically have been continued until they met the cañon of the Colorado ran out in foolish wastes of sand and inextricable disordered ranges. Here you have the significance of the Indian name for that country—Lost Borders. And you can always trust Indian names to express to you the largest truth about any district in the shortest phrases.

But there is more in the name than that. For law runs with the boundary, not beyond it; it is as fast to the given landmarks as a limpet to its scar on the rock. I am convinced most men make law for the comfortable feel of it, defining them to themselves; they shoulder along like blindworms, rearing against restrictions, turning thereward for security as climbing plants to the warmth of a nearing wall. They pinch themselves with regulations to make sure of being sentient, and organize within organizations.

1. The region of the California desert east of the Sierra Nevadas and on the northern boundaries of the Mojave Desert.

Out there, then, where the law and the landmarks fail together, the souls of little men fade out at the edges, leak from them as water from wooden pails warped asunder.

Out there where the borders of conscience break down, where there is no convention, and behavior is of little account except as it gets you your desire, almost anything might happen; does happen, in fact, though I shall have trouble making you believe it. Out there where the boundary of soul and sense is as faint as a trail in a sand-storm, I have seen things happen that I do not believe myself. That is what you are to expect in a country where the names mean something. Ubehebe, Pharanagat, Resting Springs, Dead Man's Gulch, Funeral Mountains—these beckon and allure. There is always a tang of reality about them like the smart of wood smoke to the eyes, that warns of neighboring fires.

Riding through by the known trails, the senses are obsessed by the coil of a huge and senseless monotony; straight, white, blinding, alkali flats, forsaken mesas; skimpy shrubs growing little and less, starved knees of hills sticking out above them; black clots of pines high upon rubbishy mountain-heads—days and days of this, as if Nature herself had obscured the medium to escape you in her secret operations.

One might travel weeks on end and not come on any place or occasion whereby men may live, and drop suddenly into close hives of them digging, jostling, drinking, lusting, and rejoicing. Every story of that country is colored by the fashion of the life there, breaking up in swift, passionate intervals between long, dun stretches, like the land that out of hot sinks of desolation heaves up great bulks of granite ranges with opal shadows playing in their shining, snow-piled curves. Out there beyond the borders are the Shivering Dunes, heaps upon heaps of blinding sand all crawl in the wind, drifting and reforming with a faint, stridulent rustle, and black, wall-sided box-cañons that give the stars at midday, scored over with picture-writings of a forgotten race. There are lakes there of a pellucid clearness like ice, closed over with man-deep crystals of pure salt. Long Tom Bassit told me a story of one of these which he had from a man who saw it. It was of an emigrant train all out of its reckoning, laboring in a long, hollow trough of desolation between waterless high ranges, arriving at such a closed salt-pit, too much spent to go around it and trusting the salt crust to hold under their racked wagons and starveling teams. But when they had come near the middle of the lake, the salt thinned out abruptly, and, the forward rank of the party breaking through, the bodies were caught under the saline slabs and not all of them recovered. There was a woman among them, and the Man-who-saw had cared—cared enough to go back years afterward, when, after successive oven-blast summers, the salt held solidly over all the lake, and he told Tom Bassit how, long before he reached the point, he saw the gleam of red in the woman's dress, and found her at last, lying on her side, sealed in the crystal, rising as ice rises to the surface of choked streams. Long Tom wished me to make a story of it. I did once at a dinner, but I never got through with it. There, about the time the candles began to burn their shades and red track of the light on the wine-glasses barred the cloth, with the white, disdainful shoulders and politely incredulous faces leaning through the smoke of cigarettes, it had a garish sound. Afterward I came across the proof of the affair in the records of the emigrant party, but I never tried telling it again.

That is why in all that follows I have set down what the Borderers thought and felt; for that you have a touchstone[2] in your *own* heart, but I should get no credit with you if I were to tell what really became of Loring, and what happened to the man who went down into the moaning pit of Sand Mountain.

Curiously, in that country, you can get anybody to believe any sort of a tale that has gold in it, like the Lost Mine of Fisherman's Peak and the Duke o' Wild Rose. Young Woodin brought me a potsherd once from a kitchen-midden in Shoshone Land. It might have been, for antiquity, one of those Job[3] scraped himself withal, but it was dotted all over with colors and specks of pure gold from the river-bed from which the sand and clay were scooped. Said he:

"You ought to find a story about this somewhere."

I was sore then about not getting myself believed in some elementary matters, such as that horned toads are not poisonous, and that Indians really have the bowels of compassion. Said I:

"I will do better than that, I will *make* a story."

We sat out a whole afternoon under the mulberry-tree, with the landscape disappearing in shimmering heat-waves around us, testing our story for likelihood and proving it. There was an Indian woman in the tale, not pretty, for they are mostly not that in life, and the earthenware pot, of course, and a lost river bedded with precious sand. Afterward my friend went to hold down some claims in the Coso country, and I north to the lake region where the red firs are, and we told the pot-of-gold story as often as we were permitted. One night when I had done with it, a stranger by our camp-fire said the thing was well known in his country. I said, "Where was that?"

"Coso," said he, and that was the first I had heard of my friend.

Next winter, at Lone Pine, a prospector from Panamint-way wanted to know if I had ever heard of the Indian-pot Mine which was lost out toward Pharump. I said I had a piece of the pot, which I showed him. Then I wrote the tale for a magazine of the sort that gets taken in camps and at miners' boarding-houses, and several men were at great pains to explain to me where my version varied from the accepted one of the hills. By this time, you understand, I had begun to believe the story myself. I had a spasm of conscience, though, when Tennessee told me that he thought he knew the very squaw of the story, and when

2. In gold country, a hard black stone, such as jasper or basalt, used to test the quality or authenticity of gold or silver.
3. In the Old Testament, a righteous man whose faith in God survives the test of repeated calamities; see the Book of Job. Kitchen-midden: a refuse mound containing artifacts and animal bones.

the back of the winter was broken he meant to make a little "pasear"[4] in search of the lost river. But Tennessee died before spring, and spared my confessing. Now it only needs that someone should find another sherd of the gold-besprinkled pot to fix the tale in the body of desert myths. Well—it had as much fact behind it as the Gunsight, and is more interesting than the Bryfogle,[5] which began with the finding of a dead man, clothless as the desert dead mostly are, with a bag of nuggets clutched in his mummied hands.

First and last, accept no man's statement that he knows this Country of Lost Borders well. A great number having lost their lives in the process of proving where it is not safe to go, it is now possible to pass through much of the district by guide-posts and well-known water-holes, but the best part of it remains locked, inviolate, or at best known only to some far-straying Indian, sheepherder, or pocket hunter, whose account of it does not get into the reports of the Geological Survey. But a boast of knowledge is likely to prove as hollow as the little yellow gourds called apples of Death Valley.

Pure desertness clings along the pits of the long valleys and the formless beds of vanished lakes. Every hill that lifts as high as the cloud-line has some trees upon it, and deer and bighorn to feed on the tall, tufted, bunch grass between the boulders. In the year when Tono-pah, turning upon itself like a swarm, trickled prospectors all over that country from Hot Creek to the Armagosa, Indians brought me word that the men had camped so close about the water-holes that the bighorn died of thirst on the headlands, turned always in the last agony toward the man-infested springs.

That is as good a pointer as any if you go waterless in the country of Lost Borders: where you find cattle dropped, skeleton or skin dried, the heads almost invariably will be turned toward the places where water-holes should be. But no such reminders will fend men from its trails. This is chiefly, I am persuaded, because there is something incomprehensible to the man-mind in the concurrence of death and beauty. Shall the tender opal mist betray you? the airy depth of mountain blueness, the blazonry of painted wind-scoured buttes, the far peaks molten with the alpen glow, cooled by the rising of the velvet violet twilight tide, and the leagues and leagues of stars? As easy for a man to believe that a beautiful woman can be cruel. Mind you, it is men who go mostly into the desert, who love it past all reasonableness, slack their ambitions, cast off old usages, neglect their families because of the pulse and beat of a life laid bare to its thews and sinews. Their women hate with implicitness the life like the land, stretching intermi-nably whity-brown, dim and shadowy blue hills that hem it, glimmer-ing pale waters of mirage that creep and crawl about its edges. There was a woman once at Agua Hedionda—but you wouldn't believe that either.

If the desert were a woman, I know well what like she would be:

---

4. Spanish for stroll or walk.   5. Gunsight, Bryfogle: names of two gold mines.

deep-breasted, broad in the hips, tawny, with tawny hair, great masses of it lying smooth along her perfect curves, full lipped like a sphinx, but not heavy-lidded like one, eyes sane and steady as the polished jewel of her skies, such a countenance as should make men serve without desiring her, such a largeness to her mind as should make their sins of no account, passionate, but not necessitous, patient—and you could not move her, no, not if you had all the earth to give, so much as one tawny hair's-breadth beyond her own desires. If you cut very deeply into any soul that has the mark of the land upon it, you find such qualities as these—as I shall presently prove to you.

Lost Borders, 1909

WILLA CATHER
1873-1947

In her last novel, *Sapphira and the Slave Girl* (1940), Willa Cather returned in her imagination to the Back Creek Valley of Virginia where she was born and where she lived the first nine years of her life. Though Cather is best known for her descriptions of Nebraska, this late novel suggests that transplanting, not rootedness, lies at the heart of Cather's relation to region, and that, unlike the regionalists who preceded her, Cather experienced region within the context of loss.

Born December 7, 1873, and named Wilella, Willa Cather was the first of seven children of Mary Virginia Boak and Charles Fectigue Cather. She spent her first years at Willowshade, the home of her maternal grandparents near Winchester, Virginia, in a household that included, among others, her maternal grandmother, Rachel Boak, who taught her to read and write. Her mother created a model for conventional femininity that her daughter rebelled against, even though her companion Edith Lewis recalled that in later years Cather "always said she was more like her mother than like any other member of her family" (O'Brien 42). In 1883, under pressure from his father, Charles Cather decided to emigrate to Webster County, Nebraska, and join the members of his family who had already established households there. One year of farming on the frontier proved sufficient for Charles and in 1884 the Cathers moved to the town of Red Cloud. Here Cather began formal schooling, graduating from high school in 1890, where she delivered a commencement address dressed as a boy. This action was the culmination of several adolescent years in which she identified herself as "William Cather," cropped her hair short, wore men's clothing, and declared her interest in a scientific or a medical career. Cather left Red Cloud in 1890 to attend the University of Nebraska at Lincoln. She studied Greek and Latin, joined the university's literary and debating societies, and began to write for campus magazines and Lincoln newspapers. During her years in Lincoln she began to write and publish fiction, seeing one story appear in a Boston literary weekly in 1892, and she shifted her allegiance from science to literature.

In 1896, Cather made another move, to Pittsburgh, Pennsylvania, where she accepted a job as editor and manager of a newly founded women's magazine. A year later she joined the staff of the *Pittsburgh Daily Leader*, a position she held for four years; convinced that teaching would leave her more time to write than journalism, she left her position to take a job teaching high school. This shift coincided with a decision to accept the invitation of Isabelle McClung, daughter of a prominent Pittsburgh family whom Cather had met in 1899, to move into her house and live with her. Though Cather was to spend nearly forty years with Edith Lewis, a fellow Nebraskan whom she met in

1903, and would establish a permanent household with her, the available evidence indicates that Isabelle McClung formed the great passion of Cather's life, and that Isabelle's marriage in 1916 to Jan Hambourg marked the point at which Cather's personal world broke in two. Cather lived with Isabelle from 1901 to 1906. She published *April Twilights*, a volume of verse, in 1903, and *The Troll Garden*, a collection of stories which she dedicated to Isabelle McClung, in 1905.

In 1903, S. S. McClure, publisher of *McClure's* magazine, "discovered" Cather and began actively to support her career, helping her place stories in prestigious magazines and publishing *The Troll Garden*. In 1906 Cather agreed to move to New York to join the staff of *McClure's*. Though she traveled frequently thereafter and in particular spent time in New Hampshire and on Grand Manan, a Canadian island off the coast of Maine, New York became Cather's primary residence for the rest of her life. Two years later, Cather agreed to share an apartment with Edith Lewis, several years her junior and an admirer of her fiction. After the serialization in *McClure's* of her first novel, *Alexander's Bridge*, and remembering the advice of Sarah Orne Jewett who urged her to quit journalism and devote herself to her writing, Cather resigned her position at *McClure's* in 1912 and for the rest of her life supported herself by her writing of fiction and essays. Cather's career as a writer includes twelve novels, four collections of stories, and two collections of essays. During her later years she enjoyed increasing recognition of her work. She died in New York on April 24, 1947, of a cerebral hemorrhage, and was buried in Jaffrey, New Hampshire. Twenty-five years later Edith Lewis was buried by her side.

°   °   °

Cather appropriately concludes this anthology because she signals the beginning of a different historical moment from that which produced regionalism. A nineteenth-century phenomenon and in part the fruit of the nineteenth-century women's movement, regionalism did not survive either the repression or the redirection that movement witnessed at the beginning of the twentieth century. While Jewett could live openly and unselfconsciously with Annie Fields in a "Boston marriage," Willa Cather became a woman in a Freudian context, self-conscious about her own attraction to women and aware of her deviance. But if Cather could not choose to write about women's relationships to women without a consciousness of deviance, she could choose to enter the ranks of "great" American writers because she could, as Jewett could not, imagine herself as male. In *The Country of the Pointed Firs*, Jewett's character Susan Fosdick recalls with delight the "spell o' freedom" she experienced as a child when she wore boys' clothes for a few weeks; Willa Cather, living in Red Cloud, Nebraska, in the 1880s, could choose to adopt male dress and assume a male persona for several years. This adolescent assumption of male privilege prepared Cather to imagine herself as part of an American literary tradition defined as male. Cather could aspire to enter a tradition that the regional writers either consciously rejected or felt was closed to them.

This is not to say that the values of the regionalists failed Willa Cather, or that she was unable to follow in their footsteps, but rather to recognize the implications of Cather's particular historical moment for women's ambition, particularly literary ambition. We began this volume with Stowe's first sketch, "Uncle Lot," which, in our analysis, announces the possibilities of regionalism;

we have chosen to close our volume with Cather's "Old Mrs. Harris" (1932), the late work in which we see Cather exploring her differences with the regionalists, and, with the death of Mrs. Harris, announcing the "end" of regionalism as a viable mode for the women writers of her generation.

Written on Grand Manan Island during the summer of her mother's death and apparently inspired by Cather's relationship with her mother, "Old Mrs. Harris," unlike most of Cather's other work, contains many elements that initially appear to link her to the regionalist tradition. As the story opens, Mrs. Rosen moves her lawn sprinkler from one "spot" to another, waiting for her neighbor Victoria Templeton to leave the house so that she can make a visit to Victoria's mother, old Mrs. Harris. Like numerous female characters in regionalist fiction, Mrs. Rosen hopes for a visit in which she will be able to feed Mrs. Harris, both with the cake she brings and with the visit itself. Such a visit, Cather implies, would also "feed" Mrs. Rosen, who wishes to get to know "the real grandmother" in her neighbor. Yet the grandmother is always "on her guard," and Cather writes that "Mrs. Harris and her 'things' were almost required to be invisible." Mrs. Rosen's focus on old Mrs. Harris suggests Cather's desire to rectify the grandmother's "invisibility."

Further, Cather offers the church social as a form of community which readers of regionalism will recognize, and Mrs. Harris sends her best cake to the social, expressing her own desire to participate in that community as a feeder or nurturer. Mrs. Rosen attempts to create a community with her neighbors across property lines and generations. Though Mr. Rosen and Mr. Templeton figure in the text, Cather recognizes community as a matter of women's relationships to women, for, as Mandy notes, in a crisis "poor Mr. Templeton was always called away on important business." Additionally, in choosing to tell so much of her story from Mrs. Rosen's point of view, Cather establishes empathy and mothering as central features of her narrative. Though Mrs. Rosen is "inconsolable" when the Templetons first move next door, her instincts of generosity and her spirit of justice interrupt her criticism of Victoria and enable her to empathize with all three generations of Templeton women. In feeding Vickie, Victoria, and Grandma Harris, Mrs. Rosen fulfills her desire to nurture and identifies the maternal voice and vision as dominant in "Old Mrs. Harris."

However, by indicating the limits of regionalism as a resource for her particular narrative, Cather traces the necessity for her young protagonist, Vickie Templeton, to leave behind her adopted region in order to fulfill her ambition. "Old Mrs. Harris" manifests subtle contrasts between Cather's work and the work of her New England predecessors. For example, despite the apparent similarities between Mrs. Rosen's "spot" of yard and the picket-fenced gardens of Thaxter, Jewett, and Freeman, Mrs. Rosen has imported her sense of yard and requires modern technology—the lawn sprinkler—to make it possible. In addition, although Cather includes a community social in her story, old Mrs. Harris does not attend the gathering, even though she has contributed a cake to the event. Further, although "Old Mrs. Harris" opens with a visit, the visit is not successful. Despite Mrs. Rosen's desire to get to know the "real grandmother," her empathic stance cannot overcome the barriers that dislocation from Tennessee to Colorado has placed in the way of community, and Mrs. Rosen is finally incapable of reducing old Mrs. Harris's invisibility. Moreover, while "Old Mrs. Harris" is remarkable for its balanced portrayal of the claims of each generation of women living in the Templeton household, the story nevertheless presents an image of co-existence rather than interaction. The women each follow their own generation's pattern of life, within the household they appear to compete with each other rather than to cooperate, and they rarely spend time with each other.

Finally, Cather's portrait of Mrs. Harris's "regionalist" past in Tennessee contrasts sharply with Mary Noialles Murfree's portraits and indicates a different vision of region from that which sustained the regionalist writers. In Cather's Tennessee, "the hills were full of solitary old women . . . glad to come to Miz' Harris's for good food and a warm bed," and while Mrs. Harris provided healing and comfort to the poor mountain people, she did so with full recognition that she lived in a "feudal society" that exploited such women as a source of cheap labor. And while "back there it was Grandmother's own house they lived in" and Mr. Templeton "never so much as mended one of the steps to the front porch without consulting Mrs. Harris," nothing in that environment has empowered Mrs. Harris to oppose her son Hilary's decision to sell her house and "invest" the proceeds in a move west. In Cather's Tennessee, Mrs. Harris lacked or was denied the authority to choose either to remain in the region or to carry with her the values of women's community to a new environment. Cather writes, "The road had led westward, and Mrs. Harris didn't believe that women, especially old women, could say when or where they would stop. They were tied to the chariot of young life, and had to go where it went, because they were needed." In characterizing old Mrs. Harris as having "the kind of quiet dignity that comes from complete resignation to the chances of life," Cather suggests that the values of community, empathy, nurture, and rootedness that characterize the fiction of the regionalists pose a clear danger to Vickie Templeton's developing female self. Reflecting in this story on the situation of her own generation of American women, Cather implies that while old Mrs. Harris's road may lead westward, it does not lead to college, and all that college represents. For Cather, the story of Vickie's move outside the home, beyond female community, and into the larger male-dominated world of the university represents the road of development for women of her generation.

"Old Mrs. Harris" seems to predict that Vickie's story—not Mrs. Harris's or Victoria's—will determine the shape of fiction about twentieth-century American women. Mrs. Harris has a cold and lonely "spot" under her heart which she warms with the old sweater Mrs. Rosen gives her, but neither Mrs. Harris nor, apparently, Cather can imagine that developing a relationship between Mrs. Harris and Mrs. Rosen will sustain a story. Nor does it seem that Vickie's motives for going to the University of Michigan include learning to tell old Mrs. Harris's story. Stowe, transplanted to Cincinnati, looks back to her native New England for her inspiration; she finds the source of her fiction in home, and finds home in her fiction. Cather, transplanted to Nebraska, carries home as a memory of something irrevocably lost. Dying, old Mrs. Harris comforts herself with memories of her home in Tennessee, and in the summer Mrs. Rosen secretly longs for the Adirondacks. It is Mr. Rosen, however, who finds a solution—both modern and in many ways modernist—to the problem of "losing" home: "All countries were beautiful to Mr. Rosen. He carried a country of his own in his mind and was able to unfold it like a tent in any wilderness."

Old Mrs. Harris

I

Mrs. David Rosen, cross-stitch in hand, sat looking out of the window across her own green lawn to the ragged, sunburned back yard of her neighbours on the right. Occasionally she glanced anxiously over her shoulder toward her shining kitchen, with a black and white linoleum floor in big squares, like a marble pavement.

"Will dat woman never go?" she muttered impatiently, just under her breath. She spoke with a slight accent—it affected only her *th's*, and, occasionally, the letter *v*. But people in Skyline thought this unfortunate, in a woman whose superiority they recognized.

Mrs. Rosen ran out to move the sprinkler to another spot on the lawn, and in doing so she saw what she had been waiting to see. From the house next door a tall, handsome woman emerged, dressed in white broadcloth and a hat with white lilacs; she carried a sunshade and walked with a free, energetic step, as if she were going out on a pleasant errand.

Mrs. Rosen darted quickly back into the house, lest her neighbour should hail her and stop to talk. She herself was in her kitchen housework dress, a crisp blue chambray[1] which fitted smoothly over her tightly corseted figure, and her lustrous black hair was done in two smooth braids, wound flat at the back of her head, like a braided rug. She did not stop for a hat—her dark, ruddy, salmon-tinted skin had little to fear from the sun. She opened the half-closed oven door and took out a symmetrically plaited coffee-cake, beautifully browned, delicately peppered over with poppy seeds, with sugary margins about the twists. On the kitchen table a tray stood ready with cups and saucers. She wrapped the cake in a napkin, snatched up a little French coffee-pot with a black wooden handle, and ran across her green lawn, through the alley-way and the sandy, unkept yard next door, and entered her neighbour's house by the kitchen.

The kitchen was hot and empty, full of the untempered afternoon sun. A door stood open into the next room; a cluttered, hideous room, yet somehow homely. There, beside a goods-box covered with figured oilcloth, stood an old woman in a brown calico dress, washing her hot face and neck at a tin basin. She stood with her feet wide apart, in an attitude of profound weariness. She started guiltily as the visitor entered.

"Don't let me disturb you, Grandma," called Mrs. Rosen. "I always have my coffee at dis hour in the afternoon. I was just about to sit down to it when I thought: 'I will run over and see if Grandma Harris won't take a cup with me.' I hate to drink my coffee alone."

---

1. A lightweight woven fabric.

Grandma looked troubled,—at a loss. She folded her towel and concealed it behind a curtain hung across the corner of the room to make a poor sort of closet. The old lady was always composed in manner, but it was clear that she felt embarrassment.

"Thank you, Mrs. Rosen. What a pity Victoria just this minute went down town!"

"But dis time I came to see you yourself, Grandma. Don't let me disturb you. Sit down there in your own rocker, and I will put my tray on this little chair between us, so!"

Mrs. Harris sat down in her black wooden rocking-chair with curved arms and a faded cretonne[2] pillow on the wooden seat. It stood in the corner beside a narrow spindle-frame lounge. She looked on silently while Mrs. Rosen uncovered the cake and delicately broke it with her plump, smooth, dusky-red hands. The old lady did not seem pleased,— seemed uncertain and apprehensive, indeed. But she was not fussy or fidgety. She had the kind of quiet, intensely quiet, dignity that comes from complete resignation to the chances of life. She watched Mrs. Rosen's deft hands out of grave, steady brown eyes.

"Dis is Mr. Rosen's favourite coffee-cake, Grandma, and I want you to try it. You are such a good cook yourself, I would like your opinion of my cake."

"It's very nice, ma'am," said Mrs. Harris politely, but without enthusiasm.

"And you aren't drinking your coffee; do you like more cream in it?"

"No, thank you. I'm letting it cool a little. I generally drink it that way."

"Of course she does," thought Mrs. Rosen, "since she never has her coffee until all the family are done breakfast!"

Mrs. Rosen had brought Grandma Harris coffee-cake time and again, but she knew that Grandma merely tasted it and saved it for her daughter Victoria, who was as fond of sweets as her own children, and jealous about them, moreover,—couldn't bear that special dainties should come into the house for anyone but herself. Mrs. Rosen, vexed at her failures, had determined that just once she would take a cake to "de old lady Harris," and with her own eyes see her eat it. The result was not all she had hoped. Receiving a visitor alone, unsupervised by her daughter, having cake and coffee that should properly be saved for Victoria, was all so irregular that Mrs. Harris could not enjoy it. Mrs. Rosen doubted if she tasted the cake as she swallowed it,—certainly she ate it without relish, as a hollow form. But Mrs. Rosen enjoyed her own cake, at any rate, and she was glad of an opportunity to sit quietly and look at Grandmother, who was more interesting to her than the handsome Victoria.

It was a queer place to be having coffee, when Mrs. Rosen liked order and comeliness so much: a hideous, cluttered room, furnished

2. A heavy, colorfully printed fabric used for draperies and slipcovers.

with a rocking-horse, a sewing-machine, an empty baby-buggy. A walnut table stood against a blind window, piled high with old magazines and tattered books, and children's caps and coats. There was a wash-stand (two wash-stands, if you counted the oilcloth-covered box as one). A corner of the room was curtained off with some black-and-red-striped cotton goods, for a clothes closet. In another corner was the wooden lounge with a thin mattress and a red calico spread which was Grandma's bed. Beside it was her wooden rocking-chair, and the little splint-bottom[3] chair with the legs sawed short on which her darning-basket usually stood, but which Mrs. Rosen was now using for a tea-table.

The old lady was always impressive, Mrs. Rosen was thinking,—one could not say why. Perhaps it was the way she held her head,—so simply, unprotesting and unprotected; or the gravity of her large, deep-set brown eyes, a warm, reddish brown, though their look, always direct, seemed to ask nothing and hope for nothing. They were not cold, but inscrutable, with no kindling gleam of intercourse in them. There was the kind of nobility about her head that there is about an old lion's: an absence of self-consciousness, vanity, preoccupation—something absolute. Her grey hair was parted in the middle, wound in two little horns over her ears, and done in a little flat knot behind. Her mouth was large and composed,—resigned, the corners drooping. Mrs. Rosen had very seldom heard her laugh (and then it was a gentle, polite laugh which meant only politeness). But she had observed that whenever Mrs. Harris's grandchildren were about, tumbling all over her, asking for cookies, teasing her to read to them, the old lady looked happy.

As she drank her coffee, Mrs. Rosen tried one subject after another to engage Mrs. Harris's attention.

"Do you feel this hot weather, Grandma? I am afraid you are over the stove too much. Let those naughty children have a cold lunch occasionally."

"No'm, I don't mind the heat. It's apt to come on like this for a spell in May. I don't feel the stove. I'm accustomed to it."

"Oh, so am I! But I get very impatient with my cooking in hot weather. Do you miss your old home in Tennessee very much, Grandma?"

"No'm, I can't say I do. Mr. Templeton thought Colorado was a better place to bring up the children."

"But you had things much more comfortable down there, I'm sure. These little wooden houses are too hot in summer."

"Yes'm, we were more comfortable. We had more room."

"And a flower-garden, and beautiful old trees, Mrs. Templeton told me."

"Yes'm, we had a great deal of shade."

---

3. With a seat woven of thin wooden strips.

Mrs. Rosen felt that she was not getting anywhere. She almost believed that Grandma thought she had come on an equivocal errand, to spy out something in Victoria's absence. Well, perhaps she had! Just for once she would like to get past the others to the real grandmother,—and the real grandmother was on her guard, as always. At this moment she heard a faint miaow. Mrs. Harris rose, lifting herself by the wooden arms of her chair, said: "Excuse me," went into the kitchen, and opened the screen door.

In walked a large, handsome, thickly furred Maltese[4] cat, with long whiskers and yellow eyes and a white star on his breast. He preceded Grandmother, waited until she sat down. Then he sprang up into her lap and settled himself comfortably in the folds of her full-gathered calico skirt. He rested his chin in his deep bluish fur and regarded Mrs. Rosen. It struck her that he held his head in just the way Grandmother held hers. And Grandmother now became more alive, as if some missing part of herself were restored.

"This is Blue Boy," she said, stroking him. "In winter, when the screen door ain't on, he lets himself in. He stands up on his hind legs and presses the thumb-latch with his paw, and just walks in like anybody."

"He's your cat, isn't he, Grandma?" Mrs. Rosen couldn't help prying just a little; if she could find but a single thing that was Grandma's own!

"He's our cat," replied Mrs. Harris. "We're all very fond of him. I expect he's Vickie's more'n anybody's."

"Of course!" groaned Mrs. Rosen to herself. "Dat Vickie is her mother over again."

Here Mrs. Harris made her first unsolicited remark. "If you was to be troubled with mice at any time, Mrs. Rosen, ask one of the boys to bring Blue Boy over to you, and he'll clear them out. He's a master mouser." She scratched the thick blue fur at the back of his neck, and he began a deep purring. Mrs. Harris smiled. "We call that spinning, back with us. Our children still say: 'Listen to Blue Boy spin,' though none of 'em is ever heard a spinning-wheel—except maybe Vickie remembers."

"Did you have a spinning-wheel in your own house, Grandma Harris?"

"Yes'm. Miss Sadie Crummer used to come and spin for us. She was left with no home of her own, and it was to give her something to do, as much as anything, that we had her. I spun a good deal myself, in my young days." Grandmother stopped and put her hands on the arms of her chair, as if to rise. "Did you hear a door open? It might be Victoria."

"No, it was the wind shaking the screen door. Mrs. Templeton won't be home yet. She is probably in my husband's store this minute, order-

4. A short-haired breed, bluish in color, popular in America in the late 19th century.

ing him about. All the merchants down town will take anything from your daughter. She is very popular wid de gentlemen, Grandma."

Mrs. Harris smiled complacently. "Yes'm. Victoria was always much admired."

At this moment a chorus of laughter broke in upon the warm silence, and a host of children, as it seemed to Mrs. Rosen, ran through the yard. The hand-pump on the back porch, outside the kitchen door, began to scrape and gurgle.

"It's the children, back from school," said Grandma. "They are getting a cool drink."

"But where is the baby, Grandma?"

"Vickie took Hughie in his cart over to Mr. Holliday's yard, where she studies. She's right good about minding him."

Mrs. Rosen was glad to hear that Vickie was good for something.

Three little boys came running in through the kitchen; the twins, aged ten, and Ronald, aged six, who went to kindergarten. They snatched off their caps and threw their jackets and school bags on the table, the sewing-machine, the rocking-horse.

"Howdy do, Mrs. Rosen." They spoke to her nicely. They had nice voices, nice faces, and were always courteous, like their father. "We are going to play in our back yard with some of the boys, Gram'ma," said one of the twins respectfully, and they ran out to join a troop of schoolmates who were already shouting and racing over that poor trampled back yard, strewn with velocipedes[5] and croquet mallets and toy wagons, which was such an eyesore to Mrs. Rosen.

Mrs. Rosen got up and took her tray.

"Can't you stay a little, ma'am? Victoria will be here any minute."

But her tone let Mrs. Rosen know that Grandma really wished her to leave before Victoria returned.

A few moments after Mrs. Rosen had put the tray down in her own kitchen, Victoria Templeton came up the wooden sidewalk, attended by Mr. Rosen, who had quitted his store half an hour earlier than usual for the pleasure of walking home with her. Mrs. Templeton stopped by the picket fence to smile at the children playing in the back yard,—and it was a real smile, she was glad to see them. She called Ronald over to the fence to give him a kiss. He was hot and sticky.

"Was your teacher nice today? Now run in and ask Grandma to wash your face and put a clean waist [6] on you."

II

That night Mrs. Harris got supper with an effort—had to drive herself harder than usual. Mandy, the bound girl[7] they had brought with them from the South, noticed that the old lady was uncertain and short of

---

5. An early type of bicycle with pedals attached to the front wheel.

6. A child's undershirt.

7. An indentured servant.

breath. The hours from two to four, when Mrs. Harris usually rested, had not been at all restful this afternoon. There was an understood rule that Grandmother was not to receive visitors alone. Mrs. Rosen's call, and her cake and coffee, were too much out of the accepted order. Nervousness had prevented the old lady from getting any repose during her visit.

After the rest of the family had left the supper table, she went into the dining-room and took her place, but she ate very little. She put away the food that was left, and then, while Mandy washed the dishes, Grandma sat down in her rocking-chair in the dark and dozed.

The three little boys came in from playing under the electric light (arc lights had been but lately installed in Skyline) and began begging Mrs. Harris to read *Tom Sawyer*[8] to them. Grandmother loved to read, anything at all, the Bible or the continued story in the Chicago weekly paper. She roused herself, lit her brass "safety lamp," and pulled her black rocker out of its corner to the wash-stand (the table was too far away from her corner, and anyhow it was completely covered with coats and school satchels). She put on her old-fashioned silver-rimmed spectacles and began to read. Ronald lay down on Grandmother's lounge bed, and the twins, Albert and Adelbert, called Bert and Del, sat down against the wall, one on a low box covered with felt, and the other on the little sawed-off chair upon which Mrs. Rosen had served coffee. They looked intently at Mrs. Harris, and she looked intently at the book.

Presently Vickie, the oldest grandchild, came in. She was fifteen. Her mother was entertaining callers in the parlour, callers who didn't interest Vickie, so she was on her way up to her own room by the kitchen stairway.

Mrs. Harris looked up over her glasses. "Vickie, maybe you'd take the book awhile, and I can do my darning."

"All right," said Vickie. Reading aloud was one of the things she would always do toward the general comfort. She sat down by the wash-stand and went on with the story. Grandmother got her darning-basket and began to drive her needle across great knee-holes in the boys' stockings. Sometimes she nodded for a moment, and her hands fell into her lap. After a while the little boy on the lounge went to sleep. But the twins sat upright, their hands on their knees, their round brown eyes fastened upon Vickie, and when there was anything funny, they giggled. They were chubby, dark-skinned little boys, with round jolly faces, white teeth, and yellow-brown eyes that were always bubbling with fun unless they were sad,—even then their eyes never got red or weepy. Their tears sparkled and fell; left no trace but a streak on the cheeks, perhaps.

Presently old Mrs. Harris gave out a long snore of utter defeat. She had been overcome at last. Vickie put down the book. "That's enough

8. *The Adventures of Tom Sawyer* (1876), a novel by Samuel Clemens.

for tonight. Grandmother's sleepy, and Ronald's fast asleep. What'll
we do with him?"

"Bert and me'll get him undressed," said Adelbert. The twins
roused the sleepy little boy and prodded him up the back stairway to
the bare room without window blinds, where he was put into his cot
beside their double bed. Vickie's room was across the narrow hallway;
not much bigger than a closet, but, anyway, it was her own. She had
a chair and an old dresser, and beside her bed was a high stool which
she used as a lamp-table,—she always read in bed.

After Vickie went upstairs, the house was quiet. Hughie, the baby,
was asleep in his mother's room, and Victoria herself, who still treated
her husband as if he were her "beau," had persuaded him to take her
down town to the ice-cream parlour. Grandmother's room, between
the kitchen and the dining-room, was rather like a passage-way; but
now that the children were upstairs and Victoria was off enjoying
herself somewhere, Mrs. Harris could be sure of enough privacy to
undress. She took off the calico cover from her lounge bed and folded
it up, put on her nightgown and white nightcap.

Mandy, the bound girl, appeared at the kitchen door.

"Miz' Harris," she said in a guarded tone, ducking her head, "you
want me to rub your feet for you?"

For the first time in the long day the old woman's low composure
broke a little. "Oh, Mandy, I would take it kindly of you!" she
breathed gratefully.

That had to be done in the kitchen; Victoria didn't like anybody
slopping about. Mrs. Harris put an old checked shawl round her shoulders and followed Mandy. Beside the kitchen stove Mandy had a little
wooden tub full of warm water. She knelt down and untied Mrs.
Harris's garter strings and took off her flat cloth slippers and stockings.

"Oh, Miz' Harris, your feet an' legs is swelled turrible tonight!"

"I expect they air, Mandy. They feel like it."

"Pore soul!" murmured Mandy. She put Grandma's feet in the tub
and, crouching beside it, slowly, slowly rubbed her swollen legs.
Mandy was tired, too. Mrs. Harris sat in her nightcap and shawl, her
hands crossed in her lap. She never asked for this greatest solace of the
day; it was something that Mandy gave, who had nothing else to give.
If there could be a comparison in absolutes, Mandy was the needier of
the two,—but she was younger. The kitchen was quiet and full of
shadow, with only the light from an old lantern. Neither spoke. Mrs.
Harris dozed from comfort, and Mandy herself was half-asleep as she
performed one of the oldest rites of compassion.[9]

Although Mrs. Harris's lounge had no springs, only a thin cotton
mattress between her and the wooden slats, she usually went to sleep
as soon as she was in bed. To be off her feet, to lie flat, to say over the
psalm beginning: *The Lord is my shepherd,*[1] was comfort enough.

9. See Luke 36.   1. Psalm 23.

About four o'clock in the morning, however, she would begin to feel the hard slats under her, and the heaviness of the old home-made quilts, with weight but little warmth, on top of her. Then she would reach under her pillow for her little comforter (she called it that to herself) that Mrs. Rosen had given her. It was a tan sweater of very soft brushed wool, with one sleeve torn and ragged. A young nephew from Chicago had spent a fortnight with Mrs. Rosen last summer and had left this behind him. One morning, when Mrs. Harris went out to the stable at the back of the yard to pat Buttercup, the cow, Mrs. Rosen ran across the alley-way.

"Grandma Harris," she said, coming into the shelter of the stable, "I wonder if you could make any use of this sweater Sammy left? The yarn might be good for your darning."

Mrs. Harris felt of the article gravely. Mrs. Rosen thought her face brightened. "Yes'm, indeed I could use it. I thank you kindly."

She slipped it under her apron, carried it into the house with her, and concealed it under her mattress. There she had kept it ever since. She knew Mrs. Rosen understood how it was; that Victoria couldn't bear to have anything come into the house that was not for her to dispose of.

On winter nights, and even on summer nights after the cocks began to crow, Mrs. Harris often felt cold and lonely about the chest. Sometimes her cat, Blue Boy, would creep in beside her and warm that aching spot. But on spring and summer nights he was likely to be abroad skylarking, and this little sweater had become the dearest of Grandmother's few possessions. It was kinder to her, she used to think, as she wrapped it about her middle, than any of her own children had been. She had married at eighteen and had had eight children; but some died, and some were, as she said, scattered.

After she was warm in that tender spot under the ribs, the old woman could lie patiently on the slats, waiting for daybreak; thinking about the comfortable rambling old house in Tennessee, its feather beds and hand-woven rag carpets and splint-bottom chairs, the mahogany sideboard, and the marble-top parlour table; all that she had left behind to follow Victoria's fortunes.

She did not regret her decision; indeed, there had been no decision. Victoria had never once thought it possible that Ma should not go wherever she and the children went, and Mrs. Harris had never thought it possible. Of course she regretted Tennessee, though she would never admit it to Mrs. Rosen:—the old neighbours, the yard and garden she had worked in all her life, the apple trees she had planted, the lilac arbour, tall enough to walk in, which she had clipped and shaped so many years. Especially she missed her lemon tree, in a tub on the front porch, which bore little lemons almost every summer, and folks would come for miles to see it.

But the road had led westward, and Mrs. Harris didn't believe that women, especially old women, could say when or where they would stop. They were tied to the chariot of young life, and had to go where it went, because they were needed. Mrs. Harris had gathered from Mrs. Rosen's manner, and from comments she occasionally dropped, that the Jewish people had an altogether different attitude toward their old folks; therefore her friendship with this kind neighbour was almost as disturbing as it was pleasant. She didn't want Mrs. Rosen to think that she was "put upon," that there was anything unusual or pitiful in her lot. To be pitied was the deepest hurt anybody could know. And if Victoria once suspected Mrs. Rosen's indignation, it would be all over. She would freeze her neighbor out, and that friendly voice, that quick pleasant chatter with the little foreign twist, would thenceforth be heard only at a distance, in the alley-way or across the fence. Victoria had a good heart, but she was terribly proud and could not bear the least criticism.

As soon as the grey light began to steal into the room, Mrs. Harris would get up softly and wash at the basin on the oilcloth-covered box. She would wet her hair above her forehead, comb it with a little bone comb set in a tin rim, do it up in two smooth little horns over her ears, wipe the comb dry, and put it away in the pocket of her full-gathered calico skirt. She left nothing lying about. As soon as she was dressed, she made her bed, folding her nightgown and nightcap under the pillow, the sweater under the mattress. She smoothed the heavy quilts, and drew the red calico spread neatly over all. Her towel was hung on its special nail behind the curtain. Her soap she kept in a tin tobacco-box; the children's soap was in a crockery saucer. If her soap or towel got mixed up with the children's, Victoria was always sharp about it. The little rented house was much too small for the family, and Mrs. Harris and her "things" were almost required to be invisible. Two clean calico dresses hung in the curtained corner; another was on her back, and a fourth was in the wash. Behind the curtain there was always a good supply of aprons; Victoria bought them at church fairs, and it was a great satisfaction to Mrs. Harris to put on a clean one whenever she liked. Upstairs, in Mandy's attic room over the kitchen, hung a black cashmere dress and a black bonnet with a long crêpe veil, for the rare occasions when Mr. Templeton hired a double buggy and horses and drove his family to a picnic or to Decoration Day[2] exercises. Mrs. Harris rather dreaded these drives, for Victoria was usually cross afterwards.

When Mrs. Harris went out into the kitchen to get breakfast, Mandy always had the fire started and the water boiling. They enjoyed a quiet half-hour before the little boys came running down the stairs, always in a good humour. In winter the boys had their breakfast in the kitchen, with Vickie. Mrs. Harris made Mandy eat the cakes and fried ham the children left, so that she would not fast so long. Mr. and Mrs. Temple-

---

2. May 30, originally a holiday kept in memory of those who died in the Civil War; now called Memorial Day.

ton breakfasted rather late, in the dining-room, and they always had fruit and thick cream,—a small pitcher of the very thickest was for Mrs. Templeton. The children were never fussy about their food. As Grandmother often said feelingly to Mrs. Rosen, they were as little trouble as children could possibly be. They sometimes tore their clothes, of course, or got sick. But even when Albert had an abscess in his ear and was in such pain, he would lie for hours on Grandmother's lounge with his cheek on a bag of hot salt, if only she or Vickie would read aloud to him.

"It's true, too, what de old lady says," remarked Mrs. Rosen to her husband one night at supper, "dey are nice children. No one ever taught them anything, but they have good instincts, even dat Vickie. And think, if you please, of all the self-sacrificing mothers we know,— Fannie and Esther, to come near home; how they have planned for those children from infancy and given them every advantage. And now ingratitude and coldness is what dey meet with."

Mr. Rosen smiled his teasing smile. "Evidently your sister and mine have the wrong method. The way to make your children unselfish is to be comfortably selfish yourself."

"But dat woman takes no more responsibility for her children than a cat takes for her kittens. Nor does poor young Mr. Templeton, for dat matter. How can he expect to get so many children started in life, I ask you? It is not at all fair!"

Mr. Rosen sometimes had to hear altogether too much about the Templetons, but he was patient, because it was a bitter sorrow to Mrs. Rosen that she had no children. There was nothing else in the world she wanted so much.

III

Mrs. Rosen in one of her blue working dresses, the indigo blue that became a dark skin and dusky red cheeks with a tone of salmon colour, was in her shining kitchen, washing her beautiful dishes—her neighbours often wondered why she used her best china and linen every day—when Vickie Templeton came in with a book under her arm.

"Good day, Mrs. Rosen. Can I have the second volume?"

"Certainly. You know where the books are." She spoke coolly, for it always annoyed her that Vickie never suggested wiping the dishes or helping with such household work as happened to be going on when she dropped in. She hated the girl's bringing-up so much that sometimes she almost hated the girl.

Vickie strolled carelessly through the dining-room into the parlour and opened the doors of one of the big bookcases. Mr. Rosen had a large library, and a great many unusual books. There was a complete set of the Waverley Novels[3] in German, for example; thick, dumpy

---

3. A series of romantic novels set in Scotland, written by Sir Walter Scott (1771–1832), Scottish poet and novelist.

little volumes bound in tooled leather, with very black type and dramatic engravings printed on wrinkled, yellowing pages. There were many French books, and some of the German classics done into English, such as Coleridge's translation of Schiller's *Wallenstein.*[4]

Of course no other house in Skyline was in the least like Mrs. Rosen's; it was the nearest thing to an art gallery and a museum that the Templetons had ever seen. All the rooms were carpeted alike (that was very unusual), with a soft velvet carpet, little blue and rose flowers scattered on a rose-grey ground. The deep chairs were upholstered in dark blue velvet. The walls were hung with engravings in pale gold frames: some of Raphael's "Hours,"[5] a large soft engraving of a castle on the Rhine, and another of cypress trees about a Roman ruin, under a full moon. There were a number of water-colour sketches, made in Italy by Mr. Rosen himself when he was a boy. A rich uncle had taken him abroad as his secretary. Mr. Rosen was a reflective, unambitious man, who didn't mind keeping a clothing-store in a little Western town, so long as he had a great deal of time to read philosophy. He was the only unsuccessful member of a large, rich Jewish family.

Last August, when the heat was terrible in Skyline, and the crops were burned up on all the farms to the north, and the wind from the pink and yellow sand-hills to the south blew so hot that it singed the few green lawns in the town, Vickie had taken to dropping in upon Mrs. Rosen at the very hottest part of the afternoon. Mrs. Rosen knew, of course, that it was probably because the girl had no other cool and quiet place to go—her room at home under the roof would be hot enough! Now, Mrs. Rosen liked to undress and take a nap from three to five,—if only to get out of her tight corsets, for she would have an hour-glass figure at any cost. She told Vickie firmly that she was welcome to come if she would read in the parlour with the blind up only a little way, and would be as still as a mouse. Vickie came, meekly enough, but she seldom read. She would take a sofa pillow and lie down on the soft carpet and look up at the pictures in the dusky room, and feel a happy, pleasant excitement from the heat and glare outside and the deep shadow and quiet within. Curiously enough, Mrs. Rosen's house never made her dissatisfied with her own; she thought that very nice, too.

Mrs. Rosen, leaving her kitchen in a state of such perfection as the Templetons were unable to sense or to admire, came into the parlour and found her visitor sitting cross-legged on the floor before one of the bookcases.

"Well, Vickie, and how did you get along with *Wilhelm Meister?*"[6]

"I like it," said Vickie.

Mrs. Rosen shrugged. The Templetons always said that; quite as if a book or a cake were lucky to win their approbation.

4. An historical dramatic poem written by Friedrich Von Schiller (1759–1805), German dramatist, poet, and historian.
5. Engravings based on the paintings of Raphael, Italian painter of the Renaissance (1483–1520).
6. *Wilhem Meisters Lehrjahre*, a biographical romance by Johann Wolfgang Goethe (1749–1832).

"Well, *what* did you like?"

"I guess I liked all that about the theatre and Shakespeare best."

"It's rather celebrated," remarked Mrs. Rosen dryly. "And are you studying every day? Do you think you will be able to win that scholarship?"

"I don't know. I'm going to try awful hard."

Mrs. Rosen wondered whether any Templeton knew how to try very hard. She reached for her work-basket and began to do cross-stitch. It made her nervous to sit with folded hands.

Vickie was looking at a German book in her lap, an illustrated edition of *Faust*.[7] She had stopped at a very German picture of Gretchen entering the church, with Faustus gazing at her from behind a rose tree, Mephisto at his shoulder.

"I wish I could read this," she said, frowning at the black Gothic[8] text. "It's splendid, isn't it?"

Mrs. Rosen rolled her eyes upward and sighed. "Oh, my dear, one of de world's masterpieces!"

That meant little to Vickie. She had not been taught to respect masterpieces, she had no scale of that sort in her mind. She cared about a book only because it took hold of her.

She kept turning over the pages. Between the first and second parts, in this edition, there was inserted the *Dies Irae*[9] hymn in full. She stopped and puzzled over it for a long while.

"Here is something I can read," she said, showing the page to Mrs. Rosen.

Mrs. Rosen looked up from her cross-stitch. "There you have the advantage of me. I do not read Latin. You might translate it for me."

Vickie began:

> "Day of wrath, upon that day
> The world to ashes melts away,
> As David and the Sibyl say.

"But that don't give you the rhyme; every line ought to end in two syllables."

"Never mind if it doesn't give the metre," corrected Mrs. Rosen kindly; "go on, if you can."

Vickie went on stumbling through the Latin verses, and Mrs. Rosen sat watching her. You couldn't tell about Vickie. She wasn't pretty, yet Mrs. Rosen found her attractive. She liked her sturdy build, and the steady vitality that glowed in her rosy skin and dark blue eyes,—even gave a springy quality to her curly reddish-brown hair, which she still wore in a single braid down her back. Mrs. Rosen liked to have Vickie about because she was never listless or dreamy or apathetic. A half-

7. A tragedy in verse written by Goethe, the first part of which was published in 1808 and the second in 1832.
8. An ornate typeface commonly used for printing

German.
9. I.e., day of wrath; a Latin hymn on the Last Judgment, used as part of the Requiem Mass in the Roman Catholic Church.

smile nearly always played about her lips and eyes, and it was there because she was pleased with something, not because she wanted to be agreeable. Even a half-smile made her cheeks dimple. She had what her mother called "a happy disposition."

When she finished the verses, Mrs. Rosen nodded approvingly. "Thank you, Vickie. The very next time I go to Chicago, I will try to get an English translation of *Faust* for you."

"But I want to read this one." Vickie's open smile darkened. "What I want is to pick up any of these books and just read them, like you and Mr. Rosen do."

The dusky red of Mrs. Rosen's cheeks grew a trifle deeper. Vickie never paid compliments, absolutely never; but if she really admired anyone, something in her voice betrayed it so convincingly that one felt flattered. When she dropped a remark of this kind, she added another link to the chain of responsibility which Mrs. Rosen unwillingly bore and tried to shake off—the irritating sense of being somehow responsible for Vickie, since, God knew, no one else felt responsible.

Once or twice, when she happened to meet pleasant young Mr. Templeton alone, she had tried to talk to him seriously about his daughter's future. "She has finished de school here, and she should be getting training of some sort; she is growing up," she told him severely.

He laughed and said in his way that was so honest, and so disarmingly sweet and frank: "Oh, don't remind me, Mrs. Rosen! I just pretend to myself she isn't. I want to keep my little daughter as long as I can." And there it ended.

Sometimes Vickie Templeton seemed so dense, so utterly unperceptive, that Mrs. Rosen was ready to wash her hands of her. Then some queer streak of sensibility in the child would make her change her mind. Last winter, when Mrs. Rosen came home from a visit to her sister in Chicago, she brought with her a new cloak of the sleeveless dolman type,[1] black velvet, lined with grey and white squirrel skins, a grey skin next a white. Vickie, so indifferent to clothes, fell in love with that cloak. Her eyes followed it with delight whenever Mrs. Rosen wore it. She found it picturesque, romantic. Mrs. Rosen had been captivated by the same thing in the cloak, and had bought it with a shrug, knowing it would be quite out of place in Skyline; and Mr. Rosen, when she first produced it from her trunk, had laughed and said: "Where did you get that?—out of *Rigoletto?*"[2] It looked like that—but how could Vickie know?

Vickie's whole family puzzled Mrs. Rosen; their feelings were so much finer than their way of living. She bought milk from the Templetons because they kept a cow—which Mandy milked,—and every night one of the twins brought the milk to her in a tin pail. Whichever

1. A woman's cloak or coat with capelike armpieces.
2. Opera by the Italian composer Giuseppi Verdi (1813–1901).

boy brought it, she always called him Albert—she thought Adelbert a silly, Southern name.

One night when she was fitting the lid on an empty pail, she said severely:

"Now, Albert, I have put some cookies for Grandma in this pail, wrapped in a napkin. And they are for Grandma, remember, not for your mother or Vickie."

"Yes'm."

When she turned to him to give him the pail, she saw two full crystal globes in the little boy's eyes, just ready to break. She watched him go softly down the path and dash those tears away with the back of his hand. She was sorry. She hadn't thought the little boys realized that their household was somehow a queer one.

Queer or not, Mrs. Rosen liked to go there better than to most houses in the town. There was something easy, cordial, and carefree in the parlour that never smelled of being shut up, and the ugly furniture looked hospitable. One felt a pleasantness in the human relationships. These people didn't seem to know there were such things as struggle or exactness or competition in the world. They were always genuinely glad to see you, had time to see you, and were usually gay in mood—all but Grandmother, who had the kind of gravity that people who take thought of human destiny must have. But even she liked light-heartedness in others; she drudged, indeed, to keep it going.

There were houses that were better kept, certainly, but the housekeepers had no charm, no gentleness of manner, were like hard little machines, most of them; and some were grasping and narrow. The Templetons were not selfish or scheming. Anyone could take advantage of them, and many people did. Victoria might eat all the cookies her neighbour sent in, but she would give away anything she had. She was always ready to lend her dresses and hats and bits of jewellery for the school theatricals, and she never worked people for favours.

As for Mr. Templeton (people usually called him "young Mr. Templeton"), he was too delicate to collect his just debts. His boyish, eager-to-please manner, his fair complexion and blue eyes and young face, made him seem very soft to some of the hard old money-grubbers on Main Street, and the fact that he always said "Yes, sir," and "No, sir," to men older than himself furnished a good deal of amusement to by-standers.

* * *

Two years ago, when this Templeton family came to Skyline and moved into the house next door, Mrs. Rosen was inconsolable. The new neighbours had a lot of children, who would always be making a racket. They put a cow and a horse into the empty barn, which would mean dirt and flies. They strewed their back yard with packing-cases[3] and did not pick them up.

---

3. Moving boxes.

She first met Mrs. Templeton at an afternoon card party, in a house at the extreme north end of the town, fully half a mile away, and she had to admit that her new neighbour was an attractive woman, and that there was something warm and genuine about her. She wasn't in the least willowy or languishing, as Mrs. Rosen had usually found Southern ladies to be. She was high-spirited and direct; a trifle imperious, but with a shade of diffidence, too, as if she were trying to adjust herself to a new group of people and to do the right thing.

While they were at the party, a blinding snowstorm came on, with a hard wind. Since they lived next door to each other, Mrs. Rosen and Mrs. Templeton struggled homeward together through the blizzard. Mrs. Templeton seemed delighted with the rough weather; she laughed like a big country girl whenever she made a mis-step off the obliterated sidewalk and sank up to her knees in a snow-drift.

"Take care, Mrs. Rosen," she kept calling, "keep to the right! Don't spoil your nice coat. My, ain't this real winter? We never had it like this back with us."

When they reached the Templetons' gate, Victoria wouldn't hear of Mrs. Rosen's going farther. "No, indeed, Mrs. Rosen, you come right in with me and get dry, and Ma'll make you a hot toddy[4] while I take the baby."

By this time Mrs. Rosen had begun to like her neighbour, so she went in. To her surprise, the parlour was neat and comfortable—the children did not strew things about there, apparently. The hard-coal burner threw out a warm red glow. A faded, respectable Brussels carpet[5] covered the floor, an old-fashioned wooden clock ticked on the walnut bookcase. There were a few easy chairs, and no hideous ornaments about. She rather liked the old oil-chromos on the wall: "Hagar and Ishmael in the Wilderness," and "The Light of the World." While Mrs. Rosen dried her feet on the nickel[6] base of the stove, Mrs. Templeton excused herself and withdrew to the next room,—her bedroom,—took off her silk dress and corsets, and put on a white challis[7] négligée. She reappeared with the baby, who was not crying, exactly, but making eager, passionate, gasping entreaties,—faster and faster, tenser and tenser, as he felt his dinner nearer and nearer and yet not his.

Mrs. Templeton sat down in a low rocker by the stove and began to nurse him, holding him snugly but carelessly, still talking to Mrs. Rosen about the card party, and laughing about their wade home through the snow. Hughie, the baby, fell to work so fiercely that beads of sweat came out all over his flushed forehead. Mrs. Rosen could not help admiring him and his mother. They were so comfortable and complete. When he was changed to the other side, Hughie resented the interruption a little; but after a time he became soft and bland, as smooth as oil, indeed; began looking about him as he drew in his milk. He finally dropped the nipple from his lips altogether, turned on his mother's arm, and looked inquiringly at Mrs. Rosen.

"What a beautiful baby!" she exclaimed from her heart. And he was. A sort of golden baby. His hair was like sunshine, and his long lashes were gold over such gay blue eyes. There seemed to be a gold glow in his soft pink skin, and he had the smile of a cherub.

"We think he's a pretty boy," said Mrs. Templeton. "He's the prettiest of my babies. Though the twins were mighty cunning little fellows. I hated the idea of twins, but the minute I saw them, I couldn't resist them."

Just then old Mrs. Harris came in, walking widely in her full-gathered skirt and felt-soled shoes, bearing a tray with two smoking goblets upon it.

"This is my mother, Mrs. Harris, Mrs. Rosen," said Mrs. Templeton.

"I'm glad to know you, ma'am," said Mrs. Harris. "Victoria, let me take the baby, while you two ladies have your toddy."

"Oh, don't take him away, Mrs. Harris, please!" cried Mrs. Rosen.

The old lady smiled. "I won't. I'll set right here. He never frets with his grandma."

When Mrs. Rosen had finished her excellent drink, she asked if she might hold the baby, and Mrs. Harris placed him on her lap. He made a few rapid boxing motions with his two fists, then braced himself on his heels and the back of his head, and lifted himself up in an arc. When he dropped back, he looked up at Mrs. Rosen with his most intimate smile. "See what a smart boy I am!"

When Mrs. Rosen walked home, feeling her way through the snow by following the fence, she knew she could never stay away from a house where there was a baby like that one.

IV

Vickie did her studying in a hammock hung between two tall cottonwood trees over in the Roadmaster's[8] green yard. The Roadmaster had the finest yard in Skyline, on the edge of the town, just where the sandy plain and the sage-brush began. His family went back to Ohio every summer, and Bert and Del Templeton were paid to take care of his lawn, to turn the sprinkler on at the right hours and to cut the grass. They were really too little to run the heavy lawn-mower very well, but they were able to manage because they were twins. Each took one end of the handle-bar, and they pushed together like a pair of fat Shetland ponies. They were very proud of being able to keep the lawn so nice, and worked hard on it. They cut Mrs. Rosen's grass once a week, too, and did it so well that she wondered why in the world they never did

---

8. An employee of a railroad who has charge of railroad maintenance in a particular district.

anything about their own yard. They didn't have city water, to be sure (it was expensive), but she thought they might pick up a few veloci-pedes and iron hoops, and dig up the messy "flower-bed," that was even uglier than the naked gravel spots. She was particularly offended by a deep ragged ditch, a miniature arroyo,[9] which ran across the back yard, serving no purpose and looking very dreary.

One morning she said craftily to the twins, when she was paying them for cutting her grass:

"And, boys, why don't you just shovel the sand-pile by your fence into dat ditch, and make your back yard smooth?"

"Oh, no, ma'am," said Adelbert with feeling. "We like to have the ditch to build bridges over!"

Ever since vacation began, the twins had been busy getting the Roadmaster's yard ready for the Methodist lawn party. When Mrs. Holliday, the Roadmaster's wife, went away for the summer, she always left a key with the Ladies' Aid Society and invited them to give their ice-cream social at her place.

This year the date set for the party was June fifteenth. The day was a particularly fine one, and as Mr. Holliday himself had been called to Cheyenne on railroad business, the twins felt personally responsible for everything. They got out to the Holliday place early in the morning, and stayed on guard all day. Before noon the drayman[1] brought a wagon-load of card-tables and folding chairs, which the boys placed in chosen spots under the cottonwood trees. In the afternoon the Method-ist ladies arrived and opened up the kitchen to receive the freezers of home-made ice-cream, and the cakes which the congregation donated. Indeed, all the good cake-bakers in town were expected to send a cake. Grandma Harris baked a white cake, thickly iced and covered with freshly grated coconut, and Vickie took it over in the afternoon.

Mr. and Mrs. Rosen, because they belonged to no church, contrib-uted to the support of all, and usually went to the church suppers in winter and the socials in summer. On this warm June evening they set out early, in order to take a walk first. They strolled along the hard gravelled road that led out through the sage toward the sand-hills; tonight it led toward the moon, just rising over the sweep of dunes. The sky was almost as blue as at midday, and had that look of being very near and very soft which it has in desert countries. The moon, too, looked very near, soft and bland and innocent. Mrs. Rosen admitted that in the Adirondacks, [2] for which she was always secretly homesick in summer, the moon had a much colder brilliance, seemed farther off and made of a harder metal. This moon gave the sage-brush plain and the drifted sand-hills the softness of velvet. All countries were beauti-ful to Mr. Rosen. He carried a country of his own in his mind, and was able to unfold it like a tent in any wilderness.

9. Spanish for a small river or stream.
1. Delivery cart driver.

2. Mountain range in northern New York.

When they at last turned back toward the town, they saw groups of people, women in white dresses, walking toward the dark spot where the paper lanterns made a yellow light underneath the cottonwoods. High above, the rustling tree-tops stirred free in the flood of moonlight.

The lighted yard was surrounded by a low board fence, painted the dark red Burlington colour, and as the Rosens drew near, they noticed four children standing close together in the shadow of some tall elder bushes just outside the fence. They were the poor Maude children; their mother was the washwoman, the Rosens' laundress and the Templetons'. People said that every one of those children had a different father. But good laundresses were few, and even the members of the Ladies' Aid were glad to get Mrs. Maude's services at a dollar a day, though they didn't like their children to play with hers. Just as the Rosens approached, Mrs. Templeton came out from the lighted square, leaned over the fence, and addressed the little Maudes.

"I expect you children forgot your dimes, now didn't you? Never mind, here's a dime for each of you, so come along and have your ice-cream."

The Maudes put out small hands and said: "Thank you," but not one of them moved.

"Come along, Francie" (the oldest girl was named Frances). "Climb right over the fence." Mrs. Templeton reached over and gave her a hand, and the little boys quickly scrambled after their sister. Mrs. Templeton took them to a table which Vickie and the twins had just selected as being especially private—they liked to do things together.

"Here, Vickie, let the Maudes sit at your table, and take care they get plenty of cake."

The Rosens had followed close behind Mrs. Templeton, and Mr. Rosen now overtook her and said in his most courteous and friendly manner: "Good evening, Mrs. Templeton. Will you have ice-cream with us?" He always used the local idioms, though his voice and enunciation made them sound altogether different from Skyline speech.

"Indeed I will, Mr. Rosen. Mr. Templeton will be late. He went out to his farm yesterday, and I don't know just when to expect him."

Vickie and the twins were disappointed at not having their table to themselves, when they had come early and found a nice one; but they knew it was right to look out for the dreary little Maudes, so they moved close together and made room for them. The Maudes didn't cramp them long. When the three boys had eaten the last crumb of cake and licked their spoons, Francie got up and led them to a green slope by the fence, just outside the lighted circle. "Now set down, and watch and see how folks do," she told them. The boys looked to Francie for commands and support. She was really Amos Maude's child, born before he ran away to the Klondike,[3] and it had been rubbed into them that this made a difference.

---

3. Gold-rush country in the Yukon Territory, Canada.

The Templeton children made their ice-cream linger out, and sat watching the crowd. They were glad to see their mother go to Mr. Rosen's table, and noticed how nicely he placed a chair for her and insisted upon putting a scarf about her shoulders. Their mother was wearing her new dotted Swiss,[4] with many ruffles, all edged with black ribbon, and wide ruffly sleeves. As the twins watched her over their spoons, they thought how much prettier their mother was than any of the other women, and how becoming her new dress was. The children got as much satisfaction as Mrs. Harris out of Victoria's good looks.

Mr. Rosen was well pleased with Mrs. Templeton and her new dress, and with her kindness to the little Maudes. He thought her manner with them just right,—warm, spontaneous, without anything patronizing. He always admired her way with her own children, though Mrs. Rosen thought it too casual. Being a good mother, he believed, was much more a matter of physical poise and richness than of sentimentalizing and reading doctor-books. Tonight he was more talkative than usual, and in his quiet way made Mrs. Templeton feel his real friendliness and admiration. Unfortunately, he made other people feel it, too.

Mrs. Jackson, a neighbour who didn't like the Templetons, had been keeping an eye on Mr. Rosen's table. She was a stout square woman of imperturbable calm, effective in regulating the affairs of the community because she never lost her temper, and could say the most cutting things in calm, even kindly, tones. Her face was smooth and placid as a mask, rather good-humoured, and the fact that one eye had a cast and looked askance made it the more difficult to see through her intentions. When she had been lingering about the Rosens' table for some time, studying Mr. Rosen's pleasant attentions to Mrs. Templeton, she brought up a trayful of cake.

"You folks are about ready for another helping," she remarked affably.

Mrs. Rosen spoke. "I want some of Grandma Harris's cake. It's a white coconut, Mrs. Jackson."

"How about you, Mrs. Templeton, would you like some of your own cake?"

"Indeed I would," said Mrs. Templeton heartily. "Ma said she had good luck with it. I didn't see it. Vickie brought it over."

Mrs. Jackson deliberately separated the slices on her tray with two forks. "Well," she remarked with a chuckle that really sounded amiable, "I don't know but I'd like my cakes, if I kept somebody in the kitchen to bake them for me."

Mr. Rosen for once spoke quickly. "If I had a cook like Grandma Harris in my kitchen, I'd live in it!" he declared.

Mrs. Jackson smiled. "I don't know as we feel like that, Mrs. Templeton? I tell Mr. Jackson that my idea of coming up in the world would

---

4. A crisp cotton fabric embellished with woven, flocked, or embroidered dots.

be to forget I had a cook-stove, like Mrs. Templeton. But we can't all be lucky."

Mr. Rosen could not tell how much was malice and how much was stupidity. What he chiefly detected was self-satisfaction; the craftiness of the coarse-fibred country girl putting catch questions to the teacher. Yes, he decided, the woman was merely showing off,—she regarded it as an accomplishment to make people uncomfortable.

Mrs. Templeton didn't at once take it in. Her training was all to the end that you must give a guest everything you have, even if he happens to be your worst enemy, and that to cause anyone embarrassment is a frightful and humiliating blunder. She felt hurt without knowing just why, but all evening it kept growing clearer to her that this was another of those thrusts from the outside which she couldn't understand. The neighbours were sure to take sides against her, apparently, if they came often to see her mother.

Mr. Rosen tried to distract Mrs. Templeton, but he could feel the poison working. On the way home the children knew something had displeased or hurt their mother. When they went into the house, she told them to go upstairs at once, as she had a headache. She was severe and distant. When Mrs. Harris suggested making her some peppermint tea, Victoria threw up her chin.

"I don't want anybody waiting on me. I just want to be let alone." And she withdrew without saying good-night, or "Are you all right, Ma?" as she usually did.

Left alone, Mrs. Harris sighed and began to turn down her bed. She knew, as well as if she had been at the social, what kind of thing had happened. Some of those prying ladies of the Woman's Relief Corps, or the Woman's Christian Temperance Union,[5] had been intimating to Victoria that her mother was "put upon." Nothing ever made Victoria cross but criticism. She was jealous of small attentions paid to Mrs. Harris, because she felt they were paid "behind her back" or "over her head," in a way that implied reproach to her. Victoria had been a belle in their own town in Tennessee, but here she was not very popular, no matter how many pretty dresses she wore, and she couldn't bear it. She felt as if her mother and Mr. Templeton must be somehow to blame; at least they ought to protect her from whatever was disagreeable— they always had!

v

Mrs. Harris wakened at about four o'clock, as usual, before the house was stirring, and lay thinking about their position in this new town. She didn't know why the neighbours acted so; she was as much in the dark

---

5. An organization of Christian women aimed at combating widespread alcoholism and abolishing the liquor traffic; founded in 1874. Women's Relief Corps: one of many women's societies devoted to social welfare.

as Victoria. At home, back in Tennessee, her place in the family was not exceptional, but perfectly regular. Mrs. Harris had replied to Mrs. Rosen, when that lady asked why in the world she didn't break Vickie in to help her in the kitchen: "We are only young once, and trouble comes soon enough." Young girls, in the South, were supposed to be carefree and foolish; the fault Grandmother found in Vickie was that she wasn't foolish enough. When the foolish girl married and began to have children, everything else must give way to that. She must be humored and given the best of everything, because having children was hard on a woman, and it was the most important thing in the world. In Tennessee every young married woman in good circumstances had an older woman in the house, a mother or mother-in-law or an old aunt, who managed the household economies and directed the help.

That was the great difference; in Tennessee there had been plenty of helpers. There was old Miss Sadie Crummer, who came to the house to spin and sew and mend; old Mrs. Smith, who always arrived to help at butchering- and preserving-time; Lizzie, the coloured girl, who did the washing and who ran in every day to help Mandy. There were plenty more, who came whenever one of Lizzie's barefoot boys ran to fetch them. The hills were full of solitary old women, or women but slightly attached to some household, who were glad to come to Miz' Harris's for good food and a warm bed, and the little present that either Mrs. Harris or Victoria slipped into their carpet-sack[6] when they went away.

To be sure, Mrs. Harris, and the other women of her age who managed their daughter's house, kept in the background; but it was their own background, and they ruled it jealously. They left the front porch and the parlour to the young married couple and their young friends; the old women spent most of their lives in the kitchen and pantries and back dining-room. But there they ordered life to their own taste, entertained their friends, dispensed charity, and heard the troubles of the poor. Moreover, back there it was Grandmother's own house they lived in. Mr. Templeton came of a superior family and had what Grandmother called "blood," but no property. He never so much as mended one of the steps to the front porch without consulting Mrs. Harris. Even "back home," in the aristocracy, there were old women who went on living like young ones,—gave parties and drove out in their carriage and "went North" in the summer. But among the middle-class people and the country-folk, when a woman was a widow and had married daughters, she considered herself an old woman and wore full-gathered black dresses and a black bonnet and became a housekeeper. She accepted this estate unprotestingly, almost gratefully.

The Templetons' troubles began when Mr. Templeton's aunt died and left him a few thousand dollars, and he got the idea of bettering

6. A traveling bag made of carpet.

himself. The twins were little then, and he told Mrs. Harris his boys would have a better chance in Colorado—everybody was going West. He went alone first, and got a good position with a mining company in the mountains of southern Colorado. He had been book-keeper in the bank in his home town, had "grown up in the bank," as they said. He was industrious and honourable, and the managers of the mining company liked him, even if they laughed at his polite, soft-spoken manners. He could have held his position indefinitely, and maybe got a promotion. But the altitude of that mountain town was too high for his family. All the children were sick there; Mrs. Templeton was ill most of the time and nearly died when Ronald was born. Hillary Templeton lost his courage and came north to the flat, sunny, semi-arid country between Wray and Cheyenne, to work for an irrigation project. So far, things had not gone well with him. The pinch told on everyone, but most on Grandmother. Here, in Skyline, she had all her accustomed responsibilities, and no helper but Mandy. Mrs. Harris was no longer living in a feudal society, where there were plenty of landless people glad to render service to the more fortunate, but in a snappy little Western democracy, where every man was as good as his neighbour and out to prove it.

Neither Mrs. Harris nor Mrs. Templeton understood just what was the matter; they were hurt and dazed, merely. Victoria knew that here she was censured and criticized, she who had always been so admired and envied! Grandmother knew that these meddlesome "Northerners" said things that made Victoria suspicious and unlike herself; made her unwilling that Mrs. Harris should receive visitors alone, or accept marks of attention that seemed offered in compassion for her state.

These women who belonged to clubs and Relief Corps lived differently, Mrs. Harris knew, but she herself didn't like the way they lived. She believed that somebody ought to be in the parlour, and somebody in the kitchen. She wouldn't for the world have had Victoria go about every morning in a short gingham dress, with bare arms, and a dust-cap on her head to hide the curling-kids,[7] as these brisk housekeepers did. To Mrs. Harris that would have meant real poverty, coming down in the world so far that one could no longer keep up appearances. Her life was hard now, to be sure, since the family went on increasing and Mr. Templeton's means went on decreasing; but she certainly valued respectability above personal comfort, and she could go on a good way yet if they always had a cool pleasant parlour, with Victoria properly dressed to receive visitors. To keep Victoria different from these "ordinary" women meant everything to Mrs. Harris. She realized that Mrs. Rosen managed to be mistress of any situation, either in kitchen or parlour, but that was because she was "foreign." Grandmother perfectly understood that their neighbour had a superior cultivation which made everything she did an exercise of skill. She knew well enough

7. Curlers.

that their own ways of cooking and cleaning were primitive beside
Mrs. Rosen's.

If only Mr. Templeton's business affairs would look up, they could
rent a larger house, and everything would be better. They might even
get a German girl to come in and help,—but now there was no place
to put her. Grandmother's own lot could improve only with the family
fortunes—any comfort for herself, aside from that of the family, was
inconceivable to her; and on the other hand she could have no real
unhappiness while the children were well, and good, and fond of her
and their mother. That was why it was worth while to get up early in
the morning and make her bed neat and draw the red spread smooth.
The little boys loved to lie on her lounge and her pillows when they
were tired. When they were sick, Ronald and Hughie wanted to be in
her lap. They had no physical shrinking from her because she was old.
And Victoria was never jealous of the children's wanting to be with her
so much; that was a mercy!

Sometimes, in the morning, if her feet ached more than usual, Mrs.
Harris felt a little low. (Nobody did anything about broken arches in
those days, and the common endurance test of old age was to keep
going after every step cost something.) She would hang up her towel
with a sigh and go into the kitchen, feeling that it was hard to make a
start. But the moment she heard the children running down the uncar-
peted back stairs, she forgot to be low. Indeed, she ceased to be an
individual, an old woman with aching feet; she became part of a group,
became a relationship. She was drunk up into their freshness when
they burst in upon her, telling her about their dreams, explaining their
troubles with buttons and shoe-laces and underwear shrunk too small.
The tired, solitary old woman Grandmother had been at daybreak
vanished; suddenly the morning seemed as important to her as it did
to the children, and the mornings ahead stretched out sunshiny, important.

VI

The day after the Methodist social, Blue Boy didn't come for his
morning milk; he always had it in a clean saucer on the covered back
porch, under the long bench where the tin wash-tubs stood ready for
Mrs. Maude. After the children had finished breakfast, Mrs. Harris
sent Mandy out to look for the cat.

The girl came back in a minute, her eyes big.

"Law me, Miz' Harris, he's awful sick. He's a-layin' in the straw in
the barn. He's swallered a bone, or havin' a fit or somethin'."

Grandmother threw an apron over her head and went out to see for
herself. The children went with her. Blue Boy was retching and choking, and his yellow eyes were filled up with rhume.[8]

8. I.e. rheum; runny eyes.

"Oh, Gram'ma, what's the matter?" the boys cried.

"It's the distemper. How could he have got it?" Her voice was so harsh that Ronald began to cry. "Take Ronald back to the house, Del. He might get bit. I wish I'd kept my word and never had a cat again!"

"Why, Gram'ma!" Albert looked at her. "Won't Blue Boy get well?"

"Not from the distemper, he won't."

"But Gram'ma, can't I run for the veter'nary?"

"You gether up an armful of hay. We'll take him into the coal-house, where I can watch him."

Mrs. Harris waited until the spasm was over, then picked up the limp cat and carried him to the coal-shed that opened off the back porch. Albert piled the hay in one corner—the coal was low, since it was summer—and they spread a piece of old carpet on the hay and made a bed for Blue Boy. "Now you run along with Adelbert. There'll be a lot of work to do on Mr. Holliday's yard, cleaning up after the sociable. Mandy an' me'll watch Blue Boy. I expect he'll sleep for a while."

Albert went away regretfully, but the drayman and some of the Methodist ladies were in Mr. Holliday's yard, packing chairs and tables and ice-cream freezers into the wagon, and the twins forgot the sick cat in their excitement. By noon they had picked up the last paper napkin, raked over the gravel walks where the salt from the freezers had left white patches, and hung the hammock in which Vickie did her studying back in its place. Mr. Holliday paid the boys a dollar a week for keeping up the yard, and they gave the money to their mother—it didn't come amiss in a family where actual cash was so short. She let them keep half the sum Mrs. Rosen paid for her milk every Saturday, and that was more spending money than most boys had. They often made a few extra quarters by cutting grass for other people, or by distributing handbills. Even the disagreeable Mrs. Jackson next door had remarked over the fence to Mrs. Harris: "I do believe Bert and Del are going to be industrious. They must have got it from you, Grandma."

The day came on very hot, and when the twins got back from the Roadmaster's yard, they both lay down on Grandmother's lounge and went to sleep. After dinner they had a rare opportunity; the Roadmaster himself appeared at the front door and invited them to go up to the next town with him on his railroad velocipede. That was great fun: the velocipede always whizzed along so fast on the bright rails, the gasoline engine puffing; and grasshoppers jumped up out of the sage-brush and hit you in the face like sling-shot bullets. Sometimes the wheels cut in two a lazy snake who was sunning himself on the track, and the twins always hoped it was a rattler and felt they had done a good work.

The boys got back from their trip with Mr. Holliday late in the afternoon. The house was cool and quiet. Their mother had taken Ronald and Hughie down town with her, and Vickie was off somewhere. Grandmother was not in her room, and the kitchen was empty.

The boys went out to the back porch to pump a drink. The coal-shed door was open, and inside, on a low stool, sat Mrs. Harris beside her cat. Bert and Del didn't stop to get a drink; they felt ashamed that they had gone off for a gay ride and forgotten Blue Boy. They sat down on a big lump of coal beside Mrs. Harris. They would never have known that this miserable rumpled animal was their proud tom. Presently he went off into a spasm and began to froth at the mouth.

"Oh, Gram'ma, can't you do anything?" cried Albert, struggling with his tears. "Blue Boy was such a good cat,—why has he got to suffer?"

"Everything that's alive has got to suffer," said Mrs. Harris. Albert put out his hand and caught her skirt, looking up at her beseechingly, as if to make her unsay that saying, which he only half understood. She patted his hand. She had forgot she was speaking to a little boy.

"Where's Vickie?" Adelbert asked aggrievedly. "Why don't she do something? He's part her cat."

Mrs. Harris sighed. "Vickie's got her head full of things lately; that makes people kind of heartless."

The boys resolved they would never put anything into their heads, then!

Blue Boy's fit passed, and the three sat watching their pet that no longer knew them. The twins had not seen much suffering; Grandmother had seen a great deal. Back in Tennessee, in her own neighbourhood, she was accounted a famous nurse. When any of the poor mountain people were in great distress, they always sent for Miz' Harris. Many a time she had gone into a house where five or six children were all down with scarlet fever or diphtheria, and done what she could. Many a child and many a woman she had laid out and got ready for the grave. In her primitive community the undertaker made the coffin,—he did nothing more. She had seen so much misery that she wondered herself why it hurt so to see her tom-cat die. She had taken her leave of him, and she got up from her stool. She didn't want the boys to be too much distressed.

"Now you boys must wash and put on clean shirts. Your mother will be home pretty soon. We'll leave Blue Boy; he'll likely be easier in the morning." She knew the cat would die at sundown.

After supper, when Bert looked into the coal-shed and found the cat dead, all the family were sad. Ronald cried miserably, and Hughie cried because Ronald did. Mrs. Templeton herself went out and looked into the shed, and she was sorry, too. Though she didn't like cats, she had been fond of this one.

"Hillary," she told her husband, "when you go down town tonight, tell the Mexican to come and get that cat early in the morning, before the children are up."

The Mexican had a cart and two mules, and he hauled away tin cans and refuse to a gully out in the sage-brush.

Mrs. Harris gave Victoria an indignant glance when she heard this, and turned back to the kitchen. All evening she was gloomy and silent. She refused to read aloud, and the twins took Ronald and went mournfully out to play under the electric light. Later, when they had said good-night to their parents in the parlour and were on their way upstairs, Mrs. Harris followed them into the kitchen, shut the door behind her, and said indignantly:

"Air you two boys going to let that Mexican take Blue Boy and throw him onto some trash-pile?"

The sleepy boys were frightened at the anger and bitterness in her tone. They stood still and looked up at her, while she went on:

"You git up early in the morning, and I'll put him in a sack, and one of you take a spade and go to that crooked old willer tree that grows just where the sand creek turns off the road, and you dig a little grave for Blue Boy, an' bury him right."

They had seldom seen such resentment in their grandmother. Albert's throat choked up, he rubbed the tears away with his fist.

"Yes'm, Gram'ma, we will, we will," he gulped.

VII

Only Mrs. Harris saw the boys go out next morning. She slipped a bread-and-butter sandwich into the hand of each, but she said nothing, and they said nothing.

The boys did not get home until their parents were ready to leave the table. Mrs. Templeton made no fuss, but told them to sit down and eat their breakfast. When they had finished, she said commandingly:

"Now you march into my room." That was where she heard explanations and administered punishment. When she whipped them, she did it thoroughly.

She followed them and shut the door.

"Now, what were you boys doing this morning?"

"We went off to bury Blue Boy."

"Why didn't you tell me you were going?"

They looked down at their toes, but said nothing. Their mother studied their mournful faces, and her overbearing expression softened.

"The next time you get up and go off anywhere, you come and tell me beforehand, do you understand?"

"Yes'm."

She opened the door, motioned them out, and went with them into the parlour. "I'm sorry about your cat, boys," she said. "That's why I don't like to have cats around; they're always getting sick and dying. Now run along and play. Maybe you'd like to have a circus in the back yard this afternoon? And we'll all come."

The twins ran out in a joyful frame of mind. Their grandmother had been mistaken; their mother wasn't indifferent about Blue Boy, she was sorry. Now everything was all right, and they could make a circus ring.

They knew their grandmother got put out about strange things, anyhow. A few months ago it was because their mother hadn't asked one of the visiting preachers who came to the church conference to stay with them. There was no place for the preacher to sleep except on the folding lounge in the parlour, and no place for him to wash—he would have been very uncomfortable, and so would all the household. But Mrs. Harris was terribly upset that there should be a conference in the town, and they not keeping a preacher! She was quite bitter about it.

The twins called in the neighbour boys, and they made a ring in the back yard, around their turning-bar. Their mother came to the show and paid admission, bringing Mrs. Rosen and Grandma Harris. Mrs. Rosen thought if all the children in the neighbourhood were to be howling and running in a circle in the Templetons' back yard, she might as well be there, too, for she would have no peace at home.

After the dog races and the Indian fight were over, Mrs. Templeton took Mrs. Rosen into the house to revive her with cake and lemonade. The parlour was cool and dusky. Mrs. Rosen was glad to get into it after sitting on a wooden bench in the sun. Grandmother stayed in the parlour with them, which was unusual. Mrs. Rosen sat waving a palm-leaf fan,—she felt the heat very much, because she wore her stays so tight—while Victoria went to make the lemonade.

"De circuses are not so good, widout Vickie to manage them, Grandma," she said.

"No'm. The boys complain right smart about losing Vickie from their plays. She's at her books all the time now. I don't know what's got into the child."

"If she wants to go to college, she must prepare herself, Grandma. I am agreeably surprised in her. I didn't think she'd stick to it."

Mrs. Templeton came in with a tray of tumblers and the glass pitcher all frosted over. Mrs. Rosen wistfully admired her neighbour's tall figure and good carriage; she was wearing no corsets at all today under her flowered organdie[9] afternoon dress, Mrs. Rosen had noticed, and yet she could carry herself so smooth and straight,—after having had so many children, too! Mrs. Rosen was envious, but she gave credit where credit was due.

When Mrs. Templeton brought in the cake, Mrs. Rosen was still talking to Grandmother about Vickie's studying. Mrs. Templeton shrugged carelessly.

"There's such a thing as overdoing it, Mrs. Rosen," she observed as she poured the lemonade. "Vickie's very apt to run to extremes."

"But, my dear lady, she can hardly be too extreme in dis matter. If she is to take a competitive examination with girls from much better schools than ours, she will have to do better than the others, or fail; no two ways about it. We must encourage her."

Mrs. Templeton bridled a little. "I'm sure I don't interfere with her studying, Mrs. Rosen. I don't see where she got this notion, but I let her alone."

9. A delicate fabric of cotton or silk.

Mrs. Rosen accepted a second piece of chocolate cake. "And what do you think about it, Grandma?"

Mrs. Harris smiled politely. "None of our people, or Mr. Templeton's either, ever went to college. I expect it is all on account of the young gentleman who was here last summer."

Mrs. Rosen laughed and lifted her eyebrows. "Something very personal in Vickie's admiration for Professor Chalmers we think, Grandma? A very sudden interest in de sciences, I should say!"

Mrs. Templeton shrugged. "You're mistaken, Mrs. Rosen. There ain't a particle of romance in Vickie."

"But there are several kinds of romance, Mrs. Templeton. She may not have your kind."

"Yes'm, that's so," said Mrs. Harris in a low, grateful voice. She thought that a hard word Victoria had said of Vickie.

"I didn't see a thing in that Professor Chalmers, myself," Victoria remarked. "He was a gawky kind of fellow, and never had a thing to say in company. Did you think he amounted to much?"

"Oh, widout doubt Doctor Chalmers is a very scholarly man. A great many brilliant scholars are widout de social graces, you know." When Mrs. Rosen, from a much wider experience, corrected her neighbour, she did so somewhat playfully, as if insisting upon something Victoria capriciously chose to ignore.

At this point old Mrs. Harris put her hands on the arms of the chair in preparation to rise. "If you ladies will excuse me, I think I will go and lie down a little before supper." She rose and went heavily out on her felt soles. She never really lay down in the afternoon, but she dozed in her own black rocker. Mrs. Rosen and Victoria sat chatting about Professor Chalmers and his boys.

Last summer the young professor had come to Skyline with four of his students from the University of Michigan, and had stayed three months, digging for fossils out in the sand-hills. Vickie had spent a great many mornings at their camp. They lived at the town hotel, and drove out to their camp every day in a light spring-wagon. Vickie used to wait for them at the edge of the town, in front of the Roadmaster's house, and when the spring-wagon came rattling along, the boys would call: "There's our girl!" slow the horses, and give her a hand up. They said she was their mascot, and were very jolly with her. They had a splendid summer,—found a great bed of fossil elephant bones, where a whole herd must once have perished. Later on they came upon the bones of a new kind of elephant, scarcely larger than a pig. They were greatly excited about their finds, and so was Vickie. That was why they liked her. It was they who told her about a memorial scholarship at Ann Arbor, which was open to any girl from Colorado.

In August Vickie went down to Denver to take her examinations. Mr. Holliday, the Roadmaster, got her a pass, and arranged that she should stay with the family of one of his passenger conductors.

For three days she wrote examination papers along with other contestants, in one of the Denver high schools, proctored by a teacher. Her father had given her five dollars for incidental expenses, and she came home with a box of mineral specimens for the twins, a singing top for Ronald, and a toy burro for Hughie.

Then began days of suspense that stretched into weeks. Vickie went to the post-office every morning, opened her father's combination box, and looked over the letters, long before he got down town,—always hoping there might be a letter from Ann Arbor. The night mail came in at six, and after supper she hurried to the post-office and waited about until the shutter at the general-delivery window was drawn back, a signal that the mail had all been "distributed." While the tedious process of distribution was going on, she usually withdrew from the office, full of joking men and cigar smoke, and walked up and down under the big cottonwood trees that overhung the side street. When the crowd of men began to come out, then she knew the mail-bags were empty, and she went in to get whatever letters were in the Templeton box and take them home.

After two weeks went by, she grew down-hearted. Her young professor, she knew, was in England for his vacation. There would be no one at the University of Michigan who was interested in her fate. Perhaps the fortunate contestant had already been notified of her success. She never asked herself, as she walked up and down under the cottonwoods on those summer nights, what she would do if she didn't get the scholarship. There was no alternative. If she didn't get it, then everything was over.

During the weeks when she lived only to go to the post-office, she managed to cut her finger and get ink into the cut. As a result, she had a badly infected hand and had to carry it in a sling. When she walked her nightly beat under the cottonwoods, it was a kind of comfort to feel that finger throb; it was companionship, made her case more complete.

The strange thing was that one morning a letter came, addressed to Miss Victoria Templeton; in a long envelope such as her father called "legal size," with *"University of Michigan"* in the upper left-hand corner. When Vickie took it from the box, such a wave of fright and weakness went through her that she could scarcely get out of the post-office. She hid the letter under her striped blazer and went a weak, uncertain trail down the sidewalk under the big trees. Without seeing anything or knowing what road she took, she got to the Road-master's green yard and her hammock, where she always felt not on the earth, yet of it.

Three hours later, when Mrs. Rosen was just tasting one of those clear soups upon which the Templetons thought she wasted so much pains and good meat, Vickie walked in at the kitchen door and said in a low but somewhat unnatural voice:

"Mrs. Rosen, I got the scholarship."

Mrs. Rosen looked up at her sharply, then pushed the soup back to a cooler part of the stove.

"What is dis you say, Vickie? You have heard from de University?"

"Yes'm. I got the letter this morning." She produced it from under her blazer.

Mrs. Rosen had been cutting noodles. She took Vickie's face in two hot, plump hands that were still floury, and looked at her intently. "Is dat true, Vickie? No mistake? I am delighted—and surprised! Yes, surprised. Den you will *be* something, you won't just sit on de front porch." She squeezed the girl's round, good-natured cheeks, as if she could mould them into something definite then and there. "Now you must stay for lunch and tell us all about it. Go in and announce yourself to Mr. Rosen."

Mr. Rosen had come home for lunch and was sitting, a book in his hand, in a corner of the darkened front parlour where a flood of yellow sun streamed in under the dark green blind. He smiled his friendly smile at Vickie and waved her to a seat, making her understand that he wanted to finish his paragraph. The dark engraving of the pointed cypresses and the Roman tomb was on the wall just behind him.

Mrs. Rosen came into the back parlour, which was the dining-room, and began taking things out of the silver-drawer to lay a place for their visitor. She spoke to her husband rapidly in German.

He put down his book, came over, and took Vickie's hand.

"Is it true, Vickie? Did you really win the scholarship?"

"Yes, sir."

He stood looking down at her through his kind, remote smile,—a smile in the eyes, that seemed to come up through layers and layers of something—gentle doubts, kindly reservations.

"Why do you want to go to college, Vickie?" he asked playfully.

"To learn," she said with surprise.

"But why do you want to learn? What do you want to do with it?"

"I don't know. Nothing, I guess."

"Then what do you want it for?"

"I don't know. I just want it."

For some reason Vickie's voice broke there. She had been terribly strung up all morning, lying in the hammock with her eyes tight shut. She had not been home at all, she had wanted to take her letter to the Rosens first. And now one of the gentlest men she knew made her choke by something strange and presageful in his voice.

"Then if you want it without any purpose at all, you will not be disappointed." Mr. Rosen wished to distract her and help her to keep back the tears. "Listen: a great man once said: '*Le but n'est rien; le chemin, c'est tout.*' That means: The end is nothing, the road is all. Let me write it down for you and give you your first French lesson."

He went to the desk with its big silver ink-well, where he and his wife wrote so many letters in several languages, and inscribed the sentence on a sheet of purple paper, in his delicately shaded foreign script, signing under it a name: *J. Michelet.*[1] He brought it back and

---

1. Jules Michelet (1798–1874), French historian.

shook it before Vickie's eyes. "There, keep it to remember me by. Slip it into the envelope with your college credentials,—that is a good place for it." From his deliberate smile and the twitch of one eyebrow, Vickie knew he meant her to take it along as an antidote, a corrective for whatever colleges might do to her. But she had always known that Mr. Rosen was wiser than professors.

Mrs. Rosen was frowning, she thought that sentence a bad precept to give any Templeton. Moreover, she always promptly called her husband back to earth when he soared a little; though it was exactly for this transcendental quality of mind that she reverenced him in her heart, and thought him so much finer than any of his successful brothers.

"Luncheon is served," she said in the crisp tone that put people in their places. "And Miss Vickie, you are to eat your tomatoes with an oil dressing, as we do. If you are going off into the world, it is quite time you learn to like things that are everywhere accepted."

Vickie said: "Yes'm," and slipped into the chair Mr. Rosen had placed for her. Today she didn't care what she ate, though ordinarily she thought a French dressing tasted a good deal like castor oil.

IX

Vickie was to discover that nothing comes easily in this world. Next day she got a letter from one of the jolly students of Professor Chalmers's party, who was watching over her case in his chief's absence. He told her the scholarship meant admission to the freshman class without further examinations, and two hundred dollars toward her expenses; she would have to bring along about three hundred more to put her through the year.

She took this letter to her father's office. Seated in his revolving desk-chair, Mr. Templeton read it over several times and looked embarrassed.

"I'm sorry, daughter," he said at last, "but really, just now, I couldn't spare that much. Not this year. I expect next year will be better for us."

"But the scholarship is for this year, Father. It wouldn't count next year. I just have to go in September."

"I really ain't got it, daughter." He spoke, oh so kindly! He had lovely manners with his daughter and his wife. "It's just all I can do to keep the store bills paid up. I'm away behind with Mr. Rosen's bill. Couldn't you study here this winter and get along about as fast? It isn't that I wouldn't like to let you have the money if I had it. And with young children, I can't let my life insurance go."

Vickie didn't say anything more. She took her letter and wandered down Main Street with it, leaving young Mr. Templeton to a very bad half-hour.

At dinner Vickie was silent, but everyone could see she had been crying. Mr. Templeton told *Uncle Remus* stories[2] to keep up the family morale and make the giggly twins laugh. Mrs. Templeton glanced covertly at her daughter from time to time. She was sometimes a little afraid of Vickie, who seemed to her to have a hard streak. If it were a love-affair that the girl was crying about, that would be so much more natural—and more hopeful!

At two o'clock Mrs. Templeton went to the Afternoon Euchre[3] Club, the twins were to have another ride with the Roadmaster on his velocipede, the little boys took their nap on their mother's bed. The house was empty and quiet. Vickie felt an aversion for the hammock under the cottonwoods where she had been betrayed into such bright hopes. She lay down on her grandmother's lounge in the cluttered play-room and turned her face to the wall.

When Mrs. Harris came in for her rest and began to wash her face at the tin basin, Vickie got up. She wanted to be alone. Mrs. Harris came over to her while she was still sitting on the edge of the lounge.

"What's the matter, Vickie child?" She put her hand on her granddaughter's shoulder, but Vickie shrank away. Young misery is like that, sometimes.

"Nothing. Except that I can't go to college after all. Papa can't let me have the money."

Mrs. Harris settled herself on the faded cushions of her rocker. "How much is it? Tell me about it, Vickie. Nobody's around."

Vickie told her what the conditions were, briefly and dryly, as if she were talking to an enemy. Everyone was an enemy; all society was against her. She told her grandmother the facts and then went upstairs, refusing to be comforted.

Mrs. Harris saw her disappear through the kitchen door, and then sat looking at the door, her face grave, her eyes stern and sad. A poor factory-made piece of joiner's[4] work seldom has to bear a look of such intense, accusing sorrow; as if that flimsy pretence of "grained" yellow pine were the door shut against all young aspiration.

X

Mrs. Harris had decided to speak to Mr. Templeton, but opportunities for seeing him alone were not frequent. She watched out of the kitchen window, and when she next saw him go into the barn to fork down hay for his horse, she threw an apron over her head and followed him. She waylaid him as he came down from the hayloft.

"Hillary, I want to see you about Vickie. I was wondering if you could lay hand on any of the money you got for the sale of my house back home."

2. Negro folktales written down by Joel Chandler Harris (1848–1908) and first published in book form in 1880; Uncle Remus is the narrator of the stories.

3. A card game.
4. A carpenter or cabinetmaker.

Mr. Templeton was nervous. He began brushing his trousers with a little whisk-broom he kept there, hanging on a nail.

"Why, no'm, Mrs. Harris. I couldn't just conveniently call in any of it right now. You know we had to use part of it to get moved up here from the mines."

"I know. But I thought if there was any left you could get at, we could let Vickie have it. A body'd like to help the child."

"I'd like to, powerful well, Mrs. Harris. I would, indeed. But I'm afraid I can't manage it right now. The fellers I've loaned to can't pay up this year. Maybe next year—" He was like a little boy trying to escape a scolding, though he had never had a nagging word from Mrs. Harris.

She looked downcast, but said nothing.

"It's all right, Mrs. Harris," he took on his brisk business tone and hung up the brush. "The money's perfectly safe. It's well invested."

Invested; that was a word men always held over women, Mrs. Harris thought, and it always meant they could have none of their own money. She sighed deeply.

"Well, if that's the way it is—" She turned away and went back to the house on her flat heelless slippers, just in time; Victoria was at that moment coming out to the kitchen with Hughie.

"Ma," she said, "can the little boy play out here, while I go down town?"

XI

For the next few days Mrs. Harris was very sombre, and she was not well. Several times in the kitchen she was seized with what she called giddy spells, and Mandy had to help her to a chair and give her a little brandy.

"Don't you say nothin', Mandy," she warned the girl. But Mandy knew enough for that.

Mrs. Harris scarcely noticed how her strength was failing, because she had so much on her mind. She was very proud, and she wanted to do something that was hard for her to do. The difficulty was to catch Mrs. Rosen alone.

On the afternoon when Victoria went to her weekly euchre, the old lady beckoned Mandy and told her to run across the alley and fetch Mrs. Rosen for a minute.

Mrs. Rosen was packing her trunk, but she came at once. Grandmother awaited her in her chair in the play-room.

"I take it very kindly of you to come, Mrs. Rosen. I'm afraid it's warm in here. Won't you have a fan?" She extended the palm leaf she was holding.

"Keep it yourself, Grandma. You are not looking very well. Do you feel badly, Grandma Harris?" She took the old lady's hand and looked at her anxiously.

"Oh, no, ma'am! I'm as well as usual. The heat wears on me a little, maybe. Have you seen Vickie lately, Mrs. Rosen?"

"Vickie? No. She hasn't run in for several days. These young people are full of their own affairs, you know."

"I expect she's backward about seeing you, now that she's so discouraged."

"Discouraged? Why, didn't the child get her scholarship after all?"

"Yes'm, she did. But they write her she has to bring more money to help her out; three hundred dollars. Mr. Templeton can't raise it just now. We had so much sickness in that mountain town before we moved up here, he got behind. Pore Vickie's downhearted."

"Oh, that is too bad! I expect you've been fretting over it, and that is why you don't look like yourself. Now what can we do about it?"

Mrs. Harris sighed and shook her head. "Vickie's trying to muster courage to go around to her father's friends and borrow from one and another. But we ain't been here long,—it ain't like we had old friends here. I hate to have the child do it."

Mrs. Rosen looked perplexed. "I'm sure Mr. Rosen would help her. He takes a great interest in Vickie."

"I thought maybe he could see his way to. That's why I sent Mandy to fetch you."

"That was right, Grandma. Now let me think." Mrs. Rosen put up her plump red-brown hand and leaned her chin upon it. "Day after tomorrow I am going to run on to Chicago for my niece's wedding." She saw her old friend's face fall. "Oh, I shan't be gone long; ten days, perhaps. I will speak to Mr. Rosen tonight, and if Vickie goes to him after I am off his hands, I'm sure he will help her."

Mrs. Harris looked up at her with solemn gratitude. "Vickie ain't the kind of girl would forget anything like that, Mrs. Rosen. Nor I wouldn't forget it."

Mrs. Rosen patted her arm. "Grandma Harris," she exclaimed, "I will just ask Mr. Rosen to do it for you! You know I care more about the old folks than the young. If I take this worry off your mind, I shall go away to the wedding with a light heart. Now dismiss it. I am sure Mr. Rosen can arrange this himself for you, and Vickie won't have to go about to these people here, and our gossipy neighbours will never be the wiser." Mrs. Rosen poured this out in her quick, authoritative tone, converting her *th's* into *d's*, as she did when she was excited.

Mrs. Harris's red-brown eyes slowly filled with tears,—Mrs. Rosen had never seen that happen before. But she simply said, with quiet dignity: "Thank you, ma'am. I wouldn't have turned to nobody else."

"That means I am an old friend already, doesn't it, Grandma? And that's what I want to be. I am very jealous where Grandma Harris is concerned!" She lightly kissed the back of the purple-veined hand she had been holding, and ran home to her packing. Grandma sat looking down at her hand. How easy it was for these foreigners to say what they felt!

XII

Mrs. Harris knew she was failing. She was glad to be able to conceal it from Mrs. Rosen when that kind neighbour dashed in to kiss her good-bye on the morning of her departure for Chicago. Mrs. Templeton was, of course, present, and secrets could not be discussed. Mrs. Rosen, in her stiff little brown travelling-hat, her hands tightly gloved in brown kid, could only wink and nod to Grandmother to tell her all was well. Then she went out and climbed into the "hack"[5] bound for the depot, which had stopped for a moment at the Templetons' gate.

Mrs. Harris was thankful that her excitable friend hadn't noticed anything unusual about her looks, and, above all, that she had made no comment. She got through the day, and that evening, thank goodness, Mr. Templeton took his wife to hear a company of strolling players sing *The Chimes of Normandy* at the Opera House. He loved music, and just now he was very eager to distract and amuse Victoria. Grandma sent the twins out to play and went to bed early.

Next morning, when she joined Mandy in the kitchen, Mandy noticed something wrong.

"You set right down, Miz' Harris, an' let me git you some whisky. Deed, ma'am, you look awful porely. You ought to tell Miss Victoria an' let her send for the doctor."

"No, Mandy, I don't want no doctor. I've seen more sickness than ever he has. Doctors can't do no more than linger you out, an' I've always prayed I wouldn't last to be a burden. You git me some whisky in hot water, and pour it on a piece of toast. I feel real empty."

That afternoon when Mrs. Harris was taking her rest, for once she lay down upon her lounge. Vickie came in, tense and excited, and stopped for a moment.

"It's all right, Grandma. Mr. Rosen is going to lend me the money. I won't have to go to anybody else. He won't ask Father to endorse my note, either. He'll just take my name." Vickie rather shouted this news at Mrs. Harris, as if the old lady were deaf, or slow of understanding. She didn't thank her; she didn't know her grandmother was in any way responsible for Mr. Rosen's offer, though at the close of their interview he had said: "We won't speak of our arrangement to anyone but your father. And I want you to mention it to the old lady Harris. I know she has been worrying about you."

Having brusquely announced her news, Vickie hurried away. There was so much to do about getting ready, she didn't know where to begin. She had no trunk and no clothes. Her winter coat, bought two years ago, was so outgrown that she couldn't get into it. All her shoes were run over at the heel and must go to the cobbler. And she had only two weeks in which to do everything! She dashed off.

Mrs. Harris sighed and closed her eyes happily. She thought with

---

5. A carriage or hackney for hire.

modest pride that with people like the Rosens she had always "got along nicely." It was only with the ill-bred and unclassified, like this Mrs. Jackson next door, that she had disagreeable experiences. Such folks, she told herself, had come out of nothing and knew no better. She was afraid this inquisitive woman might find her ailing and come prying round with unwelcome suggestions.

Mrs. Jackson did, indeed, call that very afternoon, with a miserable contribution of veal-loaf as an excuse (all the Templetons hated veal), but Mandy had been forewarned, and she was resourceful. She met Mrs. Jackson at the kitchen door and blocked the way.

"Sh-h-h, ma'am, Miz' Harris is asleep, havin' her nap. No'm, she ain't porely, she's as usual. But Hughie had the colic last night when Miss Victoria was at the show, an' kep' Miz' Harris awake."

Mrs. Jackson was loath to turn back. She had really come to find out why Mrs. Rosen drove away in the depot hack yesterday morning. Except at church socials, Mrs. Jackson did not meet people in Mrs. Rosen's set.

The next day, when Mrs. Harris got up and sat on the edge of her bed, her head began to swim, and she lay down again. Mandy peeped into the play-room as soon as she came downstairs, and found the old lady still in bed. She leaned over her and whispered:

"Ain't you feeling' well, Miz' Harris?"

"No, Mandy, I'm right porely," Mrs. Harris admitted.

"You stay where you air, ma'am. I'll git the breakfast fur the chillun, an' take the other breakfast in fur Miss Victoria an' Mr. Templeton." She hurried back to the kitchen, and Mrs. Harris went to sleep.

Immediately after breakfast Vickie dashed off about her own concerns, and the twins went to cut grass while the dew was still on it. When Mandy was taking the other breakfast into the dining-room, Mrs. Templeton came through the play-room.

"What's the matter, Ma? Are you sick?" she asked in an accusing tone.

"No, Victoria, I ain't sick. I had a little giddy spell, and I thought I'd lay still."

"You ought to be more careful what you eat, Ma. If you're going to have another bilious spell, when everything is so upset anyhow, I don't know what I'll do!" Victoria's voice broke. She hurried back into her bedroom, feeling bitterly that there was no place in that house to cry in, no spot where one could be alone, even with misery; that the house and the people in it were choking her to death.

Mrs. Harris sighed and closed her eyes. Things did seem to be upset, though she didn't know just why. Mandy, however, had her suspicions. While she waited on Mr. and Mrs. Templeton at breakfast, narrowly observing their manner toward each other and Victoria's swollen eyes and desperate expression, her suspicions grew stronger.

Instead of going to his office, Mr. Templeton went to the barn and ran out the buggy. Soon he brought out Cleveland, the black horse, with his harness on. Mandy watched from the back window. After he had hitched the horse to the buggy, he came into the kitchen to wash his hands. While he dried them on the roller towel, he said in his most business-like tone:

"I likely won't be back tonight, Mandy. I have to go out to my farm, and I'll hardly get through my business there in time to come home."

Then Mandy was sure. She had been through these times before, and at such a crisis poor Mr. Templeton was always called away on important business. When he had driven out through the alley and up the street past Mrs. Rosen's, Mandy left her dishes and went in to Mrs. Harris. She bent over and whispered low:

"Miz' Harris, I 'spect Miss Victoria's done found out she's goin' to have another baby! It looks that way. She's gone back to bed."

Mrs. Harris lifted a warning finger. "Sh-h-h!"

"Oh yes'm, I won't say nothin'. I never do."

Mrs. Harris tried to face this possibility, but her mind didn't seem strong enough—she dropped off into another doze.

All that morning Mrs. Templeton lay on her bed alone, the room darkened and a handkerchief soaked in camphor[6] tied round her forehead. The twins had taken Ronald off to watch them cut grass, and Hughie played in the kitchen under Mandy's eye.

Now and then Victoria sat upright on the edge of the bed, beat her hands together softly and looked desperately at the ceiling, then about at those frail, confining walls. If only she could meet the situation with violence, fight it, conquer it! But there was nothing for it but stupid animal patience. She would have to go through all that again, and nobody, not even Hillary, wanted another baby,—poor as they were, and in this overcrowded house. Anyhow, she told herself, she was ashamed to have another baby, when she had a daughter old enough to go to college! She was sick of it all; sick of dragging this chain of life that never let her rest and periodically knotted and overpowered her; made her ill and hideous for months, and then dropped another baby into her arms. She had had babies enough; and there ought to be an end to such apprehensions some time before you were old and ugly.

She wanted to run away, back to Tennessee, and lead a free, gay life, as she had when she was first married. She could do a great deal more with freedom than ever Vickie could. She was still young, and she was still handsome; why must she be for ever shut up in a little cluttered house with children and fresh babies and an old woman and a stupid bound girl and a husband who wasn't very successful? Life hadn't brought her what she expected when she married Hillary Templeton; life hadn't used her right. She had tried to keep up appearances, to dress well with very little to do it on, to keep young for her husband and children. She had tried, she had tried! Mrs. Templeton buried her face in the pillow and smothered the sobs that shook the bed.

---

6. A medicinal stimulant made from camphor-tree wood.

○ ○ ○

Hillary Templeton, on his drive out through the sage-brush, up into the farming country that was irrigated from the North Platte, did not feel altogether cheerful, though he whistled and sang to himself on the way. He was sorry Victoria would have to go through another time. It was awkward just now, too, when he was so short of money. But he was naturally a cheerful man, modest in his demands upon fortune, and easily diverted from unpleasant thoughts. Before Cleveland had travelled half the eighteen miles to the farm, his master was already looking forward to a visit with his tenants, an old German couple who were fond of him because he never pushed them in a hard year—so far, all the years had been hard—and he sometimes brought them bananas and such delicacies from town.

Mrs. Heyse would open her best preserves for him, he knew, and kill a chicken, and tonight he would have a clean bed in her spare room. She always put a vase of flowers in his room when he stayed overnight with them, and that pleased him very much. He felt like a youth out there, and forgot all the bills he had somehow to meet, and the loans he had made and couldn't collect. The Heyses kept bees and raised turkeys, and had honeysuckle vines running over the front porch. He loved all those things. Mr. Templeton touched Cleveland with the whip, and as they sped along into the grass country, sang softly:

"Old Jesse was a gem'man,
Way down in Tennessee."

XIII

Mandy had to manage the house herself that day, and she was not at all sorry. There wasn't a great deal of variety in her life, and she felt very important taking Mrs. Harris's place, giving the children their dinner, and carrying a plate of milk toast to Mrs. Templeton. She was worried about Mrs. Harris, however, and remarked to the children at noon that she thought somebody ought to "set" with their grandma. Vickie wasn't home for dinner. She had her father's office to herself for the day and was making the most of it, writing a long letter to Professor Chalmers. Mr. Rosen had invited her to have dinner with him at the hotel (he boarded there when his wife was away), and that was a great honour.

When Mandy said someone ought to be with the old lady, Bert and Del offered to take turns. Adelbert went off to rake up the grass they had been cutting all morning, and Albert sat down in the play-room. It seemed to him his grandmother looked pretty sick. He watched her while Mandy gave her toast-water with whisky in it, and thought he would like to make the room look a little nicer. While Mrs. Harris lay with her eyes closed, he hung up the caps and coats lying about, and moved away the big rocking-chair that stood by the head of Grandma's bed. There ought to be a table there, he believed, but the small tables in the house all had something on them. Upstairs, in the room where he and Adelbert and Ronald slept, there was a nice clean wooden cracker-box, on which they sat in the morning to put on their shoes and stockings. He brought this down and stood it on end at the head of Grandma's lounge, and put a clean napkin over the top of it.

She opened her eyes and smiled at him. "Could you git me a tin of fresh water, honey?"

He went to the back porch and pumped till the water ran cold. He gave it to her in a tin cup as she had asked, but he didn't think that was the right way. After she dropped back on the pillow, he fetched a glass tumbler from the cupboard, filled it, and set it on the table he had just manufactured. When Grandmother drew a red cotton handkerchief from under her pillow and wiped the moisture from her face, he ran upstairs again and got one of his Sunday-school handkerchiefs, linen ones, that Mrs. Rosen had given him and Del for Christmas. Having put this in Grandmother's hand and taken away the crumpled red one, he could think of nothing else to do—except to darken the room a little. The windows had no blinds, but flimsy cretonne curtains tied back,— not really tied, but caught back over nails driven into the sill. He loosened them and let them hang down over the bright afternoon sunlight. Then he sat down on the low sawed-off chair and gazed about, thinking that now it looked quite like a sick-room.

It was hard for a little boy to keep still. "Would you like me to read *Joe's Luck*[7] to you, Gram'ma?" he said presently.

"You might, Bertie."

He got the "boy's book" she had been reading aloud to them, and began where she had left off. Mrs. Harris liked to hear his voice, and she liked to look at him when she opened her eyes from time to time. She did not follow the story. In her mind she was repeating a passage from the second part of *Pilgrim's Progress*,[8] which she had read aloud to the children so many times; the passage where Christiana and her band come to the arbour on the Hill of Difficulty: *"Then said Mercy, how sweet is rest to them that labour."*

At about four o'clock Adelbert came home, hot and sweaty from raking. He said he had got in the grass and taken it to their cow, and if Bert was reading, he guessed he'd like to listen. He dragged the wooden rocking-chair up close to Grandma's bed and curled up in it.

Grandmother was perfectly happy. She and the twins were about the same age; they had in common all the realest and truest things. The years between them and her, it seemed to Mrs. Harris, were full of trouble and unimportant. The twins and Ronald and Hughie were important. She opened her eyes.

---

7. A rags-to-riches novel titled *Joe's Luck, or Always Wide Awake* by the American novelist Horatio Alger (1832–1899).
8. The allegory of the Christian's journey to heav-enly reward by the English religious author and preacher John Bunyan (1628–88), first published in 1678.

"Where is Hughie?" she asked.

"I guess he's asleep. Mother took him into her bed."

"And Ronald?"

"He's upstairs with Mandy. There ain't nobody in the kitchen now."

"Then you might git me a fresh drink, Del."

"Yes'm, Gram'ma." He tiptoed out to the pump in his brown canvas sneakers.

When Vickie came home at five o'clock, she went to her mother's room, but the door was locked—a thing she couldn't remember ever happening before. She went into the play-room,—old Mrs. Harris was asleep, with one of the twins on guard, and he held up a warning finger. She went into the kitchen. Mandy was making biscuits, and Ronald was helping her to cut them out.

"What's the matter, Mandy? Where is everybody?"

"You know your papa's away, Miss Vickie; an' your mama's got a headache, an' Miz' Harris has had a bad spell. Maybe I'll just fix supper for you an' the boys in the kitchen, so you won't all have to be runnin' through her room."

"Oh, very well," said Vickie bitterly, and she went upstairs. Wasn't it just like them all to go and get sick, when she had now only two weeks to get ready for school, and no trunk and no clothes or anything? Nobody but Mr. Rosen seemed to take the least interest, "when my whole life hangs by a thread," she told herself fiercely. What were families for, anyway?

After supper Vickie went to her father's office to read; she told Mandy to leave the kitchen door open, and when she got home she would go to bed without disturbing anybody. The twins ran out to play under the electric light with the neighbour boys for a little while, then slipped softly up the back stairs to their room. Mandy came to Mrs. Harris after the house was still.

"Kin I rub your legs fur you, Miz' Harris?"

"Thank you, Mandy. And you might get me a clean nightcap out of the press."

Mandy returned with it.

"Lawsie me! But your legs is cold, ma'am!"

"I expect it's about time, Mandy," murmured the old lady. Mandy knelt on the floor and set to work with a will. It brought the sweat out on her, and at last she sat up and wiped her face with the back of her hand.

"I can't seem to git no heat into 'em, Miz' Harris. I got a hot flat-iron on the stove; I'll wrap it in a piece of old blanket and put it to your feet. Why didn't you have the boys tell me you was cold, pore soul?"

Mrs. Harris did not answer. She thought it was probably a cold that neither Mandy nor the flat-iron could do much with. She hadn't nursed so many people back in Tennessee without coming to know certain signs.

After Mandy was gone, she fell to thinking of her blessings. Every night for years, when she said her prayers, she had prayed that she might never have a long sickness or be a burden. She dreaded the heart-ache and humiliation of being helpless on the hands of people who would be impatient under such a care. And now she felt certain that she was going to die tonight, without troubling anybody.

She was glad Mrs. Rosen was in Chicago. Had she been at home, she would certainly have come in, would have seen that her old neighbour was very sick, and bustled about. Her quick eye would have found out all Grandmother's little secrets: how hard her bed was, that she had no proper place to wash, and kept her comb in her pocket; that her nightgowns were patched and darned. Mrs. Rosen would have been indignant, and that would have made Victoria cross. She didn't have to see Mrs. Rosen again to know that Mrs. Rosen thought highly of her and admired her—yes, admired her. Those funny little pats and arch pleasantries had meant a great deal to Mrs. Harris.

It was a blessing that Mr. Templeton was away, too. Appearances had to be kept up when there was a man in the house; and he might have taken it into his head to send for the doctor, and stir everybody up. Now everything would be so peaceful. *"The Lord is my shepherd,"* she whispered gratefully. "Yes, Lord, I always spoiled Victoria. She was so much the prettiest. But nobody won't ever be the worse for it: Mr. Templeton will always humour her, and the children love her more than most. They'll always be good to her; she has that way with her."

Grandma fell to remembering the old place at home: what a dashing, high-spirited girl Victoria was, and how proud she had always been of her; how she used to hear her laughing and teasing out in the lilac arbour when Hillary Templeton was courting her. Toward morning all these pleasant reflections faded out. Mrs. Harris felt that she and her bed were softly sinking, through the darkness to a deeper darkness.

Old Mrs. Harris did not really die that night, but she believed she did. Mandy found her unconscious in the morning. Then there was a great stir and bustle; Victoria, and even Vickie, were startled out of their intense self-absorption. Mrs. Harris was hastily carried out of the play-room and laid in Victoria's bed, put into one of Victoria's best nightgowns. Mr. Templeton was sent for, and the doctor was sent for. The inquisitive Mrs. Jackson from next door got into the house at last,—installed herself as nurse, and no one had the courage to say her nay. But Grandmother was out of it all, never knew that she was the object of so much attention and excitement. She died a little while after Mr. Templeton got home.

Thus Mrs. Harris slipped out of the Templetons' story; but Victoria and Vickie had still to go on, to follow the long road that leads through things unguessed at and unforeseeable. When they are old, they will come closer and closer to Grandma Harris. They will think a great deal about her, and remember things they never noticed; and their lot will be more or less like hers. They will regret that they heeded her so little; but they, too, will look into the eager, unseeing eyes of young people and feel themselves alone. They will say to themselves: "I was heartless, because I was young and strong and wanted things so much. But now I know."

Ladies Home Journal, September, October 1932;
Obscure Destinies, 1932

Works Cited

Baym, Nina. *Woman's Fiction: A Guide to Novels by and about Women in America, 1820–1870*. Ithaca: Cornell Univ. Press, 1978.

Austin, Mary. "Regionalism in American Fiction." *English Journal* 21 (1932): 97–107.

———. *Earth Horizon: An Autobiography*. Boston: Houghton, 1932.

Bush, Robert. *Grace King: A Southern Destiny*. Baton Rouge: Louisiana State Univ. Press, 1983.

Cather, Willa. Preface to *The Country of the Pointed Firs and Other Stories*, by Sarah Orne Jewett. Boston: Houghton, 1925.

Cott, Nancy. *The Bonds of Womanhood: "Woman's Sphere" in New England 1780–1835*. New Haven: Yale Univ. Press, 1977.

Fields, Annie. *Authors and Friends*. Boston: Houghton, 1897.

Fields, Annie, ed. *Life and Letters of Harriet Beecher Stowe*. Boston: Houghton, 1898.

Fisher, Alice Poindexter. "Zitkala-Sä: The Evolution of a Writer." *American Indian Quarterly* 5 (1979): 229–38.

———. "The Transportation of Tradition: A Study of Zitkala-Sä and Mourning Dove, Two Transitional American Indian Writers." Diss., City Univ. of New York, 1979.

Hirata, Lucie Cheng. "Chinese Immigrant Women in Nineteenth-Century California." In *Women of America: A History*, edited by Carol Ruth Berkin and Mary Beth Norton, 223–44. Boston: Houghton, 1979.

Hull, Gloria T., ed. *Give Us Each Day: The Diary of Alice Dunbar-Nelson*. New York: Norton, 1984.

———. *Color, Sex and Poetry: Three Women Writers of the Harlem Renaissance*. Bloomington: Indiana Univ. Press, 1987.

Jewett, Sarah Orne. *Letters of Sarah Orne Jewett*, edited by Annie Fields. Boston: Houghton, 1911.

King, Grace Elizabeth. *Memories of a Southern Woman of Letters*. New York: Macmillan, 1932.

Metcalf, Eugene Wesley. "The Letters of Paul and Alice Dunbar: A Private History." Diss., Univ. of California, Irvine, 1973.

Parks, Edd Winfield. *Charles Egbert Craddock*. Chapel Hill: Univ. of North Carolina Press, 1941.

Seyersted, Per. *Kate Chopin: A Critical Biography*. Baton Rouge: Louisiana State Univ. Press, 1969; paperback reprint 1980.

Sherman, Sarah Way. *Sarah Orne Jewett: An American Persephone*. Hanover, N.H.: Univ. Press of New England, 1989.

Spofford, Harriet Prescott. *A Little Book of Friends*. Boston: Little Brown, 1916.

Sui Sin Far. "Leaves from the Mental Portfolio of an Eurasian." *Independent* 66 (1909): 125–32.

Thaxter, Celia. *Letters of Celia Thaxter*, edited by Annie Fields and Rose Lamb. Boston: Houghton, 1895.

Thaxter, Rosamund. *Sandpiper*. Hampton, N.H.: Peter E. Randall, 1963.

Venable, W. H. *Beginnings of Literary Culture in the Ohio Valley*. Cincinnati: Robert Clarke, 1891.

Young, Mary E. "Gertrude Simmons Bonnin." In *Notable American Women 1607–1950*, edited by Edward T. James, Janet Wilson James, and Paul S. Boyer, vol. 1, 198–200. 3 vols. Cambridge: Belknap, 1971.

Chronology of First Regional Publications

Harriet Beecher Stowe: "Uncle Lot," *Western Monthly Magazine*, April 1834.

Alice Cary: "Aunt Polly's Visit," *National Era*, August 1847.

Rose Terry Cooke: "Love," *Putnam's*, March 1857.

Celia Thaxter: "Among the Isles of Shoals," *Atlantic Monthly*, January 1869.

Sarah Orne Jewett: "The Shore House," *Atlantic Monthly*, September 1873.

Mary Noialles Murfree: "The Dancin' Party at Harrison's Cove," *Atlantic Monthly*, May 1878.

Mary E. Wilkins Freeman: "Two Old Lovers," *Harper's Bazar*, March 1883.

Grace Elizabeth King: "Monsieur Motte," *New Princeton Review*, January 1886.

Kate Chopin: "At the 'Cadian Ball," *Two Tales*, October 1892.

Alice Dunbar-Nelson: *Violets and Other Tales*. Boston: Monthly Review, 1895.

Sui Sin Far: "A Chinese Ishmael," *Overland*, July 1899.

Zitkala-Sä: "Impressions of an Indian Childhood," *Atlantic Monthly*, January 1900.

Mary Austin: "A Shepherd of the Sierras," *Atlantic Monthly*, July 1900.

Selected Bibliography

Mary Austin
Selected Primary Works
The Land of Little Rain. Boston: Houghton, 1903.
The Basket Woman. Boston: Houghton, 1904.
The Flock. Boston: Houghton, 1906.
Lost Borders. New York: Harper, 1909.
Western Trails: A Collection of Short Stories by Mary Austin, edited by Melody Graulich. Reno: Univ. of Nevada Press, 1987.
Stories from the Country of Lost Borders, edited by Marjorie Pryse. New Brunswick: Rutgers Univ. Press, 1987.
Selected Secondary Works
Austin, Mary. *The American Rhythm*. New York: Harcourt, 1923.
————. *Earth Horizon: An Autobiography*. Boston: Houghton, 1932.
————. "Regionalism in American Fiction." *English Journal* 21 (Feb. 1932): 97–107.
Fink, Augusta. *I-Mary*. Tucson: Univ. of Arizona Press, 1983.
Jaycox, Faith. "Regeneration Through Liberation: Mary Austin's 'The Walking Woman' and Western Narrative Formula." *Legacy* 6 (Spring 1989): 5–12.
Pearce, Thomas Matthews. *Mary Hunter Austin*. New York: Twayne, 1965.
————, ed. *Literary America, 1903–1934: The Mary Austin Letters*. Westport, Conn.: Greenwood, 1979.
Porter, Nancy. Afterword to *A Woman of Genius*, by Mary Austin. Old Westbury, N.Y.: Feminist Press, 1985.
Ruppert, James. "Discovering America: Mary Austin and Imagism." In *Studies in American Indian Literature*, edited by Paula Gunn Allen, 243–58. New York: MLA, 1983.
————. "Mary Austin's Landscape Line in Native American Literature." *Southwest Review* 68 (Autumn 1983): 376–90.
Sergeant, Elizabeth Shepley. "Mary Austin: A Portrait. *Saturday Review of Literature* 11.8 (8 Sept. 1934): 96.
Steffens, Lincoln. "Mary Austin." *The American Magazine* 72.2 (June 1911): 178–81.
Stineman, Esther Lanigan. *Mary Austin: Song of a Maverick*. New Haven: Yale Univ. Press, 1987.

Work, James C. "The Moral in Austin's *The Land of Little Rain*." In *Women and Western American Literature*, edited by Helen Winter Stauffer and Susan J. Rosowski, 297–309. Troy, N.Y.: Whitston, 1982.
Wynn, Dudley. *A Critical Study of the Writings of Mary Austin*. Graduate School of Arts and Science of New York Univ., 1941.

Alice Cary
Selected Primary Works
Clovernook: or, Recollections of Our Neighborhood in the West. New York: Redfield, 1852.
Clovernook; or, Recollections of Our Neighborhood in the West, Second Series. New York: Redfield, 1853.
Pictures of Country Life. New York: Derby, 1859.
Clovernook Sketches and Other Stories, edited by Judith Fetterley. New Brunswick: Rutgers Univ. Press 1986.
Selected Secondary Works
Ames, Mary Clemmer. *A Memorial of Alice and Phoebe Cary, with Some of Their Later Poems*. New York: Hurd, 1873.
Armstrong, M. F. "Alice and Phoebe Cary—A Remembrance." *Woman's Journal* 9 (Sept. 1871).
Cary, Phoebe. "Alice Cary." *Woman's Journal* 5 (Aug. 1871).
Fetterley, Judith, and Marjorie Pryse. "Alice Cary: 1820–1871." *Legacy* 1 (1984): 1–3.
Greeley, Horace. "Alice and Phebe Cary." In *Eminent Women of the Age*, edited by James Parton et al., 164–72. Hartford: Betts, 1868.
Kolodny, Annette. *The Land Before Her*, 178–99. Chapel Hill: Univ. of North Carolina Press, 1984.
Pulsifer, Janice G. "Alice and Phoebe Cary, Whittier's Sweet Singers of the West." *Essex Institute Historical Collections* 109 (Jan. 1973): 9–59.
Venable, W. H. *Beginnings of Literary Culture in the Ohio Valley*. Cincinnati: Clarke, 1891.

Kate Chopin
Selected Primary Works
Bayou Folk. Boston: Houghton, 1894.

A Night in Acadie. Chicago: Way, 1897.

The Awakening. Chicago: Stone, 1899.

The Complete Works of Kate Chopin, edited by Per Seyersted. Baton Rouge: Louisiana State Univ. Press, 1969.

Selected Secondary Works

Elfenbein, Anna Shannon. *Women on the Color Line: Evolving Stereotypes and the Writings of George Washington Cable, Grace King, Kate Chopin.* Charlottesville: Univ. Press of Virginia, 1989.

Ewell, Barbara. *Kate Chopin.* New York: Ungar, 1986.

Gaudet, Marcia. "Kate Chopin and the Lore of Cane River's Creoles of Color." *Xavier Review* 6 (1986): 45–52.

Grover, Dorys Crow. "Kate Chopin and the Bayou Country." *Journal of the American Studies Association of Texas* 15 (1984): 29–34.

O'Brien, Sharon. "Sentiment, Local Color, and the New Woman Writer: Kate Chopin and Willa Cather." *The Kate Chopin Newsletter* 2 (Fall 1976): 16–24.

Rankin, Daniel S. *Kate Chopin and Her Creole Stories.* Philadelphia: Univ. of Pennsylvania Press, 1932.

Seyersted, Per. *Kate Chopin: A Critical Biography.* Baton Rouge: Louisiana State Univ. Press, 1969.

Taylor, Helen. *Gender, Race, and Region in the Writings of Grace King, Ruth McEnery Stuart, and Kate Chopin.* Baton Rouge: Louisiana State Univ. Press, 1989.

Thomas, Heather Kirk. " 'Development of the Literary West': An Undiscovered Kate Chopin Essay." *American Literary Realism* 22 (Winter 1990): 69–75.

Toth, Emily. *Kate Chopin.* New York: Morrow, 1990.

Rose Terry Cooke

Selected Primary Works

Somebody's Neighbors. Boston: Osgood, 1881.

The Sphinx's Children and Other People's. Boston: Ticknor, 1886.

Huckleberries Gathered from New England Hills. Boston: Houghton, 1891.

How Celia Changed Her Mind & Selected Stories, edited by Elizabeth Ammons. New Brunswick: Rutgers Univ. Press, 1986.

Selected Secondary Works

Donovan, Josephine. *New England Local Color Literature: A Women's Tradition,* 68–81. New York: Ungar, 1983.

Downey, Jean. "A Biographical and Critical Study of Rose Terry Cooke." Diss., Univ. of Ottawa, 1956.

———. "Rose Terry Cooke: A Bibliography."

Bulletin of Bibliography 21 (May–Aug. 1955): 159–63; (Sept.–Dec. 1955): 191–92.

Kleitz, Katherine. "Essence of New England: The Portraits of Rose Terry Cooke." *American Transcendental Quarterly* 47–48 (Summer–Fall 1980): 127–39.

Newlyn, Evelyn. "Rose Terry Cooke and the Children of the Sphinx." *Regionalism and the Female Imagination* 4 (Winter 1979): 49–57.

Spofford, Harriet Prescott. *A Little Book of Friends,* 143–56. Boston: Little, Brown, 1916.

Toth, Susan Allen. "Character Studies in Rose Terry Cooke: New Faces for the Short Story." *The Kate Chopin Newsletter* 2 (Spring 1976): 19–26.

———. " 'The Rarest and Most Peculiar Grape': Versions of the New England Woman in Nineteenth-Century Local Color Literature." In *Regionalism and the Female Imagination: A Collection of Essays,* edited by Emily Toth, 15–28. New York: Human Sciences, 1985.

Westbrook, Perry D. *Acres of Flint: Sarah Orne Jewett and Her Contemporaries,* 78–85. Metuchen, N.J.: Scarecrow, 1951; revised 1981.

Alice Dunbar-Nelson

Selected Primary Works

Violets and Other Tales. Boston: Monthly Review, 1895.

The Goodness of St. Rocque and Other Stories. New York: Dodd, Mead 1899.

The Works of Alice Dunbar-Nelson, edited by Gloria T. Hull. Vols. 1 and 3. New York: Oxford, 1988.

Selected Secondary Works

Bryan, Violet Harrington. "Creating and Re-Creating the Myth of New Orleans: Grace King and Alice Dunbar-Nelson." *Publications of the Mississippi Philological Association* (1987): 185–96.

Dunbar-Nelson, Alice. *Give Us Each Day: The Diary of Alice Dunbar-Nelson,* edited by Gloria T. Hull. New York: Norton, 1984.

Hull, Gloria T. "Alice Dunbar-Nelson: A Regional Approach." In *Teaching Women's Literature from a Regional Perspective,* edited by Leonore Hoffman and Deborah Rosenfelt, 64–68. New York: MLA, 1982.

———. *Color, Sex, and Poetry: Three Women Writers of the Harlem Renaissance.* Bloomington: Indiana Univ. Press, 1987.

———. "Researching Alice Dunbar-Nelson: A Personal and Literary Perspective." *Feminist Studies* 6 (Summer 1980): 314–20.

———. "Shaping Contradictions: Alice Dunbar-

Nelson and the Black Creole Experience."
New Orleans Review 15 (Spring 1988): 34–
47.

Whitlow, Roger. "Alice Dunbar-Nelson: New
Orleans Writer." *Regionalism and the Female Imagination* 4 (1978): 51–61.

Mary E. Wilkins Freeman

Selected Primary Works

A Humble Romance and Other Stories. New
York: Harper, 1887.

A New England Nun and Other Stories. New
York: Harper, 1891.

Pembroke. New York: Harper, 1894.

By the Light of the Soul. New York: Harper,
1906.

Selected Stories of Mary E. Wilkins Freeman,
edited by Marjorie Pryse. New York: Norton, 1983.

Selected Secondary Works

Apthorp, Elaine Sargent. "Sentiment, Natural-
ism, and the Female Regionalist." *Legacy* 7
(Spring 1990): 3–21.

Brand, Alice. "Mary Wilkins Freeman: Misan-
thropy as Propaganda." *New England
Quarterly* 50 (March 1977): 83–100.

Donovan, Josephine. *New England Local Color
Literature,* 119–38. New York: Ungar,
1983.

Fienberg, Lorne. "Mary E. Wilkins Freeman's
'Soft Diurnal Commotion': Women's Work
and Strategies of Containment." *New England Quarterly* 62 (Dec. 1989): 483–504.

Foster, Edward. *Mary E. Wilkins Freeman.*
New York: Hendricks, 1956.

Glasser, Leah Blatt. "Mary E. Wilkins Freeman: The Stranger in the Mirror." *Massachusetts Review* 25 (Summer 1984): 323–
39.

———. " 'She is the One You Call Sister' ": Discovering Mary Wilkins Freeman." In *Between Women,* edited by Carol Ascher,
Louise DeSalvo, and Sara Ruddick, 187–
211. Boston: Beacon, 1984.

Hamblen, Abigail Ann. *The New England Art of
Mary E. Wilkins Freeman.* Amherst,
Mass.: Green Knight, 1966.

Hirsch, David. H. "Subdued Meaning in 'A New
England Nun.' " *Studies in Short Fiction* 2
(1965): 124–36.

Kendrick, Brent L. *The Infant Sphinx: The Collected Letters of Mary E. Wilkins Freeman.*
Metuchen, N.J.: Scarecrow, 1985.

———. "Mary E. Wilkins Freeman." *American
Literary Realism* 8 (Summer 1975): 255–57.

Pryse, Marjorie. "The Humanity of Women in
Freeman's 'A Village Singer.' " *Colby Library Quarterly* 19 (June 1983): 69–77.

———. Introduction and Afterword to *Selected
Stories of Mary E. Wilkins Freeman,* edited
by Marjorie Pryse. New York: Norton:
1983.

———. "Mary E. Wilkins Freeman." In *Modern American Women Writers,* edited by
Elaine Showalter. New York: Scribner's,
1990.

———. "An Uncloistered 'New England
Nun.' " *Studies in Short Fiction* 20 (Fall
1983): 289–96.

Quina, James H., Jr. "Character Types in the
Fiction of, Mary Wilkins Freeman." *Colby
Library Quarterly* 9 (June 1971): 432–39.

Reichardt, Mary R. " 'Friend of My Heart':
Women as Friends and Rivals in the Short
Stories of Mary Wilkins Freeman." *American Literary Realism* 22 (Winter 1990): 54–
68.

Romines, Ann. "A Place for 'A Poetess.' " *Mark-
ham Review* 12 (Summer 1983): 61–64.

Toth, Susan A. "Defiant Light: A Positive View
of Mary Wilkins Freeman." *New England
Quarterly* 46 (March 1973): 82–93.

———. "Mary Wilkins Freeman's Parable of
Wasted Life." *American Literature* 42 (Jan.
1971): 564–67.

———. " 'The Rarest and Most Peculiar
Grape': Versions of the New England
Woman in Nineteenth-Century Local Color
Literature." In *Regionalism and the Fe-
male Imagination: A Collection of Essays,*
edited by Emily Toth, 15–28. New York:
Human Sciences, 1985.

Westbrook, Perry D. *Acres of Flint: Sarah Orne
Jewett and Her Contemporaries,* 86–104.
Metuchen, N.J.: Scarecrow, 1981.

———. *Mary Wilkins Freeman.* New York:
Twayne, 1967.

Sarah Orne Jewett

Selected Primary Works

Deephaven. Boston: Osgood, 1877.

Old Friends and New. Boston: Houghton, 1879.

Country By-Ways. Boston: Houghton, 1881.

A White Heron and Other Stories. Boston:
Houghton, 1886.

Tales of New England. Boston: Houghton, 1890.

Strangers and Wayfarers. Boston: Houghton,
1890.

The Life of Nancy. Boston: Houghton, 1895.

The Country of the Pointed Firs. Boston:
Houghton, 1896.

The Queen's Twin and Other Stories. Boston:
Houghton, 1899.

*The World of Dunnet Landing: A Sarah Orne
Jewett Collection,* edited by David Bonnell
Green. Lincoln: Univ. of Nebraska Press,
1962.

Selected Secondary Works

Ammons, Elizabeth. "Going in Circles: The Female Geography of *The Country of the Pointed Firs.*" *Studies in the Literary Imagination* 16 (Autumn 1983): 83–92.

———. "Jewett's Witches." Nagel, *Critical Essays*, 165–84.

———. "The Shape of Violence in Jewett's 'A White Heron.'" *Colby Library Quarterly* 22 (Mar. 1986): 6–16.

Cary, Richard. "Jewett on Writing Short Stories." *Colby Library Quarterly* 6 (June 1964): 425–40.

———. *Sarah Orne Jewett.* New York: Twayne, 1962.

———. "The Sculptor and the Spinster: Jewett's 'Influence' on Cather." *Colby Library Quarterly* 10 (Sept. 1973): 168–78.

———, ed. *Appreciation of Sarah Orne Jewett.* Waterville, Me.: Colby College Press, 1973.

Cather, Willa. "148 Charles Street." In *Not Under Forty.* New York: Knopf, 1953.

———. "Miss Jewett." In *Not Under Forty.* New York: Knopf, 1953.

———. Preface to *The Country of the Pointed Firs and Other Stories*, by Sarah Orne Jewett. Boston: Houghton, 1925.

Donovan, Josephine. *New England Local Color Literature*, 99–118. New York: Ungar, 1983.

———. *Sarah Orne Jewett.* New York: Ungar, 1980.

Eppard, Philip B. "Local Colorists: Sarah Orne Jewett, Mary E. Wilkins Freeman, and Mary N. Murfree." In *American Women Writers: Bibliographical Essays*, edited by Maurice Duke, Jackson R. Bryer, and M. Thomas Inge. Westport, Conn.: Greenwood, 1983.

Fields, Annie, ed. *Letters of Sarah Orne Jewett.* Boston: Houghton, 1911.

Folsom, Marcia McClintock. "'Tact Is a Kind of Mind-Reading': Empathic Style in Sarah Orne Jewett's *The Country of the Pointed Firs. Colby Library Quarterly* 18 (1982): 66–78; reprinted in Nagel, *Critical Essays*, 76–88.

Fryer, Judith. "What Goes on in the Ladies Room? Sarah Orne Jewett, Annie Fields, and Their Community of Women." *Massachusetts Review* 30 (Winter 1989): 610–28.

Green, David Bonnell. "The World of Dunnet Landing." *New England Quarterly* 34 (Dec. 1961): 514–17.

Hovet, Theodore R. "America's 'Lonely Country Child': The Theme of Separation in Sarah Orne Jewett's 'A White Heron.'" *Colby Library Quarterly* 14 (Sept. 1978): 166–71.

Jobes, Katharine T. "From Stowe's Eagle Island to Jewett's 'A White Heron.'" *Colby Library Quarterly* 10 (1974): 515–21.

Matthiessen, F. O. *Sarah Orne Jewett.* Boston: Houghton, 1929.

Miller, Elsie. "Jewett's *The Country of the Pointed Firs*: The Realism of the Local Colorists." *American Literary Realism* 20 (Winter 1988): 3–20.

Nagel, Gwen L. *Critical Essays on Sarah Orne Jewett.* Boston: Hall, 1984.

———, and James Nagel. *Sarah Orne Jewett: A Reference Guide.* Boston: Hall, 1978.

Nagel, James. "Sarah Orne Jewett Writes to Hamlin Garland." *New England Quarterly* 54 (Sept. 1981): 416–23.

Pryse, Marjorie. Introduction to *The Country of the Pointed Firs and Other Stories*, by Sarah Orne Jewett, edited by Mary Ellen Chase. New York: Norton, 1981.

———. "Women 'At Sea': Feminist Realism in Sarah Orne Jewett's 'The Foreigner.'" *American Literary Realism* 15 (1982): 244–52; reprinted in Nagel, 89–98.

Renza, Louis. *"A White Heron" and the Question of Minor Literature.* Madison: Univ of Wisconsin Press, 1984.

Roman, Judith. "A Closer Look at the Jewett-Fields Relationship." In Nagel, 119–34.

Romines, Ann. "Domestic Troubles." *Colby Library Quarterly* 24 (Mar. 1988): 50–60.

———. "In *Deephaven*: Skirmishes Near the Swamp." *Colby Library Quarterly* 16 (1980): 205–19; reprinted in Nagel, 43–57.

Sherman, Sarah Way. *Sarah Orne Jewett: An American Persephone.* Hanover, N.H.: Univ. Press of New England, 1989.

Singley, Carol J. "Reaching Lonely Heights: Sarah Orne Jewett, Emily Dickinson, and Female Initiation." *Colby Library Quarterly* 22 (Mar. 1986): 75–82.

Toth, Susan Allen. "'The Rarest and Most Peculiar Grape': Versions of the New England Woman in Nineteenth-Century Local Color Literature." In *Regionalism and the Female Imagination: A Collection of Essays*, edited by Emily Toth, 15–28. New York: Human Sciences, 1985.

———. "Sarah Orne Jewett and Friends: A Community of Interest." *Studies in Short Fiction* 9 (1972): 233–41.

Westbrook, Perry D. *Acres of Flint: Sarah Orne Jewett and Her Contemporaries.* Metuchen, N.J.: Scarecrow, 1981.

Zagarell, Sandra. "Narrative of Community: The Identification of a Genre." *Signs* 13 (1988): 498–527.

Grace King

Selected Primary Works

Monsieur Motte. New York: Armstrong, 1888.

Balcony Stories. New York: Century, 1893.

Grace King of New Orleans: A Selection of Her Writing, edited by Robert Bush. Baton Rouge: Louisiana State Univ. Press, 1973.

Selected Secondary Works

Bryan, Violet Harrington. "Creating and Re-Creating the Myth of New Orleans: Grace King and Alice Dunbar-Nelson." *Publications of the Mississippi Philological Association* (1987): 185–96.

Bush, Robert. *Grace King: A Southern Destiny.* Baton Rouge: Louisiana State Univ. Press, 1983.

Elfenbein, Anna Shannon. *Women on the Color Line: Evolving Stereotypes and the Writings of George Washington Cable, Grace King, Kate Chopin.* Charlottesville: Univ. Press of Virginia, 1989.

Juncker, Clara. "The Mother's Balcony: Grace King's Discourse of Femininity." *New Orleans Review* 15 (Spring 1988): 39–46.

King, Grace Elizabeth. *Memories of a Southern Woman of Letters.* New York: Macmillan, 1932.

Taylor, Helen. "The Case of Grace King." *The Southern Review* 18 (Fall 1982): 685–702.

———. *Gender, Race, and Region in the Writings of Grace King, Ruth McEnery Stuart, and Kate Chopin.* Baton Rouge: Louisiana State Univ. Press, 1989.

Mary Noialles Murfree

Selected Primary Works

In the Tennessee Mountains. Boston: Houghton, 1884.

The Prophet of the Great Smoky Mountains. Boston: Houghton, 1885.

Selected Secondary Works

Cary, Richard. *Mary N. Murfree.* New York: Twayne, 1967.

Ensor, Allison. "The Geography of Mary Noialles Murfree's *In the Tennessee Mountains.*" *The Mississippi Quarterly* 31 (Spring 1978): 191–99.

Eppard, Philip B. "Local Colorists: Sarah Orne Jewett, Mary E. Wilkins Freeman, and Mary N. Murfree." In *American Women Writers: Bibliographical Essays,* edited by Maurice Duke, Jackson R. Bryer, and M. Thomas Inge. Westport, Conn.: Greenwood, 1983.

Parks, Edd Winfield. *Charles Egbert Craddock.* Chapel Hill, Univ. of North Carolina Press, 1941.

Wright, Nathalia. Introduction to *In the Tennessee Mountains,* by Mary Noialles Murfree, 5–33. Knoxville: Univ. of Tennessee Press, 1970.

Harriet Beecher Stowe

Selected Primary Works

The Mayflower, or Sketches of Scenes and Characters among the Descendants of the Puritans. New York: Harper, 1843.

The Minister's Wooing. New York: Derby, 1859.

The Pearl of Orr's Island: A Story of the Coast of Maine. Boston: Ticknor, 1862.

Oldtown Folks. Boston: Fields, 1869.

Sam Lawson's Oldtown Fireside Stories. Boston: Osgood, 1872.

Selected Secondary Works

Adams, John R. *Harriet Beecher Stowe.* New York: Twayne, 1963. Revised 1989.

Ammons, Elizabeth, ed. *Critical Essays on Harriet Beecher Stowe.* Boston: Hall, 1980.

Boydston, Jeanne, Mary Kelley, and Anne Margolis. *The Limits of Sisterhood: The Beecher Sisters on Women's Rights and Woman's Sphere.* Greensboro: Univ. of North Carolina Press, 1988.

Cox, James M. "Harriet Beecher Stowe: From Sectionalism to Regionalism." *Nineteenth-Century Literature* 38 (Mar. 1984): 444–66.

Crozier, Alice. *The Novels of Harriet Beecher Stowe.* New York: Oxford, 1969.

Crumpacker, Laurie. "Four Novels of Harriet Beecher Stowe: A Study in Nineteenth-Century Androgyny." In *American Novelists Revisited: Essays in Feminist Criticism,* edited by Fritz Fleischmann, 78–106. Boston: Hall, 1982.

Donovan, Josephine. *New England Local Color Literature: A Women's Tradition.* New York: Ungar, 1983.

Fields, Annie, ed. *Life and Letters of Harriet Beecher Stowe.* Boston: Houghton, 1898.

Foster, Charles. *The Rungless Ladder: Harriet Beecher Stowe and New England Puritanism.* Durham: Duke Univ. Press, 1954.

Hedrick, Joan. " 'Peaceable Fruits': The Ministry of Harriet Beecher Stowe." *American Quarterly* 40 (Sept. 1988): 307–32.

Kelley, Mary. *Private Woman, Public Stage: Literary Domesticity in Nineteenth-Century America.* New York: Oxford, 1984.

Rugoff, Milton. *The Beechers: An American Family in the Nineteenth Century.* New York: Harper, 1981.

Showalter, Elaine. "Piecing and Writing." In *The Poetics of Gender,* edited by Nancy Miller. New York: Columbia Univ. Press, 1986.

Stowe, Charles Edward. *The Life of Harriet Beecher Stowe Compiled from Her Letters and Journals.* Boston: Houghton, 1889.

Warhol, Robyn R. "Toward a Theory of the Engaging Narrator: Earnest Interventions in Gaskell, Stowe, and Eliot." *PMLA* 101 (Oct. 1986): 811–18.

Wilson, Forrest. *Crusader in Crinoline: The Life of Harriet Beecher Stowe*. Philadelphia: Lippincott, 1941.

Wolstenholme, Susan. "Voice of the Voiceless: Harriet Beecher Stowe and the Byron Controversy." *American Literary Realism* 19 (Winter 1987): 48–65.

Sui Sin Far

Selected Primary Works

Mrs. Spring Fragrance. Chicago: McClurg, 1912.

Selected Secondary Works

Ling, Amy. *Between Worlds: Women Writers of Chinese Ancestry*. New York: Pergamon, 1990.

———. "Edith Eaton: Pioneer Chinamerican Writer and Feminist." *American Literary Realism* 16 (Autumn 1983): 287–98.

Solberg, S. E. "Sui Sin Far / Edith Eaton: First Chinese-American Fictionist." *MELUS* 8 (1981): 27–39.

Sui Sin Far. "The Chinese Woman in America." *Land of Sunshine* 6 (Jan. 1897): 59–64.

———. "Leaves from the Mental Portfolio of an Eurasian." *Independent* 66 (21 Jan. 1909): 125–32.

White-Parks, Annette. Introduction to "The Wisdom of the New," by Sui Sin Far. *Legacy* 6 (Spring 1989): 34–37.

Celia Thaxter

Selected Primary Works

Among the Isles of Shoals. Boston: Osgood, 1873.

An Island Garden. Boston: Houghton, 1894.

Selected Secondary Works

Fields, Annie. *Authors and Friends*. Boston: Houghton, 1897.

Laighton, Oscar. *Ninety Years at the Isles of Shoals*. Boston: Star Island, 1971.

Rutledge, Lyman. *The Isles of Shoals in Lore and Legend*. Boston: Star Island, 1965.

Thaxter, Rosamond. *The Life and Letters of Celia Thaxter*. Hampton, N.H.: Randall, 1963.

Vallier, Jane E. *Poet on Demand: The Life, Letters and Works of Celia Thaxter*. Camden, Me.: Down East, 1982.

———. "The Role of Celia Thaxter in American Literary History: An Overview." *Colby Library Quarterly* 17 (Dec. 1981): 238–55.

Westbrook, Perry D. *Acres of Flint: Sarah Orne Jewett and Her Contemporaries*, 105–27. Metuchen, N.J.: Scarecrow, 1981.

White, Barbara A. "Celia Thaxter." *Legacy* 7 (Spring 1990): 59–64.

Zitkala-Sä

Selected Primary Works

"Impressions of an Indian Childhood." *Atlantic Monthly* 85 (Jan. 1900): 37–47.

"The School Days of an Indian Girl." *Atlantic Monthly* 85 (Feb. 1900): 185–94.

"An Indian Teacher Among Indians." *Atlantic Monthly* 85 (Mar. 1900): 381–86.

"The Soft-Hearted Sioux." *Harper's Monthly* 102 (Mar. 1901): 505–8.

"The Trial Path." *Harper's Monthly* 103 (Oct. 1901): 741–44.

Old Indian Legends. Boston: Ginn, 1901.

American Indian Stories. Washington, D.C.: Hayworth, 1921.

Selected Secondary Works

Fisher, Alice Poindexter. "The Transformation of Tradition: A Study of Zitkala-Sä and Mourning Dove, Two Transitional American Indian Writers." Diss., City Univ. of New York, 1979; partial reprint in *Critical Essays on American Literature*, edited by Andrew Wiget, 202–11. Boston: Hall, 1985.

———. "Zitkala-Sä: The Evolution of a Writer." *American Indian Quarterly* 5 (1979): 229–38.

Johnson, David L. and Raymond Wilson. "Gertrude Simmons Bonnin, 1876–1938: 'Americanize the First American.'" *American Indian Quarterly* 12 (1988): 27–40.

Young, Mary E. "Gertrude Simmons Bonnin." In *Notable American Women 1607–1950*, edited by Edward T. James, Janet Wilson James, and Paul S. Boyer, vol. 1, 198–200. 3 vols. Cambridge: Belknap, 1971.

Index